GW01044152

Rana P. B. Singh

Banaras,
the Heritage City of India

Geography, History, and
Bibliography

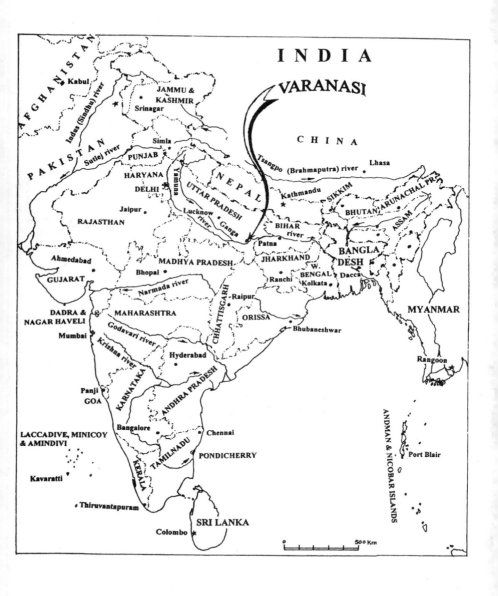

BANARAS,

THE HERITAGE CITY OF INDIA

Geography, History, and Bibliography

Rana P. B. Singh

Banaras Hindu University

INDICA

Pilgrimage & Cosmology Series: 8

Cover illustration: *Kashi standing on Shiva's trishul,*
          detail of miniature.

Cataloguing Data:
   Singh, Rana P. B. (b. 1950)
   Banaras, the Heritage City of India: Geography, History, and Bibliography.
   [Three essays and 1276 bibliographic sources]; includes bibliographical
   references, list of deities, list of *Jala tirthas* and *ghats*, list of festivals, and index.
   458 pp., 13 tables, 32 figures. 31 December 2008.
   Published by: Indica Books, Varanasi.
   1. Indian History. 2. Banaras. 3. Heritage studies. 4. Cultural geography. 5.
   Urban History.

© Rana P.B. Singh 2009

1st edition published in 2009 by

Indica Books
D 40/18 Godowlia
Varanasi - 221001 (U.P.), India

Indicabooks@satyam.net.in
www.indicabooks.com

ISBN: 81-86569-85-5

Printed in India : *First Impression*, New Delhi
                011-22481754, 09811224048

This book is dedicated to
James Prinsep (1799 - 1840),

the man whose genius discovered the name of Asoka the Great (B.C. 272-232), the Buddhist monarch, and Kanishka, another emperor, by deciphering their Brahmi and Kharoshti edicts and coins, which places him above Champollion, the decipherer of Egyptian hieroglyphs. Not only was Prinsep a great epigraphist, but he was also, at the same time, an Architect (Banaras: Mint, St. Mary's Church, Nandeshwar Kothi, etc.), Archaeologist (restorer of the minarets of Aurangzeb's masjid, Banaras), Engineer (builder of Karmanasa bridge and Circular Canal, Calcutta), Artist (Benares Illustrated, 35 plates), Cartographer (Map of Benares, 1822), Demographer (Census and Directory of Benares, 1828-31), Engraver, Scientist (Fellow of the Royal Society at 28; inventor of Evaporometer, Fluviameter, Pyrometer, Assay Balance, etc.), Journalist (editor-publisher of the Journal of the Asiatic Society, and Gleanings in Science), Chemist (Assay Master of Benares & Calcutta Mints), Musician and Actor. His works paved the path to study this holy city and are still serving as a light tower.

Varanasi: Light and Dark

Kashi : thou of many names, many glories,
    philic and phobic both.
Banaras : where juice is ready every time,
    yet people thirst all the time.
Varanasi : city between the Varana and Asi rivers,
    where people enjoy the flowing sewers.
Kashi: known as the City of Light,
    also of delight and plight.
Shmasana : the city of burning corpses,
    making pits of garbage-ashes.
Jnanavapi : where the well of wisdom lies,
    however always the rumour flies.
Holy Tirtha : the city of divine realm,
    now changing to devil's helm.
The Abode of Vishvesvara — Lord of the Universe,
    where the people are diverse.
Here Police inspector Bhairava lives,
    but all the time people weep!
Annapurna assures for giving alms,
    however the dwellers enjoy hemp!
Ganesha watches the deeds as witness,
    who can measure people's dullness!
This is Shiva's 'Forest of Bliss',
    yet the motto : to kill and kiss!
The flowing Ganga calls for eternity,
    worshippers follow the path of disparity!
Good and bad: both the apexes everywhere,
    one is free to march anywhere.
O Kashi! Bowing we to thy personality,
    bliss and wish for our stability.

Rana P.B. Singh

CONTENTS

Background; Geographical setting: topography, flood, climate; Nomenclature and related tales; Growth of population: early 19th century, 20th century, population characteristics; Religious Landscape: ethnic and social structure, archetype of an all-India, Shiva as supreme, Jain and temples, Sikhism and shrines, Christianity and churches, Muslims; sacred places; Varanasi, the mini-India; Industrial landscape; Tourist landscape; Epilogue.

Background; Early historical period; Pratiharas and Gahadavalas period; Delhi Sultanate and Mughal Eras; the story of Vishvanatha Temple: Perspectives in time; The Modern and British Period; Post-Independence Period; Battle to save the Ganga River and its riverfront; the issue of Contesting Pilgrimage.

Background; Towards Conceptualising Heritage; Battle for the Heritage Preservation; The Master Plan & Heritage Zones; Other Heritagescapes; UNESCO guidelines for Cultural Heritage and Cultural Landscape; Varanasi on the criteria of UNESCO-WHC; Old City Heritage and Riverfront Cultural Landscape; JNNURM and the Varanasi CDP: Dilemmas!; Pressures and Heritage Scenario; Deteriorating Heritagescapes and Issue of Awakening; Actions at the various levels of Governance; Concluding Remarks.

Appendices

LIST OF FIGURES

9

LIST OF TABLES

11

ACKNOWLEDGEMENTS

All my life I have felt close to place. Place speaks. Place talks. In late 1970s my inner quest mobilised my sight and vision for reading the *genius loci* of Varanasi, ultimately trying to interpret and understand the meanings, messages and milieus preserved there; this resulted into a constant march, a never ending journey. On this road while walking, people from different parts of the world joined and made our group a company of seekers, a mosaic of culture, thought and vision. The first and foremost wanderer who inspired and persuaded me to follow this path of sacred journey is my German friend Niels Gutschow whom I first met during an International Conference on 'Ritual Space in India: Studies in Architectural Anthropology', at Max Müller Foundation, Bombay (Mumbai), 22-25 February 1979; and soon we became co-pilgrims in search of the *genius loci* of sacredscapes in and around Banaras. In the same conference I met two other great personalities who worked on 'sacred space' and also on Banaras, they are Jan Pieper, and George Michell. In course of time, I intensively worked together with them and learnt different perspectives to study and understand Banaras. While marching on the above path I met Axel Michaels in an International Conference on 'Banaras as Place of Pilgrimage', University of Bern, Switzerland, 25 May 1993, with whom I again collaborated from the Indian side in his directed project on 'Visualising Sacred Space of Banaras' under the auspices of Heidelberg University (Germany) in 1999-2002. As summing up celebration the South Asia Institute at Heidelberg had organised an International Symposium on 'Visualized Space: Constructions of Locality and Cartographic Representations in Varanasi' during 22-25 May 2002, where I gave a keynote address and benefitted from scholars from all over the world working on Banaras, including so many young researchers.

Banaras: where 'always ready' (*Bana*) is the 'juice of life' (*ras*)! This 'Life-juice' flows in plenitude here in different colours, varying tones, multiple textures and layers, diverse situations, contrasting conditions, etc.; its history is rooted in my own *tour de force* during the last thirty years, 1979-2008. My first paper on Banaras was published in the proceedings-based volume in the *Art and Archaeology Research Paper Series* (London) in 1980, followed with the second paper on Varanasi dealing with geographical space and cognitive maps published in the proceedings in the *Frankfurt Social Geography Series* in 1982. Since then my path has been widened and many companions have joined at different stages, in different turnings and in different ways. During 1998-2000 under the auspices of University of Colorado Project on 'The Cultural Astronomy and Sacred Space in Banaras', I worked with the famous astrophysicist John McKim Malville, and our collaboration flourished in several publications; this helped us to understand the link between the mythological and the scientific endeavours. During 1999-2003, working in the UK-DFID project on 'Land use changes in the Peri-urban areas around Varanasi' has also helped me in reflecting upon the expansion of the city.

The first draft of this book started in the congenial and friendly environment of the VPI, Virginia Polytechnic Institute and State University at Blacksburg, USA University, during January-April of 1981 where I served as Visiting Professor in the School of Environmental and Urban Studies. I express my special thanks to Charles Good and Bradley Hertel, friends at VPI-SU, who treated me as their family member. Being visiting professor in other countries I have been benefitted by their support and accessories in preparing this book and doing researches about Banaras; affiliation to such institutions include Karlstad University (Sweden) in December 1989, May-June 1993, August 1996, May 2002, May-June 2005, May-June 2006, University of Otago, New Zealand in October 1995, Gifu Women's University, Japan in December 2004, and Gothenburg University in October 2008. At Kartstad my collaborator and friend Gerhard Gustafsson has always been immensely helpful.

I have collaborated with and was enriched by the researches and interaction with scholars and lovers of Banaras from different parts of the world who helped in shaping my ideas and expanding of horizons; noteworthy among them, according to country, are:

Austria: Armin Brugger, Wolfgang Dokonal, Grigor Doytchinov, Martin Gaenszle, Götz Hagmüller, Wolfgang Heusgen, Hasso Hohmann, Carl Pruscha, Klaus Rötzer.

Australia: Reena Tiwari, Peter Friedlander, Kama Maclean, Kiran Shinde, Yashdeep Srivastava.

Belgium: Ruth Brinkmann, Winand Callewaert, Joris Gielen, Bermijn Isabelle, Greet Van Thienen.

Canada: Christopher Justice, Anne Pearson, J. Douglas Poeteus, Hillary Rodrigues.

Denmark: Hans Helge Madsen, Erik Sand, Birgitta Schöndorf.

France: Francesco Bandarin, Ghassan Chemaly, Mathieu Claveyrolas, Catherine Clementin-Ojha, Rémy Delage, Antonio Martinelli, Emmanuelle Pucci, Serge Santelli, Dominique Varma.

Germany: Joachim Bautze, Monika Boehm-Tettelbach, Hans-Georg Bohle, Michaela Dimmers, Heike Dittmers, Joerg Gengnagel, Niels Gutschow, Harry Falk, Istvan Keul, Uwe Köckman, Hermann Kulke, Stephan Lemcke, Birgit Mayer-Koeing, Jan Piper, William Sax, Volkmar Schaefer, Stefan Schuette, Annette Wilke, Xenia Zeiler, Lena Zühlke.

Greece: Alexander Karsiotis, Demetrios Th. Vassiliades.

India: P.K. Agrawal, Jamal Akhtar, T.K. Basu, Bettina Bäumer, T.K. Biswas, K. Chandramaouli, Charles Choreo, D.P. Dubey, Vidula Jayaswal, O.P. Kejariwal, Madhu Khanna, Ananda Krishna, Nita Kumar, Ranjit Makkuni, Bhanu Shankar Mehta, K.P. Mishra, A.K. Narain, D.B. Pandey, Vishwanath Pandey, Ajay Pandey 'Pinku', Shobita Punja, Vinay Sharma, Pratibha Singh, Pravin Rana, Ramesh K. Safaya, Ritwik Sanyal, Baidya Nath Saraswati, Geeti Sen, Vinay Sharma, C.D. Singh, Tripurari Shankar, (late) Dhirendra Singh, Purushottam Singh, (late) Ram Dular Singh, Ravi Singh, Shashank Singh, (late) Sukdeo Singh, Virendra Singh, Radhika Singha, M.N.P. Tiwari, Mohammad Toha, (late) Sushil Tripathi, Vibha Tripathi, Rabindra Vasavada, T.P. Verma, (late) L.P. Vidyarthi, Ishwar S. Vishwakarma.

Israel: Ran Aaronsohn, Assa Doron, Oded Maimon, Revital Shoshany, Michael Turner.

Italy: Paolo Baldeschi, Georgio Bonazzoli, Urmila Chakraborty, Alessandra Consolaro, Vrinda Dar, Donatella Dolcini, Gian Giuseppe Filippi, Giampietro Massella, Paolo Pecile, Gianni Pellegrini, Raoul Ravenna.

Japan: Masaaki Fukunaga, Shuji Funo, Shingo Hashimoto, Taigen Hashimoto, Hiroshi Ishida, Kenkichi Kanokogi, Misako Kanno, Ryujiro Kondo, Eiichi Matsumoto, Hisayoshi Miyamoto, Hiroko Nagasaki, Shuichi Nakayama, Toshiatsu Niki, Teiji Sakata, (late) Jiro Yonekura, Yoshiharu Tsuboi, Kiwamu Yanagisawa, Yuko Yokochi, Kotani Yoshihisa.

Mexico: David Lorenzen, Natalia Gil Torner.

Netherlands: Hans Bakker, Peter Bisschop, Marten Bode, Irma Schotsman.

Norway: Kaya Borchgrevink, Knut Jacobsen, Ute Hüsken, Jon Skarpeid, Herman Strøm, Hans Christie Bjønness.

Spain: Álvaro Enterría, Bernat Masferrer, Òscar Pujol.

Sweden: Daniel Andersson, Eric Clark, Gerhard Gustafsson, Per-Olof Fjällsby, Sidsel Hansson, Marc Katz, Katri Lisitzin, Kristina Lejonhud, Kristina Myrvold, Åke Sander, Göran Viktor Ståhle, Olla Wetterberg.

Switzerland: Pierre R. Dasen, Beat Niederer, Nicolas Yazgi.

UK: Chris Bayly, Dilip Chakrabarti, Mark Dyczkowski, Julia Hegewald, Roger Housden, Richard Lannoy, George Michell, Jonathan Parry, Simon Roberts, Mary Searle-Chatterjee, Marcus Trower, Hugh Dunford Wood.

USA: Kelley Alley, Ronald Barrett, Sunther & Elizabeth Chalier-Visuvalingam, Pramod Chandra, Vasudha Dalmia, Michael Dodson, Diana L. Eck, Sandria Freitag, Paul Golding, Martin Gray, Roxanne P. Gupta, Barbara Holdrege, Cynthia Humes, Sandy Huntington, Catherine Karnitis, Chaise LaDousa, Rob Linrothe, Deryck Lodrick, Timothy Lubin, John Malville, Bharat Mehra, William (Vijay) Pinch, Sumathi Ramaswamy, Arun Rewal, Richard Salomon, Richard Schechner, Mathew Schmalz, Pravina Shukla, Amita Sinha, Rakesh Solomon, Travis LaMar Smith, Pam Strayer, L. Eugene Thomas, Richard F. Young, Luke Whitmore.

Many of the above cited persons have already worked and published on Banaras, and the others were involved in promoting studies in various pursuits, directly or indirectly. But all of them have been helpful either by discourses or sending theirs and others publication on Banaras that are incorporated in this book.

During my post-graduate and research studies, I have been fortunate enough to have great teachers like (late) R.L. Singh (1917-2001) and Kashi N. Singh, who taught, inspired and encouraged to search and re-search the deeply rooted roots in the ancient traditions of India and their usefulness and relevance today and to follow this path like a 'crossing' (*tirthayatra*) — pilgrimage into the sacred territory of Kashi. A special thanks is due to my friend Rakesh Singh (Harmony Books), who during the last fifteen years helped and encouraged me in several ways to study and write about Banaras. Likewise my publisher friend Álvaro Enterría has been an invaluable source of inspiration at various stages during the last decade; his insight and visions are scattered in several pages of this book.

Acknowledgements

I convey my sincere gratitude to all personalities mentioned above, and others whose name I missed, who helped and influenced me in different ways at several occasions in preparing this book, which took three decades of slow progress. Nevertheless, when they will go through this book they will certainly find their own views and visions highlighted and scattered everywhere.

In a sense this book is a token of small tribute and dedication to my life-partner since the last thirty-eight years, my wife Manju (Usha), who suffered and tolerated consistently much negligence and carelessness from my end, but above all constantly encouraged me to proceed for the good cause of studying Banaras. It is because of her feminine spirit and deep human values that we call her '*Annapurna*', the primordial mother. I hope she will be happy to see this book and finally grant me excuses.

Rana P.B. Singh
New F - 7, Jodhpur Colony
Banaras Hindu University
Varanasi: 15 December 2008
Paush Krishna, light fortnight 3, Samvata 2065

Preface

BANARAS, THE WORLD OF SACRALITY

The sacred bond between person and place is a reciprocal process. The human relation with nature is realised primarily while narrating the place, understanding the place and becoming part of the 'spirit of place' (*genius loci*). The essence of 'place' consists of components like location, integration of nature and habitat, framework of circulation, system of land ethic, and the dynamic nature of its changing value in tandem with the relevant belief system. Place is the central nexus where we experience the harmonic relationship between man and nature. The process of understanding a place is a walk in search of interrelationship between the physical milieu and its metaphysical values.

We are surrounded not by sense objects but by images that are invisible to everybody else. The symbolic expression of place, the set of symbols that gives the people of a culture orientation in space and time, is pervasive in Hindu culture. We find in Hinduism that places like special sites or natural scenarios, rivers, mountains, grounds, sacred buildings and sacred cities replicate the forms and processes of the cosmos. In fact, a passion for placement is basic to Hindu thought. Sacred place as 'storied place' is eulogised in Hindu mythology, or oral epics, with divine connotation — there intersects myth and *terra firma*. Banaras is such a distinct place in India.

The uniqueness and distinctiveness of a place are the special aspects of a sacred place where *genius loci* and values of human environment are deeply rooted and maintained by means of *sacred ways* — as reflected in pilgrimages and associated performances and rituals. The quality of the sacred place depends upon the human context that has been shaped by it, with respect to memories, experiences, miracles and expectations. The city of Varanasi is unique in the architectural, artistic and religious expressions of traditional Indian culture and is a living example of this culture even today. The cultural heritage of the city is 'special' and is an exceptional testimony to living traditions, to be seen and to be believed, in religious faith, rituals and myriad festivals, traditional forms of worship and belief that are still practised, asceticism, spiritual exercises, education, music, dance, handicrafts and art forms that continue to be transmitted through generations.

The paraphrasing of Samuel Johnson's (1709-1784) remarks for London is well suited to the city of Banaras: "By seeing Banaras, one can see as much of life as the whole India can show". In fact, Banaras is an archetype of all India, but it is full of complexity and contrasts resulting too difficult in comprehension for those who stand outside the Hindu tradition. Those who love this city with heart and mind will share with me the metaphorically expressions in terms of capturing space, time and tradition. Since the city of Banaras records a long experience in history as centre of pilgrimages and mystics, everywhere the *puranic* literature is given prime importance.

The old city centre and other important cultural and religious places are today enclosed within the modern city and are seriously threatened by pressures of modernisation and development. The religious, philosophical and cultural heart of India, Varanasi, or Banaras as it is popularly called, or Kashi as the ancient centre of the city was called in the religious context, is the most important pilgrimage destination of the Hindus. The Sarnath zone, which is within the wider city precincts, is extremely important for Buddhists the world over. The culture as seen and lived here is a rare heritage asset for Indians and for the citizens of the world, contributing to the cultural, philosophical and intellectual knowledge of Indian culture and the cultural community of the world.

Since the first stage of human evolution, the idea of mystical power of place has been part of human consciousness. The identification of a place as sacred is never essentially one of individual recognition; actually, the place is never 'chosen' by humans, it is merely discovered by them. In some way or another the 'spirit of place' attracts and reveals itself to a human, and that is how he or she merely 'finds' it, though the process of discovery becomes easier when one follows the *spiritual path*.

Humans have used all their senses to search for places where divine beings manifest their power. Several such stories are mentioned in ancient mythologies. We learn from history that archaic people sought meaningful ways to link reality and psychic feeling in order "to combine empirical facts with imaginative fancies and to think in rhythm with their feelings and feel in rhythm with their thinking" (Herberger 1972). Going back to history in a search for holistic theory we find the idea of *theoria* — an ancient way of grasping experience that involves all the senses and feelings and ultimately how humans express themselves: *human talk*. The will to sacred journey involves a surrender of self to the divine, a kind of soul healing.

The key is a small thing, really, but its power is great. The key is genius loci. To every place, there is a key — direct communication with the inherent meanings and messages of the place. When the key is lost, the place is forgotten. Mythologies, folk tales, continuity of cultural traditions, the quest to understand what is beyond — all are the facets of crossings. In Indian culture the crossings are the tirthas ('sacredscapes') where one transforms oneself from the physical to metaphysical. To cross is to be transformed. On the ladder to cross from one side — physical — to the other end — metaphysical — the sacred places serve as rungs. The setting of the proper ladder relies on a secret principle — that the vertical can be attained only by strict attention to the horizontal. The ladder provides the way of ascent through care and deeper quest. A spiritual walk is the ladder, sacred ways are the steps, and human understanding is the destination. Thinking together is a new vision. Going together is a new start. Walking together is a real march. Realising together is the final destination — enlightenment. Without a pilot, one gets lost in madness, illness, or death. Without a way a pilgrim or traveller gets lost in the route. The way is a 'spirit' — spirit is an eternal sight for passing on the path in the right order.

By spiritual walk, can we regain certain understandings that have been forgotten? Why not? These understandings would help us to a certain extent regain our balance inwardly (spiritually, and psychologically) and outwardly in terms of ecological cosmology. This book is an attempt to serve as a key, a way and a companion on this march towards crossing and soul healing.

The devout Hindus say that the three bridge-pillars interlinking the earth to the heaven are Prayaga (Allahabad), Kashi (Varanasi) and Gaya. This can be revealed through the experiences of their distinct images. They express this as Prayaga munde (by tonsure), Kashi dhundhe (by search in the labyrinth lanes), and Gaya pinde (by offering rice-balls to ancestors). Through these steps one can get liberation. This triadic framework of India's cultural tradition is narrated in this companion book of spiritual walking. There are many ways of expressing the vividness and contrasts of Kashi Kshetra (territory), its cultural setting and its exposures. This publication is a humble attempt to present almost all the important sites and scenes in and around Banaras, described with a view to experiencing the deeper meanings and messages. Through the present one can feel the 'process of becoming', which reminds us that:

> The future of Present is in the past,
> The future of Past is in the future,
> The future of Future is in the present;
> Ultimately, Present makes both past and future.

It is our wish that you and we will either meet in the lanes of Banaras, or, even better, that we will perform co-pilgrimage in and around Banaras while walking on the cosmic circuit.

A call for Co-pilgrimage

Banaras: where 'always ready' (Bana) is the 'juice of life' (ras)! This 'Life-juice' flows in plenitude here in different colours, varying tones, multiple textures and layers, diverse situations, contrasting conditions, etc. It is the blending or "complex mixing" of these, which makes up the mosaic of culture known as Banaras, the City of Lord Shiva.

Shiva's liquid energy flows in the form of the Ganga river, and he is represented in the iconographic form of the *linga*. The residents of Banaras believe that Lord Shiva and his associates live invisibly in the rhythm of the city, but that only the enlightened one can experience and reveal this.

Once Mark Twain famously commented (1897: 480): "Banaras is older than history, older than tradition, older even than legend and looks twice as old as all of them put together". Banaras is not the story of bricks and stones; it is in fact a living history in itself. A son of the soil and an experiential writer (Kamal Gupt 1986: 79) describes the city metaphorically in terms of capturing space, time and tradition:

> Banaras either of the past, or of the present, and would be of the future, was a historically important city of the past, and is of the present, and would be of the future. Banaras is not only a city, but also a culture in itself. Looking this city is easy, recognition difficult. Touching it is easy, capturing difficult. Making portrait is easy, transformation on the mental canvas difficult. In this way, in spite of easiness in outlook, in appearance it is a city of dignity, infinity and complexity.

Describing the historicity and inherent power of preserving continuity, Sherring (1868: 7-8) writes:

Twenty-five centuries ago, at the least, it was famous. When Babylon was struggling with Nineveh for supremacy, when Tyre was planting her colonies, when Athens was growing in strength, before Rome had become known, or Greece had contended with Persia, or Cyrus had added lustre to the Persian monarchy, or Nebuchandnezzar had captured Jerusalem, and the inhabitants of Judaea had been carried into captivity, she had already risen to greatness, if not to glory. Nay, she may have heard of the fame of Solomon, and have sent her ivory, her apes, and her peacocks to adorn his palaces; while partly with her gold he may have overlaid the Temple of the Lord. Not only is Benares remarkable for her venerable age, but also for the vitality and vigour which, so far as we know, she has constantly exhibited. While many cities and nations have fallen into decay and perished, her sun has never gone down; on the contrary, for long ages past it has shone with almost meridian splendour. Her illustrious name has descended from generation to generation, and has ever been a household word, venerated and beloved by the vast Hindu family.

From the 11th to the 17th centuries Muslim invaders destroyed the city at least four times. However, it survived and was repeatedly revived; the sites and holy spots were re-searched, the monuments were re-paired and re-built and the spirit was again re-awakened to re-unite with the primordial. In this way the eternity of life has survived in spite of several 'superimpositions', or attempts to submerge it.

The multiple personalities of Kashi are projected as:

City of light, where every day the sunrise reflects on the crescent moon-shaped Ganga River, and finally illuminates the river front;
City of delight, where high degrees of pleasure and joy are experienced;
City of plight, where ups and downs always make life full of frequent and sudden changes;
City of might, which possesses the power of feeling and attraction;
City of sight, which allows clear vision to emerge where humanity and divinity meet;
City of right, where all the human deeds are righteously assessed by the patron deity Shiva, who then blesses and curses accordingly.

23

The *Kashi Khanda* (35.10) says, "The Ganga River, Lord Shiva, and the divine city of Kashi make the Trinity of grace and perfect bliss". The Trinity is symbolised by the three hillocks as the three forks of Shiva's trident on which the city exists, viz. Omkareshvara in the north, Vishveshvara in the central part, and Kedareshvara in the south. Blessed by Lord Shiva, Bhagiratha brought the goddess Ganga to the earth, she who provides vital life to Kashi as well as to the wide range of the plains. The mythical figure Divodasa became a divine king of the city, but finally handed it over to Shiva. Lord Shiva left Mount Kailash and settled here in a variety of forms. There are more than three thousand forms of Shiva *lingas*. By Shiva's power the city has grown as a seat of knowledge. Over fifty Sanskrit schools are still preserving the ancient traditions. Many other educational institutions have grown up here as well. Presently there are seven universities or university-level institutions, viz. the Banaras Hindu University, Sampurnananda Sanskrit University, Mahatma Gandhi Kashi Vidyapith University, Central Institute of Higher Tibetan Studies, Udai Pratap (autonomous) P.G. College, Agrasen (autonomous) P.G. College, and Jamia Salfia Darul-Islamia, an Islamic university. There are also hundreds of active cultural institutes and religious establishments, traditional schools, music, dance and art forms that have spread to the world, local artisan and handicraft products in textiles, wood and metal work. The city has always played a special role, at least since the 5th century BCE in promoting education — debates and dialectics, both religious and spiritual — traditional medicine (*ayurveda*), yoga, astrology. Further, the pattern of spatial transposition of holy sites is unique in the sense that all the important holy centres of India were replicated here before the 12th century. Varanasi can, in fact, be considered a living symbolisation and a living expression of Indian culture and traditions in all its religious rituals, in its multiethnic artistic traditions, in its architectural treasures, in its life-expressions, in its particular relationship with life and death, in its traditional schools where Sanskrit and the sacred texts are still taught and in its multicultural and multi-linguist population.

The spiritual magnetism of Banaras had attracted the Buddha here in the 6th century BCE to 'Turn the Wheel of Law'. By the turn of the 3rd century BCE, the great Buddhist king Ashoka had built a monastery township that flourished till the 11th century CE. Later, due to destruction by the Muslim invaders and by fire it turned into ruins. Now, after quite some time, the restored Sarnath has become a place of pilgrimage for Buddhists, and a place of spiritual tourism for others.

In Banaras city alone, there are over 3300 Hindu shrines and temples, about 1388 Muslim shrines and mosques, 12 churches, 3 Jain temples, 9 Buddhist temples, 3 Sikh temples (*gurudvaras*) and several other sacred sites and places. This is the only place in the world where such a huge number of Hindu and Muslim sacred places co-exist.

The city is also known as the 'City of Good Death' and the place where ancestral souls can gain final release. The fires of cremation remind one of eternity, and Lord Shiva whispers the sacred verse (*mantra*) of liberation to the souls of the dead. Along the *ghats* (stairways) pilgrims perform ancestral rites to the Ganga and give donations, a rite by which they are said to get 'reservation' in Shiva's heavenly abode - not only for their own soul, but also for the wandering souls of their ancestors. For the living there are many varieties of monasteries where one can satisfy his/her spiritual quest.

The 84 ghats along the arc-shaped Ganga symbolise the integration of the 12 signs of the zodiac (division of time) and the 7 sheaths of the body or the 7 layers of the atmosphere (division of space), thus 12 x 7 = 84. Among these, there are five of special merit: Asi, Dashashvamedha, Manikarnika, Panchaganga and Adi Keshava. Yet the whole stretch of the Ganga provides shelter and means of livelihood to thousands of people, such as boatmen, *ghatias* (priests at the *ghats*), seller of ritual items and flowers, and tourists too. The sunrise at the bank of the Ganga provides a scene of transforming colourscape. Every morning around twenty thousand people take a holy dip, but the bathers number near to a million on special occasions like the full moon in October-November (*Karttika Purnima*) and on solar and lunar eclipses.

The natural setting, the spirit of place, and the continuity of cultural traditions have all blended together to create and preserve a unique lifestyle known as Banarasi. This lifestyle has manifested itself in a musical tradition known as the Banaras Gharana (style). Many great musicians and performing artists have been born here and still regularly return to visit and to perform their art for the public as tribute to the spirit of the soil. Layers of time and traditions are superimposed one upon the other, but the essence of the life has maintained its continuity. Recently some of the old festivals have been revived in the original style, despite some modern touches.

Chapter 1

GEOGRAPHICAL PERSONALITY:

SETTING, NOMENCLATURE, HUMANSCAPE AND RELIGIOUS LANDSCAPE

> "Our everyday world is, from the outset, an inter-subjective world of culture. It is intersubjective because we live in it as men among other men, bound to them through common influence and work, understanding others and being an object of understanding for others. It is a world of culture because, from the outset, the life-world is a universe of significance to us..."
>
> Alfred Schütz (1962, vol. 1: 133).

Background

Vārāṇasī, popularly called Kāśī (Kashi) or Banāras (wrongly spelt as Benares in the colonial period), known as the Cultural Capital, Heritage city of India and one of the oldest living cities of the world, records a continuous settlement history since *ca* 1000 BCE. However, the present city has grown mostly during the early 18th century. Varanasi acquired status of a 'million+ city' (as Urban Agglomeration[1]) in 1991 and recorded a population of 1,231,220 in 2001, being thus ranked 23rd in the hierarchy of million+ cities in India according to population. The city's population consists predominantly of Hindus (63%), a substantial number of Muslims (30%) and other religious groups. The main city spreads over an area of 84.55 km². Additionally, everyday about 40,000 commuters visit the city, which increases to 60,000 during festive seasons. There are *ca* 3,300 Hindu sanctuaries, and 1,388 Muslim shrines and mosques (more than in any city in the world). The existence of 4 universities and 3 deemed universities, 150

---

[1] According to the Census of India (2001): "An Urban Agglomeration is a continuous urban spread constituting a town and its adjoining urban outgrowths (OGs) or two or more physically contiguous towns together and any adjoining urban outgrowths of such towns. Examples of OGs are railway colonies, university campuses, port areas, etc., that may come up near a city or statutory town outside its statutory limits but within the revenue limits of a village or villages contiguous to the town or city. Each such individual area by itself may not satisfy the minimum population limit to qualify it to be treated as an independent urban unit but may deserve to be clubbed with the town as a continuous urban spread."

Muslim schools, *ca* 100 Sanskrit *pathashalas* (traditional schools), and 50 Inter and Degree colleges make the place a 'City of Culture and Learning'. The vividness and multiplicity, the diversity and unity are easily envisioned in its religion, culture, society and economy — altogether making a cultural mosaic, in which festivities and performances play a major role.

Banaras is not the story of bricks and stones; it is in fact a living history in itself (Singh and Rana 2002: 21). No other city of the world is like Varanasi, not even in India. Its place in Hindu mythology is virtually unrivalled. The city got its name from the two river-tributaries Varana and Asi, meeting the Ganga in the north and south, respectively. The *Kashi Khanda* (of *Skanda Purana*; 30.17-23) refers that the two rivers were created by the gods and placed in position to guard against the entrance of evil; one was named 'The Sword' (*Asi*) and the other 'The Averter' (*Varana*). The land lying between them is the holiest of all holy places in India. According to the *Vamana Purana* (II.26-29), the Varana and the Asi originated from the body of the primordial Purusha ('Man') at the beginning of time itself (cf. Eck 1982: 27). "The Varana issued from the right foot of the cosmic giant and the Asi issued from its left foot; the peer of the sacred land between these two rivers does not exist in heaven, earth, and the netherworld." That is why Varanasi is known as the 'Eternal City'.

Situated on the river Ganga in its middle reaches, it has always been a great centre of learning, religion, art and culture, attracting people from all over the world — rich and poor, men and women, young and old, and even sick and dead. Hindus perceive Banaras as such a sacred place that if one leaves this world in Varanasi then his or her soul will undoubtedly go to heaven.

1. Geographical Setting

Varanasi is located in the middle Ganga valley along the elevated crescent-shaped bank at the left of the Ganga River. Being located on a high ground, the city has rarely witnessed devastating floods, which the other cities along the river Ganga experience from time to time. By railway it is well connected with New Delhi (764 km), Kolkata (Calcutta, 677 km) and Mumbai (1476 km); it is also connected by roads and air services with different parts of India (Fig. 2).

The city of Varanasi is the headquarters of the district (Fig. 3) of the same name (Varanasi), which has been segmented into a six-tier hierarchy for administration and planning programme (cf. Table 1; see Fig. 19). Lower areal unit is included in the next higher areal unit.

28

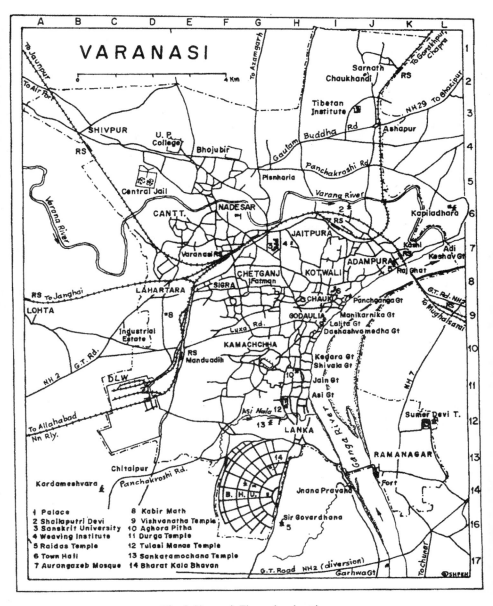

Fig. 2. Varanasi: The regional setting.

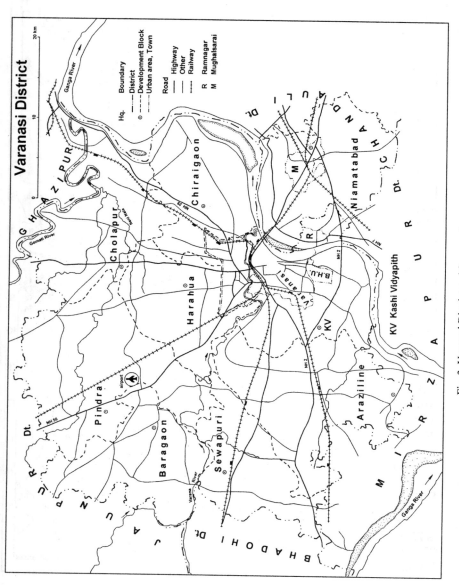

Fig. 3. Varanasi District and Surroundings.

Table 1. Varanasi, Areal Units: Extension, Area and Population, 2001.

Se	Varanasi, V – (Areal Units)	Areal extent, Lat-Long		Area, km²	Population, 2001	
		Latitude, N °	Longitude, E °		Total	% of District
1	Varanasi City, **VC**	25° 14'– 25° 22'	82° 56'– 83° 03'	83.60	1,029,961	32.72
2	V City Municipal Corporation, **VMC**	25° 14'– 25° 22'	82° 56'– 83° 03'	86.51	1,092,445	34.70
3	V Urban Agglomeration, **VUA**	25° 14'– 25° 23.5'	82° 56'– 83° 03'	115.27	1,231,220	38.49
4	V Master Plan (Opera- tive) Area, **VMP-O**	25° 13'– 25° 24'	82° 54'– 83° 04'	144.94	1,278,934	40.63
5	V Master Plan (Projec- ted) Area, **VMP-P**	25° 13'– 25° 24.3'	82° 54'– 83° 05'	179.27	1,321,568	41.98
6	V Development Region, **VDR**	25° 08'– 25° 30'	82° 48'– 83° 13'	477.34	2,483,750	78.90
7	Varanasi District (as a whole)	25° 08'– 25° 35'	82° 40'– 83° 15'	1,564.83	3,147,927	100.00

(Sources: Various reports of the Census, Statistical Office, Varanasi;
collated by the author)

The extended urban area delimited by the Census as 'Varanasi Urban Agglomeration' (VUA) consists of ten urban sub-units, viz. a Municipal Corporation (MC), an Out Growth (OG), four Contiguous Towns (CT), two Notified Areas (NA), one Municipal Board (MB), and one Cantonment Board (CB). According to the Comprehensive twenty year Master Plan of Varanasi: 1991-2011, the Varanasi Development Region (VDR) consists of the six areas (cf. Table 7; and see Fig. 19). For the 2011 Master Plan the VUA (Fig. 4) is planned to expand over an area of 144.94 sq. km.

Topography. The average height of the city from mean sea level is 77 m which is around 72 m in the south along the Asi stream, and 83.84 m at the high ground near the confluence of the Varana to the Ganga river in the north (known as Rajghat plateau). This plateau is 15.24 m high above the surrounding areas, being bounded by an abrupt

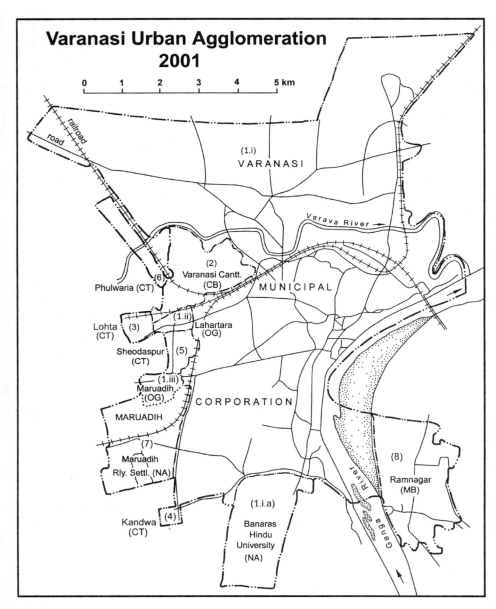

Fig. 4. Varanasi Urban Agglomeration, 2001: Areal units

break of slope with a cliff. The land away from the Ganga slopes towards the Varana, which meets to the Ganga near Adi Keshav Ghat that records a height of 73.17 m. The level of the land gradually drops down towards the interior from the crescent shaped kankar (lime concretion) ridge, which is bounded on the west roughly by the present Asi-Raj Ghat route via Godaulia and Chowk. The average elevation of the high kankar ridge is over 76.21 m (Singh, R.L. 1955: 18). The land hemmed in between the Vidyapith-Durgakund road on the east and Grand Trunk road on the west forms a low divide between the Ganga and Varana and is still studded with numerous tanks (Singh, Pramod 1985: 10). The river Varana, west of Chaukaghat meanders through a low land subject to floods but the land north of the Varana rises gradually. The nature and the character of the bank of the Ganga River has made the position of Banaras so stable and enviable, making it one amongst the few cities of the world which shows little shifting in its site. The city proper is built on a high ridge of kankar that forms the left bank of the Ganga for a distance of 5.7 km, being quite above normal flood level. To a large extent no doubt the city owes its importance to its peculiar site.

Flood. Flood is a common feature of both the rivers, Varana and Ganga. Though most of the area of the city is above the normal flood level of the Ganga, yet at the time of peak flood half of the city comes under water. It is obvious from the records of the peak flood occurrences in the city that in 1916, 1948, 1972 and 1982 the flood level reached to 73.93 m, 73.2 m, 73.5 m and 73.1 m, respectively. In these peak years flood caused a great devastation in the city. The minimum flood level recorded so far was 62.4 m; and the danger limit of flood level is 71.26 m. During the last severe flood, 25 August to 5 September 1982, the floodwater of swirling Ganga spread in the crowded market of Godaulia, reaching up to Gurubagh. During this period electricity supply was cut off in the affected areas, and all the educational institutions were closed for a month. The whole life of the city came to a standstill. Disposal of the dead bodies became a problem in the city as Manikarnika Ghat, where cremations take place, was submerged under 7.6 m of water (Singh, Pramod 1985: 11).

Climate. The city enjoys sub-tropical monsoon climate, recording three distinct seasons: the cold from November to February, the hot from March to mid-June, and the rainy from mid-June to September, while October is regarded as a transitional month (cf. Table 2). The highest monthly temperature is recorded in May, varying between 32°C and 41°C. With the advent of March, temperature rises very rapidly till the maximum is reached in May. Here the temperature rises over 41.5°C, reaching highest up to 45.4 in 2008. The mean monthly temperature in March is 24.3°C.

Relative humidity is quite high during the main monsoon months (July to September) amounting to between 82% and 85%, while in August it reaches to 88%. During December to January relative humidity ranges between 75% and 80% due to the approach of western disturbances. In late April and May when hot and dry winds (*loo*) start to blow, these keep the mean relative humidity sufficiently low and it never exceeds over 50%. Severe dust storms, called locally as '*andhi*' and the gusty-dusty hot wind (*loo*) are among the chief weather phenomena in the area during the dry summer months. The velocity of the wind in this season rises up to more than 50 km/per hr.

The monsoon reaches Varanasi by about 15 June. The mean monthly temperature falls below 33.7°C, however it continues to be above 29.05°C. The summer monsoon retreats by the end of September and the sky becomes clear once again. The temperature begins to fall after the middle of October, and days are warmer than nights. The normal annual rainfall in Varanasi city is around 1000 mm. The annual number of rainy days is 48 days, out of which 42 days occur during the monsoon season (June to September), recording 84 percent of the total annual rainfall. The highest rainfall recorded in recent history was 1845.06 mm in 1948 when flood level also reached to 73.2 m crossing the danger limit of 71.26 m. On average seven days of thunderstorms are usually recorded during July-August. The maximum visibility is recorded in March and April while minimum is in winter. Annual maximum visibility is 4-10 km, which is recorded for 143 days, while minimum visibility is up to half km recorded for a week. Visibility is an important factor in traffic and tourist movement (cf. Singh and Rana 2002: 27).

Table 2. Varanasi: Climatic Characteristics, 2006.

No.	Month	Temperature, C°					Relative Humidity %	Total month relative rainfall	Air pressure (mb)	Mean wind speed (km/h)
		Max.	Min.	Average	Highest of the month	Lowest of the month				
1.	Jan	21.83	6.49	14.16	28.0	2.4	88.74	0.54	1007.46	2.3
2.	Feb	27.00	9.61	18.30	32.3	3.9	74.61	0.97	1004.72	2.9
3.	Mar	32.59	14.00	23.30	37.8	5.4	56.39	1.20	1003.10	3.7
4.	Apr	37.16	19.81	28.48	43.5	15.5	39.93	2.90	999.89	4.0
5.	May	38.61	25.37	31.99	44.0	15.4	62.00	43.50	994.25	4.4
6.	Jun	34.97	25.83	30.40	39.6	23.9	79.00	267.50	990.23	4.9
7.	July	32.86	25.65	29.25	34.8	23.7	87.55	307.00	990.50	4.0
8.	Aug	33.55	25.79	29.67	35.6	23.0	88.92	322.70	993.05	3.3
9.	Sept	30.50	23.51	27.00	34.9	21.2	89.80	302.40	996.30	3.0
10.	Oct	33.71	19.87	26.79	35.6	16.1	81.06	0.00	1001.02	1.7
11.	Nov	29.36	16.17	22.77	33.4	9.4	79.80	0.00	1005.40	1.6
12.	Dec	25.63	7.53	16.58	28.1	5.6	81.16	0.00	1006.17	1.7
	Monthly average	31.48	18.30	24.89	35.63	13.79	68.35	104.06	999.34	3.1

(Source: Dept. of Geophysics, Banaras Hindu University, Varanasi)

Considering the weather condition, the winter (November to early March) is recommended for visiting Banaras City and the region. During the period between December and January fog is a common phenomenon. The period between January and February records the finest weather when the temperature varies between 13°C and 17°C (cf. Table 2). Sometimes when there is a snowfall in the northwest Himalaya the wind blowing down is particularly cold and this makes the temperature fall to around 5°C. Relative humidity reaches a maximum of 80% at 08.30 hrs and minimum to 24% at 17.30 hrs. Occasionally, the area faces severe hailstorms in the winter, more commonly in February. The weather is generally mild and dry with light and pure air and azure-blue sky. The patches of stratocumulus clouds are driven away from the sky. The serenity of weather is, however, broken by the passage of 'western disturbances', which give some rainfall in the winter.

2. Nomenclature and related Tales

The city of Varanasi has been designated by different names at different times in different contexts. Observes Eck (1983: 25): "The names express the various powers and attributes of the city and reveal the dimensions of its sacred authority". Of course, the two names Kashi and Varanasi are the most common and were in use in early antiquity. By the turn of the 2nd century CE the words Kashi and Varanasi became synonymous for the holy city. However, as a reference to an administrative territory only Kashi had been used. To make it clear, in the Puranic era the word Kashipuri was used to denote the city of Kashi (cf. Dubey, 1985/ 1993).

Kashi. The word Kashi means 'concentration of cosmic light'. Kashi is the oldest name and was first used in the Atharva Veda (V.22.4), a ca 15th century BCE text: "Kashi shines and illumines the universe. Kashi makes moksha (liberation) dawn on everybody by giving wisdom". In the period of the Mahabharata Kashi refered to the sacred city and its territory (cf. Altekar, 1937: 58-59), which is similar to the present area of Kashi Kshetra delineated by the Panchakroshi Yatra circuit. Kashi is also interpreted as a derivation of Kasha, who was the 7th king of the earliest known dynasty ruling over Kashi, which would have been thus named after him. According to another version, it is said that the area was dominated by a tall silver flowering grass, called *kasha* (Saccharum spontaneum), and that is how it received the name Kashi. The *Kashi Khanda* (26.27) mentions that Shiva, being settled on the three high peaks in Varanasi, spreads light all around the city, thus the name Kashi. The rays of the early-morning sun spread across the river and strike the high-banked face of this city, which devout Hindus call Kashi — the Luminous, the City of Light.

Varanasi. This is the capital city of the historical past, lying along the western bank of the Ganga river. In all the puranic literature and treatises this name has been popularly eulogised in this context (cf. Sircar 1967: 104, 106-107). The city lying between the Varana river in the north and the Asi stream in the south is known as Varanasi (Varana + Asi). A myth establishes that the two rivers Varana and Asi are respectively originated from the right and left legs of Vishnu lying at

Prayaga (Allahabad). According to a myth of the 15th century, the two rivers were created by the gods and placed in position to guard against the entrance of evil. The northern one was named 'The Averter' (Varana) and the southern river was named 'The Sword' (Asi). In the early Puranas the Varana river is called Varanavati or Varanasi, and the old city would have then got its name as it was settled along the river.

Banaras. The Buddhist literature like the *Jatakas* frequently referred to Varanasi as Banarasi or Banaras. This is in fact a Pali version that became more popular during the period of the Mughal emperor Akbar (1556-1605) as reported by Abdul Fazl, the court historian of the emperor (cf. *Ain-e-Akbari*, II.169, III.333). The name Banaras is still frequently used by the masses. In the colonial rule the British misperceived the name and spelt it as Benares, Bunarus, and Benaras, etc. In both Muslim and British India, the city was called 'Banaras' (cf. Singh and Rana 2002: 29). One of the etymologies explains the word Banaras as: '*Bana*', 'readymade', and '*ras*', 'the juice of life'; thus Banaras means 'the place where juice of life is always readymade' — high and low, both. The bad image goes back to the 12th century CE. In an epithet Hemachandra (*Kumaracharita*, 3.59) referred to this place as 'seat of thieves' (*thaganam sthanam*). A similar viewpoint was held by Pt. Damodara (*Ukativyakti Prakarana*, 38.28-30), who says that there was no dearth of thieves in the city during the 12th century.

Avimukta. According to the *puranic* literature (e.g. MtP, 179.54; SKP, IV.26-27; SP, IV.22.21) Lord Shiva said "Because I never forsake it, nor let it go, this great place is therefore known as Avimukta ('never forsaken')". This refers to the myth that the city was never abandoned, even in the cosmic dissolution, and additionally suggests that the spirit of the city itself is the bestower of liberation to everybody, irrespective of caste, creed, hierarchy or class (cf. KuP, I.29.59-60; SP, IV.23.21-22). Even at present pilgrims follow the sacred journey of the Avimukta territory. The name Avimukta is often used to emphasise the fact that people should never leave this place. According to one of the myths the Sun advised Shiva to dwell in this city and he conferred the name Avimukta upon Banaras. Today it has fallen into disuse, and it is only referred to in the mythologies.

Anandavana. The *Kashi Rahasya* (6.40, 14.39) mentions that Shiva himself explains: "My *lingas* are everywhere there, like little sprouts arisen out of sheer bliss" (also see, *Skanda Purana*, VI.26.35). Thus it is called *the Forest of Bliss* (Anandavana, or Anandakanana). The remnants of the five old forests are now preserved as the names of the neighbourhoods. The *puranic* sources describe the 'Forest of Bliss' as a garden paradise, sprinkled with the waters of the heavenly Ganga. Here everything exists and bestows bliss. Therefore all those who crave for supreme bliss or *mukti* (liberation), and all varieties of living beings, desire to come and live here. The fascination and the enchantment of Varanasi goes far back in time and are deeply rooted in the hearts of devout Hindus. The city today is so dense that it is difficult to imagine it as a Forest of Delight. The name actually refers to this place in the idyllic times of its mythological beginnings.

Rudravasa. The 'City of Shiva'. From ancient time the city has been known as the resort of Lord Shiva. Varanasi is first of all Rudravasa because Rudra (Shiva) lives in and protects it (SKP, IV.11.114, 21.97, 81.8). In the common feelings of the people, in Varanasi everything is pervaded by Shiva, even the pebbles and dust are saturated with him: "*Kashi ke Kankara Shiva Shankara*" (the very pebbles of Kashi are Shiva). This prevalence of Shiva in Varanasi naturally made it Shankarapuri ('the abode of Shiva'; KP, I.28.61). It is also believed that everyone who lives here is a form of Shiva (*Rudrarupina*). Says the *Kashi Khanda* (30.102b), "a man who adores all those stationed in Kashi belonging to the different castes and the different stages of life with great faith and the belief that they are the Lord himself, attains the benefit of the direct worship of Rudra-Shiva".

Mahasmashana. 'The Great Cremation Ground'. The whole of Kashi is a cremation ground. Shiva is the controller and divinity of the cremation place. The *Skanda Purana* (IV.30.103-104) explains the word as follows: '*Maha*', great, '*sma*' means a corpse, and '*shana*' means final rest; when the dissolution of the universe comes, even the great beings lie here as corpses and therefore this place is called *Mahasmashana*". In Puranic myth Lord Shiva said: "Avimukta is a famous crematorium; assuming the form of Death-god at this place I destroy the world" (cf. PdP, III.33.14, and KuP, I.29.27). It is also said that the great (*maha*) five gross elements (*bhutas*, viz. earth, water, air, fire, and sky) all live here like corpses, hence the name. Even at present there are two cremation ghats along the Ganga river, i.e. Harishachandra and Manikarnika. All together, more than 38,000 corpses are cremated here in a year. People from different parts of India come here to die with a view to receiving relief from transmigration. Here death is an auspicious event, almost a festival.

During the colonial British rule the popular name Banaras was distorted as 'Benares', or 'Benaras', and it is something of a surprise to Indians that people in the West still prefer to spell it in its distorted form. This shows either their ignorance, unwillingness to accept the facts of history, or maybe their vested interest to disrespect Indian culture. By the efforts of Dr Sampurnananda, the then Chief Minister of Uttar Pradesh, the Govt. of India on 24th May 1956 has officially restored and declared the name of the city as 'Varanasi'. A railway station in the northern outskirts of the city now represents Kashi. Nevertheless millions of pilgrims and devout Hindus in all parts of the country continue to call the holy city as Kashi.

3. Sacred Territories: layers

The manifestation of a transcendental element may be translated into a parallelism between the *macrocosmos* (cosmos/ heaven) and the *microcosmos* (temple/ human body). In between these two polarities one can also perceive a mediating spatial-sacred structure given by the (built) environment that is called *mesocosmos*. The holy city of Varanasi is considered as a *mesocosmos* in which the human complexity of the *microcosmos* and the cosmic-temporal stability of the *macrocosmos* meet. This is visualised and well exemplified by the five pilgrimage circuits where all the above three layers of the cosmos are represented, and merged into a form of *mandala*. Varanasi is one of the celestial-archetypal cities where the material environment expresses the parallelism between *macro-*, *meso-*, and *micro-* cosmos, regrouping them to form a sacred spatial system and link all the sacred sites and divinities and their shrines by a path or route (Fig. 5). The five pilgrimage circuits of Varanasi (Kashi) symbolise the parallelism of the five heavenly gross elements (i.e. sky, earth, air, water, and fire) with the five basic parts of the human body (i.e. head, legs, face, blood, and heart, respectively), transcendental power and the associated sheath and the corresponding sacred number of shrines/images on the route (cf. Singh and Rana 2006: 46-48).

The location of shrines and deities along the sacred routes is depicted over a cognitive pilgrimage map as *mandala* prepared by Kailashnath Sukul, head of a renowned family in the Kalabhairav mohalla of the city, in CE 1876 (cf. Fig. 6); it measures 79 x 92 cm and is printed on cloth, using four engraved stone slabs as printing blocks (cf. Pieper, 1975: 215). Of course, many of these goddesses and their shrines are described in different contexts too; their full and systematic listing is given in the Khh (72.3-13 and 97-99). Of course this pilgrimage map is not a scaled map, however it records a very close correspondence with the modern map based on topographical survey (see Fig. 5), which obviously shows a positive correspondence.

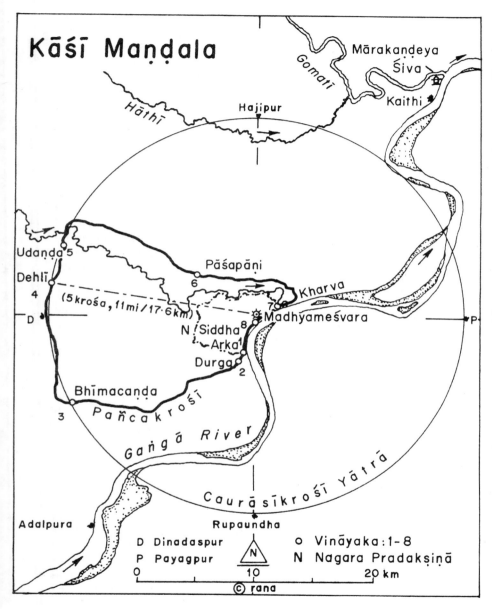

Fig. 5. Kashi Mandala: Spatial View

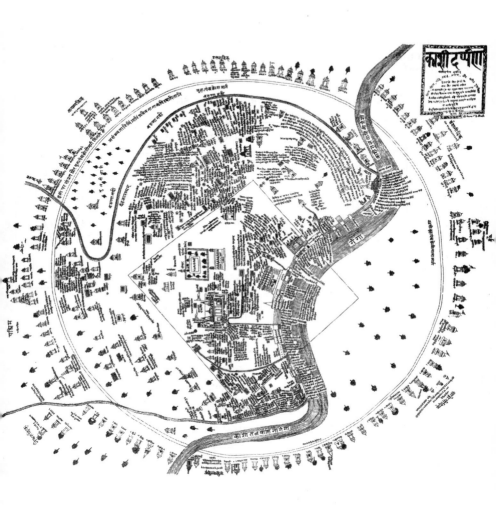

Fig. 6. Kashi Mandala (cognitive view):
Kashi Darpana, after Kailashnath Sukul 1875.

4. Growth of Population

It is a difficult task to estimate the population of the ancient past, however by following the crude method of geometric progression and adjusting the results in accordance to the historical and literary sources, a tentative outline of population growth of Varanasi is presented here (Table 3).

Table 3. Varanasi: Projected Population, 1500 BCE – CE 2001.

Year	Population	Growth rate, %
2001	1,231,220	82.5
1901	215,223	12.9
1800	190,583	12.1
1700	170,966	13.7
1623	110,304	– 26.6
1600	150,280	12.2
1500	133,965	11.1
1400	120,540	11.0
1300	108,625	10.7
1200	98,105	11.2
1100	88,245	69.8
1000	51,960	69.8
CE 500	30,595	62.6
0	18,815	54.8
BCE 500	12,150	48.5
1000	8,180	46.1
1500	5,600	—

The life of courtesans in Varanasi as described in Damodara's *Kuttanimatam* (*ca* 735-810), written in CE 8th century, refers the peaceful and harmonic life pattern. After the passage of time, during the rules of Pratihara (9th century) and Chedis (10th century) again the city had flourished. During CE 01-1000 the city recorded a very high growth of population. From about 8,000 inhabitants in 1000 BCE it went up to about 90,000 in CE 1100. By this period the city had extended south-wards and got divided into many neighbourhoods. Of course, in CE 1013 Ahmed Nialtagin invaded the city and demolished many temples, however again during the 12th century under the Gahadavalas (1137-1183) the city recorded peace and growth. But in 1194 Qutb-uddin Aibak invaded the city and demolished the temple of Vishvanatha as well as the main Vishnu temple. The city was invaded again in 1197 by Sultan Ahmed, and in 1248 by Mohammad Ghori, followed by destruction of temples by Firoz Shah in 1375. According to earlier estimates, by CE 1300 the population of Banaras had already crossed 100,000 persons. In 1526 after defeating Ibrahim Lodi, Babur also demolished many temples in Varanasi.

In 1623 the city had badly suffered to plague; and according to literary sources one-third of the population had died (cf. Motichand 1985: 210). This was the time when the great *bhakta*-poet Tulasi died. According to an estimate the population of the city in 1600 was around 150,280, but it fell down to 110,304 in 1623 (a loss of 26.6%). However, in the following years the population recorded an unprecedented growth — by 1700 reaching to 170,966 (cf. Table 3).

The rapid growth and recovery of population had its root in history as Varanasi was an important river port and the cotton, silk (tussore) and other manufactures of the city were famous (Kosambi 1970: 123), all which attracted a large mass of population to settle here. The city of Varanasi records an enormous diversity in urban economics and urban culture during Mughal rule; it was also a major manufac-turing and commercial centre (cf. Hambay 1982: 438).

In 1700 primate cities like Delhi, Agra and Lahore had lost their regional status, but Varanasi and Lucknow had achieved a comparable degree of dominance (cf. Naqvi 1968; also Bayly 1983: 112). In the late 17th century communications with the Deccan improved and a large body of Deccani and Western Indian teachers began to come and settle in Varanasi (Bayly 1983: 186).

Population in the early 19th Century

In mid 18th century, the city had grown in different ways mostly under the patronage of Marathas; especially after 1735 with the support of Peshavas many *ghats* were constructed along the Ganga river. The *mahalas* (neighbourhoods) like Chaukhambha and Thatheri Bazar were developed in 1765 by cutting the woodlands covering the area. By the early 19th century Varanasi grew to be one of the northern India's largest cities (Varady 1989: 231). Based on folklore, James Prinsep had described the forest territories of the city. He opined that before the palace of Man Singh, the Commander-in-chief of Akbar (1556-1605), there was no palatial building in the city (Prinsep 1832: 11; also Singh 1955: 10).

Table 4. Varanasi City: Caste Structure, 1827-28 (based on Prinsep)

Religion / Caste	Persons	%
Hindus	122,446	67.5
Shudras	60,302	33.2
Brahmins	32,381	17.8
Kshatriyas & Bhumihars	14,292	7.9
Vaishyas	8,300	4.6
Hindu Fakirs (*Sadhus*)	7,171	4.0
Muslims	31,248	17.2
Julahas	10,000	5.5
Sheikh, Saiyyad, and Pathans	10,000	5.0
Fakirs & Chandals	1,200	0.7
Others	10,048	5.5
Children & Visitors (not mentioned)	26,387	14.5
Omissions	1,401	0.8
TOTAL	181,482	100.0

In 1828-29 James Prinsep (1832: 472) for the first time took a detailed census of the city. He had also tried a cross-check taking into account the consumption of salt, but he was aware of the inaccuracy (cf. Bhattacharya and Bhattacharya 1965: 278). According to him in 1827-28 there were 30,205 houses, scattered in 369 *mahalas*. The city was inhabited by 181,482 persons, excluding 11,876 native population and 7,092 Europeans in Secrole (Cantonment), thus altogether the total population reached to 200,450, but he had presented the details of only the main city. Bishop Heber (1828, I: 270) believed that in the year mentioned, the population of Varanasi was larger than in any European city. However Hamilton (1820: 306) grossly exaggerated the population to 582,000, which may not be accepted.

According to Prinsep the population density per house varied between 4.5 and 7.0 people, with an average of 6.0. The one and two-storied houses together recorded about 81 per cent of total houses. In addition to these houses, Prinsep had observed ruins of houses, or spaces marked out for buildings, numbered to 1498. He had also recorded 174 gardens and ponds, etc., 1000 Shivalas (Shiva temples) and other Hindu temples, and 333 mosques. Prinsep had made a detailed survey of the caste structure of the city (cf. Table 4); accordingly there were 67.5 per cent of Hindus divided into five groups, 17.2 per cent Muslims divided into four groups, and 14.5 per cent children and other visitors not mentioned. Excluding these numbers he had also mentioned the omission of 1401 persons (0.8 per cent); thus the total population reached to 181,482 in the main city, excluding Secrole area. The castes were further identified with reference to the dominance of their occupation.

Population in the 20th Century

After Prinsep's survey (1827-28, 1829) the next census was taken in 1853 recording a slight decrease (185,984 persons in City and Cantt.). This tendency continued in the following decade, but the growth recovered in 1872 at the rate of 8.07 per cent. The first reliable and detailed census was taken in 1881 recording 218,573 persons, followed by population in 1891. Subsequently, at decade intervals, the counting of population was started. Since then the population has been growing continuously, except for a short break during the following decades (1891-1921) when the population of the city declined by 11.2 %, mainly due to unfavourable natural conditions.

During the following three decades (1891-1921), the population of the city declined by 11.2 per cent mainly due to several unfavourable factors like poor harvests, droughts, irregularities of weather, floods, epidemics and the post-war effects of World War I. In fact, during 1901-1925, Varanasi was one of the most deadly cities in northern India recording high population and unsanitary conditions (Arnold 1989: 248). The city and its environs suffered severe epidemics in 1878, 1884, 1889, 1897, 1926, 1930, 1934, 1944-45 and 1951-52 (Joshi, 1965: 353). On the other side, surprisingly thousands of persons from eastern India and the Deccan came to this city in 1901-02 to get escape from the plague, believing that the dreaded disease could never enter into such a sacred place (Nevill 1909: 27). Alas! their belief was not proved, and calamities occurred ultimately.

45

Since 1921 the city has recorded constant growth of population (Table 4), reaching to 1,026,467 persons in 1991, recording a growth of + 28.77 per cent in 1981-91. During 1821-31 the growth rate was 3.81 per cent, while it reached to 28.10 during 1931-41. In fact, "in the first half of the decade the falling prices consequent upon the depression of 1931 must have given a stimulus to the city-ward population" (Singh 1955: 56). The closing impacts of World War II had also encouraged city-ward march of population. The post-war developments, the influx of rural population for employment and immigration of refugee population due to India's partition at the time of independence in 1947 were responsible for a very rapid growth during 1941-51 (i.e. 39.02%). However the abrupt situation had changed in course of time. In the succeeding decades the growth rate recorded a tendency to decline due to stage of settlement. That is how during 1951-61 the growth rate slightly declined. This tendency had continued till 1971-81 (Table 5). However, again during 1981-91 the growth rate became slightly higher, mainly due to the impact of the tendency of rural to urban migration in search of better livelihood and employment opportunities in the city. The city was conferred the status of metropolis (Urban Agglomeration) in 1991. The decline resulted from urban sprawl in peri-urban areas, which were not counted as part of the city. The heavy influx of migration from rural to urban in search of better livelihood has supported the high growth rate of population, recording around 32.5% in 1991-2001. The birth rate in 1991-2001 was 27 persons/ per 1000 population. The family welfare programmes have had a strong impact resulting in decrease of birth rate, and on the other end increasing health facilities have improved life and longevity. In 2001 the population of the city reached 1.23 millions (cf. Table 5). A little over one-third of the population is Muslim, while their share was only 17 per cent in 1828-29. Muslims are mostly engaged in weaving *saris* and carpets.

Like most of the developing societies the city of Varanasi also records a typical pattern of age-sex structure. A little less than 40% of the total population belongs to the age of 0-14 years. Only one quarter of the total population falls under 25-44 years of age, and only 3.5% of the population was recorded to be above 65 years of age. The male-female ratio observed was 896 females/ per 1000 males, which is higher than the average of the State. The average literacy in Varanasi is recorded as 54% of the total population, but it was 63.25 for males and 48.355 for females (as per the Census 2001). In the old-settled central part of the city the density of population reaches to 1600 persons/ha, and nearby areas recorded 750 persons/ha; however the outer areas record a density of 200 to 300 persons/ha.

Recent acceleration in population growth can be attributed to the widening development gap between rural and urban areas in the country. And since there is no visible change in the rural development policy, urban explosion would continue in the next decades. However, the city has grown at a slower rate than other large cities of the country. In 1961 it ranked 12th among the large cities of India. In subsequent decades its rank came down to 15th in 1971, 18th in 1981, 22nd in 1991 and 23rd in 2001. This happened because industrialization, which worked as the engine of growth, almost bypassed Varanasi. In comparison to other metropolises, its growth is slower mostly due to lack of services related to administrative-capital and diversified industrial developments.

Table 5. Varanasi City (since 1991 VUA): Population Growth, 1853 - 2001

Decadal year	Population	Growth rate, %
1853	185,984	—
1865	173,352	- 6.79
1872	187,347	8.07
1881	218,573	16.67
1891	223,375	2.20
1901	215,223	- 3.64
1911	205,420	- 4.55
1921	200,022	- 2.63
1931	207,650	+ 3.81
1941	266,002	28.10
1951	369,799	39.02
1961	505,952	36.82
1971	635,175	25.54
1981	815,366	28.37
1991	1,030,863	29.48
2001	1,231,220	19.44

(Source: Based on Census of India reports)

[Decadal figures given in table 3 are not comparable. The 1991 and onwards population figures relate to the Varanasi Urban Agglomeration (VUA), which consists of seven urban units of different categories including the Varanasi Municipal Corporation. The figures for earlier years relate to the Municipal Corporation only].

Table 6. Varanasi, Municipal and Urban Area addition:
Population Growth, 1991-2031.

Units / Year	1991	2001	2011*	2021*	2031*
Municipal Area	929,270	1,103,951	1,367,278	1,640,216	1,835,197
Urban area Addition	101,593	127,269	205,558	344,502	511,962
VUA, Varanasi Urban Agglomeration	1,030,863	1,231,220	1,572,836	1,984,718	2,347,159
Decadal growth, VUA,%	29.48	19.44	27.75	26.19	18.26

(Source: Based on Census of India reports. *Low projection estimates)

Varanasi Urban Agglomeration (VUA), i.e. metropolis, is constituted of seven urban units of different characteristics and status as defined by the Census of India 1991 and 2001. The details of the population of these units are given in Table 7. It is estimated that the growth of Varanasi UA would reach 27.75 per cent in 2011. Thereafter, it will taper off to 26.19 per cent in 2021 and 18.26 in 2031. Due to family planning measures and peoples' awakening towards population the speed of growth will be reduced.

Table 7. Varanasi Urban Agglomeration: Population Characteristics, 2001

Urban unit (Uttar Pradesh code 67)	Population, 2001	Decadal Growth Rate, %			
		1961-71	1971-81	1981-91	1991-01
VARANASI U.A. (Varanasi Dt.)	**1,231,220**	25.54	28.37	29.48	19.44
(1) **Varanasi**	1,103,951	23.04	22.45	28.95	17.58
i. Varanasi (MC)	1,091,917	23.89	22.45	28.57	10.83
ii. Lahartara (OG), Ward 91	5,223	——	——	53.46	67.03
iii. Maruadih (OG), Ward 92	6,811	——	——	76.34	35.33
(2) Varanasi Cantt. (CB)	17,259	81.99	65.73	1.64	18.03
(3) Lohta (CT)	19,706	——	——	44.71	52.56
(4) Kandwa (CT)	7,555	——	——	98.50	21.80
(5) Sheodaspur (CT)	11,420	——	——	85.43	50.08
(6) Phulwaria (CT)	11,971	——	——	61.87	22.60
(7) Maruadih Rly. Sett. (NA)	18,739	——	85.38	17.56	- 23.45
(8) Ramanagar (MB)	40,619	7.17	35.13	28.26	34.87
§ Banaras Hindu University (NA), [included in Varanasi MC]	10,788	40.90	26.12	- 6.63	- 6.24
Mughalsarai U.A. (Chandauli Dt.) [closely adjacent urban area]	**116,308**	35.69	141.94	32.19	27.11
(1) Mughalsarai (MB)	88,387	28.14	25.38	38.42	32.85
(2) Mughalsarai Rly settlement (NAC)	27,921	43.32	40.80	18.79	11.79

(Source: Census of India 2001, Series-1, INDIA.
Registrar General of India Office, New Delhi, 2003).

It is estimated that the decadal growth rate of Varanasi UA will be increased slowly from 16.64 to 26.19 per cent from 2001 to 2021; however, most likely the growth rate will decline to 18.26 by 2031 (cf. Table 5). The earlier estimates by R.L. Singh (1985) are therefore not fitting to the present estimates. In fact, R.L. Singh has not considered the case of Mughalsarai and Ramnagar, the two satellite towns, for his estimates. At present the Varanasi UA spreads over 144.96 sq.km, thus recording a density of 7,081 persons/ sq.km, while it was 9,434 persons/ sq. km in 1981. The decline of density is the result of the growth of residential colonies outside the UA area together with an increase in the defined area of the UA in 1991. According to the Census of 2001, of the total population (1,231,220) only a little over a quarter (26.6%) was employed, in which industry and manufacturing recorded 10.72%. Trade and commence (6.8%) and other services (5%) were the other main categories of employment. Among the population engaged in industry and manufacturing about half were in spinning and weaving, followed by metal and manufacturing (15%), printing and publishing (6.2%), and electrical machinery (5.02%).

5. Religious Landscape

5.1. Ethnic and Social Structure

Owing to different immigrants who came to this city for solace, peace and sacred merit, Sanskrit education, and as a consequence of various invasions, Varanasi developed a diversified community structure while preserving its regional characteristics. In this manner Varanasi has evolved a mosaic of social-cultural spaces, representing the whole of India (Fig. 7). Brahmins from different parts of the country came and settled around the important Hindu temples. The priests of the Vishvanatha temple and also of the major temples of the Omkareshvara Khanda (in the northern part) are Sarayuparina Brahmins. The priesthood of the southern segment, Kedara Khanda, is controlled by the Gauda Brahmins from South India; however Bhadaini and Asi area are mostly under the priesthood of Sarayuparina. South Indians are mostly concentrated in the Kedara Khanda, but the Tamil people are around the Vishalakshi temple and Hanuman Ghat. Maharastrians are settled in Durgaghat, Chowkhambha and Brahmanal area, and Gujaratis are concentrated in Hatakeshvara (Haraha Sarai), Bhaironath and near Kath-ki-Haveli and Soot Tola.

Sikhs have occupied many pockets of the city like Bari Ash Bhairo, Gurubag, Agastyakunda and Chaitanyamath at Visheshvarganj. Sindhis have established Sadhubela Ashram at Bhadaini and pilgrims' rest houses at Agastyakunda, Kamachha and Assi. Recently Sindhis have settled in Gulab Bag, Maldahia, Orderly Bazar and Kamla Nagar. Bengalis are concentrated in Jangambari, Ramapura, Bangalitola, Sonarpura and Bhelupura areas. Several areas of Varanasi have also been dominated by different minority groups like Kashmiris and Punjabis in Lahori Tola, Nepalis in Dudhvinayaka and Nepali Khapra.

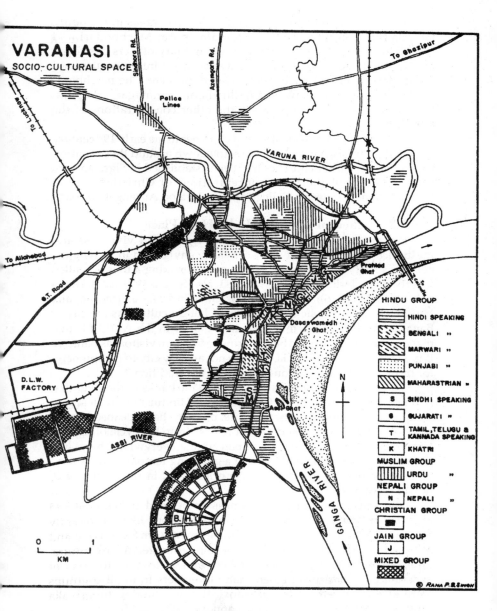

Fig. 7. Varanasi: Socio-Linguistic structure.

Muslims are settled mostly in the suburban areas in the north, i.e. Alaipur, Jaitpura, Adampura, Kamalpura, Machhodari and Nakhighat. During the Muslim rule the military officers destroyed the notable Hindu temples and converted them into mosques, and the neighbouring areas have been settled by them. The neighbourhoods of Lallapura, Nawabganj, Bhadaini, Daranagar, Alaipura, Aurangabad and Madanpura are the other concentrations of the Muslims.

The opening of missionaries and churches in the early 19th century attracted a Christian population to settle down around those centres. Of course, the earlier churches had been established in Sigra and the Cantonment, but the main concentrations of Christians are at Ramkatora near Queen's College and in Sigra on Aurangabad road.

5.2. Archetype of an All-India Holy Place

Perceived as a site of 'vigour and rigor', and vividness and multiplicity, diversity and unity are easily envisioned in its religion, culture, society and economy — altogether making a mosaic, called 'microcosmic India' (cf. Eck, 1982: 283, also Singh, 1994: 223). Diana Eck writes (1982: 6), "There are few cities in India as traditionally Hindu and as symbolic of the whole of Hindu culture as the city of Banaras. And there are few cities in India, or in the world for that matter, as challenging and bewildering to Western visitors as Banaras. It is a city as rich as all India. But it is not an easy city to comprehend for those of us who stand outside the Hindu tradition."

Varanasi: the city that is a prayer. On the banks of the river that is almost a faith, the flowing Ganga, stands Hinduism's greatest city: Varanasi. For several thousand years, pilgrims have cleansed themselves of their sins here and sought release from the cycle of rebirth. Hinduism, deep and mystical, is perceptible everywhere here: in a decorated doorway, in a glimpse of a glittering temple, in the sound of a sacred bell, in the chant of the priests and in the fragrance of flower oblations.

The sense and spirit of holiness embedded in Banaras has attracted people from various sects and religions like Vaishnavas, Shaivas, Tantrics, Buddhists, Jains, and even Muslim Sufis. For many of the adherents, this is a special place of pilgrimage. In the course of time, people from all parts of India came and settled here to have the experience of that spirit. Later, many foreigners from all countries were also attracted to this paradoxical city, bringing to light its universal character. Says Richard Lannoy (2002: 58), "Banaras, in its unimaginable antiquity, belongs not just to Hindus, but to Muslims, Sikhs, Buddhists, Jains and Christians. But it also belongs to everybody. … A sacred city dreamed into existence over the ages, it is also a state of mind. As an old saying puts it: *Banaras is wherever you are*."

The process of spatial transposition of holy centres of India has started in the 6th century and reached its climax by the 13th century, the Gahadavala period. All the pan-India and regionally prominent sacred sites have been replicated in Varanasi (Fig. 8). Mythological literature has been created to manifest the power of holiness in those sites, which finally resulted in making this city the 'holiest' for Hindus that preserved the '*wholeness*'. This together with the mosaic of ethnic and social structure further helped in the formation of Varanasi as the 'cultural capital of India'. The sites of the four *dhams* (abode of gods) — the holy centres in the four cardinal directions of the country, i.e. Badrinath in the north, Jagannath Puri in the east, Dvaraka in the west and Rameshvaram in the south — are re-established in Varanasi in archetypal form as their representative around the nuclei of the presiding deities at Matha Ghat (Badrinath), Rama Ghat (Puri), Shankudhara (Dvaraka) and Mir Ghat (Rameshvaram).

Other religio-cultural places of India have also been conceived in the different localities of Varanasi — Kedaranath at Kedar Ghat, Mathura at Bakaria Kund or Nakhi Ghat, Prayag (Allahabad) at Dashashvamedha Ghat, Kamaksha (Assam) at Kamachha, Kurukshetra at Kurukshetra Kund near Asi, Manasarovar Lake at Manasarovar near Shyameshvara, etc. The process of spatial transposition has promoted a sense of awakening and a notion of 'national consciousness' among the dwellers of Varanasi to perceive this city as a 'mini-India' or the 'cultural capital of India'. Similarly other sacred centres are spatially manifested in Varanasi. There are also 12 churches, 3 Jain temples, 9 Buddhist temples, 3 Sikh temples (*gurudvaras*) and several other sacred sites and places. This is the only place in the world where such a huge number of Hindu (*ca* 3300) and Muslim (1388) sacred places co-exist.

5.3. Shiva, the supreme: Shiva Linga, the Mandala

The frame of the cosmic reality, according to ancient Hindu thought, consists of the three fundamental states called evolution (*shrishthi*), existence (*sthiti*), and involution (*samhara*) that act in an infinite cyclic process. Each one of these phases is controlled by a god, named Brahma (the creator), Vishnu (the preserver), and Shiva (the one who completes the cosmic cycle and re-starts it); these three gods

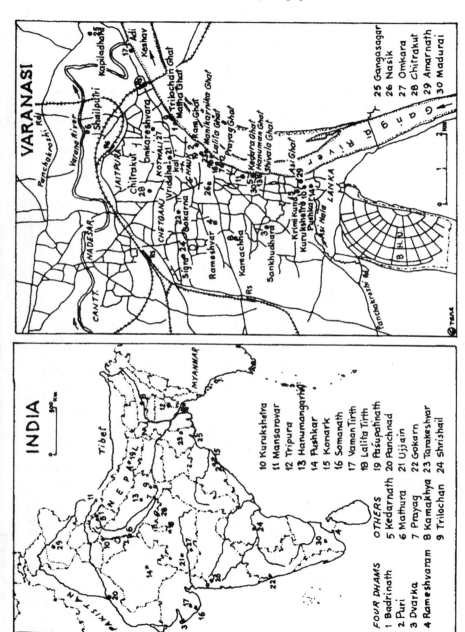

Fig. 8. Varanasi: An archetype of All-India.

form a kind of Trinity (*trimurti*). Shiva, being the last to complete the cycle from which a new cycle starts, is known as *Mahadeva*, the Supreme Divinity. The iconographic form of Shiva, the *Linga*, represents the unity of the three states of the cosmos (Fig. 9).

Śiva Liṅga Maṇḍala

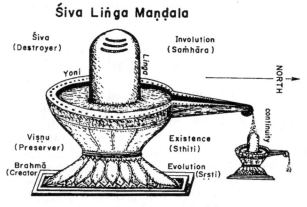

Fig. 9. Shiva Linga as Mandala.

The *Agni Purana* (53.3-5), an early 6th century text, mentions that "the *linga* should extend progressively in the Brahma and Vishnu portions. That for Brahma should be four sided, that for Vishnu eight, sixteen, thirty-two, or sixty-four sided, and that for Shiva should be round". The *linga* consists of the three parts. The first is a square base of three-layers at the bottom showing the three mythical realms (*lokas*), symbolising evolution — the place of Brahma. The second is an octagonal round form in the middle showing the eight directions, symbolising existence or perseverance — the place of Vishnu; and the third is a cylinder at the top with a spherical end, symbolising involution or completion of the cosmic cycle — the place of Shiva. The *Agni Purana* (53.5) has further elaborated on the vertical position of the *linga*; it says:

> … from the foot up to the knees should be Brahma's portion, from the knees up to the navel it should be Vishnu's portion, and from the navel up to the top of the head should be Shiva's portion. The portion assigned to Brahma is buried in the ground, that for Vishnu is within the *pithika*, and that for Shiva is above the *pithika*.

This icon shows the supreme state of integrity, the ultimate form of Shiva — the *linga* itself is a symbol of the cosmic *mandala*. As Sadashiva (eternal reality) Shiva is represented as a *linga*, standing also for 'total knowledge'. As Rudra, the destroyer, his consort is Kali. As Bhairava, the terrible destroyer, his consort is Durga. As a jovial god living in the Himalaya, his wife is Parvati. As possessor of all forms of divine power, Shiva stands at the centre of everything that is moving. That is why he is called *Ishvara*, derived from *I-chara*, i.e. *I*, the centre, and *chara*, the rhythm of movement. Shiva is also depicted as cosmic dancer, *Tandava Nartakari*, the one who keeps up the rhythm of the world in the cosmos.

In the cosmogonic frame it is believed that the city of Kashi lies on the trident of Lord Shiva in his own realm, and whatever Kashi we perceive is the shadow of the cosmic Kashi. Shiva is the patron deity of Varanasi and presents himself in all his forms at different locations, worshipped by devotees on different occasions and also daily by devout Hindus. The *Kashi Khanda*, a 15th century text, mentions about 1188 temples in Varanasi, of which 540 are directly of Shiva, 56 of Vishnu, 16 of Bhairava, 96 of Devi (the goddess who in different forms is Shiva's consort), and 72 of Vinayaka (Ganesha), Shiva's son. According to the *Linga Purana* (II.14.1-3), in the manifest form Shiva's presence is in all the five senses of cognition (hearing, feeling, seeing, tasting, and smelling) and the five gross elements of organic life (earth, water, fire, air, and space), and he dwells in each with his five organs of actions (excretion, reproduction, apprehension, locomotion, speech). The sacred mantra honouring Shiva is composed of five syllables, "*(Om) Na-mah-Shi-va-ya*", denoting the five above characteristics. Thus, Shiva represents the ultimate reality of unity between Man (humanity) and the Cosmos (divinity).

5.4. Jains and their temples

After the Mahabharata War (ca 1400 BCE), changes and transformations in Hinduism had took place. At this moment Jainism appeared as an alternative reformation movement. The Jain literature refers to Banaras as a Jain Tirtha (holy place) because here were born 4 of the Jain Tirthankaras (the 'ford-makers'). In the 8th century BCE Parshvanatha was born around Bhelupur in Varanasi; he established the triad-principle of the *mahavratas* ('great vows'): *ahimsa* (non-violence), *asteya* (non-stealing) and *aparigraha* (non-accumulation). The main Jain images excavated at this site belong to the 9th-11th centuries. Parshvanatha was followed in the 6th century BCE by Mahavira, a younger contemporary of the Buddha, who also visited Varanasi during his 42nd year of itinerant teaching. The birthplace of Suparshvanatha, the 7th Tirthankara, is also described in the Jain literature, though its location and identification have still not been confirmed. The temple of Suparshvanatha in Bhadaini (house no. B 2/ 89) commemorates that incident. It is believed that the present Jain temple in Sarnath, near the Dhamekha Stupa, was built to commemorate the birthplace of Shreyamshanatha, the 11th Tirthankara. He was born in the nearby village of Simhapur. The birthplace of the 8th Tirthankara Chandraprabhu is identified with Chandravati. This is an ancient village lying on the Varanasi-Ghazipur road at 23 km northeast from Banaras, at the western bank of Ganga River. There are two Jain temples belonging to the *Svetambara* and *Digambara* groups of the Jains. These temples were built in 1892 and 1913, respectively.

5.5. Sikhism and their holy shrines

Sikhs themselves have a clear articulate history of their community, which they refer to as the *panth*, meaning 'path' or 'way'. The world 'Sikh' itself means 'disciple'. Sikhs are known as a special community called into being through the work of Guru Nanak (1469-1539), the founder, and his successors. Says Guru Nanak, "What terrible separation it is to be separated from God and what blissful union to be united with Him". In northwest India Nanak was a leading Sant (saint) during the medieval period of Muslim suppression, and was very much influenced by Kabir and Raidas, two leading saints living in Banaras. The original teachings of Guru Nanak, *Guru Grantha Saheb*, were compiled by the 5th Guru, Arjan (1581-1606) and given the name *Adi Granth*, 'the original text'. Nanak's writings synthesise Hindu devotionalism and the Sufi tradition of Islam.

Legends suggest that Nanak visited Banaras two times, most probably in 1502 and 1506; first in his youth when he was on pilgrimage as described in the *janam-sakhis*. Later he came to have discourses with saints living in Banaras and also to convey his messages in 1506 on the day of the *Maha Shivaratri* festival; he stayed in a garden at Luxa, which later came to be known as the Guru Bagh, where he impressed the learned scholars of Banaras through his deeper message and synthesising of religions (Myrvold 2007: 85). The *Adi Granth* consists of the hymns of Guru Nanak and of the first five gurus as well as poems by great earlier saint-poets and singers such as Kabir and Raidas. The Guru-ka-Bagh (the *gurudvara* at Gurubagh) commemorates the locality where Guru Nanak stayed and the Asu Bhairava

Sangat (Nichibagh), the place where the 9th Guru Tegh Bahadur (1664-1675) had stayed in 1666. Asu Bhairava had also been the residence of Guru Govind Singh (1675-1708), the 10th and last guru. During his period of stay Guru Tegh Bahadur gave a few lessons of teachings at Dhupachandi, Jagatganj, where in course of time a *gurudvara* has been built in memory of the incident. Legends also relate that Guru Govind Singh sent his five disciples to Varanasi to get Sanskrit education, and the school is still continuing under the name of *Nirmal Sanskrit Mahavidyalaya* in Lahori Tola. The *Guru Nanak Sanskrit Vidyalaya* in Bisheshvarganj is also dedicated to his memory. There are three more sacred sites, *Sangats*, associated with the Sikh community. There is another monastery at Ramanagar, which possesses an authentic copy of the *Guru Grantha Saheb*. Finally, a palatial *gurudvara* was also constructed near Augharnath-ka-Takia. The majority of Sikhs arrived in the city during the years surrounding India's partition in 1947, either as migrant traders or refugees from Western Punjab in the present Pakistan (Myrvold 2007: 36). Their present population is around 5,000 people.

5.6. Christianity and Churches

Banaras came under the direct political control of the East India Company in the time of Warren Hastings, by the end of the 18th century. By serving the cause of Sanskrit teaching and Hindu theology through establishing a Sanskrit School in 1791 (by Jonathan Duncan), the East India Company established a strong foothold for Christianity in the city. This step helped to popularise the Christian faith and to prepare pandits for assisting the British judges in deciding cases involving the Hindu Law. The first English Seminary, named Anglo Indian Seminary, was established in 1830, and this encouraged the arrival of Christian missionaries. Christianity had very little impact on the high castes Hindus. Among the poorer and illiterate group of downtrodden masses, especially the untouchables, some accepted Christianity as a route to prosperity. However, in course of time, the end of colonial rule and the Hindu awakening have all worked to check the expansion of Christianity. Presently, there are twenty-two important churches in Banaras, viz. St. Mary Cathedral (Cantt.), Methodist Red Church (Nadesar), Catholic Church (Cantt.), David's Church (Teliabagh), St. Paul Church (Sigra), Bethlehem Gospel (Mahmoorganj), St. Thomas (at Godaulia), Church of Banaras (Cantt.), CNI Red Church (Cantt.), CNI Church (Ramkatora), Pentecostal Church (Newada, Sunderpur), Pilgrims' Mission (Cantt.), St. Joseph (Lohta), St. Francis Assisi (Nagwa,

Lanka), St. John Church (D.L.W.), St. John Baptist (Marhauli), Fatima Church (Mawaiya), St. Thomas the Apostle (Benipur), Evangelical Church of India (Kakarmatta, DLW), New Life League (Cantt.), Internal Life (Indiranagar, Sundarpur), and Nav Sadhna Chuch (Shivpur).

5.7. Muslims' Sacred Places and Sites

Muslims constitute 29.7% (i.e. 365,672) of the total population of Varanasi City (1.23 million in 2001) and have earned a significant place in the society, culture, landscape and traditional economy of the city. The invasions of Mahmud of Ghaznawi in 1021-1030 CE had opened the door to Muslim settlement in Varanasi. With reference to spatial, functional and numerical perspectives, the Muslim sacredscapes of Banaras may be grouped into 7 types. They are: *masjid* (mosque) 415, *mazar* (religious-cultural sites) 299, *imamchauk* (the crossing sites for *taziya*) 197, *takiya* (burial ground) 88, *idgah* (place of special prayer) 11, *imambara* (the burial site for *taziya*) 3, and others 375. The total number of sacred places reaches to 1,388 of which about 30 per cent are mosques.

6. Varanasi, the Mini India

Banaras is a mosaic of Indian culture, representing all the diversity and distinctiveness of the regional cultures of India. Superimposition of various traditions has taken place upon the course of time. People from all parts of India, speaking different languages and dialects and carrying their own traits, taboos and traditions have settled in this city while preserving their own culture inwardly, and becoming part of the mosaic culture of the city outwardly. This synthesis of diversity in regional identity, language and tradition converges to form the personality of an all-India city, Banaras. Unity and integration among diversity and multiplicity are the unique traits this city presents. Mythology says that even those who came to disturb the city, ended up settling here and became an integral part of its culture. Ultimately they accepted Vishvanatha Shiva as their main deity.

The city has possessed a strong force of spiritual magnetism, the special power of *genius loci*, and the sacred bondage between person and place called *mysterium tremendum*. This power always enhances the sensitivity to the *'crossings'* from this world to the world beyond, where humanity meets divinity. It is not a surprise why the city has found its place in all the great Indian epics, *Puranas* and other ancient · Hindu as well as Buddhist literature. This is the city preferred by the gods, demi-gods, godlings, sages, kings and the common men, who worshipped Shiva and established their mark in the form of a *linga* named after the person who consecrated it. That is why there are around 3,300 Shiva *lingas* in the city. The city is believed to be out of this world, and one must try to see it through the eyes of a Banarasi, 'a dweller of Banaras'. Only by walking one can realise that. A Britisher, settled and transformed himself into a Banarasi, suggests, "You have to try and get lost in the maze of lanes and then find your own way out".

Fig. 10. Four Faces of Kashi: the cartoonist's view.

It is said "by seeing Varanasi, one can see as much of life as the whole of India can show"; but it is not an easy city to comprehend for the outsider. The life style of Banaras is distinct in nature; it is referred to as *banarasipan*. It is an art of living, both passionate and carefree, what the Banaras dwellers call *masti* ('joie de vivre'), *mauj* ('delight, festivity') and *phakarpan* ('carefreeness'). The life style can be represented with the help of sketches (Fig. 10): washing clothes while drying wet clothes in the sun, grinding a narcotic hemp (*Cannabis Indica*) to make a special cold drink (*thandhai*), a hippy smoking and discoursing with an Indian mystic, and life in the lanes of Varanasi showing scenes of a wandering widow (*rand*), a wandering bull (*sand*), steep stairways (*sidhi*) and a wandering ascetic (*sanyasi*). This illustrates a common proverb about Banaras: "Avoid wandering widows, bulls, ascetics, and steep stairways; then only you can stay in Kashi" (*"rand, sand, sidhi, sanyasi, inse bache to seve Kashi"*).

6.1. Banaras as a superb blending of the Spiritual and the Material

Varanasi in comparison to cities of its size is a balanced multi-functional city with six sporadic industrial areas at Ramnagar, Chandpur, DLW, Lahartara, Lohta and Shivpur. The urban morphology of the city shows a complex pattern where traditions are maintained and modernity is introduced in an often discordant way. The areas with the highest density of religious and heritage properties have also the highest density of commercial wholesale and retail outlets. These commercial activities range from gold and silver jewellery, saris, typical food products of the city, utensils, jute and bamboo carpets, handicrafts, publishers and book shops, stationery articles and handmade paper, etc. — and the lanes are still called by the category of wares they trade in. And it is here that one finds some of the oldest and most important shrines of Hindu deities like Kal Bhairava, Dandapani Bhairava, Vishveshvara, Annapurna as well as several *kundas* (water tanks). It is here that one finds products for the enjoyment of man's material life, and here that one is *en route* to the cremation *ghat* — life and death, material enjoyment and spiritual quest, immanent and transcendent uniquely juxtaposed together.

7. Industrial Landscape

Out of a total of inhabitants of 1,231,220 (in 2001) in Varanasi UA, only 26.64% were recorded as employed, in which only 10.72% were engaged as industrial and manufacturing workers.[2] Earlier the city had attracted artisans, potters, and weavers who initiated household industrial establishments like ivory work and making of idols, silken brocades, utensils and *zarda*. Even at present the people engaged in household industries (like spinning and weaving) constitute a very high share of workers (50%), more than that of Kanpur, the industrial hub of Uttar Pradesh (cf. Table 8). Among the occupational structure of employed workers, the two predominant groups that share the maximum number of the male working population are trade and commerce (17.25%) and household industry (23.50%). The other occupations include manufacturing (16.15%) and transport, storage and communication (6.14%). The demand for various ritualistic items and souvenirs by the pilgrims and tourists promote the structure of household industries.

---

[2] According to the Census of India 2001, those workers who had worked for the major part of the reference period (i.e. 6 months or more) are termed as *Main Workers*. And, those workers who had not worked for the major part of the reference period (i.e. less than 6 months) are termed as *Marginal Workers*.

The small scale and household industrial sectors consist of the major share of industrial workers and commuters. These industries mostly include spinning and weaving, followed with textiles, hosiery, chemicals and soap, food, printing and publishing, utensil, fencing net, tobacco, golden and silver foil making, etc. Spinning and weaving is the oldest and most important household industry, employing more than half of the industrial workers.

Table 8A. Varanasi City: Employment Profile, 2001

Category	No. of Employees	% Share
Not Employed, UE	890,878	73.52
Total Employed, TE (*Main Workers*)	314,933	26.00
Manufacturing	128,930	10.64
Trade and Commerce	82,035	6.77
Other Services	60,466	5.00
Transport &, Communications	24,235	2.00
Agriculture	12,239	1.01
Construction	7,028	0.58
Marginal Workers, MW	5,938	0.49
TOTAL (UE + TE + MW)	1,211,749	100.00

Table 8B. Varanasi: Distribution of Industrial Workers, 2001

Category	No. of Employees	% Share
Spinning and Weaving	65,368	50.70
Metal and manufacturing	19,223	14.91
Food and food products	4,938	3.83
Timber & wood workers	4,487	3.48
Printing & Publishing	7,981	6.19
Manufacturing & Machinery	4,435	3.44
Textile	1,354	1.05
Zarda and Tobacco	1,147	0.89
Chemical products	2,669	2.07
Transport equipment	1,405	1.09
Electricity Machinery	6,472	5.02
Miscellaneous	9,451	7.33
TOTAL	128,930	100.00

(Source for both tables: VDA, Vision 2025 Draft Final Report. Feb. 2004)

During the post-independence period several large scale factories have been developed in and around the city, especially along G.T. Road (N.H. 2) between Mughalsarai and Parao, e.g. Hari fertilisers, Woollen Mill, Engineering units, Agricultural equipment manufacturing plants, etc. With the establishment of Diesel Locomotive Works (D.L.W.) in 1961 in the western part of the city, another industrial landscape has also emerged. The factory manufactures diesel locomotives and employs more than 10,000 workers. Encompassing about 200 ha of land there has developed a well-planned colony of 3,000 quarters. Asia's leading designer and manufacturer of diesel and electric locomotives, this unit supplies locomotives not only to the whole of India but also to Asian, East African and other markets.

An Industrial Estate has been developed at the west of the city at Lohta, where small-scale industries have sprung up. These incorporate manufacturing of chemicals, plastic goods, iron bars and metal equipments, etc. The city has recently developed a specialised industrial wing of bead and carpet manufacturing. No industrial zone is identifiable as such. The city has grown haphazardly in a natural unchecked process. Some newly planned residential have also been erected, with assistance of the Town Planning Organisation, Vikas Pradhikaran, Avas Vikas Parishad and private colonisers.

8. Tourist Landscape

The diversities, contrasts and distinctive features of Varanasi have played a major role in attracting tourists from India and abroad. Varanasi is one of the top individual tourist destinations in India and about 7 per cent of all the international tourists coming to India pay a visit to Varanasi. Like any other heritage city, Varanasi is also the product of a unique set of historical, cultural and functional circumstances and presents itself to particular group of people (i.e. devout Hindus) as a distinct sacred place (for pilgrimage). Every year over 2.5 millions devout Hindus (domestic) pay a visit to this holy city and perform rituals and pilgrimages. The multiplicity and distinctiveness of this city has also attracted a huge mass of tourists. Arrivals to Varanasi in recent years show a continuous increase of national tourists/pilgrims and also of international tourists. In 2007 the city recorded a little over 2.5 million domestic tourists and around four hundred thousands international tourists, respectively recording an increase of 74.4% and 38.5% over the previous year (Table 9).

Table 9. Influx of International Tourists:
World, India, U.P., and Varanasi (Vns)
(World data in million, and the rest in thousands)

CE	1990	1992	1994	1996	1998	2000	2002	2004	2006	2007
World	448.3	503.1	546.5	594.8	625.2	698.3	714.2	779.3	846.2	898.4
India	1330	1868	1886	2288	2361	2642	2384	3457	4008	5662
U.P.	400	560	571	680	760	850	813	963	1174	1329
Vns	46	28.3	69.2	134.1	132.6	123.8	86.2	121.9	289.0	400.3
Vns %	3.5	1.5	3.7	5.9	5.6	4.7	3.6	3.5	7.2	7.1
% AC	+96.6	-0.4	72.6	281.0	- 2.4	+10.3	- 20.5	+11.2	+ 74.4	+ 38.5

Note: Vns, Varanasi; Vns %, share of Varanasi in India;
   % AC, Annual variation of tourists in Varanasi.

(*Source*: WTO, Annual Report, Dept. of Tourism,
UP Tourism Statistics, and Tourist Bureau Varanasi)

Tourists' arrivals in recent years in Varanasi (Table 10) show a continuous increase of domestic tourists, and a tendency to decrease in international tourists during 1998-2001. Still the volume of international tourists in Varanasi is considerably high, as it is almost double to some states of India.

It is obvious that the major international catastrophes have directly affected the inflow. The terrorist attack on the World Trade Center, New York on 11 September 2001, which produced an atmosphere of insecurity and fear, had directly checked the inflow of international tourists. Thus in 2002 there was a decline of 20.5% in tourist influx in Varanasi (cf. Table 10). This had a severe and multiple bad affect, resulting in a great loss of number of tourists. The estimated number of international tourists to Varanasi in 2001 was 130,000; it means that there was loss of 65,000. This threat had a strong inverse impact in the following year, i.e. a loss of 20.5%. In 2002, the tourism industry in Varanasi gained a little but again faced great loss in 2003 due to the spread of SARS disease in Southeast countries. However, since 2004 the tourist flow to Varanasi has recorded an appreciable growth. A good number of foreign tourists visit the city and live in cheaper guest houses, and in many cases their data are not recorded.

Under the current Master Plan the idea of Heritage Zoning and its special plans are taken into account, and five areas are identified as heritage zones — their package for cultural tourism and heritage planning is in process. Recently, the increasing pace of modern facilities of transport and organisation and package programmes, together with the increasing consciousness of religious activities as good means of healing and solace, have promoted a drastic increase of domestic visitors, especially since the turn of this century (Table 10).

Table 10. Banaras/ Varanasi: Tourist Influx

Year	Domestic		International		TOTAL	
	Total	Growth, %	Total	Growth, %	Total	Growth, %
1990	79,512	+ 24.6	46,021	+96.6	125,533	+18.6
1991	109,924	+ 38.3	28,436	- 38.3	138,360	+ 10.3
1992	98,738	- 10.2	28,342	- 00.3	127,080	- 8.2
1993	130,370	+ 32.0	40,119	+ 29.4	170,489	+ 34.2
1994	179,669	+ 37.8	69,156	+ 72.4	248,825	+ 49.9
1995	118,969	- 33.8	116,529	+ 68.5	235,498	- 5.4
1996	157,768	+ 32.6	134,091	+ 15.1	291,859	+ 23.9
1997	166,492	+ 5.5	135,779	+ 1.3	302,271	+ 3.6
1998	287,606	+22.7	132,588	- 2.4	420,194	+ 39.0
1999	341,974	+ 18.9	112,141	- 15.4	454,115	+ 8.1
2000	431,901	+ 26.3	123,786	+ 10.4	555,687	+ 22.4
2001	454,832	+ 5.3	108,546	- 12.3	563,378	+ 1.4
2002	496,539	+ 9.2	86,267	- 20.5	582,806	+ 3.4
2003	534,269	+ 7.6	89,658	+ 3.9	623,927	+ 7.1
2004	597,543	+ 11.8	121,942	+11.2	719,485	+ 15.3
2005	792,630	+ 32.6	165,714	+ 35.9	958,344	+ 33.2
2006	1,455,492	+ 83.6	289,010	+ 74.4	1,744,502	+ 82.0
2007	2,552,365	+ 75.4	400,320	+ 38.5	2,952,685	+ 69.3

(Sources: FRO (LIU), Varanasi, UP Tourism, and Dept. of Tourism; collated by the author)

Among the international tourists to the city Japan maintains its predominance, although in percentile share it has tendency of decline. Due to long historical and cultural linkages, recognition of Buddhism and cultural ties, the Japanese prefer to visit this city from where the first message of Buddha was proclaimed. France, U.K., U.S.A. and

Germany are the other countries that record a high share of tourists. Economic development and an increased Buddhist consciousness have encouraged pilgrimage to Sarnath and Varanasi from the Buddhist countries of Southeast and East Asia (viz. Thailand, Sri Lanka, Myanmar; cf. Table 11).

Table 11. Nationality-wise Foreign Tourists' arrival in Varanasi

Country	1986		2000		2006	
	Total	% of total	Total	% of total	Total	% of total
Japan	1,248	2.10	18,568	15.00	35,490	12.28
France	2,318	3.90	13,888	11.22	26,358	9.12
U.K.	4,160	7.00	13,121	10.60	24,219	8.38
U.S.A.	4,873	8.20	8,108	6.55	21,271	7.36
Germany	2,258	3.80	8,665	7.00	17,948	6.21
Mauritius	4,754	8.00	3,340	2.70	13,497	4.67
Italy	1,545	2.60	3,342	2.70	12,688	4.39
Thailand	2,496	4.20	1,438	1.16	10,289	3.56
Australia	1,457	2.45	4,295	3.47	9,711	3.36
Sri Lanka	2,674	4.50	1,659	1.34	9,017	3.12
Netherlands	2,674	4.50	1,232	1.00	7,514	2.60
Poland	2,377	4.00	1,139	0.92	7,081	2.45
Switzerland	1,188	2.00	3,095	2.50	6,705	2.32
Spain	980	1.65	2,008	2.44	6,243	2.16
Canada	1,248	2.10	2,191	1.77	5,838	2.02
Malaysia	1,426	2.40	718	0.58	5,809	2.01
Israel	327	0.55	591	0.47	3,699	1.28
Iran	3,209	5.40	87	0.07	3,410	1.18
Saudi Arab	1,070	1.80	62	0.05	260	0.09
Other Countries	19,145	32.21	34,231	27.65	61,963	21.44
Total	59,427	100.00	123,786	100.00	289,010	100.00

(Source: FRO (LIU), Varanasi, UP Tourism, and Dept. of Tourism; collated by author).

The city of Varanasi and its surrounding region (Kashi Kshetra) are visited by thousands of Hindu and Buddhist pilgrims, Jains, Sufi saints and foreign visitors each day. Known the world over as the 'sacred city' and 'the ancient most continuously living city', Varanasi and its region is rich in architectural and cultural heritage (both tangible and intangible: temples, shrines, palaces, *maths*, mosques, ashrams; and fairs, festivals, musical performances, wrestling traditions, handicrafts, silk weaving, sari, Rama Lilas), natural aesthetics (e.g. the crescent form half moon-shaped northerly flow of the Ganga). The local religious and cultural life of Varanasi together with its built architectural heritage and the natural landscape of the Ganga river constitute an immense resource for heritage and sustainable tourism, both Indian and foreign.

This city is very important, especially for pilgrimage tourism where the visitors enjoy a morning boat ride, walk through narrow lanes (*gali*), feel the Banarasian spirit and visit Sarnath where Lord Buddha gave his first sermon and established his community (*sangha*). Sarnath is the second most important tourist attraction after the *ghats* of Varanasi. By attracting many tourists who are followers of Buddhism, Sarnath indirectly supports tourists' growth in Varanasi. The number of Indian tourists is continuously increasing since 1998, but the tendency of international visitors changes according to the global happenings (cf. Table 10).

In spite of rise of prices and lack of infrastructural facilities in comparison to the West, the quest for experiencing awe, wonder and the mystical image of India, the beautifully blended together 'spirituality' (*yoga*) and 'materialism' (*bhoga*) in Varanasi, the number of tourists from abroad has been constantly increasing. The media, films, internet and websites have further strengthened the desire to visit this city; another reason is also cheap flights and cheap travel agency programmes. Of course, till the turn of the century UK and USA recorded the highest position in the number of tourists, but by 2006 the situation turned towards Japan and France, together recoding a little over one-fifth of the total visitors (Table 11). Recently Israel, Spain, Italy and Germany have recorded more incoming of tourists. Various studies and cultural programmes promoted by French and Spanish organisations and governmental institutions are praiseworthy in this direction.

9. Epilogue

Varanasi, an ancient and sacred city, gives solace to millions of Indians and a sense of wonder to thousands of foreigners each day and year. Its soul lies in its history; the mind in learning and the body in Ganga. If Ganga would go, Varanasi would lose its very being. It is the body that houses the mind as well as the soul. Unfortunately, Ganga, whose waters purify the impure, is on the way to lose its identity as a river. Ganga is today the most polluted major river of India and one of the most polluted rivers of the world. It is a sad reflection on Indian urban planning and let-loose industrialization, that the river has been converted into a drain to carry urban and industrial effluents. To paraphrase Carl Jung: "The people of India will never find true peace until they can come into a harmonious relationship with and cultivate deeper feelings of reverence for the Ganga River, which is the cradle and identity of India's culture and civilization since time immemorial" (cited by Swan, as in Singh, 1996: 105).

With the growth of global tourism and a widespread interest in seeing culture in the mirror of history and tradition, religious heritage resource management becomes a critical issue in two primary ways: 1) protection and maintenance of sacred sites, and 2) the survival and continuity of pilgrimage ceremonies that preserve centuries-old human interactions with the earth and its mystic powers. Fostering a rediscovery of forgotten (or almost forgotten) common cultural heritage and practices at sacred places that centred on reverence to and harmony with the Earth as source and sustainer of life, the conservation and preservation of such holy sites would be a strong step in this direction (Singh, 2006: 233). The *'Riverfront Heritage and the Old City'* of Varanasi is in the process of getting inscribed in the UNESCO World Heritage List. Let us hope that we will succeed in a very near future. (For details, see chapter 3 of this book).

Varanasi has been a sacred city of scholarship and wisdom. To continue and re-enforce the intellectual and spiritual tradition of the city universities like Banaras Hindu University, Sampurnanand Sanskrit University, Mahatma Gandhi Kashi Vidyapeeth and Central Institute of Tibetan Studies have been set up in relatively recent times. But the city appears to be losing its serenity and sacredness. Ganga, its soul, is polluted. Today it is so polluted that many people have started wondering if it is still suitable for bathing — the most important ritual that pilgrims perform. The city has become so congested that it is difficult to reach the *ghats* and more difficult to have the *darshan* ('auspicious sight') of Vishvanatha. In the words of a devout pilgrim, "The people of Varanasi, nay the world community have to take action against the pollution of Ganga. A movement to bring Ganga back to what it was before it was converted into a sewer drain and to modernize the city while preserving its heritage has to be launched. The past is there to inspire; the future is there in dreams; the present is the time to act. Some saints have given a lead. Let us hope that the caravan would lengthen and a time will come, sooner than later, to make Varanasi what it deserves to be."

10. References (not cited in the Bibliography)

Sanskrit References (all cited in the Bibliography, chapter 4)

Schütz, Alfred 1962. *Collected Papers*. Vol. 1 and 2. Martinus Nijhuff, The Hague.

Sircar, D.C. 1967. *Cosmography and Geography in Early Indian Literature*. Indian Studies: Past & Present, Calcutta.

Chapter 2

BANARAS:

TRANSFORMATION ON THE CRADLE OF TIME

"Reviewing the history of Benares over the last two centuries, the city has clearly lacked an overarching focus (if that is not a contradiction in terms). There can be no question of there being anything like the focus, apex or axis in the way that, anciently, the symbolism of the Cosmic Pillar or the Cosmogram served. Could there be some pristine and shining Image which lifts everyone clear of complexities and 'communalism', which surpasses the humdrum limitations of an ageing city? ... By now the hidden order of Benares is only just discernible, a substructure almost completely buried under the detritus of the ages, and only with the greatest diligence can we have direct experiential access to it."

Richard Lannoy 2002: 367-368

Background

Banaras is a city where the past and the present mingle so beautifully that the joy of visiting it and even living in it is unforgettable. It has now become a large city with more than a million people, but the basic culture of the city has remained alive. Today Varanasi is a complex web of old and new, stability and change, industry and agriculture, and business and spirituality. To be in Varanasi is an extraordinary experience, an experience in self-discovery, an eternal oneness of the body and soul. It is a city where experience and discovery reach the ultimate bliss. Varanasi or Kashi, popularly known as Banaras, is one of the oldest living cities of the world. Its history goes back to several millennia. Mark Twain (1897: 480), the famous American litterateur once wrote: "Banaras is older than history, older than tradition, older even than legend and looks twice as old as all of them put together. ... It has had a tumultuous history, both materially and spiritually. It started Brahminically, many ages ago; then by and by

Buddha came in recent times 2,500 years ago, and after that it was Buddhist during many centuries — twelve, perhaps — but the Brahmins got the upper hand again, then, and have held it ever since." The older city was spread in the territory between the Varana (in the south) and the Gomati (in the north); the latter meets the Ganga *ca* 20 km north from the Varana. Reading the pages on the historical growth of this city gives an understanding of the growth of Indian civilisation itself.

During the first millennium BCE there developed an established habitation in the Banaras area based on commercial transaction with the nearby rural areas, as exemplified by the excavations at Rajghat, Sarnath, Bairat, Akatha and Baigar (Chakia). The suitable contact-point location (where water is available throughout the year) along the river Ganga had helped accessibility and transport. References in the ancient mythologies mention the existence of Banaras as a port town and later as a political, administrative, educational, and religious centre. It is commonly accepted that the oldest core of Banaras was definitely in the northern part, which was mostly occupied by small peasantry villages, with an elongated projection along the Ganga to a little north of Raj Ghat, and expanded up to the confluence of the Gomati to the Ganga rivers (village Kaithi). Most of the ruins of the past lie north of the present Maidagin-Kashi Railway Station Road and near the confluence of the Varana river with the Ganga. The two rivers that once sandwiched the city were the Varana and the Asi which is now reduced to a dirty *nala* (drain), hence the name Varanasi.

1. Early Historical Period

Possessing the spirit of divinity, the myths and traditions have maintained the vibration of life in Varanasi since time immemorial. Of course, archaeologically it has been proven that since *ca* 800 BCE the city has continuously been inhabited by humans; the more recent excavations date the settlements to about 1200 BCE (cf. Jayaswal 2000-02). However, some historians of religions opine that the "ancient site of Varanasi can not be pushed further back than the 8th century BCE" (Bakker and Isaacson 2004: 19). The early literary evidence that confirms the archaeological findings is provided in Patanjali's *Mahabhasya* (MbP 4.384). That is why the city is metaphorically known as one of the 'oldest living cities in the world'. While a number of cities and cultures have risen and disappearêd, Varanasi continued to grow and to follow its ageless traditions of religious discourses, learning, and arts and crafts. Shushruta, the father of Indian surgery, was educated in Banaras.

A little before the Mahabharata War (*ca* 1400-1200 BCE) Krishna had introduced natural symbolism in worship; this was an indication of reformation in Vedic Hinduism. According to mythological sources, Kashi had been an Aryan settlement at least since the post-Vedic period (about 1500 BCE). Of course, it was more famous as a seat of learning, and also a centre of cottage industries and textile manufacturing even in pre-Buddhist times.

The first reference of the Vedic battle between Pratardana and Videha (ref. *Rig Veda*, RgV 10.179.2) was an example of two regional cultures. The essence of the battle is detailed out in a historical novel by Shivprasad Singh, i.e. *Vaishvanar* ('the Primordial Fire', 1996; here after referred as, VS:). According to mythology Dhanvantari was the 7th in the lineage of Manu, the primordial man described in the Brahminical creation theory. Dhanvantari, known as the father of Indian medicine, was one of the earliest kings of this city (cf. VyP 92.33.28; and BdP 3.63 and 119-141). No details about his son, Bhimaratha, are given in the mythologies. The myth tells that Dhanvantari's grandson Divodasa was once exiled from the city and thus made another capital city at the confluence of the river Ganga and the Gomati, which was described as Markandeya Tirtha in the *Mahabharata* (Aranyaka 82.68-70), and identified today with Kaithi (Kitagiri), lying 28 km northwest from Varanasi city. Divodasa first defeated the Haihayas, another group; but his son Pratardana was defeated by a non-Aryan chieftain Kshemaka who had threatened Brahminical rituals. After passage of time Pratardana's son Alarka killed Kshemaka and re-established the Brahminical code of rituals under the guidance of the Brahmin sage Bharadvaja. One of the *puranic* myths tells that Pratardana had destroyed his opponent Haihayas ruled by their king Vitahavya, and re-established the kingdom of Kashi (Sherring 1868: 381). The story of Divodasa and his son Pratardana refers to the threats of migration groups from the west who had made conquest for settling down in the Ganga Valley (Singh, Rana 2004: 42). This is in accordance to the *Mahabharata* (13.31.19), which refers that Divodasa was driven out of Varanasi after an attack by the hundred sons of Haihaya.

The mythology of Divodasa has two main sources, viz. the *Mahabharata*, and the *Puranapanchalakshna* (based on the *Vayu Purana* and *Brahmanda Purana*), which significantly differ from one another. However, the common elements in both the stories are: (1) Divodasa, king of the Kashi tribe (Kashiraja), rules Varanasi, (2) Divodasa is forced to give up this city, (3) Divodasa had an enemy who had a hundred sons, and (4) only after Divodasa had left Varanasi, a son was born to him, named Pratardana (Bakker and Isaacson 2004: 188, for detailed discussion, see pp. 187-194).

The later version of the Divodasa story refers to the battle between the patron deity Shiva and the king Divodasa (cf. *Brahmanda Purana*, 2.3.67-68; also *Vayu Purana*, 92; both dated *ca* 9th-10th centuries). Divodasa is described as a man of unusual purity and of strict integrity who resisted the encroachments of Brahminism on its first approach to Banaras, but eventually was obliged to succumb to it, and to surrender his crown to the Brahminic followers (worshippers of Shiva). According to another interpretation Divodasa might had been a Tantric, follower of indigenous belief systems! However, this all is a matter of debate.

The story further continues that due to catastrophic drought and epidemic in mid 17th century BCE, the Aryans migrated from the west to the Ganga Valley and succeeded in superimposing their culture at the place of the indigenous culture. For the first time in history a great war by the Yadu clan of Haihaiyas spread from Gandhara (Afghanistan) to Saptasindhu (northwest part of India). This was the first dark spot on human migration when all the codes of human values lost their hold and one brother killed the other one (cf. VS: 194).

The conflict between sage Vashishtha (a Brahmin) and sage Vishvamitra (a Kshatriya) is a metaphorical narration of the battle between Brahminical rigidity and the challenges against it (cf. *Atharva Veda*, 12.1-69). For the cause of humanity Vishvamitra immerged himself into a long state of torturing, arduous austerities, fasting, and humiliation from the predominant Brahmins; however finally he succeeded to acquire the power of supreme bliss and ultimately was accepted by Vashishtha. To commemorate it he manifested the most sacred *mantra* of the Vedas — still having the same status today — called Gayatri (RgV, 3.62.10), which says:

> Let us obtain the adorable splendour of the Sun; may He arouse our minds.

By this prayer Vishvamitra succeeded in challenging the supremacy of the Vedic gods like Indra, Varuna, Vayu, Agni, Mitra, etc. and finally started a kind of hermitage school to teach the holistic knowledge of life with yoga, law, administration, science, astronomy, and health (cf. VS: 345). The conflict of Vashishtha and Vishvamitra symbolises the two phases of Aryan civilisation. Ultimately Vishvamitra prophesied the image of Universal Man (*Vishvamanusha*) who can constantly shed light upon humanity through the use of spiritual resources, as echoed in the words of Trishoka Kanva (cf. RgV, 8.45.42):

> Bring that divine wealth,
> Which does Vishvamanusha have?
> Let's take work to get that wealth,
> And have that ambrosia forever.

Dhanvantari, grandfather of Divodasa, honoured as the first Vishvamanusha, had accepted suffering as his destiny to save humanity. As the 'self' is completely merged into superconsciousness, 'self' is in the service to others. He by churning the ocean of milk received the *amrita* (ambrosia) and presented it to human beings.

Most of the times battles in the ancient past turned into acceptance of each other's codes, rituals, ways of performances and also the divinities. One of the earliest mythologies narrates that Vishnu was performing austerities to please Shiva who by his persuasion accepted the city of Kashi as his abode. This is the example of acculturation between two groups. Of course, on the human side there are examples of battles between the adherents of Vishnu and Shiva, but again it was settled down. Its climax was reached in the early medieval period through the worship of Harihara (joint form of Vishnu and Shiva), as narrated by the saint poet Tulasi. Moreover, examples of battles challenging Brahminism (either by gods or men) and its ideologies were also found in the Vedic literature, including the *Rig Veda* (10-12th century BCE). The ancient literatures describe the settling process and the conquest and conflicts that went together, until finally peace was established in a unitary manner. Amidst the battles the light of peace spread by the Vedic seers is the real message for compassion and the welfare of humanity.

It was at this stage that Jainism was introduced as a reformation movement. In the 8th century BCE Parshvanatha, the 23rd Tirthankara and the leading prophet of Jainism was already born near a mythical tank in Varanasi (presently identified with the Parshvanatha Jain temple in Bhelupura) and the influence of Jainism was recorded. The main Jain images excavated at this site belong to the 9th-11th centuries BCE; however a few of the images dated back to the 5th century. His father Ashvasena was described as the king of Kashi (Motichandra 1985: 39). Later on Mahavira (599-527 BCE), the last Tirthankara, a younger contemporary of the Buddha, also made his imprint on the cultural arena though his visit to the city in his 42nd year of itinerant teaching. The birthplace of Suparshvanatha, the 7th Tirthankara, is also described in the Jain literature, though its location and identification have still not been confirmed. Traditionally, the temple of Suparshva-natha in Bhadaini commemorates that incident. It is believed that the present Jain temple in Sarnath, near the Dhamekha Stupa, was built to commemorate the birthplace of Shreyamshanatha, the 11th Tirthankara. The birthplace of the 8th Tirthankara Chandraprabhu is identified with Chandravati, an ancient village lying on the Varanasi-Ghazipur road at 23 km northeast from Banaras at the western bank of Ganga River. That is how it is known as a Jain *tirtha*. A huge mound (ruins of a fort) near the bank of Ganga at this site was eroded during the flood in 1912, and that is how a huge stone cage was recovered that contains copper inscriptions of the Gahadavala king Chandradeva (1085-1100). The copper plate found at this site, dated 1091 CE (Samvata 1148) mentions the chief fort of the Gahadavala dynasty and a temple of the patron deity Chandramadhava (a form of Vishnu). Oral history narrates that this site had a glorious history in the past, but during the Mughal period (14th to 16th century) the site was turned into ruins by the Muslim rulers.

Walking near the confluence of the Varana and the Ganga, through the area known as Rajghat plateau, one can have a glimpse of the ancient site. Presently the area is occupied by grounds of the Annie Besant College, the Krishnamurti Foundation, and the Gandhian Institute. The epic *Mahabharata* has a passing reference to the city, but on the other hand the *Jataka Tales*, written after the *Mahabharata*, record vivid descriptions of the city. This is further supported by the literary description given in the *Shatapatha Brahmana*, dated *ca* 9th century BCE, which mentions the rich pastoral life and habitation in the Rajghat area. The *Jataka Tales*, 6th to 3rd century BCE, refer to Banaras as the site of manifestation of previous Buddhas, the last one being the Gautama Buddha (563-483 BCE).

The archaeological findings and the C[14] dating of some of the wares excavated from the earliest level (upper part of IA layer, sample No. TF-293) in the vicinity confirm the existence of urban settlements in the period during 1000-500 BCE. Because of frequent use of clay, mud and wood for building, human habitations were least resistant to the flooding of the river and as such physical and material evidence of earlier occupation appears to have vanished. Such evidence was unearthed at Kamauli village, lying 4 km northeast from Rajghat across the Varana river. Here microlithic tools associated with a kind of Red Ware, datable to the 5th and 3rd millennium BCE were obtained underneath the sterile deposits at about 4 m, just below the Sunga levels (200 BCE to the beginning of Christian era (Narain and Roy 1976 I; Fig. 11).

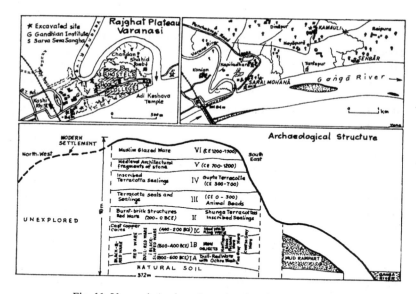

Fig. 11. Varanasi: Ancient site and archaeological structure.

Archaeological investigation is further supported by Robert C. Eidt (1977: 1332) on the basis of scientific analysis of chronosequence of non-occluded/occluded phosphate ratios of the vertical profile of anthrosols in the Rajghat area of Varanasi, dated from 800 BCE to CE 800 (Fig. 12). The results support the fact that residential settlement during this time span was uninterrupted. This further supports a claim that the site is the original centre of one of the oldest continuously occupied modern cities in the world. Moreover the results of phosphate fractionation further indicate that the residents combined small farming with pastoral life. The archaeological remains (e.g. pottery, terracotta, iron implements, artefacts, seals, etc) found in the area are datable to the

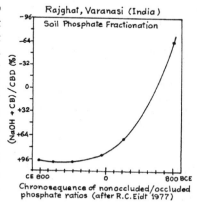

Fig. 12. Varanasi, Rajghat: Soil phosphate and chronosequence curve (after Eidt 1977).

ca 9th century BCE, and include evidence of Black Slipped Ware Culture. This indicates that the population of the city was small and spatially dispersed. Probably copper and iron working appear to have engaged a section of the society. The evidence further indicates to domestication of animals, a further sign of pastoral economy. The evidences at Aktha site further extend the settlement to *ca* 1200 BCE (cf. Jayaswal 1998).

The Puranic myth of Divodasa, a story of the struggle for power in the ancient period, also sheds light on the religious and political changes (cf. KKh 43). During this period the worship of *Yaksha*, a demigod (vegetal deity) and *Surya* (the sun) was prevalent (see Motichandra 1985: 31-33). The offshoots of this tradition are still recognisable in the form of *Bira* images, and solar discs and shrines. The later Jain and Buddhist literature refer to the visits of Tirthankara Parshvanatha and Mahavira, and the Buddha several times for learning, meditation and discourses. These accounts also mention the crafts, fabrics and mercantile goods such as perfumes, wood and ivory articles. Banaras was also mentioned as a famous halting station on the ancient northerly route, *Uttarapatha*, which had connected Rajagriha in the southeast and the sea coast to as far as Taxila (now in Pakistan) in the northwest (cf. *Vinayapitaka* 1.262; *Dhammapada* 1.126; Motichandra 1985: 48). During the Mauryan period this was a famous route and it grew in importance; later during the Muslim rule this road was renovated and revived, and it is presently known as the Grand Trunk Road, National Highway No. 2. The Buddha also walked on this great path and it figures importantly in Kipling's classic *Kim*. The city was a known centre of trade and commerce. It commanded an ideal position on the Ganga, linking the fertile Magadha (western Bihar), Anga (eastern Bihar) and Vanga (Bengal) regions with a number of developed cities of the West and Northwest on the one hand and Central India and Deccan on the other.

From Pali texts such as *Anguttaranikaya* and *Dighanikaya* and several *Jatakas* we can form some idea of Banaras in Buddhist times, during which the city-territory was generally known as Kashi. These sources mention the structure, condition, and components of early Banaras, especially the six beautiful gates surrounding the city, perhaps linked to the market areas of the city, the moats along the main protecting rampart walls, and the rest-houses for pilgrims and visitors. The archaeological excavations at Rajghat to the north of the present city inform on the earliest form of Banaras (cf. Jayaswal 1998). It is evident that by the turn of the 8th century BCE the city was established near the confluence of the Ganga and Varana, dominated by mud houses planned in a rectangular design, protected by a massive earthen wall. But by the turn of the 2nd century BCE burnt bricks became common for building. Other materials used in building construction included limestone concrete (*kankar*), burnt brick, mud, and wood (Singh, B.P. 1985). The plan of the city clearly showed open spaces between adjacent houses as well as segregating lanes. Sanitary arrangements were also developed in various phases by lining vertical pits with terracotta rings. At many places wells were situated close to main buildings. Houses of this period mostly had three to four rooms and an inner courtyard. Existence of ditches and drains near house-blocks indicate a functioning sewerage system (Singh 2005: 23). More recent excavations by the Department of Ancient Indian History, Culture and Archaeology, B.H.U. in Aktha village, about 3 km southwest of Sarnath, has pushed back the horizon of Kashi's culture to about 1200 BCE (Jayaswal 2000-02).

The excavations of Rajghat indicate the first use of brick traceable to the 3rd century BCE, from which time houses were built of both burnt and unburnt mud brick. Terracotta tiles and iron nails were also found. The lower portions of walls indicated dwellings without any regular formation, but with brick-lined wells and drains. There was no indication of structures with a religious purpose. Similar architectural remains were exposed for the next period, coinciding with the 1st-3rd centuries CE. Here, however, the walls of the houses were oriented approximately to the cardinal directions. A lesser number of domestic structures were noticed at the later level coinciding with the 4th-7th centuries. Noteworthy here were two square *kunds* (tanks) with widening sides, a brick-edged platform, kitchen with oven and storage jars, an apsidal structure (a shrine?), and another structure with large circular brick platforms. An outstanding feature associated with all these phases at the site was a rammed clay embankment rising more than 10 metres, presumably to shield the settlement from the Ganga floods (Biswas 2005: 43).

At the end of the 5th century BCE there was a short period in which the Shishunaga and Nandas ruled over the kingdom of Kashi. However, by the 4th century BCE the Mauryan dynasty took the rule. Ashoka (272-242 BCE), the great Mauryan king, had favoured Buddhism especially — even if also promoting and helping other religious and sects — and visited Sarnath (cf. *Jataka* 4.15), where under his patronage there developed a Buddhist township with many monasteries, *stupas* and shrines. After the downfall of the Mauryas, the glory of the city declined till the rule of the Kushanas in the 1st century CE. The inscriptions of the Kushana king Kanishka, dated 3rd century CE, refer to the persistence of Buddhism together with the animistic religion of Yaksha. In this period, Shaivism, which was closely associated with asceticism, received recognition as a popular religion. The city had not yet become apparently the prominent sacred place (*tirtha*) so famous in the following centuries. A number of clay seals discovered at the Rajghat mounds testify to the prosperity of the township. Rajghat is a site that was "settled for about 600 years (*ca* 800-200 BCE) but was abandoned for a considerably long time and was reoccupied only during the late medieval times" (Singh, B.P. 1985: 3). The archaeological layout of the houses, lanes and drainage channels shows a developed pattern of planning, as it is visible even today in the old parts. The city of Banaras from the Kushana to the beginning of the Gupta period was rich in artistic finds, as exemplified by the images of Bodhisattvas, Yakshas, and Nagas (cf. Vishwakarma 1987: 140-175). While describing the grand pilgrimage the *Mahabharata* also mentions Vrishabhadhvaja Shiva sanctuary, with its annexe bath pool Kapilahrida — presently called Kapiladhara.

While the Sarnath site preserves specimens of *stupas, viharas,* temples, and votive shrines spanning a period of almost a thousand years, the same cannot be said of Banaras itself where there is a dearth of such architectural evidence. All we have are wall panels, doorjambs, columns, and capping superstructure slabs discovered haphazardly in different parts of the city. Significantly, none of these remains is of any great size, suggesting that they come from modestly scaled shrines consecrated to different religious cults. Among such pieces are two inscribed stone pillars, perhaps from a temple porch (see BHU Museum BKB 225 and 29). One is incised with the name of its donor, Damasvamini, and a date equivalent to 478 CE. It is adorned with carvings of Vishnu, Vamana, Kevala Narasimha, and an unidentified deity (a goddess?) holding a lotus stalk. Its companion displays icons of Vishnu, Varaha, Narasimha, and Kapila — all forms of Vishnu (Biswas 2005: 45). Stone icons recovered from different parts of the city testify to the profusion of acculturating Buddhist, Jain, Hindu and animistic (e.g. Yaksha) cult divinities that received worship in ancient Kashi.

The Gupta period (*ca* 320-550 CE) was a time of great religious vitality and transformations. It is known as India's Golden Age. The Vaishnava tradition of Hindu religion was introduced, and cults like Skanda, Surya and folk and village guardians were also revived and given recognition. Architectural fragments of this period are scattered in and around the city. If one travels on the Panchakroshi road, one will find ample proof of the Gupta temples — surviving as fragmentary sculptures or with their architectural remains studded in the walls of these resurrected temples. The clay seals from this period give evidence of business, educational institutions and the importance of forests (cf. VyP 29.383; Jayaswal 1937: 123). During this period many of the earliest Puranas were composed. In literature the theology, symbolism and manifestations of Shiva became prominent and the earliest Puranas like the *Vayu*, *Markandeya*, and *Matsya* speak of the greatness of Shiva, his consort, many of his forms and the series of territories devoted to him. The Varanasi Stone Pillar Inscription of Buddhagupta found in Rajghat, dating from the Gupta year 159 (CE 478), testifies to the foundation of a Krishna temple in the city and other pious activities that promoted the establishment of religious monuments (cf. Biswas and Jha 1985: 43; also Bakker and Isaacson 2004: 25-26).

The use of burnt brick for building storehouses, temples, and shrines was prevalent in the Banaras of the Gupta period. Besides continuing the structural conditions of the earlier period with necessary modifications, this period is also credited with an impressive and peerless trade and warehouse complex. Iron nails for making joints, wooden beams, and stone pieces were also common. The houses at this time may be categorised into three major groups. The first group consists of mud houses with bamboo thickets for making walls and grass and weeds for roof, used by the poorer people and the artisan class. Later, such houses used fired clay tiles and bricks in addition to mud. The second group belonged to the merchant community and is represented by multi-storeyed houses of four to five rooms, the use of stone in the basement, an inner courtyard, and in some instances an attached warehouse complex. The third category of houses belonged to a higher class. Such dwellings were distinguished by their large size, three to five storeys in height with multiple rooms for different functions, several gates, and water pools or wells. Admittedly, the existence of houses of this type is mostly supported by literary sources but lacks archaeological evidence. By this time the city had expanded following a rough rectangular plan. The main road ran north-south, parallel to the Ganga. With buildings on either side, this road was regarded as one of the main thoroughfares, passing through the heart of the city. There were also side lanes similarly lined with residential structures. While there is evidence to demonstrate that Banaras was divided by many wide roads and lanes, there was no well-planned design (Singh 2005: 23-24).

Varanasi finally was established and recognised as a great sacred place (*tirtha*) in the late Gupta period. The association of the Shiva *lingas*, the Ganga river, and a few of the *ghats* was given religious-ritual meaning as described later in terms of its material position. Banaras was also able to maintain its glory as an old centre of trade, banking and commerce. During the first half of the 7th century, in the reign of Emperor Harsha of Kannauj (r. 606-48) the Chinese Buddhist pilgrim, Hsüan-tsang (Xuan Zang) arrived in the city and described it as thickly populated, prospering and an important seat of learning. He describes the city as a conglomerate of congested houses separated by narrow lanes, gardens and groves, and water pools with lotus flowers. He notices a predominance of Shiva temples, numbering twenty, and shrines with beautifully carved stone and wooden pillars and roofs. He also remarks on one particular Shiva *linga* that was about 30 metres high and clad with copper plate (Fleet 1963). This, in fact, was a Maurya-period Buddhist pillar, a fragment of which survives to this day under the name of Lat Bhairav, presently only 1.5 m tall. Furthermore, Xuan Zang described the nearby Buddhist township of Sarnath, with its many *stupas*, commemorative pillars, temples and shrines, eight divisions of residential quarters for the monks, surrounding wall, three water pools and numerous wells, a deer park and a forest tract.

By the turn of the 8th century widespread clearing of the forest took place and Banaras started expanding south of the present Dashashvamedh Road. This area was first settled by Hindu sages who were engaged in scholastic pursuits and who founded several small hermitages (*ashrams*). These *ashrams*, mostly associated with sacred places, were established under patronage, not only to consolidate Hindu worship but also to disseminate *shastric* knowledge. Besides, there was major expansion and transformation of landscape to the north of the city, which continued up to the 12th century.

The arrival and preaching of Adya Shankaracharya (*ca* CE 788-820) marks the revival of Brahmanical thought, which finally uprooted Buddhism from this soil (*Shankaradigvijaya* 6.81-84). It was here that Shankaracharya completed his main portion of the *Brahmasutra* (7.1). Shankara established the non-dualistic Shaiva doctrine that promoted the formation of the adherents' group, further segmented into 'ten' groups (*dashanami*). For the spatial expansion and dissemination of his ideas he established sacred sites (*pithas*) in the four corners of India, viz. Sharada at Shringeri (in the south, Karnataka), Kalika at Dvaraka (in the west, Gujarat), Jyotira at Badrinath (in the north, Uttarakhand) and Govardhana at Puri (in the east, Orissa). It is strongly believed that

81

he had also built his seat in Kashi, which in course of time converted into a large monastery known as Jangamabari Math. Further, after the passage of time this monastery became the headquarters of Virashaivism of the Lingayata sect. One of the inscriptions possessed by the monastery mentions that a yogi and Shaiva Jayanandadeva had founded the math in CE 574. During the Mughal period (1526-1707) many of the emperors donated grants of villages and landed properties to this monastery (cf. Sinha and Saraswati 1978: Appendix 7; 264-266). This points to the glories and recognition of the power of the monastery. The main *linga*, Chandramaulishvara, is said to have been installed by Shankara himself.

2. Pratiharas and Gahadavalas Periods

In the early medieval period, Banaras had passed from one ruler to another — from the Maukharis of Kannauj to the Gurjara Pratiharas (9th century). In the mid-10th century Banaras was under the rule of the Pratihara dynasty and had expanded southwards. At the turn of the 11th century the city came under the sway of the Kalachuris, a period that is generally acknowledged as the golden era in the city's history. Finally in the early 11th century it went under Gangeyadeva, king of Kannauj, descendant of the Kalachuris. Their first king Chandradeva is said to have acquired the kingship of Kanyakubja, i.e. Kannauja by his valour of arms after quelling the unrest among the people. Kanyakubja being a traditional seat of empires since the time of the Maukharis, it might have been their capital of honour; but Varanasi seemed to be their most favoured capital. There are about ninety inscriptions of the Gahadavalas, and a majority of them record donation of land to Brahmins after bathing in the Ganga river at Varanasi. This shows that they mostly lived in Varanasi and its environs. Karna was the most illustrious ruler of the Kalachuri dynasty. He is credited to have erected a Shiva temple at Varanasi, known as Karnameru, at a place that is still known as Karnaghanta. Varanasi and Allahabad were his favourite cities and at Allahabad he is said to have constructed a *ghat* called Karna Tirtha on the banks of Ganga. It is also said that the Kashmiri poet Bilhana or Chauras (*ca* 11th century) stayed with him at Varanasi for some time.

The Gahadavalas provided strong Hindu leadership and saw themselves as the protectors of the *tirthas*, especially four of the great *tirthas* of their realm, the most important of which were Kashi and, farther west along the Ganga, ancient Kannauj (cf. Niyogi 1959: 200-

02, 234-36). Kannauj was the city which, for three centuries, had been the political heart of North India, following the Gupta age. Now, Kannauj and Kashi became not only the recipients of the religious patronage of the Gahadavalas, but the administrative centres of their empire as well (Eck 1982: 80-81). With the Gahadavala kingdom, the city of Kashi came into political prominence for the first time in nearly two thousand years. Not since the days when Kashi vied with other North Indian kingdoms for prestige in the 6th and 7th centuries BCE had this been an imperial capital. Now Kashi entered a golden age. The Gahadavalas were liberal and eclectic in their religious patronage. In their inscriptions the kings described themselves as 'great worshippers of Shiva', the Lord of Kashi (Niyogi 1959: 196). Shiva is referred to as Krittivasa in some inscriptions, indicating that the great temple of Krittivasa was at its height in this period. Nonetheless, the most famous of these kings, Govindachandra, had two queens who espoused and patronized Buddhism. For the most part, however, the Gahadavalas were worshippers of Vishnu, and in one inscription, Govindachandra (1114-1154), the greatest in the history of this dynasty, is praised as an incarnation of Vishnu, commissioned to protect Vishnu's favourite abode, the city of Varanasi (Niyogi 1959: 202-3). He had defeated the Muslim invaders two times during 1114-1118, and patronised the Hindu religion. Queen Kumar Devi, wife of Govindachandra, came from a Vajrayani (Tantric) Buddhist family. She restored several buildings at Sarnath and built a new *vihara* (hostel for monks) there.

The Rajghat Plateau had once served as the centre of the royal capital of Gahadavala dynasty, and at the patron temple of Adi Keshava, the 'Original Vishnu', the king Govindachandra made numerous ritual donations, including the gift of the tax revenues of a small village to the support of some particular Brahmin or temple. An inscription dated CE 1093 refers to this Vishnu temple and the associated *ghat* named after him. Govinclachandra left over fifty inscriptions recording such charitable donations to temples of Shiva, Vishnu, and Surya (Eck 1982: 81). In the days of Govindachandra the city was known as an important centre for learning Vedas, Sanskrit grammar, philosophy and medicine. Perhaps later in this period the *Kashi Khanda* became attached to the *Skanda Purana* as a major canto.

Govindachandra was indeed a great patron of learning, and perhaps the most important thing he did in his entire reign was to appoint the learned Brahmin Lakshmidhara as his chief minister. Almost single-handedly, Lakshmidhara inaugurated a new era in Hindu religious literature by compiling one of the earliest, most reputable, and most extensive digests (*nibandhas*) of literature on *dharma*, composed in 14 volumes, known as the *Krityakalpataru*, 'The Magical Wishing Tree of Duties' (cf. *Epigraphica Indica* 2.1, 9.59). Later compilers of digests borrowed extensively from this pioneering work (Eck 1982: 81-82). Here he brought together quotations from the vast literature of the Epics, Puranas, and Dharmashastras, topic by topic, covering such subjects as the duties of householders and kings, the establishing of divine images, the rites of worship, the rites for the dead, the giving of charitable donations, and, of course, the visiting of *tirthas*. In one of its volumes, he mentions the scriptural references to over 350 shrines in Kashi, to the development and demarcation of the holy territory of the Panchakroshi (an archetypal cosmic circuit) and also points out the close connections between the scholars of Banaras and Kashmir. He had also advanced his theory of Hindu *tirtha*, which is grounded both on an inner level (archetype and body symbolism) and an outer one (spatial affinity and orientation). Govindachandra gave Lakshmidhara the lofty epithet of 'Spokesman for Reflection upon All Knowledge' (*sarvavidya-vichara-vachaspati*) (Niyogi 1959: 230).

Another scholar of the period, Pt Damodara Bhatta's work the *Uktivyakti Prakarana* expresses the culture and social life of the people, mentioning the condition of houses and the use of space, farming and cooking of rice and wheat, gardens and groves and fruits, cows and oxen, the king and the people, economy and business, and religious life and taboos. Anandadhara's *Madhavanalyakhyana* also describes the glories as well as the defiled culture of the period.

Banaras under the Gahadavalas was at its zenith. The three sacred zones, surrounding the present Ornkareshvara, Vishveshvara, and Kedareshvara Temples were fully developed and inhabited by traders and migrants from different parts of the country. A chain of shrines linked by pilgrimage routes delineated these three segments. Various occupational groups with artisans, craftsmen, and other service people settled on the western margin of the ridge that lined the Ganga and also along the streams that lay inland. Most of the ponds and lakes were converted into *jalatirthas* (water-front sacred sites) associated with both Puranic and other deities, or even special deities belonging to a particular social group. This development led to the diffusion and spread of miscellaneous types of settlements from the limit of Rajghat in the north to Asi Nala in the south and Pishachmochan and Baijnattha in the west. The Gahadavala king Govindachandra is credited for the development of proper *ghats* along the Ganga, as well as several sacred wells, gardens, groves, and pools. Madanpura, a neighbourhood in the then southern part of the city, was inhabited by the people in the name of the Gahadavala ruler, Madanpal (r. 1104-1114). Later, another ward, Govindpura, was founded by Dalel Khan during the reign of Govindachandra. The glories and prosperities of the Gahadavalas are exemplified by the 84 inscriptions (mostly on copper plates, except the one on stone) found in the middle Ganga valley — the stronghold of their kingdom. Out of the total, 41 were directly referring to donations and gifts of the king, and were found in Varanasi city and its environs.

After the demolition of the Rajghat fort in 1194 by Qutbuddin Aibak and Shahabuddin, the inhabitants of the area had to shift toward the west and southwest. Most of the main deities at the time were situated to the west and southwest of Rajghat. The great Patan Darwaza standing to the south of Matsyodari (now Machhodari) near Gai Ghat was the main gate to the river port, with most of the city's population located to its north, southeast, and southwest. Numerous groups of people also settled around sacred places in Pakka Mahal, areas which had been forested in pre-Gahadavala times. People also lived in small wards in the peripheral areas of the city, including a Muslim community descended from the military men of Malik Afzal Alvi, the then general of Salar Masud Ghazi who invaded Banaras in 1034-35.

With the spread of Shaivism across northern India the religious prestige of Banaras continued to increase. Shiva, the principal divinity of Banaras, was recognised as Mahadeva, the Great God, or *Ishvara*. Thus there spread hundreds of temples and shrines with the suffix '*ishvara*', such as Tarakeshvara (built in 1792 by Ahilyabai Holkar), Ratneshvara (built in 1828 by Baijabai), Samrajeshvara (built in 1843 by Rajendra Vikram Shah, king of Nepal), etc., all being dedicated to some particular manifestation of Shiva. With the growth of the city's population, augmented by migrants from different parts of the country, the city must have acquired a cosmopolitan character. A large number of temples and shrines were established and several places within the urban territory became *tirthas* (holy spots) of varying sizes and glories. It was during this period that the well-known Avimukteshvara *linga* came to be replaced by that of Vishveshvara. Even so, the Adi Keshava (Vishnu) Temple seems to have served as the cult shrine for the royal family. The noted scholar of this era, Lakshmidhara, describes no less than 350 temples in the city, thereby confirming the growth of Banaras as the pre-eminent religious nucleus of northern India under the Gahadavalas. During this era the city expanded up to Lolarka Kund in the south, where lies the famous solar disc. Here Queen Goshala Devi performed sacred baths and donated villages to the Brahmins.

The inscriptions of this period mention seven *ghats* along the Ganga.

In the Gahadavala period Vajrayana Buddhism had reached its climax. Their followers were mostly engaged in enjoying liquor, non-vegetarian food, sex and terrible gestures. Innumerable variety of deities and divinities were introduced in this period. There were example of conflicts among Brahminical Hindus and Vajrayani Buddhists. The battle between these two groups is narrated in the various mythologies. The sense of animosity, the culture of cheating, the dominance of prostitutes and brothel culture were the offshoots of such downfall.

The Tantric rituals were transferred to left-handed black magic (*vamacharas*), and even soldiers from the royal court were involved in such activities. Such practitioners were called Kapalikas. In some of the monasteries (*mathas*) on auspicious occasions like *Chakra puja* there also performed animal sacrifices and even human ones (Singh, SP BM: 80). Such seats received the protection of the royal soldiers because both the *sadhakas* and soldiers tried to bring the people against Chandradeva, the peace-loving king of the half-territory whose palace was across the Varana river. Day-by-day the Tantrics were increasing in number.

A sect of Buddhism practising Tantrism, called Vajrayanis, dominated the territory of Rishipattan (modern Sarnath) which was formerly surrounded by dense forest, Mahavana (Singh, S.P. BM: 53, 54). In this Mahavana, the Buddhist Vajrayanis were performing their sacrifice and rituals of Panchamakaras with the help of *mans* (meat), *mina* (fish), *madira* (wine), *mudra* (physical postures), and *maithuna* (sex). [Note the *Pancha*, five; and *makara,* the letter *m*]. This promoted terror among the people, who were scared of such rituals performed in that central tract of forest. Even today some of Aghoris, follower of the left-hand Tantrism, practice such rituals.

Jayachandra, the grandson of Govindachandra Gahadavala, was a rival of the Chahamana king Prithviraja. Both of them wanted to establish their hegemony over the whole North India; both wasted their efforts in this rivalry and both were losers. Taking advantage of their internal conflict, Qutbuddin Aibak, a slave-general of Muhammad Ghori, after vanquishing Prithviraj, defeated Jayachandra in 1193-94 and beheaded him. His army sacked and looted the city, destroying nearly one thousand temples in Banaras City alone and raising mosques on their foundation using the debris of the temples (Niyogi 1959: 193). It took 1,400 camels to haul away the plunder. The glorious century of Govindachandra ended in catastrophe (Eck 1982: 82). The second invasion by Qutbuddin Aibak in 1197-98 that records the defeat of King Harishachandra, son of Jayachandra, marks the end of the glories of the Gahadavalas (cf. Motichandra 1985: 126).

3. The Delhi Sultanate and Mughal Eras

In the late 12th century conflicts among Chandelas, Gahadavalas and Chahamanas started, especially for their ascendancy of power. Alas, they were unaware about the turning of the wheel of time of cycle which was ended by the invasion of Sultan Muizuddin Muhammad bin Sam (generally known as Shihabuddin or Muhammad Ghori) in 1192-94, and finally by the defeat of the Hindu king Harishchandra, the last Gahadavala king. This opened the door for the Muslim rule. A book of that period, *Jayachandra Prabandha*, describes the glories, pitfalls, diplomatic relations and political corruption. With the second invasion of Banaras by Aibak in 1197 the glory of the Gahadavalas was lost forever. Mosques like Dhai Kangure, Chaubisa Khambha, Bhadaon and Ganje Shahida are representative of this period; they were built with the debris of the Hindu temples demolished in the recent past, mostly at the same sites.

In 1206 Aibak became the emperor at Delhi and reigned till 1210; he issued an order for the destruction of temples. This was the period when the major Shiva temples in Banaras, like Vishvanatha, Krttivasheshvara, Avimukteshvara, Kala Bhairava, Adi Mahadeva, Siddheshvara, Kumbhishvara, Hiranyaksheshvara, Yajnavalkeshvara, Baneshvara, Balishvara, Kapaleshvara, Kapileshvara, etc. were demolished. In this way the Delhi Sultanate was established and the entire Ganga valley came under Muslim domination.

After about sixteen years after the first destruction by Aibak, in the period of Iltutamish (1211-1226) a revolt took place in the city which slowed down the speed of destroying the temples. However, the processes of demolishing of temples and the construction of new temples were going on together in parallel (Motichandra 1985: 182). It was said that in the period of Iltutamish the temple of Vishveshvara was rebuilt. An inscription of that period mention that a well known devotee and merchant from Gujarat, named Vastupala, had donated hundred thousands rupees as gift to Vishveshvara. A *muhalla*, Hajidaras, named after him, still exists in the city. Iltutamish died in Banaras where his tomb is still stands in *muhalla* Qazzaqpura. In the period of Allauddin Khilzi (1292-1316) the process of destruction of Hindu temples continued. However, it is surprising to note that in 1296 a saint Padmasadhu built a grand temple of Padmeshvara facing temple of Padmeshvara facing Vishveshvara. However, during the reign of the Sharqi Sultans this temple of Padmeshvara was destroyed and Lal Darwaza Mosque (Atala) was built up at Jaunpur with the same materials in CE 1447 (cf. Pathak 2007-08: 172). The inscription on the wall of this mosque refers that it was made with the remains of the Padmeshvara temple. Based on inscriptional information, it is obviously noted that during 1296-1447 the temple of Vishveshvara was the sacrosanct landmark in the city. This is a clear indication of a change in the attitude of fanatic Muslim rulers. In this period Manikarnika Ghat was constructed in stone in 1302; this is confirmed by inscriptional evidence, which makes this *ghat* the first for which we have a date. Another inscription mentions that on 24th July 1302, a person named Vireshvara built Manikarnikeshvara Temple, which was commemorated by giving the same name to the adjacent *ghat* (Motichandra 1985: 183).

During the 14th century the city was divided into two broad segments. The 'Deva Varanasi' was spread over in the southern part surrounding Vishvanatha temple. The 'Yavana Varanasi', predominantly occupied by Muslims, was situated in the northern part. This spatial segmentation has prevailed even today. In spite of great turmoil and dominance of Muslim culture and Islam, the city of Varanasi maintained its glory as the city of Shiva through the system of rituals and performances. Everywhere there were monasteries and houses of various sects, and also everywhere deceitful people and swindlers were flourishing.

According to local tradition Jalaluddin Ahmad was in charge of Banaras during the reign of Ghiasuddin Tughluq (1321-1325), and he founded a *muhalla* named Jalaluddinpura. Following the sack of the city by the forces of Muhammad Ghori, again in the late 14th century Firoz Shah Tughlaq (1351-1388) destroyed many temples (Elliot and Dowson 1905, II: 222-224). In November 1353, Firoz Shah Tughluq marched against Ilyas Hazi, who had declared himself Sultan Samsuddin and included Banaras into his dominion (Joshi 1963: 45). It was only after reaching Banaras that Firoz could collect Government dues from the people of Varanasi. In 1394 Mohammad Shah Tughluq established the dynasty of Sharqi Sultans in Jaunpur; they imposed heavy taxes on the pilgrims visiting Varanasi (Pathak 2007-08: 272). In the 15th century, the city came under the rule of the Sharqi kings of Jaunpur, and temples were again destroyed, and their blocks hauled away for the construction of a mosque in Jaunpur. During the moments of calm, Hindus rebuilt temples and *lingas* but these were again destroyed by the next wave of invaders. After the passage of time, the city came under the rule of the Lodis (1451-1526), who had seized power from the Sharqis, and again a major part of the city was destroyed by Sikander Lodi.

The main revolutionary and reformer in this period was Ramananda (1299-1411), who challenged the rigid rule of Brahminic social hierarchy and propounded devotionalism (*bhakti*) as a way to God. He told that there is no line defining purity and pollution in the eyes of God. It is the human intention and wish for supremacy that produced a hierarchical order; all those who worship God are only 'devotees' (*bhaktas*), irrespective of caste, creed and ways of worship. Additionally, he raised and awakened the low caste people (including untouchables). The best known propagator of Ramananda's noble thought was Kabir (1398-1518). Kabir was known as a great challenger of superstitions, who struck at the root of caste distinctions, idolatry and all the external paraphernalia of religious life. Kabir and Banaras were an integral part of a social revolution in the 15th century. Says Kabir (*Bijaka* 25. 83, cf. Singh & Hess 1977: 26):

> Pandits read *Puranas, Vedas*.
> Mullas learn Muhammad's faith.
> Kabir says, both go straight to hell
> if they don't know Rama in every breath.

Kabir never tried to adjust with the situation, rather he followed the path of challenging the evils existing both among the Hindus and Muslims. Kabir emphasised the universal integrity and its understanding through the path of love. Even Mullahs were impressed by his revelation as "he may be saying the plain truth exemplified by deep experiences, therefore whenever he spoke people were attracted to hear him silently, whatever their status were — high or low!" He proclaimed that "all the paths merged into the path of love, either Hinduism or Islam; it is our convenience to put them under dogmatic limitations that nurture disparate identity and belonging". One of his close friends, Raidas/Ravidas (1418-1547), a cobbler saint, said "there is no authority in caste and kin, he who practices devotion crosses over the world". Another contemporary saint and founder of Sikhism, Nanak (1469-1539) is also said to have paid several visits to Varanasi and have had discussions with Kabir and Raidas. These saint-poets and reformers taught the idea of a formless ultimate being.

In the 15th century the Brahminical belief systems were laden with a dominance of rituals, superstitions, folk totemism, oracles, performances of fasts and festivals, variety of sects and groups, and Tantra's distortion as black magic. In fact, the Brahminical religion became more like a loose assemblage of many contrasting and desperate ideologies based on personal whims. The Brahmin priests became more materialist, desperate and victims of worldly pleasures and corruption. On the other end Islam was a well organised religion promoting a strict following of its rules, thus no freedom for escape was given to the person who had once accepted Islam. The sympathetic attitude to living beings, respect to mankind, tolerance, non-violence, etc., all such norms of Hinduism had to face the rules and system which were against this conception. Nevertheless, the Hindus learnt how to adjust and survive in the new situation, of course after a great sacrifice.

During the Sultanate period from *ca* 1200 until the reign of Akbar (r. 1556-1605), the history of the city cannot be easily reconstructed. However, many of the mosques and tombs that still survive were built during the Sultanate period, presumably with both local and imported craftsmen and labour, thus providing employment. The fact that few temples of this or earlier periods have survived is significant. Certain sultans were less tolerant than others. Not until the Mughal emperor Akbar ascended the throne did Hindu patrons again begin to build religious edifices. Man Singh and Raja Todarmal, the two senior Rajput ministers in the court of Akbar, participated actively in repairing the temples and *ghats* of Banaras. One of the oldest *ghats*, called Adi Vishveshvara Ghat, named after the Vishveshvara Temple in its close vicinity, was partly constructed in stone by the king of Bundi in 1580, which led to its renaming as Bundi Parkota Ghat (Hegewald 2005: 68). It is commonly accepted that in the regime of Akbar the Christian priests started visiting north India, and during his time already in Goa the Portuguese missionaries established a few churches.

Akbar visited Jaunpur to crush the rebellion of Ali Quli Khan in 1566, and after quelling the rebellion, he marched towards Chunar and Banaras on 24 January 1566. Immediately after Akbar's departure, Ali Quli again revolted against the Emperor and sent troops to Ghazipur and Jaunpur. In such a period of turmoil Iskander and Bahadur attacked Banaras and plundered the whole city (Srivastava 1972: 94). Akbar decided to stay for sometime to see the rebellion quelled, and finally he marched from Jaunpur on 3

March 1566 (Abul Fazl's *Akbarnama*, p. 397). In the following year, 1567, Akbar made a second visit to the holy city but was not welcomed by the local people who shut their doors against the Emperor. Humiliated by this behaviour, he issued a general order to plunder the city of Banaras. The order was countermanded, but it was too late by then (ibid.: 435).

Like Mirza Chin Qulij, the *fauzdar* of Banaras, who rebelled during Jahangir's reign (*ca* 1611) but was killed, Jahangir's son Khurram (later known as Shahjahan) also rebelled against his father but was compelled to return to Banaras in 1624 (Elliot & Dowson 1867, IV: 394; also Fisher and Hewett 1884: 218). Abdul Hamid Lahori (the author of the *Badashahnama*, the official history of Shahjahan's reign) has described this incidence in detail. A Persian inscription found in Banaras, dated 1618, mentions that in Jahangir's reign Khwajah Muhammad Salef, the *fauzdar* of Banaras, had sponsored and supervised the building of a mosque, and also founded a neighbourhood called after him as Muhalla Khwajapura (Fisher and Hewett 1884: 132). During the reigning period of Shahjahan an order was issued that new temples under construction at Banaras should be pulled down without delay. The Subedar of Allahabad reported to the Court about the destruction of 76 temples in Banaras in 1632 (Elliot & Dowson 1867, VII: 36). In 1657 Banaras was attacked by Shuja, younger brother of Aurangzeb and then in-charge of Bengal, but he was defeated by his brother Dara Shikoh. But Shuja did not squander the chance when Dara Shikoh was defeated at the hands of Aurangzeb in the struggle for succession. He seized Banaras and ejected Ramdas, the commander of the fort, exacted forcefully a loan of 3 lakh rupees from the city and proceeded to Jaunpur (cf. Sarkar 1928: 184).

A great sigh of relief was surely heaved in the late 16th century when Mughal Emperor Akbar granted more religious freedom. The Rajputs Man Singh and Todarmal, the two senior ministers in the court of Akbar, participated actively in repairing, rebuilding and in new construction of temples and *ghats* in Banaras during this part of the Mughal period. It is commonly believed that the Vishveshvara temple was rebuilt in 1585 for a third time at a third site (see the model view, Fig. 3) under the supervision of Narayana Bhatta, the noted scholar and compiler of the *Tristhalisetu* ('Bridge to the Three Sacred Places': Kashi, Prayag, and Gaya). Unfortunately, still no inscriptional source was found to prove the testimony and this interpretation. In most instances, except of course many mosques constructed in the city, Islam had largely been associated with destruction and forcible conversion of sacred buildings in Banaras. It was Raghunath Tandan, the finance secretary of the Mughal emperor Akbar, who initiated the firm construction in stone of the previously unbound sand embankment of Panchaganga Ghat. In the 17th century Raja Man Singh, the king of Amber, made Manasarovar Ghat firm using stone slabs. Because of its pre-eminent ritual importance Manikarnika Ghat is an exception with respect to the early date of its secure building in stone. Little information with regards to the architecture of other *ghats* is available before the 16th century. Based on inscriptional evidence, Panchaganga Ghat, which is one of the five most sacred bathing places on the Ganga, as well as Adi Vishveshvara Ghat, were clad in stone in 1580 (Hegewald 2005: 68).

During the 15th century the culture and people of Kashi faced serious threats, but in the late 16th century, they enjoyed an era of peace under the reign of Akbar (r. 1556-1605) who was liberal in tolerating Hindu religion. Akbar is often adduced as an example of the tolerant ruler, whose policies demonstrate that though he himself was a Muslim, the state was not Islamic. Some have even pointed to him as a 'secular' ruler, when scarcely any monarch in Europe was such at this time, and his advocacy of a new faith, the *Din-i-ilahi*, which combined elements from various religions, exemplifies the ecumenism with which he is associated. Due "to diffuse, individualistic system, putting stress, on the one hand, on concrete ritual acts of worship of the physical, symbolic representations of divine persons and forces, and on the other hand, on broad, speculative, and free thinking about eternal questions of right morality, and the nature of the universe" (Cohn 1971: 67), Hinduism had reached to the cliff of devastation. In this context Kabir took the lead to provide a path but succeeded only marginally, while Tulasi succeeded well. Tulasi (1547-1623) followed a different form of *bhakti* (devotionalism) based on incarnation and anthropomorphic vision of God. He had been preceded by Vallabha (1479-1531), who was born near Chunar, a town 40 km southeast of Banaras, and who studied and passed many years in Banaras. It is no doubt that Tulasi was disturbed with the defiled condition of the city, as he narrated it at many places. Tulasi felt that such happenings were due to the inauspicious moment of time, as there lays the shadow of Saturn at constellation Pisces (cf. *Kavitavali* VII. 177). At the outset of one of the sections of his work, *Vinaya Patrika* ('Petition to Rama') Tulasi praises Kashi and its Lord,

Shiva. Although as devotee of Rama one might call Tulasi a Vaishnava, the poet consistently displays a non-sectarian spirit in his apprehension of the Divine (Eck 1982: 88). He begins one hymn to Kashi:

> Serve with love all life through Kashi,
> > the wish-giving cow of this Dark Age,
> It banishes woe, affliction, sin, disease,
> > and it amasses all things auspicious.
>
> (Allchin 1966: 22-23)

The magical wish-giving cow of which Tulasi writes is the bestower of all desires. At the close of his last collection, the *Kavitavali*, Tulasi blesses Kashi as that place where all men are as Shiva and all women as Parvati. And he takes his leave with a note of mourning for the plague which was then causing great suffering to the citizens (Allchin 1964: 197-204).

The greatest mistake of Tulasi was his submissive nature and the glorification of the conservative ideas of Brahmins, and also denying the acceptance of the *dalits*. Being born in a traditional Brahmin family and having being nurtured along these lines, he was unable to escape from the social and cultural evils thrust upon by the Brahmins. Of course, he succeeded in establishing an ideal order of society and culture, however he failed measurably to challenge the social hierarchy based on purity-pollution grading and the exploitative strategies of the landlords and Brahmin priests. Tulasi lived through the best days of the Mughal period in Banaras.

The late medieval period in the history of Banaras saw the rise and spread of a new wave of popular *bhakti* devotionalism in North India. In this movement, the classical Sanskrit literature yielded to a vibrant new poetic literature composed in the languages of the common people. Despite its reputation as a stronghold of Hindu orthodoxy and conservatism, Banaras participated in the vibrant devotional resurgence during the 14th to the early 17th centuries. Among the active poets and reformers the most notable were Vallabha, Ramananda, Kabir, Raidas, Tulasi, Chaitanya and Guru Nanak. Kabir, indeed, was one of the greatest poets in the whole Indian literature, whose colloquial songs are still sung today (cf. Medhasananda 2002: 16). Tulasi retold the epic story of the *Ramayana* in vernacular Hindi, naming it the *Ramacharitamanasa*, which remains to this day the single most popular classic, the 'Bible' of the Hindi-speaking people. The greater part of this great epic was completed in Banaras.

During the period of Jahangir (1602-1627) Banaras was not in the limelight. In the late 16th century Ralph Fitch (1583-1591), an English traveller, paid a visit to the city and described its social and cultural life. He also described various taboos, images, rituals, ways and means of religious performances, and other cultural activities. Fitch went on to describe the rites he saw people performing along the riverbank:

> And by breake of day and before, there are men and women which come out of the towne and wash themselves in Ganges. And there are divers old men which upon places of earth made for the purpose, sit praying, and they give the people three or foure straws, which they take and hold them betweene their fingers when they wash themselves; and some sit to marke them in the forheads, and they have in a cloth a litle rice, barlie, or money, which, when they have washed themselves, they give to the old men which sit there praying. Afterwards they go to divers of their images, and give them of their sacrifices. And when they give, the old men say certaine prayers and then all is holy.

(cf. Foster, 1921: 20)

With the passing of time, during the reign of Akbar's grandson Shahjahan (1627-1657), the imperial policy changed again, trying to blend Persian and Indian cultures. It was reported that in the early years of his reign many new temples had either been constructed or were in the process of construction in north India. While the *shariat* might allow the continued existence of ancient places of worship of other religions under the regime of a Muslim ruler, construction of new ones challenged the very core of the Islamic state. Shahjahan wasn't one to ignore this challenge. That is how finally he ordered that "whatsoever idol-temples had been recently built be razed to the ground." By his order, about seventy-six temples under construction and seventy existent temples were ultimately destroyed. However, in this period by the initiatives of the great scholar Kabindracharya (1627-70), the *zakat* tax on the Hindu pilgrims was withdrawn by the king.

Dara Shikoh (1614-1657), son of Shahjahan and elder brother of Aurangzeb, was disappointed by the biased policies and vested interests of Muslim rulers. He had tried his best to protect the existence and maintenance of Hindu temples in Banaras. In his capacity as governor he issued royal orders (*farmans*) on these lines. One of such *farmans* ordered the Brahmin priest Panda Bhimarao Lingiya (*Lingayat*) that clearly expresses his views (cf. Pandey 1975: 20):

> O! The existing authorities and the assistants (*ahalgaras*, officials). With the courtesy of the Emperor and his expectations, this news has reached before me. That means, the *farman* issued by the Emperor that refers to the receipts (gifts) etc. offered to the temples of Banaras, including Vishveshvara, to be noted that this was granted to them by the Hindu trusts. Meanwhile, an order is issued from myself that is in honour of the crown, to be followed that the offerings and gifts presented or possessed by the Lingiyas, to be left to their occupancy without any interference. Date 4 of the month Safar 30 Julus Mubaraq, i.e. 1067 Hizri (CE 1658).

After murdering his two elder brothers, Dara Shikoh and Murad Bakhsh, and younger brother Shah Shuja, and imprisoning his father Shahjahan, Aurangzeb (r. CE 1657-1707) succeeded to get hold of the crown. He was even more fundamentalist than other preceding Mughal emperors in his disdain for the temples and shrines of the Hindus. At the first two years of his reign he had shown interest in maintaining peace and law and order with an aim to improve his cruel image. Soon afterwards (1659) he had ordered that "according to the Islamic rules no old temples should be destroyed; however no new temples should be built. ... Such arrangements should be made that no one illegally interferes in the religious activities of the (Hindu) Brahmins". Sarkar (1928, vol. 3: 249-250) suggested that Aurangzeb intended nothing less than to establish an Islamic state in India, an objective that could not be fulfilled without "the conversion of the entire population to Islam and the extinction of every form of dissent". He further suggests that the *jizya* (poll-tax) on non-Muslims, which Aurangzeb had re-instituted in 1679, was aimed at forcibly converting Hindus to Islam, though he was unable to marshal evidence to substantiate this view. In 1659 by his order the temple of Krittivasheshvara was demolished and its place the Alamgiri Mosque was built; its date of construction was mentioned in the inscription dated Hijri 1068 (1659).

As soon as Aurangzeb established his authority on the imperial throne, he prohibited Hindu teaching and learning. On 18th April 1669, he came to know that in spite of his orders people, including Muslims, were going to Banaras for education. Immediately he issued orders to the Provincial Governors for the demolition of Hindu schools and temples. To prove their loyalty and over-enthusiasm the splendorous temples of Vishvanatha and Veni Madhava were razed down, and mosques were constructed on their foundations using their remains; Aurangzeb got to know about this on 2nd September 1669. In his zeal for crushing the religious places of the Hindus, Aurangzeb even tried to rename the city 'Muhammadabad', and coins were also issued bearing that name, but the name did not stick (Altekar 1947: 250).

Fortunately, on 12th December 1665, before these sad happenings, the French Traveller Jean-Baptiste Tavernier, a dealer in jewels, had paid a visit to Banaras and described the architectural beauty and grandeur of Vindu Madhava temple at the riverside, which he called a 'great pagoda'. His account is notable because the temple was demolished in 1673 by the armies of Aurangzeb. The French traveller Jean-Baptiste Tavernier's narration describes:

> Returning to the pagoda at Benares. The building, like all the other pagodas, is in the figure of a cross having its four arms equal. In the middle a lofty dome rises like a kind of tower with many sides terminating in a point, and at the end of each arm of the cross another tower rises, which can be ascended from outside. Before reaching the top there are many niches and several balconies, which project to intercept the fresh air; and all over the tower there are rudely executed figures in relief of various kinds of animals. Under this great dome, and exactly in the middle of the pagoda, there is an altar like a table, of 7 to 8 feet in length, and 5 to 6 wide, with two steps in front, which serve as a footstool, and this footstool is covered with a beautiful tapestry, sometimes of silk and sometimes of gold and silk, according to the solemnity of the rite which is being celebrated. The altar is covered with gold or silver brocade, or some beautiful painted cloth. From outside the pagoda this altar faces you with the idols upon it; for the women and girls must salute it from the outside, as, save only those of a certain tribe,

they are not allowed to enter the pagoda. Among the idols on the great altar one stands 5 or 6 feet in height; neither the arms, legs, nor trunk are seen, only the head and neck being visible; all the remainder of the body, down to the altar, is covered by a robe which increases in width below. Sometimes on its neck there is a rich chain of gold, rubies, pearls, or emeralds. This idol has been made in honour and after the likeness of Bainmadou [Veni Madhava], formerly a great and holy personage among them, whose name they often have on their lips. On the right side of the altar there is also the figure of an animal, or rather of a chimera, seeing that it represents in part an elephant, in part a horse, and in part a mule. It is of massive gold, and is called Garou [Garuda], no person being allowed to approach it but the Brahmans. It is said to be the resemblance of the animal which this holy personage rode upon when he was in the world, and that he made long journeys on it, going about to see if the people were doing their duty and not injuring anyone. At the entrance of the pagoda, between the principal door and the great altar, there is to the left a small altar, upon which an idol made of black marble is seated, with the legs crossed, and about two feet high.

(as in Mahajan 1994: 75-76)

Tavernier (1665) has also described the sandstone column of Lat Bhairava which was then preserved to a height of more than 10 metres, standing on the edge of Kapalamochana Kund in the northern part of the city. British scholar John Irwin (1984) interprets this relic as the stump of a lofty Buddhist column associated with the *stupa* and other religious structures that once stood beside the road running from Kashi to Sarnath, as noticed by the Chinese Buddhist pilgrim Xuan Zang (Hsüan-tsang) in CE 636. He has further argued that the column may actually predate Ashoka's reign, but since it is impossible to examine its original sandstone surface for any inscription, this opinion cannot be confirmed. Most likely, Lat Bhairava forms a counterpart to Ashoka's column at Sarnath, without doubt the most celebrated ancient monument in the Banaras area, even if now broken. Its quadruple-lion capital is now displayed in the Archaeological Museum, only a short distance from its original find spot. The Lat Bhairava has acquired considerable notoriety since it was the site of the Hindu-Muslim riot of 1809, one of the worst in the city's history. Presently it is worshipped as a manifestation of Bhairava, whose polished metallic face protrudes out of the orange cloth that is presently draped over the column; Lat Bhairava stands within an *idgah* compound still in use.

There is no major religious sanctuary in the city of Banaras that pre-dates the time of Aurangzeb in the 17th century. The only temple complex which was saved from the destruction is at Kandwa (i.e. Kardameshvara), because of its location in the countryside making it nearly inaccessible during that period. The city of Puranic glory and beauty as it was known in the 12th century had completely disappeared by the end of the 17th century. The sacred city could not be destroyed, but it could certainly be defaced.

Despite the discouraging, repeated ruination of the period, Banaras continued to be an important centre of intellectual life and religious thought. However, the traditions of learning for which the city was famous could not easily be broken, for they were independent of the rise and fall of temples. During the latter part of this period, the French scholar and medical doctor, François Bernier, visited Banaras, which he called the Athens of India, and recorded his observations in a letter to one Monsieur Chapelain (Eck 1982: 84):

> The town contains no colleges or regular classes, as in our universities, but resembles rather the schools of the ancients; the masters being dispersed over different parts of the town in private houses, and principally in the gardens of the suburbs, which the rich merchants permit them to occupy. Some of these masters have four disciples, others six or seven, and the most eminent may have twelve or fifteen; but this is the largest number. It is usual for the pupils to remain ten or twelve years under their respective preceptors...
>
> (Bernier 1914: 334)

Some of the notable structures in the city and its neighbour-hood associated with the Sultanate and Mughal periods are the shrines and *idgah* at Bakaria Kund (Fig.13), the Arhai Kangura mosque, and the mosque at Panchaganga Ghat. Other architectural vestiges masked by groves and orchards are to be found in the area south of the Varana near Rajghat fort and even north of the Varana up to Sarnath.

Fig. 13. An old scene of Bakaria Kund and the ruins of Hindu temple
(after Sherring 1868: p. 282).

The early Muslim settlers of Banaras might have occupied some
vacant spaces in the southern portions of the city, particularly in the
present Shiwala mohalla. The westward limit of urban growth during
these centuries was marked by the present Durgakund-Bhelupura
Road and Ramapura and Godaulia-Jagatganj Roads, and on the north
by the Varana river. This is quite clear from the present distribution
of the Muslim population and their old structures. Before the arrival
of the Muslims the Hindu city lay mainly to the east of the present
Assi-Godaulia and Godaulia-Jagatganj Roads.

Most of the Mughal rulers interpreted the rules ordained in their
holy book the *Quran* at different degrees according to their ideology
and choice. Since "God Almighty himself in the *Quran* commanded
the complete degradation of the non-Muslim" (*yan yad yaham saghrun*;
cf. Sale's *Quran*, p. 152), slaying, plundering and imprisoning of the
non-Muslim became routine, and profusely exemplified in the pages
of Mughal history of mass destruction, killing and conversion.

On the name of *moksha*, the Brahmin priests of the temple of
Kashi Karvat were religiously murdering innocent and devout
Hindus (cf. Justice 1997: 43-45). This place was used by the *pandas*
and *pujaris* (priests) to persuade pilgrims to commit ritual suicide
during the medieval period (16th-17th centuries). According to local
sources these *pandas* would throw innocent devotees from the upper

during the medieval period (16th-17th centuries). According to local sources these *pandas* would throw innocent devotees from the upper part of the well, where they would fall on a big sword kept there. Their wealth was then taken by the *pandas*. By the description of Mallik Muhammad Jayasi, a contemporary of Akbar (r. 1556-1605), and Alexander Hamilton (1744) it was clear that the tradition of killing people or ritualistic suicide was already in practice. The gesture performing the specific ritual prescribed to lay down the body on the ground and slowly fall into the well by turning your body (*'karvat lena'*); that is how the temple is named Kashi Karvat. Although the ancient books of law (*dharmashastras*) generally condemn suicide, some books like the *Smritis*, epics and *Puranas* exceptionally allowed it. The *Matysa Purana* (183.77) refers that by committing suicide by fire in Kashi one gets liberation from transmigration. Drowning in the Ganga river was also a common tradition. Later on by the orders of Shahjahan (r. 1627-1657) and Aurangzeb (r. 1657-1707) the tradition was banned. A similar tradition was also existing at Prayag (Allahabad) and Gaya, as all the three places have been associated with the ancestral rituals and symbolised as doorways to the *Svarga* (heaven). After 1680 the Marathas appear to have replaced the Rajputs as major donors at pilgrimage places like Banaras, Allahabad, Puri and Gaya.

Two texts of this period, Varadaraja's *Girvanapada-Manjari* (1600-50) and Dhundhiraja's *Girvanavanga-Manjari* (1702-04) describe the glories and defiled culture of Brahmins in Banaras. The later text vividly describes the cruelty, fanaticism and inhuman deeds of the Muslim rulers, and also the greed of the Brahmins. The text describes this period as 'an era of falsehood' (*Kaliyuga*). During the reign of Bahadur Shah (1707-1712) Banaras remained a part of the Mughal Empire. In his regime the people of Kaswar *pargana* (Banaras) rose in rebellion against the Emperor and drove the Mughal garrison out of Banaras. Later Banaras came under the control of Farrukh Siyar (1713-1719), who visited Banaras in 1713 to impose a levy of one lakh ruppes on Rai Kripa Nath of Banaras. In 1713, he sent an army led by Mamur Khan to punish *zamindars* who were slaughtered and women and children captured. Those who persisted were buried alive and those who submitted were pardoned and rewarded (Khairuddin 1875: 2; cf. Pathak 2007-08: 274). A special tax, called *zazia*, which was imposed upon the Hindus by Aurangzeb, was withdrawn in 1720 by the initiatives of the king Savai Jaisingh.

The age-old traditions of learning and discourses for which the city was famous could not easily be broken, for they were independent of the rise and fall of temples. As Richard Lannoy (1999: 10) writes:

> Banaras has repeatedly been destroyed and then rebuilt from nothing but rubble. It has not lodged its history in buildings. The real past of Banaras is a past of mind, upon which no body sets any store other than in its capacity to inspire the present. Its imperishable elements are moments of human experience. In fact, despite pitiably few material remains from its more ancient past, the eternal moments of the city are recorded in the written word, embodied in extraordinarily durable, still potent, sacred sites, and evoked by a few surviving art treasures of exceptional quality.

It is also notable that the extensive religious networks within which Banaras was embedded have constituted the primary identity of the city since the early medieval period, and in fact were specific to the particular historical contingencies that have marked each historical period (Freitag 2005: 36). Thus it is noted that "both Guru Nanak and Chaitanya (Bhakti leaders in Punjab and Bengal in the medieval period, respectively) visited Banaras in order to expound their gospel"; and this pattern is to be interpreted as a marker of the city's pre-eminence in shaping South Asian religious thought (Altekar 1947: 43). Indeed, literary specialists as well as religious leaders and teachers set themselves up in Banaras and received disciples and students there for centuries: the perception of Banaras as a centre of Hindu thought continued even in the face of actual ebbs and flows shaped by political instability at any particular time. This perception of Banaras as a seat of Hindu learning extended the aura provided by a *tirtha* (sacredscape). This made the city irresistible to those interested in serving as patrons and charitable contributors, thus enabling wealth to be directed toward a range of practices (and practitioners) as well as the built environment of this urban place. While the architecture that shaped the modern city is clearly tied closely to the interplay of political power and patronage, here we might note that charity and patronage also had other important implications, from the heavy emphasis on education to the extraordinary scale of support provided to Brahmins and widows (Freitag 2005: 36).

4. The story of Vishvanatha Temple: Perspectives in time

Only a year after becoming emperor in 1657, Aurangzeb issued an order (*farman*) proclaiming himself a true propitiator of Islam on 9 April 1669. On that date, according to *Ma'sîr-i-Ālamgîrî*, "The Emperor ordered the governors of all provinces to demolish the schools and temples of the infidels and strongly put down their teaching and religious practices" (cf. Sarkar 1928: 186). Aurangzeb's *Fatawâ-i-Ālamgîrî* truly mentions that the noblest occupation for Muslims is *jihad* (war against non-Muslims). This meant that military service provided the best career for a Muslim, and it was the business of the kings and commanders to declare every war a *jihad*. The practice of the military profession was made identical with the fulfilment of a religious duty [*Fatawâ-i-Ālamgîrî*, Matba al-Kubra, Egypt, 1310 H., vol. V, pp. 346-48, cf. Mujeeb 2003: 71]. Saqi Mustaad Khan, the author of *Ma'sîr-i-Ālamgîrî* writes: "His majesty, eager to establish Islam, issued orders to the governors of all the provinces (imperial *farman* dated April 9, 1669) to demolish the schools and temples of the infidels and put down with the utmost urgency the teaching and the public practice of the religion of these misbelievers." Soon after "it was reported that in accord with the Emperor's command, his officers had demolished the temple of Vishvanatha at Kashi" on 18 April 1669. This was the period when the Maratha chief Chhatrapati Shivaji took refuge for a few days in 1666 with the help of the local people in Banaras, after escaping from imprisonment in Agra. This fact is a proof of the people's feelings against the government.

This news further irritated Aurangzeb (Pandey 1975: 20). Jadunath Sarkar has cited several sources regarding the subsequent destruction of temples which went on all over the country, and right up to January 1705, two years before Aurangzeb died (Sarkar 1928: 186-89). By this order once again around a thousand temples including the city's greatest temples like Vishveshvara, Krittivasa and Vindu Madhava, were razed and their sites were forever sealed from Hindu access by the construction of mosques (Sukul 1977: 29). However, according to some leftist historians, the image of Aurangzeb as a temple-breaker may not withstand scrutiny, since there is some evidence to show that, like his predecessor Mughals, he continued to confer land grants (*jagirs*) upon Hindu temples, such as the Jangambadi Shiva temple in Banaras, Someshvaranatha Mahadev temple in Allahabad and Umananda temple in Gauhati (cf. Ali 1968: 30-32).

Fig. 14. Western part of the ancient Vishvanatha temple in the early 19th century (Prinsep, 1833).

103

The medieval temple of Vishvanatha stood near the bend of Chauk Road close to the mosque of Bibi Raziyya (r. 1236-1240), but nothing of it now survives. Bibi Raziyya's mosque, occupying a central location in the ancient city, erected over the dismantled Vishvanatha temple, shows an act that effectively 'islamicised' a site particularly holy to the Hindus. This mosque was built from previous materials, in particular. pillars of an older Hindu temple, and consists of two chambers connected by a three-arched opening; and four pillars in the middle of each chamber carry a set of lintels on which rest the slabs of the ceiling, devoid of any dome (Rötzer 2005: 53). At the next site, occupied by the present Aurangzeb mosque, only traces of Raja Todarmal's temple, rebuilt around 1585 in Chunar sandstone less than 100 metres to the south of old Vishvanatha Temple, can be seen. The qibla wall rises above the plainly visible remains of the temple, which was not completely demolished — in fact, merely crushed (cf. Figs. 14, 15).

It is not easy to establish the original appearance of the temple built by Raja Todar Mal and Narayana Bhatta. As for the overall plan of the monument, we have James Prinsep's hypothetical reconstruction published in 1833, partly based on the description of the deities worshipped there as imagined in the *Kashi Khanda*. Prinsep's plan visualizes the temple as a *mandala* (cosmogram) of 3 by 3 square chambers, the central and larger one reserved for Vishveshvara (Fig. 16). One finds this reconstruction unconvincing since it accords neither with the observable architectural evidences, nor with the temple building practice of the day. This may be compared with the slightly earlier monument erected at the pilgrimage site of Brindavan on the Yamuna river by Raja Man Singh of Amber, another of Akbar's Rajput military commanders. Dedicated to Govindadeva,

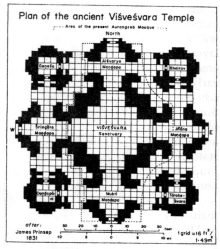

Fig. 15. Varanasi: Ancient Vishveshvara temple plan (Prinsep, 1833).

Fig. 16. Vishvanatha temple: Model view of the 1594 plan.

the Brindavan temple of 1591 graphically demonstrates how Mughal building techniques were placed at the service of Hindu ritual requirements. Though its octagonal spired sanctuary was later demolished, a part of the temple still stands. This includes a *mandapa* of majestic proportions roofed with a dome raised more than 14 metres high on lofty pointed arches. Transepts leading to side porches with external colonnades give the temple an almost perfect cruciform layout. (The great Chaturbhuja Mandir at Orchha in central India erected by Bir Singh Bundela (r. 1592-1627) of Bundelkhand in the early 17th century presents a complete version of the Govindadeva scheme since its octagonal spired sanctuary is still intact.) Bir Singh Bundela, a Rajput of eminence, had been a loyal supporter and friend of Emperor Jahangir from his tumultuous princely days. As Jahangir ascended the throne, Bir Singh was happily ensconced in his home state of Orchha in Bundelkhand at the north-western tip of Madhya Pradesh, and easily patronised and promoted the building of grand temples at important places (cf. Michell 2005).

We would expect to find a similar arrangement of architectural features in Raja Todar Mal's monument in Banaras, since both this and the Govindadeva Temple at Brindavan were almost contemporary projects. (The same may have also been true of the great Bindu Madhava Temple erected at the turn of the 17th century by Raja Man Singh above Panchaganga Ghat in Banaras) (Michell 2005: 81). It is also speculated

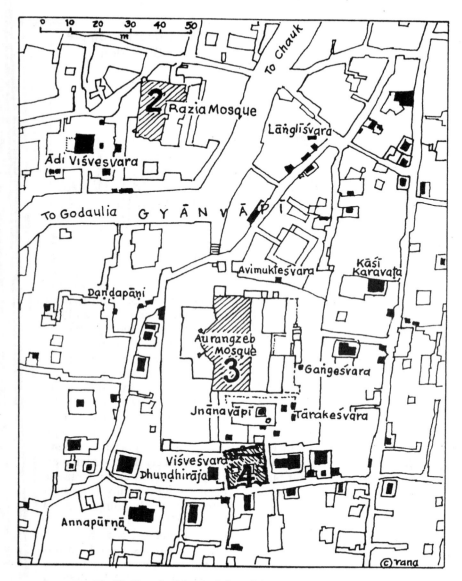

Fig.17. Changing historical sites of the Vishvanatha temple:
(1) Unknown, before *ca* 7th century CE (!), (2) *ca* 7th century to 1194,
(3) From 1594 to 1669, and (4) Since 25 August 1777 to the present.

106

ELEVATION OF THE TEMPLE OF VISHVESHVUR AT BENARES
Drawn on Stone by L. Haghe from a Sketch by James Prinsep Esqr. by C. Hullmandel

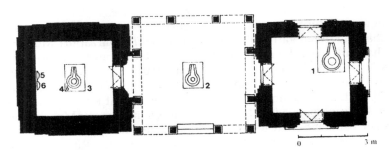

Fig. 18. Vishvanatha Temple, architectural design of the front view,
after Prinsep 1833.

107

that Bir Singh Bundela was the major source behind the construction of the Vishvanatha temple, most probably around 1623 in the regime of Jahangir! Unfortunately there is no evidence to support it.

During her reign Razia Sultana (1236-1240) had built a mosque on the deserted site of Vishvanatha temple, which had been earlier demolished by Aibak in *ca* 1194. By the end of the 13th century the Vishvanatha temple was re-built in the compound of Avimukteshvara and existed till the next destruction (of course partial) under the rule of the Sharqi kings of Jaunpur (1436-1458). But in 1490 Sikandar Lodi completely demolished it. Only after a gap of about ninety years, in *ca* 1585 with the support of Todar Mala, one of the senior courtiers of Akbar, the great scholar and writer Narayana Bhatta (1514-1595) had re-built it again, most likely on the structural plan of the previous temple of the 13th century. In 1669 even this temple was demolished by the order of the bigot Mughal emperor Aurangzeb, and today the Jnanavapi mosque stands on its site. As it would have been only a little additional trouble for Aurangzeb to order the demolition of the entire temple, one can only assume that the back portion was consciously spared as a warning and insult to the feelings of the city's Hindu population (Michell 2005: 80). And, only a century later on 25 August 1777 by the patronage of Queen Ahilyabai Holkar of Indore the present temple of Vishvanatha was completed (cf. Fig. 18, compare Fig. 19). Ahilyabai's temple typifies the revivalist idiom that spread across north India during the course of the 18th century (Michell 2005: 81).

5. The Modern and British Period

In 1719 the emperor Farrukh Siyar was murdered and Muhammad Shah ascended the throne of the Mughal Empire. He appointed one of his courtiers Murtaza Khan as overseer of the Banaras region (including three *sirkars*, consisting of Banaras, Jaunpur, Ghazipur, Azamgarh, Ballia and Chunar *tahsil* of Mirzapur). Murtaza Khan entrusted the management of these territories to Mir Rustam Ali (a relative) against the payment of 500,000 rupees annually with the right to retain the surplus revenue for himself (Srivastava 1952: 42). In 1722, Muhammad Amin, known as Saadat Khan Burhan al-Mulk, was appointed as Nawab of Awadh by the emperor Muhammad Shah. Being too effete to carry on the administration, in 1728 Murtaza Khan leased his *jagir* to Saadat Khan and allowed Rustam Ali to continue to manage the estate on agreement of paying 8 lakh rupees annually, which he retained the charge till 1738. Mansaram (1732-

1739), a Gautam Bhumihar ['martial land-owning Brahmins'] *zamindar* of Thithria (now called Gangapur), 11 km southwest of Banaras city, was a close worker in the revenue office of Rustam Ali (Srivastava 1954: 186). As part of his job Mansaram had to negotiate on behalf of his employer Mir Rustam Ali with the Nawab. He gained the confidence of Mir Rustam Ali and was able to supplant his employer in his position as revenue contractor (Srivastava 1954: 186; also cf. Oldham 1870). He continued as a confidential adviser and obedient servant of Mir Rustam Ali, and he dealt on his behalf with Saadat Khan, the Nawab. But through cunningness, and by presenting him a slave girl and jewelleries, Mansaram managed to convince Safdar Jang, a nephew of the Nawab, to arrest Mir Rustam Ali and have him posted in his place by obtaining a *sanad* (royal grant), immediately after the death of Saadat Khan in 1739 (Cohn 1987: 487). Of course, the *sanad* for three *sarkars* was issued in the name of Mansaram's son Balwant Singh by Safdar Jang under the authority of Saadat Khan, however it did not include the Kotwali of Banaras, governorship of Jaunpur fort and mint at Banaras (Oldham 1876: 88-91). Finally Rustam Ali was taken prisoner on grounds of arrears of revenue to the *Kotwal* of Banaras, where he ultimately committed suicide (Pathak 2007-08: 276).

On the 10th June 1738 Mansaram was made *amil* (tax official) or superintendent of revenue collection for the present districts of Jaunpur, Banaras, and part of Mirzapur by the Nawab. Thus Mansaram became the founder of the new dynasty in Banaras, popularly known later as 'Kashiraj'. In 1739, just before he died, he was able to get his son, Balwant (Balband) Singh, recognized as the zamindar of most of the Banaras province, and to get him granted the title of *Raja* ('king' as a honorific title). After Mansaram's death in 1739 this right was confirmed by the emperor in Delhi and the Nawab of Awadh on behalf of his son, Balwant Singh (r. 1739-1770). In 1758 his charge was extended to the present districts of Ballia and Ghazipur (cf. Nevill 1922: 137-145 and 195-204).

Banaras was one of the fastest growing cities during the years 1750-90. It became the commercial capital of north India after the decline of Murshidabad and the collapse of the Jagat Seths in Bengal in 1757. It received immigrant merchant capital from the whole of north India and stood astride the growing trade route from Bengal to the Maratha territories. Yet this was also a city which benefited from the sustained agricultural performances of the rich and stable tracts which surround it (Bayly 1983: 104). In this period, the more elevated ritual specialists such as the *pandas* (river priests) and *pujaris* (hereditary temple priests) formed close-knit bodies inhabiting separate residential areas. In this process, by 1750 the Gosains, a merchant-trader-soldier community of Brahmins, became the largest property owners in Banaras (Bayly 1983: 126). There were considerable *math* (monastery) buildings in the city between 1760 and 1800. The census records 500 *maths*, but 18th-century property deeds in the hands of Chaukhambha and Dashashvamedha families suggest that in addition a large proportion of house property was owned by Gosains and Bairagis (ibid.: 126-27 fn. 50).

It was from the 17th century that large colonies of Maharashtrian Brahmins began to settle here, and with them came Vedic learning as well. After 1680 the Marathas replaced the Rajputs as major donors to the three holy places, Banaras, Allahabad and Gaya — together known as 'tristhali', i.e. 'the three holy spots making three pillars in the bridge to the heavens'. A fresh wave of cultural renaissance overtook Banaras during the 18th century under the influence of the Marathas (1734-1785), who substantially rebuilt the city. The city, which had sheltered the rebel Maratha hero, Shivaji, in his challenge to Mughal power, now became the recipient of the gratitude, the wealth, the skill and energy of the Marathas. The noted historian Altekar (1947: 24) writes: "Modern Banaras is largely a creation of the Marathas". Bajirao Peshva I (1720-40) patronised the construction of Manikarnika and Dashashvamedha Ghats and the nearby residential quarters. A number of *ghats*, water pools along with the noted temples of Vishvanatha, Trilochana, Annapurna, Sakshi Vinayaka and Kala Bhairava were rebuilt under Maratha patronage. Queen Ahilyabai of Indore built the present Vishvanatha temple in 1775-76. As one after another *ghat* was added, the temples rose, the city regained its gaiety, and its educational system was revitalised.

After the death of his father Mansaram, his successor Balwant Singh (r. 1739-1770) obtained the power cleverly from the Nawab in 1740 and established a fiefdom independent state, which for about forty years remained a centre of attention and a source of trouble for the rising East India Company. Balwant Singh expanded and consolidated his hold on the Banaras province. In 1752 he shifted his headquarters from Gangapur (Thithria) to Ramnagar, on the other side of the Ganga river, where in 1763 he built a fort, which is still a palace of their family, laying on the other side of Banaras. When he died and was succeeded by his son, Chet Singh (1770-1781), the family was established as the paramount political power in the region.

Soon afterward Chet Singh paid the Company two million rupees and agreed to provide troops, and in exchange he was allowed to run the province as his own kingdom. However in 1775 Banaras was ceded to the East India Company by the Nawab of Awadh, Asaf-ud-daula, but the British did not exercise any direct political authority except to establish a resident until 4 September 1782 when they fully declared the State of Banaras as a part of the Company.

The tension between the two powers reached its acme in 1781, when Chet Singh usurped the throne and put Lord Warren Hastings in serious trouble; he was then driven into exile where he finally died. After Chet Singh's rebellion against the Company in 1781, Warren Hastings undertook some changes in the government of the *raja*, but he allowed 19-years old Mahip Narayan Singh (r. 1781-1795), Balwant Singh's only daughter's son, to continue to rule much as did his predecessor. Mahip Narayan Singh had already made secret overtures to Hastings during his stay at Banaras and Hastings finally appointed him as successor of Chet Singh, fixing 40 lakhs (4 millions) rupees as the amount of revenue. In 1722 the revenue demand was 9 lakhs; but, it increased to 40 lakhs in 1783 (Altekar 1947: 66).

The final phase started with the appointment of Jonathan Duncan at Banaras as resident in 1787, where he stayed up to 1795, with authority from the Council in Calcutta to run the revenue system on behalf of the *raja*. Theoretically, his appointment did not affect the *raja*'s sovereignty over his domain. However, at first the *raja* of Banaras had full rule, but much of the real administrative power was in the hands of the British resident and two European assistants. During Duncan's time as resident, a revenue settlement was carried out in 1793 which, although based on the principles of revenue settlement then practised in Banaras, had a fixity and regularity of type not known in the area for fifty years (cf. Cohn 1987: 350; also Shakespear 1873; Mishra 1975, ch. 2).

But finally in 1794 Banaras came under British administration with a limited jurisdiction known as the 'Banaras State'. The sovereignty of the Banaras Raj completely ends with the extension of all the Bengal regulations of 1793 to Banaras, and the declaration of the permanent settlement of land revenue in 1795. A provincial court of appeal with three European judges and a European register was established for the four inferior courts in Banaras City. The new raja, Mahip Narayan Singh, was a minor and inexperienced, and mismanagement by him and by his advisers and officials led to the taking over of the administration by the British in 1795. The rajas of

Banaras kept a sizeable area as their own *jagir* (landed property). With his capital and the experience he had gained by this time the raja was able to get control of a large number of tax officials (cf. Oldham 1870: 100-105). His son and successor Udit Narayan Singh (r. 1795-1835) was also known as 'raja' but served as care-taker under the control of the British. He did not have a son; therefore he adopted his brother's son Ishwari Narayan Singh (r. 1835-1889) as his successor. In fact, Mahip Narayan Singh and his descendants continued to be nominal kings and real zamindars for more than a century.

Following the tradition of succession Ishwari Narayan Singh adopted as his successor his brother's 34-years old son Prabhu Narayan Singh (r. 1889-1931) to rule the state.[3] In 1910 Lord Minto's Government took the unusual step of creating a new Indian state by investing Prabhu Narayan Singh, the then *Maharaja*, with full ruling powers. The newly created Banaras State was not given jurisdiction over the city of Banaras, which continued to be under British administration (Altekar 1947: 67). Pleased by his good services to promote the cause of the British and considering his popularity, he was crowned with the title of 'His Highness'. In his regime, several of the *parganas* that were earlier ceded to the British were transferred to Banaras State but their control and administration was in the hands of the British. Apart from services to the state, Prabhu Narayan Singh was the key personality behind the construction of several schools, hospitals, water pools and irrigation dams. Moreover, he gave an enthusiastic support to the establishment of the Banaras Hindu University in 1914-16.

The reputation of the Ahilyabai's Vishvanatha temple, built in 1777, attracted later rulers from other places in India to contribute to its splendour; even the British contributed. In 1781, Warren Hastings instructed Ali Ibrahim Khan, the Magistrate of Banaras, to erect an ornate gateway to the temple, called a *naubatkhana* ('drum house'), as documented in the inscribed panel set into its walls. This building project encouraged other powerful figures to act as patrons. Following this trend the 24-bayed pavilion with Mughal styled fluted columns and lobed arched brackets sheltering the sacred Jnanavapi, or Well of Wisdom, immediately north of the temple, was contributed by Rani Baijabai, widow of Daulat Rao Scindia of Gwalior in 1828. A decade later in 1839 the

---

[3] According to popular belief, the kings of Banaras did not have sons due to the curse of a *sadhu* (Aghori Baba Kinaram, 1627-1755); see the story in Rudra Kashikeya 1967: 141-147, and for translation, see Golding and Singh 1997: 178-186. The curse was lifted by his successor some years ago.

embossed gold sheets cloaking the spires and dome were added by the Sikh Maharaja Ranjit Singh of Lahore (Michell 2005: 81-82).

The 18th century was a period when new politico-cultural alignments emerged, which profoundly affected the processes of construction of most of the architectural landmarks that anchor the contemporary city. This widespread transformation became possible, in part, because of the fact that much of the religious architecture of the city had been razed in *ca* 1660s by the bigoted Mughal emperor Aurangzeb. Of course his attempt to superimpose an Islamic layer above the Hindu basement of Banaras was only partially successful in his own life, but after a century an integrated frame of alternative collaboration emerged by accepting the various patches and locales of Muslim settlements and their culture. In fact, by the early 18th century, like some of the important holy cities such as Allahabad and Ayodhya, Banaras had been a *'mughalising'* city owing much to the cultural patterns established first by the Mughals and then fostered by the Nawabs of Awadh's court (Freitag 1989: 9). By the early 19th century, a Hindu tradition had been 'reinvented' to serve certain goals cherished by the triumvirate of power-holding groups in Banaras.

In the 18th century cities like Allahabad, Banaras and Gaya received the special privileged status of holy places. In theory, they were the property of the gods and all men could worship there. Out of their religious pre-eminence derived a sense of the 'public' (Derrett 1975 II: 25, 45). In practice, of course, private property existed in Banaras and other holy cities. Yet the central part of Banaras north of Dashashvamedh Ghat was commonly regarded as an area of particular reverence. There was considerable concern to keep the 'holy mile' (*pakka mahal*) free from undesirable groups. These included not only the representatives of the earlier Muslim authority but even the *raja* and his collaterals (Bayly 1983: 182).

The urban area of Banaras continued to expand along the riverfront southward and westward through the 19th century. Masonry bridges were built on the Ganga and the Varana river; many ponds like Benia, Maidagin and Machhodari and Godaulia Nala (drain) were drained and replaced by parks or streets, while many houses were demolished to widen the roads in the centre of the city. Broad roads were cut through the city where formerly there had been narrow lanes. The Dashashvamedha-Luxa Road was built running west from the river toward the Cantonment train station (now called Varanasi Junction). The north-south artery called Chauk was cleared through the business district. Slowly the city came to have its present shape.

James Prinsep (1799-1840), who was the British Assay Master of the Mint in Banaras from 1819 to 1830, published the first map (in 1822, cf. Figs. 19 and 20) and reliable census of the city, which concluded that 68% of the population was Hindu and 18% was Brahmin; among the Brahmins, 35% were Maharashtrian in origin. According to the 1827 survey of James Prinsep there were 333 mosques and no less than 1,000 temples in Banaras. The mosques were distributed generally in the northern part of the city comprising the present Jaitpura and Adampura wards, the chief area of Muslim settlement. A few mosques were also scattered in other centres of Muslim population, such as Lallapura and Madanpura. Magnificent temples were naturally numerous along the Ganga. Small shrines, however, were common in the angles of the streets and under the shadow of lofty houses. Many temples and shrines were covered with beautiful and elaborate carvings of flowers and animals. The house of every well-to-do family in the city contained a small temple or shrine [?], called *thakurbari*, or place of family worship. It was in these *thakurbaris* that all religious performances on auspicious and ceremonial occasions took place.

The sacred territory of Varanasi has been dramatically associated with water bodies. The whole city had hundreds of water ponds (Hindi: *talab*, Sanskrit: *kund*) which even as late as the mid-19th century formed a series of streams dividing the city into five forest tracts (*Vana*). From north to south these were Maha Vana, Daru Vana, Ananda Vana, Harikesh Vana and Bhadra Vana (cf. Fig. 16). Till the 12th century Banaras was centred in the north around the confluence of the Ganga and the Varana. As the city continued to spread and prosper, the surrounding land was strained to supply the rising needs of the city and its visitors. Even in the late 18th century the picture of the riverfront shows a coverage of green lush trees. By that time the urban centre of the city had already shifted southwards after clearing the forest. By the turn of the 19th century the region's resource base was becoming strained, and the dwellers retained only memories of the once luxuriant woods. Of course patches of woodlands remained at different places till even the mid-20th century. One central neighbourhood came to be known as the Ban Kati, the 'Cut Down Forest' as memorial of the past (cf. Eck 1982: 29).

Many of the water ponds connected with each other during heavy rains (July-September) by following the lowlands. The sacred topography of the city thus followed the seasonal rhythm of nature. The map of Varanasi made by the British scholar James Prinsep in

1822 (Fig. 16) clearly shows how numerous these ponds and tanks were. His drawing shows how in the north Maha Vana and Daru Vana were divided by the stream linking Mandakini and Matsyodari, further meeting Rinamochana and finally flowing into the Varana river. The overflow of water connected Bhulotana Garha, Benia Talab, Suraj Kund and Misir Pokhara, and finally met the Ganga at Dashashvamedha Ghat. Of course, today these water bodies are filled up only during heavy rains or floods, such as in the years 1948, 1978 and 1992, when the channels again came to the surface, reminding us of the presence of the old water bodies and their routes.

The early 19th century sources refer, albeit briefly, to several incidences of harmonious civic sense between Hindu and Muslim dwellers. On various occasions of celebrations and festive processions, e.g. marriage of Lat Bhairava and the Bharat Milap of Nati Imli, both communities took an active part and also divided the offerings. Of course these festivals were more celebratory and multitudinous in nature and only secondarily religious. The tension and suspicion between the two groups was mostly based on the issue of ownership of the Jnanavapi mosque that contains the major walls of the earlier Hindu temple of Vishvanatha, demolished and converted into mosque in 1669. In 1809 the seed of unprecedented riots between Hindus and Muslims arose, on the line of the earlier tension that ocurred after the demolition of the temple in 1969. The Muslim community was leaded by two weaver brothers, *julahas*, and the Hindus under the leadership of the Rajputs. The dispute started on the issue of the construction of a shrine on the land between the temple and the mosque. Muslims razed the newly built temple of Hanuman, and attempted to loot the Vishvanatha temple. By the skilful interference of the then city magistrate W.W. Bird the battle came to an end. In the same year Muslims had also broken down the pillar of Lat Bhairava, but major disturbances did not happen. The British strategy of 'divide and rule' was one of the causes of such consequential developments. In course of time, with the rise of fanaticism and fundamentalism, riots became a common scene (cf. Freitag 1989: 206).

In *ca* 1825 Rani Baijabai (Scindia) of Gwalior had built the Ratneshvara Temple in Gujarati style at Manikarnika Ghat, which only three years later partly submerged and since then stands there as a unique landmark. This temple built in five-spired (*pancharatha*) consists of inner sanctum, half-form of pavilion, and four pillars stand in three directions. This temple represents an example of

Fig. 19. The City of Banaras, after Prinsep, 1822).

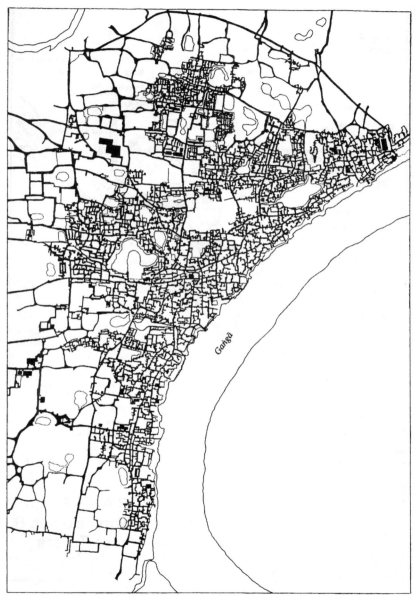

Fig. 20. The City of Banaras, Street Plan, redrawn on the map by Prinsep, 1822.

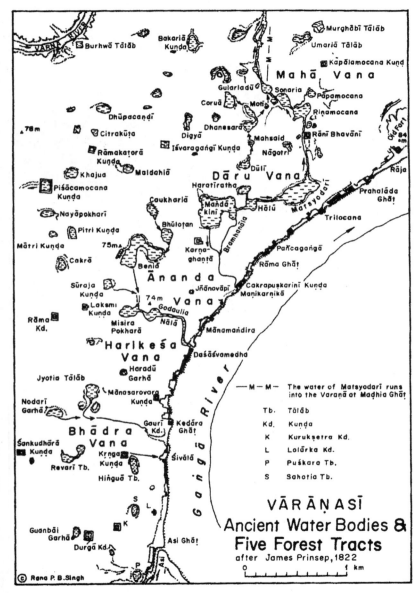

Fig. 21. Varanasi: Ancient Water landscape and Forest Kshetra
(after Prinsep, 1822).

118

Chalukya temple and is full of artistic decorative scenes. The stones are locked in notching that gives a look of the monolithic structure.

By the mid-19th century, the majority of temples' foundations in Banaras were led by the princely estates from central India — covering a period of 150 years (Nevill 1909: 237). The tradition was strongly developed by the houses of Sindhia and Holkar which ruled the dominant Maratha states. Both of these houses built huge stone bathing wharves (*ghats*) in Banaras and established 'colleges' of dependent Brahmins there. The Marathas immigrants in Banaras accounted for about 30,000 people, including traders, Deccani Brahmins and the retainers of the many noblemen, by the end of the 18th century (Bayly 1983: 137).

Immediately after getting direct control over the city of Banaras in 1810 the British introduced a form of house tax to cover the costs of administration and for the support of the local police, watch and ward (cf. Heitler 1972, and Bayly 1983: 320). This taxation was on the line of a tax supporting neighbourhood police (*chaukidari*), which was introduced in 1795. With a view to keeping the pre-British structure of community organisation, there was a strong protest against this tax. The British had to withdraw this tax in 1867, when the provinces of the Municipalities Act of 1850 were applied to the city. Under this Act a new improvement programme was introduced, including an octroi tax on imports that proved to be the 'backbone' of municipal income (Singh, B.N. 1941: 79). In this strike about 300,000 persons stopped their work, and additionally did not take food for a day. Brahmins had used their usual ways of conviction: if the rest of the Hindu mass would not join in this agitation, they would commit suicide! This strategy finally worked to awaken the Hindu masses.

The picturesque description of Banaras in 1841 by Macaulay (1910: 157-158) in his *Essays on Clive and Hastings,* points to crucial aspects of the city's history in the late 18th and early 19th century:

> A city, which, in wealth, population, dignity, and sanctity, was among the foremost of Asia… [with a huge population crowded into a] labyrinth of lofty alleys, rich with shrines, and minarets, and balconies, and carved oriels… The schools and temples draw crowds of pious Hindus from every province where the Brahminical faith was known… Commerce had as many pilgrims as religion. All along the shores of the venerable stream lay great fleets of vessels laden with rich merchandize. From the looms of Benares went

forth the most delicate silks that adorned the balls of St. James's [and of Versailles]; and in the bazaars, the muslins of Bengal and the sabers of Oude [Awadh] were mingled with the jewels of Golconda and the shawls of Cashmere.

This paragraph shows that the city was situated in far-flung networks both commercial and cultural, with a built environment that reflects the socio-political power structures that have characterized the last three centuries. Especially interesting is the description of the city's simultaneous positioning within South Asia's power networks (we have seen the influence of the Marathas, especially) and its connections to cultural consumption in western Europe (which leads inexorably through European expansion to the presence of imperial Britain). Freitag (2005: 31) analysed the processes and conditions involved in the maintenance of this urban personality, noting at least three reasons:

> First is the city's place in trade: it has long been positioned astride trade routes connecting various regions of the subcontinent and beyond. More, it continuously produced goods desired by far-flung consumers, ranging from cloth (muslins and silk) to perfumes and ointments and, by our period, brass sculpture, while at the same time importing crucial elite products such as gold, jewels, horses and elephants.
>
> Second is the city's pre-eminent religious position for Hindus (and, before them, for Buddhists). Pilgrimage to the holy places constructed through the 18th century reflected a much longer tradition, so that though the city's built environment was almost wholly new in the 18th century, it reflected long-standing assumptions about the city's role as a *tirtha*. Education reinforced this public understanding about the importance of Banaras: patrons and students flocked to pre-eminent Hindu religious thinkers based there. Indeed, there is a sense in which anyone wanting to make an impression on South Asian religious thought felt the need to present himself in Banaras.
>
> The third explanation for the unique influence of Banaras relates to the perception held by rulers throughout the subcontinent that having a presence in the city provided recognition of one's political importance and legitimacy. Taken together, these three related but distinct impulses secured the city's place in the dramatically changing political

realities from the 18th century to the present. It is worth noting that all three aspects also required networks and flows of ideas, goods and persons. If we wish, then, to understand modern Banaras as evoked by its built environment, we need to contextualize the cityscape in much larger frames of reference.

Banaras in the early decades of the 19th century was a typical north Indian city. Streets were not wide enough for a wheeled carriage, particularly in the densely settled residential areas. They were generally at a lower level than the entrances of the houses and shops that lined them. The Grand Trunk Road passed through the northern outskirts of the city and the Ganga was not yet bridged near Rajghat. The Varana also was not bridged at Chaukaghat or near the Civil Courts, while the old bridge constructed during the Muslim period was in ruins. In the southern portion of the city there were two main thoroughfares: the Durgakund-Kamachha road and Bhelupura road which served the outer zone; and the Asi-Madanpura-Godaulia road, running almost parallel to the Ganga, that continued as far as Rajghat via Thatheri Bazaar. The Godaulia-Chauk and Godaulia-Luxa roads, as seen today, did not exist. Among the notable radial arteries of the city were the Jagatganj-Maidagin and Chetganj roads. The riverside and inner zones of the city were approached by numerous narrow lanes as we can see to this day.

About one-third of the city's houses were *pakka*, either built of Chunar sandstone or of brick. The majority of the *pakka* houses were lofty, with two or three storeys; several went up to five or six storeys. Their exteriors and inner courtyards were richly embellished with verandas, galleries, projecting oriels windows, and broad overhangs supported by carved brackets. Walls were richly painted in a deep red colour with designs of flowerpots, men and women, bulls, elephants, and gods and goddesses in various forms. As regards their orientation, it was only natural that wherever possible houses faced towards the Ganga. Almost all the habitations between Chauk Road and the Ganga were of *pakka* construction. A few *pakka* examples were, however, scattered farther away from the built-up area, particularly along the outer roads of the city, in the gardens and groves where the wealthy inhabitants of the city had their evening resorts. These indicate the tendency at this time to segregate resort dwellings from the more crowded, fully built-up inner zone of the city. We may note here that the remaining two-thirds of the houses of Banaras were *kachcha*, having mud-walls and tiled and bamboo roofs with projecting eaves. Such dwellings were either clustered in over-crowded zones of compact settlement along well-drained sites in the inner city, or were scattered in the outer zone where they constituted smaller hamlets. In addition to such residential structures there were innumerable temples and mosques, exemplifying the religious character of the city.

Freitag (1989: 220-221) mentions that "In the 1890s, while the rest of the province rioted over the issue of Cow Protection, the collective violence in Banaras was directed at state-mandated technology. ... By 1980 the attendant tax increased to fund the scheme had been levied in Banaras. ... This intrusion of tax-financed technology exacerbated the perceptions of hardship which had originated with a grain shortage. Particularly hard hit by the great rise in grain prices, Muslim weavers experienced 'grave' reductions in circumstances from the falling off in the demand for those rich fabrics for which Banaras was famous." In late 1890 the Municipal Board took a decision to construct waterworks in Bhadaini (one of the southern neighbourhoods). At this site existed a temple of local importance which the Municipal Board ordered to demolish, rejecting the appeal to protect the temple by the local residents. This resulted into a violent eruption. About six thousand people assembled at the temple for protest and ultimately the mob tored up the water-supply pipes and rushed through the city to destroy street-lamps, railway structures and such amenities symbolising the British rule. In this assemblage few high class/ caste Hindus took part, except poor Brahmin priests. This incidence shows the conflict between sacred and secular activities. The gap between lower-class and upper-class residents of the city widened even more in the early 20th century (Freitag 1989: 223). This tendency helped the British to rule the city and make their presence stronger.

In 1852, in response to the rumour that the Hindu prisoners were being converted by force to Christianity, Hindu masses (under the leadership of Brahmins) gathered at Bhonshala (probably Gai) Ghat and demanded the release of prisoners. The shopkeepers observed a partial strike but later the city life returned to normal (Saletore II: 173), by the usual British way of suppression, dissension and arresting the leaders. This event illustrated the discontentment of the people against the British, an incident precursor of the struggle for freedom that broke out five year later in 1857, the first fight for freedom, called 'Sepoy Mutiny' by the British.

During the last *ca* 70 years of suppression and rule by the British, the common mass of Banarasis were disappointed and distressed. The whole city was changed into military camps, and the society was living always under terror and suspicion. The prices of daily consumable goods rose drastically high. The seeds of rebellion started growing. In May 1857, in many of the military camps in north India, including in Banaras, rebellion rose against the British, mainly due to the rumour that gun-powder used in the cannons had substance of cow fat. Hindu felt it as an insult to their religion, which fanatic Muslim thought to enjoy this incidence. Of course, the rebellion was finally suppressed. However, in the late night some fanatic Muslims attacked the Vishvanatha temple, but with the support of Rajputs the authorities succeeded to get control and maintained peace. The main credit of this happening was given to Mr F.B. Gabbins, the then city magistrate. There was no obvious loss in Banaras in the rebellion of 1857. On the other front Mr Gabbins had formed a committee to enquire into the disputes that arose about the pilgrimage route of Panchakroshi and its path; he took the support of Pathaka Svami, a renowned saint of the region. The contributions of Mr Gabbins in reinventing and re-establishing the pilgrimage routes had been a landmark in the history of cultural preservation (cf. Singh 2002: 38).

A great Hindu reformist, Dayananda Saraswati (who founded the Arya Samaj in 1868) paid a visit to the city in 1869 and had religious debates with the leading authorities, representing Hindu orthodoxy. But the traditionalist Brahmins and their Hindu followers did not pay much attention to him, therefore he was only partially successful in propagating his message (Joshi 1962: 72). According to a common folk tale Dayananda was declared defeated in one of the debates when he was asked an explanation of a wrongly quoted verse from the *upanishads*. Dayananda was shocked with this immoral behaviour of the scholarly Brahmins. After this experience he did not tried again to have such debates in Banaras.

Banaras during the 19th century was also remarkable for its commercial and business activities. The city was the great mart in which the shawls of the north, the diamonds of the south, and the muslins of the eastern provinces were gathered, and it had very considerable silk, cotton, and woollen industries of its own. Swords, shields, and spears from Lucknow and Monghyr and those European luxuries that were becoming popular in India circulated from Banaras to distant parts, from Bundelkhand to Gorakhpur and Nepal, mainly through the riverine arteries. Many specialised market areas were developed inside the city. The general market was called Chauk, but it occupied a different site from the present Chauk. The main cloth market was in Kunj Gali. There were two grain-markets: one at Trilochan and the other at Khojwa. The latter is still in existence even today. There was a temporary grain market near Prahlad Ghat, mainly used as a transit station for goods coming from the other side of the Ganga. Here stood the customs house to exact duty on articles of trade. The main vegetable market was at Chaukhamba, and the grocery mart was at Dinanath Gola. Besides these we note the hardware market of Thatheri Bazaar, the basketwork market of Raja Darwaza, the horse *sarai* in Aurangabad, the meat market in Khassi Tola, and the ghee market at Gheehutta. The *pan* (betel) market, a speciality of Banaras even today, was also prominent. Moreover, there were some smaller marketplaces with retail shopping parades in the northern wards; for instance, Purana Qila market (near the old fort) in Rajghat, Koila Bazaar (charcoal market) in the northeast of Machhodari, Kazi-ki-Mandi, Hanumanganj, Ausanganj Bazaar in Jaitpura, and the Chetganj market. Among the storehouses in the heart of the city we may mention Babu Ram ka Bara and Rup Singh ka Bara.

The city was well served by its public guards involving about 500 people stationed at night at the sixteen gates of the different urban wards. There were, however, practically no public utility services. For water supply the people had to depend on the Ganga itself or on the wells distributed almost everywhere within the urban area, though these were generally inadequate in the *pakka mahals* (built-up areas). Many houses had a well in the courtyard or near the entrance, so that even those not belonging to the household might make use of it. Both the Cantonment and Civil Stations were established in the north-western suburb of the city, the former on the south and the latter on the north of the Varana. Several palatial buildings, with beautiful gardens attached, enjoyed isolated locations on the outer margins of the city. Only a few settlements could be seen south of the Asi Nala. The urban area of the city continued to develop along the river under the British rule.

Mark Twain (1897: 496), who visited Banaras in 1895, describes the riverfront as:

> The Ganges front is the supreme show-place of Benares. Its tall bluffs are solidly caked from water to summit, along a stretch of three miles, with a splendid jumble of massive and picturesque masonry, a bewildering and beautiful

confusion of stone platforms, temples, stair-flights, rich and
stately palaces — nowhere a break, nowhere a glimpse of
the bluff itself; all the long face of it is compactly walled
from sight by this crammed perspective of platforms, soaring
stairways, sculptured temples, majestic palaces, softening
away into the distances; and there is movement, motion,
human life everywhere, and brilliantly costumed — stream-
ing in rainbows up and down the lofty stairways, and
massed in metaphorical flower-gardens on the miles of great
platforms at the river's edge.

Many educational institutions were established in Banaras in the
19th and 20th centuries. British rule brought a major change in the
ancient pandit-student pattern of learning that had predominated in
Banaras for 2,500 years. By the approval of the British Governor-
General Warren Hastings in 1791, Jonathan Duncan, a British resident
in Banaras, founded a Sanskrit College, and in 1853 the present
buildings of the college were built in Gothic style, now called
Sampurnananda Sanskrit University. The oldest local educational
initiative goes back to Jay Narayan Ghosal, a rich landlord from Bengal,
who with the British support founded a school in 1814. In 1898 Annie
Besant (1847-1933), the founder of the Theosophical Society in India
started a Central Hindu College, a campus which proved to be only
the nucleus of a growing university. On similar lines in 1904, the great
pandit and reformer Madan Mohan Malviya (1861-1946) began
campaigning for a modern Hindu university which would provide a
platform of productive interaction between classical cultural traditions
and the modern sciences; presently it spreads over an area of 554.5
ha, consisting of 198 departments, *ca* 2,200 teachers, over 18,000
students and *ca* 8,000 non-teaching employees.

A Scot vibrant town planner Patrick Geddes (1854-1932) became
involved in the planning of Banaras and also the Banaras Hindu
University in 1914-15. His original plan was to develop a university
based on an organic concept as is the case with Indian philosophy,
and in close association with nature. It was Geddes's doctrine that
every part of the social and cultural heritage must be unlocked for
the common man (Lannoy 2002: 343). Geddes became involved in
the planning of Banaras Hindu University in 1915. To his son
Alasdair he outlined the main gist of his architectural plan, with "a
long series of one-story courtyards, each a quad for its department,
with shade and ventilation through by open verandas communi-

cating. All simply built within their temple scheme... To build in mud and bamboo in first place... some day to be replaced by something statelier in carved wood or stone, or in brick sometimes" (Lannoy 2002: 344). But all his dreams and concrete plans for making a temple of higher education in the Sacred City vanished as he was kicked from the plan (Boardman 1978, cited in Lannoy 2002: 344). Till date Geddes's report and plans are not available! However, his basic outline of a semi-circular plan succeeded in giving final shape to the Banaras Hindu University. In 1916, the Viceroy of India, Lord Hardinge, laid the foundation stone of what would become one of the largest and most beautiful universities in Asia. In the late 19th and early 20th centuries many educational institutions were established in Banaras.

Christian missionaries also brought major changes to the urban landscape. In 1816, the Baptist Society became the first Christian body to introduce a mission in the holy city. The Church Missionary Society of the Church of England had started to work in Banaras in 1817, and opened one church at Sigra and another in the centre of the city near the present Girjaghar in Godaulia crossing. The London Missionary Society was located in the British Cantonment since 1820. Later in the century, the Wesleyan Missionary Society launched its Banaras mission, and the Zenana Bible and Medical Mission started a hospital for women. These attempts of the Christian missions never had a chance of gaining momentum in Banaras; of course by 1848 the Christian communities had already settled in different parts, mostly the northern, of the city. In 1848 under the supervision of Bishop Hartman from Rome a 'Trippeet Diesis' (region) for managing and expanding the Christian activities was established. That is how in the same year a fully established church, St. Mary Cathedral, was opened, which even today is an active church. The thought behind these missions was that if they would succeed in converting the Brahmins of Kashi (Banaras) to Christianity, then the whole of India would very easily turn Christian. But they hardly managed to convert any Brahmin of the city. Sherring (1868: 357) has already confessed: "it appears that Christianity has been more successful in many places in India than in Benares". In a similar vein Greaves (1909: 116) also noted that, "the Indian Christian community numbers about 800 (in Benares) including the Children in Sigra orphanage and the girl's Boarding School. Numerically this does not appear to be a great achievement for nearly a century of work". The Christian arena in 1895 was described by Mark Twain (1897: 498) as:

Benares is a religious Vesuvius. In its bowels the theological forces have been heaving and tossing, rumbling, thundering and quaking, boiling, and weltering and flaming and smoking for ages. But a little group of missionaries have taken post at its base, and they have hopes. There are the Baptist Missionary Society, the Church Missionary Society, the London Missionary Society, the Wesleyan Missionary Society, and the Zenana Bible and Medical Mission. They have schools, and the principal work seems to be among the children. And no doubt that part of the work prospers best, for grown people everywhere are always likely to cling to the religion they were brought up in.

The Municipal Board was instituted in 1867 under the Municipal Act XXVI of 1850, with a view to introducing a general improvement in the existing condition of the city. In continuation of such improvements, the site of the Maidagin tank gradually came to be replaced by a park known as Company Garden, north of the present Maidagin-Kashi Station Road. Opposite the garden, to the south of the road, the Town Hall was built in 1875, as a result of the efforts of the Maharaja of Vizianagram. It is surrounded by a large open space that lends itself to public meetings and other functions in the centre of the city. The Machhodari tank was drained into the Ganga through an underground channel and its site was turned into a park with a small tank in the middle. Close by, a new market, Bisheshvarganj, was established in 1830, north of the main road, which has today grown to be the greatest grain market in the city. Likewise, Godaulia Nala and the contiguous tanks and depressions were filled, and Dashashvamedha Road appeared as a great landmark in the cultural landscape of the city. Similar efforts were made to dam the Benia Talao and the adjoining low lying areas, but these did not succeed until 1903.

The introduction of various branches of the Northern and Northeastern Railways along with the construction of the railway bridge near Rajghat, installation of waterworks, and provision of improved sewerage and drainage works in the last quarter of the 19th century greatly modified the urban fabric of Banaras. The effects of contacts with social, educational, and political European ideas, which had already begun to be felt in the 19th century, became prominent and boldly marked the urban landscape in the course of the 20th century.

The architectural contributions of the Ramnagar Maharajas continued through the 19th century. Temples and palaces built by members of the ruling family served as punctuation both within the city, as it expanded outward and accommodated increasing numbers of British administrators, and across the river in Ramnagar itself. This building contribution may have culminated with the Sumeru Devi temple, a royal foundation of the late 18th century: the role of the Maharaja's family as cultural leaders was marked by the renewed use of sculpture to tell a story in this temple. The built environment was but one facet of cultural patronage that still marks the contributions of the dynasty, long after privy purses have been abolished.

By their order on 4 April 1911, the British restored the Bhumihar dynasty to its status as ruler (*'raja'*) of a proper princely state of Banaras, and in the process recognized a cultural role that continued even after Independence. However, although this recognition may have restored the Maharaja's (Prabhu Narayan Singh) official status, it actually marked yet another shift in power-holding. The British intended their recognition of the Maharaja to stem the nationalist tide; yet, if we use the evidence of the built environment to gauge developments of the early 20th century, what we find is that the patrons increasingly were such as Shiva Prasad Gupta, who sponsored the 1936 Bharat Mata temple. Others of his generation of leaders, including Maharaja Prabhu Narayan Singh, put their energies into hospitals, schools, and water treatment plants, marking a whole new arena for patrons pursuing civic recognition (Freitag 2005: 41). After the passing away of the Maharaja on 19 August 1931, his son Aditya Narayan Singh succeeded the crown, but only eight years later he expired on 4 April 1939. In his own life he had adopted a 7-year old boy Vibhuti as his son and successor on 24 June 1934. By the consent and approval of the British administrator of the State of Banaras its political agent Kifaiatullah Khan had appointed the king's adopted son Vibhuti Narayan Singh (b. 5 Nov. 1927, d. 25 Dec. 2000) as king on 5 April 1939, when he was only 11½-years old (Pandey 1975: 89-91). On 15 October 1948 the state of Banaras merged into the Republic of India, thus the 37-years old Banaras kingdom (1911-1948) ended.

6. Post-Independence Period

India received independence from British rule on the 15th of August 1947, and declared itself a democratic republic state on the 26th of January 1950. Since 1947 no substantive change in the urban fabric and city morphology is recorded. On 15th October 1949 the district of Banaras assumed its present form and area by the merger of the erstwhile Banaras State (Kashiraj), and the city of Banaras became the district headquarters. In 1948, 1978 and 1982, the city faced catastrophic flood damage when the flood level reached 73.2 m, 73.5 m, and 73.1 m, respectively; the danger level of flooding is 71.3 m. During this period, areas around Godaulia, the Godaulia-Luxa road and Lanka near the Banaras Hindu University were under floodwater. Tourism also began to have an impact.

In the 1960s and the 1970s Institute of Tibetan Studies, and many Buddhist monasteries like the Chinese, Thai and Japanese were established at Sarnath. In the 1990s many 'star' hotels, mostly in the Mall area, were constructed to respond to the increasing influx of foreign tourists. The Diesel Locomotive Works (DLW) factory was set up in 1961 with technical collaboration from USA; this is the only heavy industry unit in the district. In 1992 a new Hindu Observatory was opened in the compound of Sanskrit University. Five institutions, viz. Sampurnanand Sanskrit University, Mahatma Gandhi Kashi Vidyapith, Central Institute of Higher Tibetan Studies, the Parshvanatha Jain Institute, and Jamia Salfia Darul-Islamia have been given the official status of Deemed University by the University Grants Commission. In 1999 four road bridges, two on the Varana river (at the Mall, and at Pulkohna on City-Sarnath Rd), one on the Ganga river in the south of the city for passing the by-pass diversion of the GT Road (NH 2) and one on the Asi drain (Lanka-Ravindrapuri Rd), were constructed. In 1999 four road bridges were constructed: two on the Varana at the Mall and at Pulkohna, on City-Sarnath Road; one on the Ganga to the south of the city serving as a bypass diversion of the Grand Trunk Road (NH2); and one on the Asi Nala (Lanka-Ravindrapuri Road).

For the first time in history Banaras also became a target of terrorism. Recently, on 7th March 2006, four bombs went off in an act of terrorism; around 20 people were reported killed, and many more were injured. One of the bombs was planted in the Sankatamochan Hanuman Temple, a shrine dedicated to Lord Hanuman, while another was placed on a platform of the Varanasi Cantonment Railway Station, the main railway station in the city. An Islamic group, Lashkar-e-Kahab, claimed responsibility for the terror attacks. On 23rd November 2007 the city faced another bomb blast. The bomb was placed in the civil court area, which resulted in the death of more than 20 people and over 100 injured. India TV news channel received an e-mail 5 minutes before the bomb blast saying that within the next 5 minutes there will be bomb blasts in different cities of Uttar Pradesh. A terrorist organization called HUJI took the responsibility of the bomb blasts.

7. Battle to save the Ganga River and its riverfront

For the first time in history the idea of using the Ganga river as a resource for irrigation and hydropower was initiated by the British engineer Sir Probe T. Courtly in 1839. He made a survey of the source area and prepared a plan for a dam and a canal. Since the opening of the Upper Ganga Canal in 1855 at Haridvar, engineering officials realised that every year after the rainy season, in September-October, the canal had to be cleaned to clear the boulders and shingle by blocking the entire flow of the river water to the branch stream and to the irrigation canal (Alley 2002: 109). In 1912 near Haridvar (Bhimagoda) the construction of a permanent dam started. All over north India the Hindus made an agitation against this dam, and finally in 1914 an agreement between the British government and the Hindu community was made. But the agreement was not followed in the succeeding years, resulting in a further agreement in 1916 with the assurance by the British that "the constant flow of the Ganga will be continued. No change will be made without prior permission of the Hindu community." In course of time it was realised that because the water flow was blocked the pure water did not reach downstream, provoking impurity. To improve the flow and make it constant a parallel channel was planned. At this juncture All-India Hindu Sabha together with similar organizations started a protest under the leadership of Madan Mohan Malviya. A similar meeting was also held in 1916. This protests movements and public awareness continued from time to time, and later reached Varanasi.

In 1926 the Kashi Tirtha Sudhar Trust was established with the object of repairing, improving and rebuilding the *ghats* of Banaras; the trust consisted of Hon'ble Raja Sir Motichand as president and Thakur Shiva Shankar Singh as Hon. Secretary. The surveys were made under the guidance of the Executive Officer of the Municipal Board Mr Asharfi Lal, who also served as the first secretary of the Trust. By their initiative, within a short span of time a sum of Rs 50,000 was raised for carrying out the preliminary survey of the *ghats*, and by 1930 most of their plans got implemented. Finally, the report of the work done was published in book form along with appendices carrying various proposals, surveys, architectural designs and recommendatory measures. Their published report, *Benares and its Ghats* (KTST, 1931), was appreciated and supported by the then Viceroy and Governor Lord Irwin.

Time passed, and the country became independent in 1947. In the name of comprehensive and integrated development again in 1972 the Indian government planned massive dams on the Ganga river. And, in 1986 with the financial support of the Soviet Union the ambitious Tehri Dam Project was started. This dam consists of a chain of three other smaller dams. By the inspiration and under the leadership of Sundarlal Bahuguna, all over India constant agitation started against the Tehri Dam. From a sacred perspective, Hindus also felt that the construction of such a massive dam and channels to divert the stream together with stopping the natural runway water near the source are directly a great threat to Hindus' belief and cultural traditions.

A sensitive walker has expressed that "a walk along the *ghats* presents another image too, one of poverty and crowding. And, another is of filthy and polluted scenes created by the garbage piles, sewerage, breeding diseases, drains carrying human waste directly to the stream, occasionally floating corpses and also pouring toxins from India's burgeoning industrial sector". The standard of purity set for the Ganga by the environmental ministry of India is a maximum biochemical oxygen demand (BOD) of three parts per million or three milligrams per litre. Tests conducted along the Ganga report a BOD of over 5.5 parts per million and faecal coliform counts of 5,000 to 10,000 per 100 litres (cubic centimetres) of water, while the limit for the latter is only 3,000 per 100 litres of water. At some of the sewage outlets the faecal coliform counts exceed 100,000 per 100 litres. In 1986 the *Central Ganga Authority* (CGA) was created, which unveiled a master plan for the clean-up with its highly touted *Ganga Action Plan* (GAP) with a budget of 293 million rupees (equivalent to 18.5 million US dollars) for the first five years. It started its functioning in 1988. The Second Phase was planned for the period of 1994-1999 with a budget of Rs 491 million rupees (equivalent to 16.5 million US dollars), but has never been implemented. The Third Phase, including the budget of the Second Phase, is in process with a budget of Rs 2080 million rupees (equivalent to 45.3 million US dollars), and it was expected to be implemented by the end of 2009. These proposals include pollution prevention, checking and diversion of sewage outlets, increasing the capacity of treatment plants and over 30 related schemes. Founded in 1982, the *Swatcha Ganga Campaign* (SGC), an

NGO for 'cleaning the Ganga movement', is a widely publicised and propagated institution in this area. Both of these bodies make their own *claims* for the great success, and always *blame* each other for obstacles and misuse of money! To different degrees, both agencies seem more concerned with creating a reputation at the local, national and international levels than with taking swift and decisive action to clean up the Ganga river. The clean-up campaign of the Ganga has failed miserably in almost all respects. There is a lack of public participation and a lack of awareness of the river's problems. At the same time there has also been a failure to revive the old theological ethics of harmony with nature and the spirit of sustainability.

According to newspaper reports around half of the money granted, which comes about 378 million rupees (i.e. 16.8 million US dollars), has gone into the pockets of officials. The clean-up campaign of the Ganga has failed miserably in almost all respects. There has also been a failure to revive the old theological ethics of harmony with nature and the spirit of sustainability. Presently many NGOs are involved in similar programmes. However, they appear to be more concerned with political show and propaganda, and more interested in receiving grants and engendering cheap popularity. A mass awakening of awareness in the context of old cultural values would promote a new spirit of sustainability. Such a revival, however, need not turn into fundamentalism nor should it cause any damage to secular life.

The disposal of human wastes and other pollutants in the Ganga has been prohibited sine time immemorial. According to the *Brahmapurana*'s *Prayashchittatattva* (2.535), a *ca* 10th century CE text, "One should not perform fourteen acts in and around the holy waters of the river Ganga, i.e., excreting in the water, brushing and gargling, removing all clothes from the body, combing the hair, throwing hair or dry garlands in the water or throwing remains of a *puja* (*nirmalya*), playing in the water, laughing and joking, taking alms and donations, having erotic enjoyment, having sense of attachments to other holy places, praising other holy places, washing clothes, throwing dirty clothes, thumping water and swimming" (cf. Jagannath 2007: 13, compare the *Ganga Lahiri*: 1, p. 23). The *Padma Purana* (*Bhumi-khanda*, 96.7-8) states that persons who engage in such unsociable activities and engage in acts of environmental pollution are cursed and will certainly go to hell.

To paraphrase Carl Jung: "The people of India will never find true peace until they can come into a harmonious relationship with and cultivate deeper feelings of reverence for the Ganga River, which is the cradle and identity of India's culture and civilisation since time immemorial."

8. The Issue of Contestation to Pilgrimage

By the early medieval period (*ca* 10th century CE) Banaras/ Kashi was considered an important holy city together with Prayaga (Allahabad) and Gaya — all together called *tristhali*. The glory of Banaras reached an extent that people from all parts of India started coming, including many learned Brahmins who settled down here. In spite of the destruction of the city at least four times (during 12th-17th century) the eminence of Kashi had not fallen down. During the British period and under the patronage of the Marathas and Peshvas a large number of temples and water pools were built up. By the turn of the 18th century the cosmological frame referring to archetypal descriptions took shape. The Ganga river and its water have always been sacred and the most holy to the Hindus.

The riverfront has been famous for purification and ancestor-rites; the rituals are managed by the specialised priests called *pandas* or *ghatias* (also called *Gangaputras*). These *pandas* have been well known for their exploitative attitude, cheating and falsely making records. Taking benefit of the religious beliefs and the faith of the pilgrims they have often cheated and looted them. A group of citizens, merchants and rich people appealed to Warren Hastings, the British Governor General, who in 1787 issued an order to punish them and banned their violent and corrupt deeds. In spite of this, in the early 19th century they again recovered power and thus the image of the religious arena of Banaras fell down. Parallel to the *pandas*, the *tirtha-purohits* ('priests at the sacred site') also came as another group and started maintaining their separate organisation. In the early 18th century many Maharashtrian Brahmins settled in Banaras and later succeeded to have their hold in the religious activities. This resulted in a battle between the two groups. Both groups started fighting and filing court cases against each other. In 1717 a decision from the court was given in favour of the Panchadravida Brahmins of Maharashtra. But only two years later both groups agreed upon having their share on the basis of regular control (cf. Nevill 1905: 68-71). During 1730-1735 several such examples of group fights were noticed (cf. Motichandra 1985: 369-370). Before 1803 the donations and income received by the *pandas* were deposited into the government treasury, but afterwards an order was passed that *pandas* have right to keep hold of such gifts and donations. Taking benefit of such conflicts other groups and even associates like Bhaderias also started their independent possession and control. Several cases concerning conflicts among these groups were filed in the court.

The first indisputable record of an attempt by the citizens to protect the holy places, especially Allahabad, Banaras and Gaya, was the protest in 1725. This protest was against the raising of an additional pilgrim tax; such an echo of the battle was also recorded in 1664 (!) in Banaras. "The British in turn were faced with a series of popular reactions, beginning with the famous strike against the proposed house tax in 1809," and stretching forward to the protest against the construction of municipal water works on the holy Ganges in 1889 (Bayly 1983: 183).

9. References (not cited in the Bibliography)

The Puranic and epical textual references, and also the references directly mentioning Varanasi are given in Chapter 4, Select Bibliography. Other references are given below:

Ali, M. Athar 1968. *The Mughal Nobility under Aurangzeb*. Asia Publishing House, Bombay.

Derrett, J.D.M. 1975. *Essays in Classical and Modern Hindu Law*. 2 vols. E.J. Brill, Leiden.

Elliot, Henry M. and Dowson, John 1867. *The History of India as Told by its Own Historians*. 2 vols. John Murray, London. Reprinted, Low Price Publications, New Delhi, 2001.

Jayaswal, K.P. 1933. *History of India, 150 AD to 350 AD*. Motilal Banarasidass, Lahore.

Mujeeb, Mohammad 2003. *The Indian Muslims*. Sundeep Publ., New Delhi. Originally: George Allen and Unwin, London, 1967.

Sarkar, Jadunath 1928. *History of Aurangzeb*. 4 vols. Calcutta. Reprinted in 1972 by Orient Longman, New Delhi.

Srivastava, Ashirbadi Lal 1954. *The First Two Nawabs of Oudh*. 2nd ed. Shiva Lai Agarwala and Co. Ltd., Educational Publishers, Agra.

Srivastava, Ashirbadi Lal 1972. *Akbar, the Great, Political History (1542-1605)*, vol. 1. Shiva Lal Agarwal and Co., Agra.

Chapter 3

Varanasi, the Heritage city of India:
Master Plan, JNNURM and issue
of inscription in UNESCO WHL

Background

The word 'heritage' is commonly used in a broad sense involving both natural and cultural milieu, and in a more extended form it also refers to the ideas, beliefs, and ways of life that people value and use when faced with change — above all the link to an intimate relationship between the human psyche and the mystery of nature. Religion is a major factor and has the capacity to endow space with sacred meaning. All the sacred spaces vary according to the special sense attached to them, depending on how 'sacred' the space is — persons, cultures or faiths, and the intensity of attraction at a sacred place as centre of pilgrimage. In India, the holy centres, sacred sites and centres of pilgrimage are almost identical, and together in a complex way represent the archetype-mysticism built structure, historicity and faithscape — to be understood and explained through the framework of heritage ecology. Therefore, to know our past and to link the past with present and future, the preservation of heritage environment becomes necessary. Cultural heritage is to be seen as the embodiment of human feelings that developed within the historical-cultural processes, therefore it should be studied for understanding a deeper and hidden truth while interpreting it in terms of intrinsic meanings and reverence. ·

In Indian tradition, heritage is defined as 'dharohara', which is derived from 'the mother earth' (dharâ-), and 'endeavour of identity through time' (-ihara). That is how it is explained in terms of the 'root' ('shrota') and 'identity' ('asmita') — a framework of continuity of interconnectedness and a personality of culture. As a representation of the memories and glories of the past, the concept of heritage is a way of viewing the past and its association with places. Thus ancient sites, monuments, antiquities and sacredscapes are, symbolically, the places of learning, and the 'repositories of knowledge about former understanding of our planet and our relationship with it'. In a broad sense such heritage refers to the places where the spirit of nature and culture meet, and are additionally symbolised and maintained by people's attachment to the rituals (sacred and secular, both) performed there.

We want to possess the sacred without owing the ordinary. Trying to receive power from the heritage sites we want the direct experience of body touch, e.g. festivities, or celebrations. As a result, inevitably we look *beyond* everything without seeing it for what it is. That is why a preparatory and special rite and mode of human psyche are prescribed before entering to the territory of sacredscape. Only then one can get a close experience of touch and feeling. However, only those can get that experience who have deep faith. The reverence and faith of people to the cultural heritagescape and an integral part of their traditions should be respected and added to the strategy of heritage conservation together with sustainable development. The nearby inhabitants and their belief in the sacredness of heritage sites should be made part and parcel of the conservation programme.

1. Towards Conceptualising Heritage

Heritage is not an old concept; it appeared in recent years with respect to cultural tourism. The ancient sites, monuments and antiques, the ancient places of learning, all of which give knowledge about the past, fall under the heritage category. The main principle behind declaring a place as 'heritage site' is to understand our past better and to maintain a relationship between the memories of past, the existence of present and the prospects of future. In the General Conference of the UNESCO, 1972, the World Heritage Trust Convention was formed with the intention to foster "preservation and restoration of outstanding culture and natural areas of the world". By the end of January 1992, the WHL (World Heritage List of the UNESCO) counts 360 sites in 80 countries, with more being added annually from widely separated geographical regions of the world. By 2001 the WHL enlisted 690 sites from 122 countries as heritage. On the occasion of Habitat II, 1996, the World Heritage Centre (UNESCO) had launched its *Programme for the Safeguarding and Development of the Cities of Asia for the 21st Century*. This aims to promote cultural heritage conservation as part of an integrated, sustainable urban development strategy in each participating city. Presently thirty countries of Asia are co-operating in this programme.

In April 1991, the World Heritage Committee had laid down specific criterions for the selection of cultural monuments, sites and natural heritage. In general, a cultural monument possesses a great architectural influence and aesthetics, and a natural site exemplifies a stage of the earth's evolutionary process (cf. UNESCO-IUCN 1992: 12).

The bases of **Cultural Monuments & Sites** accepted as heritage are:

* The city should have unique artistic accomplishments and master-pieces.
* There should be considerable influence on architectural, cultural or monumental developments at a certain period.
* The site may provide evidence of a civilisation which has disappeared.
* The city should have eminent examples of a particular type of architectural construction significant of a historical period.
* The site should constitute an outstanding example of a traditional way of life and human habitat representing culture.
* There should be direct or indirect association with events, ideas or beliefs of exceptional universal significance.

The bases of **Natural Sites** accepted as heritage are:

* They are representative of a Biological evolution.
* They illustrate a stage in the Earth's evolution or on-going geological processes.
* The sites contain natural habitat of endangered species.
* They constitute remarkable natural formations of areas of exceptional natural beauty.

In the above context three basic meanings, in historical context, to the understanding of heritage sites proposed by Arpin (1993: 553) are:

1) a *political* meaning — to assure responsibility for the decisions,
2) a *cultural* meaning — to save culture rootedness and sense of continuity, and
3) a *didactic* meaning — to promote citizen's participation.

Out of 878 heritage sites in the world (as in November 2008), 29 heritage sites (Cultural 24, Natural 5) from India are included in the World Heritage List. Of course, the Indian government has declared

150 places as national heritage sites on the basis of the criteria adopted by the Archaeological Survey of India (ASI). The UNESCO committee consists of the three types of programmes, which include research and documentation, training and awareness, and conservation and sustainable planning. Presently a proliferation of international agencies attests the global character of concern for tangible heritage and its preservation; these include the International Council of Museums (ICOM), the International Council of Monuments and Sites (ICOMOS), the International Centre for the Study of the Preservation and Restoration of Cultural Property (ICCROM), the International Institute for Conservation of Historic and Architectural Works (IIC-HAW), the World Heritage Centre (WHC) of the UNESCO, and Sacred Sites International Foundation (SSIF). Efforts to develop heritage programmes and heritage resource conservation are promoted by these agencies in different ways and on priority basis in various parts of the globe. In India, the Archaeological Survey of India (ASI), the Indian National Trust for Art, Culture and Heritage (INTACH) and Indian Heritage Society (HIS) are the prime organisations responsible for protection, conservation and preservation of heritage sites. Recently, the Department of Tourism at the Centre and also its counterparts in all the States are promoting various programmes for sustainable heritage tourism. The recently established government body named the Indian Tourism Council aims to co-ordinate between ASI, INTACH and various NGOs dealing with the issue of sustainable tourism. In the current IX Five-Year Plan (1996-2001), the government has also proposed a National Council for Culture (NCC) to develop a mechanism for conservation of heritage and for environmental cleanliness and promotion of sustainability. However, this institution has not yet started its functioning, even in the on-going programmes under the XI Five-Year Plan (2006-2011).

Both history and heritage make a selective use and connotation of the past. In most of the cases, the symbolic representations or the visual artefacts are deliberately transformed into a commodity for the satisfaction of the contemporary consumption, and this is commonly referred as 'heritage resource'. This 'commodification' process and its marketing are the basic reality of heritage tourism. To preserve, conserve and maintain the continuity of the essence of heritage is related to the intrinsic nature of heritage planning. This leads to the concept of 'place making' that refers to "the art and practice of building communities in which all human beings transform the places they find themselves into the places where they live". Historic buildings, monuments and associated landscapes are of enormous value in creating places of character — in place-making. Their value stretches at least in three contexts, viz. aesthetic value, community value, and economic value. The three layers (time, city, planning) within the triad nature of their components, ultimately reached to the end process of heritage planning where placemaking exists as pivot.

2. Battle for Heritage Preservation

The history of preservation and renovation of *ghats* goes back to the early 1930s when a religious trust, Kashi Tirtha Sudhar Samiti, KTSS (founded in 1926), realising the serious threats to the riverfront, made an improvement and development plan with a starting fund of then Rs 50,000. This project was supported by the Viceroy and Governor-General of India, Lord Baron Irwin. The trust prepared a book with a detailed account of the *ghats* and an improvement plan (1931), with an estimated cost of Rs 3 millions. But this amount had never been allocated, and that is how the whole project was not fully implemented. The second attempt was made during the early 1960s by the American Academy of Banaras (known as American Institute of Indian Studies since 1970), taking Rewan Palace — where the Academy was first housed — and its adjoining *ghat* as a pilot project. This project was successful, and later the building was transferred to Banaras Hindu University. The third wave of conservation and preservation was started in the late 1980s under the sponsorship of Indian National Trust for Art and Cultural Heritage, INTACH, under the direction of the historians of art Anand Krishna and Kalyan Krishna (father and son, both from Banaras Hindu University). By their support the whole palace of Raja Ghat was completely restored, renovated and preserved as fitting into its original form. INTACH has further supported the restoration and cleaning of Manikarnika Ghat. Since then, no such sponsored and community-based restoration and renovation has taken place, except for some individual attempts, mostly musical and cultural performances and exhibitions. Since May 2006, a new local committee of INTACH chapter (Varanasi) has been formed, but it has not yet taken any pilot project in this direction, neither promoted any programme for heritage inscription in UNESCO WHL or even documentation of heritage properties. Civil society bodies and government authorities in Banaras are agreeing that to achieve a more positive attitude towards architectural heritage certain processes will have to be set into motion. However, there doest not exist till date any integrating force or institution to produce mass awareness, consciousness and cultural revolution (cf. Dar 2005: 142). It is felt that more evaluation and detailed listings need to be made of the existing heritage of the city, i.e. systematic and comprehensive documentation. There are no such strong legal procedures and acts that take care of heritage restoration, preservation and management.

The idea of enlisting natural and cultural sites along the Ganga in the UNESCO WHL was discussed in a National Seminar on 'Natural and Cultural sites along the Ganga for Inscription in the World Heritage List' held at IIC New Delhi: 7-8 April 1989 under the auspices of the National Academy of Sciences (NAS, Allahabad), which was chaired by M.S. Swaminathan, then President of the IUCN (The World Conservation Union) and also of NAS. In this Seminar Varanasi was not presented; moreover, the proceedings turned into a mere academic exercise that lacked a manifesto for such action programme. But the attention for enlisting Riverfront Varanasi in the UNESCO WHL was firstly drawn by a letter dated 18 May 1992 addressed to the President of the ICMS by the present author. Resultantly its associated body IUCN forwarded that appeal to the Ministry of Human Resource development (Govt. of India), who further passed on it to the Department of Culture, and notified the request for appropriate action (ref. No.F.17-19/92-UU, dated 01 June 1992). Time passed, its memory was lost, but somewhere the spirit of awakening remained. Afterwards no attempt was made, except that after a decade again re-thinking started in this direction in late 2001 (cf. Singh, Rana et al. 2001), again led by the present author with the collaboration of Kautilya Society, an NGO working for the cultural development in Varanasi. The city administration, including the Commissioner, and Varanasi Development Authority, took an active role in preparing the documents for proposals, which resulted into three volumes by April 2002. Since then no progress, no survey and no such activities have taken place, except the highlighting of some news in the newspapers.

The post-World War II craze for master planning led to the creation of Banaras Improvement Trust in 1948. The first **Master Plan of Varanasi** was prepared in 1951. To further institutionalise the planning and development activities, the Varanasi Development Authority (VDA) was created in 1974. The revision and modification of the Master Plan were made in 1973 and 1982 when new plans were prepared. Unfortunately, not a single one of these plans was implemented; all of them were delayed and recommendations were made for further revision. In 1982 the VDA made an assessment of the earlier plans of the city. Taking in view the past efforts, a comprehensive Master Plan of Varanasi 1991-2011 was prepared by the VDA, with assistance of Town & County Planning Organization (TCPO), Government of India, during which time the population of Varanasi Agglomeration is expected to double that of 1991. The latest plan was submitted on 26th February 1996, when for the first time the concept of heritage planning and preservation of heritage zones was proposed. This plan was approved and accepted by the State Government in February 2001 (Singh 2005: 29). In this plan five cultural zones have been identified for special care and planning. However, due to the lack of public awareness and active participation, the complex web of bureaucracy, and the rise of individualism and consumerism, there seems to be little hope for the proper implementation of these plans.

To consider and workout the city development with emphasis on assessing the prospects for rejuvenating Varanasi, a National Seminar was organised during 11-12 August 2000 by the Central and State authorities. In this Seminar, the Ministry of Urban Development, Govt. of India announced a moderate budget of Rs 5.07 billion (*ca* US $112.7 million) for the total improvement and transformation of the city. No progress has been made on its implementation and further assessment. Time will be the only judge of the rationality and achievements of this project. After six and half years of gap, a two-days Conference, 12-13 February 2007, was jointly organised by the UNESCO and the city of Varanasi on 'The Riverfront Heritage Cities: Issues of Development' to consider the issue of 'The Riverfront Ghats and Old City of Varanasi'. This was attended by the UNESCO delegation and a few selected people from the local administration, scholars and stakeholders. Of course various aspects were discussed and the possibility of Indo-French collaboration has been sought out, but like preceding conferences it also became a memorable show that has no frame for implementation and action programmes. Of course the local INTACH was involved, but it failed to seek cooperation with various NGOs and the people directly concerned with riverfront heritage. No follow up programmes have been chalked out. This Conference turned out to be a rich people performance for their own recreation and a potential visit abroad.

Under the leadership of the French architect Prof. Serge Santelli, a workshop programme of the students of the School of Architecture, Paris was organised during January-February 2006 and 2007, i.e. completing two terms. A group of French and Indian students of architecture and design, anthropology and urban planning visited the city for eight to ten weeks and worked on different aspects of the cultural and architectural heritage of Varanasi. It was the guidance and inspiration of Serge Santelli during 1987-89 that the pioneer work on architecture of Banaras was prepared by French scholars (cf. Couté and Léger 1989). It is expected that in the near future a compendium of the architectural and heritage of Banaras, based on these researches, be released.

Above all, it is important to contextualise the protection of Banaras within the central emotional role that the city plays in the country's consciousness. The existing national and international consciousness of Banaras needs to be directed towards the city's architectural heritage. In responding to the Government of India invitation to prepare an effective Conservation and Management Plan, it is essential that all stakeholders should be involved and that all the important aspects of the city's unique heritage be considered, namely: (1) the tangible heritage, especially the built architectural heritage (temples, shrines, palaces, monasteries, mosques, ashrams, water bodies, etc.) and art and craft heritage (paintings, folk art forms, silk weaving, wood, metal crafts, etc.); (2) the intangible heritage, covering the local religious and cultural life of the city and related activities (pilgrims' rituals, traditional schools, music, forms of dance and folk theatre, study centres, monastery and ashram life, religious teachings, etc.); and (3) the cultural landscape heritage, in particular the unique identification of the natural setting of the Ganga with the specific religious importance of the *ghats* area and the religious buildings and places there, as well as the natural preservation of the eastern riverbanks and the rural area beyond it (Dar 2005: 142).

3. The Master Plan and Heritage Zones

As the city has grown in area, population, business and administrative functions, its influence extends beyond the municipal limits. From a city with a single core (CBD, i.e. Chauk), it has now acquired the character of an Urban Agglomeration (UA) spread over an area of 115.27 km². And then there is a much larger area called Varanasi Urban

Region over which it has no formal control but to which it sends its products and from which it draws its food and other requirements. What happens in the region has implications for the city and its people and *vice versa*. With further improvement of the GT road (National Highway 2) into a super highway, the future expansion of the city will continue to be on all sides surrounding the city.

In 1982 the Varanasi Development Authority (VDA, formed in 1974) made an assessment of the earlier plans of the city. And, under its direction, the Town & County Planning Organisation (TCPO) prepared a comprehensive Master Plan of Varanasi 1991-2011, during which time the population of Varanasi Agglomeration is expected to double (cf. Table 12). The five-tier areal units are defined on the basis of administration and planning strategy, taking **Varanasi Development Region**, VDR (as in Master Plan 2011) as the outer limit. From lower to higher hierarchy they are: Varanasi City Municipal Corporation 84.55 km², Varanasi Urban Agglomeration, VUA 112.26 km², Varanasi Master Plan - Operative Area 144.94 km², Varanasi Master Plan - Projected Area 179.27 km², and the outer most Varanasi Development Region, VDR 477.34 km² (Fig 22).

Under the Master Plan 2011 the expanded area proposed for Greater Varanasi is 179.27 km², however the land use categories planned do not fit the standard norms of ecological balance in the minimum threshold. The most noticeable change during the 1991-2011 plan is the expansion of the area of the city (+112%). The major changes since 1991 as in the Master Plan 2011, introduced after 1988, indicate a catastrophic increase of land under government and semi-government uses (+390.50%), and public and community facilities (+190.63%). The increasing pace of population results to increase area under residential uses up to 253.63% over 1988 (cf. Table 12). This catastrophic change spoils the ecological system of land use; the most crucial group is parks and open ground that records a decrease of over 60% in comparison to 1999. Similarly a great loss of agriculture and open land within the master plan area, at a rate of above 40%, is again a great warning. In addition to the city's population, everyday about 40,000 commuters visit the city; this numbers increases to 60,000 during festive seasons.

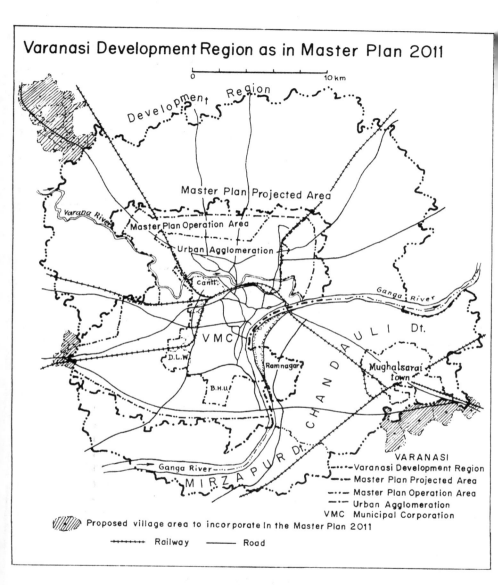

Fig. 22. Varanasi, Development Region: Development Plan, 2011-2021.

Table 12. Varanasi Master Plans, MP:
Land Use, **I**: 1961-91, and **II**: 1991-2011

Se	Land Use Category	1988		I: MP, as in **1999**		II: MP, as in **2011**		Change,
		Area, ha	% of area	Area, ha	% of area	Area, ha	% area	**I – II**, %
1.	Residential	2,615.64	46.16	5,457.24	37.65	9,254.61	51.62	+69.58
2.	Commercial	176.08	3.11	475.10	3.28	618.23	3.45	+30.13
3.	Industrial	195.31	3.45	981.37	6.77	656.19	3.66	-33.13
4.	Public & Community facilities	261.05	4.61	450.42	3.11	1,309.07	7.30	+190.63
5.	Recreation (Park/ Open ground)	53.04	0.94	2,705.76	18.67	948.47	5.49	-64.95
6.	Services & Utilities	—		—	—	103.97	0.58	—
7.	Govt. & Semi-Government	56.69	1.00	292.18	2.01	1,433.15	7.99	+390.50
8.	Tourism (area) & Heritage zone	—	—	—	—	423.73	2.37	—
9.	Transport & Communication	914.30	16.13	1300.27	8.97	1,460.35	8.15	+12.31
10.	Other (agriculture & open space)	1,393.79	24.60	2,832.06	19.54	1,683.45	9.39	-40.56
	TOTAL Area	**5,665.90**	100.00	**14,494.40**	100.00	**17,927.22**	100.00	**+ 23.68**

(Source : *Varanasi Master Plan—2011*.
Varanasi Development Authority, and Town & Country Planning Organisation,
Varanasi, Uttar Pradesh. 13 July 2001; 50pp + 1 Map; ref. page 5)

For the first time in the history of Master Plans for Varanasi,
some strategies of urban heritage and heritage zoning were proposed
in the recent Master Pan (1991-2011; Table 12) to maintain and
preserve the religious and cultural symbols of the ancient glory of
Varanasi, and to identify necessary facilities and infrastructure and
various heritage complexes (cf. Rana and Singh, 2000: 150-154). A
little over 2% of the total area is proposed under tourism and heritage
zone. More emphasis has been laid on the government and semi-
government uses.

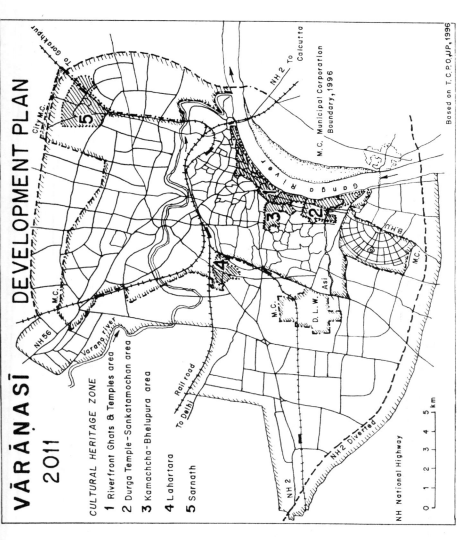

Fig. 23. Varanasi, Development Plan 2011.

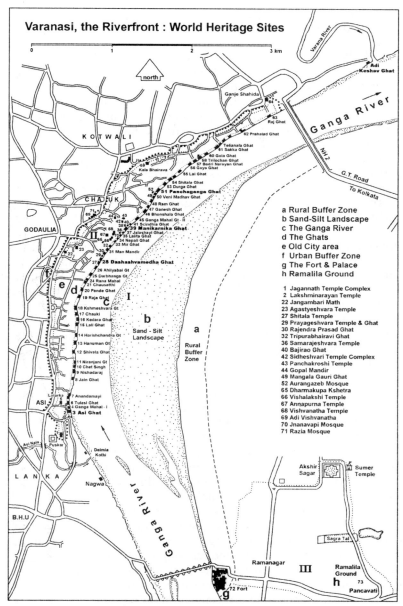

Fig. 24. Riverfront Varanasi, World Heritage Site

According to the zoning plan, five heritage zones can be identified in Varanasi (Fig. 23):

1. Riverfront Ghats (stairways to the riverbank)

The riverfront heritage covers the portion of the city stretching within 200 m from the river bank. Eighty-four riverfront *ghats* cover a length of 6.8 km along the crescent-shaped bank of the River Ganga, *Ganga-ji* (Ganges, devotionally called Ganga-Ji), from the confluence of Asi drain in the south to the confluence of the Varana river in the north (Fig. 24). Here the riverfront is overlooked by lofty palatial buildings built mostly by kings and lords from different parts of India between 18th and 20th centuries, and the area along the *ghats* is dominated by various shrines and temples. One of the most impressive buildings is the Darbhanga Palace, presently called 'Brij Rama Palace'. The *ghats* of Varanasi (cf. Figs. 25, 26 and 27) represent one of the finest ensembles of monumental architecture linked with the everyday activities of the pilgrims and the local people, and they are a symbol of the heritage tradition of India. Almost all visitors (tourists and pilgrims) take part in the on-site package scenic tour programmes (whether at a luxury or a humble level), of which the Ganga *ghats* are the most popular. The *ghats* are the nexus of the major rituals and festivals ('the intangible cultural heritage resources') in the holy city, from where all rituals start by taking a sacred bath and get concluded by giving a donation, like thanks giving (cf. Singh 2007: 61).

In order to absorb the population growth in the old city centre, new buildings are being constructed either by demolishing old structures or by building on them. Since most of the heritage sites are in these densely inhabited narrow lane areas, two U.P. State Government orders (no. 320/9-A-32000-127, of 5 February 2000, and 840/9-A-3-2001, of 11 April 2001) state that, "in all the towns situated along the Ganga river, no development activities can take place 200 metres from the riverbank". It specifically prohibits new construction on the riverfront *ghats* unless these buildings are temples, *maths* and *ashrams* (monasteries) and only if these have approved construction plans or are only being renovated. The order goes on to say that all other old buildings that are within 200 metres from the *ghats* can only be renovated (cf. Singh 2007: 62). These orders have been passed with the aim to save the river Ganga from pollution, and to protect the buildings categorised as heritage monuments, which are an integral part of the cultural and religious

Fig. 25. A scene of Dashashvamedha Ghat area in the early 19 Century, after Prinsep 1833.

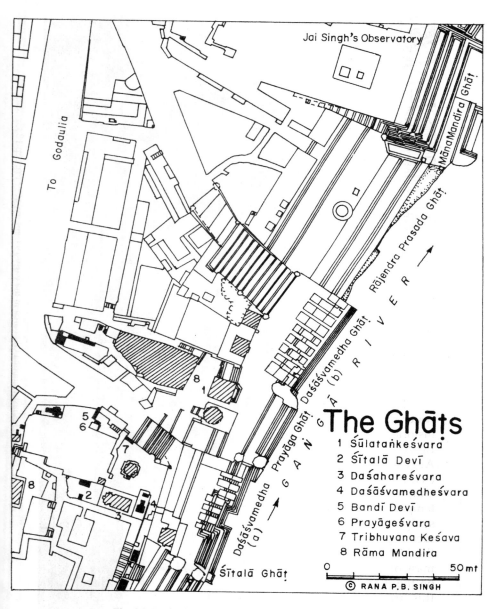

Fig. 26. Dashashvamedha and nearby Ghats: surface plan.

Fig. 27. Riverfront Varanasi: a scene of the main ghats: Ahilyabai to Shitala Ghats.

life of the city. Overall these orders aim to protect the integrity, sacredness and the ancient glory of cities along the Ganga. The crescent-moon shaped riverbank is a landscape temple in the form of an amphitheatre, where the *ghats* form the platforms, the water the altar and the sun is God.

2. Durgakund-Sankatmochan Area

This area contains about twenty temples and shrines and the water pools of Durgakund and Kurukshetra *kundas*, which are two historic sacred tanks dating from the late 18th century (Singh 1994). Every Tuesday, and more frequently in the month of *Shravana* (July-August) and *Ashvina* (September-October), especially the nine nights (*Navaratri*) in the light fortnight, worshippers perform rituals in the Durga temple. This was built on the orthodox model of Hindu temples, but without an excessive display of minute carvings and sculptures. Towards the east near the Ganga river is the oldest sacred pond in Varanasi, Lolarka Kund, which was referred to in the *Mahabharata* (2nd century BCE) and which still attracts a large mass of pilgrims, especially on its annual day of celebration falling on the *Bhadrapada* (August-September) 6th of the light fortnight. In this area also stand the temples of Tulasi Manas Mandir and Sankatmochan Hanuman Mandir.

151

3. Kamachcha-Bhelupura Area

This area records some of the old monasteries, ancient shrines and an ancient heritage site associated with the Jain Tirthankara Parshvanath, together with many monuments and buildings of the British period (18th-19th centuries). The historically notable temples and shrines in this zone are: Kamachha Devi, Krodhan Bhairava, Angareshi Chandi, Vatuka Bhairava and Vaidyanath Shiva. The Dvarakadhisha (Krishna) temple and sacred pool of Shankhudhara are other heritage sites.

4. Kabir Math (Lahartara) Area

This site was the birthplace of Kabir, a great saint-poet and social reformer of the 16th century. There are several monasteries in this area related to the life of Kabir. The Kabir Temple Complex is coming up as a great heritage and centre of solace and learning. Under the heritage complex development programme by the UP Government, a development plan has been prepared and some works have already been started.

5. Sarnath

This archaeological heritage site was famous for its sanctity, beauty and natural scenery (Fig. 28), qualities that attracted the Buddha to give his first sermon here in 528 BCE. Following Muslim invasions and the downfall of the Gahadavalas Kings, the site was left in ruins and only came to light in 1793. The principal site includes a well-preserved commemorative *stupa* (a decorated masonry tumulus) which dominates the site, the foundations of a reliquary *stupa*, the ruins of the temple complex and ancient monasteries, and a myriad of small votive *stupas* (cf. Fig. 29). The on-going development plan is in accord with heritage conservation, environmental sensibility, public involvement and user feelings, as befitting a most important centre of heritage tourism. It is sad to record that there is lack of co-ordination between Japanese donors and the Indian institutions involved in planning.

6. Other Heritagescapes

There are many other sites, areas and monuments in Varanasi which urgently require restoration and preservation and inclusion in the sustainable heritage tourism programmes. These include the Hindu Observatory at Man Mandir Ghat, the Amethy temple at Manikarnika Ghat, the Sumer Devi temple at Ramnagar and adjoining tank, and

152

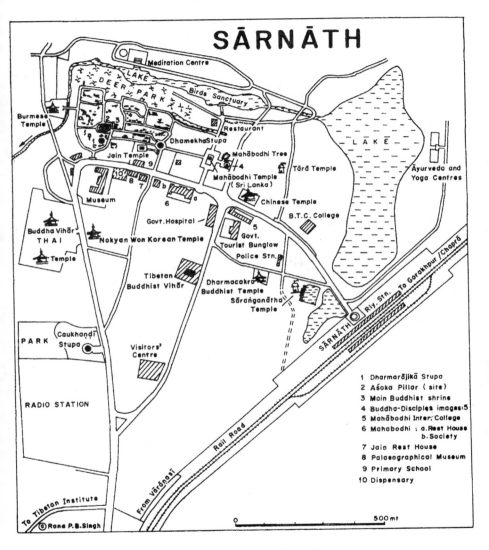

Fig. 28. Sarnath: Places of attraction.

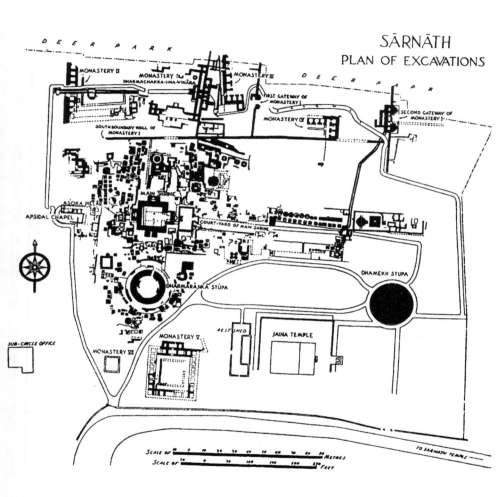

Fig. 29. Sarnath: Archaeological area and remains.

many others. Varanasi is famous for its series and layers of sacred circuits, among which the Panchakroshi is the most popular. This pilgrimage circuit representing the cosmo-spatial *mandalic* territory (*kshetra*) of Kashi is a unique attribute of Varanasi. The total route covers 88.5 km (25 *krosha*, i.e. 5 *krosha* x 5 parts) and is divided into five parts marked by overnight stops. At these five spots there are 44 *dharmashalas* (rest houses) for pilgrims. In every intercalary month, *malamasa* (e.g. the last one was from 17 May to 15 June 2007, and the forthcoming will cover from 15 April to 14 May 2010; falling every 3rd year), over 45,000 devotees perform this pilgrimage (cf. Singh, Rana 2002). Under the recently initiated heritage development project, a part of the Master Plan, partial works like improvement of roads, cleaning of the water pools and repairing of some of the roads are being completed. On the ground of pilgrimage-tourism this cosmic circuit should be given special emphasis, so as to promote sustainable heritage tourism.

Among the above five sections, of course the Riverfront City is being in the process of getting enlisted in the UNESCO Heritage List as 'mixed cultural landscape'. Due to lack of public awareness and active participation, the complex web of bureaucracy, rising corruption, and the rise of both individualism and consumerism, there seems to be little hope for the proper implementation of the plans. Ultimately there is an urgent need to re-vitalise the city with re-establishing the ecological order by promoting civic sense and active public participation. The Ganga is so polluted now that only the most faithful would venture to take bath in it. The Ganga River as an environmental milieu is not simply a water stream that flows across the land. The Ganga is what the Hindu culture knows to be true — and knows this in a certain way. It is not simply a question of how the river matters to society at present (in a strict sense), it is more important to see the meanings and cultural values which have been sustained for centuries. It is our moral obligation to revere this deeper attitude and maintain it in the context of the present needs, searching for a balanced relationship between man and nature within the microcosm of the Ganga river. This ideal brings together both Hindu culture and the vision of a sustainable society (cf. Singh, 1996: 100). The Ganga was declared as "National River" by the Prime Minister on 5th November 2008 as a first step for its preservation and conservation.

The impact of urban sprawl and neighbouring effect is constantly marked by the expansion and growth of two towns across the Ganga river, i.e. Ramnagar and Mughalsarai, lying only at 5 km and 18 km east of the main city, and recording a population of 40,619 and 116,308 in 2001, respectively (cf. Table 13). During 1991-2001 they recorded a growth of 35 and 23%, and are expected according to the Master Plans to grow up to 30 and 38 % in 2001-11, respectively. It is further estimated that both towns will be directly linked as a continuous urban space by 2031. This tendency will further intensify the demographic and economic pressure on the city of Varanasi.

Table 13. Varanasi Region: Population across the Ganga from Varanasi

Year	Ramanagar (MB)		(a) Mughalsarai Nagar Palika		(b) Mughalsarai Rly. Settlement		Mughalsarai UA (a) + (b)	
	Popula-tion	Growth, %	Popula-tion	Growth, %	Popula-tion	Growth, %	Popula-tion	Growth, %
1931	12,493	——	3,545	——	——	——	3,545	——
1941	12,953	3.68	5,567	57.04	——	——	5,567	57.04
1951	14,022	8. 25	7,332	31.70	8,153	——	15,485	178.16
1961	16,088	14.73	10,600	44.57	10,486	28.62	21,086	36.15
1971	17,242	7.17	13,583	28.14	15,029	43.32	28,612	35.69
1981	23,298	35.13	48,063	25.38	21,161	40.80	69,224	141.94
1991	30,118	29.27	66,529	38.42	24,976	18.02	91,505	32.19
2001	40,619	34.87	88,387	32.85	27,921	11.79	116,308	27.11
2011*	46,647	23.00	114,469	38.00	37,025	25.00	151,494	30.25

(*Based on Master Plan; source: VDA, Vision 2025 Draft Final Report. Feb. 2004)

4. UNESCO guidelines
for Cultural Heritage and Cultural Landscape

According to the **Operational Guidelines** (2005) of the World Heritage Committee of UNESCO, a property designated as 'cultural heritage' nominated should:

i. represent a masterpiece of human creative genius (monument, group of buildings or site);

ii. exhibit an important interchange of human values, over a span of time or within a cultural area of the world, on developments in architecture or technology, monumental arts, town-planning or landscape design;

iii. bear a unique or at least exceptional testimony to a cultural tradition or to a civilisation which is living or which has disappeared;
iv. be an outstanding example of a type of building or architectural
or technological ensemble or landscape which illustrates (a)
significant stage(s) in human history;·
v. be an outstanding example of a traditional human settlement, land-
use or sea-use which is representative of a culture (or cultures), or
human interaction with the environment especially when it has
become vulnerable under the impact of irreversible change; and
vi. be directly or tangibly associated with events or living traditions,
with ideas, or with beliefs, with artistic and literary works of outstanding universal significance (the Committee considers that this
criterion should preferably be used in conjunction with other criteria).

Additionally, it would be more plausible to have one more criterion from the natural heritage to be taken into consideration for
identifying cultural heritage:
vii. contains superlative natural phenomena or areas of exceptional natural beauty and aesthetic importance.
The 'Riverfront cultural and heritage landscape and Old City
Heritage of Varanasi' fully accord with all the above criteria of WHC
UNESCO 2005 (i to vi and vii).
There appeared a number of 'imbalances' and 'gaps' on the world
heritage list of UNESCO till 1994, including the over-representation
of historic towns, religious buildings, and European sites. With a
strategy to solve it, the concept of cultural landscapes was introduced
in 1992 and a 'global strategy' was framed; however, after passage of
time the spatial and typological alleged imbalances have grown further
(cf. Aa 2005: 37). Even if being one of the founding members, India
has not been fully represented, mostly due to lack of seriousness from
the side of government authorities and community organisations; the
'Riverfront heritagescape of Varanasi' is an example of a site not being
finally proposed for getting enlisted, in spite of fulfilling all the world
heritage criteria (ibid.: 24; cf. Singh, Dar and Rana 2001).

5. Varanasi on the criteria of UNESCO-WHC

i. *Representing a masterpiece of human creative genius*
There are several examples of architectural masterpieces attached
with inherent meanings, archetypal representations and continuity
of performances and rituals. The micocosmic temple of Panchakroshi

that places 273 deities in three-dimensionality as replica of the originally existing images and shrines along the five sacred routes in the
city is a unique example (Gutschow 2005). Built in 1936 Bharat Mata
('mother India') temple, the interior of which is dominated by a
remarkable 90-square-metre map of India carved in a relief out of
marble blocks set into the floor, is an example of perceiving the nation
as a goddess, as eulogised in the ancient mythologies. Other distinct
and unparallel examples include the temples of Gurudham, Kardameshvara, Vrisabhadhvajeshvara, Amethy, Mahamaya, Lolarka water
pool, and some others too (cf. Michell and Singh 2005).

One of India's earliest, most picturesque and one of the finest
Gothic Revival structures in Perpendicular style, the building of
Sanskrit University, Varanasi, dates from 1848-52. Of course the
Sanskrit University (earlier college) was founded in 1795, but later it
shifted to the present building. This is the only institution in the whole
world that is based on Sanskrit language and ancient Indian tradition.
It has also the richest collection of ancient manuscripts, kept in the
Sarasvati Vidya Library. Presently the building and the collections in
the library are both facing the problem of destruction and loss.

ii. *Exhibiting interchange of human values in architecture and monuments*

Varanasi is the only city in India where textually described cosmogonic frame and geomantic outlines are existent in their full form and
totality, thus the city becomes universally significant even today. The
city is a mosaic of the various religious groups and their traditions. In
the city alone, there are over 3300 Hindu shrines and temples, about
1388 Muslim shrines and mosques, 12 churches, 3 Jain temples, 9
Buddhist temples, 3 Sikh temples (*gurudvaras*) and several other sacred
sites and places. Here Hinduism, Buddhism, Jainism, Sikhism,
Christianity and even Islam have their distinct traditions, and on the
other end they together conform the harmonious life and culture of
the city called 'Banarasian'. The life style of Banaras is unique in nature,
and is referred to as Banarasipan. It is an art of living, both passionate
and carefree, what the Banaras dwellers call *masti* ('*joie de vivre*'), *mauj*
('delight, festivity') and *phakarpan* ('carefreeness'). Here the deepest
spirit of place, involving sacred ecology, spatial manifestation and
historical events presents itself in its optimal form. Layers of time and
traditions are superimposed one upon the other but the essence of
life has maintained its continuity. That is how the city is known as the
'cultural capital of India', or microcosmic India. Teaching and

training of Sanskrit and Ayurveda (the traditional system of Indian Medicine) has been present here since at least the 5th century BCE, and is still in practice prominently.

iii. *Testimony to cultural tradition in history*

The city has two remnants of a holy past: the first one being Sarnath where Buddha gave his first sermon, 'turning the wheel of law' in *ca* 528 BCE. Later during the 3rd century BCE king Ashoka built a monastery township there which continued its existence till the 12th century CE and was later destroyed. The second one is the Rajghat Plateau, where the archaeological findings and the C[14] dating of some of the wares excavated from the earliest level (upper part of IA layer, sample No. TF-293) refer the existence of urban settlements in the period during 1000-500 BCE. The archaeological investigation is further supported by Robert Eidt (1977) on the basis of scientific analysis of chronosequence of non-occluded/occluded phosphate ratios of the vertical profile of anthrosols in the Rajghat area of Varanasi. The results support the fact that residential settlement during this time span was uninterrupted. This site has been the original centre of one of the oldest continuously occupied modern cities in the world. The site evidences indicate small farming and domestication of animals, a sign of pastoral economy. This is only the far past. After this, the whole history of Banaras is a 'testimony to cultural tradition in history', as it was one of the main centres of Hindu culture and civilisation.

iv. *Outstanding example of architectural ensemble and landscape*

The unique crescent-shaped arc of the Ganga river has attracted people from various parts of India to come, settled and make their own distinct imprint along the 7 km bank of the river as clearly visualised in the architectural grandeur and the cultural landscapes. The existence of 84 *ghats* along the Ganga river points to archetypal connotations, e.g. 12 division of time x 7 *chakra* (sheaths), or layers in the atmosphere; likewise the number 84 refers to the 84 *lacs* (hundred thousands) of organic species as described in Hindu mythologies. This development records a sequential growth during the last two thousand years. Since sunrise to sunset, the cultural landscape along the Ganga river is dominated by ritual scenes and religious activities, a supportive system for other profane functions that are dependent on this. The view of the riverfront from the river is clearly an outstanding example of architectural ensemble and landscape.

v. *Example of a traditional habitat, culture and interaction*

Since the past people from different cultures, religions and territories came and settled here while maintaining their own distinct traditions in their own community, and also developed a harmoniously integrated culture of traditions lost elsewhere, which is still visible on different festive occasions. Of course, occasionally there also happen religions conflicts, tensions and contestations; however, during natural calamities like flood, water logging, heavy rains, or human induced occurrences like bomb blasts and riots, people from such diverse ideologies, like Hindus and Muslims, work together to save the city and thus prove that this is a city of humanity and universality. There are fourteen tombs of Muslim Sufi saints which are regularly visited by Hindus and Muslim, who perform their own rituals side-by-side.

vi. *Example of the continuity of living traditions of life (tangible)*

Since ancient times the natural and cultural landscapes of the city, closely associated with the traditional way of life, have retained an active social role in contemporary society. The city is a place of pilgrimage and a holy site for sacred baths in the Ganga River, for having a good death and getting relief from transmigration, for learning and receiving spiritual merit, etc. The city has still maintained its traditions. In spite of several downfalls and upheavals, traditions are fully alive even today. The presence of 'dying homes', charitable homes and pilgrims' rest houses are some of the city's unique characteristics. Additionally, silk weaving and sari making, metal, wood and terracotta handicrafts, toy making, particular painting forms, etc., bear witness to the continuity of historico-cultural traditions. Banaras is considered to be a veritable jungle of fairs and festivals with respect to variety, distinction, time, sacred sites, performers, overseers and side-shows. The popular saying that there 13 festivals happen in the 7 days of a week express that richness. "Every day is a great festival in Banaras" — so says the tradition. Recently some of the old festivals have been revived in their original style, despite some modern touches. This lifestyle has also manifested itself in a musical tradition known as the Banaras Gharana (style). Many great musicians and performing artists have been born here and still regularly return to visit and to perform their art for the public as tribute to the spirit of the soil. The names of Ravi Shankar, (late) Bismillah Khan, (late) Kishan Maharaj and many others make obvious the richness of the Banaras musical culture.

vii. *Beauty of natural phenomena & aesthetic importance*

The city represents a unique natural shape along the Ganga river which forms a crescent shape, flowing from south to north for about 6.8 km; the city has grown on the left bank in circular form around it. The area along the right side is a flood plain, preserving the natural ecosystem. Thus, together the two sides represent the cultural and natural beauty, which is unique in the whole course of the Ganga river. This is described in ancient mythology and religious literature, that became part of the religious and ritual activities that are still prominent. The eastern edge of the city faces the rising sun, which makes the *ghats* of Banaras sacred and unique for all Hindu rituals. This aesthetic harmony between the river and the city is unique in its presentation.

6. Old City Heritage and Riverfront Cultural Landscape

All the criteria, according to Article 2 of the UNESCO World Heritage Convention of 2003 and 2005, which relate to the domain of intangible cultural heritage, are already part of age-long traditions in Varanasi. This includes oral traditions of ritual performances, folk music and songs; performance arts like traditional dance, music and theatrical performances on special festive occasions throughout the year; social practices in celebrating festivals and events; knowledge and practices concerning nature (like naturopathy, alternative medicine, yoga) and the universe (classical astronomy and astrology); and traditional craftsmanship like toy and pot making, silk embroidery, etc. Moreover, other characteristics as defined in the above Article also are a part of life in Varanasi, continued and maintained since the past, being transmitted from generation to generation; being constantly recreated by communities and groups, in response to their environment, their interaction with nature, and their history; providing communities and groups with a sense of identity and continuity; promoting respect for cultural diversity and human creativity; being compatible with international human rights instruments; and complying with the requirements of mutual respect among communities, and of sustainable development.

Article 1 of the World Heritage Convention of 2003 clarifies its purpose for safeguarding the intangible cultural heritage by ensuring respect for the intangible cultural heritage of the communities, groups and individuals concerned, raising awareness at the local, national and international levels about the importance of intangible cultural heritage, and securing mutual appreciation thereof, and ultimately providing international cooperation and assistance. Nevertheless it is to be noted that all these plans have to pass through governmental and bureaucratic procedures. Thus many times they suffered delays, obstacles, as well as lack of priority — given to other choices for political or personal motives — in spite of the urgency of the matter and its universal importance. One can cite the example of the administrate building complex of Chandigarh (built in the late 1950s by the Swiss architect and urban planner Charles-Édouard Jeanneret-Gris, known as Le Corbusier, 1887-1965) which is now in process of getting proposed for inscription in the UNESCO WHL in 2009.

The Ganga riverfront with its *ghats* fully fulfil the criteria of Cultural Landscapes as designated in Article 1 of the Convention, and specifically that of cultural landscape "that retains an active social role in contemporary society closely associated with the traditional way of life, and in which the evolutionary process is still in progress", and associative cultural landscape "by virtue of powerful religious, artistic, cultural associations of the natural element".

The conservation of most heritage properties faces intense pressure. Even if these properties are presently in the same physical condition as in the last couple of decades and their architectural characteristics are being maintained without many legal and administrative measures, their architectural integrity is now being threatened. In the name of development, old structures are modified or demolished, even where these structures are made of stone and are not weak. The ownership is often collective or remote (like *maths, ashrams, havelis,* palaces, etc.), and renovation work is expensive. Unless stringent measures are taken for protection, there is a high probability that new structures, using new building materials, will increasingly replace old architectural shapes and material. Recent construction work and events in the old city demonstrate that even when ownership is in a single proprietor's hands, he usually prefers rebuilding rather than renovating. Besides these risks, the buffer zones and the skyline of the old city, whose status quo is preserved at this moment, are also being threatened by encroachments and the rising heights of buildings.

According to the **Master Plan** (1991-2011), under the Clause 2.9.2 Use Zone S-2 (Core Area/Heritage Zone), all the heritage monuments will be protected by the laws and construction permits will be issued as per the norm of 'the distance-regulation'. This plan is the first of its kind to be officially approved by the govt. of Uttar Pradesh (ref.

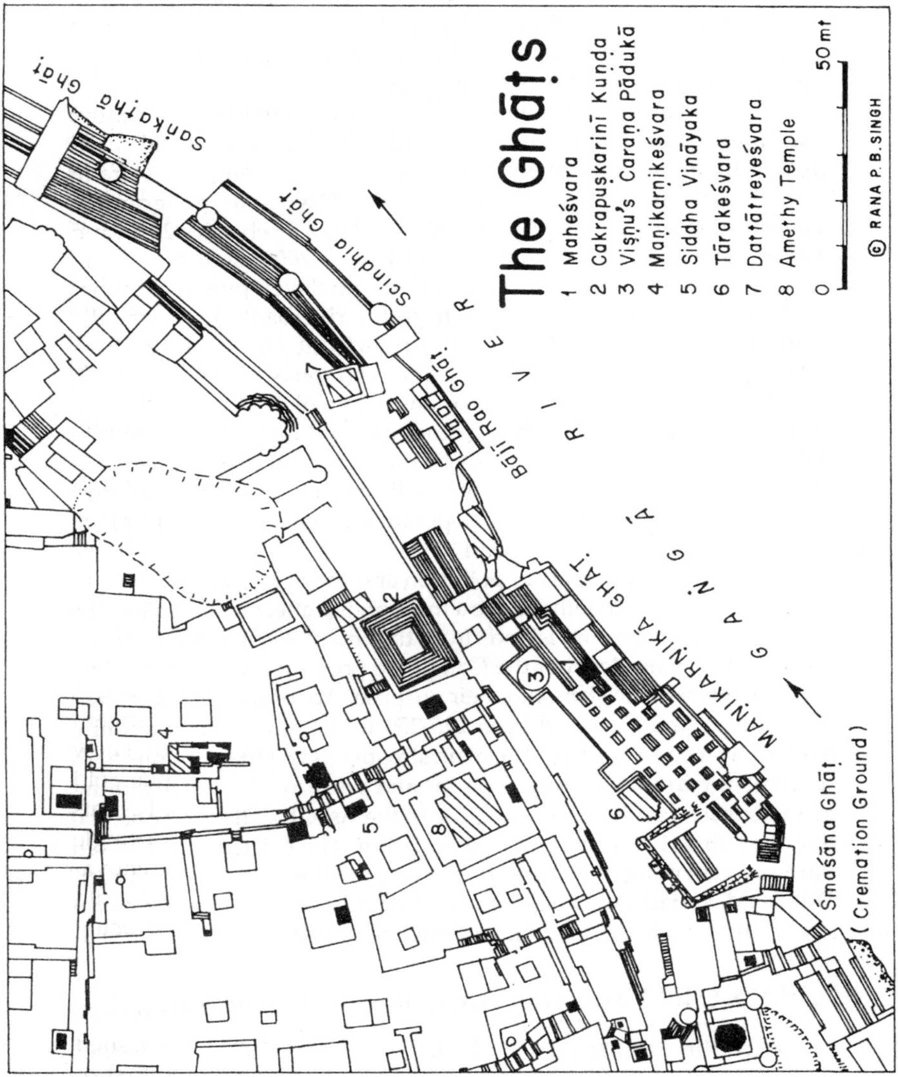
The Ghāṭs
1 Maheśvara
2 Cakrapuṣkariṇī Kuṇḍa
3 Viṣṇu's Caraṇa Pādukā
4 Maṇikarṇikeśvara
5 Siddha Vināyaka
6 Tārakeśvara
7 Dattātreyeśvara
8 Amethy Temple
0
50 mt
© RANA P. B. SINGH
Saṅkaṭhā Ghāṭ
Scindhia Ghāṭ
Bājī Rao Ghāṭ
RIVER
GAṄGĀ
MAṆIKARṆIKĀ GHĀṬ
Śmaśāna Ghāṭ
(Cremation Ground)

Fig. 30. Manikarnika Ghat and environs: spatial view.

No. 2915/9-Aa-3-2001-10Maha//99, dated 10 July 2001). For the first time, heritage protection issues have been discussed in this Plan and heritage zones and sites have been identified. The Plan has been revised in order to implement the policy of preservation of heritage sites and to channelise the development of the city in the context of environment and heritage protection.

In order to absorb the population growth in the old city centre, new buildings are being constructed either by demolishing old structures or by building on them. Since most of the heritage sites are in these densely inhabited narrow lane areas, two state government orders (order number 320/9-A-32000-127, dated 5 February 2000, and order number 840/9-A-3-2001, dated 11 April 2001) state that, in all the towns situated along the Ganga river, no development activities can take place within 200 metres from the riverbank. It specifically prohibits new construction on the riverfront *ghats* unless these buildings are temples, *maths* and *ashramas* (monasteries) and only if these have approved construction plans or are solely being renovated. The order goes on to say that all other old buildings that are within 200 metres from the *ghats* can only be renovated. A recent example of renovation and conservation of the Manikarnika Ghat with the support of JAICA (Japan International Cooperation Agency) is an example of work in progress (cf. Figs. 30 and 31).

The increasing impact of pollution and the decreasing volume of water in the Ganga together have a multiplying effect in Varanasi. The appearance of huge sand islands from the end of April and the increasingly lower water level of the Ganga are proving a big threat to the very existence of the *ghats* and their purpose. About three decades ago the width of the river had been 225-250 m, however it has recently reached to around 60-70 m. The main stream has lost the previous high speed of its current due to less volume and pressure of water, resulting in an increased pollution level. Close to the Asi Ghat, the first one, the river has already left the bank about 7-8 m. The existence of *ghats* in Varanasi is in danger because the existence of the Ganga is in danger. This trend is constantly increasing, and already some *ghats* at the down stream are now in 2008 facing the problem of sinking and fracturing.

7. JNNURM and the Varanasi CDP: Dilemmas!

According to the census of 2001 a little over 27.8% of India's total population (1.029 billion; projected over 2 billions by 2071) lives in urban areas, and it is expected that its share will be close to

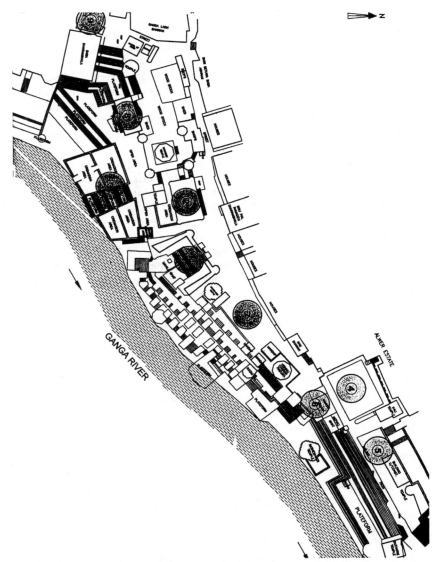

Fig. 31. Manikarnika Ghat, Varanasi, the Heritage Planning sites:
(1) Janana Ghat, (2) Raised Cremation Platform, (3) Cremation Platform,
(4) Manikarnika Kund, (5) Heritage Corner, (6) Takht Hazara, (7) Ramalila Maidan,
(8) Birla Dharamshala, and (9) Toilet facilities and Waiting Room.

165

45% by 2050. To handle India's rapid urban growth and sprawl and its consequential problems a comprehensive and sustainable development strategy was designed and inaugurated by the Prime Minister of India, Dr. Manmohan Singh, on 3rd December 2005. This is named Jawaharlal Nehru National Urban Renewal Mission (JNNURM), which will work for a period of 7 years beginning from 2005-06 under the central Ministry of Urban Development/ Ministry of Urban Employment and Poverty Alleviation, under the 74th Constitution Amendment Act (CAA), 1992. The main components under the mission include urban renewal, water supply and sanitation, sewerage and solid waste management, urban transport, re-development of inner city areas, development of heritage areas, preservation of water bodies, slum development, basic services to urban poor and street lighting. In the first phase, the Mission is being executed in 63 cities with a population of 'one-million and above', State capitals and 23 other cities of religious and tourist importance. With an estimated provision of Rs 614.6 billion [1 US $ = Rs 49 as per November 2008] for 7 years, the Mission is the single largest Central Government initiative in the urban sector. The Prime Minister emphasised the importance of cities that are internationally known for heritage, tourism and pilgrimage and maintained their historical and cultural glories, like Varanasi, Amritsar, Haridwar, Ujjain, etc.

The Mission has to work on improving urban infrastructure and urban basic services. The JNNURM plans to trigger a deeper process of reform at the state and city level, viz. (i) using fiscal flows to all sort of service utilities and local governments to change and reform, (ii) decentralisation as potential to spark change and create incentives with the support of effective regulation, and (iii) promoting citizens' demand by making service delivery provision directly to the grass level.

The primary objective of the JNNURM is to create productive, efficient, equitable and responsive cities. In line with this objective, the Mission focuses on: (i) Integrated development of infrastructure services, (ii) Securing linkages between asset creation and maintenance for long-run project sustainability, (iii) Accelerating the flow of investment into urban infrastructure services, (iv) Planned development of cities including the peri-urban areas, outgrowths (OG), and urban corridors, (v) Renewal and redevelopment of inner city areas, and (vi) Decentralization of urban services to ensure their availability to the urban poor. In view of these issues the future vision for Varanasi city is to keep and develop it as an "economically vibrant, culturally rich tourist city". Under this programme the City Development Plan (CDP) was prepared by the Municipal Corporation (MC) within a month through a hired agency, Feedback Ventures (FV) of New Delhi, and was submitted to the Central Government in September 2006.

For implementing the Mission's objectives of equitable, sustainable and rationally service delivery mechanism through community participation and involvement of Urban Local Bodies (ULBs) for individual cities, comprehensive City Development Plans (CDP) are prepared. The CDP aims to provide a rational perspective and vision for the development of the city where lessons be learnt from the past, problems of the present be critically examined and solved, and prospects of the future be made reality. The Varanasi CDP was submitted on 22 August 2006, and the evaluation report on it was released on 12 October 2006. It is quite surprising that the CDP was prepared only within two months on the basis of secondary sources and giving over-emphasis on the structural plan with financial allocations.

The Varanasi CDP submitted to the JNNURM lacks the survey and understanding of the present ground realities faced by the city. Of course, the report recognises that "the process of CDP being a multi disciplinary platform includes various stakeholders who work towards the development of the city. As the stakeholders know the city better and are responsible citizens, their views are important at every step, while preparing the CDP", but in fact, the city authorities had been least concerned with this objective. In the later half of 2006, meetings for this purpose were held for an hour in the forenoon (i) on 6 June with people involved in sari (silk lion-cloth) industry, (ii) on 8 June with Weavers Association, (iii) on 13 June with Sankatmochan Temple trust, and also (iv) on 20 July having discussions with District Industrial Association and INTACH (Indian National Trust for Art, Culture and Heritage). Using their usual colonial setup of complicated bureaucracy, and neglecting the active involvement of the people, stakeholders and scholars who have been working life-long on various aspects of Varanasi, the Municipal Corporation (MCV) and Varanasi Development Authority (VDA) had succeeded in formulating the CDP that was finally submitted to the government. That is how after four hours of discourses with stakeholders, in which only two persons in each group were represented, the city authorities took only two months

(5 July to 5 August 2006) for assessment and documentation of the CDP under the contract of a private agency, Feedback Venture of New Delhi (FV 2006) and had it finalized.

In the spirit of JNNURM, the making of Varanasi CDP had claimed to follow the two-stage procedures: *consultation* for the purpose of making the people understands the existing situation, followed with *participation* process for involving the people to take *decisions*. However, at no stage the first draft had been put before the public, thus their claim for transparency and active public participation is not at all justified. In the appraisal report of the Varanasi CDP the above issues are mildly mentioned and further clarifications were asked for. In a bureaucratic way the list of NGOs and persons attending the meetings were submitted, and that is how the CDP has been approved (cf. Rao 2006). This whole CDP report (3 parts and annexure; and appraisal report) turned to be a mere good-looking report, lacking the contemporary surface realities like complexity of land use and space allocation, priority concerns, the Ganga riverfront heritage planning that attracted the attention of UNESCO WHC, civic amenities, etc.

Surprisingly, the appraisal report at the end appreciated the "vision of the CDP in making the city an economically vibrant, cultural rich tourist destination", adding further that "the vision lays emphasis on heritage and cultural preservation" (Rao 2006: 13), but nowhere in the CDP these aspects are considered as measures of urban planning, preserving cultural heritage, and promoting religious (like pilgrimages) or sustainable heritage tourism. Since 2001 the city has recorded a mass movement to have the 'Riverfront and Old City Heritage and Cultural Landscape' enlisted in the World Heritage List by the UNESCO. Following the guidelines and identifications of the current Master Plan, 1991-2011, thematic surveys and documentations of the state and conditions of heritage buildings and the regional perspectives were prepared under the auspices of Varanasi Development Authority, and reports were sent to the government (see full report: Singh, et. al. 2002; also Hohmann 2006). Of course, no progress has yet been noticed, again primarily due to lack of bureaucratic and governmental support, and also of strong public involvement. In the meantime some architects, urban planners and conservationists from Austria, Germany and France with the assistance of their students and the collaboration of Indian colleagues have prepared detailed inventories and documentations, including some major publications (cf. Michell and Singh 2005, and Gutschow 2005). To fill up the blanks under the key issues in the Varanasi CDP a few sentences and a chart have been added that refer to planning the riverfront heritage and the old city heritage zones while integrating heritage conservation with developmental activities (cf. FV 2006: 140). The critical issues of environmental deterioration, preservation of cultural heritage (tangible and intangible), demographic pressures and illegal encroachments along the riverfront heritage zone are not given a single reference. Additionally, the legislation system and need for citizens' awareness about these subjects are not taken into consideration in the CDP.

8. Pressures and Heritage Scenario

Development Pressures

Like most urban areas in India, Varanasi too has to affront intense development pressures. The impact of these pressures is harder in the old city centre where every inch is constructed, where population density is extremely high (400 to 500 persons/ ha) and where the city is bursting at its seams. The development pressures can be grouped under the following categories: population, shrinking spaces, modifying urban spaces, traffic, tourism and pilgrimage, and environmental pressures; these will be described below.

Population Pressure

According to the Census of 2001, the population of the city was around 1.23 million, which is projected to reach 2.35 million by 2031. The first census made in 1828-29 by James Prinsep recorded a total of 181,482 persons. Since 1921 the city has recorded constant growth of population. The heavy influx of migration from rural to urban in search of better livelihood has supported the high growth rate of population, recording around 32.5% in 1991-2001.

There is an estimated 30,000 floating population in the city every day. The riverfront and old city heritage zone of the city is densely populated (above 500 persons/ ha), and it is here that development pressures are altering irreversibly the socio-cultural fabric of the city. The built heritage of the city, which is a priceless non-renewable resource, is seriously threatened today. The state and city administration have initiated efforts towards the protection and management of heritage zones, and this is making some inroads in stopping destruction in these zones but it is still far from slowing the process of their degradation.

Shrinking spaces

With population growth, the demand for utilising every inch of free space is increasing. This is creating pressures for substituting the existing spacious architectural forms with optimal space utilisation plans. Parks are becoming smaller and giving way to concrete residential or commercial structures. Trees are increasingly felled, making them a heritage at risk. The existing legislation is unable to prevent open spaces, even inside temple complexes, from being encroached upon. These constructions are increasingly suffocating an already thickly populated and constructed area. Legislations are also unable to prevent the conversion of public pilgrim resting places or buildings, called *'dharamshalas'*, from being converted into private residential accommodations. These trends are often increasingly disturbing and destroying the existing architectural beauty and harmony of heritage properties.

Modifying urban spaces

The modification of urban spaces in the old city centre of Varanasi could also negatively alter the religious and cultural life for which the city is considered sacred and destroy the tourist attractions — both of which are the major sources of earning for its population. Many of these built-up areas are potential heritage buildings. They are either part of a collective ownership (like temples, ashrams, etc.) or are occupied by tenants, thereby making their maintenance or renovation difficult. In fact, when parts of these buildings collapse, they are often replaced by new, cheap construction alternatives. And these are often utilised as for accommodation of visitors or other tourism structures that are potentially incompatible with the religious exigencies of the city and the urban carrying capacity of a congested city centre and are thus bound to have a hard impact on the long-term sustainability of the cultural assets of the city. This trend, over the next years, will definitely contribute to a slow destruction of the heritage buildings, leading to a transformation of the architectural façade of the old city, altering its skyline and affecting the aesthetic and sacred harmony of the *ghats*. The city is fortunate that many of the modifications being presently carried out in and around heritage properties are not always irreversible, but some single cases of demolition, or so-called 're-construction', are indeed irretrievable. We are presently touching the tip of the iceberg.

One such case is an old palace on one of the most photographed and important *ghats* of the city. This palace was sold to a chain of hotels, and some parts were being demolished in order to make a five star hotel. The demolition activity could not be stopped because no permits were earlier required in the city for destroying any property, leave alone heritage properties. The Varanasi Development Authority, on the complaint of a local NGO and subsequent proof provided by it, has recently taken a very positive step in the direction of preserving the architectural heritage of the city. The authority has made it compulsory for owners of heritage properties (as idenfied and recorded by VDA) to have special demolition permits before modifying any part of the existing structure. It has, furthermore, decisively disallowed further demolition of the palace and cancelled the construction approval given to the owners prior to this. In some cases demolition was stopped by the court.

Traffic loads and pressure

Increasing population and motorisation is leading to traffic congestion, not only at peak hours but at most times of the day. This leads to noise pollution and smog. Since roads in the old city cannot be widened, it is important that many of the roads in the city centre should become pedestrian pathways and walking areas; Godaulia-Dashashvamedha road to be cited as an example. Another very disturbing fact is that motorcycles have taken possession of the lanes in Banaras. They provoke tension, congestion and sound pollution, e.g. Thatheri Gali, Kedar Ghat lane, Bhikharidas lane, etc. Some traffic has been converted to one-way circulation but more roads need to become one way so as to make traffic flow much smoother.

These trends and events are strong indicators that unless stringent and positive intervention takes place through legislation, monitoring and impact evaluations, the current trends of architectural degradation will become irreversible. The aim of this proposal for nominating the heritage centres of the city in the UNESCO World Heritage List is also the first step in a positive direction.

Tourism and Pilgrimage Pressures

Varanasi has always been the most important destination of domestic religious tourism and thus the unsustainable tourism pressures do not emerge from this segment of tourists, except for their increasing number. Every year more than a million pilgrims come to this city, and all of them bathe in the Ganga river, followed by worship in various temples. Tourism and related activities are a major source of earning for the local population, but it is important to maintain a sustainable tourism development that is in harmony with the existing cultural and religious atmosphere of the city. Some efforts to this end are being taken by the concerned authorities through promoting specific kinds of activities and the organisation and re-vitalisation of religious festivals.

The city of Varanasi and its surrounding region (Kashi Kshetra) is visited by thousands of Hindus, Buddhists, Jains, Sufis and foreign visitors each day. Known the world over as the 'sacred city' and 'one of the ancient most continuously living cities', Varanasi and its region is rich in architectural and cultural heritage (comprising temples, shrines, palaces, *maths*, mosques, ashrams; and fairs, festivals, musical performances, wrestling traditions, handicrafts, silk weaving, sari, Rama Lilas), natural aesthetics (e.g. the crescent half moon-shaped northerly flow of the Ganga). The local religious and cultural life of Varanasi together with its built architectural heritage and the natural landscape of the Ganga river constitute an immense resource for heritage and sustainable tourism, both for Indian and foreign visitors. The six months ranging from October to March have always been the main season for international tourists but recent tendency shows a continuous pattern throughout the year (cf. Tables 10 and 11 in chapter 1). In fact, the religious, cultural, natural, architectural and artisan heritages of Varanasi and related economic activities like pilgrimages, rituals and religious teaching, art and music, tourism, hospitality structures, silk and carpet weaving, metal craft, schools and universities, etc. form the backbone of the economy of the city of Varanasi.

Among international tourists visiting Varanasi, more than 40% is shared by four countries, viz. Japan, France, UK and Germany. While the Japanese come to the city mostly because of its association with the Buddha, who in 528 BCE gave his first sermon in Sarnath, the British are mostly attracted by the colonial tales of India, the Germans follow their indological perceptions and the French are guided by their aesthetic quests for selecting this city as destination point. There has been an increasing influx of tourists from Australia, Italy and Switzerland (cf. Table 11, page 66). The foreign tourism inflow is largely seasonal, concentrating in the months of July-September and then throughout the winter months from November to March. There are also many foreigners who are regular yearly visitors, staying for fixed periods of four to six months each winter. The kind of tourists or foreign students who stay in guest houses spread throughout the city usually want to learn the local culture and try to integrate themselves with the local population. These tourists are adventurous and ready to adapt to local customs. They usually come to live and breathe the cultural atmosphere of Banaras or to learn music, dance, yoga, ayurveda, etc. This tourism is a soft-impact tourism and often socially, environmentally and culturally harmonious and sustainable.

The hard-impact mass luxury two-day tourism, that views the local culture as a museum, is the new major threat to the local urban and cultural environment that is the real tourism attraction. The pressure for developing this kind of tourism in the old city is immense. Since heritage zones naturally attract tourists, there is an increasing trend in the city to utilise heritage properties for hotel business and commercial purposes targeted at satisfying the exigencies of only foreign tourists. Where heritage properties are in spacious areas, such activities are in harmony with their surroundings. The negative impact of such tourism on the local culture and economy multiplies when such hotelier structures are inside densely populated heritage zones of the city, like the *ghats*, where they are in disharmony with the spiritual and religious atmosphere of the place and where they also overburden the carrying capacity of the urban and cultural environment, water resources, sewage systems, etc. This kind of tourism does not bring economic benefit to the city but only to the luxury hotelier structures. Since this kind of tourism brings greater economic benefits to the owners, the trend is to increasingly utilise heritage structures and the river to suit these ends. Unless counter measures are taken, this tendency will spread like wildfire.

Environment Pressures

The rich abundance of clay has kept the eco-system of the river still intact but increasing urban and industrial pressure and pollutant agricultural run-offs have started stretching the sustainable limits of the river system to the maximum. The river eco-system is facing pressures from the increasing population in the riverfront heritage zone and also from other parts of the city whose sewage flows directly into the river. It is also facing pressure from the pollutant agricultural run-offs from villages around the city. However, approximately 80% of the pollution in the River Ganga in Varanasi is urban waste. The river and the underground water are also the source of drinking water for the population that lives in the heritage zones. The river faces additional pressures on the days of religious festivals when millions of devotees bathe in the Ganga. Besides these, the increasing use of plastics and un-dissolvable materials clogs drains and contaminates the river water. In order to tackle these problems, broad based policy initiatives are required and must be supported by strict implementation, monitoring and impact evaluation of environmental legislation.

Of course, there are several Environmental Legislations in India, at both Central and State levels; their rational implementation is a crucial issue. The Acts at the Central level include dealing with water pollution, air pollution, noise pollution, marine pollution, hazardous wastes, radiation, pesticides, forest and wild life conservation. The state of Uttar Pradesh has already passed some acts, but nothing related directly to the major environmental issues. Around 60% of the total overall pollution concentrates in the Riverfront and nearby Old City heritage zone of Varanasi. The population density in this area is more than 500 persons/ ha, and the average number of persons per house is around 10. This zone is practically devoid of parks and open spaces. The disposal of solid wastes at every street corner is an obnoxious scene. Still there is domestic use of coal and wood, in addition to the burning corpses in the areas of the two cremation *ghats* (Manikarnika and Harishchandra). Due to contamination of water, water borne diseases are common in this area. Recently the dissolved oxygen has dropped to such an alarmingly low degree that it has already reached to septic levels.

Other likely threats do not apply to this city because it is not vulnerable to earthquakes or natural disasters.

9. Deteriorating Heritagescapes: Scenario and the Issue of Awareness

The threatening impact of consumerism has resulted into loss of heritage buildings at dangerous limits. A report (cf. Yadav 2005) has described the situation as alarming to culture and society. Based on perceptual surveys and interviews, the report reflects that it is a matter of mystery how the people of this holy city are not conscious and concerned, while this city had awakened the society in the past. The heritagescapes of the city are subject to illegal encroachment, unauthorised possession, unethical destruction and change in the basic structure, carelessness for the neighbourhood and lack of community sense, and so many associated issues that together make the situation havoc. Groups of mafias are so active and rooted into the system that the common society is terrorised and keeps itself desperate, rarely thinking about the need for awareness and mass movements. The rich people, with support from such mafias, purchase the disputed properties and replace the structure with what they like, completely transforming its heritage vale, use and its contextual image in the community. Remember, it is the moral duty of the local people to maintain the existence and continuity of age-old traditions and the architectural beauty that we inherited from the past. The above report further mentions that the rich people involved in such business have developed a favourable alliance with VDA which compensates them by protecting their interest. Of course, there are no such laws concerning the sale and purchase of heritage properties, their protection, renovations and maintenance. According to VDA those who purchase such buildings are free to make use of them as they like.

However, the sensitivity to the heritage and cultural values is not completely lost; there is still hope for a change for the better. The cases of Hotel Ganges View and Banaras Art Culture may be taken as model examples of rational renovation, preservation and maintenance and use that suits to the present requirement. Another example of 'heritage awakening walk' (*dharohar chetna march*) took place on 21 April 2008 when a group of eleven people performed a 'site survey and understanding march' to visit Lolark Kund in Bhadaini. It was realised that on the name of heritage preservation and renovation, repairing and changes are made which in no way suit the architecture, landscape and the structure of the walls, e.g. use of artificial tiles, stone blocks, paints, and fencing and locking of the neighbourhood, and cementing the natural floor surrounding the sacred trees and the sacred fire pit (*havan kund*). In fact, the political leaders performed such renovations for their own interest to gain popularity. In no way support from the architectural and conservation experts was taken. Such visits should be regularised and further enlarged into mass movements under the slogan 'Save Kashi, Save your Culture' (*Kashi bachao, sanskriti bachao*).

Since the late 1990s, mainly due to loose administration and lack of administrative control from the VDA (Varanasi Development Authority), there has been a spate of illegal encroachments and opening of restaurants and guest houses along the riverfront *ghats*, partial conversion of the houses into shops or paying guest houses, silk and handicrafts shops, and also transformation of heritage buildings for more economic benefits. The well known heritagescape of Mir Ghat is now changed into a commercial hotel, and the hospice nearby has been turned into a guest house. The huge fig-tree that once gave shadow and shelter to the ghat died, and no one thought of replacement. The Prayageshvara temple at Prayag Ghat (built in

1934) is slowly becoming part of private property and is subject to destruction of the main architecture and colour symbolism. Similarly the architectural beauty and the symmetry of the adjacent platform at Panchaganga Ghat have recently been destroyed by the renovation and repairing works. The opening of the Disneyland-type four storied Dolphin Restaurant-cum-hotel next to the Manmandir Observatory, a protected monument by the ASI, is one of such examples of illegal construction and the worst threat to heritage building. No legal or public agitations were made to stop such developments.

While Banaras is one of the unique cities in the world where the traditional lifestyle is best preserved, it is paradoxically also one of the cities where architectural heritage is least protected. There is no law that forbids private owners to make drastic changes to their historic buildings or even completely destroy them just to achieve a clear land property. There is indeed an ordinance that forbids new constructions within a 200 metre distance from the riverside, but this is little policed and extensively disrespected (Dar 2005: 140). Taking advantage of the loopholes of the law, and encouragement through the ideology of 'making identity and getting protection under the umbrella of religion', many illegal and immoral buildings and constructions are already growing in the other side on the sand-silt strip of the Ganga river. There is no concern for the moral code (*dharma*) or spiritual feeling for nature (*adhyatmik anubhuti*). This, in fact, is a shameful threat to the basic essence of the cultural beauty and identity of Banaras.

In a special meet of the VDA on 13 August 2008 the issue of enlisting heritage zone/s of Varanasi in the UNESCO World Heritage List was discussed. This issue is now victim of confusion in understanding and framing, confrontation in the political arena, and contradiction in the bureaucratic system. Through the newspapers it is proclaimed that 'Varanasi needs to be declared a heritage City', keeping aside the criteria and guidelines of UNESCO WHL that refers to cultural landscape and mixed (natural and cultural) heritage. On these guidelines only the 'Riverfront and Old City of Varanasi' fits to be nominated in the Heritage List, as discussed in the sequence. Without critically and strictly following the Unesco Criteria, everything belonging to the old tradition should not be projected as heritage as it leads to confusion at a global scale. Also, in the name of beatification (e.g. constructing fly-over bridges, and new roads) and minor repairing of heritage properties (selected buildings), sometimes ugly, unscientific and destructive repairing are performed on the name of heritage conservation. Such issues attract politicians who take the opportunity for their electoral support by confusing people, which finally results in confrontation, of course for a shorter period. Rarely, in the case of Varanasi, the bureaucracy has properly maintained coordination with local NGOs, politicians, social activists, and researchers and intellectuals. Again another governmental meeting was held on 18 August 2008 at Lucknow, the State's headquarters, and several ideas were chalked out, but no action and follow-up plans crystallised.

In a recent meeting held at Lucknow (5 September 2008), under the chairmanship of the chief secretary of government of Uttar Pradesh, the authorities have reconsidered the issue of inscribing heritage zones of Varanasi in the Unesco WHL, and nominated INTACH (New Delhi) as advising and coordinating agency. In no way the earlier submitted 3 detailed and illustrated reports (2002, see Singh, Rana P.B. 2002a, b, c, ref. N: 1, 2, 3 in chapter 4) have been taken into consideration. In fact, together these three reports consist of 166 heritage sites illustrated with detailed surface plans, architectural designs, and cross-sections. And the third report has already been distributed among scholars, institutions and architect-planners, belonging to different parts of the world, concerned with Varanasi. The recommendations include assignment to the VDA for preparing phase-wise action programmes and preparation of pilot projects and management plan, taking the support of the state departments of housing, tourism, and culture. It is to be noted that the local branch of INTACH is not involved in the documentation, protection, preservation and conservation of the architectural heritage. However, it is to be remembered that in the 1980s INTACH successfully renovated and preserved the architectural grandeur of the palace of Raja Ghat, the only example of such work still date. The new committee of INTACH Varanasi, working since May 2006, has not taken any initiative in this context for the moment.

Sometimes misleading news are also propagated, like the one (4 April 2008) saying that "according to unofficial news Varanasi is also accepted to be inscribed as Heritage city by UNESCO, declaration waited" (cf. *Thats Hindi* 2008). In fact, this is completely false, as no such official proposal has been submitted. Under the auspices of VDA the Kautilya Society, an NGO in service of culture and heritage, has prepared three such reports that refer to 'Varanasi: Inscribing Heritage Zones for WHL UNESCO' during March-April 2002 [see chapter 4, *Bibliography* 'N', p. 344]. The third report was widely circulated among the architects and scholars directly concerned with such studies, collaborative programmes and also those served the WHL and ICOMOS for heritage inscription in countries like Austria, France, Japan, Nepal, and Italy. Already six years have passed after submission of the final report, and no 'management plan' or 'operational time schedules' has been finalised yet nor any such attempt made. The present author has presented papers on these issues in four international conferences held abroad, but the issue has not attracted the local intellectuals. In the situation of political crises and lack of awakening it becomes now an herculean task to revive the 'heritage conservation plan' and activate public movement for this noble purpose.

Whenever some queries or clarification are asked from the parliament, human rights commission, or Unesco Representative in India concerning the heritage enlisting, for a few days the VDA authorities feel awakened to take up some action programme and making a proposal. However after some time those issues are kept out of concern, in view of other priorities. Additionally, intermittently the senior officials of VDA are transferred to other places so that no follow-up action is implemented. The incoming officials watch and learn the situation and peoples' willingness for five-six months, but when they plan to start they are transferred to other centres.

Based on a survey (2006-7) concerning understanding the public participation and resultant action (PPRA), it is obviously noted that in order to achieve a long term self-sustained maintenance of the healthy life in Varanasi, an extensive programme of public awareness should be conducted to communicate and educate about the value of public hygiene, health and heritage and their potential socio-economic and cultural benefits, that can be enhanced by the harmonious integration between the old heritagescape and the modern constructs. This strategy will help stakeholders to participate in sustainable operations, management and maintenance plans effectively and successfully. With this approach of marching from a development culture based on physical infrastructure to a development culture based on accumulation and sharing of knowledge, we need to realise that sustainable planning is possible only by active public awareness and participation. Of course, this is true everywhere, but it is more true in Varanasi, where the root of underdevelopment is none other than lack of knowledge, awareness and participation.

The passive fatalism and uncooperative acceptance of 'made-elsewhere' policies that has previously characterized urban planning in Varanasi, now can be reversed by the methodology of participated programme design, implementation and evaluation that the local development institutions have illustrated and recommended too.

10. Actions at the various levels of Governance

The declaration of Varanasi as a heritage city in the World Heritage Cities List implies that specific heritage-conservation related actions should be taken at the following governance levels:

At the City (District) Level

It is suggested that the City (District) Administration:

1) Draft and ratify a Manifesto committing itself to the conservation and protection of the city and accepting its responsibilities as the guardian of a World Heritage Site. This manifesto must include, among others, the following points:

* All proposals for development will give importance to the protection of the cultural and historic fabric of the Heritage City.

* Planning and demolition permits for the heritage city will be in accordance with the declaration of the identified precincts of the city as a heritage site.

* All pressure for change and development will be in such a way as to preserve and enhance the cultural, historic, architectural and artistic fabric and landscape of the Heritage City.

2) All built heritage assets of the city must be identified and documented through a survey, listing, mapping, architectural plans of individual buildings, historical evidence, visual photography, etc. of the same.

3) A specific conservation plan must be drafted and must be made an integral part of the development plan of the city.

4) A Conservation Cell must be created within the local Development Authority, without whose approval no demolition or renovation of listed heritage will be permitted. The Cell must comprise administrative officers, local political representatives, concerned local organisations and experts. The Conservation Cell must approve all interventions in, on or around the listed sites. All

intervention in the listed heritage sites must be in accordance with national and international norms and specifications laid down in a Charter drafted and ratified by the Conservation Cell. The Cell will continuously update concerned conservation by-laws and development plans. The Conservation Cell must nominate local organisations for systematic and continuous monitoring of listed heritage assets of the city.

5) Specific by-laws must be formulated for the development and preservation of listed heritage sites, their skylines and surrounding areas. The Conservation Cell must be part of the process of formulating these by-laws.

At the State Level

It is suggested that the State Ministries and concerned institutions:

1) Draft and approve legislations for the heritage zones of Banaras that are binding on citizens, government and political institutions alike.

2) Promote local efforts to involve stakeholders in policy making processes.

3) Give the same weight to conservation as to development, on the principle of co-existing sustainability.

4) Draft tourism development plans that are environmentally-sustainable — natural, cultural and urban areas, put utmost attention on restricting hard-impact tourism and on the carrying capacity of heritage zones.

5) Make continuous impact evaluations of conservation efforts, policies and laws.

6) Promote training and development of technical capacity in the field and scope for adjustment and alterations.

At the National level

It is suggested that the National ministries and concerned national institutions:

1) Make legislations to foster a climate of conservation and appropriate administrative and financial measures.

2) Sustain legal, administrative, technical, and economic development

and social-cultural measures that support the specific characteristics of the Heritage City.

3) Channelise part of the national funds for conservation of important heritage sites.

4) Have a holistic approach to development of heritage sites satisfying both economic and social-cultural objectives.

11. Concluding Remarks

Heritage is the mirror of mankind's growth, progress and prospects; it is very important that it should be preserved. One has to remember that modern way of life and science, and ancient wisdom and its messages can work together to help in searching a harmonious and peaceful path of mankind's integration with nature. In order that this heritage become a resource for development, it needs to be first documented, then protected, maintained and finally utilized according to specific heritage guidelines and legislations. Only then, combined with an increased citizens' awareness and participation, will policy efforts and interventions become sustainable — environmentally, socially and culturally. We may separate ourselves from the web of our heritage in the pursuit of modernity and secularism, but it would always be at the cost of our hearts and souls (cf. Singh 1993: 306).

It is notable that the initiative taken by local NGOs, experts and eminent citizens of the city to propose the nomination of the old city centre of Varanasi for inclusion in the UNESCO World Heritage List has activated the present sensitive and positive city administration to propose comprehensive measures for the preservation of the cultural heritage of Varanasi. A mass movement of awakening (*chetna march*) in the context of old cultural values would promote a new spirit of sustainability. Such a revival, however, needs not turn into fundamentalism nor should it cause any damage to secular life.

In our temporal frame we have to give respect to the past, search solutions in the present, and make directions for the future. This should apply to the issue of urban sprawl beyond the corporation boundary and interlinks with the surrounding areas (peri-urban), which were not considered in preparing the CDP. Remember, a thing is right when it tends to preserve the integrity, stability and beauty of the site as a living organism. In order that this heritage becomes a resource for development, it needs to be first documented, then protected, maintained and finally utilised according to specific heritage guidelines and legislations. Only then, combined with an increased stakeholder awareness and participation, will policy efforts and interventions become sustainable — environmentally, socially and culturally. Mahatma Gandhi rightly warned us: "There is enough on earth for everybody's need, but not enough for one person's greed".

Chapter 4

Banaras / Kashi / Varanasi
A Selected Bibliography

This *Bibliography* (1276 entries) is classified into 16 groups:

A. Books, mostly in English, with select annotation: 317

B. Research Papers & Essays (mostly English): 491

C. (i). Persian Works, Translated: 4, C (ii). Urdu Sources: 4

D. The Sanskrit sources on Kashi/ Varanasi (selected): 59

E. Books/ articles in Hindi: 99

F. Marathi Sources: 2

G. Bengali Sources: 3

H. Published Reports/ Government Documents: 26

I. Electronic Publications: 16

J. Film (English): 10

K. Japanese Sources (in Japanese): 12

L. Unpublished Dissertations, selected: 69

M. Unpublished Reports: 10

N. Unpublished Reports (Varanasi: Inscribing Heritage Zones for WHL UNESCO): 03

O. Unpublished (Undergraduate) Fieldwork Projects, The University of Wisconsin Program: College Year in India: 152

(prepared & © by Rana P. B. Singh)

A. Books (mostly English; with select annotation)

Ackerman, Michael 1999. *End Time City.* Photographs by Michael Ackerman; with a conversation between Michael Ackerman and Alexis Schwarzenbach and a text by Christian Caujolle. Scalo, Zurich-Berlin-New York. ISBN: 3-908247-13-6.

Adriaensen, Rob; Bakker, Hans T. and Isaacson, Harunaga 1998. *The Skandapurana: Vol. I Adhyaya 1 - 25.* Critically edited with Prolegomena and English synopsis. Egbert Forsten, Groningen. Hb 2 figures, appendix, index to prolegomena, index to the synopsis and appendix, index to the text passages, & bibliography. xiv + 349 pp. Hb. ISBN: 90-6980-106-X.

This is a pioneering masterpiece and the only critical edition of the *Skandapurana*, from chapter 1 to 25. The first part deals with prolegomena, containing chapters on introduction, testimonia (various myths and stories of leading sages and scholars of the preceding periods), Puranic parallels (contexts to Puranas like *Vayu*, *Matsya*, *Linga*, *Brahmanda*, and *Skanda*), the *Mahabharata*, language and style, manuscript transmission, editorial procedures, presentation of text and critical apparatus, and the synopsis. The second part, Synopsis, contains the English translation. The third part contains the critical edition of chapters 1 to 25 of the *Skandapurana*, in original Sanskrit with layers of footnotes giving variant forms of metres and their interpretation.

Agrawal, J.J. Vijaya Kumar (compiler) 1984. *Glimpses of Varanasi.* Printed and published by: Ratna Printing Press, Varanasi for Kashi Jaycees Youth Club. xviii + 110pp. (English, 17 articles) & 77pp (Hindi, 15 short articles).

The topics covered in the English section are: Sacred Kashi, the Ganga, temple of Vishvanatha, contribution to medicine, music and dance, silk and brocades, temples and images, religious institutions, Sarnath, ghats, tourist places, historical events, cultural legacy, and general information. The Hindi section covers topics like lanes, music, carefreeness, Banarsian-ness, reminiscences, inside history, fairs and festivals, widows and hospices, and pilgrimages in Kashi.

Agrawal, Yashodhara 2004. *Silk Brocades (India Crest)*. 3 + 141 pages, illustrated with 124 colour plates. Lustre Press/ Roli Books Pvt Ltd, New Delhi. Hb, ISBN-13: 978-8174362582.

An excellent book of masterly colour illustrations of silk brocades, presenting the historical perspective, ancient and medieval silk fabrics, expansion of silk brocades industry, development of patterns, brocade weaving, southern and western Indian brocades, brocades of north India, and Varanasi: a special reference (pp. 121-141).

Agrawala, Vasudeva Sharan 1984. *Varanasi Seals and Sealings*. Edited with notes by Prithvi K. Agrawala. 1ˢᵗ ed. Indian Civilisation Series. Prithvi Prakashan, Varanasi.

Studying the seals and sealings found in the archaeological excavations at Rajghat, the book present the full catalogue with description and cross-cultural references. This is the only book on this topic.

—— 1986. *Sarnath*. Archaeological Survey of India, Calcutta. 4ᵗʰ ed. 14 b & w photographs + 1 site map, 29 pp. First published in 1956. Reprinted almost every year.

The fist and only standard guide of the archaeological sites, remains and the site museum and its collected sculptures. The selected site remains and the museum objects are described in detail.

Aiyangar, K.V. Rangasami (ed.) 1942. *Krityakalpataru* (of Bhatta Lakshmidhara). Vol. III *Tirthavivechankandam*, ed. B. Bhattacharya. Gaekwad's Oriental Series, Vol. XCVIII, Baroda.

The only publication of this treatise with a detailed commentary and introduction. The commentator rightly opines that the above digest is the most important and complete treatise of the early 12ᵗʰ century, the period ascribed to be the golden era in the history of Banaras (the time of the Gahadavala ruler Govindacandra, 1104-1154). The treatise contains fourteen parts, but only theis one is dealing with sacred places. Mostly based on the *Linga Purana* about 350 sacred places were described by Lakshmidhara.

Ali, Subhan 1852. *History of Benares*. The Indian Press, Benares.

Of course dated, this represents the earliest attempt to highlight the major events of history of Banaras city and its estate, mostly on the basis of popular tales and oral traditions.

Allchin, F.R. (ed.) 1964. *Kavitavali* (of Tulasi, 1547-1623). English translation with critical introduction. George Allen & Unwin Ltd., London.

[This book's description on Banaras is examined elsewhere; cf. Singh, Rana P.B. 2004: pp. 112-128].

Allchin, F.R. (ed.) 1966. *Vinaya-Patrika* (*The Petition to Lord Rama*; of Tulasi, 1547-1623). English translation with introduction, notes and glossary. George Allen & Unwin Ltd., London.

[This book's description on Banaras is examined elsewhere; cf. Singh, Rana P.B. 2004: pp. 112-128].

Alley, Kelly D. 2003. *On the Banks of the Ganga: When Wastewater Meets a Sacred River*. University of Michigan Press, Ann Arbor MI. 2 maps, 12 figs. xiv + 296pp. Glossary, bibliography, index. Pb ISBN: 0-472-06808-3, HB ISBN: 0-472-09808-X.

This is the final report of a nine-year project, presenting the inter-sections of culture, ecology and religion that concern the environ-mental anthropology and ecological future of the region. In focus-sing the contested notions of purity and pollution and the cultural politics of waste management in the sacred city of Banaras, the book demonstrates the power of ethnographic research to elucidate environmental debates, covering geographical personality, issue of purity and pollution, the power of the Ganga, purity and unclean-liness, purity and flow, defilement and fouling, judicial activism, institutional management, contesting water quality, transcendence and immanence, paradigm of discourses and related issues like perceptions, ethics, awareness, legal outlooks and public conscious-ness. The various meanings of the Ganga in Banaras, from the binary of sacred vs. secular, pure vs. polluted, etc. are narrated meticulously.

All-India Kashiraj Trust (ed.) 1981. *Varanasi, An Introduction to the Greatness of the City*. Kashiraj Trust, Ramnagar Fort, Varanasi. 74pp.

This is a compiled introductory book prepared on the occasion of the 5th World Sanskrit Conference held at B.H.U., Varanasi: 21-26 October 1981. It gives a short introduction to Puranic names, early history, major historical events, genealogy of the kings of Kashi, tourist places, important temples and pilgrimages, religious insti-tutions, festivals, and bibliography.

Altekar, Anant Sadasiv 1937. *History of Banaras: From Prehistoric Times to Present Day.* Cultural Publications, Banaras. ii + 76pp. First published in *The Journal of Banaras Hindu University*, vol. 1 (1): 47-75, and vol. 1 (2): 253-286 pp.

—— 1947. *Banaras and Sarnath: Past and Present.* Revised reprint of his earlier work, 1937. Banaras Hindu University, Varanasi. ii + 76pp., 6 b & w figures and photographs.

The first attempt to present a short history of the city in a systematic way. Even to date, this is considered to be one of the best treatments of the history of Banaras, covering ancient to British periods.

Alter, Joseph S. 1992. *The Wrestler's Body. Identity and Ideology in North India.* University of California Press, Berkeley. 2 figures, 15 b & w photographs, appendix, bibliography, index, xvi + 306pp. ISBN: 0-520-07697-4. http://ark.cdlib.org/ark:/13030/ft6n39p104. Reprinted in 1997: Munshiram Manoharlal Publ., New Delhi, ISBN: 81-215-0799-5.

This study established 'the body of the wrestler' as a focal symbol in the rubric of 'ethical nationalism'. Wrestlers feel that a reform of the Indian national character is imperative, and that moral reform on this scale can only be achieved through a discipline of the individual body. The book explains how the wrestlers advocate their way of life as an ideology of national health. Everyone is called on to become a wrestler and build collective strength through self-discipline. The book documents the story of a way of life organised in terms of physical self-development, with case studies from Banaras, Delhi and Mussoorie.

Aly, S.H. 1957. *Varanasi: The Holy City (Kashi).* 67pp. Mata Prasad, Allahabad.

Ambasth, R. S. and Tripathi, B. D. 1984. Eds. *River Ecology and Human Health.* (Proceedings of the National Seminar). National Environmental Conservation Association, Dept. of Botany, Banaras Hindu University, Varanasi. vi + 107pp.

This proceedings contains 16 short scientific articles, all related to river ecology, especially the Ganga. The topics covered are environmental conservation, water pollution, monitoring and management, physico-chemical characteristics, ecological investigations, liminology, effluent outfall, ecosystem, perception and awareness, impacts on mammals, and bacteriological assessment.

(Anonymous) 1882. *History of the Province of Benares*. 200pp. Carruthers, London and The Medical Hall Press, Benares, by E. J. Lazarus & Co., Part I and Part II. First published 1875.

A type of Souvenir publication for general understanding.

Armstrong, William (Old Resident of New York) 1875. *Benares Guide-book for the Use of Tourists and Others Visiting Benares: With Sketch Map of City and Suburbs*. Published by Printed by E.J. Lazarus & Co. London at the Medical Hall Press, Benares. 128 pp.

Bahadur, P. 1976. *Technical Feasibility of Ground Water Development in Varanasi District*. T.M. no. 6, G.W.I.O., Lucknow.

Baker, Deborah 2008. *A Blue Hand: The Beats in India*. Illustrated. 246 pp. The Penguin Press, New York, London and New Delhi. Hb, ISBN-13: 978-1594201585.

Drawing from extensive research in India, undiscovered letters, journals, and memoirs, the acclaimed biographer Deborah Baker has woven a many layered literary mystery out of Allen Ginsberg's odyssey. On 11 December 1961, Allen Ginsberg, a 37-year old poet from Newark, left New York by boat for Bombay, India. He brought with him his troubled lover, Peter Orlovsky, and a plan to meet up with poets Gary Snyder and Joanne Kyger. This book follows him and his companions as they travel from the ashrams of the Himalayan foothills to Delhi opium dens and the burning pyres of Banaras. They encounter an India of charlatans and saints, a country of spectacular beauty and spiritual promise and of devastating poverty and political unease.

Bakker, Hans T. and Isaacson, Harunaga 2004. *The Skandapurana: Vol. IIA Adhyaya 26-31.14, The Varanasi Cycle*. Critical edition with an Introduction, English synopsis & Philological and Historical Commentary. Egbert Forsten, Groningen. 5 maps, 1 Fig., bibliography, index to the synopsis, index of text passages, index to the introduction, commentary and appendix, xv + 345 pp. Hb ISBN: 90-6980-152-3.

This book is in continuation of the only critical edition of the *Skandapurana: Vol. I Adhyaya 1-25* by Adriaensen, Bakker, and

Isaacson (1998, *op. cit.*), and deals with the Varanasi cycle. The introduction covers the glorifying narrative of Varanasi and its association with the *Skandapurana*, the religious history of Varanasi up to the Islamic conquest and the New Beginning, followed by the critical edition of the text in Sanskrit. The next section covers synopsis and commentary dealing with celestial prelude, prehistory, in the divine palace, in the divine garden, the myth of Yaksha Pingala, and appendix. In the editors' commentary through their field study they have highlighted the contemporary spatial perspectives and associated symbolic cosmogony, which rarely people from the field of Indology attempt to interpret.

Barker, Robert 1777. *An Account of the Brahmins Observatory at Benares.* W. Bowyer & J. Nichols, London. 12pp.

Barrett, Ron 2008. *Aghor Medicine. Pollution, Death, and Healing Northern India.* Foreword by Jonathan P. Parry. University of California Press, Berkeley and London. xxii + 216 pages, 6 x 9 inches, 10 b & w photographs, 4 line illustrations, 1 map, 3 tables. Hb ISBN: 978-0-520-25218-9.

For centuries, the Aghoris have been known as the most radical ascetics in India: living naked on cremation grounds, meditating on corpses, engaging in cannibalism and coprophagy, and consuming intoxicants out of human skulls. In recent years, however, they have shifted their practices from the embrace of ritually polluted substances to the healing of stigmatized diseases. In the process, they have become a large, socially mainstream, and politically powerful organization. Based on extensive fieldwork for doctoral dissertation (2002, Emory University), this lucidly written book explores the dynamics of pollution, death, and healing in Aghor medicine. The author successfully and lucidly examines a range of Aghor therapies, from ritual bathing to modified Ayurveda and biomedicines, and clarifies many misconceptions about this little-studied group and its highly unorthodox, powerful ideas about illness and healing. The book moves seamlessly between an ethnography of religion and medical anthropology, and quite marvelous are the stories of suffering and renunciation, of collective experience that turn Indian hierarchy and discrimination upside down. The narratives and descriptions are clear and direct, and the interpretations balanced and scupulously documented.

Basu, Tarun Kanti 1991. *Varanasi, the Luminous City*. T.K. Basu, Varanasi. 142pp., illustrated. 2nd ed. 1999.

A short introduction to the city by one of the most experienced tour guides; however it lacks the wide coverage and systematic description of the places and spots. This is a casual guidebook for one-day western tourists, not for serious tourists and pilgrims.

Bauer, Marchel and Christoph 1980. *Der Tod Benares*. Spee-Buchverlag GmbH, Trier; in German.

An introductory guidebook in German. [See; Gutschow and Michaels 1993].

Bautze, Joachim Karl 2007. *Das Koloniale Indien. Photographien von 1855 bis 1910.* 281 photographs, 320pp. Fackelträger-Verlag, Köln. Hb, ISBN-13: 978-37716-4347-8. [in German].

There appear several photographs of the British period presenting different scenes of Banaras.

Bayly, Christopher A. 1983. *Rulers, Townsmen and Bazaar: North Indian Society in Age of British Expansion, 1770-1870.* Cambridge University Press, Cambridge. Conclusion, notes, bibliography, glossary, index, xiv + 490pp. Hb ISBN: 0-521-22932-4.

This book traces the evolution of towns and merchant communities in Banaras Region from the decline of Mughal domination to the consolidation of the mature Victorian empire following the 'Mutiny' of 1857. This is a pioneer work of social history in the 18th and 19th centuries, emphasising the understanding of the origins and the composition of the Indian 'middle classes' who came to dominate the modern history of India. The focus of chapters deals with society, economy, rise of corporations, political stability, colonial economy: its indigenous origin and its crisis, conflicts and their impacts, urban sprawl, merchants, and trade and society after the great rebellion.

Bedi, Rajesh and Keay, John 1987. *Banaras. City of Shiva*. Brajbasi Printers Pvt. Ltd., New Delhi.

A photographic book, mostly colour, that covers the religious landscape, riverfront scenes and also temples' activities.

Berglund, Henrik 2000/ 2004. *Hindu Nationalism and Democracy. A Study of the Political Theory and Practice of Bhartiya Janta Party*; [published PhD thesis; supervisor: Prof. Björn Beckman, Dept. of

Political Science, Stockholm University, SE-10691 Stockholm, Sweden]. Dept. of Political Science, Stockholm University: Stockholm Studies in Politics Pub. 73. 210pp. ISBN: 91-7265-198-9. Ref. chapter 7, "BJP in Varanasi", pp. 157-174. Reprinted, 2004; Shipra Publs., Delhi.

Bernier, Francois 1914. *Travels in Moghul Empire, AD 1656–1668*. Translated by A. Constable, 2nd ed. revised by V.A. Smith. Oxford University Press, London.

In the purview of Medieval history, the author has described the travels and conquests of the Mughal rulers in the middle Ganga Valley.

Bhatia, Suresh 2007. *Sarnath, Varanasi and Kausambi. A Pilgrim's Guide Book*. Indica Books, Varanasi. 126pp. Pb, ISBN: 81-86569-77-4.

This guidebook deals with three Buddhist places: Sarnath, Varanasi and Kausambi, giving however more emphasis on Sarnath, the place where the Buddha "turned the wheel of *dharma*". The author explains the Four Noble Truths of Buddhism, expounded in Sarnath for the first time, the significance of 'sacred sites', the history of the Buddhist kings and the records of the Chinese pilgrims. He describes the main archaeological sites, monuments and temples of Sarnath. A picture of Varanasi and its ancient Buddhist heritage is also presented. The last part describes the rediscovery of Kausambi and its Buddhist heritage.

Bhattacharya, Brajmadhaba 1999. *Varanasi Rediscovered*. Munshiram Manoharlal, New Delhi. 12 maps, 40 b & w illustrations, notes and index, xvi + 315pp. Hb ISBN: 81-215-0860-6.

This is a collection of reminiscences of an old author who once lived in Banaras, and who ambitiously thought at the end of his life (around 85-years old) to write a book, covering almost every aspect of the city. However, his assertions are not supplemented by other sources, and in many instances mistakes and errors are introduced under claim of originality. This is neither a travelogue, nor a documented analysis, but rather an unsystematic mixture of several aspects of the city. It is therefore, a book to be read with care and consciousness.

Bhattacharya, B.C. 1924. *The History of Sarnath or the Cradle of Buddhism*. Tara Printing Works, Banaras.

An early attempt to describe the development and growth of Buddhism and the history of Sarnath, describing the Jataka sources, archaeology and tales.

Bilas, Ram 1988. *Rural Water Resource Utilisation and Planning. A Geographical Approach in Varanasi District.* Concept Publs. Co., New Delhi. (Revised doctoral thesis). Appendices, bibliography, index, 31 figs., 58 tables, 176pp. + 23 b & w photographs. ISBN: 81-7022-027-0.

Based on his doctoral thesis, this book presents a case study of Varanasi district with emphasis on geographical setting, water resource potentiality and its utilisation pattern, rural domestic water supply, water for agriculture, planning and management of water resources, and finally summary and conclusion. This monograph appraises the total water resource and its utilization for agricultural, domestic and industrial purposes. Various consequences due to specific reasoning, like development of hardness and salinity caused by water logging, increased use of fertilizers, and dumping of industrial waste are also taken into account for making a rational use of water supply plan. The water supply needs for various uses in 1991 is also projected, and ways and means to meet these requirements are suggested.

Bisschop, Peter C. 2006. *Early Saivism and the Skandapurana. Sects and Centres.* Edited by H. T. Bakker. Groningen Oriental Studies. Egbert Forsten, Groningen. [originally a doctoral dissertation in theology, University of Groningen, 2004].

Biswas, Taran K. and Jha, Bhogendra D. 1985. *Gupta Sculptures, Bharat Kala Bhavan.* 107 pp., illust. Books & Books, New Delhi. ISBN: 81-85016143.

This is a collection of iconographic pictures, and photographic illustrations of the Gupta sculptures preserved in the Bharat Kala Bhavan of the Banaras Hindu University.

Bjerkan, Lise 2002. *Faces of a Sadhu. Encounters with Hindu Renouncers in Northern India.* Published doctoral thesis. Norwegian University of Science and Technology, Faculty of Social Sciences and Technology Management. 368pp. ISBN: 82-471-5095-6. Website: http://urn.ub.uu.se/resolve?urn=urn:nbn:no:ntnu:diva-24 <accessed: 01 March 2007>.

India is a continent of paradoxes and contradictions-desperate poverty and immense wealth, purity and impurity, caste and class, heat and cold, monsoon and drought, mosques and temples, *ahimsa* and violence, secularism and fanaticism, sacred cows and holy men. Enigmatic customs and practices raise an apparently never-ending line of questions with either no answers or a multitude of them. To visualize and understand all together Banaras has no alternative, especially for the variety of *sadhus*. The book throws light on the cultural and religious traditions, the practice of renunciation, and the life-style adopted by men and women of all ages. The narration helps to understand their stories as to how they left behind the world of domestic demands, obligations and dependency and entered what is often described as a state of peace (*shanti*) and eternal happiness (*ananda*).

Bonner, Georgette; Soni, Jayandra and Soni, Luitgard (eds.) 1993. *Alice Boner Diaries: India 1934-1967.* 300pp. Motilal Banarasidass Pub., Delhi. Hb, ISBN: 81-208-1121-6.

Alice Bonner (1889-1981) was a sculptor and painter who settled in Varanasi in 1936 and became one of the outstanding scholars and interpreters of Indian sculpture and temple architecture. In her commemorative honour there is a permanent gallery named after her in the Bharat Kala Bhavan (museum in the B.H.U.). She has written many small pieces about her vision and perception of Banaras, scattered in the following pages: 32-48, 52-55, 56-60, 64-92, 92-97, 99-109, 111-113, 115-117, 126-128, 135-141, 173-175, 179-188, 190, 192-195, 199-202, 206-208, 211-212, 214, 218, 234-245, 246-273, 276-278, 285-286, 287, and 289-291.

Booker, Y. A. 2004. *Incident at Varanasi.* 244pp. Temple House/Sidharta, Victoria (Australia).

Brooke, Arthor 1850. *History of the Rise of the Bengal Army.* 2 vols. London.

There are several instances of scenes and narrations of Banaras that deal with political economy, administration and military and the historical background.

Burford, Robert and Smith, Robert 1840. *Description of a View of the Holy City of Benares, and the Sacred Ganges.* Now Exhibiting at the Panorama, Leicester Square (London, England). Published by Printed by T. Brettell & Co., London. 12pp.

Buyers, William 1852. *Travels in India: Comprising Sketches of Madras, Calcutta, Benares, and the Principal Places on the Ganges*; Also of the Church of England, Baptist, London Society, and Other Missionary Stations, with Observations on the Origin, Customs, and Worship of the Hindoos. J. Blackwood, London. 548pp.

Callewaert, Winand and Robert Schilder 1997. *Benares. Stad van Goden, Hart van India*. Uitgeverij Peeters, Leuven (Belgium). In *Flemish*. Select bibliography, glossary, index, viii + 135 pp. + 91 b & w and colour photographs. ISBN: 90-6831-956-6.

Written from the perspective of a common visitor, this books covers almost every aspect of Banaras, covering cosmology, sacred city, Siva's home, Bhairava as watch guard, Ganesha, Annapurna, the pilgrimage journeys, Hanuman, the *pandas*, the *ghats*, the weavers, feelings of personalities like Dr Mehta, and a young female student from Belgium, architecture, etc.

Cape, Charles Phillips 1910. *Benares: The Stronghold of Hinduism*. 262pp. Charles H. Kelly Publs. By R.G. Badger, London.

An early attempt to describe the religious history of the city that developed as the stronghold, or cultural capital, of the Hindus.

Chakrabarti, Dilip K. 2006. *Archaeological Geography of the Ganga Plain: The Lower and the Middle Ganga*. 350pp. + 60 plates + maps. Permanent Black, New Delhi; Book No. A006. Hb. ISBN: 81-7824-016-5

This book discusses the ancient historical geography of the lower and middle (central) part of the Ganga plain, i.e. Banaras Region, successfully integrating archaeology, history, landscape studies and geography. Its basis is a field-study of the distribution of archaeological sites in the region. The geographical issues which have been considered here are the location of sites, the historical linkages of different areas, the problems of political geography, and the routes. The last time an archaeologist tried to understand the ancient historical-geographical situation of the Ganga plain in its totality was in the closing decades of the nineteenth century. In a sense this work is the first attempt to update and recast the classical work by Alexander Cunningham and his group in the late 19th and early 20th centuries. Section VIII 'Along the Ganga from Ballia to Banaras and beyond' especially deals with the Banaras Region.

Chakravarti, P.M. 1957. *Banaras and Sarnath*. Orient Publishers, Banaras.

A popular introduction to the city and Sarnath.

Chakravorty, P.M. 1969. *Banaras - The Most Ancient City of the World*. Orient Publishers, Varanasi. 114pp.

Based on his earlier work, the author has attempted to establish this city as the most ancient city of the world! However, he fails to provide historical, archaeological and chemical proofs to justify his ambitious hypothesis.

Chandra, Rai Govind and Prakash, Vidya (eds.) 1968. *Varanasi at a glance: a Souvenir*; issued on the eve of the XXIV session of All India Oriental Conference, Varanasi. All India Oriental Conference, Varanasi.

Chandramouli, K. 1995. *Kashi, The City Luminous*. Rupa & Co., New Delhi. 13 appendices, references, glossary, index, illustrated, xviii + 490pp. ISBN: 81-7167-236-1.

An exploratory and ambitious attempt by an experienced engineer to analyse the energy that keeps the city of Kashi vibrating, the spirit which keeps it growing and the sacred essence that keeps it ever charming. So many aspects in unsystematic order are highlighted to narrate the vividity of the city of Kashi.

——2006. *Luminous Kashi to Vibrant Varanasi*. Indica Books, Varanasi. 13 appendices, notes, references, glossary, index, illustrated, 486pp. ISBN: 81-86569-56-1.

This is a revised and expanded version of the author's earlier publication (1995). The author claims that the city's uniqueness and multiple symbolism are to be analysed in the context of contrast, i.e. old and new, where spirituality and materialism go together. Altogether there are fifty short pieces that deal with various aspects, including thematic history, people's faith, mythical stories, devotionalism of medieval periods, the saint tradition, sacred places, deities, tradition of debates, landscape, tourism, craft and silk weaving, music, wresting tradition, education, impression of travellers, etc. The book lacks a concise focus or systematic orientation, but gives a lot of information on many aspects. In fact, it is written as a tribute to the sacred city that was once experienced and dwelt upon by the author, a senior executive who served several industries in the country.

Chalier-Visuvalingam, Elizabeth 2003. *Bhairava: terreur et protection. Mythes, rites et fêtes à Bénarès et à Katmandou;* (in French). Dieux, Hommes et Religions (Gods, Humans and Religions, Vol. 4, Gen. Editor: Fragnière Gabriel). P.I.E. Peter Lang, Bruxelles. 268pp., illus. Pb, ISBN: 90-5201-173-7.

Substantive portions of this D.Litt. dissertation deal with Banaras (e.g. pp. 53-94 and 171-182).

Chatterjee, Gopal Chander 1893. *Yatindra Charitam, Or, A Short Life of Swami Bhaskarananda Saraswati of Benares.* Kahinoor Press, Calcutta.

Chiefala, Captain Niccola 1826. *Descrizione della citta di Benares* (in Italian). Livorno, Rome.

The first Italian description of the city, its history, landscape, culture, people, festivals, and religious institutions.

Chrintine, Etchezaharreta and Dabadie, Séverine (with photographs by Dabadie, Séverine) 2006. *A Day in Kashi.* Pilgrims Publishers, Varanasi. xx + 276pp, 108 colour photographs with captions, and 100 without captions, 5 maps (by Rana P.B. Singh). Translated from French. ISBN: 81-7769-388-3. [Also available in French and Spanish].

Claveyrolas, Mathieu 2003. *Quand le temple prend vie. Atmosphère et dévotion à Bénarès* ["When the temple comes to life. Atmosphere and Devotion in Banaras"] (in French). Collection Monde Indien Sciences sociales: 15th-20th siècle. CNRS Editions, 15 rue Malebranche, FR-75000 Paris. 5 figures, 24 b & w and 16 colour photographs, bibliography, glossary, index, 416pp. ISBN: 2-271-06117-2.

This is a piece of research on the microcosmos of the Sankatmochan Hanuman temple; it further gives cross-sectional links to the ethnographic, religious, psychological and lifeworld themes that evolved and maintained Hindu culture. The ten chapters are arranged into five parts. The first part, 'the housing, the temple and neighbourhood', describes the social and administrative frame and the scene of landscape transformation. The second part, 'theosphere and devotees', examines the spatial structure, devotees and visitors and the associated wrestling tradition. The third part, 'the environment and the divine', deals with space and devotionalism, the sanctuary of Rama, chanting and citations of religious stories, sensitivity and territoriality, and euphemisms. The fourth part, 'the temple atmosphere and devotees', narrates the activities, festivities, involvement, impact of change and maintenance of orthodoxy, and the tradition of bhakti. The fifth part, 'the evolutionary atmosphere of Hindu paradise', deals with the natural landscape, change of vegetal cover, sentiments and emotion, and construction of eternity. [Compare with another work in German: Keul, István 2002]

Cohn, Bernard S. 1987. *An Anthropologist among the Historians and Other Essays*. Oxford University Press, New Delhi. [7th impression 2001]. Part IV, 'The British in Benares', comprising 8 essays published earlier: pp. 320-631; details of these essays cited under 'B. Research Papers', in sequence. ISBN: 019-562616-8.

The themes covered by the eight essays [cf. list of essays, cited separately in this bibliography] are initial impact of British on the region, structural change in rural society (1596-1885), the British and the colonial society in nineteenth century, Indian status to British contract, political system in eighteenth-century Banaras region, recruitment and training of British civil servants, law and change, and anthropological notes on law and disputes.

—— 1996. *Colonialism and its Forms of Knowledge: The British in India*. Princeton University Press, Princeton.

Many portions and passages deal with Banaras.

Cohen, Lawrence 1998. *No Aging in India: Alzheimer's, The Bad Family, and Other Modern Things*. Bibliography, glossary, xxv + 367 pp. + 4 b & w figures. University of California Press, Berkeley and Los Angeles. Pb ISBN: 978-0-520-22462-9.

From the opening sequence, in which mid-19th-century Indian fishermen hear about the possibility of redemption in an old woman's madness, this book captures the reader with its interplay of story and analysis. Drawing on more than a decade of ethnographic work, the author links a detailed investigation of mind and body in old age in four neighbourhoods of Banaras, with events and processes around India and around the world. This compelling exploration of senility — encompassing not only the aging body but also larger cultural anxieties — combines insights from medical anthropology, psychoanalysis, and postcolonial studies. Bridging literary genres as well as geographic spaces, Cohen responds to what he sees as the impoverishment of both North American and Indian gerontologies — the one mired in ambivalence toward demented old bodies, the other insistent on a dubious morality tale of modern families breaking up and abandoning their elderly. He shifts our attention irresistibly toward how old age comes to matter in the constitution of societies and their narratives of identity and history. A tour-de-force in the analysis of body and society. The book is an exemplar of critical and cultural analysis.

Consolaro, Alessandra 2003. *Madre India e la parola. La lingua hindi nelle università nazionali di Varanasi* ('Mother India and the Word: Hindi as National Language and the National University of Varanasi'); in Italian; revised doctoral thesis from Dept. of Oriental Studies, University of Torino. Edizioni dell'Otro, Alessandria (Italy). Notes on each page, 4 figures, 1 table, glossary, bibliography, index, 474pp. Pb, ISBN: 88-7694-654-3.

The subject matter is arranged in eight chapters, describing introduction to problem and methodology, the language and its national identity, scholastic tradition and institutions, Banaras Hindu University and its national image, the role of Hindi as national language and the role of B.H.U., the national consciousness and movement at level in 1920, growth and development of Kashi Vidyapith, Hindu and Hindustani: the role of KVP, and conclusions: assessing Ramchandra Shukla and Premchand, and revolutions.

Couté, Pierre-Daniel et Léger, Jean-Michel (eds.) 1989. *Bénarès. Un voyage d'architecture. An Architectural Voyage.* (in French and English). 74 photographs and 72 architectural designs, bibliography, 152pp. Editions Créaphis, Paris; with the support of the French Embassy at New Delhi. ISBN 2-907150-09-X. [See also; Gutschow, Niels 2005].

This book (printed in French and English, side by side) was published together with the exhibition: 'Benares, an Urban Space' inaugurated on 15th October 1989 at Man Singh Palace, Banaras, as part of the Festival of France in India. This project was sponsored by the French Ministry of Foreign Affairs, the C.N.R.S., and the Paris-Belleville School of Architecture. The book, the only of its kind, unveils the diversity of Banaras with respect to the forms, religious architecture, water architecture, architecture and techniques, architecture and practices, emphasising ways of life: palaces or houses, traditional housing, pilgrims rest houses, gardens and water bodies.

Curwe, F. (trans.) 1875. *The Balwantnamah.* (English translation from Persian). Indian Press, Allahabad.

This book describes the history, glories, administration and revenue systems of the state of Banaras in the period of its king Balwant Singh Raja (1740-70), son of Mansa Ram, a Bhumihar of Gangapur (Thithria) who seized the governorship of Banaras in 1738 with the approval of Nawab Sadat Khan and declared his son as king of an independent state.

Dalmia, Vasudha 1997. *The Nationalization of Hindu Traditions. Bhârtendu Harischandra and Nineteenth-century Banaras.* Bibliography, index, xii + 490 pp. Oxford University Press, Delhi. Pb, 1999. ISBN: 0-19-564856-0.

This book studies how a dominant strand of Hinduism in north India — the tradition which uses and misuses the slogan 'Hindi-Hindu-Hinduism' — came into being in the late 19th century. It examines the life and writings of one major Hindi writer of the 19th century — the playwright, journalist and polemicist Bhartendu Harishchandra (often called the Father of Modern Hindi) — as its focal point for an analysis of some of the vital cultural processes through which modern India, as we experience it today, came to be formed.

Daniélou, Alain 1987. *Way to the Labyrinth: Memories of East and West.* 356pp. New Directions Publishing Co., New York. Pb, ISBN-13: 978-0811210157.

Daniélou was an amazing forerunner of the modern western traveller in India. He had the good fortune to hook up with a wealthy lover who helped him travel and live in style in India in the first half of the 20th century. He describes their pleasant lives in a rented Maharaja's palace on the banks of the Ganga in Banaras, narrating a fascinating account of life in Varanasi and beyond, where the couple learned languages, music, and entertained *tout le monde.* The book presents a compelling look at Westerners' first real entry into the literati life of Banaras as well as into high Indian art and culture, and also provides a glimpse into the disappeared world of the 1930s-1940s. His personal odyssey brought him back to Paris with a newfound ambition to bring Indian classical music to the world's attention and preserve it.

Dar, S.L. and Somaskandan, S. 1966/2007. *History of the Banaras Hindu University*. Banaras Hindu University Press, Banaras. xiii + 864pp + pasted 254 b & w photographs. Foreword by N.H. Bhagwati, Vice-Chancellor. Reprinted with a new *Foreward* by Prof. Panjab Singh, VC, and two *Appendices*: 'Banaras Hindu University-Retrospect and Prospect': Vishwanath Pandey, and 'Banaras Hindu University, Architectural Plan: Symbolism and Meaning': Rana P.B. Singh. Banaras Hindu University Press, Varanasi, 2007.

The only book on the history of Banaras Hindu University; it lacks however the viewpoints of landscape transformation, architectural planning, and recent changes. The thematic chapters are Malviya's dream, idea into action, Bhartiya Vishvavidyalaya, progress of the movement, Annie Besant and her proposed university, Malviya's revised scheme, prince of beggars, the Hindu University Society, educational scope of the university, second collection campaign, and after, fulfilment of government's condition, enactment of B.H.U. bill, the Banaras Hindu University act, university site and the holy Kashi, the foundation stone laying ceremony, the first court meeting, university starts functioning, the first convocation, the years 1919-1921, visit of the Prince of Wales, onward march 1922-30, difficult times, Malviya retires, a true successor, silver jubilee, August 1942 and after, years of consolidation, early post-independent years, progress amidst vicissitudes, and Malviya centenary and after.

Das, Asok Kumar 1992. *Paintings from Royal Albums: Mughal masterpieces from the Bharat Kala Bhavan, Varanasi*. Lalit Kala Akademi, New Delhi.

Davis, Cuthbert Collin (ed.) 1948. *The Benaras Diary of Warren Hastings*. 40pp. Camden Miscellany, London, vol. 18. Offices of the Royal Historical Society, London for the British Museum, and British Library. Transcribed from British Museum, Add. ms. 29,212, fos. 1-83 and Add. ms. 29,233, fos. 23 sqq.

Davis, John Francis 1871. *Vizier Ali Khan, Or, The Massacre at Benares: A Chapter in British Indian History.* 98pp. Spottiswoode & Co., London.

Denton, Lynn Teskey (late, 1949-1995) 2004. *Females Ascetics in Hinduism.* Ed. By Steven Collins. State University of New York (SUNY) Press, Albany. x + 218pp., 8 tables, notes, glossary, bibliography, index. Pb ISBN: 0-7914-6180-7.

This posthumous book provides a vivid account of the lives of women renouncers in the frame of institutionalised asceticism — women who renounce the world to live ascetic spiritual lives in India — based on her study of Banaras. The author approaches the study of female asceticism by focussing on features of two *dharmas*, two religiously defined ways of life: that of women-as-householder and that of the ascetic, who, for various reasons, falls outside the realm of householdership. The book explores the renouncers' social and personal backgrounds, their institutions, and their ways of life. In six chapters, it covers the themes of religious life; life of a woman who is not a householder; unity and diversity: basis; unity and diversity; sectarian affiliation, spiritual path and ascetic mode; socio-religious aspects of female; and sainthood, society and transcendence.

Derné, Steve 1995. *Culture in Action: Family Life, Emotion, and Male Dominance in Banaras, India.* State Univ. of New York Press, Albany. xiv + 232pp., fieldwork in urban India, notes, bibliography, index. ISBN: (Hb) 0-7914-2425-1, (Pb) 0-7914-2426-X.

This book explores the interconnections between male dominance, joint-family living, Indian emotional life, and a cultural focus on group pressures, based on interviews of Hindu men about women, marriage, and family, to develop an understanding of how culture works in Banaras. Derné emphasizes the Hindu focus on the social group, but shows that men often distance themselves from group culture by marrying for love, separating from their parents, or embracing closeness with their wives. The author's suggestion that Indian men's cultural focus on the group limits men's and women's strategies for breaking cultural norms offers a new approach to understanding how culture constrains. He shows how the child-rearing practices and emotional tensions associated with joint-family living shape Indians' group emphasis. This approach suggests that the Hindu focus on the group is intimately connected with male dominance.

Dhapola, T.S. 1979. *Mid-term Parliamentary Election in Varanasi: A Behavioural Study*. Rupa Psychological Centre, Varanasi. 150pp.

Dodson, Michael S. 2007. *Orientalism, Empire and National Culture. India, 1770-1880*. Cambridge Imperial and Post-Colonial Studies Series. 288pp. Palgrave Macmillan Ltd., Hampshire UK. Hb ISBN: 978-1-4039-8645-0.

Orientalist research has most often been characterized as an integral element of the European will-to-power over the Asian world through the histories of knowledge — Sanskrit erudition and forms of legitimacy. This study, profusely illustrated with case studies from Banaras, seeks to nuance this view, and asserts that British Orientalism in India was also an inherently complex and unstable enterprise, predicated upon the cultural authority of the Sanskrit pandits, its principal Indian intermediaries. In exploring the evolution of Sanskrit intellectual culture at Benares College, the author reveals a complex, layered world of knowledge production in an increasingly important outpost of the British Empire, *1770-1880*. The 'common ground' of Benares College possessed, to be sure, an uneven political topography, but it was a topography full of surprising landmarks-especially for those who assume an easy congruence between trajectories of power and knowledge in Europe's engagement with its Others. By revealing the unacknowledged roles which this 'traditional' intelligentsia played within elements of the colonial state apparatus, this book traces the conflicts and ambiguities within Orientalism, from the consolidation of Britain's fledgling Indian empire to its links with the emergence of early forms of Indian national identity and inherently anti-colonial cultural movements. At the end, the book also presents a glimpse of linkages among Sanskrit, authority, and national culture.

Doron, Assa 2009. *Caste, Occupation and Politics on the Ganges: Passages of Resistance*. Ashgate, Aldershot, Hampshire.

Based on detailed fieldworks among the boatmen of Banaras, the contents deal with the anthropology and social behaviour of the people maintaining their traditional occupation while also keeping pace with the modern impact of tourists. In marriage and death rites boatmen serve as important functionaries, and on special occasions of sacred bathing serve as carriers. Boatmen make their own lifeworld that has different niches and compartments for the

202

Hindu clients or visitors from abroad, that is how they are called as cultural brokers working for ritual economy, and sometimes priests for folk celebrations. The realities of social life and daily interaction within the local community suggest that agency and the plurality of context produce dynamic, multiple and overlapping identities.

Dutta, Vijay Ranjan 1973. *Micro Level Political Elite: A Study of the Social Background of Varanasi.* 62pp. Gandhian Institute of Studies, Varanasi.

Dwivedi, Prem Shankar 1990. *Wall Paintings of Mahamaya Temple in Varanasi.* 110pp, 25 b & w photographs with short stories from texts, bibliography. Kala Prakashan [B 33/33-A-1 New Saket Colony], Varanasi.

This is a pioneering attempt to document the four layers of wall paintings in the Mahamaya temple (House No. K 6/ 7/ 78-3), in Ishwargangi locality, while describing the different settings, poses, motives, backgrounds, associations and styles. The local, Avadhi, Nepali, Company, Rajasthani and Mughal schools of painting are depicted on the wall in different compositions, mostly around the goddess at the centre. At the beginning the book introduces the tradition of mural art and its tradition in Varanasi. [See also, Dwivedi, 1993]

—— 1993. *Durga Theme in Varanasi Wall Paintings.* 195pp., 20 b & w photographs with narration. Eastern Book Linkers, Delhi. ISBN: 81-85133-82-4.

This is a revised and updated version of the author's book published in Hindi (1985), which was based on his doctoral dissertation. The themes covered include Banaras and its contributions to the art of painting and historical context, Durga and her symbolism and associated festivities, Durga in Indian art, painting and sculpture, tradition and characteristics of wall painting and scenes from Banaras, case studies of the wall paintings from different places and shrines in Banaras, specific cases of paintings and their codification, and annotated catalogue of Durga related paintings in Bharat Kala Bhawan, the museum in Banaras Hindu University. [See also, Dwivedi, 1990].

Eck, Diana L. 1982. *Banaras. The City of Light.* Penguin India, New Delhi (Indian Reprint). Glossay, notes, bibliography, index. 60 b & w photos and 7 maps. 446pp., illustrated. Published originally in 1982 by Alfred Knopf, New York. ISBN: 0-394-51971-X; in 1983 by Routledge, London. Indian reprint: 2000, Penguin Books India (P) Ltd., New Delhi.

The best introductory book, coherent and comprehensive in scope, linking mythology, historicity, sacrality, physical landscape, cultural institutions and the religious landscape from different perspectives. The nine chapters deal with introduction, historical perspective, city of Shiva, sacred circles of all the gods, the River Ganges and ghats, seasons and times, city of all India, city of good life, and city of death and liberation. There are six appendices, dealing with sources of study, sacred zones, selected Shiva Lingas, cycle of goddesses, other deities of Kashi, and the calendar.

—— 1989. *Banaras. Stadt des Lichts.* Insel Verlag, Frankfurt am Main (in German). Translation of the author's earlier book, *Banaras. The City of Light* (1982), cited above.

—— 1993. *Encountering God. A Spiritual Journey from Bozeman to Banaras.* Beacon Press, Boston. xvi + 259pp., notes, select readings, index. ISBN: 0-8070-7302-4. Reprinted 1995; Penguin Books India (P) Ltd., New Delhi.

For all of us, the religious differences with our neighbours can seem bewildering and strange; the deeply held beliefs of Buddhists, Muslims, Hindus, and others call into question our own fundamental faiths. Diana Eck, a lifelong Methodist as well as an expert in the religions of India, understands this, and in this book, she lets us learn from the story of her personal encounters with the many non-Christian friends and teachers whose insights challenged her to examine her Christian faith anew. Eck insists that the spiritual questions she explores in this book — Who is God? How are we to pray? What are we to believe in the face of inexplicable suffering? — find deeper, more meaningful answers when we strive to see how other believers respond. In fact, interreligious dialogue — relying on imagination, empathy, respect, and forgiveness — is essential if we are to reach the peace that eludes us at home and abroad. This book is a valuable lesson in how to begin this dialogue.

Eden, Emily 1930. *Up the Country. Letters Written to her Sister from the Upper Provinces of India.* Rev. ed. 1984. Virgo Press Ltd., London: 24-30 (1887), Banaras.

Edgerton, Eleanor 1980. *A Year in Benares.* Priyamvada Press, Delhi. 151 pp.

Ewen, Robert C. 1886. *Benares, A Handbook for Visitors.* Baptist Mission Press, Calcutta.

Falk, Harry 2006. *Asokan Sites and Artefacts: A Source-book with Bibliography.* Philipp von Zabern, Mainz. 295pp. 724 Farb- und 117 Schwarzweißabb. (Monographien zur indischen Archäologie, Kunst und Philologie, Bd. 18). ISBN 3-8053-3712-4/ 978-3-8053-3712-0.

Two substantive chapters deal with Sarnath ⁻Ashokan built space and plans, and other artefacts.

Fisher, F.H. and Hewett, J. P. 1884. *Statistical, Descriptive, and Historical account of the North-western Provinces of India.* Vol. XIV, Part I-Benares. Government Press, Allahabad.

Fitzjames, E. 1880. *Preliminary Report on the Sewerage and Water Supply of the City of Benares.* Government of NW Provinces and Oudh, Public Works Dept. North-Western Provinces and Oudh Press, Allahabad.

Forrest, G.W. 1910. *Selections from the Papers of the Governor Generals of India, Warren Hastings.* 2 vols. Oxford University Press, London.

Foster, George 1798. *A Journey from Bengal to England through the Northern Part of India, Kashmir, etc.* vol. 1. John Murray, London.

Foster, William (ed.) 1921. *Early Travels in India, 1583-1619.* Oxford University Press, London. Reprinted, New Delhi, 1968.

Freitag, Sandria B. (ed.) 1989. *Culture and Power in Banaras. Community, Performance, and Environment, 1800-1980.* 5 maps, 17 figures, bibliography, index, xviii + 290pp. Hb ISBN: 0-520-06367-8. University of California Press, Berkeley, also Oxford University Press, Delhi. For the full book on web: http://ark.cdlib.org/ark:/13030/ft6p3007sk/

Banaras is a complex world, with differences in religion, caste, class, language, and popular culture. The diversity of the ten essays of this book embraces those differences, dealing with the public arenas, Hindi drama, folk music, settlement guardians, Muslim weavers, linguistic identity, popular protests, land use changes, and ecology and cosmology of disease. These essays focus on the cultural activities that constitute Banarsis' work and leisure; these activities reveal power relations in a particular urban space and how those relations change over time. The articles examine everyday activities to learn about shared values and motivations, processes of identity formation, and self-conscious constructions of community. Essays are arranged into three parts. Part I examines the performance genre and the audiences; Part II focuses on the areas of neighbourhood, leisure and work, and Part III links the experiences within Banaras to a series of 'larger world'.

Gaenszle, Martin and Gengnagel, Jörg (eds.) 2006. *Visualised Space in Banaras: Images, Maps, and the Practice of Representations.* (Ethno-Indolgoy: Heidelberg Studies in South Asian Rituals (General Editor: Axel Michaels), ISSN: 1860-2053, Vol. 4). Otto Harrassowitz Verlag KG, Wiesbaden. 358 pp. 80 figures. Hb, ISBN 3-447-05187-6. Reprinted, 2008: Oxford University Press, New Delhi; ISBN: 978-019-569570-4.

This book is the proceedings of a conference held at Heidelberg in June 2002. The thirteen research papers based on intensive field studies deals with Early development of the Avimuktakshetra, Spatial patterns of goddesses, Navadurga's spatial cycle, Transcendence and translocality in the two maps of the city, Maps and processions associated with the Pancakroshi Yatra, Sense of nationalism in enshrining the map of India, Panoramic view, Authorship and identification of copies and versions of views, Visualizing cities by modern citizens, Children space in the neighbourhood and the home, Social landscape of the washermen, Appropriations of Nepali places, and Visions of a new Banaras in the early twentieth century. The present volume deals with the multiple ways this urban site is visualised, imagined, and culturally represented by different actors and growth. The forms of visualisations are manifold and include buildings, paintings, drawings, panoramas, photographs, traditional and notional maps, as well as verbal and mental images. The major focus is on visual media, which are of special significance for the representation of space. But this cannot be divorced from other forms of expressions, which are part of the local lifeworld ('*Lebenswein*'). The contributions look at local as well as exogenous construction of the rich topography of Kashi and show that these imaginations and constructions are not static but always embedded in social and cultural practices of representation, often contested and never to be complete. (All the essays are cited separately in this bibliography.)

Ganeri, Anita 1993. *Benares*. 46pp. Silver Burdett Press, London. Pb, ISBN 0875185738, 9780875185736.

This book provides a look at the key city of the Hindu religion, with explanations of the city's history and the traditions that bring it into the modern day.

Ganguly, Rita 2003. *Bismillah Khan and Banaras*. 136pp. South Asia Books, New Delhi. Hb. ISBN-13: 978-8170206798.

Garstin, J. 1801. *An Account of the Hindoo Temple of Vissvisshoor, Or Bissinaut at Benares*. 6 aquatints (incl. plan and section) by T. Medland. Calcutta.

Gengnagel, Jörg 2008. *Visualized Texts–Sacred: Spaces, Spatial Texts and the Religious Cartography of Banaras*. Habilitationsschrift, Philosophische Fakultat der Universitat Heidelberg. (Ethno-Indology. Heidelberg Studies in South Asian Rituals; General Editor: Axel Michaels, ISSN: 1860-2053, Vol. 7). Otto Harrassowitz Verlag KG, Wiesbaden.

'Gol', Miguel Gómez Andrea 1999. *A Pilgrimage to Kashi. Baṇaras, Varanasi, Kashi*. Indica Books, Varanasi. 86pp., multi-colour cartoon illustrations; also available in French, Spanish, German, Japanese and Hindi (all these 2008).

The first and the only cartoon book which covers the good and bad of the city along with funny scenes and traditions, narrating in pictures the history, mythology and culture of the strangest and most fascinating city in India.

Glucklich, Ariel 1997. *The End of Magic*. Oxford University Press, New York & Oxford. viii + 256pp. Hb. ISBN 10: 0-19-510880-4.

Throughout history, magic has been as widely and passionately practiced as religion. But while religion continues to flourish, magic stumbles towards extinction. What is magic? What does it do? Why do people believe in magic? The author finds the answers to these questions in the streets of Banaras, India's most sacred city, where hundreds of magicians still practice ancient traditions, treating thousands of Hindu and Muslim patients of every caste and sect. Through study and interpretation of the Banarasi magical rites and those who partake in them, the author presents fascinating living examples of magical practice, and contrasts his findings with the major theories that have explained (or explained away) magic over the last century. These theories, he argues, ignore an essential sensory phenomenon which he calls 'magical experience': an extraordinary, though perfectly natural, state of awareness through which magicians and their clients perceive the effects of magic rituals. The book opens the cross-cultural comparison and theoretical discussion on the cutting edge in the field of social sciences theory and methodology as well as to a number of fundamental questions that ritual, belief, and magic, pose for the fields of philosophy and religious studies, linking the inherent 'spirit of place' and the 'human consciousness' to experience and its continuity.

Gokhale, Namita 2006. *Shakuntala, the Play of Memory*. Penguin Books India, New Delhi. 208pp. Pb. ISBN: 97-90-14-206227-1.

A novel taking the background of Banaras and its ghats. "One can almost feel the heat of the burning pyre on the ghats of Banaras. ... The rhythm of life along the Ganges poignantly comes to life" ‾ *Pioneer*.

Golding, Paul R. with Virendra Singh 1997. *Tales of Banaras. The Flowing Ganges*. Book Faith India, Delhi. xxii + 191pp., 10 figures, glossary after chapters, postscript. ISBN: 81-7303-054-5.

This book presents the life and lore of India's sacred city on the Ganges, based on the translation of 13 original Hindi stories (out of 17) by Rudra Kashikeya, pen name of Shiv Prasad Mishra. All these stories are set in the British period, and based on the popular tales and folklore of the period. This collection of wistful and interconnected tales presents the inner life of the otherwise inscrutable Banaras shrouded in morning mists and evening smoke. In addition to revealing the mythology, customs and history of

Banaras, these evocative psychological tales are also notable for their human tragedies of unrequited love and nostalgia for a romantic past that is gone with the flowing Ganga.

Goodman, Hananya (ed.) 1993. *Between Jerusalem and Banaras*: *Comparative Studies in Judaism and Hinduism.* SUNY Press, Albany. Hb, ISBN 0791417166, 9780791417164. Reprinted, 1997: Sri Satguru, Delhi. Hb. ISBN: 81-7030-522-5.

Some of the papers describe Hinduism and its facets, taking Banaras as a symbolic reference to these aspects.

Greaves, Edwin 1909. *Kashi: The City Illustrious or Benares.* The Indian Press, Allahabad. Reprinted by Asian Education Service, New Delhi, 2003; 19 b & w photos, vii + 154pp. + vi index. Hb, ISBN: 81-206-1694-4.

Once a classic and early comprehensive description of the city's history, culture, traditions and landscape.

Greeven, Richard 1898. *The Bungled Miracle, a Legend of Benares.* Medical Hall Press, Benares. 77pp.

Gupta, Kalpna 2006. *Adolescent Girls, Urban Society and Family Life. Study with reference to Varanasi, India.* 195pp. Sunrise Publications, New Delhi. Hb, ISBN: 81-87365-32-3.

Gupta, Subhadra Sen 2003. *Varanasi, A Pilgrimage to Light.* 159pp., illustrated. Rupa & Co. Publishers, New Delhi. ISBN: 81-29101-65-3.

A sketchy and popular description, covering most of the aspects that the author has thought to be important, lacking historical context, field observations and deep experiences.

Gunnell Wood, W. 1915. *An Estimate and Design for the Construction of a Road Bridge to Carry the Grand Trunk Road over the River Ganges.* The Pioneer Press, Allahabad.

An architectural and engineering report.

Gutschow, Niels 2005. *Benares - The Sacred Landscape of Varanasi.* 498 pp. with 732 ill., mostly in colour, 280 x 270 mm, hardcover. Edition Axel Menges GmbH: Esslinger Strasse 24 D-70736 Stuttgart-Fellbach. Germany. ISBN 3-936681-04-X.

This book is a comprehensive view of the complex world of sacred place that materialises in the shape of *lingas*, deities, ponds, wells or rivers. Thousands of these places represent *tirtha*, crossings between this world and the other. Concerning location of sacred places at which to profit from divine energy, Banaras represents the entire universe of India: the four abodes of Vishnu at the four corners, the seven sacred cities, the twelve *lingas* of light, etc., all these and many more. The book opens up a new view: visually compelling photographs focus on sacred objects like *lingas* as the objects of worship, and also of ritual acts that transcend as art. [See also Couté, Pierre-Daniel et Léger, Jean-Michel (edited) 1989].

Gutschow, Niels and Michaels, Axel 1993. *Benares. Temple und religiöses Leben in der heiligen Stadt der Hindus*. DuMont Buchverlog, Köln. (Taschenbücher 294). 10 maps, 58 b & w Photographs, 10 colour photos, 258pp. (In German). ISBN: 3-7701-2849-4.

The first, the most compact and a master piece handbook for pilgrimage-tourism, especially sacred journeys, the holy spots and their related symbolism. The issues expressed include sacrality and its place in Hinduism, historical development, the Ganga and the ghats, inside the temples and shrines, the religious landscape, the tradition of yatras and associated deities, and selected areas around the city, e.g. Sarnath and Ramnagar.

Hall, Fitzedward 1868. *Benares, Ancient and Medieval: A Monograph*. Published by Printed by Stephen Austin, London. 23 pp.

Hansen, Kathryn 1992. *Grounds for Play: The Nautanki Theatre of North India*. University of California Press, Berkeley. Illustrations, appendix, notes, bibliography. xvii + 354pp. Reprinted: Manohar, New Delhi. Hb, ISBN-13: 978-0520072732. http://ark.cdlib.org/ark:/13030/ft9v19p2qq/ ; available on web: http://www.escholarship.org/editionsview?docId=ft9v19p2qq&brand=eschol

In the 19th century the traditional theatre of Banaras had a major impact on the social and cultural life and the independence movement. The book explains various aspects, like introducing Nautanki through a decentred approach, Nautanki in relation to conventional anthropological guideposts, social history of the community of theatre and recitational practices, segmentation into lineages related to authors and texts, meanings and contradictions, political authority and community identity, gender difference, resonances with historical conditions, pulse of musical life, and finally implications to wider contexts.

Hansson, Sidsel 2001. *Not Just any Water. Hinduism, Ecology and the Ganges Water Controversy*; [published PhD thesis, supervisor: Prof. Tord Olsson, History of Religions, Lund University]. Lund Studies in African & Asian Religions vol. 13, Lund University, Lund (Sweden). No tables, no figures, glossary, 159pp.

This is a study of the religious life and behaviour as modified by, or rather constructed by the concerns of everyday life. The field study covers the period between July 1996 and April 1998, interviews with 85 persons at the riverside Banaras. The subject matter is arranged into five chapters, consisting of introduction and background, urban scene: ritual and natural spaces, purity and gender along the ghat, the tradition of bathing in the Ganga and changes, and analytical outlook of everyday life along the riverfront. This is followed by conclusive remarks, glossary and bibliography.

Harder, Kelsie B. 1963. *The Bathing and Burning Ghats of Benares*. Ohio Valley Folk Research Project, The Ross County Historical Society, Columbus OH.

Hasso, Hohman; Fink, Wolfgang J., and Strempfl-Ledt, Gertraud F. (eds.) 2006. *ISG Magazin, Spec. Issue: Weltkulturerbe Varanasi* (Internationales Städteforum Graz Forum der historischen Städte und Gemeinden; Hauptplatz 3, A-8010 Graz, Austria), 4 (December): pp. 1-16; 24 colour photos and 6 masps and figures; six short essays. In German and English.

This issue attempts to present in brief the Austrian efforts concerning the inclusion of Varanasi on UNESCO's World Cultural Heritage list. This report, representing an outcome of the project carried out jointly between ISG and the Graz University of Technology concerning the historical preservation of the heritage zones of Varanasi, has to be seen in conjunction with both earlier and parallel projects, including the basic works carried out by Rana P.B. Singh (B.H.U., Varanasi) and Niels Gutschow (Germany). The issues highlighted include the consideration of Riverfront Varanasi as

Heritage Zone for enlishing in the UNESCO's Heritage List, the heritage zoning of the Ghats, distinctive personality of the Riverfront, Ghats and Palaces, French contribution of Benares Workshop, and a case study of Nilkanth/Vishvanath Singh Lane. A detailed map of the Riverfront Ghats is also presented.

Hastings, Warren, Esq. 1782. *A Narrative of the Insurrection which Happened in the Zamendary of Benares.* Calcutta (including appendix). Reprinted in Roorkee, 1853.

—— 1782. *A Narrative of the late Transactions at Benares.* 132pp. Pre-1801 Imprint Collection (Library of Congress). J. Debrett (succeffor to Mr Almon), London.

Havell, Ernest Binfield 1905, *Benares, the Sacred City.* Blackie & Sons Ltd, London. Thaper Spink & Co., Calcutta (reprinted, 1968) and Pilgrims Book House, Varanasi (reprinted, 1999). Illustrated, viii + 226pp.

The variety of religious landscapes and Hindu sacred places are described. The emphasis is on the religious history from the Vedic period to the early 20th century, the ghats and their architecture, and the temples and their architecture. Of course dated.

Heber, (Bishop) Reginald 1849. *Narrative of a Journey through the Upper Provinces of India, from Calcutta to Bombay, 1824-1825.* Carey, Lea, and Carey, Philadelphia, and John Murray, London; 2 vols.

Herbert, Jean 1957. *Banaras, Guide to Panch Kroshi Yatra.* 30pp with several sketches. Saturday Mail, Calcutta.

The first book by a foreign scholar based on his experience, explaining in systematic order all the sites and shrines along the Panchakroshi pilgrimage circuit.

Hertel, Bradley R. and Humes, Cynthia A. 1993. Eds. *Living Banaras, Hindu Religion in Cultural Context.* SUNY Press, Albany/ New York. 41 illustrations, Appendices, bibliography, index, xii + 320pp. Hb ISBN: 0-7914-1331-4. Reprinted 1998; Manohar, Delhi. Hb. ISBN: 81-7304-258-6.

An anthology with an introduction, the book consists of nine unlinked essays that deal with Ramlila of Ramnagar, theatrical presentation of medieval epic of *Ramacharitamanasa* of Tulasi, Hanuman worship and wrestlers, mythology and religious contexts, Dandi monastic mendicants, Goddess Vindhya in Banaras, Sun worship at Lolark Kund, and identity of cultural community. The book provides in-depth ethnographical views of contemporary popular religious practices that need special attention for deeper understanding.

Hodges, William 1786. *Select Views in India. Drawn on the Spot in the Years 1780-1783, and Executed in Aquatint.* Edwards, London.

—— 1793. *Travels in India, 1780-1783.* John Murray, London. 154pp. John Murray, London. 2nd facsimile edition, reprinted by Munshiram Manoharlal Publishers, New Delhi. Hb. ISBN: 81-215088-51.

These two books contain many paintings of Banaras by the first British landscape artist to come to India.

Hooker, Roger Hardham 1978. *Journey into Varanasi.* 75pp. Church Missionary Society, London. ISBN: 0852730225.

—— 1979. *Voices of Varanasi.* 119pp. Church Missionary Society, London. ISBN: 0852730268.

Howard, Wayne 1966. *Veda Recitation in Varanasi.* x +401pp., transcriptions, tables, photos, bibliography, index. Motilal Banarsidass, Delhi. Also: South Asia Books, Columbia MO. Hb, ISBN:0836408721.

This book narrates the historical background and the continuity of the tradition of Banaras that has been a major centre of orthodox Hindu learning. The Vedic reciters of Banaras are renowned for their fidelity to tradition. Pandits with ancestral ties to Maharashtra, Madhya Pradesh, Uttar Pradesh and Gujarat as well as South India continue to preserve and transmit their modes of chanting in this city of pilgrims, Ganga *ghats* and shrines. The author has successfully resolved some of the tangled misconceptions about the variations in style found among the reciters, and has answered questions about their accuracy and their authenticity.

Hughes, A.J. 1889. *Water Supply and Sewerage of Benares.* Northwest Provinces and Municipal Works-Project, Irrigation Branch. Northwest Provinces and Oudh. Allahabad. December.

Hultzch, E., and Konow, Sten (eds.) 1907-08. *Sarnath Inscription of Kumaradevi*. Vol. 9, Epigraphica Indica and Record of the Archaeological Survey of India. Office of the Superintendent of Government Printing, India, Calcutta.

Ivekovic, Rada 2001. *Bénarès : essai d'Inde*. (In French). L'Harmattan, Paris. 182pp. ISBN: 2-7475-0183-3.

This book, written during a stay of the author in the beautiful city of Banaras, is walking music. Beyond stereotypes, India is the place that allows one to discover suddenly oneself as another. Based on traditional festivals, short chapters present an event, meeting, a character, or some philosophical question: initiation, language, the teacher, the 'game', time, and so on.

Jagannath, Panditraja 2007. *The Flow of the Ganges. Ganga Lahiri.* Sanskrit text, English and Hindi translation. English version by Boris Marjanovic, and Hindi version by Svami Avimukteshvarananda Sarasvati. B & w and colour illustrations. Indica Books, Varanasi. Pb, ISBN: 81-86569-62-6.

Jain, Shashi Prabha 2005. *Benares Ki Rasoi: Cuisine of Benares.* Softcover, xii + 126p., Tables; Plates; 22cm. Rupa & Co., New Delhi. 2nd edn. ISBN: 9788171676101.

This book is an expert culinary guide to the exotic recipes from the ancient living city of Banaras. The cuisine of this city is a unique blend of purity, simplicity and refinement. The book is a valuable storehouse of delectable fare from from cool drinks like Mango Panna, Kanji and various kinds of sherbet including *falase, kaaseru* and *bel* to appetisers like corn fritters, Raj Kachori, Nagori Tikkias to main dishes like Kachnar ki kali ki tarkari, Kofta, Arbi Dum along with Channa Dal with gourd, Kevati etc. These can be combined with a wide selection of rice preparations and Indian breads. To complete a perfect meal, the book has an exciting collection of preserves, chutneys and of course the famous sweet dishes including Malpua, Srikhand, Phirni, Kulfi and Chandra Kala. The book presents a happy convergence of the cuisines of eastern U.P. and Bihar.

Jayaswal, Vidula 1998. *From Stone Quarry to Sculpturing Workshops: A Report on Archaeological Investigations around Chunar, Varanasi and Sarnath.* Agam Kala Prakashan, Delhi. xviii + 260pp. + 107 b & w photographs and 36 figures. ISBN: 81-7320-033-5.

This monograph is derived from a report based on eight years of detailed archaeological investigations, exploration and their interpretation to link and reflect upon the hidden history of the past, emphasising systematically the introduction of the subject matter and methodological orientation, Chunar as a quarry area, Varanasi-Sarnath region — exploration of route of transportation of sandstone, Tilmapur — the satellite settlement of Sarnath, Asapur — the stone carving site, Kotwa — the sculpturing site, deduction, and finally the reference bibliography. At the end, this research monograph consists of four appendices, dealing with sculpturing process as a study in the past, some recently noticed Kharosthi epigraphs in U.P., a note on the recently found inscriptions in Chunar area, and soil analysis of the abandoned channel.

Jhingran, Sharad and Dutta, Reena 1992. *Traditional Designs from Varanasi for Artists and Craftsmen.* 108pp. Vyapar Setu, Varanasi and New Delhi.

Joshi, Esha Basanti (ed.) 1965. *Uttar Pradesh District Gazetteers: Varanasi.* Government Press, Allahabad.

This is an updated and re-written version of the old Gazetteer, covering history, population, economy, revenue, agriculture, etc. illustrated with statistics.

Justice, Chistopher 1997. *Dying the Good Death. The Pilgrimage to Die in India's Holy City.* SUNY Press, Albany, NY. Glossary, notes, references. 45 figures and 1 map. xxii + 268 pp. ISBN: 0-7914-3262-9. Reprinted 1997; Sri Satguru, Delhi. Hb. ISBN: 81-70305-57-8.

This book is based on fieldwork conducted in Banaras's hospices, so called 'mansions of liberation' and deals with the experiences of the individuals and families in the context of social taboos and religious beliefs. The book also has clear implications for the potential ways in which we may choose to face the ends of our lives. (Compare: Parry, J.P. 1994, *Death in Banaras*; Cambridge University Press).

Kapera, Constance 1966. *The Worship of Kali in Varanasi, An Inquiry.* Motilal Banarasidass Publs., Delhi.

Kapur, Anuradha 1992. *Actors, Pilgrims, Kings and Gods. The Ramlila at Ramnagar.* x + 250pp., 62 b & w photographs, 22 figures, notes, glossary, index. Seagull Books, Calcutta. ISBN: 81-70460-46-8.

The Ramlila at Ramnagar (Banaras) is a unique theatrical and religious event, a month-long enactment of the Ramayana story which is now an annual tradition. The performance covers a whole town and involves an entire community, from its Maharaja to its thousands of common people. Men, women and children follow the course of the processional Performance, accompanying Rama from his exile to his triumphant return to Ayodhya to partake of the joy and glory of Ramarajya. The book presents the rich and lively experience of the Ramlila with its *svarupas*, effigies, masks, *ramayanis*, *vyasas*, gods, goddesses, demons and monkeys; with its theatrical gimmickry and spectacle and marvels; with its thronging, surging, crowds. Performers and spectators are part of a seamless ceremony; and the readers can re-live this whole experience through the vivid pages of the author's diaries.

Katz, Marc J. 1993/ 2006. *The Children of Assi: The Transference of Religious Traditions and Communal Inclusion in Banaras.* Department of Religious Studies, Publ. Series. Vol. 12, University of Göteborg, Göteborg (Sweden). 13 b & w photos, 21 maps and figures, notes, glossary, bibliography, xx + 514 pp. ISBN: 91-88348-11-3. Reprinted 2006, one page new foreword pasted; and with addition of index by subject: pp. 515-544, by name: pp. 545-548; Pilgrims Publishing, Varanasi. Hb, ISBN: 81-7769-499-5; Pb, ISBN: 81-7769-498-7.

This is a published doctoral dissertation, reprinted identically together with index of subject and names. This is a work of interdisciplinary approach on the issue of developmental psychology of religion, by taking participatory observations and experiences in the cultural arena for more than two years. The book examine the role of the theatrical dramas (*Lilas*) based on the *puranic* stories of Rama and Krishna, and acceptance in the cultural traditions-their transformation and transference from one generation to another. The subject matter is arranged into four parts, successively The Lila, The Lila and the Devis of Assi, Festivals of the street and the children of Assi, and Equalising the children of Assi. The book ends with conclusion, six appendices, bibliography, glossary and index. All the statistics are dated to 1986-88, thus it completely lacks the scene of change and contemporary perspective that has been noticeably strong, however the methodology and the

216

conclusions are challenging and fresh even after two decades. This book attempts to link 'locality' to 'universality' with illustrations from a southern neighbourhood of Varanasi City, however it succeeded only marginally.

Kaye, George Rusby 1920. *A Guide to the Old Observatories at Delhi, Jaipur, Ujjain, Benares*. 108pp. Superintendent government printing, India, New Delhi.

—— 1982. *The Astronomical Observations of Jai Singh*. Archaeological Survey of India, New Delhi. Reprint in different format and setting.

Kedia, Kusum Lata 1986. *Local Finance in an Indian State: A Study of Municipal Finance of Varanasi*. 332pp. Uppal Publishing House, Varanasi and Delhi.

Kedar, B. and Z. Werblowsky 1998. Eds. *Sacred Space: Shrine, City, Land.* The Israel Academy of Sciences and Humanities, Jerusalem.

Some of the essays directly deal with Banaras; and there are several passing on references.

Kennedy, James 1884. *Life and Work in Benares and Kumaon, 1839-1877; with an introductory note: Sir William Muir*. T. Fischer Unwin, London. Reprinted by Asian Education Service, New Delhi and Madras, 1993. 11 line sketches, xxiv + 392pp. Hb. ISBN: 81-206-0751-1.

As a missionary Kennedy paid visits to Banaras during 1839-1840, 1854-1857, and 1859-1868 and vividly described the culture, traditions and religious arena of the city, especially in chapters 2 to 9, 14-15, 17, and 19. The narrations mention Scenes of first impression, Hindu society, Riverfront landscape and rituals, The beggars, Christian missionaries' activities and plans, Interaction with the native culture and Studying the culture, Climatic conditions, Issue of poverty, inside and other side of the 'sacred city', Mughal invasions and Muslim culture, Macaulay's impact on education, British rule and alliances in promoting Christianity, Hindus' family life including marriage, Religious performances, Sacred bathing, Schooling system, Voyaging in the Ganga, Village life, Christian community of the city, European life in the cantonment area, Caste systems, and Muslims.

Kesavan, Mukut (text), and Seth, Sanjeev (photographs) 1989. *A Journey down the Ganga*. Lustre Press Pvt. Ltd., New Delhi.

Keul, István 2002. *Hanuman, der Gott in Affengestalt. Entwicklung und Erscheinungsformen seiner Verehrung*. de Gruyter Verlag, Berlin and New York. (Series: Religionsgeschichtliche Versuche und Vorarbeiten, 47). 25 b & w and 24 colour photographs, 8 maps, appendices, bibliography, index, x + 350 pp. In German; published doctoral dissertation. ISBN: 3-11-017187-2.

This is a comprehensive and complete documentation of Hanuman temples, images and varieties of rituals associated with him. The detailed ethnographical and religious surveys of the four Hanuman temples located in the four parts of the city, i.e. Hanuman Phatak (north), Hanuman Ghat (east), Dvarkadhisha (Krishna) temple at Sankhudhara (west), and Bankati Hanuman (south), are described meticulously. The phenomenological narration of the ceremony of installating a Hanuman image at Assi Ghat is presented in all details. The subject matter covers introducing Hanuman in Banaras, the epic and *puranic* traditions of Hanuman worship and impact of *bhakti* movement and the present status, spatial perspective of temples and shrines of Hanuman, a text with translation referring the ritual frame of installing Hanuman image, and finally, the role of Hanuman in society and culture. [Compare another work in French: Claveyrolas, Mathieu 2003].

Keyserling, Count Hermann A. 1925. *Indian Travel Diary of a Philosopher*. Translated from German by J. Holroyd-Reece. Reprinted, Bhartiya Vidya Bhavan, Bombay, 1969. 2nd Ed. With Kapur Surya Foundation, New Delhi, 1999. Chapter 13 'Benares': 130-218. [Keyserling, 1880-1946].

Khanna, Ashok and Kumar, Ramesh 1988. *Banaras: The Sacred City*. Lustre Press, New Delhi.

A photographic book from the perspective of life and religious landscape.

Kinsley, David 1996. *Health, Healing, and Religion: A Cross-Cultural Perspective*. Prentice Hall, Upper Saddle River. xi + 212pp.

This is an ambitious book explaining with specific examples how healing is related to religious and moral concerns, as well as how healers and religious specialists overlap. It contains extended discussion of healing centres at Pishachmochan (Banaras) and Balaji Temple near Bharatpur.

Krishna, Anand; Krishna, Vijay and Mookerjee, Ajit 1966. *Banaras Brocades: Historical Background*. Crafts Museum, Delhi. 97pp.

The book illustrates the distinct aspects and specialities of the Banaras silk, emphasising varieties of textiles types and silk product like organzine, kimkhab, kaldbattu, and referring to the historical growth in the Gahadvala period, impact of Mughal painting, links to Gujarat, impact of Jaunpur and Ahmedabad, role of Sir George Watt, role of Mathura, and Jain history in developing these brocades.

Krishna, Anand and Krishna, Madhu (24 pp text by them) 2003. *Banaras in the Early 19th Century: Riverfront Panorama*. Panorama of Banaras viewed from across the Ganges from the Ramnagar side by 'a native artist'; 12 gouaches on paper, affixed to card, 52 x 31 cm. © Photography copyright by the British Museum, London. Pilgrimage and Cosmology Series: 4. Indica Books, Varanasi. ISBN: 81-86569-29-4.

From the late 18th century onwards, both amateur and professional European painters were drawn to paint the panoramic scenic beauty of *ghats* of Banaras. The *ghats* are a vast area of space for the religious and cultural life of the city. These were gradually stone-paved and steps leading to the river were built; this trend mainly started in the second half of the 16th century. This great architecture movement was initiated by the Rajputs and subsequently followed by Maratha donors. In the present illustration folder, the core of this chain of *ghats* was already built while the flanks were yet to come. These paintings, covering the whole river front as it was at that time, are the work of a 'Company School' local painter, working in a localised tradition of British landscape watercolour. The scenes are mostly naturalistic and present an authentic account of the riverfront.

Köckmann, Uwe 1982. *Hindutradition und Stadtentwicklung. Varanasi: Analyse einer gewachsenen ungeplanten Pilgerstadt am Ganges*. Studienverlag Dr. Brockmeyer, Bochum. 4 figures, 6 tables, bibliography, summary in English (pp. 100-106), x + 115pp. + 1 folded map. ISBN: 3-883-39-239-1.

Analysing the structure of the holy city of Banaras, the characteristics of seven structural components are site and arrangement, size, existence, genesis, architecture and town planning, legal position and competence and other functional aspects. The book ends with the concluding remark by Spate (1950) that "The streets are crowded with priests, mendicants, and touts, and their pilgrims prey, and through the turmoil the sacred bulls of Siva lounge arrogantly. In Christian countries the odour of excessive sanctity has not infrequently a commercial taint, but in Benares it is all-pervading".

KTST, Kashi Tirtha Sudhar Trust 1931. *Benares and its Ghats*. KTSS, President: Hon'ble Raja Sir Motichand, and Hon. Secretary: Thakur Shiva Shankar Singh. Indian Bookshop, Theosophical Society, Benares. Map 1, sectional drawings 6, b & w photographs 77; v + xxx + 154pp.

The KTST was established in 1926 to conserve, preserve and repair the riverfront heritage of Banaras. This is the first attempt of its kind that published the story of their projects and works during 1926-1930, emphasising the riverfront Banaras, history, present status and condition with photographs and illustrations, and also recording suggestions and recommendations for improvement and preservation of the riverfront heritage. These are still useful in understanding the riverfront heritage and its planning.

Kumar, Nita 1988. *The Artisans of Banaras: Popular Culture and Identity, 1880-1986*. Princeton University Press, and Indian reprint, Oxford University Press, Delhi. 300pp. (Revised doctoral thesis, University of Chicago). xx + 279pp., 6 tables, 6 b & w photographs, appendices, glossary, bibliography., index. ISBN: 0-691-05531-9. Reprinted by Orient Longman, Hyderabad and New Delhi, 1995, ISBN: 81-250-0362-2.

This book deals with contemporary cultural tradition and its growth, and the way leisure time is used by Hindu and Muslim artisans-the weavers, metalworkers, woodworkers, and also the cultural aspects of working-class life. The analysis in the book turns away from the usual models of Hindu-Muslim conflict by seeing divisions based on occupation, income level, education, and urban neighbourhood as more relevant for the construction of identity than those based on religion or community.

—— 1992. *Friends, Brothers and Informants: Fieldwork Memoirs of Banaras*. University of California Press, Berkeley. xii + 260pp., 15 b & w photographs, 1 map, glossary, index. ISBN, Hb: 0-520-07138-7, Pb: 0-520-07139-5.

This is a personal and evocative account of fieldwork experiences, confronting the dilemma of how a class-sensitive Indian intellectual adapts to the field and builds deeply affecting relationships with strangers. She discloses what it is like to be a Western-trained Indian researching her own culture, offering her fieldwork memoirs in all their spontaneity and candour. One sees Banaras through her eyes when she first arrives: unfamiliar people, inhospitable lodgings, unhygienic food, overwhelming filth, and the inscrutability of a proud old city. But the story end in a different way, blended with 'outsidedness' in reflection and 'insidedness' of lifeways. The author, ultimately, shows that the recognition of the personal dignity and freedom of others remains the anthropologist's most elusive goal.

—— 2000. *Lessons from Schools. The History of Education in Banaras*. Sage Publications, New Delhi and Thousand Oaks CA (USA). Glossary, bibliography, index. 232pp. ISBN: 0-7619-9378-9 (US-Pb); and ISBN: 81-7036-846-4 (India, Pb).

This book describes the history of education (1840-1940) set in the social contexts of castes, occupational groups, religious communities, gender, and urban life. An underlying theme is the dynamics of the interaction between a colonial power advocating state control over education and indigenous educational systems of considerable heterogeneity patronising a variety of institutions and system of learning.

Kumar, Suphal 1999. *Dateline Varanasi*. Kashi Patrakar Sangh, Varanasi. 10 figures, xii + 146 pp.

The first attempt to collect news items from the newspapers as written and flashed by the author, a professional journalist and wanderer in the lanes of the city.

Kushawaha, R. and Singhvi, Laxmi Mall 1977. *Working of Nyaya Panchayats in India: A Case Study of Varanasi District*. For the Institute of Constitutional and Parliamentary Studies (New Delhi, India). 149pp. Young India Publications, New Delhi.

Lal, Makkhan and Gopal, Lallanji 1984. *Archaeology of Population*. Banaras Hindu University, Varanasi.

Lambert, G.B. 1927. *List of Darbaris, Benares Division*. Corrected up to 31 January 1927. Govt. Secretariat, United Provinces, Allahabad. 117pp.

Lannoy, Richard 1999. *Benares Seen From Within*. Callisto Books, Bath (UK) & Indica Books, Varanasi, & University of Washington Press, Seattle. 640pp., profusely illustrated with b & w and colour photographs and diagrams. ISBN: 1 902716 00 0.

A saga, the author's *magnum opus* and the outcome of his life-long (1953-1998) implication with Banaras in a creative way of seeing through human eyes of insights and deeper understanding, and converting them with the eyes of camera, capturing pilgrimages, the temples and gods, the lanes, the city life, craft, wisdom and grace, and the Buddha and his sermon township of Sarnath. This is an unparalleled production.

—— 2002. *Benares: A World within a World. The Microcosm of Kashi Yesterday and Today*. Pilgrimage & Cosmology Series: 2. Indica Books, Varanasi. Glossay, bibliography, index. 420pp. ISBN: 81-86569-25-1.

This book contains the revised text of the photographic book by Richard Lannoy, *Benares Seen from Within* (1999), including a small quantity of b & w photographs. Some of the paragraphs have been replaced from the original version with substantial additions. Lannoy's survey extends up to the present, describing the city as the last cosmic city and the centre of the world. Other chapters include the cosmogram, Banaras as state of mind, interconnectedness of things, forest of bliss, pilgrimages, the Ganga, Hinduism in practice, abode of Gods, Shiva and Lat Bhirava, death and regeneration, glimpses of history, renunciates, wisdom and grace, and night thoughts.

Lata, Prem and Singh, Rana P.B. 1991. *Sarnath. Cultural Heritage, Museum, Tourism*. Tara Book Agency, Varanasi. 96pp., 18 tables, 7 figures, 20 b & w photographs. ISBN: 81-85403-79-1.

This book, consisting of seven chapters, deals with: historical outline of site museums in India, cultural-historical background, the background and exhibits in the Sarnath Museum, arrangement and management of Sarnath museum, tourist and places of attraction, and visitors and their cognition. At the end a selected bibliography is given.

Leckie, Daniel Robinson 1800. *Journal of a Route to Nagpore and Benares: Contains a day by day account of the journey undertaken in the year 1790.* John Stockdale Publs., London, 1800.

Lejonhud, Kristina 2003. *Indian Villages in Transformation. A Longitudinal Study of Three Villages in Uttar Pradesh.* Karlstad University Studies, ISSN: 1403-8099, 2003: 11. Karlstad University, Karlstad (Sweden). (Doctoral Dissertation in Human Geography). 12 maps and figures, 35 b & w photos, 196pp. Pb, ISBN: 91-85019-27-5.

This work is a doctoral dissertation in which the author has put more than a decade long patient observations, analyses, and interpretations to describe village transformation. She tries to scan the process of rural transformation in India by undertaking a detailed longitudinal case study of three villages, viz. Chamaon, Pachhimpur, and Shahabuddinpur (Chamaon Gram Sabha, Varanasi). The whole work is organised into three parts and ten chapters. In the first part a general backdrop is provided wherein introduction, research framework, and methodological considerations are discussed. The second part outlines the analytical details of the villages under study. And, the last part is an attempt to bring out the changes that have taken place in these villages especially in the last decade. This work demonstrates how the (human) geographers can extend the horizons of village study by including external connections and relations.

Lill, Bernhard 1991. *Zwischen Bombay und Benares.* (In German). Frederking & Thale, Berlin.

Lutgendorf, Philip 1992. *The Life of a Text: Performing the Râmacaritamânas of Tulsidas.* 33 illustrations, glossary. Bibliography, index, xvi + 470 pp. University of California Press, Berkeley. ISBN: 0-520-06690-1.

This book contributes to the growing body of research on the cultural contexts of sacred literature and narrative structure, focussing the various ways in which it is performed by examining them in the context of older practices and then tracing the rise-especially during the 18th and 19th centuries-of the *Ramacaritamanas*, the pre-eminent text of the public performance in the arena of Banaras. The book is an unique presentation of the sacred text in the context of Hindi and Hindu culture. the book breaks new ground by capturing the range of performance techniques in vivid detail and tracing the impact of the epic in its contemporary cultural context.

Macaulay, Thomas Babington 1910. *Essays on Clive and Hastings*, edited by Charles Robert Gaston. The Athenaeum Press, Boston: pp. 157-58 for description of Banaras.

Macleod, Norman 1870. *Days in North India*. J.B. Lippincott & Co., Philadelphia: ref. pp. 9-43 for Banaras.

Madsen, Hans Helge 1993. *Hvor Guderne Leger. Om byers tilblivelse*. (Where Gods Play. About Pluralism and Process of Cities' Growth). Rosinate/ Munksgaard, Kobenhavn; ref. : pp. 61-70. (in Dutch).

Mahajan, Jagmohan 1994. *Ganga Observed. Foreign Accounts of the River*. (Selected and edited). 20 b & w figures, bibliography, index, 152pp. Virgo Publs., New Delhi. Reprinted in 2003: Indica Books, Varanasi. ISBN: 81-86569-40-5.

It is not a wonder that the river Ganga has caught the imagination of the multitude of foreign visitor's to the country through the ages. Travellers of different nationalities and regions visiting India from abroad could not but take note of the Ganga. They have left fascinating accounts of the river scene observed for over two millennia. The information provided by them is vast and varied. Besides exhaustive extracts from the foreign travellers' accounts included in this anthology, the book is also illustrated with some of the fascinating sketches of the river-scene made by landscape artists among them as they went up and down the river, including several scenes of riverfront Banaras.

—— 2007. *Varanasi Vista: Early Views of the Holy City*. Size: 44 x 29 cm. 90pp. Hb, ISBN: 81-86569-71-5. Indica Books, Varanasi.

Varanasi has attracted pilgrims from all over India for over 2500 years. A number of landscape artists, almost entirely from Britain, began coming to India towards the end of the 18th century, and made superb sketches of Varanasi when they visited the city. The views of Varanasi by the visiting landscape artists (including the Daniells, and Prinsep) gave not only the outside world but also the Indians themselves the first ever visual impressions of the scenic splendours of the holy city. Until then no such visual record existed because of the lack of the genre of landscape painting in an otherwise rich Indian art. Assembled from public and private art collections in India and abroad, these views are now being published together, along with a short survey of travellers' accounts of their visits to Varanasi, for the first time. [Available also in Spanish, French and Japanese].

Majumdar, B. 2006. *A Guide to Sarnath*. Pilgrims Books, Varanasi. ISBN 81-7769-079-5.

Makkuni, Ranjit and Khanna, Madhu 2003. *The Crossing Project: Living, Dying and Transformation in Banaras*. [Preamble for 4-vols. set Exhibition Catalogue]. Colourful 174pp. Sacred World Foundation, San Francisco. ISBN: 81-88934-14-3.
Web: http://www.sacredworld.com

Mann, Paul 1996. *The Burning Ghats*. Ballantine Ivy Books, New York.

Marshall, P. J. 1965. *The Impeachment of Warren Hastings*. Oxford University Press, Oxford.

May, Canon Peter 1958. *Banaras and Bethlehem: Some Aspects of the Christian Faith in Relation to Hinduism*. Christian Faith in relation to Literature & Society, Madras.

McDonald, Ian 2006. *River of Gods*. [A novel set around Varanasi]. 597 pp. Simon & Schuster, (Pyr Publs.), London. Hb, ISBN-13: 978-1591024361

This ambitious portrait of a future India from a British author offers multitudes: gods, castes, protagonists, cultures, mostly set in and around Varanasi. Nine disparate characters, including a cop, a scientist and a stand-up comic, act out their related dramas — be they personal, political or of the mystery-thriller variety — in successive chapters within each of the book's five sections. In the India of 2047, genetically engineered children comprise a new caste, adults can be surgically transformed into a neutral gender, a water war has broken out as the Ganges threatens to run dry, AIs are violently destroyed if they approach levels akin to human intelligence, and something strange has just appeared in the solar system. The deliberate pace and lack of explanation require patience at the outset, but readers will become increasingly hooked as the pieces of richly detailed world fall into place.

Medhasananda, Swami 2002. *Varanasi at the Crossroads. A Panoramic View of Early Modern Varanasi and the Story of its Transition.* The Ramakrishana Mission, Institute of Culture, Kolkata. Notes, glossary, bibliography, index, xxxvi + 1044 pp., 97 b & w photographs. ISBN: 81-87332-18-2.

This work is based on an in-depth study of a vast corpus of source-materials, both primary and secondary, epigraphic, literary and archival, viz., documents, correspondences, administrative reports, charts, maps and plans in addition to non-official records, diaries, memoirs, reminiscences, minutes of civil bodies, visual materials and even testimonials. A number of such materials have been explored and utilised for the first time. Photographs concerning this study, some of which are rare, are another important feature of this work. Based on an objective evaluation of available materials, this work is a welcome addition to the growing corpus of regional history, especially that of cities, and provides the reader with an example of a devoted study derived more from a serious quest to identify the 'personality' of the sacred city of Kashi.

Mehrotra, Raja Ram 1977. *Sociology of Secret Languages.* viii + 102 pp. Indian Institute of Advanced Study, Shimla. Chapter 2 (on Banaras) reprinted in Singh, Rana P.B. 1993, *Banaras (Varanasi)*: pp. 197-214.

The book seeks to provide, in a multidimensional and multi-level frame, an authentic account of the special and secret languages of some small, cohesive, and closed groups in relation to their socio-cultural matrix. The four studies included delineate how the language disguise helps the speakers to carry on their profession legitimate or illegitimate, and also to maintain and reinforce their group exclusiveness and we-feeling.

Michell, George and Singh, Rana P.B. 2005. Eds. *Banaras, The City Revealed*; photographs by Clare Arni. Marg Publications, Mumbai. A de luxe library edition, 305 x 241 mm, 152 pages with 133 illus-trations (mostly colour); ISBN: 81-85026-72-6, LC: 2005-318067.

Existing books on Banaras vary from evocative photographic treatments of the city and its picturesque riverside frontage to studies of present-day religious beliefs and practices. None of these, however, deals with the architecture and art of the city within a specific historical context. Much of Banaras's surviving architecture is no earlier than the 18th-19th centuries, a time when Banaras enjoyed unparalleled peace and prosperity. This volume takes a close look at the city's diverse buildings. Here can be found chapters dealing with the riverside palaces that overlook the Ganga and the steps (*ghats*) that lead down to the water; the different styled temples and shrines dotted throughout the city and the mosques and tombs that serve the city's sizeable Muslim population; the mansions and gardens of the city's elite, as well as its sacred reservoirs and wells. Nor is the British contribution to the city overlooked. Maps of the city provide precise locations of the buildings described. Since the ancient buildings of Banaras are now under threat, the book serves as a timely document in the struggle to preserve the city's unique architectural heritage.

Mishra, Kamala Prasad 1975. *Banaras in Transition (1738-1895): A Socio-Economic Study*. Munshiram Manoharlal Publ. Pvt. Lt., New Delhi. (Revised doctoral thesis, SOAS, London). viii + 231p + 1 map.

This book traces the rise and growth of the Banaras Zamindari into a major regional power within the state of Awadh by the middle of the 18th century, and its coming into the Company's orbit in the 1770s, finally resulting in the establishment of direct British administration. It describes and analyses the process of change in the political and administrative system of the Zamindari with special reference to the effect it produced on the socioeconomic structure of the Banaras region during the period 1738 to 1795. This study is based on the records of the East India Company, supplemented by some European accounts and private papers preserved in various libraries and archives of Great Britain and India. The author has also applied the methods and findings of allied disciplines, such as social anthropology, to his work and has asked new questions of old material in a productive and invigorating way. The book contains chapters on important aspects of socio-economic history, such as politics, land management, village economy, trade, banking and currency. The book thus presents a lively approach to the study of a Zamindari in transition.

Mishra, Pankaj 2000. *The Romantics*. Picador India, New Delhi. vi + 280pp. ISBN: 0-330-39277-8.

This is a travelogue-novel on the perception and reflections of the Western visitors in Banaras, having a luminous intelligence about love, literature and politics in Banaras. However, one will be disappointed if the hard realities of today and the spectacular and long experiences of Banaras are compared with the characters and scenes moving in the novel. This is an attempt to see the two faces of Banaras through the lenses of the West and the East, giving an impression that the culture of Banaras is like mixed vegetables — *hotchpotch* (potpouri) — where it is difficult to describe the taste of anyone of them, however all together result in a unique taste. Here all the vegetables are blended in the colour of western viewpoint as the author perceived and believed it.

Mishra, S.N. and Bedi, Rajesh 1981. *Banaras.* Roli Books International, Singapore and New Delhi.

A photographic book with short introduction and captions.

Misra, Chhote Lal 2007. *Playing Techniques of Tabla: Banaras Gharana.* Eastern Book Corporation, New Delhi. Hb, ISBN: 81-7391-929-1.

The *Tabla* is the most popular Percussion instrument of North India. Each sound on the Tabla has an onomatopoetic syllable to represent it. There are many books available on the subject of Tabla and writers have written, focusing their on areas. The book explains the controversy in technical words and some specific clarifications in practical/experimental aspect, which is essential for the students. The book is divided into two parts: part I deals with theory of music and school (Gharana), its parts and technical words associated with its playing, and part II emphasises the issues of traditional compositions and their varieties and their links and correspondences to light and classical music.

Mitra, Swati 2002. (Editor & Publisher), *Varanasi City Guide.* Series Editor: Sona Thakur. Supported by U.P. Tourism, Govt. of U.P. Glossary, index, 216pp. Eicher Goodearth, New Delhi. ISBN: 81-87780-04-5.

A photographic and sketchy guidebook for rich Indian or Western tourists. Short introduction of most of the aspects are given, covering themes like religious symbolism and divine images, tourists sites, e.g. *ghats*, temples, lanes, Ramnagar and Sarnath, life and people, and practical information.

Mookerjee, Ajit 1966. Ed. *Banaras Brocades: Essays by Rai Ananda Krishna and Vijay Krishna.* Craft Museum, New Delhi.

Moon, P. 1947. *Warren Hastings and British India.* London.

Mukherjee, Neela and Jayaswal, Meera 2006. *Chained by Food: Marginalized Voices from Peri-urban India: Poor Households as Food Producers and Consumers in Peri-urban India.* Annexes, References, Index, 136 p., tables. Concept Publ. Co., New Delhi. ISBN 81-8069-238-8.

This book consists of three essays that deal with suburban farming systems in Varanasi. Chapter 3 describes 'Livelihood strategies and role of horticulture producers — Varanasi' and Chapter 5 refers to 'Food preparation and consumption practices — Varanasi'. Finally with a comparative analysis with case studies from Faridabad, the authors narrate the implications of this research under 'Policy inferences and recommendations'. This book provides an integrated picture of issues related to poverty, agriculture, urbanization, food safety and food security in the peri-urban India. Based on field-research, the book presents the perspectives of the farmers — both as producers and consumers on the role of agriculture, food production and consumption practices, quality of life and the effectiveness of the existing support networks available to them. The findings highlight the pivotal role peri-urban agriculture plays in societal and cultural issues.

Mukherjee, Suroopa 2006. *Across The Mystic Shore.* [A novel dealing with 'By the side of Varanasi']. New Delhi.

Murdoch, John and Sherring, Matthew Atmore 1897. *Kasi Or Benares, the Holy City of the Hindus: The Holy City of the Hindus.* Christian Literature Society for India, Christian Literature Society for India, London and Madras. 2nd ed. 40pp.

Muthiah, K.S. & Co. 1911. *Smiling Benares.* Raithby & Co., Madras.

—— (an Old resident) 1918. *All about Benares: Containing a Sketch from the Vedic Days to the Modern Times, with Many Illustrations, and a Map of Benares and Its Environs.* K. S. Muthiah, Madras. 164pp.

Myrvold, Kristina 2007. *Inside the Guru's Gate. The Ritual Uses of Texts among the Sikhs in Varanasi.* Lund University Studies, ISSN: 0284-8651. Lund University, Lund, Sweden. (Doctoral Dissertation in Indic Religions, Centre of Theology & Religious Studies). 536pp. Pb, ISBN: 978-91-974897-7-5.

This work aims to direct the focus towards a deeper understanding of contemporary religious worship and oral performance traditions in Sikhism. Based on field work in a Sikh congregation at Varanasi (Northern India), the study investigates how local Sikhs perceive, use and interact with the *Guru Granth Sahib*, the holy scripture, and other religious texts accredited *gurbani* status, i.e. words being uttered by their human Gurus, through a wide spectrum of practices. From the perspective of ritual and anthropological theories, the study analyzes the discursive and ritual means by which local Sikhs create and confirm conceptions of the Guru's presence and agency in the world. The study argues that ritual uses of the *Guru Granth Sahib* and the living performance traditions of mediating the scriptural words are the means by which the Sikhs personify and bring the scripture to life, as an agentive Guru, and make its teaching perpetually alive and relevant to changing contexts in a human and socially conditioned world.

Nair, P. Thankappan 1999. *James Prinsep. Life and Work.* Vol. I *Background and Benares Period.* Firma K.L. Mukhopadhyaya Pvt. Ltd., Calcutta. xxxii + 280pp. Subject index: xiii-xv, 13 b & w illustrations. ISBN: 81-7102-085-2.

James Prinsep (1799-1840), a veritable genius, discovered the name of Ashoka the Great (B.C. 272-232), the Buddhist monarch, and Kanishka, another emperor, by deciphering their Brahmi and Kharoshti edicts and coins, placing him above Champollion, the decipherer of Egyptian hieroglyphs. Not only was Prinsep a great epigraphist, but he was also, at the same time, an Architect (Benares: Mint, St. Mary's Church, Nandeshwar Kothi, etc.), Archaeologist (restorer of the minarets of Aurangzeb's Masjid, Benares), Engineer (builder of Karmanasa bridge and Circular Canal, Calcutta), Artist ('*Benares Illustrated*', 35 plates), Cartographer (Map of Benares, 1822), Demographer (*Census and Directory of Benares*), Engraver, Scientist (Fellow of the Royal Society at 28; inventor of Evaporo-meter, Fluviameter, Pyrometer, Assay Balance, etc.), Journalist (editor-publisher of the *Journal of the Asiatic Society,* & *Gleanings in Science*), Chemist (Assay Master of Benares & Calcutta Mints), Musician and Actor. This book deals with his family background, personal life and works at Benares. The book is divided into three chapters; the two chapters narrate the story of Prinsep in Calcutta, and his life and work. The third chapter (pp. 108-279) elucidates various faces of his life and his contributions to Benares, including Prinsep's will, his disassociation with the Asiatic Society, Benares directory and other activities.

Namasivaya, Swami 1932. *Guide to Benares.* Benares.

Narain, Avadh Kishor and Roy, T.N. (eds.) 1976. *Excavations at Rajghat. 1957-58, 1960-65. Part I-IX.* Banaras Hindu University Press, Varanasi.

Narain, Avadh Kishor and Gopal, Lallanji (eds.) 1969. *Introducing Varanasi.* Banaras Hindu University, Varanasi.

A special publication on the occasion of the Indian Science Congress, aiming to provide a general but authentic background to the important aspects of Banaras.

Narain, Vishnu Anugrah 1959. *Jonathan Duncan and Varanasi.* Firma K.L. Mukhopadhyaya Pvt. Ltd., Calcutta. 240pp.

Nevill, Herbert Andrews 1914, 1928 and 1936. *Benares: A Gazetteer.* District Gazetteers of the United Provinces of Agra and Oudh — Supplementary Notes and Statistics. Vol. XXVI — *Benares Division*, B, C and D Volumes the Government Press, Allahabad.

Nevil, Major Herbert Andrews 1915. *Benares: The Hindus' Holy City : A Guide to Places of Interest with History and Map.* Caxton Printing Works, Bombay. 55pp.

Nicholls, George 1848. *Sketch on the Rise and Progress of the Benares Sanskrit College.* George Nicholls, Allahabad.

Nicholls, George 1907. *History of Sanskrit College.* United Province Government Press, Allahabad.

Niyogi, Roma 1959. *History of Gahadavala Dynasty.* Oriental Book Agency, Calcutta. 283pp.

Oldham, Wilton 1870/ 1876. *Historical and Statistical Memoir of the Ghazeepoor District*. Parts I (1870) & II (1876). Government Press, Allahabad.

An excellent description of administrative, political, revenue and territorial systems of the state of Banaras, illustrated with sketches and statistics.

Oldham, Wilton 1873. *Tenant Right and Auction Sales in Ghazeepoor and the Province of Benares*. Dublin.

Pandey, Badri Prasad 1981. *Banaras Brocades: Structure and Functioning*. Institute of Gandhian Studies, Varanasi. Appendices, iv + 172pp.

This is a research document based on an empirical and participatory survey about the Banaras brocades, going through the historical outline, the master weavers and their family background, ownership of looms, employment and wages, techniques and training, output and marketing, capital and loaning system, working and living conditions, perspective, problems and prospects, and finally the conclusions and suggestions.

Pandey, Rajendra 1979. *Kashi through the Ages*. Sundeep Prakashan, Delhi.

Pandey, Raj Bali 1969. *Varanasi: the Heart of Hinduism*. Orient Publs., Varanasi.

Parekh, Manu 2005. *Banaras. Painting the Sacred City*. Penguin/ Viking, New Delhi. 143pp. Photographs and paintings. ISBN: 067-005824-6.

Banaras, the religious capital of India, has fascinated Manu Parekh, one of India's leading modern painters, ever since his first visit there in 1979. Over the next decade and a half, he kept returning to Banaras and produced a series of works in which he has attempted to capture the essence of the world's oldest living city, a sacred place where the mundane and the sublime coexist. The *ghats* where the faithful gather and the funeral pyres blaze; the narrow, busy lanes where everyday life carries on; the boats ferrying pilgrims on the Ganga; evening lights in the shrines by the river-all these provide the images and symbols that Manu Parekh uses to create powerful and dramatic compositions. The book includes 75 of his paintings of the city.

Parker, Rev. Arthur 1895. *A Hand-book of Benares*. 85pp. J. Lazarus & Co., Banaras. Republished in 1901 by Travancore Government Press, Trivendrum.

This book is based on the author's own experiences and understanding, and is considered to be the most authentic description of the period. Widely cited by Mark Twain, it has four parts, the first dealing with the historical tradition, the British influence and the Buddhist period; the second part emphasises the relationship among Shiva, the holy city and Hindu traditions; and the third part describes various *ghats*, mosques, Dufferin Bridge, and provides hints to travellers, and finally describes places including Sarnath, Queen's College and Golden Temple.

Parry, Jonathan P. 1994. *Death in Banaras*. Cambridge University Press, Cambridge. Indian Reprint: Motilal Banarasidass, New Delhi. Preface, glossary, 14 b & w plates, 2 figures, 6 maps, 9 tables, notes, references, index, xxvi + 314pp. Hb ISBN: 0-521-46625-3.

This is a study of priests and other sacred specialists who serve them: about the way in which they organise their business, and about their representations of death and understanding of the rituals over which they preside. All the three levels are informed by a common ideological preoccupation with controlling chaos and contingency. The book is centrally concerned with concepts of body, person, culture and religious practice in contemporary Hinduism, together with ideas about hierarchy, renunciation and sacrifice. [see, Laidlaw, James 1996. The Uses and Abuses of Theology: Comments on Jonathan Parry's *Death in Banaras*. Review Article. *South Asia Research*, 16: 31–44.]

Pathak, B.D. 1977. *Geology and Ground Water Conditions of Varanasi District, U.P.* Bulletin of the Geological Survey of India (G.S.I.), Series-B: Engineering Geology and Ground Water, Pub. No. 41. G.S.I., Calcutta. 56pp.

Payne, Peggy 2001. *Sister India*. Penguin Books India, New Delhi. vii + 275pp. ISBN: 0-14-302761-1.

A novel set amidst the turmoil of religious violence in modern day Banaras, a compelling and poetic evocation of contemporary India. Another attempt to see the increasing impact of tourists and cultural mixing between the West and the East, touching issues like threat of culture, Hindu-Muslim relationship, superseding over old values by materialism, the drastic rise of tourists guesthouses and lifeways of cheating.

Pearson, Anne Mackenzie 1996. *"Because it Gives me Peace of Mind". Ritual Fasts in the Religious Lives of Hindu Women.* SUNY Press, Albany, NY. xviii + 315 pp., 17 b & w photographs, notes, glossay, bibliography, index. ISBN: 0-7914-3038-3.

Based on her doctoral thesis at McMaster University (Supervisor: Prof. David Kinsley) that analyses her data collected during 1984-1989. This is the first book-length study that explores the history and nature of *vrats*-votive fasting rites-the role these rites play in the religious lives of Hindu women in North India, especially in Banaras, and the meanings these women attribute to them.

Pinch, William R. 1996. *Peasants and Monks in British India.* University of California Press, Berkeley. 2 maps, xi + 242pp. ISBN: 978-0-520-20061-6.

In this compelling social history, the author tackles one of the most important but most neglected fields of the colonial history of India: the relation between monasticism and caste. The highly original inquiry yields rich insights into the central structure and dynamics of Hindu society — insights that are not only of scholarly but also of great political significance. There are several illustrations and events concerned with Banaras.

—— 2006. *Warrior Ascetics and Indian Empires.* Cambridge University Press, Cambridge. Cambridge Studies in History and Society, No. 12. 11 illustrations, vii + 278pp. Hb, ISBN-13: 978-0-521-85168-8.

Using the life of Anupgiri Gosain, a Hindu ascetic who lived at the end of the 18th century, to explore the subject, the author demonstrates that Hindu warrior ascetics were not only pervasive in the medieval and early modern Indian past, but were also an important component of the South Asian military labour market and crucial to the rise of British imperialism. There are several illustrations and events concerned with Banaras.

Pintchman, Tracy 2005. *Guests at God's Wedding. Celebrating Kartik among the Women of Benares.* State University of New York Press, Albany NY. xii + 241pp, table 1, figures 25 b & w photographs, notes to the chapters, references, index. ISBN: 0-7914-6595-0 (Hb), 0-7914-6596-9 (Pb).

This book integrates six papers of the author (cf. *cited separately in this bibliography*), having being rewritten, incorporated and substantially updated. The book deals with the sacred Hindu month of Kartik (October-November) as it is celebrated in the city of Banaras, highlighting Kartik-related practices, stories, songs, and experiences particular to women. During Kartik, Hindu women living in and around Banaras meet daily to enact a form of ritual worship, or *puja*, in which they raise the playful Hindu deity Krishna from childhood to adulthood throughout the month, ultimately marrying him to the plant-goddess Tulasi (holy Basil). The author explores how women who perform Kartik *puja* understand and celebrate both Kartik and Krishna in ways that are linked to the desires, hopes, fears, and social realities characteristic of many Hindu women living in the rather conservative social milieu of this holy city and the environs. The book meticulously synthesises the *shashtrik* (textual) and the *paramparik* (oral) traditions that together make the lifeways of the Hindu world, especially the feminine.

Prasad, Onkar 1985. *Folk Music and Folk Dances of Banaras*. Anthropological Survey of India, Calcutta, Memoir No. 71.

Prasad, Raghunath 1929. *Views of Benares presented by the Maharaja of Benares*. Kashiraj Trust, Varanasi [s.n.].

Presler, Henry Hughes 1941. *Social Thought in Benares*. Lucknow Pub. House, Lucknow.

Prinsep, James 1831, 1833. *Benares Illustrated in a Series of Drawings*. Lithographed in England by Eminent Artists. I to III Series. Baptist Mission Press, Calcutta; and Smith, Elder & Co., London 1834. Reprinted with introduction by O.P. Kejariwal 1996: Vishwavidyala Prakashan, Varanasi. Hb, ISBN 81-7124-176-X

Still considered the most influential publication in terms of views from the sacred city of Banaras in early 19th century by James Prinsep (1799-1840). Some of the original watercolour surfaced only very recently and it seems that Prinsep made many more watercolours which were not reproduced in this book. As no copyright then existed, Princep's lithographed watercolours were the most influential in illustrating the Western view of Banaras (cf. Bautze 2006: p. 214). All the thirty-five lithographed prints are described with meticulous views and describing the conditions prevailed in those days.

Rai, Govind Chandra and Prakash, Vidya (eds.) 1968. *Varanasi at a Glance: a Souvenir issued on the eve of the XXIV session of All India Oriental Conference.* All India Oriental Conference, Varanasi.

Rai, Subas 1997. *Clique Formation and Academic Deterioration in Indian Universities: A Case of Banaras Hindu University.* Bhavan Book Service, Varanasi. 110pp. ISBN: 81-870900-06.

With an intentional attempt to narrate the 'dark side' of the B.H.U. the book narrates the stories of downfalls and corruptions, manoeuvring and fraud happened in the appointments, publications, promotions, and also financial bungling. Several case studies also been mentioned.

Rao, Raja 1960. *The Serpent and the Rope.* [A novel with several scenes on Varanasi]. Orient Paperbacks, Delhi; reprinted 1968.

The first metaphysical-cum-autobiographical novel on this city by a great laureate that tells the story of a search for spiritual truth in Europe and India. It was written after a long silence during which Rao returned to India. He renewed the connection with his roots in the modern rendering of the Mahabharata legend of Satyavan and Savithri. The work also dramatized the relationships between Indian and Western culture. Ramaswamy, a young Brahmin studying in France, is married to a French college teacher, Madeleine, who sees her husband first as a guru. As Ramaswamy struggles with commitments imposed on him by his Hindu family, his wife becomes a Buddhist in her spiritual quest and renounces wordly desires. She leaves her husband to find her own true self. Banaras is rooming everywhere in this novel. The serpent in the title refers to the illusion and the rope to the reality.

—— 1989. *On the Ganga Ghat.* (A short novel based on Banaras). Vision Books, New Delhi. ISBN: 81-2220-149-0.

A strong compact and compassionate *tour-de-force* of the contra-diction and the brittle enchantments of Banaras, narrating its strange characters and their confused metaphysics that are finely linked and etched in these short stories. A masterpiece from a philosopher-novelist that portrays the lifeworld and lifeways of Banaras, an ultimate destination of millions of Hindus who come to this city to die at the bank of the Ganga.

Rathaur, Manjula 1990. *Unmarried Working Women: Marriage and Career. A Study of College and University Teachers of Varanasi.* 118pp. Stosius Inc/Advent Books Division, New Delhi. Hb, ISBN: 81-70271-34-7.

Ratnakar, Pramesh 2005. *Banaras and Sarnath.* 96pp. Roli Books, New Delhi. Pb, ISBN: 81-74360-51-4.

Ratnakar, Pramesh and Deo, Krishna 1993. *Banaras: Shiva's Eternal City.* Lustre Press, New Delhi.

Ray, Anil 1978. *Students and Politics: A Case Study of Benares Hindu University, India.* South Asia Books, New Delhi. Hb, ISBN: 0883867893, 9780883867891.

Rehold, Leah 2005. *A Hindu Education: Early Years of Banaras Hindu University.* Oxford University Press, Delhi. xviii + 237 pp. Hb. ISBN: 0-1956-7483-9.

This book explores the complex inter-relationships between religion, education, identity formation, and resistance patterns, with a case study of the B.H.U. It re-examines the general view of most modern scholarship on religious nationalism grounded in the assumption that nationalism thrives only in modern, secular cultures. It also offers a different perspective on university education in colonial India.

Rivière, Jean M. 1982. *Lettres de Bénarès.* (In French) 236pp. Spiritualités Vivantes, Serie Hindouisme. Albin Michel, Paris. Pb ISBN: 2-2260-1317-2.

Having a deep knowledge of India and its religions, the author presents Banaras from a spiritual point of view. In all times and in all places, there were sacred sites: "Just as the *chakras* of the human body are the focal points of cosmic forces with the body, even these places are sacred *chakras* of the earth, points of communication between the invisible and the world of men". In this context, the author describes vivid scenes of the city.

Rodrigues, Hillary Peter 2003. *Ritual Worship of the Great Goddess: The Liturgy of the Durga Puja with Interpretations.* xvi + 417 pp., illus., bibliogr. State University of New York (SUNY) Press, Albany NY. Pb, ISBN-10: 0791454002.

This is the first-hand description of the Durga Puja, the Hindu celebration of the Great Goddess, Durga, in Banaras. During a nine-day period every autumn, Hindus in India and throughout the world worship the Great Goddess, Durga-the formidable deity who is loved like a mother. One of the most dramatic and popular of these celebrations is the Durga Puja, a rite noted for its visual pageantry, ritual complexity, and communal participation. In this book, Hillary Peter Rodrigues describes the Bengali style of Durga Puja practiced in the sacred city of Banaras from beginning to end. A romanization of the Sanskrit litany is included along with an English translation. In addition to the liturgical description, the author provides information on the rite's component elements and mythic aspects covering the wide range of sources that come together in these rituals: thus *vedic* and *puranic* sources are complemented by elements from the devotionalist tradition and Tantric symbolism. There are interpretive sections on *puja*, the Great Goddess, women's roles in the ritual, and the socio-cultural functions of the ritual. The author maintains that the Durga Puja is a rite of cosmic rejuvenation, of empowerment at both the personal and social levels, and a rite that orchestrates manifestations of the feminine, both divine and human.

Rohatgi, Kamla and Rohatgi, S. P. 1991. *Buddhism and Sarnath.* Bhartiya Kala Prakashan, Delhi.

Roy, P.B. 1955. *Banaras: The Soul of Hinduism. A handy historical guide to Ancient and Modern Banaras.* Saturday Mail Publications, Calcutta.

Sachs, Sebastian 2008. *Benares-heilige Stadt der Hindus am Ganges: Heilige Stadt der Hindus am Ganges.* Published by GRIN Verlag, Berlin. [in German]. ISBN: 363891-9803, 978-363891-9807. 32pp.

Sanyal, Suprakash 1979. *Benares and the English East India Company, 1764-1795.* Calcutta: World Press. 249pp.

Saletore, G.N. 1955 a. *Banaras Affairs (1788-1810).* U.P. State Records Series, Selections from English Records No. 1 and 2.. Govt. Central Records Office, U.P., Allahabad.

—— 1955 b. *Press List of Pre-Mutiny Records, Banaras Correspondence (1776-1789)*. Vol. I. 109pp. U.P. State Records Series. Govt. Central Records Office, U.P., Allahabad.

Saltzman, Devyani 2006. *Shooting Water. A Mother-Daughter Journey & the Making of a Film*. Afterword by Deepa Mehta. Penguin Books India, New Delhi. xiv + 256 pp., 2 maps, & 15 b & w photographs. ISBN-10: 0-14400-102-0.

"In late December 1999, Devyani Saltzman, daughter of international award-winning film-maker Deepa Mehta, travelled to Banaras to work with her mother on '*Water*', the final film of the Elements Trilogy after Fire and Earth. Since her parents' divorce when she was eleven years old, Devyani had spent her life navigating between two religions, two traditions, two cultures, and two people-belonging to both and to neither at once. *Water* would be mother and daughter's second chance. But after only a week of shooting, the film-about the oppression of Hindu widows-became the target of a series of politically motivated attacks by Hindu fundamentalists. Protestors destroyed the sets, burned effigies of Deepa, and made threats on her life. *Water* was shut down. What began as a journey to heal deep wounds from the past turned into a five-year odyssey to complete a film." Transformative and inspiring story of Devyani's life-changing experiences tells the inside realities of the Banaras mindset (esp. pp. 21-93). After passing the first of four weeks peacefully and pleasantly, the team faced all the troubles and turmoil resulting from the vested interests of politicians and Hindu fundamentalists; thus finally the film making was stopped. However, the film was finally made in another setting near Colombo (Sri Lanka) and received international recognition. The film portraits the obnoxious life of windows in the holy city of Banaras during the 1930s.

Sanjiva, B. Rao 1913. *George Sydney Arundale, His Life and Work in the Central Hindu College, Benares*. Theosophical Publishing House, Benares and Madras. 219pp.

Sanyal, Ritwik and Widdess, Richard 2004. *Dhrupad: Tradition and Performance in Indian Music*. xxii + 396pp.; CD. SOAS Musicology Series. Ashgate Publ., Aldershot and Burlington, Vt. Hb, ISBN 13: 978-0-7546-0379-5.

Dhrupad is the oldest style of classical vocal music performed in north India that has preserved its historical style, and Banaras is one of its main centres since the past and still maintains that tradition, e.g. by celebrating Dhrupad Mela. There are several descriptions about the Banaras tradition.

Sanyal, Suprakash 1979. *Benares and the English East India Company, 1764-1795*. The World Press Private Ltd., Calcutta.

Sarasvati, B.N. 1975. *Kashi: Myth and Reality of a Classical Cultural Tradition*. 8 b & w photographs, glossary, index, xii + 81pp. Institute of Advanced Studies, Simla.

How do the inhabitants of Kashi look at themselves? How do they organise and interpret 'sacred'? How do they cultivate excellence in purely secular pursuits, and how do they restore equilibrium between 'sacred' and 'secular' in their inner structuring and societal behaviour? What makes them a coherent cultural group possessing a distinct style of life? How do they attain unity and continuity in traditions? How do they modernise their traditions, and to what extent? This book aims to present a non-conventional approach to studying the 'self-view' of a classical cultural tradition in trying to answer these questions.

Saxena, Kavita 1995. *Life and Status of Professional Women: a Study of Varanasi*. Radiant Publications, New Delhi. 123pp. ISBN: 8170272076.

Saxena, V.N., et. al. 1979. *Ground Water Potential of Different Blocks of Varanasi District*. T.M. no. 24. D.P.A.P., G.W.I.O., Lucknow.

Schaumann, J.S. 1964. *Wall Paintings of Banaras*. (27 leaves of photographs of mural paintings and decoration on separate paper inserted). 186pp. Banaras Hindu University, Varanasi.

Schechner, Richard 1989. *Performative Circumstances from the Avant Garde to Ramlila*. 337 pages, 37 illustrations. Seagull Books, Calcutta. Pb. ISBN: 81-7046-01-82.

This collection of essays studies a wide range of performative circumstances, covering aboriginal initiation rites and rituals, traditional dance and theatre forms in Asia, Africa and Australia, and *avant garde* experiments all over the world, tracing the movement from ritual to theatre and back, and offering a fresh perspective for the new theatre. The author provides the best aesthetic so far for acting and the workshop-rehearsal process, drawing upon his studies of the Ramlila of Ramnagar, the Chhau of Purulia and Seraikella, texts like the *Natyasastra*, contemporary anthropological theory, and his exposure to different cultures.

Schilder, Robert and Callewaert, Winand 2000. *Banaras. Visions of a Living Ancient Tradition.* Hemkunt Publ. (P) Ltd., New Delhi. 128pp., b & w and colour photographs.

This is a good combination of literary narratives and capturing the life in camera based on long experiences of vision, perspectives and understanding, with text narration and illustrated with photographs. Typical scenes and characteristics of landscape and people of Banaras are portrayed that cover pilgrimage, Shiva and Ganesha, death, riverfront, architecture, weavers and Sarnath, and also the dark side of the culture.

Schütte, von Stefan T. 2003. *Soziale Netzwerke als räumliche Orientierungssysteme. Konstruktionen von Raum und Localität der Wäscher von Banâras*. Studien zur Geographischen Entwicklungsforschung (Studies in Development Geography) 23. Verlag für Entwicklungspolitik, Saarbrücken GmbH. 5 tables, 8 figures, 13 maps, 21 b & w photographs, English summary (232-245), bibliography, xviii + 264pp. ISSN: 1618-3657. ISBN: 3-88156-770-4.

This study deals with the washermen ('*Dhobi*') of Banaras and the ways they collectively order their living spaces and their community life. It is based on one year's empirical research and seeks to discover how traditional forms of social organisation in urban India continue into the 21st century and to what extent these still shape everyday life, social interactions, and spatial perceptions. It is argued that the example of the washermen in Banaras is an eligible case which demonstrates the actual significance of traditional orientation systems that help to build social security, dignity, opportunity, and collective action and go hand in hand with a distinctive spatial framework. It thus gives a secular outlook on Banaras and the various ways in which the city is ordered and perceived according to the needs and aspirations of a subordinated caste group. The Dhobi's place in Banaras needs to be contended, and it is made possible via '*tat*' as a social system and a social identity, where power and prestige are expressed and key-issues are debated.

Searle-Chatterjee, Mary 1981. *Reversible Sex Roles: The Special Case of Banaras Sweepers*. Pergamon Press, Oxford. 12 tables, 2 maps, 7 figues, 15 b & w photographs, appendix, viii + 112pp. Pb, ISBN: 0-08-025780-1; 9780080257808.

This is the first authentic and still valid document on the untouchable group of Sweepers in Banaras, who live in localities surrounded by a high wall forming an enclave into which persons of other castes rarely enter. This pioneering work covers topics like the frame and method, the setting of sweepers in the sacred city, the lifeways of sweepers, working structure and money received, unpaid work, their kinship and social links, community and recreation, self-respect and the body, education and occupational mobility, trade unionism and involving leadership, direction of changing aspirations and attitudes, and finally conclusions pertaining to mobility and sex roles. This is an inside story of *dalit* society.

Sen, Rajani Ranjan 1912. *The Holy City: Benares*. M.R. Sen for Minto Press, Chittagong. Reprinted with new setting, 40 colour and 43 b & w new photographs. Bibliography, index. Shubhi Publications, Gurgaon; 2005. ISBN: 81-8290-003-4. 180 pp.

This book was first published in 1912, and is now reprinted with a new setting, replacing most of the photographs with new ones. This guidebook describes the culture, holy sites and places, monuments and temples, the riverfront, the fort, etc. — what the author had once observed. Additionally, the history, geography and various sects and cults are also taken care of. The book is a good source to understand the city in the early twentieth century. The chapters include the general tour to the city, astronomical observatory and its uses, the monasteries and religious sects, old remnants scattered in the city, the historical offshoots and related objects, the Buddhist site of Sarnath, Shiva and associated temples in the different quarters of the city, water bodies and holy wells, the ghats, and Ramnagar and related history of Maharajas.

Seshadri, P. 1930. *Benares*. 3rd ed. Published by Printed by S.N. Tandon at the City Press, Cawnpore.

Shakespear, A. 1873. *Selections from the Duncan Records*. Medical Hall Press, Benares, 2 vols.

This book describes the administrative and revenue systems of implementation of permanent settlement under the direction of Jonathan Duncan (1787-1795 in Banaras), one of the most famous of eighteenth-century British civil officers. [See also Mishra 1975, ch. 2].

Sharma, N.K. 1975. *Varanasi, The City of Burning and Learning*. Ambika Puri, Varanasi.

A popular narrative by a well-known local tourists' guide.

Sharma, R.C. 1964. *Brass and copperware industry in Uttar Pradesh with special reference to Varanasi*. Manager of Publications Division of the Govt. of India, Delhi.

Sharma, Ramesh Chandra and Ghosal, Pranati (eds.) 2006 a. *Jain Contribution to Varanasi*. x + 166 pp. 11 b & w photos; index; 23 cm. D.K. Printworld (P) Ltd., New Delhi. Hb, ISBN: 81-246-0341-3.

This book incorporates thirteen short papers, presented in a two-day seminar, on multiple aspects of Jain traditions related to Varanasi. It covers themes like Jain contribution, nativity and mark, Sarnath and its Jain images, sculptural art, Jain culture, Kashi and Banarasidass, function of Jain institute, and sources of Jain literature.

—— (eds.) 2006 b. *Vaishnava Contribution to Varanasi*. x + 166 pp. 15 b & w photos; index; 23 cm. D.K. Printworld (P) Ltd., New Delhi. Hb, ISBN: 81-246-0342-1.

This book incorporates fifteen short papers, presented in a two-day seminar, on multiple aspects of Vaishnava traditions related to Varanasi. It covers scattered themes like Mahabharata, Vaishnava Bhakti, Vaishnava Images, Ideology of Kabir, Vaishnava adoration, Lilas, Pushtimarg Vaishnava, Haveli music, an antiquarian perspective, Vaishnava art, symbols, and Bhagavat Bhaktas.

—— (eds.) 2006 c. *Sakta Contribution to Varanasi*. xii + 148 pp. 24 b & w photos; index; 23 cm. D. K. Printworld (P) Ltd., New Delhi. Hb, ISBN: 81-246-0343-X.

This book consists of fifteen papers, presented in a one-day seminar, on multiple aspects of Sakta traditions practised in Varanasi. Having some links to philosophical and religious leanings, the contents expose the iconographic, ritualistic and artistic rendering of the Mother Goddess as found in Varanasi. Saktism has also been a forceful current in the cultural stream of this holy city. This is evidenced by several Devi temples, sacred places, cosmic designs, fairs and festivals associated with the worship of goddesses. Unfortunately, there is neither a catalogue of the goddess shrines, nor their locations. All the papers are without any linking introduction, and completely lack coherence, integrity and new interpretations. This gap is fulfilled by an authoritative paper (cf. Singh, Ravi and Singh, Rana 2006: 41-68), which was also presented in the above seminar.

Shepherd, Frances and Sahai, Sharda 1992. *Play Tabla: A Manual for the Benares Style of Tabla Playing*. Trentham, New York. 68pp. ISBN: 094-808027-2.

Sherring, Matthew Atmore 1863. *Benares and Its Antiquities*. Medical Hall Press, Benares. 34pp.

—— 1868. *Benares. The Sacred City of the Hindus in Ancient and Modern Times*. Illustrated, 424pp. Trübner & Co., London. Cheap Publ, Delhi (reprinted, 1990), South Asia Books, New Delhi (reprinted, 1996), Hb, ISBN 8186142886, 9788186142882; and Pilgrims Book House, Varanasi (reprinted, 2000). ISBN: 81-7303-2351.

The first compendium on the sacred city dealing with history, architecture, growth of Hinduism, religious landscape, rituals, ethnic structure, Buddhist ruins, and fairs and festivals. Of course dated, but still a classic that covers the long span of time and vast area of space in describing the religious landscape and performative culture of Banaras with fineness of details and microcosmic authentic observation.

—— 1872-1881. *Hindu Tribes and Castes as Represented in Benares*. Thacker, Spink & Co., London and Calcutta. Reprint Cosmo Publications, Delhi in 1974; 3 vols.

The author discusses the Brahmanical Tribes, the Kshatriya or Rajpoot Tribes, the Agnikulas or Fire Races, Aboriginal Tribes of Benares.

—— 1897. *Index to Hindu Tribes and Castes as Represented in Benares*; Compiled by Nânak Chand. Asiatic Society of Bengal, Calcutta. 112pp.

Showeb, Mohammad 1986. *Education and Mobility among Harijans: A Study Based on Students, Government Employees and Traditionally Employed Chamars of Varanasi.* 161pp. South Asia Books, Varanasi. Hb, ISBN: 81-850720-00.

—— 1994. *Silk Handloom Industry of Varanasi: A Study of Socio-economic Problems of Weavers.* Ganga Kaveri Publ. House & Gandhian Institute of Studies, Varanasi. 82pp. ISBN:81-856941-17.

Shukla, Pravina 2008. *The Grace of Four Moons: Dress, Adornment, and the Art of the Body in Modern India.* Indiana University Press, Bloomington and Indianapolis. 528 pages, 49 b&w photos, 25 colour photos, 2 maps. Photographs by her husband and fellow professor Henry H. Glassie. Hb ISBN: 978-0-253-34911-8.

Because clothing, food, and shelter are basic human needs, they provide excellent entries to cultural values and individual aesthetics. Everyone gets dressed every day, but body art has not received the attention it deserves as the most common and universal of the material expressions of culture. The book aims to document the clothing decisions made by ordinary people in their everyday lives. Based on fieldwork conducted primarily in the city of Banaras for doctoral degree (1998, University of California), the author conceptualizes and realizes a total model for the study of body art — understood as all aesthetic modifications and supplementations to the body. She urges the study of the entire process of body art, from the assembly of raw materials and the manufacture of objects, through their sale and the interactions between merchants and consumers, to the consumer's use of objects in creating personal decoration. Aims to document the clothing decisions made by ordinary people in their everyday lives.

Singh, Bhola Nath (compiled) 1941. *Benares, a Handbook: Prepared for the Indian Science Congress 28th Session.* Indian Science Congress Association and Banaras Hindu University, Banaras. 178pp.

Singh, Bhagwati Sharan 1988. *Varanasi.* National Book Trust, India, New Delhi. xx + 96pp.

This is a short introduction of the city in the series 'India-The Land and the People', sketching the city's eternal spirit, medieval saints and philosophers, cultural heritage, culture, people, architecture, and reminiscences.

Singh, Birendra Pratap 1985. *Life in Ancient Varanasi (An Account Based on Archaeological Evidence).* Sundeep Prakashan, Delhi. Introduction, conclusion, bibliography, index, xx + 326pp., 38 line figures, and 37 plates. ISBN: 81-757406-39.

A revised doctoral dissertation that is based on analysis archaeological findings, like the ground plans and their structures, utensils, dress, ornaments, coiffure, toilet accessories, objects bearing on food habits and kitchen equipments, and economic life. The introduction provides the evolution of the city with special reference to its plans and archaeological structures, building maters, and further narrating the mythology and history. At the end the main findings and the resume of the work are presented in 'conclusion'. This is the only book of its kind.

Singh, Chandramani and Ahivasi, Devaki 1981. *Woollen textiles and costumes from Bharat Kala Bhavan, Varanasi, Banaras Hindu University.* Banaras Hindu University, Varanasi. [mostly deals with Kashmir shawls].

Singh, Charu Sheel 2007. *Kashi, A Mandala Poem.* Adhyayan Publishers & Distributors, New Delhi. ISBN: 978-81-8435-029-6.

Kashi is the divine city, the abode of Lord Shiva Himself. Civilizations have come and gone, ages have withered away but Kashi has proved its eternal credentials by withstanding the ravages of time. Throughout the historiographical narratives available on Kashi in different *Puranas* and other books, one has altogether missed a poetic *avatara* of Kashi in English. This is the first poem of its kind that evokes Kashi with *mandala* auguries that ultimately take their figural posture into the body of a Sri-Cakra, the genealogical ambience of the goddesses who enfold Shiva in the form of a *bindu* surrounded by peripheries of multiple kinds. The poem is full of the richness of experience and range of metaphorical imagistic repertoire.

Singh, Jai Ram 1980. *Sarnath, Past and Present.* Atmatosh Prakashan, Varanasi. 16 b & w photographs, 5 maps, 6 appendices, bibliography, index, x + 115pp.

Giving as introduction to the general history of Varanasi, the five chapters deal with the importance of Sarnath as the sacred site where the Buddha turned the Wheel of Law, nomenclature, history down the ages, excavations at Sarnath, and finally Sarnath today.

Singh, Nand Lal, (ed.) 1961. *Mahamana Malviyaji Birth Centenary Commemorative Volume.* 25th December. The Secretary, All-India Malviya-ji Centenary Celebration Committee.

Singh, Prahlad 1978. *Stone observatories in India, erected by Maharaja Sawai Jai Singh of Jaipur, 1686-1743 A.D., at Delhi, Jaipur, Ujjain, Varanasi, Mathura;* assisted by Pandit Kalyan Dutt Sharma. Bharata Manisha, Varanasi.

Singh, Pramod 1985. *Environmental Pollution and Management (Case of Varanasi).* Chugh Publications, Allahabad. (Revised doctoral thesis). Appendices, bibliography, index, 18 b & w photographs + 24 maps, xxiv + 243pp.

This is the first book-length study of the environmental problems of Varanasi, describing the general problems, and accounting various issues and facets of pollution, i.e. water, air, noise, land, population, social aspects, and finally environmental management and preventive measures.

Singh, Raghubir 1988. *Banaras, Sacred City of India.* Introduction and 96 photographs. Size: 12.5 x 10.5 x 1 inches. 120pp. Thames & Hudson Ltd., London. Hb, ISBN-10: 0500241325; ISBN-13: 978-0500241325.

In this book, starting with an introduction and illustrated with 96 colour photographs, the renowned photographer Raghubir Singh [1942-1999] reflected the broad cultural and geographic diversities and distinctions of Banaras, from a lone bather jumping into the Ganga river to the tens of thousands of worshipers that gathered at the *ghats* of this city. The beauty, mystery and life scenes of Banaras were caught by his camera with the elegance of a painter.

Singh, Ram Bali 1975. *Rajput Clan Settlement in Varanasi District (Middle Ganga Valley).* National Geographical Society of India, Varanasi, Res. Pub. 12. (Revised doctoral thesis). 52 maps, xx + 134pp. ISBN: 81-86187-11-1.

The rural habitat and landscape of Varanasi district (of which Varanasi is the HQ) is analysed with reference to geographical personality, population characteristics, distribution and evolution of rural settlements, cultural geography of pre-Rajput period, the historical models of growth, morphological structure, and finally clan areas and territorial growth.

247

Singh, Ram Dular (ed.) 1986. *Bengal and Varanasi, A Study of Cultural Synthesis & National Integration (Bengal's Contribution to Varanasi)*. Bibliographical Society of India, Varanasi. 154pp.

This is a collection of 22 short essays on the focal theme that deal with different aspects of Bengal and its association with Banaras, including education, temple construction, culture, monastic tradition, historical links, literary tradition, trade and commerce, women's life, art and paintings, medical science, and the spirit of place.

—— (ed.) 1997. *Encyclopaedia Kashika*, Vol. I (*Journals and Journalism*-1775-1800). Bibliographical Society of India, Varanasi.

Singh, Ram Lochan 1955. *Banaras, A Study in Urban Geography*. Nand Kishore & Bros. Banaras (India). Bibliography, index, 36 maps/figs., xvi + 184pp + 22 b & w photographs.

Based on the author's doctoral thesis at LSE London, this is the pioneering and only book of its kind on contemporary Banaras in geographical context, that covers themes like historical development, evolution of cultural landscape, demographic features, functional zones, social and public institutions, public utility services, *umland* of Banaras, and finally planning and improvements of Banaras.

Singh, Rana P.B. 1989. *Where Cultural Symbols Meet. Literary Images of Varanasi*. Tara Book Agency, Varanasi. 254pp. 13x18cm. Hb, ISBN: 81-85403-36-8.

The book presents vivid scenes of topophilia and topophobia related to landscape and people as projected in creative contemporary writings: Kabir, Tulasi, Ghalib, Bhartendu, Rudra, Raja Rao, Bismillah, Shiv Prasad Singh, and Kashinath Singh. It also narrates the intrinsic realities, non-sensuous happenings in the life of dwellers. [See for an elaborated and expanded version: Singh, Rana P.B. 2004].

—— 1991. *Pancakroshi Yatra, Varanasi. Sacred Journey, Ecology of Place, and Faithscape*. Tara Book Agency, Varanasi. ii + 50pp. 15 x 20 cm. ISBN: 81-85403-84-8.

The contextual milieu, cultural metaphor, and cosmogonic meaning associated with the sacred territory and pilgrimage are explained to understand the distinctiveness and diversity of sacredscapes. [For an enlarged and comprehensively expanded version, see Singh, Rana P.B. 2002].

—— (ed.) 1993. *Banaras (Varanasi). Cosmic Order, Sacred City, Hindu Traditions.* 62 figs/maps, 344pp. 18 x 24 cm. Tara Book Agency, Varanasi on behalf of the Varanasi-Studies Foundation. ISBN 81-85403-92-9.

An anthology of 20 essays (mostly reprinted here) by leading authors from all parts of the world, and covering varied aspects such as survey of Sanskrit sources, early mythology, pilgrimages, riverfront ghats, death and deathscapes, Shiva's universe, Bhairava, ghosts and sins, the *pandas*, Hindu rituals, five *melas*, Sarnath, Ramanagar and Ramlila, milk bovines, demographic profiles, role of educational institutions, and Varanasi as heritage city. The authors include Diana Eck, Hans Bakker, D.P. Dubey, Rana P.B. Singh, M. Kaushik, Jonathan Parry, E-C. Visuvalingam, R.R. Mehrotra, Nita Kumar, William Sax, D.O. Lodrick, and U. Kockmann. At the end historical chronology and bibliography (494 entries) are also given.

—— 1993a. *Varanasi Region. An Insight Guide to Tourist Places.* 54pp. 15 x 20cm. Tara Book Agency, Varanasi.

A first attempt to prepare a guidebook for tourists in contemporary time. Late a detailed and exhaustive guidebook was developed. [For the enlarged and rewritten version, see Singh, Rana P.B. and Rana, Pravin S. 2002/ 2006].

—— 2002. *Towards the Pilgrimage Archetype. Pancakroshi Yatra of Banaras.* Pilgrimage & Cosmology Series: 3. 222pp, 72 figs/maps. 13x18cm. Indica Books, Varanasi. ISBN: 81-86569-30-8. [This is the 2nd revised and expanded edition].

Assuming itself as the centre of the cosmos, Kashi (Varanasi/ Banaras) has preserved its mandalic system, which is experienced and revived by the millions of devout Hindu by pilgrimages. This is the first book-length study on Panchakroshi and its associated inner sanctum, Antargriha Yatra. At least since the 16th century the pilgrimages of these two circuits are continuously walked by pilgrims. The contextual milieu, cultural metaphor, and cosmogonic meaning associated with the sacred territory and pilgrimage are narrated to understand the distinctiveness and diversity of sacredscapes.

—— 2003/ 2008. *Where the Buddha Walked. A Companion to the Buddhist Places of India.* Pilgrimage & Cosmology Series: 5.

320pp., 110 maps & figs. 13 x 18cm. Indica Books, Varanasi. ISBN: 81-86569-36-7. 2nd ed. 2008.

This book describes all the places where the Buddha walked, with emphasis on the Sacred Ways & Spiritual Walks and the Buddha and his Message, in search of the spirit of the places. The places described, in its historical, cultural and contextual contexts, include: Lumbini (birthplace), Kapilavastu (childhood place), Kushinagar (nirvana place), Shravasti (the place of Great Miracles), Kaushambi (the ruins site), Sarnath (the First Sermon), Vaishali (offered honey here), Kesariya (night halt), Sankisa (descended from the heaven), Bodh Gaya (Enlightenment); Rajgir (tamed a mad elephant), and Nalanda (monastic University and its ruins).

—— 2004. *Cultural Landscapes and the Lifeworld. The Literary Images of Banaras*. Pilgrimage and Cosmology Series: 6. 398pp., 55 figures. 13 x 18cm. Indica Books, Varanasi. ISBN: 81-86569-45-6.

This is the first book describing the literary images of a single city, based on individuals' writings on Banaras. The literary images and the cultural traditions as described in the fictions and regional writings are interpreted in the purview of cultural symbols and the alive traditions, which have maintained its continuity since the past. Each of the fifteen essays describes a time and its culture, illustrated with *puranic* sources, as expressed in the writings of Kabir, Tulasi, Mirza Ghalib, Bhartendu Harishchandra, Rudra 'Kashikeya', Shivprasad Singh, Bhishm Sahni, Raja Rao, Abdul Bismillah, Kashinath Singh, and Pankaj Mishra. Of course, it cannot be claimed that this will be the end-product of literary images, but surely the work will be helpful in understanding the complexity and multiplicity of belief systems and historical perspectives of metaphor, symbolism and milieu.

—— 2008. *Banaras, the Heritage City of India: Geography, History, and Bibliography*. Also, historical chart, a list of 1100 shrines and divinities and their locations, and Hindu Festivals, 2006-15. Pilgrimage and Cosmology Series: 8, 458 pp.; 13 statistical tables, 32 figures; 1267 entries. Indica Books, Varanasi. Hb ISBN: 81-86569-85-5.

This is the first attempt of its kind on the holy city of Varanasi. The section on Geography covers the general background of the topography, climate, soils, vegetation, and humanised landscape. The

250

History section gives a general brief outline of history, from the ancient to the modern, including a chronological chart. The issue of inscribing the heritagescapes, especially of the '*riverfront ghats*', on the line of UNESCO Heritage criteria, has also been fully described. The Bibliography (1270 entries), classified into 16 groups, is by far the most complete about the city of Banaras/ Varanasi/ Kashi. Additionally, chart of cultural happenings in North India parallel with Banaras, the Hindu almanac and festivals for 2006-2015 are added.

—— 2010. *Kashi & Cosmos. Sacred Geography and Ritualscape of Banaras*. Pilgrimage and Cosmology Series. 450pp., 150 figures. 15 x 20 cm; in process.

This book is a collection of all the research papers published by the author during 1980-2007; all are updated, revised and re-written to fit into the sequence and the subject matter, along with several new chapters to interconnect the themes. This is an encyclopaedic book on Varanasi/ Kashi. The chapters cover themes like Banaras and its Images, Geographical Personality (physical landscape and climatic characteristics), Transformation on the cradle of Time (evolution), The Ghats: the Riverfront Heritagescape, Pilgrimage mandala and cultural astronomy, Sacred Journeys and Associated Deities, Panchakroshi Yatra: Cosmic Circuit and Journey, Sacred Geography of Goddesses, Sun shrines and the Sacredscapes, The Festivals and Ritualscape, Sacrality and Perceptual World, Literary Images: Change and Continuity, Modern Varanasi as revealed in Singh's the *Street Turns Yonder*, Demographic Profile and James Prinsep's Census, The Buddhist Sacredscape (Sarnath), Heritage Tourism: Scenario and Perspectives, The Muslim Sacredscape, and Selected Bibliography. At the end there are several Appendices, consisting of Historical Outline, Festivals & Roman Dates, 2001-2016, List of Kashi's Divinities (1200), List of Devas by Muhallas, List of Pilgrimage Routes and Images, Sacred Journeys and Sites: GPS values of 450 sites, List of Existing 324 Shiva Lingas, as ref. KKh, and List of Lost 200 Shiva *lingas*, as ref. KKh.

Singh, Rana P.B. and Rana, Pravin S. 2002/ 2006. *Banaras Region. A Spiritual and Cultural Guide*. Indica Books, Varanasi. Pilgrimage & Cosmology Series: 1. 111 Maps/ Figs., 402pp. 13 x 18cm. ISBN 81-86569-24-3. [2nd revised reprint, 2006].

This is a compendium and encyclopaedic handbook of cultural tourism in Varanasi, covering details of the history, culture and traditions of the one hundred sites and places. The book is arranged into three parts: Inside Varanasi City, Sites around Varanasi (the sites lying less than 80 km), and Sites of Varanasi Region (the places in the range of 100-300 km, like Allahabad, Ayodhya, Chitrakut, Khajuraho, and Gaya) — all illustrated with maps and special information about the utilities and facilities available. Through guiding into 'Sacred Ways & Spiritual Walks', the book calls for co-pilgrimage.

Singh, S[achchida] N[and] 1986. *Geography of Tourism and Recreation. (With special reference to Varanasi)*. xx + 200pp., 21 figures, 16 tables, appendices, bibliography, and 41 tiny size b & w photographs, index. Inter-India Publications, New Delhi. ISBN: 81-210-0065-3.

This is the published form of a doctoral dissertation, dealing with attributes of tourism and related infrastructure that facilitates and attract the tourists to Varanasi. The contents are arranged into nine chapters, dealing with review of tourism and geography, personality of the city, transport and communication, humanised landscape, tourist attractions, tourist facilities, functional analysis of tourist data, tourist cognition and scenic beauty, finally planning perspectives, and summary and conclusion. The first three thematic chapters lack synthesis and integration with the later themes. Chapter eight dealing with tourist cognition is substantially based on and copied from an earlier publication, i.e. Singh, R.L. and Singh, R.P.B. 1980, without reference. Only a marginal attempt is made to analyse the rich religious and heritage resources of the sacred city; in fact, more emphasis is given on data than on the spirit and message involved therein.

Singha, Radhika 1998. *A Despotism of Law: Crime and Justice in Early Colonial India*. xxix, 342 pp. Oxford University Press, Delhi. ISBN: 0-19-56404-97.

Sinha, Kunal 2004. *A Banarasi on Varanasi*. Bluejay Books (an imprint of Srishti Publ.), New Delhi and Kolkata. 13 x 18 cm. ISBN: 81-88575-24-0.

Sinha, Surjit and Saraswati, Baidya Nath 1978. *Ascetics of Kashi. An Anthropological Exploration.* N.K. Bose Memorial Foundation, Varanasi. 37 b & w photographs, chart of historical chronology, appendices, index, xii +286pp., illustrated.

This is a pioneering study of ascetics and their organisations, with emphasis on defining asceticism and its organisation, the different sects like Shaiva, Vaishnava and miscellaneous, the festival of Kumbha, interaction between ascetics and householders, and future prospects of asceticism, and also dealing in the context with the individual attitudes of life, caste and cult, spiritual pursuit, and impact of modernisation

Sittapati, P. and Purushottam, V. (ed. and trans.) 1973. *Kashiyatra Charitra: Enugula Veeraswamy's Journal.* Andhra Pradesh Government Oriental Manuscripts Library and Research Institute (State Archives), Hyderabad.

Spilsbury, Louise and Spilsbury, Richard 2007. *Living on the Ganges River.* Raintree, London. ISBN: 1410928209.

Smith, Captain Robert 1840. *Description of a View of the Holy City of Benares and the Sacred Ganges.* London.

Srivastava, Harish Chandra 1974. *The Genesis of Campus Violence in Banaras Hindu University Varanasi.* Indian International Pub., Allahabad. 106pp.

Ståhle, Göran Viktor 2004 (December 17). *The Religious Self in Practice at a Hindu Goddess-Temple: A Cultural Psychological Approach for the Psychology of Religion.* [This is a case study of the Durga Temple, Varanasi]. Division of Psychology of Religion, Dept. of Theology, Uppsala University, Uppsala (Sweden).

Sukul, Kubernath 1974, *Varanasi Down the Ages.* K.N. Sukul, Patna. Printed at Bhargava Bhushan Press, Varanasi. 21 b & w photographs, 1 map pasted, appendix, viii + 328pp.

The only book dealing with overall cultural and educational history of the city with emphasis on ancient Kashi and its kingdom, trade and commerce, agriculture and crafts, music and dancing, education and physical culture, growth of religion, religious set-up, monastic institutions, saints and monks, fairs and festivals, riverfront ghats, the scene in 19th century, and finally the cultural arena.

Sundaram, V.A. 1942. *Benares Hindu University 1916-1942*. Silver Jubilee Edition. Banaras Hindu University Press, Varanasi.

Tagare, G.V. (translated and annotated by), 1996, 1997. *The Skanda-Purana, Book IV: Kashi-Khanda*. Vols. 58, Parts X, Chapters 1 to 50. Motilal Banarasidass Publs. Pvt. Ltd., Delhi. Index, x + 544pp. ISBN: 81-208-1364-2.

This is the only translation of the *Kashi Khanda*, a 14th century puranic text, known as the encyclopaedia on Varanasi, and covers 50 cantos (*purvardha*). This volume refers to the stories of Vindhya, Agastya, seven holy cities, Celestial Damesels and the Sun, stellar world, world of various gods, Brahma hymn to Kashi, the Ganga, Bhairava, Dandapani, Jnanavapi, religious student, characteristics of women, Avimukta, Kala, King Divodas, Sixty-four Yoginis, and various form of Sun-god (Aditya), e.g. Lolarka, Uttararka, Samba, Draupada, Mayukha and Khakhola. This is also available in 2 Volumes in Hindi, published by Sampurnanand Sanskrit University, Varanasi (1991-1994).

—— (translated and annotated by), 1996, 1997. *The Skanda-Purana, Book IV: Kashi-Khanda*. Vols. 59, Parts XI, Chapters 51 to 100. Motilal Banarasidass Publs. Pvt. Ltd., Delhi. Index, x + 574pp. ISBN: 81-208-1365-0.

This translation of the second part of the *Kashi Khanda* covers the next 50 cantos (*uttarardha*), with the stories of Sun-gods Arun and Vriddha, Dashashvamedha, Shiva's attendants, Pishacha-mochana, Ganesha and Vinayakas, Divodasa, Panchanada, Bindumadhava, Jyesthesha, various forms of Shiva lingas, Durga, Omkaresha, Trilochana, Kedara, Dharmesha, Vishveshvara, the Ganga and Varana confluence and Manikarnika, Durvasa, Daksha, Sati and Her body, Amritesha, Vyasa, holy sites of Varanasi, and Index to Kashikhanda. This is also available in 2 Volumes in Hindi, published by Sampurnanand Sanskrit University, Varanasi (1996-1998).

Tavernier, Jean-Baptiste 1889. *Travels in India*. Translated from the original French edition of 1676 with a biographical sketch of the author, notes, appendices, etc. by V. Ball, 2nd edition, edited by William Crooke (Macmillan, London), 2 Vols. Reprint of the 1925 edition, New Delhi, 1977.

Thomas, Olivier Germain 1986. *Retour à Bénarès*. (In French). Albin Michel, Paris. 139pp. ISBN: 2-2260-2641-X.

As writer, producer at France culture, and tourist, the author has travelled India intensively during the last 20 years. In the spirit of that temptation, adventures and sensitivity he has described the rituals, death ceremonies, sacred rituals and the special places of veneration and their associated life.

Times of India, 2000. *The Times Guide to the City of Varanasi*. Bennett, Coleman & Co. Ltd, Delhi. 112pp., 1 map, illustrated. 2nd short edition, 2001.

A pocket pictorial catalogue book on Varanasi giving in short some sense of the city, also giving addresses and telephones of shops and restaurants; however it lacks the view of a guidebook.

Toutain, Pierre 1985. *Benares*. UBS Publishers Distributors, New Delhi. (French)

Twain, Mark 1898. *Following the Equator. A Journey around the World*. American Publishing Co., Hartford, Connecticut. ISBN: 0404015778. OCLC 577051.

The American humanist Samuel Langhorne Clemens, better known by his pen name Mark Twain (1835-1910), famous for his travel-ogue writings and his sensitivity to culture, had visited Banaras for a week in 1865 (!). He portrayed the scenes of Banaras in this accomplished book that contains four chapters/essays (50-53) dealing with the vivid life, landscape and cultural scenes of Banaras.

TTK Series 1988. *Varanasi. A TTK Guidebook* (Compiled by the Editorial Staff). T.T. Maps & Publications Pvt. Ltd., Madras (Chennai). 7 maps, 9 photographs, 74pp. Pb. ISBN: 81-7053-057-1.

A short guidebook for casual visitors, like one-day tourists, not for pilgrims.

Vaish, Devi Charan Lal 1972. *The Rise of British Power and the Fall of Marathas*. Upper India Pub. House, Allahabad. 703pp.

Valentia, George Viscount 1809. *Voyages and Travels in India, Ceylone, the Red Sea, Abyssinia and Egypt, 1802-1806*. Vol. I. John Murray, London.

Velden, Wieke Theresia van der 1991. *Silent Voices: Gender, Power, and Household Management in Rural Varanasi, India.* Centrale Huisdrukkerij, Vrije Universiteit, Amsterdam. 195pp.

Ventós, Alex 2002. *Cenizas de Benarés : Ashes of Benares : [fotografías].* [In Spanish] Belacqva, Madrid. Hb, ISBN: 8495894297, 9788495894298

Véqaud, Yves 1985. *Bénarès.* [In French]. Champ Vallon. 112pp. ISBN: 2-903528-60-8.

Verma, T.P.; Singh, D.P. and Mishra, J.S. (eds.) 1986. *Varanasi through the Ages.* Proceedings of an All-India Seminar. Bhartiya Itihas Samkalan Samiti, Varanasi, Publ. No. 4. (Essays in English and Hindi). 19 figures, 19 b & w photographs, 372pp.

This anthology is based on an All-India Seminar held at B.H.U. during 1-4 August 1985, and contains 54 presentations without revision, expansion, or editorial polishing. The articles are in a haphazard manner, and several times repetitious too. The essays, both in English (21) and Hindi (33), are arranged into eight sections, dealing with history, art and architecture, society and culture, economy, religion, literature, geography, and miscellaneous. The book lacks selected bibliography and index at the end.

Vidyarathi, L.P., Saraswati, B.N. and Jha, M. 1979. *The Sacred Complex of Kashi (A Microcosm of Indian Civilisation).* Concept Publ. Co, Delhi. 320pp., illustrated.

Based on a project work, this book deals with the in-depth purview of sacrality in geographic context, beliefs and practices, specialist priests and social composition, and also the impact of modern changes. The main focus of major factors of the sacred complex, viz. the institution of pilgrimage and the sacred specialists who cater to its religious and secular needs. This book provides a socio-religious study of the sacred complex of Kashi.

Vijayabhaskararavu, Vadapalli 2004. *The Walking Shiva of Varanasi: Life, Legends & Teachings of Trailingaswami.* 177pp., illustrated. Richa Prakashan, Delhi. ISBN: 81-90120085.

Wilson, Henry 1985. *Benares.* (80 Colour photographs). 95pp. Thames & Hudson Ltd., London. Hb, ISBN 0500241236, 9780500241233.

Winkler, von Josef und Schwichtenberg, Christina (Illustrators) 2008 (Juli). *Domra: Am Ufer des Ganges* (Taschenbuch). Suhrkamp Neuauflage Auflage Verlag, Frankfurt am Main. 283 Seiten. ISBN-13: 978-3518395943. [in German].

Yadava, K.N.S. 1992. *Rural Urban Communication and Rural Development*. 173pp. Shipra Publications, New Delhi. ISBN: 81-85402116.

Yusuf Ali, A. 1900. *A Monograph on Silk Fabrics produced in the North Western Provinces and Oudh*. Allahabad.

Zahir, M. Abdul 1966. *Handloom Industry of Varanasi*. Banaras Hindu University Press, Varanasi.

B. RESEARCH PAPERS & ESSAYS (mostly English)

Adam, Rev. M.T. 1833. 'Benares'; in, *The Missionary or Christians New Year's Gift*. Seley & Sons (et. al.), London.

Agarwal, D.K., et al. 1976a. Bacteriological Study of Ganga Water at Varanasi. *Indian Journal of Medical Research*, vol. 64 (no. 3): pp. 373-383.

—— 1976b. Physico-chemical Characteristics of Ganga water at Varanasi. *Indian Journal of Environmental Health*, vol. 18 (3): pp. 201-206.

Agarwal, D.K.; Kaur, P.; Katiyar, G.P. and Agarwal, K.K. 1980. Pattern of care during pregnancy and lactation in Sunderpur (An urban slum area of Varanasi). *Indian Journal of Public Health*, 24 (2), Apr-Jun: 82-87.

Agrawal, Madhoolika; Singh B.; Rajput M.; Marshall F. and Bell J.N.B. 2003. Effect of air pollution on peri-urban agriculture: a case study. *Environmental Pollution*, 126 (3), December: 323-329. doi:10.1016/S0269-7491(03)00245-8.

Agrawala, Prithvi K. 1971. The triple Yaksha statue from Rajghat. *Chhavi, Golden Jubilee Volume*. Bharat Bala Bhavan (Banaras Hindu University), Varanasi: pp. 139-148.

—— 1977. Some Varanasi Images of Ganapati and their iconographic problem. *Artibus Asiae*, vol. 39 (no. 2): 139-155.

Ahamed, Sad; Sengupta, Mrinal Kumar & twelve co-authors 2006. Arsenic groundwater contamination and its health effects in the state of Uttar Pradesh (UP) in upper and middle Ganga plain, India: A severe danger. *Science of the Total Environment*, vol. 370 (2-3), 1 November: 310-322. doi:10.1016/j.scitotenv.2006.06.015.

Ahmad, Q. 1961. An historical account of the Banaras mint in the later Mughal period, 1732-61. *The Journal of the Numismatic Society of India* (Varanasi), vol. 23.

Ahmed, Sara 1994. The rhetoric of participation re-examined: The state, NGOs and water users at Varanasi, Uttar Pradesh, India. *The Environmentalist* (Springer Netherlands, ISSN: 0251-1088), 14 (1), March: 3-16. DOI: 10.1007/BF01902655.

—— 1995. Whose concept of participation? State-Society dynamics in the cleaning of the Ganges at Varanasi; in, *Water and the Quest for Sustainable Development in the Ganges Valley*, eds. Graham Chapman and M. Thompson. Mansell, London & New York: 141-160.

Alley, Kelly D. 1992. On the banks of the Ganga. *Annals of Tourism Research*, vol. 19 (Winter): pp. 125-127.

—— 1994. Ganga and Gandagi: Interpretations of Pollution and Waste in Banaras. *Ethnology*, 33 (Spring): 127-145.

—— 1998. Idioms of degeneracy: assessing Ganga's purity and pollution. In, *Purifying the Earthly Body of God: Religion and Ecology in Hindu India*, ed. Lance E. Nelson. SUNY Press, Albany, NY : pp. 297- 330.

Allman, T. D. 1981. The eternal city of Benares. *Asia* (New York), vol. 4 (2), July-August: 44-49 and 54.

Alter, Joseph S. 1993. Hanuman and the moral physique of the Banarasi wrestler. In, Hertel and Humes, eds. *Living Banaras* (SUNY Press, Albany): 127-144.

Archer, Mildred 1971. Banaras and the British; in, Krishna, Anand (ed.), *Chavi, Golden Jubilee Volume*. Bharat Kala Bhavan, Banaras Hindu University, Banaras: pp. 70-74, figures 179-185.

—— 1980. "Many portraits of and around Banaras"; in her, *Early Views of India. The Picturesque Journeys of Thomas and William Daniell 1786-1794. [The Complete Aquatints with 258 illustrations, 33 in colour and 3 maps]*. Thames & Hudson, London. 240 pp. ISBN: 0-500-01236-5. [For Banaras, see pp. 23, 71-101].

Archers, William G. 1971. Banaras and British Art; in, Anand Krishna (ed.), *Chavi. Golden Jubilee Volume*. Bharat Kala Bhavan, Banaras Hindu University, Varanasi: 43-47, figures 123-132.

Arni, Clare 2005. The Urban Setting: A Panorama [colour photographs]; in, *Banaras, The City Revealed*; eds. George Michell and Rana P.B. Singh. Marg Publs., Mumbai: 8-18.

Arnold, David 1989. The ecology and cosmology of disease in the Banaras region; in, Freitag, S. B. (ed.) *Culture and Power in Banaras* (University of California Press, Berkeley): 246-267.

Askari, S.H. 1954. Chait Singh and Hastings from Persian sources. *Indian Historical Records Commission, Proceedings*, vol. 30, pt. 2.

Bakker, Hans T. 1993. Early mythology relating to Varanasi; in, Singh, Rana P.B. (ed.) *Banaras/ Varanasi* (Tara Book Agency, Varanasi): 21-28.

—— 1996. Construction and Reconstruction of sacred Space in Varanasi. *Numen*, 43 (1): 32-55.

—— 1998. The Sacred Centre as the Focus of Indological Research: The History of India's most holy tîrtha, Vârânasî, reconsidered; in, Vacek, Jaroslav & Dvorák, Jan (eds.) *Trends in Indian Studies. Proceedings of the ESIS*. Karolinum, Charles University Press, Prague: 9-20.

—— 2006. The Avimuktaksetra in Varanasi: Its Origin and Early Development; in, Gaenszle, Martin and Gengnagel, Jörg (eds.) *Visualised Space in Banaras*. (Heidelberg Studies in South Asian Rituals, Vol. 4). Harrassowitz Verlag, Wiesbaden: 23-39.

Balfour, H. 1897. The life-history of an Aghori fakir. *Journal of the Anthropological Institute* (London), 26: 340-57.

Banerjee, Priyatosh 1955. An inscribed stone slab from Paharia (Banaras). *Journal of the Asiatic Society, Letters*, XXI (No. 1). web http://www.ibiblio.org/radha/p_a026.htm

Banerji, Adris. 1945. Some sculptures from Rajghat, Benares. *The Journal of the Ganganatha Jha Research Institute*, 3 (1), Nov.: 1-9.

—— 1963. Eastern Expansion of the Ghadavla Kingdom. *Journal of the Asiatic Society*, 5 (3-4): 105-111.

Barker, R. 1777. An account of the Brahmin' Observatory at Benares. *Philosophical Transactions of the Royal Society of London*, vol. LXVII.

Barrett, Ronald L. 2005. Self-mortification and the stigma of leprosy in Northern India. *Medical Anthropological Quarterly* (American Anthropological Assoc.), 19 (2): 216-230. doi:10.1525/maq.2005.19.2.216.

Barrett, Ronald L. and Balaban, V. 2000. Fire and water: Holi in Banaras. *Emory Magazine*, 76 (4): 76-87.

Barrow, H.W. 1893. On Aghoris and Aghoripanthis. *Journal of the Anthropological Society of Bombay*, 3: 197-251.

Bäumer, Bettina 2001. Tântrik Pandits in Varanasi: a brief survey. In, Axel Michaels (ed.) *The Pandit. Traditional Scholarship in India.* (Festschrift Parameswara Aithal). Manohar Publ., New Delhi: 99-103.

Bautze, Joachim K. 2006. Examples of Unlicensed Copies and Versions of Views from Benares: T4cii- Authorship and Identification; in, Gaenszle, Martin and Gengnagel, Jörg, eds. *Visualised Space in Banaras.* (Heidelberg Studies in South Asian Rituals, Vol. 4). Harrassowitz Verlag, Wiesbaden: 213-232.

Bayly, Christopher A. 1978. Indian Merchants in a 'Traditional' Setting, Banaras 1780-1820; in, Hopkins, A. and Dewey, C. (eds.), *The Imperial Impact.* Athlone Press, London: 151-173.

—— 1981. From ritual to ceremony: death ritual and society in hindu north India since 1600; in, Whaley, Joachim (ed.) *Mirrors of Morality: Studies in the Social History of Death.* Europa, London.

—— 2000. Orientalists, Informants and the Critics in Banaras, 1790-1860; in, Malik, J. (ed.) *Perspectives on Mutual Encounters in South Asian History, 1760-1860.* E.J. Brill, Leiden.

Berwick, D. 1986. Benares: City of Light, Cityt of Dark; in his, *A Walk along the Ganges.* Century Hutchinson, London: pp. 120-121.

Bhatnagar, Tarun; Mishra, C.P., Mishra R.N. 2003. Drug prescription practices: a household study in rural Varanasi. *Indian Journal of Preventive & Social Medicine*, vol. 34 (No. 1 & 2), Jan.-June: 33-39.

Bhattacharyya, Raghunath 1986. Lokamata Maharani Bhavani. In, Singh, Ram Dular, ed. *Bengal and Varanasi.* Bibliographical Society of India, Varanasi: 1-19.

Bilas, Ram 1980. Ground water resources of Varanasi District, India: an assessment of condition, use and quality. *The National Geographical Journal of India* (NGSI, B.H.U., Varanasi. ISSN: 0027-9374/1980/0535), 26 (1-2): 81-93.

Bilas, Ram and Kayastha, S.L. 1983. Rural water supply and related problems in Varanasi District. *National Geographer* (Allahabad), vol. 18 (1): 77-86.

Bilas, Ram and Singh, Rana P.B. 1981. Rural water supply and the problem of health in village India: case of Varanasi District. *Geographia Medica* (Budapest), vol. 11: 65-85.

Bishnoi Indira and Singh, Vibha 2007. Awareness of DWCRA programme among rural women (Varanasi). *International Journal of Rural Studies* (IJRS, ISSN 1023–2001), vol. 14 (1), April: 1-5.

Bisschop, Peter C. 2002. On a quotation of the *Skandapurana* in the *Tirthavivecanakanda* of Lakshmidhara's *Krityakalpataru*. Study in the *Skandapurana* V. *Indo-Iranian Journal*, 45 (3): 231-243.

—— 2004. Siva's Ayatanas in the various recensions of the *Skandapurana* 167; in, Bakker, Hans T. (ed.) *Origin and Growth of the Puranic Text Corpus*. Motilal Banarasidass, New Delhi: 65-76.

Biswas, T.K. 2005. Vestiges of the Past; in, Michell, George and Singh, Rana P. B. (eds.) *Banaras, The City Revealed.* Marg Publs., Mumbai: 42-49.

Bloom, Shelah S.; Wypij, David and Das Gupta, Monica 2001. Dimensions of Women's Autonomy and the Influence on Maternal Health Care Utilization in a North Indian City (Varanasi). *Demography*, 38 (1), February: 67-78.

Bourne, Samuel 1976. "Many old photographs of Banaras"; in his, *The Last Empire. Photography in British India, 1855-1911*. Preface by The Earl Mountbatten of Burma with text by Clark Worswick and Ainslie Embrace. Gordon Fracer Gallery Ltd., London & Bedford. ISBN: 0-900406-74-7. [For Banaras, see pp. 62, 69, 111].

Brunton, Paul 1934/ 1999. The wonder-worker of Benares. Chapter 11, in his, *A Search in Secret India*, pp. 189-205. Srishtl Publisher & Distributor, New Delhi. ISBN: 81-87075-45-0. 3rd ed. 2003 by Rider, an imprint of Random House, London.

Burglund, Henrik 2000. Chapter 7: BJP in Varanasi, pp. 157-174. *Hindu Nationalism and Democracy. A Study of the Political Theory and Practice of Bhartiya Janta Party*. Dept. of Political Science, Stockholm University: Stockholm Studies in Politics, No. 73. ISBN:

91-7265-198-9. 210pp. (Published doctoral thesis; Supervisor: Prof. Björn Beckman, Dept. of Pol.Sc., Stockholm University, SE-10691 Stockholm).

Caracchi, P. 1983. La Râmlîlâ di Râmnagar (Benares): vitalità di una tradizionne. *Annali dell'Istituto Universitario Orientale di Napoli*, vol. 43: 109-134. (in Italian).

Carnegy, Patrick. 1876. The Bhars of Audh and Banáras. *The Journal of the Asiatic Society of Bengal*, 45 (1): 297-308.

Casolari, Marzia 2002. Role of Benares in constructing political Hindu identity. *Economic and Political Weekly* (a weekly from Sameeksha Trust Publication, Mumbai; http://www.epw.org.in), vol. XXXVII, No. 15, April 13-19: 1413-1420.

Chakraverty, Anjan 1999. Banaras lithographs: an art of the bourgeoisie. *Nandan* (Vishva Bharati, Santiniketan), 19: 38-49.

—— 2001. Gods and men, Demons and violence-Nineteenth century lithographs of Banaras. *Kala Dirgha* (Lucknow), No. 2, April: 39-43.

—— 2005. Siva in the nineteenth century Banaras lithographs; in, Das, Sadananda and Furlinger, Ernst (eds.) *Sâmrasya: Studies in Indian Art, Philosophy and Interreligious Dialogue*. D.K. Printworld (P) Ltd., New Delhi: 179-198.

Chalier-Visuvalingam, Elizabeth 1986/ 1993. Bhairav: Kotwal of Varanasi; in, Verma, T. P. et el., (eds.) 1986, *Varanasi Through the Ages*. Bhartiya Itihas Samkalan Samiti, UP, Varanasi: 241-260. Reprinted in, Singh, Rana P.B. (eds.) 1993, *Banaras/ Varanasi*. Tara Book Agency, Varanasi: 163 -177.

—— 1989. Bhairava's royal Brahmanicide: The problem of the Maha-brahmana; in, Hiltebeitel, Alf (ed.) *Criminal Gods and Demon Devotees*. State University of New York Press, Albany: 157-229.

—— 1994. Union and unity in Hindu Tantrism; in, Goodman, Hananya (ed.) *Between Jerusalem and Banaras*. SUNY Press, Albany.

Choudhary, Seema; Mishra, C.P. and Shukla, K.P. 2003. Nutritional status of adolescent girls in rural area of Varanasi. *Indian Journal of Preventive & Social Medicine*, vol. 34 (1 & 2), Jan.-June: 53-61.

Chaudhary, U.K.; Srivastava, N.K. and Mohan, D. 1998. Convex bank potential of river pollution management ('the Ganga river, Varanasi'); in, Sivakumar, M. (Siva) and Chowdhury, Robin N. (eds.) *Environmental Management*. Vol. 1 *Engineering the Water Environment and Geo-Environment*. [Proceedings of the 2nd International Conference on Environmental Management. ISBN: 0-08-042847-9]. Elsevier, Amsterdam and New York: pp. 609-619.

Ciotti, Manuela 2006. In the past we were a bit 'Chamar': education as a self- and community engineering process in northern India. *Journal of the Royal Anthropological Institute*, 12 (4): 899-916. doi: 10.1111/j.1467-9655.2006.00369.

—— 2007. Ethnohistories behind local and global bazaar: Chronicle of a Chamar weaving community in the Banaras region. *Contributions to Indian Sociology*, 41 (3): 321-354. DOI: 10.1177/006996670704100302.

Clémentin-Ojha, Catherine 2000. Être un brahmane smârta aujourd'hui. Quelques points de repère à partir d'une enquête ethnographique à Bénarès. *Bulletin de l'École française d'Extrême-Orient* 87: 317-339.

Cocari, Diane M. 1989a. Protection and identity: Banaras's Bir Babas as neighbourhood guardian deities; in, Freitag, S.B. (ed.) *Culture and Power in Banaras* (University of California Press, Berkeley): 130-146

—— 1989b. The Bir Babas of Banaras and the deified dead; in, Hiltebeitel, Alf (ed.) *Criminal Gods and Demon Devotees*. SUNY Press, Albany: 251-269. (Reprinted by Manohar, New Delhi, India).

Cohen, Lawrence 1995. Toward an Anthropology of Senility: Anger, Weakness and Alzheimer's in Banaras, India. *Medical Anthropology Quarterly*, 9 (3): 314-334.

—— 1995. The Pleasures of Castration: the Postoperative Status of Hijras, Jankhas, and Academics; in, Abramson, P. and Pinkerton, S. (eds.) *Sexual Nature, Sexual Culture*, pp. 276-304. Chicago: University of Chicago Press,

—— 1995. Holi in Banaras and the Mahaland of Modernity. *Global Learning Quarterly, GLQ*, 2 (3): 399-424.

Cohn, Bernard S. 1960. The initial British Impact on India, a case study of Banaras region. *Journal of Asian Studies* (Ann Arbor), 19 (4), August: 418-431.

———— S. 1961. From Indian status to British contact. *Journal of Economic History*, December: 613-627.

———— 1962 a. Political Systems in Eighteenth Century India: The Banaras Region. *Journal of the American Oriental Society*, 82 (no. 3), July-September: pp. 312-320. doi:10.2307/597642.

———— 1962 b. The British in Banaras: A Nineteenth century colonial Society. *Comparative Studies in Society and History*, 4 (no. 2), January.

———— 1964. The role of Gosains in the economy of eighteenth and nineteenth century upper India. *Indian Economic and Social History Review*, 1 (4): 175-182.

———— 1965. Anthropological Notes on law and disputes in North India. *American Anthropologist*, 67 (no. 6, pt. 2), December.

———— 1966. The Recruitment and Training of British civil servants in India, 1600-1860; in, Brabanti, Ralph (ed.) *Asian Bureaucratic Systems: Emergent from the British Imperial Tradition*. Duke University Press, Durham.

———— 1969. Structural change in Indian rural society, 1556-1885; in, Frakenberg, R.E. (ed.) *Land Control and Social Structure in Indian History* (University of Wisconsin Press, Madison).

———— 1987. Some Notes on Law and Change in North India; in his book, *An Anthropologist among the Historians and Other Essays*. Oxford University Press, New Delhi: 554-574. [First published in 1959].

Colebrooke, Edward 1887. Warren Hastings in Benares, 1781. *Asiatic Quarterly Review*, Ser. 1 (3), Oct.: 279-312.

Consolara, Alessandra 2000. I temple delle università 'nazionali' di Benares: un esempio di politicizzazione di simboli religiosi e letterari. *Culture*, 1: pp. 95-114. (in Italian).

Courtney, Sheleyah A. 2006. Creating a living goddess: Status, sacrality and urban contests of desire in Varanasi. *The Australian Journal of Anthropology* (ISSN: 1035-8811; AAS Sydney), 17 (2), August: 127-146.

2007. The Storm of Deepa's Water: From Violent Tempest in Varanasi to Glacial Account of Hindu Widowhood. <Film review article>. *The Australian Journal of Anthropology* (ISSN: 1035-8811; AAS Sydney), 18 (1), April: 115-120.

Daasmahapatra, S.K. 2007. Some French traveller's account of Varanasi (in relation to its remote past as a centre for dissemination of knowledge, ancient sciences & technologies). *Gavaksha.org* (a language, linguistic & culture e-journal), vol. 1 (1), September: 111-122.

Dalmia, Vasudha 1996. Sanskrit Scholars and Pandits of the Old School: The Banaras Sanskrit College and the Constitution of Authority in the Late Nineteenth Century. *Journal of Indian Philosophy*, 24 (4): 321-337. [Reprinted in: *Orienting India. European Knowledge Formation in the Eighteenth and Nineteenth Centuries. Three Essays*, New Delhi, 2003: 29-52.]

—— 2001. Vernacular histories in late 19th century Banaras: Folklore, Puranas and the New Antiquarianism. *The Indian Economic & Social History Review* (Sage, New Delhi), vol. 38 (1), January-March: pp. 59-79.

—— 2006. Visions of a New Banaras in the Early Twentieth Century; in, Gaenszle, Martin and Gengnagel, Jörg, eds. *Visualised Space in Banaras*. (Heidelberg Studies in South Asian Rituals, Vol. 4). Harrassowitz Verlag, Wiesbaden: 325-347.

Dar, Vrinda 2005. Threats and Prospects; in, Michell, George and Singh, Rana P.B. (eds.) *Banaras, The City Revealed*. Marg Publs., Mumbai: 138-143.

Das, Debadyuti; Mohapatra, Pratap K.J.; Sharma, Sushil Kumar, and Sarkar, Ashutosh 2007. Attractiveness of Varanasi as a tourist destination: perspective of foreign tourists. *International Journal of Tourism Policy* (IJTP), vol. 1 (2): 111-133.

Das, Devendra Nath 1887. Worship in Benares; in his, *Sketches of Hindoo Life*. Chapman and Hall, London: 1-16.

Derné, Steve 1992a. Beyond Institutional and Impulsive Conceptions of Self-. Family Structure and the Socially Anchored Real Self. *Ethos*, 20: 259-288.

—— 1992b. Commonsense Understandings as Cultural Constraint. *Contributions to Indian Sociology* (n.s.) 26: 195-221.

—— 1993. Equality and Hierarchy between Adult Brothers: Culture and Sibling Relations in North Indian Urban Joint Families; in, Nuckolls, Charles ed. *Siblings in South Asia: Brothers and Sisters in Cultural Context.* Guilford, New York: 165-189.

—— 1994a. Hindu Men Talk about Controlling Women: Cultural Ideas as a Tool of the Powerful. *Sociological Perspectives*, 37: 203-227.

—— 1994b. Arranging Marriages: How Fathers' Concerns Limit Women's Educational Achievements; in Mukhopadhyay, Carol Chapnick and Seymour, Susan eds. *Women, Education and Family Structure in India.* Westview Press, Boulder CO: 83-102

—— 1995. Structural Realities, Persistent Dilemmas, and the Construction of Emotional Paradigms: Love in Three Cultures; in, Wentworth, William and Ryan, John eds. *Social Perspectives on Emotion*; vol. 2. JAI Press, Greenwich, CT.

—— 1998. Feeling Water: Notes on the sensory Construction of Time and Space in Banaras. *Man in India*, 78 (1-2), May-June: 1-7.

Devi, R. 1975. Bihar's response to the rising of Chait Singh of Banaras. *Journal of the Bihar and Orissa Research Society*, 61,1/4 (Jan.-Dec.1975): 123-130.

Dodson, Michael S. 2002. Re-Presented for the Pandits: James Ballantyne, 'Useful Knowledge', and Sanskrit Scholarship in Benares College during the Mid-Nineteenth Century. *Modern Asian Studies* (Cambridge University Press), 36: 257-298. doi:10.1017/ S0026749X02002019.

—— 2005. Translating Science, Translating Empire: the power of language in Colonial North India. *Comparative Studies in Society and History*, 47 (4): 809-835.

—— 2007. Contesting Translations: Orientalism and the interpretation of the Vedas. *Modern Intellectual History* (ISSN: 1479-2443; EISSN: 1479-2451. Cambridge University Press), vol. 4 (1): 43-59. doi: 10.1017/S147924430600103X.

Doharey R.K.; Sujan, D.K. and Mishra S.K. 2002. Awareness of environmental pollution among the rural and urban school children in Varanasi district. *Progressive Agriculture*, 2 (1): 49-53 [8 Ref].

Doron, Assa 2005. Encountering the 'Other': Pilgrims, Tourists and Boatmen in the City of Varanasi. *The Australian Journal of Anthropology*, 16 (no. 2): 157-178.

—— 2006. The Needle and the Sword: Boatmen, Priests and the Ritual Economy of Varanasi. *South Asia: The Journal of South Asian Studies*, N.S. (Routledge Taylor & Francis, London; ISSN 0085-6401), vol 29 (no. 3), December: 345-367. DOI: 10.1080/00856400601031955.

—— 2008. Ferrying the Gods: the Narrative and Practice of Devotion in the sacred City of Banaras. *Sites: a Journal of Social Anthropology and Cultural Studies*, 5 (2).

Doytchinov, Grigor and Hohmann, Hasso 2004. Zussammenabeit Graz-Benares. Das Kulturerbe der Stadt Varanasi (Benares) in Indien. *Magazin ISG* (Internationales Städteforum Graz; Forum der historischen Städte und Gemeinden; Hauptplatz 3, A-8010 Graz, Austria), 4 (December): 2-7. [in German, and summary in English].

Dube, Kamla Kant 1968. Tourism and pilgrimage in Varanasi. *The National Geographical Journal of India* (NGSI, B.H.U., Varanasi. ISSN: 0027-9374/1968/0265), 14 (pts. 2-3): 176-185.

—— 1994. Urban sprawl of Varanasi: Problems and planning; in, Singh, H. H., et al. (eds.) *Patterns of Urban Change in India*. Indrasini Devi Publs., Varanasi: 215-222.

Dube, Kamla Kant and Dwivedi, Jyotsana 1994. Characteristics of Rural-Urban fringe in Indian Cities: A case study of Varanasi; in, Singh, H.H. et al. (eds.) *Patterns of Urban Change in India*. Indrasini Devi Publs., Varanasi: 183-199.

Dubey, Devi Prasad 1985/ 1993. Varanasi: A name study. *Archiv Orientalni* (Academia, Praha), 53 (4): 347-354. Revised and expanded version published in, Singh, Rana P.B., ed. 1993, *Banaras/Varanasi* (Tara Book Agency, Varanasi): 29-36.

DuBois, Emily 1986. Banaras Brocade Weaving. *Art Textrina*, 3 (May). Charles Babbage Research Centre, Winnipeg, Canada.

Dwivedi, Prem Shankar 2005. The Mahamaya Temple Murals; in, *Banaras, The City Revealed*; eds. George Michell and Rana P.B. Singh. Marg Publs., Mumbai: 98-105.

Eck, Diana L. 1978. Kasi. City and Symbol. *Purana* (Varanasi), 20 (2): 169-192.

—— 1980. A Survey of Sanskrit Sources for the Study of Varanasi. *Purana* (Varanasi) 22 (1): 81-110. Reprinted in: Singh, Rana P.B. eds. 1993, *Banaras/ Varanasi* (Tara Book Ag., Varanasi): 9-19.

—— 1985. Banaras: Cosmos and paradise in the Hindu imagination. *Contributions to Indian Sociology*, NS (New Delhi), 19 (1): 41-55.

—— 1993. Kashi, the Luminous. *Parabola*, vol. XVIII (4), Winter: 26-29.

—— 1998. The imagined landscape: patterns in the construction of Hindu sacred geography. *Contributions to Indian Sociology* (Sage Publs., New Delhi), 32 (2): 165-188. doi: 10.1177/006996679803200202.

Eidt, Robert C. 1977. Detection and examination of anthroposols by phosphate analysis. *Science*, 197 (30 September): pp. 1327-1333.

Feys, J. 1984a. Exploring Kashi. *Sevartham*, 9: 79-98.

—— 1984b. Banaras, City of Light: Review article. *Sevartham*, 9: 127-141.

Forrest, G.W. 1999. 'Benares', Chapter XI, in his book, *Cities of India, Past and Present*. English Edition Publ. & Dist., Mumbai (originally: A. Constable & Co. Ltd, Westminster): 249-270.

Freitag, Sandria B. 1980. Sacred symbols as mobilising ideology: the North Indian search for a 'Hindu' community. *Comparative Studies in Society and History*, 22 (4): 597-625.

—— 1989a. State and community: Symbolic popular protest in Banaras's public arenas. In, Freitag, S.B., ed. *Culture and Power in Banaras* (University of California Press, Berkeley): 203-228.

—— 1989b. Community and state in public arenas: the Banaras example. In, Freitag, S. B. *Collective Action and Community: Public arenas and the emergence of communalism in north India* (University of California Press, Berkeley), Chapter 2: pp. 19-52.

——— 2005. Power and Patronage: Banaras in the 18ᵗʰ and 19ᵗʰ centuries; in, *Banaras, The City Revealed*; eds. George Michell and Rana P.B. Singh. Marg Publs., Mumbai: 30-41.

——— 2006. Visualizing Cities by Modern Citizens: Banaras Compared to Jaipur and Lucknow; in, Gaenszle, Martin and Gengnagel, Jörg, eds. *Visualised Space in Banaras.* (Heidelberg Studies in South Asian Rituals, Vol. 4). Harrassowitz Verlag, Wiesbaden: 233-251.

Fukunaga, Masaaki 1991. A note on the understanding sacralisation as spirit of place in Varanasi. *National Geographical Journal of India,* vol. 37 (1-2): 173-177.

Gaenszle, Martin and Gengnagel, Jörg 2006. Introduction: Visualizing Space in Banaras; in, Gaenszle, Martin and Gengnagel, Jörg, eds. *Visualised Space in Banaras: Images, Maps, and the Practice of Representations.* (Ethno-Indolgoy: Heidelberg Studies in South Asian Rituals, Vol. 4). Harrassowitz Verlag, Wiesbaden: 7-20.

Gaenszle, Martin (with Sharma, Nutan Dhar). 2002. Nepali Kings and Kâshî: On the Changing Significance of a Sacred Centre. *Studies in Nepali History and Society,* vol. 7, (1): 1-33.

——— (with Sharma, Nutan Dhar) 2006. Nepali Places: Appropriations of Space in Banaras; in, Gaenszle, Martin and Gengnagel, Jörg, eds. *Visualised Space in Banaras.* (Heidelberg Studies in South Asian Rituals, Vol. 4). Harrassowitz Verlag, Wiesbaden: 303-323.

Gengnagel, Jörg 2000. Visualisierung religiöser Räume. Zur Kartographie von Benares. In: Pezzoli-Olgiati, Daria & Stolz, F. (eds.) *Religiöse Kartographie, Cartographie religieuse. Organisation, Darstellung und Symbolik des Raumes in religiösen Symbolsystemen.* Peter Lang, Bern: 217-234. (In German)

——— 2003. Mapping sacred spaces: Aspects of cartography in the 19ᵗʰ century Benares. In, *Creating and Representing Sacred Spaces,* eds. Michael Dickhardt and Vera Dorofeeva-Lichtmann. Göttinger Beiträge zur Asienforschung (Heft 2-3, 2003, special double number, ISSN 1618-310X). Peust & Gutschmidt, Göttingen: 247-263 (3 colour maps).

——— 2005 a. *Kâshîkhandokta*: On texts and processions in Varanasi. In: Gengnagel, Jörg & Srilata Raman & Ute Hüsken (eds.) *Words and*

Deeds. Hindu and Buddhist Rituals in South Asia. Wiesbaden, Harrassowitz (Ethno-Indology. Heidelberg Studies in South Asian Rituals 1): 65-89.

—— 2005 b. Wenn Pilger vom rechten weg abkommen: Ein Fallbeispiel aus Benares (Nordindien). In, *Die Welt der Rituale. Von der Antike bis heute*; (hrsg.) Claus Ambos, Stephan Hotz, Gerald Schwedler, und Stefan weinfurter. Wissenschaftliche Buchgesellschaft, Berlin: pp. 121-128. [in German].

—— 2006. Maps and Processions in Banaras: The Debate Concerning the Panchakroshiyatra; in, Gaenszle, Martin and Gengnagel, Jörg, eds. *Visualised Space in Banaras.* (Heidelberg Studies in South Asian Rituals, Vol. 4). Harrassowitz Verlag, Wiesbaden: 145-163.

Gesler, Wilbert M. and Pierce, Margaret 2000. Hindu Varanasi. *Geographical Review* (AGS, New York), vol. 90 (2), April: pp. 222-237.

Gitlin, Todd 2004. A skull in Varanasi, a head in Baghdad. *American Scholar* (Washington DC), 73 (4. Autumn), September: 61-64. Reprinted in, Zeleski, Philip (ed.) 2005, *The Best American Spiritual Writing.* Houghton Mifflin, New York: 74-78. Also, web: http://www.toddgitlin.net/articles/varanasi.html

Gopalkrishnan, K. 1985. The Ganga: India's poisonous pilgrimage. *Hindustan Times, Earthscan Bulletin*, 8 (no. 4): 3-4.

Gupta, A.K. 2003. Role of pollutants and corridor vegetation in composting at Varuna river corridor. *Nature Env. Polln. Techno.*, 2 (3): 317-321 [16 Ref].

Gupta, Charu 2001. Mapping the Mother Nation: The Bharat Mata temple at Banaras; in, Gupta, Charu, *Sexuality, Obscenity and Community: Women, Muslims and the Hindu Public in Colonial India* (Permanent Black, Delhi): 198-203.

Gupta, Nirmala 2006-07. Dara Shukoh and theologians of Benaras. *Prajñâ* (Banaras Hindu University magazine), vol. 52 (1 2), spec. vol. "Kashi Gaurav Visheshank", vol. I: 305-324.

Gupta, Roxane P. 1995. the Kina Rami: Aughars and Kings in the age of cultural conflict; in, *Bhakti Religion in North India*, ed. D. N. Lorensen. SUNY Press, Albany: 133-142.

Gupta, V.M.; Jain R. and Sen, P. 2001. Study of interspouse communication and adoption of family planning and immunization services
in a rural block of Varanasi district. *Indian Journal of Public Health*,
45(4): 110-115.

Gustafsson, Gerhard; Singh, Rana P.B.; Lejonhud, K. & Vålvik, K.I.
2000. Change and continuity in village India: crisis and prospects
in Chamaon, Varanasi. *FENNIA, International Jl. of Geography*
(Geogr. Soc. of Finland, Helsinki). Vol. 178 (No.2): 203-214.

Gutschow, Niels 1977a. Urban space and ritual. *Storia della Citta* (Rivista
Internazionale di storia urbana e territoriale), Electa Editrice (Roma),
5: 73-75.

—— 1977b. *Benares. Geoordneter Raum-Ordered Space.* Darmastadt
im Mai: 47-73 (and 13pp. of figures and plates). Mimeographed.

—— 1994. Varanasi/Benares: the centre of Hinduism. *Erdkunde, Archiv
für Wissenschaftliche Geographie* (Berlin), Bd. 48 (3), September:
194- 209.

—— 2005. The Panchakroshi Temple; in, *Banaras, The City Revealed*;
eds. George Michell and Rana P. B. Singh. Marg Publs., Mumbai:
92-97.

—— 2006. Panoramas of Banaras; in, Gaenszle, Martin and Gengnagel,
Jörg, eds. *Visualised Space in Banaras*. (Heidelberg Studies in South
Asian Rituals, Vol. 4). Harrassowitz Verlag, Wiesbaden: 191-211.

Hegewald, Julia A.B. 2005. Ghats and Riverside Palaces; in, Michell,
George and Singh, Rana P.B. (eds.) *Banaras, The City Revealed*.
Marg Publs., Mumbai: 66-77.

Hamner, Steve; Tripathi, Anshuman; Mishra, Rajesh Kumar; Bouskill,
Nik; Broadaway, Susan C.; Pyle, Barry H., and Ford Timothy E.
2006. The role of water use patterns and sewage pollution in
incidence of water-borne/enteric diseases along the Ganges river
in Varanasi, India. *International Journal of Environmental Health
Research*, 16 (2), April: 113-132. doi: 10.1080/09603120500538226.

Hansen, Kathryn 1983a. Sultana the Decoit and the Harishchandra: Two
popular dramas of the Nautanki tradition of North India. *Modern
Asian Studies*, 17 (2): 313-331.

—— 1983b. Indian Folk Traditions and the Modern Theatre. *Asian Folklore Studies*, vol. 42 (1): 77–89.

—— 1986. Nautanki Chapbooks: Written Traditions of a Folk Form. *India Magazine*, January: pp. 65–72.

—— 1989. The birth of Hindi drama in Banaras, 1868-1885; in, Freitag, S. B. (ed.) *Culture and Power in Banaras* (University of California Press, Berkeley): 62-92.

Harrison, Barbara Grizzuti 1993. Shiva's Holy City. *New York Times Magazine*, May 16: pp. 85-93.

Heiderer, Tony 1990. Sacred Space, Sacred Time. *National Geographic*, May: pp. 106-116.

Hein, Norvin 1959. The Ram Lila. In, Singer, Milton, ed. *Traditional India, Structure and Change*. The American Folklore Society, Philadelphia.

Heitler, R. 1972. The Varanasi house tax hartal of 1810-1811. *Indian Economic and Social History Review* (New Delhi), 9: 239-257.

Hertz, Frederick 1991. Banaras: Pilgrimage places and the transformation of death. *Site Saver* (The Newsletter of Sacred Sites International Foundation, Berkeley, CA, USA), 1 (3), Summer: 1, 3.

Hess, Linda 1983. Rama Lila: the audience experience. In, Thiel-Horstmann, Monika, ed. *Bhakti in Current Research*. Dietrich Reimer, Berlin: 171-194.

—— 1993. Staring at frames till they turn into loops: an excursion through some worlds of Tulasidas. In, Hertel, Bradley and Humes, Cynthia, eds. *Living Banaras*. SUNY Press, Albany: 73-102.

Hohmann, Hasso, et. al. (eds.) 2006. Special issue on Heritage & Culture of Varanasi. *ISG Magazin* (Internationales Städteforum Graz. Forum der historischen Städte und Gemeinden, Graz, Austria; eds. 4 (December): 1-16. [7 maps, 24 colour photos].

Hollick, Julian C. and Tomalin, Emma 2002. Making a Radio Documentary on the River Ganges. *Contemporary South Asia*, 11 (2), July.

Horne, Charles. 1873. Notes on the age of the ruins chiefly situated at Banáras and Jaunpúr. *The Journal of the Asiatic Society of Bengal*, 42 (1): 160-164.

Housden, Roger 1996. Sacred City: Banaras; in, Housden, Roger: *Travels through Sacred India*. Thorsons, An imprint of HarperCollins Publ., San Francisco: 118-136.

Huberman, Jenny 2005. 'Consuming Children': Reading the impacts of tourism in the city of Banaras. *Childhood, A Global Journal of Child Research* (Sage, London), 12 (2), May: 161-176. DOI: 10.1177/0907568205051902.

——— 2006. Shopping for People, or Shopping for People?: Deciphering the Object of Consumption among Tourists in Banaras; in, Cook, Daniel Thomas (ed.) *Dramaturgies of Value in Market Places*. Palgrave Macmillan, New York: 50-68

——— 2008. Deciphering the Object of Consumption Among Tourists in Banaras; in, Trentmann, Frank and Cook, Daniel T. (eds.) *Lived Experiences of Public Consumption: Studies of Culture and Value in International Market Places*. Palgrave Macmillan, New York.

Humes, Cynthia Ann 1993. The goddess of the Vindhyas in Banaras. In, Hertel, Bradley and Humes, Cynthia, eds. *Living Banaras*. SUNY Press, Albany: 181-204.

Irwin, John 1983. The Lat Bhairo at Benares (Varanasi): Another Pre-Ashokan Monument?. *Zeitschrift der Deutschen Morgenländischen Gesellschaft* (Wiesbaden), 133 (3): 321-352.

——— 1984. The Lat Bhairo of Benares: another pre-Ashokan monument; in, Bridget Allchin, ed., *South Asian Archaeology* 1981 (Cambridge University Press, Cambridge): pp. 225-30.

Jain, Sudarshan Lal 2004. Jain Parva and Festivals of Kashi. *Fairs and Festivals of Kashi, Seminar Proceedings*, 1-3 August 2003, eds. R.C. Sharma, et al. Jnana Pravaha, Varanasi: 53-58.

Jayakar, Pupul 1967. Naksha Bandhas of Banaras. *Journal of Asian Trade History*, No. 7: 22.

Jayapal, Pramila 2000. Life and death in Varanasi. In, her *Pilgrimage. On Women's Return to a Changing India*. Seal Press, Seattle WA: pp. 129-142.

Jayaswal, Vidula 2000-02. Aktha: a satellite settlement of Sarnath, Varanasi (Report on the excavations conducted in the year 2002).

Bharati (*Bulletin of the Dept. of A.I.H.C. & Archaeology, Banaras Hindu University, Varanasi*), 26: 61-180 (figures 32, and b & w plates 16).

—— 2008a. Settlement pattern of ancient Varanasi, with special reference to non-urban sites; in, Paddaiya, K. (ed.) *Proceedings of the Centenary Celebration of Prof. H.D. Sankalia*. (Organised by the Deccan College, Pune: 10-12 December 2007). Deccan College, Pune.

—— 2008b. Urban and non-urban cultural levels of Varanasi, as revealed by the archaeological findings; in, Ray, Ranjana (ed.) *Proceedings, International Seminar on Biological and Cultural Diversity in South Southeast Asia and the Development Consequences*: 21-23 November 2007. Asiatic Society, Kolkata.

Jayaswal, Vidula and Kumar, Manoj 2005-06. excavations at Ramnagar discovery of a supporting settlement of ancient Varanasi. *Puratatva* (*Bulletin of the Indian Archaeological Society*, New Delhi), 36: 85-92.

Jha, Magna Nand 1974. Sacred performances at Kashi. *Journal of Social Research* (Ranchi), 17 (no. 1): 23-28.

Joshi, M.N. 1983. James Prinsep on temple architecture; in, K.V. Raman et al. (eds.) *Srinidhih: Perspective in Indian Archaeology, Art and Culture*. Madras: 423-429.

Joshi, Nilakanth Purushottam 1989. Varanasi Shilapattas and similar slabs in medieval sculptures of Central India, a preliminary study. *Samskrit Sandhan* (Journal of the National Institute of Human Culture, Varanasi), vol. 2: 143-159.

—— 1990. Varanasi-Silapatts, a unique depiction of Varanasi in sculpture". In, Chitta Prasad Sinha, (ed.) *Archaeology and Art*, Vol. 2, Delhi: 390-394.

—— 1992. Devapattas: a less known chapter of medieval Hindu iconography; in, Maxwell, T.S. (ed.) *Eastern Approaches. Essays on Asian Art and Archaeology*. Oxford University Press, Delhi: 133-140 + plates 46-50.

—— 2000. Varanasi Citrapati: A painted scroll. *Samskrit Sandhan, Journal of the National Research Institute of Human Culture* (Varanasi), vol. XIII: pp. 92-99.

Justice, Christopher 1995. The 'natural' death while not eating: a type of palliative care in Banaras, India. *Journal of Palliat Care*, 11 (1), Spring: 38-42.

Kane, Pandurang Vaman 1974. *Kashi*. Chapter 13, in *History of Dharmashastra*, vol. 3, 2nd ed. Oriental Series B, no. 6. Bhandarkar Oriental Research Institute, Poona.

Kapur, Anuradha 1985. Actors, pilgrims, kings and gods: the Ramalila at Ramanagar. *Contributions to Indian sociology, NS* (New Delhi), 19 (1): 57-74.

—— 1991. Râjâ and Prâjâ: Presentational Conventions in the Râmlilâ at Râmnagar. In, Thiel-Horstmann, M. (ed.) *Râmâyana and Râmâyanas*. Harrasowitz, Wiesbaden: 153-68.

Kaushik, Meena 1976/ 1993. The symbolic representation of death. *Contributions to Indian sociology, NS* (New Delhi), 10 (2): 265-292. Reprinted in, Singh, Rana P.B. 1993, (ed.), *Banâras (Varanasi): Cosmic Order, Sacred City, and Hindu Traditions*. Tara Book Agency, Varanasi: 123-139.

Kaul, Ashok Kumar 2004-2005. Power behind the frame: Ensemble of essences. *Gandhian Perspectives, An Interdisciplinary Journal of Social Sciences* (Gandhian Institute of Studies, Varanasi), vol. XX No. 2 July-Dec. 2004 & vol. XIII No. 1 Jan.-June 2005: 141-152.

Kay, W. 1853. The Benares College. *The Missionary*, 3 (9), Sept: 236-246.

Kayastha, S.L. and Prasad, N. 1957. True azimuth and distance of world capitals from Varanasi. *The National Geographical Journal of India* (NGSI, B.H.U.Varanasi. ISSN: 0027-9374/1957/0036), 23 (pts.3-4): 11-14.

Kayastha, S.L. and Singh, S.N. 1977. A study of preferences and behaviour pattern of tourists in Varanasi. *The National Geographical Journal of India* (NGSI, B.H.U.Varanasi. ISSN: 0027-9374/1977/ 0454), 23 (pts.3-4): 143-150.

—— 1983. Tourism in Varanasi: a functional analysis. *The National Geographical Journal of India* (NGSI, B.H.U.Varanasi. ISSN: 0027-9374/1983/0590), 29 (pts. 1-2): 4-17.

Keul, István 1998. Ein Gott macht Karriere. Hanumanverehrung in Benares. *Zeitschrift für Religionswissenschaft*, 6: 23-45. [in German].

Khanna, Madhu 2002. Representing Banaras, Living, Dying and Transformation: the Crossing Project. *Evam* (Samvad India foundation, New Delhi), vol. 1 (1 & 2): 57-72.

King, Christopher R. 1989. Forming a new linguistic identity: the Hindi movement in Banaras, 1868-1914; in, Freitag, S.B. (ed.) *Culture and Power in Banaras* (University of California Press, Berkeley): 179-202.

—— 1994/ 1999. The Hindi-Nagari movement; in his, *One Language Two Scripts. The Hindu Movement in Nineteenth Century North India*. Oxford University Press, New Delhi: pp. 126-172.

Kittoe, M. 1852. Memo on some ancient gold coins found near Benares, in 1851, and submitted by the Government of India for the inspection of the members of the Asiatic Society. *The Journal of the Asiatic Society of Bengal*, 21: 390-400.

Köckman, Uwe 1993. The Role of Educational Institutions in the Awakening of Hindu Nationalism in 19th Century Varanasi; in, Singh, Rana P.B. (ed.), *Banâras (Varanasi): Cosmic Order, Sacred City, and Hindu Traditions*. Tara Book Agency, Varanasi: 289-296.

Kremmer, Christopher 2007. Swimming in Varanasi; in his, *Inhaling the Mahatma*. Harpercollins Publ. India and India Today, New Delhi: 348-378.

Krishan, Y. 1992. A new interpretation of "Pañca-Ganesha" sculptures. *Artibus Asiae*, 52, (no. 1-2): 47-53.

Krishna, Anand 1982. The Gupta style of sculpture from the city of Banaras; in, Baümer, Bettina (ed.) *Rupa Pratirupa (Alice Bonner Commemoration Volume)*. Biblia Impex Pvt. Ltd., New Delhi: pp. 87-98.

—— 1995. Company painting at Banaras court; in, Goswamy, B.N. (ed.) *Indian Painting-Essays in honour of K.J. Khandalavala*. New Delhi: 245.

—— 2007. Banaras: a Brief Cultural History; in Gupta, R.C., et al. (eds.) *Souvenir. Third International BHU Alumni Meet, & International*

Seminar on Education in the 21st Century and Mahamana's Vision, 6-7 January 2007. BHU in association with Mahamana Malviya Mission, Varanasi: 70-76. [Originally distributed as mimeographed copies on 17 July 1978].

Krishna Menon, A.G. 1989. Cultural identity and urban development: The Indian experience. *Urban India* (NIUA, New Delhi), 9 (1): 1-15.

Kumar, Lalit 1990-91. Some unpublished post-Gupta sculptures from Banaras c.600 - 650 A.D. *Pragdhara. Journal of the U.P. State Archaeological Org.* (Lucknow), vol. 1 (no.1): pp. 127-129 + 1 plate.

Kumar, Nita 1987. The Mazars of Banaras: a new perspective on the city's sacred geography. *The National Geographical Journal of India* (NGSI, B.H.U., Varanasi. ISSN: 0027-9374/1987/0735), 33 (3): 263-267.

—— 1986. Open space and free time: Pleasure for the people of Banaras. *Contributions to Indian Sociology, NS* (Sage, New Delhi), 20 (1): 41-60. doi: 10.1177/006996686020001003.

—— 1989. Work and leisure in the formation of identity: Muslim weavers in a Hindu city. In, Freitag, S. B., ed. *Culture and Power in Banaras* (University of California Press, Berkeley): 147-170.

—— 1991. Widow, education and social change in twentieth century Banaras. *Economic and Political Weekly*, 26. 17 (27 April): WS-19-25.

—— 1993. Patronage, identity and cultural change: Five Melas of Banaras. In, Singh, Rana P.B., ed. *Banaras/ Varanasi*. Tara Book Agency, Varanasi: 225-233.

—— 1995. The many faces of the Modern in Banaras; in, Preben Kaarsholm, ed. *From Post-Traditional to Post-Modern? Interpreting the meaning of Modernity in Third World Urban Societies.* International Developmental Studies, Occassional Paper no. 14, Roskilde University: pp. 160-176.

—— 1998. Sanskrit Pandits and modernisation of Sanskrit Education in the Nineteenth and Twentieth centuries; in, Radice, William (ed.) *Swami Vivekananda and the Modernisation of Hinduism* (Oxford University Press, Delhi): 36-60.

—— 2003. The Ganga at Banaras; in, Baviskar, Amita (ed.) *Waterlines*. (The Penguin Book of River Writings). Penguin Books India, New Delhi: pp. 111-123.

—— 2002. History and the Nation: the learning of history in Calcutta and Banaras; reprinted in Kumar, Nita (2007) *The Politics of Gender, Community, and Modernity. Essays on Education in India.* Oxford University Press, New Delhi: 49-70.

—— 2003. Making the Nation: Ansari women in Banaras; reprinted in Kumar, Nita (2007) *The Politics of Gender, Community, and Modernity. Essays on Education in India.* Oxford University Press, New Delhi: 171-178.

—— 2006. The Space of the Child: The Nation, the Neighbourhood, and the Home; in, Gaenszle, Martin and Gengnagel, Jörg, eds. *Visualised Space in Banaras.* (Heidelberg Studies in South Asian Rituals, Vol. 4). Harrassowitz Verlag, Wiesbaden: 255-278. Reprinted in Kumar, Nita (2007) *The Politics of Gender, Community, and Modernity. Essays on Education in India.* Oxford University Press, New Delhi: 238-264.

Kumar, R.; Pai, K.; Kumar, P.; Pandey, H.P. and S. Sundar 2006. Sero-epidemiological study of kala-azar in a village of Varanasi district, India. *Tropical Medicine and International Health*, 11 (1), January: 41- 48. doi:10.1111/j.1365-3156.2005.01538.x

Kumar, R.; Kumar, P.; Chowdhary, R.K., et al. 1999. Kala-azar epidemic in Varanasi district, India. *Bulletin of the World Health Organization* (WHO, Geneva), 77: 371–374.

Kumar, S. Vijaya 1983. Kashi: Its meaning and significance in the light of Advaita-Vedanta and the Purana. *Purana* (Ramanagar Durg, Varanasi), 25 (1): 114-128.

Kumra, V.K. 1995. Water quality in the river Ganges; in, *Water and the Quest for Sustainable Development in the Ganges Valley*, eds. Graham Chapman and M. Thompson. Mansell, London & New York: 130-140.

Kumra, V.K. and Singh, B.L. 2001. A study of slum environment in Varanasi; in, Nag, P.; Kumar C.S. and Sengupta, S. (eds.) *Environment, Population and Development.* Concept Publ. Co., New Delhi: 264-274.

LaDousa, Chaise 2002. Advertising in the periphery: Languages and schools in a North Indian city. *Language in Society* (Cambridge University Press), 31 (2), April: 213-242. doi:10.1017/S0047404501020164.

───── 2004. In the mouth but not on the map. Visions of language and their enactment in the Hindi Belt. *Journal of Pragmatics* (Elsevier, New York), 36 (4), April: 633-661. doi:10.1016/S0378-2166(03)00089-4

───── 2005. Disparate markets: Language, nation, and education in North India. *American Ethnologist* (American Anthropological Assoc. ISSN: 0094-0496), 32 (3), August: 460-478. doi:10.1525/ae.2005.32.3.460.

───── 2006. The Discursive Malleability of an Identity: A Dialogic Approach to Language "Medium" Schooling in North India. *Journal of Linguistic Anthropology* (American Anthropological Assoc. ISSN: 1055-1360), 16 (1), June: 36-57. doi:10.1525/jlin.2006.16.1.036.

───── 2007. Of Nation and State: Language, School, and the Reproduction of Disparity in a North Indian City. *Anthropological Quarterly*, 80 (4): 925-959. doi: 10.1353/anq.2007.0066.

Laidlaw, James 1996. The Uses and Abuses of Theology: Comments on Jonathan Parry's Death in Banaras. Review Article. *South Asia Research*, 16 (1): 31-44.

Lannoy, Richard 2002. Benares as Tirtha. *IIC Quarterly* (India International Centre, New Delhi), 28 (Winter 2002, Spring 2002): 376-386.

Lee, Christopher R. 2000. 'Hit it with a stick and it won't die': Urdu Language, Muslim Identity and Poetry in Varanasi, India. *The Annual of Urdu Studies* (University of Wisconsin, Madison), 15 (1): 337-351.

───── 2005. Adab and Banarsipan: Embodying Community among Muslim Artisans in Varanasi, India. *Comparative Islamic Studies* [Print ISSN: 1740-7125; Electronic ISSN: 1743-1638, Equinox Publishing], vol. 1 (2), December: 177-196.

Lodrick, Deryck O. 1979/ 1993. On religion and milk bovines in an urban Indian setting. *Current Anthropology* (Chicago), (20) 1: 241-242. Reprinted in Singh, Rana P.B. (ed.) 1993, *Banaras/ Varanasi* (Tara Book Agency, Varanasi): 225-233.

London, Christopher W. 2005. Churches and Civic Monuments: The British Contribution; in, *Banaras, The City Revealed*; eds. George Michell and Rana P.B. Singh. Marg Publs., Mumbai: 126-137.

Lorenzen, David N. 1978. Warrior Ascetics in Indian History. *Journal of the American Oriental Society*, 98 (1): 61-75.

—— 2006. Marco della Tomba and the Brahmin from Banaras: Missionaries, Orientalists, and Indian Scholars. *The Journal of Asian Studies* (AAS, Cambridge University Press), 65 (1): 115-143. doi:10.1017/S0021911806000088.

Lutgendorf, Philip 1989a. Rama's Story in Shiva's City: Public Arenas and Private Patronage; in, Freitag, S.B. (ed.) *Culture and Power in Banaras* (University of Caifornia Press, Berkeley): 34-61.

—— 1989b. The View from the Ghats: Traditional Exegesis of a Hindu Epic. *Journal of Asian Studies* (Ann Arbor), 48 (2): 272-288.

Lütt, Jürgen 1976. The movement for the foundation of the Banaras Hindu University; in, *German Scholars on India: Contributions to Indian Studies*, ed. The Embassy of the FRG, New Delhi. Vol. 2. Nachiketa Publs., Bombay: 160-195.

Macleod, Norman 1870. Benares; in his, *Days in North India*. J.B. Lippincott, Philadelphia: 9-43.

Malik, Dipak 1996. Three riots in Varanasi: 1989-1990, 1991 and 1992; in, Bidwai, P.; Mukhia, H. and Vanaik, A. (eds.) *Religion, Religiosity and Communication*. Manohar Publ. & Distr., New Delhi: 157-166.

Malville, John M. 2004. The geometry of self-organised system: From chaos to Pilgrimage; in, Khanna, Madhu (ed.) *ºita: The Cosmic Order*. D.K. Printworld, New Delhi for the IGNCA, New Delhi: pp. 175-210.

Malville, John M. and Singh Rana P.B. 1995. Visual Astronomy in the mythology and ritual of India: the Sun temples of Varanasi. *Vistas in Astronomy* (Pergamon, Oxford, UK), Vol. 39 (4): pp. 431-449.

—— 2000. The Sun and its temples at Varanasi: Meaning and pattern in the three worlds of Kashi; in, Malville, J.M. and Gujaral, L. (eds.) *Ancient Cities, Ancient Skies.* Aryan Publs., New Delhi *for* IGNCA: pp. 81-98.

—— 2004. Pilgrims to Kashi: Self-Organized Patterns in Space and Time; in, Choudhary, P.K. (ed.) *Sociology of Pilgrims.* Kalpaz Publs., Delhi: pp. 163-176.

Marcus, Scott L. 1989. The rise of a folk music genre: Birha; in, Freitag, S.B. (ed.) *Culture and Power in Banaras* (University of California Press, Berkeley): 93-113.

Marriott, McKim 1996. Wai, a Southern Benares. Paper presented at the *14th European Modern South Asian Conference,* August 21-24, Copenhagen University, Denmark.

McGregor, Stuart 2001. On the Evolution of Hindi as a Language of Literature. *South Asia Research (Sage Journals, London)* 21: 203-217

Mecking, Ludwig 1913. Benares, ein kulturgeographisches Charakter-bild. *Geographische Zeitschrift* (Leipzing; A. Hettner, ed.) 19: 20-35 und 77-96. [in German].

Menon, R. 1983. Widows of Varanasi. *India Today* (a weekly from New Delhi), 15 February: 80-86.

Michaels, Axel 2000. Konstruktionen von Translokalität und Zentralität. Eine religiöse Karte von Benares; in, Pezzoli-Olgiati, Daria & Stolz, F. (eds.), *Cartografia religiosa, Religiöse Kartographie, Cartogra-phie religieuse.* Peter Lang, Bern. [In German].

—— 2006. Mapping the Religious and Religious Maps: Aspects of Transcendence and Translocality in Two Maps of Varanasi; in, Gaenszle, Martin and Gengnagel, Jörg, eds. *Visualised Space in Banaras.* (Heidelberg Studies in South Asian Rituals, Vol. 4). Harrassowitz Verlag, Wiesbaden: 131- 143.

Michell, George 2005. Temple Styles; in, Michell, George and Singh, Rana P.B. (eds.) *Banaras, The City Revealed.* Marg Publs., Mumbai: 78-91.

Minkowski, Christopher 2002. Nilakantha Caturdhara's Mantrakasi-khanda. *Journal of the American Oriental Society*, 122 (2), Apr.-Jun: 329-344. [Iranian Studies in Honor of Stanley Insler on His Sixty-Fifth Birthday].

—— 2004. Nilakantha's instruments of war: Modern, vernacular, barbarous. *Indian Economic & Social History Review* (Sage Publ.), 41 (4): 365-385. doi: 10.1177/001946460404100402.

Mishra, C.P.; Tiwari, I.C. and Mishra, R.N. 2007. Work performance of Primary Health Centres in Varanasi district.. *Indian Journal of Preventive & Social Medicine* (IMS, BHU, Varanasi), 38 (1-2), Jan.-June: 96-103.

Mishra, Pankaj 2006. Benares: Learning to Read; in his, *Temptations of the West. How to be Modern in India, Pakistan and Beyond.* Picador, London: 3-27.

Mishra, Sunita 2007. Safety aspects of street foods: A case study of city of Varanasi in India.

Indian Journal of Preventive & Social Medicine (IMS, BHU, Varanasi), 38 (1-2), Jan.-June: 32-35.

Misra, R. 1972. A comparative study of net primary productivity of dry deciduous forest and grassland of Varanasi, India; in, Golley, P.M. and Golley, F.B. (eds.) *Papers from a Symposium on Tropical Ecology with an emphasis on Organic Productivity.* University of Georgia Press, Athens, GA USA: pp. 245-267.

Misra, R.N. 1984. Banaras Yaksha legends and the Rajghat image. *Bhâratî*, 15 (1971-1984): 132-136.

Mishra, R.N.; Mishra, C.P.; Sen, P. and Singh, T.B. 2005. Nutritional Status and Dietary Intake of Pre-School Children in Urban Slums of Varanasi. *Indian Journal of Community Medicine*, vol. 26 (2), 2001-04 - 2001-06.

Mohapatra, P.; Mohapatra, S.C.; Agrawal, D.K.; Agarwal, K.N and Gaur, S.D. 1990. Nutritional Status of Antenatal Women in Rural Areas of Varanasi, Uttar Pradesh. *Man in India*, 70 (1), March: 85-91.

Monti, Alessandro 2002. The hero as a holy man: the plea for a communal Hindu identity; in, Monti, Alessandro, ed. *Hindu Masculinities across the Ages: Updating the Past.* L'Harmattan Italia, Torino (Italy): 247-270.

Muir, John 1851. The Benares Sanskrit College. *Benares Magzine*, 5 (25), February: 94-108.

Mukherjee, B.; Singh, J.N. and Mukherjee, K.L. 1967. Changes in agricultural landscape in Varanasi District during the past fifty years. *The National Geographical Journal of India* (NGSI, B.H.U., Varanasi. ISSN: 0027-9374/1967/0249), 13 (4): 187-193.

Nag, Prithvish and Kumra, V.K. 1986. Environmental problems in Varanasi. *Indian Journal of Regional Science* (IIT, Kharagpur, India), 18 (1): 25-32.

Narain, A.K. 1981. History and Archaeology of Varanasi. *Souvenir: 68th Indian Science Congress.* Banaras Hindu University (January 1-7): 1-5.

Nayak, A.K.; Raha, P. and Das, A.K. 1995. Organochlorine Pesticide residues in middle stream of the Ganga waterwater. *Bullelin of Environmental Contamination & Toxicology*, 54 (1): 68-75.

Östör, Åkos 1994. "Forest of Bliss": Film and Anthropology. *East-West Film Journal*, vol. 8 (2): 70-104.

Pandey, Gyanendra 1989. The Colonial Construction of Communalism: British Writings on Banaras in the 19th Century; in Guha, Ranajit (ed.) *Writings on South Asian History and Society*, Subaltern Studies, Vol. 6 (Oxford university Press, Delhi: 132-168; reprinted in Das, Veena (ed.) *Mirrors of Violence. Communities, Riots and Survivors in South Asia* (Oxford university Press, Delhi, 1990): 94-134.

Pandey, Rajendra 1962. Geography of Kashi. *Journal of Madhya Pradesh Itihas Parishad* (Bhopal), 4: 79-84.

Pandey, Rajendra Bihari. 1960. Studies in the history of Kâshî: economic life. *The Journal of Oriental Research Madras*, 29 (1959/1960): 1-34.

Parkhil, Thomas 1993. What's taking place: Neighbourhood Ramlilas in Banaras; in, Hertel, Bradley and Humes, Cynthia (eds.) *Living Banaras.* SUNY Press, Albany: 127-144.

Parry, Jonathan P. 1979. Religion and social structure: a case study of the Doms of Banaras. *Contributions to Indian Sociology*, (ns.) 10 (2): 265-292.

—— 1980. Ghost, Greed and Sin: The Occupational Identity of the Banaras Funeral Priests. *Man, N.S.,* (RAIGI, London), 15 (1-2): 88-111. Reprinted in Singh, Rana P.B. (ed.) 1993, *Banaras/ Varanasi* (Tara Book Agency, Varanasi): 179-196.

—— 1981. Death and Cosmogony in Kashi. *Contributions to Indian Sociology N.S.* (New Delhi), 15 (1-2), 337-365. Reprinted in Singh, Rana P.B. (ed.) 1993, *Banaras/ Varanasi* (Tara Book Agency, Varanasi): 103-121.

—— 1982. Sacrificial Death and Necrophagous Ascetic. In, M. Bloch & J. Parry (eds.), *Death and the Regeneration of Life.* Cambridge University Press, Cambridge: 74-110.

—— 1985a. The Aghori Ascetics of Banaras. In, Burghart, R. & Cantlie, A. (eds.), *Indian Religion.* Croom Helm, London/New York: 51-78.

—— 1985b/ 1993. Death and digestion: the symbolism of food and eating in north Indian mortuary rites. *Man, NS* (RAIGI, London), 20 (4): 612-630. Reprinted in, Singh, Rana P. B. (ed.) 1993, *Banaras/ Varanasi.* Tara Book Agency, Varanasi: 141-154.

—— 1988. Comment on Robert Gardner's "Forest of Bliss". *Society for Visual Anthropology Newsletter,* 4 (2), Fall: 4-7. doi:10.1525/var.1988.4.2.4.

Pathak, R.K. & Humes, C.A.1993. Lolark Kund: Sun and Shiva Worship in the City of Light; in, Hertel, Bradley R. and Humes, Cynthia A. (eds.), *Living Banaras* (SUNY Press): 205-244.

Pathak, Shreya 2007-08. Banaras in the 18th Century: a historical study. *Prajñâ* (Banaras Hindu University magazine), vol. 53 (1 2), spec. vol. "Kashi Gaurav Visheshank", vol. II: 271-282.

Pathak, Vinita; Tripathi, Brahma D. and Mishra, Virendra K. 2007. Dynamics of traffic noise in a tropical city Varanasi and its abatement through vegetation. *Environmental Monitoring and Assessment* (Springer, NL, On line ISSN: 1573-2959), December 18. doi: 10.1007/s10661-007-0060-1.

Pathak, V.S. 1957-58. Religious sealings from Rajghat. *Journal of the Numismatic Society of India* (B.H.U., Varanasi), 19-20 (II): 168-179.

—— 1959. Kashi in inscriptions (AD 700-1300). *Journal of the Research of the Universities of Uttar Pradesh: Uttarbharati,* 6 (2): 53-58.

Peggs, James 1848. India's cries to British humanity, related to Ghat murders, etc. *The Calcutta Review*, 10 (July-December): 404-436.

Pieper, Jan 1979. A Pilgrim's Map of Benares: Notes on Codification in Hindu Cartography. *GeoJournal* (Dordrecht; ISBN online: 1572-9893), vol. 3 (2), March: 215-218. doi 10.1007/BF00257710.

Pintchman, Tracy 1999. Celebrating Karttik in Benares. *Dak: The Newsletter of the American Institute of Indian Studies* (Summer): 8-11. Reprinted in her *Guests at God's Wedding* (SUNY Press, Albany, 2005).

—— 2003. The Month of Kartik and Women's Ritual Devotions to Krishna; in, *The Blackwell Companion to Hinduism*. Blackwell, Oxford: 327-42. Reprinted in her *Guests at God's Wedding* (SUNY Press, Albany, 2005).

—— 2003. The Month of Karttik as a Vaishnava Mahotsav: Mythic Themes and the Ocean of Milk. *Journal of Vaishnava Studies* 7/2 (March 1999): 65-92. Reprinted in her *Guests at God's Wedding* (SUNY Press, Albany, 2005).

—— 2003. Women's Songs for the Marriage of Tulsi and Krishna in Benares. *Journal of Vaishnava Studies* 12/1 (Fall): 57-65. Reprinted in her, *Guests at God's Wedding* (SUNY Press, Albany, 2005).

—— 2004. Courting Krishna on the Banks of the Ganges: Gender and Power in a Hindu Women's Ritual Tradition. *Comparative Studies in South Asia, Africa, and the Middle East*, 24/1 (Spring): 18-28. Reprinted in her *Guests at God's Wedding* (SUNY Press, Albany, 2005).

—— 2005. Domesticating Krishna: Friendship, Marriage, and Women's Experience in a Hindu Women's Ritual Tradition; in, *"Alternative" Krishna Traditions: Krishna in Folk Religion and Vernacular Literature*, ed. Guy Beck (State University of New York Press, New York: 43-63. Reprinted in her *Guests at God's Wedding* (SUNY Press, Albany, 2005).

Pollock, Sheldon 1993. Ramayana and Political Imagination in India. *Journal of Asian Studies*, 52 (3): 261-197.

—— 1996. The Sanskrit Cosmopolis, 300-1300 CE: Transculturation, Vernacularization, and the Question of Ideology; in, Houben, Jan

E.M. (ed.) *Ideology and Status of Sanskrit: Contributions to the History of the Sanskrit Language.* E.J. Brill, Leiden: 197-248.

Pradhan, S. 2006. Ancient Varanasi keeps its peace, proves its mettle. *Combating Communalism,* 12 (114).

Prinsep, James 1828. Abstract of a Meteorological Journal Kept at Benares during the Years 1824, 1825, and 1826. *Philosophical Transactions of the Royal Society of London,* vol. 118: pp. 251-255.

—— 1832. Census of the population of the city of Benares. *Asiatic Researches* (Calcutta), vol. 1: 470-498.

Protopapas, Jan 1998. Tradition in transition: Sanskrit education in Varanasi, India. *World and I* (Washington DC), 13 (9), September: 200-210. Also see the Web, Article # 17823: http://www.worldandi.com/specialreport/1998/september/Sa17823.htm

Pugh, Judy F. 1983. Astrological Consoling in Contemporary India. *Culture, Medicine and Psychiatry,* 7 (1): 1-21.

—— 1983a. Into the Almanac: Time, Meaning, and Action in North Indian Society. *Contributions to Indian Sociology,* N.S. (Sage, New Delhi), 17 (1): 27-49. DOI: 10.1177/006996683017001002.

—— 1983b. Astrology and fate: The Hindu and Muslim Experiences. In, Keyes, C.F. and Daniel, E.V., eds. *Karma: An anthropological Inquiry.* University of California Press, Berkeley: 131-146.

—— 1984. Concepts of Person and Situation in North Indian Consoling. *Contribution to Asian Studies* (Leiden), 18: 85-105.

—— 1988. Divination and Ideology in the Banaras Muslim Community; in, Ewing, Katherine P. (ed.) *Shari'at and Ambiguity in South Asian Islam.* University of California Press, Berkeley (CA).

—— 1991. The semantics of pain in Indian culture and medicine. *Culture, Medicine and Psychiatry* (Elsevier, New York), 15 (1), March: 19-43. DOI: 10.1007/BF00050826.

Putman, John J. (photographs by Singh, Raghubir) 1971. The Ganges, River of Faith. *National Geographic* (Washington D.C.), 140 (4), October: 445-483.

Putterman, Daniel M. 1992. Fighting for the Goddess by cleaning the soul of the sacred Ganges. *Trilogy* (Lexington, KY, USA), 4 (4): 14-23.

Qanungo, K.R. 1937. Some side lights on the history of Benaras. *Historical Records Commission Report*, 14: 65-66.

Raha, P.; Singh, S.K.; and Banerjee, H. 2003. Organochlorine Pesticide residues in ground water in world oldest existing civilized city, Varanasi, India. *Indian Journal of Agriculture, Environment & Biotec*, 1 : 94-107.

Rai, L.C. 1978. Ecological studies of Algal communities of the Ganges in Varanasi. *Indian Journal of Ecology*, 5 (1): 1-6.

Rai, Seema 1992. Housing and health in Varanasi Urban Agglomeration. *Population Geography* (Panjab University, Chandigarh), 14: 37-44.

Raman, Navneet 2006. City development plan: A case of Varanasi. *Context: Built, Living and Natural*, (DRONAH, Gurgaon, HR, India), vol. 3 (3), December: 143-149.

Ram Bilas 1980. Ground water resources of Varanasi district, India: an assessment of condition, use and quality. *National Geographical Journal of India* (Varanasi), vol. 26 (pt. 1-2); 81-93.

Ram Bilas and Singh, Rana P.B. 1981. Rural water supply and the problem of health in village India: case of Varanasi district. *Geographia Medica* (Budapest), vol. 11: 65-85.

Rama Rau, Santha (photographs by Heiderer, Tony) 1986. Banaras: India's City of Light. *National Geographic* (Washington D.C.), 169 (2), February: 214-251.

Ramaswamy, Sumathi 2006. Enshrining the Map of India: Cartography, Nationalism, and the Politics of Deity in Varanasi; in, Gaenszle, Martin and Gengnagel, Jörg, eds. *Visualised Space in Banaras*. (Heidelberg Studies in South Asian Rituals, Vol. 4). Harrassowitz Verlag, Wiesbaden: 165-188.

Rana, Pravin S. and Singh, Rana P.B. 2000. Sustainable Heritage Tourism: Framework, Perspective and Prospect. *National Geographical Journal of India* (NGSI, Varanasi), vol. 46: pp. 141-158.

—— 2004 a. Panchakroshi Yatra of Kashi: Divine typology, and Pilgrims' Characteristics. *Fairs and Festivals of Kashi, Seminar Proceedings*, 1-3 August 2003, eds. R.C. Sharma, et al. Jnana Pravaha, Varanasi: 27-38 (+ 1 map).

—— 2004 b. Behavioural Perspective of Pilgrims and Tourists in Banaras; in, Raj, Aparna (ed.) *The Tourist - A Psychological Perspective*. Kanishka Publishers, New Delhi: pp. 187-206.

Ray, Aniruddha. 1989. Revolt of Vizir Ali of Oudh at Benares in 1799; in, *Proceedings of the Indian History Congress*, Forty-Ninth Session, Karnatak University, Dharwad: 331-338.

Roberts, Paul William 1994. "It is not my fire that burns you here" Benares 1992. Chapter 13, pp. 299-358; in his, *Empire of the Soul. Some Journeys in India*. Riverhead Books, New York. ISBN:1-57322-635-1.

Robinson, Phil 1877. The Banaras riots of 1809-1811. *Calcutta Review*, 65: 92-119.

Rodrigues, Hillary P. 1993. Some Puranic myths of the Durgakund Mandir in Varanasi. *Purana* (Varanasi), 35 (2), July: 185-201.

Rötzer, Klaus 2005 a. Mosques and Tombs; in, Michell, George and Singh, Rana P.B. (eds.) *Banaras, The City Revealed*. Marg Publs., Mumbai: 50-65.

—— 2005 b. Houses and Mansions, Caravanserais and Dharmashalas; in, Michell, George and Singh, Rana P.B. (eds.) *Banaras, The City Revealed*. Marg Publs., Mumbai: 106-115.

—— 2005 c. Wells, Tanks and Gardens; in, Michell, George and Singh, Rana P.B. (eds.) *Banaras, The City Revealed*. Marg Publs., Mumbai: 116-125.

Rötzer, Klaus and Deokar, Khandu 1994. Mughal Gardens in Benares and its Neighbourhood in the Eighteenth and Nineteenth Centuries; in, Delvoye, Françoise (ed.) *Confluence of Cultures: French Contributions to Indo-Persian Studies*. Manohar, New Delhi: pp. 131-160.

Roy, T.N. 1986. Antiquity and material culture of Varanasi as revealed through archaeological excavations; in, Verma, T.P., el. al., (eds.) *Varanasi Through the Ages*. Itihas Samkalan Samiti, UP, Varanasi: 24-30.

Rushby, Kevin 2002. Kashi, and Slowly across the Ganges; in his travelogue book, *Children of Kali*. Constable, London: 231-246, and 258.

Sahni, Daya Ram 1907. Benares inscription of Pantha. *Epigraphia Indica and records of the Archaeological Survey of India* [Education Society's Press, Bombay], 9 (8): 113-119.

—— 1924. Manikarnika Ghat (Benares) stone inscription of Viresvara. *The Indian Antiquary*, 53: 209-211.

Saraswati, Baidyanath 1974. Studying sacred complex in Kashi. *Journal of Social Research* (Ranchi), 17 (1): 6-13.

—— 1984. Shastra and society (case of Vishvanath temple). *Man in India* (Ranchi), 64 (1): 3-20.

—— 1985a. The Kashivasis Widows. *Man in India* (Ranchi), 65 (2): 107-120.

—— 1985b. Kashi Pilgrimage - The End of an endless Journey; in, Makhan Jha (ed.) *Dimensions of Pilgrimage. An Anthropological Appraisal* (Based on the Transactions of a World Symposium on Pilgrimage). Inter-India Publications, New Delhi: 91-104.

Sarma, K.V. 1971. The manuscripts collection of the Jade family of Varanasi and the literary output of the Jade authors. *Vishveshvaranand Indological Journal*, vol. 9 (2), Sept.: 347-356.

Sawyer, Dana W. 1993. The Monastic Structure of Banarasi Dandi Sadhus; in, Hertel, Bradley R. & Humes, Cynthia A. (eds.), *Living Banaras* (SUNY Press, Albany): pp. 159-180.

Sax, William S. 1993. The Râmnagar Râmlîlâ: Text, Performance, Pilgrimage; in, Singh, Rana P.B. (ed.) *Banaras/ Varanasi* (Tara Book Agency, Varanasi): 257-273.

Schechner, Richard 1982a. Ramlila of Ramnagar and America's Oberammergau: Two Celebratory Ritual Dramas; in, Turner, Victor (ed.) *Celebrations: Studies in Festivity and Ritual*. Smithsonian Institute Press, Washington D.C.: 89-106.

—— 1982b. Ramlila of Ramnagar: An Introduction. *Quarterly Journal of the Nation Centre for the Performing Arts* (Bombay), 11 (3-4): 66-98.

—— 1983. Ramlila of Ramnagar: An Introduction; in, Schechner, Richard (ed.) *Performative Circumstances*. Seagull Books, Calcutta: 238-288.

—— 1985. Ramlila of Ramnagar; in, Schechner, Richard (ed.) *Between Theatre and Anthropology*. University of Pennsylvania Press, Philadelphia: 151-211.

—— 1993a. Striding Through the Cosmos: Movement, Belief, Politics and Place in the Ramlila of Ramnagar; in, Schechner, Richard.(ed.) *The Future of Ritual*. Routledge, London/New York: 131-183.

—— 1993b. Crossing the Water: Pilgrimage, Movement, and Environmental Scenography of the Ramlila of Ramnagar; in, Hertel, Bradley R. and Humes, Cynthia A. (eds.) *Living Banaras* (SUSP, Albany): 159-180.

Schechner, Richard and Hess, Linda 1977. The Ramlila of Ramnagar (India). *The Drama Review* (New York), 21 (3): 51-88.

Schmalz, Mathew N. 1999. Images of the Body in the Life and Death of a North Indian Catholic Catechist. *History of Religions*, 39 (2), special issue on 'Christianity in India' (Nov.): 177-201.

—— 2001. *Ad Experimentum*: Theology, Anthropology and the Paradoxes of Indian Catholic Inculturation; in, Barnes, Michael (ed.) *Theology and the Social Sciences*. Orbis Books, Maryknoll NY: 161-180.

—— 2002a. The Silent Body of Audrey Santo. *History of Religions*, 42 (3), Nov.: 116-142.

—— 2002b. Charismatic Transgressions: The Life and Work of an Indian Catholic Healer; in, Dempsey, Corinne G. and Raj, Selva J. (eds.) *Popular Christianity in India: Riting Between the Lines*. SUNY Press, Albany: 163-187.

—— 2006. The Death of Comrade Moti: Practicing Catholic Untouchable Rage in a North Indian Village; in, Morrill, Bruce T.; Ziegler, Joanna E. and Rodgers, Susan (eds.) *Practicing Catholic: Ritual, Body, and Contestation in Catholic Faith*. Palgrave Macmillan, New York.

Schulz, Siegfried A. 1969. Demetrios Galanos (1760-1833): A Greek Indologist. [He lived in Banaras, and referred many incidences]. *Journal of the American Oriental Society*, Vol. 89 (2), Apr.-Jun.: 339-356.

Schütte, von Stefan 2003. Soziale Räume der Sicherheit-Die Wäscher von Banaras und ihr Þäþ. In, *Geographie in Heidelberg. Ein Überblick anläßlich des Jahres der Geowissenschaften 2002*, eds. A. Schulte, W. Gamerith & K. Sachs. Selbstverlag, Heidelberg: 64-65. [In German].

Schütte, Stefan 2006. The Social Landscape of the Washermen in Banaras; in, Gaenszle, Martin and Gengnagel, Jörg, eds. *Visualised Space in Banaras*. (Heidelberg Studies in South Asian Rituals, Vol. 4). Harrassowitz Verlag, Wiesbaden: 279-301.

Schweid, Richard 2006. Another Time Around; in his book, *Hereafter Searching for Immortality*. Thunder's Mouth Press, New York: pp. 93-108, and 207-208.

Scidmore, Eliza R. 1888. The Bathing and Burning Ghats at Benares. *The National Geographic Magazine* (Official Journal of the National Geographic Society, Washington DC, U.S.), vol. 1 (February): pp. 118-128.

Searle-Chatterjee, Mary 1979. The Polluted Identity of Work. A Study of Benares Sweepers; in, Wallmann, S. (ed.), *Social Anthropology of Work*. London: 269-286.

―― 1990. The Muslim hero as defender of Hindus: Mythic reversals and ethnicity among Banaras Muslims; in, "Person, Myth and Society in South Asian Islam", ed. P. werbner, Special Issue, *Social Analysis*, 28 (July): 70-81.

―― 1993. Religious division and the mythology of the past; in, Hertel, Bradley and Humes, Cynthia (eds.) *Living Banaras* (SUNY Press, Albany): 145-158.

―― 1994. 'Wahabi' sectarianism among Muslims of Banaras. *Contemporary South Asia*, vol. 3 (2): pp. 83-93.

Sen, S.N. 1943. The Sanskrit memorandum of 1787. *Journal of the Ganganatha Research Institute* (Allahabad), November: 32-47.

―― 1944. Sanskrit college at Benares. *Journal of the Ganganatha Research Institute* (Allahabad), May: 315.

Shashtri, Bapu Deva 1864-65. Notes on Banaras Observatory. *Transactions of the Benares Institute* (for the Session 1864-65): 191-196.

Shastri, M.H. 1912. Dakshini Pandits at Benares. *Indian Antiquary* (Calcutta), 41 (1): 7-13.

Sherring, M.A. 1897. Index to Hindu tribes and castes as represented in Benares. *The Journal of the Asiatic Society of Bengal*, 65, 3 (1896), spec. no. (1897): 1-112.

—— 1866. Description of ancient remains of Buddhist monasteries and temples, and of other buildings, recently discovered in Benares and its vicinity. *The Journal of the Asiatic Society of Bengal*, 35 (1): 61-87.

—— 1885. 'Benares and its antiquities; in, *Transactions of the Benares Institute for the Session 1864-65*. Medical Hall Press, Benares.

Sherring, M.A. & Charles Horne. 1865. Description of the Buddhist ruins at Bakariya Kund, Benares. In: *The Journal of the Asiatic Society of Bengal*, 34, (1): 1-13.

Showeb, Mohd. 2004-2005. The Julahas: An Ethnographic and Socio-Economic profile of Madanpuria Weavers of Benaras. *Gandhian Perspectives, An Interdisciplinary Journal of Social Sciences* (Gandhian Institute of Studies, Varanasi), vol. XX No. 2 July-Dec. 2004 & vol. XXI No. 1 Jan.-June 2005: 66-75.

Shukla, Kamlesh Kr and Yadava, K.N.S. 2006. The Distribution of the Number of Migrants at the Household Level. *Journal of Population and Social Studies* (Nakhorn Patham, Thailand), vol. 14 (2), Jan.

Shulman, David 1998. Ambivalence and longing: Vyasa's curse on Kashi. In, Kedar, Benjamin Z. & R.J. Zwi Werblowsky (eds.), *Sacred Space: Shrine, City, Land*. New York University Press, New York: 192-214.

Simon, Beth 1993. Language choice, religion, and identity in the Banaras community. In, Hertel, Bradley and Humes, Cynthia, eds. *Living Banaras*. SUNY Press, Albany: 245-268.

Singh, Abha 1986. Agricultural population in the urban centres of Varanasi City Region: a geographical analysis. *The National Geographical Journal of India* (NGSI, B.H.U., Varanasi. ISSN: 0027-9374/1986/0680), 32 (1): 40-48.

Singh, Basant 1962. Distribution of cultivable waste and possibility of its reclamation in Chakia (Banaras). *The National Geographical Journal of India* (NGSI, B.H.U., Varanasi. ISSN: 0027-9374/1962/0137), 8 (1): pp. 59-72.

Singh, Onkar and Maurya, S.P. 1981. Process of agricultural mechanisation in Chakia Development Block (Dist. Varanasi). *The National Geographical Journal of India* (NGSI, B.H.U., Varanasi. ISSN: 0027-9374/1981/0561), 27 (3-4): 141-155.

Singh, R.L. 1956. The trend of urbanisation in the umland of Banaras. *The National Geographical Journal of India* (NGSI, B.H.U., Varanasi. ISSN: 0027-9374/1956/0018), 2 (2): 75-83.

—— 1957. Typical rural dwellings in the umland of Banaras. *The National Geographical Journal of India* (NGSI, B.H.U., Varanasi. ISSN: 0027-9374/1957/0041), 3 (2): pp. 51-64.

—— 1973. Social factors in the morphogenesis of Varanasi; in, Singh, R. L. (ed.) *Urban Geography in Developing Countries*. National Geographical Society of India, Varanasi: 3 - 27.

—— 1974. Evolution of clan territorial units through land occupance in the Middle Ganga Valley. *The National Geographical Journal of India* (NGSI, B.H.U., Varanasi. ISSN: 0027-9374/1974/0381), 20 (1), March: 1-19.

—— 1976. Origin, growth and morphological structure of Varanasi; in, Alam, S.M. and Pokshishevsky, G. (eds.) *Urbanisation in Developing Countries*. Osmania University, Hyderabad: 475-500 + 6 figures.

—— 1985. Ecology of urban habitat and environmental planning in India. *The National Geographical Journal of India* (NGSI, B.H.U., Varanasi. ISSN: 0027-9374/1985/0672), 31 (4), December: 280-290.

—— 1986. Varanasi, A Geographical analysis of the national city. *Souvenir, XII National Seminar of IASLIC* (December 28-31), eds. H.N. Prasad and J.B. Subramaniam; Dept. of Library and Information Science, Banaras Hindu University, Varanasi: 1-7.

Singh R.L. and Singh, Rana P.B. 1980. Cognising urban landscape of Varanasi: a note on the cultural synthesis. *The National Geogra-*

phical Journal of India (NGSI, B.H.U., Varanasi. ISSN: 0027-9374/ 1980/0537), 26 (3-4) : pp. 113-123.

Singh, R.L. and Singh, Ujagir 1963. Road traffic survey of Varanasi. *The National Geographical Journal of India* (NGSI, B.H.U., Varanasi. ISSN: 0027-9374/1963/0168), 9 (3-4): 139-160.

Singh, Ram Bali 1969. Rural settlement types and their distributions: examples from Varanasi District, India. *The National Geographical Journal of India* (NGSI, B.H.U., Varanasi. ISSN: 0027-9374/1969/ 0282), 15 (2): 91-104.

Singh, Rana P.B. 1980. Socio-cultural space of Varanasi. *Art & Archaeology Research Papers* (AARP, London, UK), special publication on '*Ritual Space in India*', vol. 17: 41-46.

—— 1982. Image of Varanasi city: reflection on Geography of Tourism. *Frankfurter Wirtschafts- und Sozialgeographische Schriften* (Frankfurt/Main, Germany), Heft 41: 161-174.

—— 1985. The personality and lifeworld of Varanasi as revealed in Shivaprasad Singh's novel: a study in literary geography. *The National Geographical Journal of India* (NGSI, B.H.U., Varanasi. ISSN: 0027-9374/1985/0673), 31 (4): 291-318.

—— 1986. Shiva's universe in Varanasi; in, Verma, T.P.; Singh D.P. and J.S. Mishra (eds.) *Varanasi Through the Ages*. Bhartiya Itihas Samkalan Samiti, Varanasi, Pub. 4: 303-311.

—— 1987 a. Toward myth, Cosmos, Space and Mandala in India, a search in the Geography of Belief Systems. *The National Geographical Journal of India* (NGSI, B.H.U., Varanasi. ISSN: 0027-9374/1987/0737), 33 (3), September: 305-326.

—— 1987 b. The pilgrimage mandala of Varanasi/Kashi: a study in sacred geography. *The National Geographical Journal of India* (NGSI, B.H.U., Varanasi. ISSN: 0027-9374/1987/0751), 33 (4), December: 493-524.

—— 1988 a. Interplay of sacred space and sacred time in Hindu belief system. *Spiritual Attitudes and Environment (Geistenshaltung und Umbelt)*, ed. Werner Kreisel. Abhandlungen zur Geschichte der Geowissenschaften und Religion/Umwelt-Forschung, Band 1. Alano Edition herodot, Aachen (Germany): pp. 439-454.

—— 1988 b. The Image of Varanasi: sacrality and perceptual world. *National Geographical Journal of India* (NGSI, B.H.U., Varanasi. ISSN: 0027-9374/1988/0754), 34 (1), March: 1-32.

—— 1989. Banaras/ Varanasi-From Culture and Architecture to tourism and environment: Review of 5 Books. *The National Geographical Journal of India*, 35 (pts. 3-4): 281-290.

—— 1990a. Literary images, cultural symbols and intimate sensing: the Ganga river in Varanasi. *The National Geographical Journal of India*, 36 (1-2): 117-128.

—— 1990b. Time and Hindu rituals in Varanasi, A study of Sacrality and Cycles; in, Gopal, L. and Dubey, D.P. (eds.) Pilgrimage Studies: Text and Context (Society of Pilgrimage Studies, Allahabad): 66-72 and 5pp. Hindu calendar. Reprinted also, *Geographia Religionum* (Berlin, Germany), Bd. 8: 123-138.

—— 1991. Panchakroshi Yatra, Varanasi: Sacred Journey, Ecology of Place and Faithscape. *The National Geographical Journal of India*, 37 (1-2): 49-98.

—— 1993 a. Varanasi: The Pilgrimage mandala, geomantic map and cosmic numbers; in, Singh, Rana P.B. (ed.) *Banaras (Varanasi)*. (Tara Book Agency, Varanasi): pp. 37-64.

—— 1993 b. The Ganga Ghats, Varanasi: The Riverfront landscape; in, Singh, Rana P.B. (ed.) *Banaras (Varanasi)*. (Tara Book Agency, Varanasi): pp. 65-102.

—— 1993 c. Shiva's Universe in Varanasi;. in, Singh, Rana P.B. (ed.) *Banaras (Varanasi)*. (Tara Book Agency, Varanasi): pp. 155-162.

—— 1993 d. Sarnath: Cultural history, museum and tourist sites; in, Singh, Rana P.B. (ed.) *Banaras (Varanasi)*. (Tara Book Agency, Varanasi): pp. 235-256.

—— 1993 e. Varanasi: Demographic Profile-From ancient to late 1820s and the present state; in, Singh, Rana P.B. (ed.) *Banaras (Varanasi)*. (Tara Book Agency, Varanasi): pp. 279-288.

—— 1993 f. Varanasi: A World heritage city: The frame, historical accounts; in, Singh, Rana P.B. (ed.) *Banaras (Varanasi)*. (Tara Book Agency, Varanasi): pp. 297-316.

—— 1993 g. Banaras (Varanasi): A Selected Bibliography (495); in, Singh, Rana P.B. (ed.) *Banaras (Varanasi)*. (Tara Book Agency, Varanasi): pp. 317-341. [* This was the first attempt to prepare a 'Bibliography on/of Banaras'. Compare, Gengnagel, Jörg and Michaels, Axel (compiled) 2003, *Banaras Bibliography*, which copied and rearranged these sources without citing this original source.]

—— 1993 h. Cosmic layout of Hindus' sacred city, Varanasi. *Architecture & Behaviour* (Lausanne, Switzerland), 9 (2): 239-249.

—— 1994 a. Water symbolism and sacred landscape in Hinduism: A study of Benares. *Erdkunde, Archiv für Wissenschaftliche Geographie* (Bonn, Germany), Band 48 (3), September: 210-227.

—— 1994 b. Modern Varanasi: Place and Society in Shivprasad Singh's novel *Street Turns Yonder*; in, Simpson-Housley, Paul and Preston, Peter (eds.) *Writing the City: Eden, Babylon and the New Jerusalem*. Routledge, London (UK): pp. 220-240.

—— 1994 c. Time and Hindu rituals in Varanasi. *Geographia Religionum* (Berlin, Germany), Bd. 8: 123-138.

—— 1994 d. The sacred geometry of India's holy city, Varanasi: Kashi as Cosmogram. *National Geogr. Jl. of India*, vol. 40: 189-216. Reprinted in revised form: Malville, J.M. and Gujral, L. (eds.) 1999, *Ancient Cities, Ancient Skies*. Aryan Publ. for the IGNCA, New Delhi: pp. 59-80.

—— 1994 e. Varanasi: Cosmic order and cityscape. I. Sun images and shrines. *Architecture + Design* (New Delhi), Vol. 11 (6), November-December : pp. 75-79.

—— 1995 a. Varanasi: Cosmic order and cityscape. II. Ganesh images and shrines. *Architecture + Design* (New Delhi), Vol. 12 (1), January-February : pp. 99-101.

—— 1995 b. Varanasi: Cosmic order and cityscape. III. Shiva's universe and pilgrimage journeys. *Architecture + Design* (New Delhi), Vol. 12 (2), March-April : pp. 83-85.

—— 1995 d. Sun shrines, images and alignment at Varanasi. *The Ley Hunter* (Cornwall, UK), No. TLH 123, Summer: pp. 20-26.

—— 1996 a. The Ganga River and the spirit of sustainability in Hinduism; in, Swan, James and Swan, Roberta (eds.) *Dialogues with the Living Earth. New Ideas on the Spirit of Place.* Quest Books, Wheaton, IL, USA : pp. 86-107.

—— 1996 b. Varanasi: Shiva's universe and pilgrimage journey. *The Ley Hunter* (Cheltenham, UK), No. TLH 125, Autumn : pp. 24-29.

—— 1997 a. Sacred space and pilgrimage in Hindu society: the case of Varanasi; in, Stoddard, R.H. and Morinis, Alan (eds.) *Sacred Places, Sacred Spaces. The Geography of Pilgrimages. Geoscience & Man,* vol. 34. Louisiana State University Press, Baton Rouge, USA: 191-207.

—— 1997 b. Sacredscape and urban heritage in India: Contestation and perspective; in, Shaw, Brian and Jones, Roy (eds.) *Contested Urban Heritage. Voices from the Periphery.* Ashgate, London (UK): pp. 101-131.

—— 1998. Sacred journey, Sacredscape and Faithscape: an experience of Panchakroshi pilgrimage, Varanasi (India). *The Pennsylvania Geographer* (Johnstown, PA, USA), Vol. 36 (1): pp. 55-91.

—— 2000 a. Sacredscape, Faithscape and Cosmic Geometry: A Study of Holy Places of north India; in, Esteban, C. and Belmonte, J.A. (eds.) *Astronomy and Cultural Diversity.* (Proceedings, Oxford VI & SEAC 99 Int'nal Conf., June 21-29, 1999, La Laguna, Spain). OAMC. Santa Cruz de Tenerife: pp. 99-106.

—— 2000 b. Kashi as Cosmogram: Sacred Geometry of Varanasi; in, Malville, J.M. and Gujral, L. (eds.) 1999, *Ancient Cities, Ancient Skies.* Aryan Publ. for IGNCA, New Delhi: pp. 58-81.

—— 2002. The Holy city and the Cultural Tradition of Pilgrimage Mandala in India: Cosmic Geometries of Kashi (Varanasi) and Gaya; in, Hashemi, M.R. and Papoli-Yazdi, M. (eds.) *Cultural Approach in Geography at the turn of New Millenium.* University of Mashhad Press, Mashhad, Iran.

—— 2004 a. The Ganga Riverfront in Varanasi, a Heritage Zone in Contestation. *Context: Built, Living and Natural* (DRONAH, Gurgaon, HR, India), vol. 1, no. 1, September: pp. 25-30.

—— 2005a. Growth of City, Banaras; in, Michell, George and Singh, Rana P.B. (eds.) *Banaras, The City Revealed.* Marg Publs., Mumbai: 22-29.

—— 2006. Ghats and Palaces of Varanasi. *ISG Magazin* (Internationales Städteforum Graz; Forum der historischen Städte und Gemeinden; Hauptplatz 3, A-8010 Graz, Austria; eds. Hohmann, Hasso, et. el.), 4 (December): 9-11.

—— 2007 a. Banaras Hindu University, Architectural Plan: Symbolism & Meaning; in, Gupta, R.C. et al. (eds.) *Souvenir. Third International BHU Alumni Meet, & International Seminar on Education in the 21st Century and Mahamana's Vision,* 6-7 January 2007. BHU in association with Mahamana Malviya Mission, Varanasi: 50-57. Also reprinted in, Dar, S.L. and Somaskandan, S. 1966/ 2007. *History of the Banaras Hindu University.* Banaras Hindu University Press, Banaras: pp. 884-895.

—— 2007 b. Banaras (Kashi): Setting the Culture & Breathe of India; in, Gupta, R.C. et. al. (eds.) *Souvenir. Third International BHU Alumni Meet, & International Seminar on Education in the 21st Century and Mahamana's Vision,* 6-7 January 2007. BHU in association with Mahamana Malviya Mission, Varanasi: 77-93.

—— 2008. The Sacred River Ganga (Ganges) at Varanasi. *The Gatekeeper Magzine* (Gatekeeper Trust, Devon, UK), Issue 25, April: 5-8.

—— 2008. Kashi as Cosmogram: The Panchakroshi Route and Complex Structures of Varanasi; in, Malville, John M. and Saraswati, B.N. (eds.) *Pilgrimage and Complexity.* DK Printworld, Delhi for IGNCA: 87-98.

—— 2009. Representation of Kashi through the Cartographic Art in the 19th Century. In, *Contribution of Banaras to Indian Art and Culture* (Proceedings of a National Seminar, 22-24 March 2004); eds. Ananda Krishna and Mukul Raj Mehta. Indian Institute of Advanced Studies, Simla.

Singh, Rana P.B.; Dar, Vrinda and Rana, Pravin S. 2001. Rationales for including Varanasi as Heritage City in the UNESCO World Heritage List. *The National Geographical Journal of India,* 47 (pts. 1-4): 177- 200.

Singh, Rana P.B. and Fukunaga, Masaaki, 2000. Performing pilgrimage and pilgrimage-tourism: an experience of the Pancakroshi Yatra, Varanasi; in, Dubey, D.P. (ed.) *Pilgrimage Studies. The Power of Places.* Society of Pilgrimage Studies, Allahabad: 183 - 205.

Singh, Rana P.B. and Malville, John M. 1995. Cosmic order and City-scape of Varanasi (Kashi): The Sun images and cultural astronomy. *The National Geographical Journal of India*, 41 (1), March: pp. 69-88.

—— 2005. Pilgrimage-Tourists to Varanasi (Kashi): Critique of the Theories, and a Search for Self-Organised Patterns in Space and Time; in, George, Babu P. and Swain, Sampad K. (eds.) *Advancements in Tourism Theory and Practice: Perspectives from India.* Abhijeet Publications, Delhi: 01-24.

Singh, Rana P.B. and Ram Bilas 1980. Rural water supply and problem of health in village India, case of Varanasi District; in, Yuihama, Shogo and Singh, Rana P.B. (eds.) *Changing Scene of Rural Habitat in Developing Countries.* 24th International Geogr. Congress, Tokyo/ Okayama (Japan): pp. 95-109.

Singh, Rana P.B. and Rana, Pravin S. 2001. The Future of Heritage Tourism in Varanasi: Scenario, Prospects and Perspectives. *National Geographical Journal of India*, 47 (pts. 1-4): 201-218.

Singh, Rana P.B. and Sen, Chandra 2001. The Structure of Peri-Urban Agricultural Environment in Varanasi Development Region. *The National Geographical Journal of India*, 47 (pts.1-4): 61-72.

Singh, Rana P.B.; Singh, Ravi S. and Rana, P.S. 2002. Sacred Geography of Goddesses in Kashi (Varanasi). *Journal of Geography*, vol. 3 [Theme: Social Geography, eds. H.N. Sharma and A.K. Bhagabati; Dept. of Geography, Gauhati University, Guwahati, AS, India], October: pp. 11-35.

Singh, Rana P.B. and Singh, Ravi S. 2008. Urban Fabric of Varanasi, a Holy city: Growth and Perspective; in, Misra, R. P. (ed.) *Million Cities of India.* Concept Publ., New Delhi.

Singh, Ravi S. and Singh, Rana P.B. 2006. Goddesses in Kashi (Varanasi): Spatial Patterns and Symbolic Orders; in, Gaenszle, Martin and Gengnagel, Jörg (eds.) *Visualised Space in Banaras.* (Heidelberg

300

Studies in South Asian Rituals, Vol. 4). Harrassowitz Verlag, Wiesbaden: 41-68.

Singh, S.K.; Raha, P. and Banerjee, H. 2006. Banned Organochlorine Cyclodiene Pesticide in Ground Water in Varanasi, India. *Bullelin of Environmental Contamination & Toxicology*, 76 (6): 935-941. DOI: 10.1007/s00128-006-1008-9.

Singh, Surendra Kumar 1971. The impact of electricity on agricultural development in the Banwaripur group of villages (Varanasi): a case study. *The National Geographical Journal of India* (NGSI, B.H.U., Varanasi. ISSN: 0027-9374/1971/0324), 17 (2-3): 99-112.

Singh, Ujagir 1955. A sample study in land utilisation near Sarnath (Banaras). *The National Geographical Journal of India* (NGSI, B.H.U., Varanasi. ISSN: 0027-9374/1955/0006), vol. 1 (1), September: 47-58.

Singha, Radhika 1993. 'Providential' Circumstances: The Thuggee Campaign of the 1830s and legal innovation. *Modern Asian Studies* (Cambridge University Press), 27 (1): 83-146.

——— 1998a. Civil Authority and Due Process: Colonial Criminal Justice in the Banaras Zamindari, 1781-1795; in Anderson, Michael R. and Guha, Sumit (eds.) *Changing Concepts of Rights and Justice in South Asia*. Oxford University Press, Calcutta and New York (SOAS studies on South Asia series): 30-81.

——— 2000. Settle, mobilize, verify: identification practices in colonial India', *Studies in History*, 16 (2): 151-198.

Sinha, Amita 1991. The Conservation of Sacred Sites: Sarnath, a case study. *Landscape Research*, 16 (3): 23-30.

Slawek, Stephen M. 1988. Popular kirtan in Benares: Some 'Great' Aspects of a Little Tradition. *Ethnomusicology: Journal of the Society for Ethnomusicology*, 32 (2): 77-92.

Smith, Vincent A. 1909. Benares; in, *Encyclopaedia of Religion and Ethics*. Vol. II. Edinburg/New York: 465-469.

——— 1909. Identification of the Ashoka Pillar N. E. of Benares City described by Hiuen Tsang. *Zeitschrift der Deutschen Morgenländischen Gesellschaft*, 63: 337-345.

Stratton, Mark 2005. India special: All human life — and death — is here. *Independent on Sunday*, FindArticles.com, 20 March. Web: http://findarticles.com/p/articles/mi_qn4159/is_20050320/ai_n13460085.

Sukul, Kuber Nath. 1970. Original sites of some important temples of Varanasi. *The Journal of the Ganganatha Jha Research Institute*, 26, 1/3 (Jan.-July): 717-724.

Sultana, Parveen 2004. Muslim Fairs and Festivals in Kashi. *Fairs and Festivals of Kashi, Seminar Proceedings*, 1-3 August 2003, eds. R.C. Sharma, et al. Jnana Pravaha, Varanasi: 69-74.

Tagare, G.V. 1991. Pilgrimages at Kâshî: Past and Present. *Journal of the Oriental Institute*, vol. 41: 13-16.

Tiwari, Reena 2008. Being a Rhythm Analyst in the City of Varanasi. *Urban Forum* (Springer Science+Business Media B.V.). <8 figures>. Online publication, 22 May. doi: 10.1007/s12132-008-9037-6.

Thomas, L. Eugene 1990. The ecological and cultural setting: a cross-cultural investigation of successful ageing. *Pharmacopsychoecogica* (Varanasi), 2: 57-62.

—— 1991. Dialogues with three religious renunciates and reflections on wisdom and maturity. *International Journal of Ageing and Human Development*, 33: 211-227.

—— 1992. Identity, ideology and medicine: Health attitudes and behaviour among Hindu religious renunciates. *Social Science and Medicine*, 34: 499-505.

Tomalin, Emma and Hollick, Julian Crandall 2002. Making a radio documentary series about the river Ganges. *Contemporary South Asia*, 11 (2): 211-226.

Tripathi, L.K. 1963. The Kardameshvara temple at Kandwa, Varanasi. *Bharati* (B.H.U., Varanasi), 1962-63 (No. 6): 137.

Tripathi, Vibha and Upadhyay, Prabhakar 2005-06. Anai: a settlement in the Varuna region. *Puratatva* (*Bulletin of the Indian Archaeological Society*, New Delhi), 36: 93-102.

Trower, Marcus 2007. 'Part I: India, 1998-99: Kushti Man, The Fall, The Whole World Loses Something, 5000 Bethaks and 3000 Dands, and A Tight Loincloth <all in/of Banaras>'; in his *The Last Wrestlers. A Far-flung Journey in Search of a Manly Art*. Ebury Press (div. of Random House), London: 3-97.

Tully, Mark 2007. Varanasi: the unity of opposites; in his *India's Unending Journey: Finding Balance in a Time of Change*. RIDAR Random House Group, London: pp. 248-268.

Upadhyay, Basudev 1974. Some bibliographical notes on Sacred Kashi. *Journal of Social Research* (Ranchi), 17 (1); 42-48.

Vassiliades, Demetrios Th. 2000. Demetrios Galanos (1760-1833), The First Greek Indologist. In his book, *The Greeks in India. A Survey in Philosophical Understanding*. Munshiram Manoharlal Pvt. Ltd, New Delhi: pp. 138-161.

Varady, Robert G. 1989. Land use and environmental change in the Gangetic plain. Nineteenth century human activity in the Banaras region; in, Freitag, S.B. (ed.) *Culture and Power in Banaras* (University of California Press, Berkeley): 229-245.

Venis, Arthur. 1894. Benares copper-plate grants of Govindachandra of Kanauj. *Epigraphia indica*, 2: 358-363.

Verma, Ganeshilal 1974. Hindi Journalism and Socio-Political Awakening in the North-West Provinces and Oudh in the last three decades of the nineteenth century. *Journal of Indian History*, 52 (April): 377-387.

Verma, Ratnesh 2004. Role of government to promote fairs and festivals of Varanasi; in, Sharma, R.C. et. al. (eds.) *Fairs and Festivals of Kashi, Seminar Proceedings*, 1-3 August 2003. Jnana Pravaha, Varanasi: 37-45.

Verma, Thakur Prasad 1984. The temples of Banaras. *Bharati* (B.H.U., Varanasi), 1971-1984, No. 15: 194-205.

Visuvalingam, Sunthar 1992. Between Mecca and Banaras: Towards an acculturation model of Hindu-Muslim relations. *Islam and the Modern Age*, 24 (1): 20-62.

Visuvalingam, Sunthar and Chalier-Visuvalingam, Elizabeth 1993. Death and Sexuality in Hinduism and Islam: The Marriage of Lât Bhairo and Ghâzî Miyâ. *Islam and the Modern Age* (Zakir Husain Institute of Islamic Studies, Jamia Milia Islamia, Jamia Nagar, New Delhi), Vol. 24 (no.1), February: 20-69.

——2006. Bhairava in Banaras: Negotiating Sacred Space and Religious Identity; in, Gaenszle, Martin and Gengnagel, Jörg, eds. *Visualised Space in Banaras*. (Heidelberg Studies in South Asian Rituals, Vol. 4). Harrassowitz Verlag, Wiesbaden: 95-128.

Wakankar, Vishnu Shripad 1986. Rock Art of Varanasi Region (Plates I VII); in, Verma, T.P.; Singh, D.P. and Mishra, J.S. (eds.) *Varanasi Through the Ages*. Bhartiya Itihas Samkalan Samiti, Varanasi, Pub. 4 : 91-104.

Ward, Geoffrey (Photographs by Raghubir Singh) 1985. Benares, India's most holy city, faces an unholy problem. *Smithsonian* (Washington, DC), 16 (6), September: 82-93.

Wayman, Frederick F. 1866. Benares; chapter III in his, *From Calcutta to the Snowy Range: Being a Narrative through the Upper Provinces of India to the Himalayas*. Tinsley Brothers, London: pp. 49-81.

White, David G. 2005. The Goddess in the Tree: Reflections on Nim-Tree Shrines in Varanasi; in, Krishna, Naval and Krishna, Manu (eds.), *The Ananda-Vana of Indian Art : Dr. Anand Krishna Felicitation Volume*. Varanasi: Indica Books, Varanasi: 575-586.

Wilke, Annette 1993. Durga-Puja in Benares. *Unipress* (Bern), 78: 19-25.

Wilke, Annette 2006. The Banaras Navadurga Cycle and its Spatial Orientation; in, Gaenszle, Martin and Gengnagel, Jörg (eds.) *Visualised Space in Banaras*. (Heidelberg Studies in South Asian Rituals, Vol. 4). Harrassowitz Verlag, Wiesbaden: 69-94.

Williams, J.L. 1793. Further particulars respecting the observatory at Benares. *Philosophical Transactions of the Royal Society of London*, vol. LXXXIII.

Williams, Philippa 2007. Hindu-Muslim brotherhood: Exploring the dynamics of communal relations in Varanasi, North India. *Journal of South Asian Development* (Sage Publ., New Delhi and London), 2 (2), October: 153-176.

Wikström, Owe 1996. Darsan (to see) Lord Shiva in Varanasi. Visual processes and the representation of God by seven ricksha-drivers. *Scripta Instituti Donneriani Aboensis*, vol. XVI: pp. 105-117.

Wiesner, Ulrich 1978. Defining the Pasupati temple style: Deopatyan culty image Varanasi; in his, *Nepalese Temple Architecture: Its Characteristics and its Relations*. Brill, Leiden (ISBN: ISBN: 9004056661): 01-09.

Worswick, Clark and Embree, Ainslie (text authors) 1976. Many old photographs of Sarnath, ghats and Ramanagar, cf. pp. 62-111); in, *The Last Empire. Photography in British India, 1855-1911*. Gordon Fracer Gallery Ltd., London & Bedford. Preface by The Earl Mountbatten of Burma. ISBN: 0-900406-74-7.

Wright, H.R.C. 1959. The emancipation of opium cultivators in Benares. *International Review of Social History* (International Institute for Social History, Netherlands), 4 (3): 446-460.

Yanagisawa, Kiwamu and Funo, Shuji 2004. Relationship between Spatial Formation of Varanasi City (Uttar Pradesh, India) and Pilgrimage Routes, Temples and Shrines. *Journal of Architecture, Planning and Environmental Engineering (Transactions of AIJ)* [ISSN: 1340-4210, Tokyo], Vol. No. 583: 75-82. [In Japanese, with summary in English].

——— 2002. Spatial formation of Varanasi, India: an analysis of the urban structure, pilgrimage roads, mohallas as community, composition of block and houses. *Proceedings of the 4th International Symposium on Architectural Intercharge in Asia* (held on 17-19 September 2002), Chongqing, China: 216-221.

Yun-Hua, Jan. 1966. The Korean record on Varanasi and Sarnath. *Vishveshvaranand Indological Journal*, 4 (2), Sept.: 264-272.

Zeiler, Xenia 2004. The Ten Mahavidyas' Yatra — A contemporary pilgrimage in Banaras. *Beiträge des Südasien-Instituts der Humboldt-Universität zu Berlin*, (Berlin, ISSN 0943-8742), Heft 13: pp. 105-119.

C (i). Persian Works, Translated

Curwen, F. 1875. Trans. *Bulwuntnamah* of Khai-ud-din. Allahabad.

Hoey, W. 1888. Trans. *Memoirs of Delhi and Faizabad* (*Tarikh-i-Farah-Bakhsh* of Muhamma Faiz Bakhsh), 2 vols. Allahabad.

Jarrett, H.S. 1949. Trans. *Ain-i-Akbari* of Abul Fazl Allami, vol. II, ed. by J. Sarkar. 2nd Ed. Calcutta.

Nota Manus 1926. Trans. *Seir-ul-Mutakherin* of Ghulam Hussain Khan, 4 vols. Calcutta and Madras.

C (ii). Urdu Sources

Farid, Hazi Muhammad 1974. *Tarikh Masarah Banaras*. Varanasi Press, Dalmandi (Varanasi).

Isharat, Amritlal 1968. *Sukham Waran Banaras*. Banaras.

Nomani, Abdus Salaam 1952. *Tazkara Mashaikh Banaras*. Akram Hussain Press, Banaras.

—— 1968. *Tarikh Asar-e-Banaras*. Maktabe Nadawatal Maurrif, Banaras.

D. SANSKRIT SOURCES on Kashi/ Varanasi (selected)

AgP, *Agni Purāṇa*, 1957. Anandashram Sanskrit series no. 41, Poona. Dated *ca* CE 8th century. Ref. to Varanasi: 112.

AsD, *Aṣṭādhyāyī* of Pāṇini, 1897. Ed. S.C. Bose. Chowkhambha Oriental series, Benares. Dt. *ca* 500 BCE, Ref.: IV.2.113, 116; 3.84.

AtV, *Atharva Veda*, 1895. Venkateshvara Press, Bombay. Dt.: *ca* 1000 BCE, Ref.: V.22.4.

BgP, *Bhagavata Mahāpurāṇa*, 1971. Sanskrit & English transl. Ed. G.L. Gosvami, 2 vols., Gita Press, Gorakhpur. Dt.: *ca* CE 14th century, Ref.: X.66

BP, *Brahma Purāṇa*,1954. Gurumandala Granthamalaya No. XI, 2 vols., Calcutta.

BP, *Brahma Purāṇa*, 1976. Ed. Taranisha Jha. Hindi Sahitya Sammelan, Prayag.

BhP, *Brahmāṇḍa Purāṇa*, 1976. Ed. J.L. Shastri. Motilal Banarasidass, Delhi. Dt. *ca* 4th century. Ref. Varanasi: 2.3.67, 207.

Bch, *Buddhacaritam* of Aśvaghoṣa, 1893. Ed. Cowel. Clarendon Press, Oxford. Dt.: CE 1st Century, Ref.: 15.44, 101.

BvP, *Brahmavaivarta Purāṇa*, 1935. Anandashrama Sanskrit Series No. 102, Poona.

DbP, *Devī Bhagavata Purāṇa*, 1955. Chowkhambha Sanskrit Series, Banaras. Dt.: *ca* 8th century, Ref.: VII.24.13-24.

GL, *Gaṅgālaharī* of (Paṇḍitarāja) Jagannātha, 1982. Thakur Prasad & Sons, Banaras. Dt.: *ca* CE 17th century, Ref.: 52 verses honouring the Ganga. [See Jagannath 2007].

GnM, *Gīrvāṇamañjarī* by Varadarāja (CE 1600-1660), 1964. Gaekwad Sanskrit Series Publs., Baroda. Dt.: *ca* 1650.

GBr, *Gopatha Brāhmaṇa*, 1991. Ed. Deinke Gaastra. E.J. Brill, Leiden. Dt.: *ca* 4th century BCE, Ref. 12.9.

HvP, *Harivaṁśa Purāṇa*, 1897. Trans. Manmatha Nath Dutta. Elysium Press, Calcutta. Dt. *ca* CE 3rd century (known as an appendix to the *Mahābhārata*), Ref.: I.29.

KKh, *Kāśī Khaṇḍa* (of *Skanda Purāṇa*), 1961. Gurumandala Granth-malaya No. XX, vol. IV, Calcutta. 100 chapter containing 11,624 verses.

KKh, *Kāśī Khaṇḍa* (of *Skanda Purāṇa*), 1991-1998. Editor: Karunapati Tripathi. Sampurnananda Sanskrit Vishvavidyalaya, Varanasi. 4 vols. Sanskrit and Hindi translation and commentary. Dt. *ca* 12th-14th century. Contains 100 chapters and 11,624 verses.

KKM, *Kāśī Kedāra Māhātmya* (an appendix to the *Brahmavaivarta Purāṇa*) 1939. Translation: Vijayananda Tripathi, Ed. Krishna-chandra Sahityacarya. Acyuta Granthamala, Kashi. Dt. *ca* 16th century.

KKT, *Kṛtyakalpataru*, by Lakshmidhara, 1942. Ed. K.V. Rangaswamy Aiyangar. Gaekwad's Oriental Series Vol. XCVIII. Oriental Institute, Baroda.

KPM, *Śrī Kāśī Pañcakrośī Māhātmya*, 1906. Victoria Press, Bombay.

KM, *Kāśī Māhātmya* (from the *Patāla Khaṇḍa* of the *Padma Purāṇa*), 1939. Nawal Kishore Press, Bombay. Dt. *ca* 13-14th century.

KmN, *Kāśī Mokṣa Nirṇaya* by Sureśvara, 1931. Sanskrit text with Hindi, Ed. A.D. Upadhyaya. Sri Gaurishankar Ganerrivala, Gorakhpur.

KmV, *Kāśī Mitra Vicāra* by Sureśvara, 1936. Ed. Gopinath Kaviraj. The Prince of Wales Sarasvati Bhavan Text No. 67. Government Printing, Allahabad.

(*Śrī*) *Śrī Kāśī Pañcakrośī Māhātmya*, 1906. Victoria Press, Banaras.

KR, *Kāśī Rahasya* (an appendix to the *Brahmavaivarta Purāṇa*), 1957. Gurumandala Granthamalaya, No. XIV, vol. III, Calcutta. Dt. *ca* CE 16th century. Ref. 26 chapters.

Kāśī Tattva Bhāskara, 1917. Ed. Munshi Harijana Lal. Hitacintak Press, Banaras.

Kāśī Yātrā Prakāśa, 1913. Candraprabha Press, Banaras.

KuP, *Kurma Purāṇa*, 1972. Sanskrit text and English translation. Ed. A.S. Gupta. All India Kashi Raj Trust, Varanasi. Dt. *ca* 7th-8th century. Ref. I.29-34; II.31-35.

KuM, *Kuttanīmatam*, by Damodāra Gupta, 1961. Ed. Jagannatha Pathaka. Indological Book House, Varanasi. Dt. *ca* 8th century. Ref. verses 3-18.

KYP, *Kāśīyātrā Prakāśa*, 1881. By Gorā-jī Dikṣita, published by Nand Kumar Mishra, printed in Sudharavasa Press.

LP, *Liṅga Purāṇa*, 1973 Ed. J.L. Shastri. English Trans. 2 Vol. Motilal Banarasidass, Delhi. Dt.; earlier part-*ca* CE 8th century, later part-*ca* 12th century. Ref. canto 92: 190 verses.

MbH, *Mahābhārata*, 1933-1959. Ed. V. S. Sukthankar (and others), 19 vols. Bhandarkar Oriental Research Institute, Baroda. Dt.: *ca* BCE 4th century. Ref. III.26.14; III.82.69; V.115; VI.10.30; VI.14.6; XIII.31; XIII.154.23 and 168.25.

MbP, *Mahābhāṣya* (of Patañjali) 1880-1885. Ed. by Kielhorn. Venkateshvara Press, Bombay, 4 vols. Dt. *ca* BCE 2nd century. Ref. II.V.3.35, IV.1.54, IV.3.72.

Maṇikarṇikāṣṭakam, 1888. By Śrī Gaṅgādhāra Kavi in *Kavya Sangraha*; vol. I. Jivananda Vidyasagar Bhattacharya, Calcutta.

Mdp, *Mudgala Purāṇa*, 1976. Shri Venkateshvara Press, Bombay.

MkP, *Mārkaṇḍeya Purāṇa*, 1904. Transl. & Ed. F.E. Pargiter. Reprinted, Indological Book House, Delhi, 1969. Dt.: *ca* CE 7th century, Ref.: VII-VIII.

MtP, *Matsya Purāṇa*, 1907. Anandashrama Sanskrit Series No. 54, Poona. Dt. *ca* 8th-10th century. Ref. 180,-185; 411.

NdP, *Nāradīya Purāṇa*, 1923. Venkateshvara Press, Bombay. Dt.: *ca* CE 9th century. Ref.: Uttarabhaga, II. 48-51, *ca* CE 12th century.

PP, *Padma Purāṇa*, 1894. Anandashrama Sanskrit Series No. 131, 4 vols., Poona. Dt. *ca* 12th-13th century. Ref. I.33-37; IV.235-236; V (*Sṛṣṭi Khaṇḍa*).14; VI (*Uttara Khaṇḍa*).235-236, 278.

PbC, *Prabodha Candrodaya* by Kṛṣṇa Miśra, 1955. Sanskrit Granthamala 14. Chowkhambha Vidya Bhavan, Varanasi. Dt. *ca* CE 1080.

PY, *Pañcakrośīyātrā*, 1884. Nepali Shri Haihara Pandita. Jyohari Bazar, shop of Pali Jitman Singh, Banaras, Printed at Vajracandra Press.

PYM, *Śrī Pañcakrośīyātrā Māhātmyam*, 1895. By the order of Bengali Shah, printed at Shri Satyanarayana Press.

RvS, *Ŗg Veda Saṁhitā*, 1940. Ed. Shripada Sharma. Svadhyayamandala, Anudha. Dt.: *ca* BCE 1500, Ref.: 1.130.7; 10.179.2.

RgV *The Hymns of the Ŗg Veda*, ed. J.L. Shastri, trans. R.T.H. Griffith, Rev. ed., 2 vols. Motilal Banarasidass, Delhi, 1973. Dt.: *ca* BCE 1500, Ref.: 1.130.7; 10.179.2.

SaB, *Śatapatha Brāhmaṇa*, 1882. Transl. J. Eggeling. Sacred Books of the East, vols. 12, 26, 41, 43, 44. The Claredon Press, Oxford. Reprinted, Motilal Banaridass, Delhi, 1989. Dt.: *ca* BCE 1500. Ref.: Vol. 5: 4.7.1; 13.5.4.21; 14.3.1.22; 14.14.

SuP, *Saura Purāṇa*, 1892. Venkateshvara Press, Bombay. Dt. *ca* CE 10th century, Ref. II.1.6; IV.22-27; V.44.

SkP, *Skanda Purāṇa*. Dt. *ca* CE 9th century, Ref. 29.1-5, 62-73, 74-76, 91-97, 180-241; 30. 61, 64-65, 66-75. See, Bakker, 1993.

SP, *Śiva Mahāpurāṇa*, 1960-65. Gurumandala Granthmalaya No. XX, 5 Vol., Calcutta.

SvP, *Śiva Mahāpurāṇa*, 1962. Pandita Pustakalaya, Banaras. Dt. *ca* CE 12-13th century, Ref.: Kotirudra Samhita: 22-23; also II.1.6, III.9, and V.44.

TC, *Tīrthacintāmaṇi*, by Vācaspati Miśra, 1912. Bibliotheca India, New Series No. 1256. Asiatic Society of Bengal, Calcutta. Dt. *ca* 1460.

TdS, *Tīrthenduśekhara*, by Nāgeśa Bhaṭṭa, 1936. Ed. Gopinath Kaviraj. Sarasvati Bhavan Granthamala No. 66-67. Rajakiya Mudranalaya, Allahabad.

TP, *Tīrthaprakāśa* (a section of *Viramitrodaya* of Mitra Mishra). Chowkhambha Sanskrit Series, no. 239, Varanasi. Dt.: *ca* 1620.

TS, *Tristhalīsetu*, by Nārāyaṇa Bhaṭṭa, 1915. Anandashrama Sanskrit Series, No. 78, Poona.

TvK, *Tīrthavivecana Kāṇḍa* (Part III of *Kŗtyakalpatāru* by Lakṣmīdhāra) 1942. Ed. K.V. Rangaswamy Aiyangar. Gaekwad's Oriental Series Vol. XCVIII. Oriental Institute, Baroda. Dt. *ca* 1100.

UvP, *Uktivyakti Prakaraṇa* by Paṇḍita Damodāra Śarmā, 1953. Ed. Jivavijaya Muni. Singhi Granthamala, no. 39. Singhi Jain Shashra Vidyapith. Bhartiya Vidya Bhavan, Bombay. Dt.: *ca* CE 1134-1150.

VmP, *Vāmana Purāṇa*, 1985. Ed. A. S. Gupta. All-India Kashi Raj Trust, Varanasi. Dt.: *ca* CE 8-9th century, Ref.: 3.26.

VyP, *Vāyu Purāṇa*, 1959. Gurumandala Granthamalaya, No. XIX, Calcutta. Dt.: CE 2-3rd century, Ref.: Canto 92.

VsP, *Viṣṇu Purāṇa*, 1990. Gita Press, Gorakhpur. Dt. CE 7th century.

—— 1840. Trans. In English: *The Vishnu Purana* by H.H. Wilson. Reprint, 3rd Ed. Punthi Pustak, Calcutta. Ref. V.24.

VtK, *Vividha Tīrthakalpa* by Jinaprabhu Suri, 1934. Ed. Jinavijaya Muni. University Press, Shantiniketan. Dt.: *ca* 1350.

E. Books/ articles in Hindi:

Agarwal, Kunwarji 1986. *Kasi ka Rang Parivesh*. (The Colour State of Kashi). Banaras.

Ansari, Ibadurrahman 1971. *Varanasi men Banarasi Sari Udyog: Ek Arthik Sarvekshan*. (Banarasi Sari Industry in Varanasi: An Economic Survey). Kashi Vidyapith Publs., Varanasi.

Bade Guru 1964. *Vah Banaras*. (Splendid Banaras). Bhartiya Bhasha Parishad Prakashan, Kashi.

Bismillah, Abdul 1986. *Jhini Jhini Bini Chadariya*. (The Threadbare Woven Shawl). A novel. Raj Kamal Prakashan, New Delhi.

Chaturvedi, Sitaram and Mukherjee, Vishwanath (eds.) 1962. *Yah Banaras Hai*. (This is Banaras). Thalua Club, Varanasi.

Chediram, Master Sri Ram 1983. *Holi ki Halchal*. (Celebration of Holi). Bharati Pustak Bhavan, Varanasi.

Devatirtha, Ananta (Kashthajihva Svami) 1997. *Panchakroshi Sudha. Sarvabhartiya Panchakroshi Marga*. (Nectar of Pancakroshi). Kashiraja Trust, Durg Ramanagar, Varanasi. 128pp.

Dikshit, Sudhakar (n.d.). *Naya Vishvanath Mandir Kyon?* (in Hindi) (Why a New Vishvanath Temple?). Published by Sri Sitaram Khemka, Sri Kashi Vishvanath Mandir (New), Varanasi.

Dube, Girja Prasad 1989. *Varanasi men Dakshina Bharatiya*. (The South Indians in Varanasi). Bohra Publ. & Distributors, Allahabad.

Dubey, Jagadish Narayan (ed. & trans.) 1984. *Kashi Rahasyam*. (Kashi Rahasya, Hindi version). Adarsh Prakashan Mandir, Varanasi.

Dwivedi, Prem Shankar 1985. *Durga (Varanasi ke Bhitti Chitron Men)* [Durga in the Wall Paintings of Varanasi]. Prem Shankar Dwevidi, Naria, Varanasi.

Ghalib, Mirza (CE 1797-1869) 1827. *Ciraghe-e-Dair*. (Light of the Lamp). [108 stanzas in Persian]. In, Ghalib Gaurava, ed. H.C. Nayyar. Banaras Hindu University, Varanasi, 1969: 136-150.

Giri, Kamal; Tiwari, Marutinandan, and Singh, Vijai Prakash 2003. *Kashi ke Mandir aur Murtiyan* (Temples and Images of Kashi). Jila Sanskitic Samiti, Varanasi.

Gupt, Balmukund 1935. *Kashi ya Banaras*. (Kashi or Banaras). Benares.

Hams: 1933. Kashi Visheshanka, Ed. Premchand, Vol. 4, Nos. 1-2, October-November; (*Hams*, a monthly magazine). Sarasvati Press, Banaras City: 01-222pp.
Fortysix short essays on various aspects; this is the first such attempt to have an anthology.

Harishankar 1996. *Kashi ke Ghat. Kalatmak evam Sanskritik Adhyayan*. (The Ghats of Kashi. A Study of Art and Culture). Vishvavidyalaya Prakashan, Varanasi.

Harishcandra, Babu Bhartendu 1872. *Panchakroshi Marga ka Vichar*. (Views on the route of Pancakroshi). Printed in the Medical Hall Press, Banaras, Samvata 1929. 8pp.

—— 1885. *Premajogini*. (Love-lorn Femate Ascetic). Bhartendu Granthavali, vol. I, Ed. Brajratnadas. Kashi Nagiri Pracarini Sabha, Kashi (reprinted 1989): 319-354.

Jauhari, Renu 2004. *Bharatiy Sangit ke Jagat men Varanasi ka Yogadan*. 320pp. Classical Publising Company, New Delhi. ISBN: 81-70543827.
Development of Hindustani classical music in Varanasi, Uttar Pradesh, India; a study with special reference to the Tabla players, their development and future.

Jha, Kashinath 1964. *Kashi Mahima Prakash Ya Kashi Khanda Sar*. (Summary of the Kashi Khanda). Master Khelarilal & Sons, Varanasi.

Joshi, Nilakanth Purushottam 1989. *Gwalior Sangrahalay ka Varanasi Shilapatta* (The Varanasi stoneslab of the Gwalior museum). *Puratan*, vol. 6: 151-153.

Kashyap, Prashant 2006. *Gahadavalon ka Itihas* (History of the Gahadavalas). Vishvavidyalaya Prakashan, Varanasi. ISBN: 81-7124-504-8.
After Niyogi 1959, the first thorough attempt to analyse the history of the Gahadavala dynasty, 11-12th centuries, mostly based on inscriptions, and religious contexts.

Kaul, Ashok 2002. The other side of Banaras: An untold story of EPW. *Hindustan* (a Hindi daily newspaper), Special *"Subah-e-Banaras"*, 30 May, Thursday: p. 4.

Kaviraja, Gopinatha 1964. *Kashi ki Sarasvat Sadhana.* (Intellectual Meditation of Kashi). Bihar Rastrabhasha Parishad, Patna.

Kishori, Sarit 1995. *Varanasi ke Sthan Namon ka Sanskritik Adhyayan.* (Cultural Study of Place Names of Varanasi). Vishvavidyalaya Prakashan, Varanasi.

Kumar, Kranti (ed.) 1998. *Ganga: Ek Gadya-Padya Samgraha.* (Ganga: a Collection of Essays and Poems). Triratna Nyasa, Sarnath (Varanasi). [Out of 26 essays six are in English, the rest in Hindi, and some in Sanskrit].

Lala, Munshi Harijana 1917. *Kashi Tattva Bhaskara (Kashi Varshik Yatra).* (Annual Sacred Journeys of Kashi). Shivadayalamala, Vishnudasa, Kashi. Hitacintaka Press, Ramaghat, Varanasi.

Lala, Brajabihari 1914. *Varanasi Adarsh (Arthat Kashi ki Adhyay Suchi).* (Description of deities, tirthas, and sacred sites and the rules of pilgrimage). Published by B.L. Pavagi. Hitacintaka Press, Ramaghat, Varanasi.

Mehta, Bhanushankar 2004. *Dhan Dhan Matu Ganga.* (Hail to thy Glory Mother Ganga). Vishvavidyalaya Prakashan, Varanasi. pp. xxiv + 271. ISBN: 81-7124-376-2.

—— 2006. *Ghode pai Hauda Hathi par Jin.* (Howdah on the Horse and Saddle on the Elephant). Anurag Prakashan, Varanasi. ISBN: 81-89498-12-8.
Collection of stories in the historical context of the British period, by the noted writers of Hindi literature.

Mishra, Ajay 2004. *Pakka Mahal.* (a novel on the neighbourhood of Pakka Mahal, Banaras). Vani Prakashan, New Delhi.

Mishra, Jitendra Nath 2004. *Shri Chitakut Ramalila. Kashi Atit evam Vartman.* (Chitrakut Ramalila. Present and Past of Kashi). 58/100 Ramalila Bhavan, Lohatia (Varanasi).

Mishra, Kaushal Kishore 1986. Ed. *Varanasi Visheshank.* (Sanmarg's Annual Special Number on Varanasi). Sanmarg Office, Varanasi. 69 essays on various aspects. 339pp. (size 22 x 28cm).

—— 1987. Ed. *Tirth Visheshank*. (Sanmarg's Annual Special Number on Pilgrimage). Sanmarg Office, Varanasi. 73 essays on various aspects. 410pp. (size 22 x 28cm).

—— 1989. Ed. *Vrat, Parv evam Tyohar Visheshank*. (Sanmarg's Annual Special Number on Hindu Rituals & Festivals). Sanmarg Office, Varanasi. 77 essays on various aspects. 452pp. (size 22 x 28cm).

Mishra, Tej Narayan 1992. *Banaras men Kampani Shaili ki Chitrakala*. (Company style painting in Banaras). Kala Prakashan, Varanasi.

Motichandra, 1962. *Kashi ka Itihas*. (History of Kashi). Bombay. 2nd ed. 1985, 3rd ed. 2003, Varanasi: Vishvavidyalaya Prakashan.

Mukherjee, Vishvanath 1958. *Bana Rahe Banaras*. (Long Live Banaras). Bharatiya Jnanapith Publication, Varanasi.

—— 1978. Ed. *Yah Banaras Hai*. (This is Banaras). Thalua Club, Varanasi. 2nd ed. 1983.

Panchakroshimahatmyam 1885. Published by the order of Bengali Shah, printed at Satyanarayan Press; available at north of Jnanavapi Library at the shop of the editor of Satyanarayan Press, Bengali Shah. 20 folio (42pp.).

Panchakroshiyatra 1884. Published by the order of Nepali Harihara-pandita and printed at Vrajacandra Yantranalaya; available at the shop of Jitaman Singh. Samvata 1941. 21 folio (41pp.)

Pandey, Anand Kumar 2006. *Vaitarini se Vaishvanar tak ki Yatra* (Journey from Vaitarini to Vaishvanar). Vishwavidyala Prakashan, Varanasi. ISBN: 81-7124-493-9.
The book narrates the contextual and background stories of the writings of Shivprasad Singh, who wrote three novels on Varanasi.

Pandey ['Arya'], Banarasilal 1975. *Maharaja Balvant Singh aur Kashi ka Atit*. (King Balawant Singh and the Past of Kashi). Narayana Prakashan, Varanasi.

Pandey, Banarasilal 1991. *Kashi ke Aitihasik Muhalle*. (Historical Neighbourhoods of Kashi). Sri Kavipuskara Sahitya Sodh Sansthan, Varanasi.

Pandey, Govind Narayan and Upadhyay, Divyamurti (ed.) 1993. *Shri Ramalila: Ramnagar ka Shri Ramlila par Adharit.* (Ramalila, Based on the Ramalila of Ramnagar). Srimati Gyanavati Pandey, Allahabad.

Pandey, Shrinivas (ed.) 2007. *Prajna. Kashi Gaurav-I.* (Prajna: Glory of Kashi-I). Banaras Hindu University Patrika, yr 52 (Pts. 1-2), 2006-07. 38 essays in Hindi, and 7 essays in English; 380pp.

—— (ed.) 2008. *Prajna. Kashi Gaurav-II.* (Prajna: Glory of Kashi-II). Banaras Hindu University Patrika, yr 53 (Pts. 1-2), 2007-08. 33 essays in Hindi, and 3 essays in English; 304pp.

Pandey, Uma 1980. *Varanasi: Bharat ka Sanskritik Kendra.* (Varanasi: the Cultural Capital of India). Mcmillan Co. of India Ltd., Madras.

Patel, Sudhendu 1998. *Kashi Katha.* (The Story of Kashi). Rajasthan Praurh Shiksha Samiti, Jaipur.

Prasad, Babu Sadhucharana 1903. *Bharat Bhraman.* (Journey in India). Vol. I. Kashi Bhraman (Journey in Kashi). Hitacintaka Press (Kashi Yajneshvara Yantranalaya), Banaras.

Premchand 1933. (Ed.) *Hamsa, Kashi Ank.* (Hamsa, Kashi number). October-November Issue. Saraswati Press, Varanasi.

Raghava, Rangeya 1976. *Loi ka Tana.* (The Warp of Quilt). A novel on Kabir's life. Rajpal & Sons, Delhi. 3rd ed.

Rai, Kaushal Kumar 1984. Ed. Uttar Pradesh: *Sanyuktanka – Kashi Ank.* (Uttar Pradesh: Joint Varanasi Number). Information and Public Relation Dept., Govt. of U.P., Lucknow.

Ramakrishna 1994. *Kashi: Atit ki Jhankiyan.* Vinod Kumar, Varanasi.

Ramakrishnaji, Sri Pandit 1913. Ed. *Kashi: Varshik Yatra Prakash.* (Kashi: Reflection on Annual Sacred Journeys). Chandraprabha Press, Banaras.

'Rudra', Shivprasad Mishra 1967. *Bahati Ganga.* (Flowing Ganga). Collection of 17 stories about British Period. Radhakrishna Prakashan, Varanasi.

Sarasvati, Dandi Svami Shivananda 1988. *Kashi Mahima.* (The Glory of Varanasi). Dharmasangha, Varanasi.

316

—— 1989. *Panchakroshi Darshanyatra.* (Glimpse of the Pancakroshi Pilgrimage). Dharmasangha, Varanasi.

—— 1990. *Kashi Darshan* (Glimpses of Kashi). Dharmasangha, Varanasi.

—— 1991. *Kashi Panchakroshi Yatra Mahatmya.* (Glory of Kashi's Pancakroshi Yatra). Dharmasangha, Varanasi.

—— 1998. *Kashi Gaurava* (Kashi ki Panchakroshi yatra 'mahatmya' Kasha ka itihas Kashi mahatmya vartman men prachalit Varanasi ki sampurn yatra). (The Glory of Kashi). Dharmasangha, Varanasi.

—— 2001. *Kamadhenu Kalikashi Panchakroshi Parikrama Mahatmya.* (The Glory of the Kamadhenu-form Kashi Pancakroshi Yatra). Dharmasangha (Durgakund), Varanasi.

Saraswati, Baidyanath (ed.) 2000. *Bhoga-Moksha Samabhava: Kashi ka Samnajika-Sanskritik Svarup.* [Enjoyment-Liberation United: Social-Cultural Forms of Kashi]. Co-editors: Krishnanath, Satyaprakash Mittal and Ram Lakhan Maurya.
57 essays that deal with religion, sects and the cultural traditions that make the city a mosaic of Indian culture. xiii + 362pp. Hb. ISBN: 81-246-0151-8.

Sarraf, Mukund Lal 1980. *Kashi Sarvangin Sundar Kaise Bane.* (How to Make Kashi Overall Beautiful). Kashi Tirtha Sudhar Samiti, Varanasi.

Shankar, Gauri 1970. *Ek Harijan Basti.* (An Untouchable Locality). Navachetan Prakashan, Varanasi (for the Gandhian Studies Institute).

—— 1973. *Varanasi Nagar ke Saggadavan.* (Load carriers of Varanasi). Gandhian Studies Institute, Rajghat, Varanasi.

Sharma, Narayanapati 1904. *Kashi Darpan Yatra.* (Kashi's Pilgrimages). Venkateshvara Press, Bombay.

Shrivastava, Saritakishori 1995. *Varanasi ke Sthan Namon ka Sanskritik Adhyayan.* (A Cultural Study of the Place names of Varanasi). Vishvavidyalaya Prakashan, Varanasi.

Shukla, Prayag 2005. *Kalpana: Kashi Anka.* 376pp., illus. Badarivishala Pannalala Pitti Trasta, Hyderabad. Pb, ISBN: 81-75255897.

Contributed articles in Hindi on Varanasi, Hindu pilgrimage center; compiled for an unpublished special issue of a discontinued serial *Kalpana*; includes literary pieces.

Singh, Harihar and Rai, Suresh Chandra 1984. *Kashi Hindu Vishvavidyalay ka Vikas Kram: Ek Bhaugolik Samiksha.* (Growth of Banaras Hindu University: A Geographical Analysis). *Prajna* (a biannual from B.H.U., Varanasi), vol. 29 (2) & 30 (1): 199-208.

Singh, Kashinath 1972. *Apna Morcha.* (Our Front). Prakashan Sansthan, New Delhi.
A novel on the students and educational crisis during 1970s Banaras.

—— 2002. *Kashi ka Assi* (Kashi's Assi). Raj Kamal Prakashan, New Delhi.
A novel on the culture of a neighbourhood in Banaras.

Singh, Pratibha 2004. *Shiva-Kashi: Pauranik Paripekshya aur Vartman Sandarbh* (Shiva-Kashi: Pauranic Background and Present Context). Vishvavidyalaya Prakashan, Varanasi.

Singh, Pratibha 2008. Kashi ki Panchakroshi Yatra ('Kashi's Panchakroshi Yatra'). *Durvachna: Souvenir celebrating 100th year of Ganeshotsava.* Nutan Balak Ganeshotsava Samaj Seva Mandala, Varanasi: 141-148. [Also consists of 2 figures].

Singh, Raghavendra Pratap 1987. *Varanasi aur Bhartiya Rashtriya Congress,* 1947-74. Northern Book Centre, New Delhi.

Singh, Ramabachan 1994. *Varanasi. Ek Paramparagat Nagar.* (Varanasi, A Traditional City). Bhartiya Vidya Bhavan, Varanasi.

Singh, Rana P.B. 2008. Kashi ke Vinayakon ka Bhuvainyasika Prarup ('Spatial Patterns of the Vinayakas of Kashi'). *Durvachna: Souvenir celebrating 100th year of Ganeshotsava.* Nutan Balak Ganeshotsava Samaj Seva Mandala, Varanasi: 71-76. [Includes also 2 maps].

Singh, Rana P.B. and Rana, Pravin S. 2008. Varanasi ka Bhaugolika Parivesh ('Geographical outline of Varanasi'). *Durvachna: Souvenir celebrating 100th year of Ganeshotsava.* Nutan Balak Ganeshotsava Samaj Seva Mandala, Varanasi: 45-54.[Also includes 6 tables & 3 Figures].

318

Singh, Ravi Shankar & Singh, Pratibha 2008. Kashi (Varanasi) men Hindu Deviyan ('Hindu Devis in Kashi'). *Durvachna: Souvenir celebrating 100th year of Ganeshotsava.* Nutan Balak Ganeshotsava Samaj Seva Mandala, Varanasi: 149-158.

Singh, Shivaprasad (late) 1974. *Gali Age Murati Hai.* (The Street Turns Yonder). Vani Prakashan, New Delhi, 2nd ed. 1991.
A novel on modern Varanasi.

—— 1988. *Nila Chand.* (Blue Moon). Vani Prakashan, New Delhi.
A novel on medieval Varanasi.

—— 1996. *Vaishvanara.* (The Primordial Fire). Vani Prakashan, New Delhi.
A novel on ancient Varanasi.

Singh, Shukdev (ed.) 1992 *Varanasi Jal Sansthan Shatabdi Samaroh Smarika,* 1892-1992. (Souvenir of the Century Celebration of Water Works, 1892-1992). Varanasi Jal Sansthan, Varanasi.

Sukul, Kuberanath 1968 (Samvata 2025). *Varanasi ka Adhidaivik Baibhav.* (The Divine Glory of Varanasi). Maheshvari Press, Varanasi. 36 + 6 pp.

—— 1974. *Kashi ke Yatra Kram.* (Sequence of Sacred Journeys of Kashi). Rama Ugraha Pandey, Varanasi.

—— 1977 (Samvata 2034). *Varanasi Vaibhav.* (The Glory of Varanasi). Rastrabhasha Parishad, Patna.

Tripathi, Ramapratap 1952. *Puranon me Ganga.* (The Ganga in the Puranas). Hindi Sahitya Sammelan Prayag.

Tripathi, Vishambharnath 'Bade Guru' 2007. *Aj bhi Vahi Banaras Hai.* [Banaras is the Same Today]. National Book Trust, New Delhi. Publ. ID 5239. [Tripathi, 1932-1988].

Upadhyaya, Baladeva 1994. *Kashi ki Panditya Parampara (Kashistha samskrta vidvanon jivancharit evam sahityak avadanon ka pramanik vivaran)* [1200-1980]. Vishvavidyalaya Prakashan, Varanasi. Reprinted 2002.
An authentic and comprehensive historical account of the Sanskrit Pandits of Varanasi with their biography and works, literary contributions and attainments, intellectual traditions, and reminiscences.

Upadhyaya, Baikunthanatha 1975. *Sri Kashi Panchakroshi Dev-Yatra.* (Kashi's Pancakroshi Divine Journey). Sri Bhrigu Prakashan, Varanasi. 62pp.

—— 1982-92. *Kashi Rahasya.* In 7 parts. Bhrigu Prakashan, Varanasi.

—— 1992. *Kashi Khanda.* In 5 parts. Bhrigu Prakashan, Varanasi.

Vajhe, Bhau Shastri 1951. *Sri Kashi Yatra Prakash (Kashi Mahatmya tatha Itihas).* (The Light of Kashi's Pilgrimage/ Glory of Kashi and its History). 2nd Ed. Hitacintaka Press, Varanasi.

Verma, Balamukunda 1935. *Kashi ya Banaras.* (Kashi or Banaras). Tara Printing Works (Yantranalaya), Banaras.

Verma, T.P.; Singh, D.P. and Mishra, J.S. (eds.) 1986. *Yugo Yugon men Kashi.* (*Varanasi Through the Ages*). Proceedings of an All-India Seminar. Bhartiya Itihas Samkalan Samiti, Varanasi. (Essays in Hindi and some in English).

Vishvakarma, Ishvar Sharan 1987. *Kashi ka Aitihasik Bhugol.* (Historical Geography of Kashi: From the earliest times to CE 12th century). Ramananda Vidya Bhavan, New Delhi.

Vyasa, Kedaranath 1987. *Kashikhandokta Panchakroshatmak Jyotiraling Kashi Mahatmya.* (The History and Glory of Kashi as the Panchakrosha-Form Siva linga as described in the Kashi Khanda). Kashi Sodha Samsthan, (CK 35/ 8 Jnanavapi, Varanasi), pub. by himself.

Yadav, Rahul 2005. The hover around danger on the heritage (of Varanasi). *India Today* (Hindi weekly, New Delhi), 5 September: pp. 52-53.

F. MARATHI SOURCES

GC, *Guru Charitra* (of Sarasvati Gangadhara), 1990. Trans., ed. & revised by Ramachandra Krishna Keshava Bhikaji Dhavale, Girgaon (Bombay), 14th edn., Shaka 1912. Dt.: CE 1538, Ref.: 41.136-400: Kashi Mahatyma and the sacred Yatras.

Deo, Vishvanath N. 1933. *Devi Sri Ahalyabai Holkar Charita*. Indore.

G. BENGALI SOURCES

Chakravarti, Manmathanatha B.S. 1933. *Sachitra Kashidhama*. (Holy Kashi illustrated with photographs). Shilpa O Sahitya Bibhaga, Calcutta.

Ghoshal, Jayanarayan 1906. *Kashi Parikrama*. (Pilgrimage to Kashi). Bangiya Sahitya Parishad, Calcutta.

Maitra, Akshay Kumar 1990. *Rani Bhavani*. Sahityaloka, Calcutta.

H. Published Reports/ Government Documents

Census of India 1895. *District Census Statistics 1891, Benares District, North-Western Provinces and Oudh.* North-Western Provinces and Oudh Government Press, Allahabad.

Census of India 1961. *Report on the Population Estimates of India* (1820-1830). Eds. Durgaprasad Bhattacharya and Bibhavati Bhattacharya (of the Socio-Economic Research Institute, C-19, College Street Market, Calcutta - 12. PRG.37 (N). Office of the Registrar General, India, New Delhi. Manager of Publications, Delhi, 1965. xxxix + 395pp. For Banaras, James Prinsep's survey, 1827-1829, see pp. 241-278, and 280-281.

Census of India 1961. *District Census Handbook, District Varanasi.* Uttar Pradesh, 53. Superintendent, Printing and Stationery U.P. (India), Lucknow. 1965.

Census of India 1971. *District Census Handbook, District Varanasi.* Series 21, Uttar Pradesh, Part X-A, Town and Village Directory. Ed. D.M. Sinha, Directorate of Printing, Registrar General Office of India, Lucknow, 1972.

Census of India 1981. *District Census Handbook, District Varanasi.* Series 21, Uttar Pradesh, Part X-A, Town and Village Directory. Directorate of Printing, Registrar General Office of India, Lucknow, 1985.

Census of India 2001. *District Varanasi.* Population by Religion. Outprint by Assistant Director Mr. Anand Nigam, New Delhi.

Clark, S. 1869. *Report of the Lunatic Asylums at Bareilly and Benares During 1868.* Government Printing for the North-Western Provinces (India), Allahabad.

Bhatta, B.R. 1923. *Report on the industrial survey of the United Provinces: Benares district.* Government Press, Allahabad.

Fitzjames, Frank 1880. *Preliminary report on the sewerage and water supply of the city of Benares.* North Western Provinces and Oudh Government Press, Allahabad.

IPHD 1918. *The Sanitary Survey of Benares Municipality*. Benares (city), India Public Health Department (IPHD), India Benares (city), Public Health Department. A.C. Chakravarty, Benares. 44pp.

Ishrat, Amrit Lal (ed.) 1965. *A Descriptive Catalogue of Persian Manuscripts in the Benaras Hindu University*. Banaras Hindu University Press, Varanasi.

Janki Prasad 1944. *Final settlement report of district Chakia, Benares State*. Benares State Press, Banaras.

Lambert, G.B. 1927. *List of darbaris, Benares division*. Government Secretariate of United Provinces, Allahabad.

Maharaja of Benares 1865. *Report from the Deputy Superintendent of family Domains, on the subject of the revision of Settlement now in hand of Pergana Bhudohee*. Estate of Benares, Varanasi. [s.l.]:[s.n.].

—— 1920. *Memorial to his honour the Lieutenant-Governor of the United Provinces of Agra and Oudh*. Pioneer Press, Allahabad.

Narain, A.K. and Roy, T.N. 1976. *Excavations at Rajghat* (1957-1958; 1960-1965). Part 1. Banaras Hindu University, Varanasi.

—— 1977. *Excavations at Rajghat* (1957-58; 1960-65). Part 2. Banaras Hindu University, Varanasi.

Narain, A.K. 1977. *Excavations at Rajghat* (1957-58; 1960-65). Part 3. Banaras Hindu University, Varanasi.

Porter, F.W. 1887. *Final Report on the Survey and Revision of Records recently Compiled for the Benares District*. Govt. Press, Allahabad.

Prasad, Janki 1944. *Final settlement report of district Chakia, Benares State*. Benares State Press, Banaras.

Raghunath Prasad 1929. *Views of Benares presented by the Maharaja of Benares*. Estate of Benares, Varanasi [s.n.].

Sahni, Daya Ram 1914/ 1972. *Catalogue of the Museum of Archaeology at Sarnath*. Superintendent, Government Printing, India, Calcutta. Reprinted in 1972 by Indological Book House, New Delhi.

Singh, Prahlad 1978. *Stone observatories in India, erected by Maharaja Sawai Jai Singh of Jaipur, 1686-1743 A.D., at Delhi, Jaipur, Ujjain, Varanasi, Mathura, assisted by Pandit Kalyan Dutt Sharma*. Bharata Manisha, Varanasi.

Shivanand, V., ed. 1992. *Catalogue of Kannada palm-leaf manuscripts and other research documents in North India, Kashi, Kedar (U.P.), Arrah (Bihar), Calcutta (W.B.)*. Banaras Hindu University, Varanasi. [in Kannada].

VSV-SBL 1888. *Catalogue of Sanskrit Manuscripts in the Sanskrit College Library, Benares, with Full Index*. Varanaseya Sanskrit Vishwavidyalays, Saraswati Bhavan Library, Saraswati Bhavan Library. By the Order of Government at the Government Press, N.W.P. and Oudh, Allahabad. 539pp.

Wood, W. Gunnell 1915. *An Estimate and Design for the Construction of a Road Bridge to carry the Grand Trunk road over the River Ganges at Benares*. Pioneer Press, Allahabad.

I. ELECTRONIC PUBLICATIONS

Dimmers, Michaela and Gengnagel, Jörg (compiled) 2002. *Index of Kashikhanda. Compiled by Michaela Dimmers & Jörg Gengnagel.* Electronic Publications of the Varanasi Research Project II. University of Heidelberg-South Asia Institute. URL: http://www.benares.uni-hd.de/KKh-Index/Intro-KKh.htm.

FV: Feedback Venture, New Delhi 2006 (August). *Varanasi City Development Plan under JNNURM* (Cover Page, Part 1, Part 2, Part 3 Annexure). Accessed on 15 January 2008, Web: http://www.jnnurm.nic.in/toolkit/varanasi.htm

Gengnagel, Jörg and Mayer-König, Birgit (eds.) 2003. *Descriptive Catalogue of mainly Visual Material on Varanasi kept in the Banaras Archives of the South Asia Institute* Electronic Publications of the Varanasi Research Project III. University of Heidelberg, South Asia Institute. URL: http://www.benares.uni-hd.de/ben-archive.pdf.

Gengnagel, Jörg and Michaels, Axel (eds.) 2001. *Kailashanatha Sukula's Mirror of Kashi (Kashidarpana, 1876). A historical map of Varanasi based on the Kashikhanda and related texts.* University of Heidelberg-South Asia Institute. Publications of the Varanasi Research Project I. URL: http://www.benares.uni-hd.de/map.htm

—— (compiled) 2003. *Banaras Bibliography.* Updated in October 2003. http://www.sai.uni-heidelberg.de/abt/IND/publikation/bibbanaras/bibbanaras.htm
[* This is a re-setting of an earlier publication, without mentioning the original source, from where it is directly copied; see: Singh, Rana P.B. 1993 g. Banaras (Varanasi): A Selected Bibliography (495); in, Singh, Rana P.B. (ed.) *Banaras (Varanasi).* Tara Book Agency, Varanasi: pp. 317-341.]

Gutschow, Niels 1999. *Pilgrimage and Space. The definitory purpose of pilgrimage routes. (Case studies from Bhaktapur, Kag and Muktinath (Nepal) and Varanasi).* Internatiomnal Conference on Pilgrimage and Complexity, IGNCA, New Delhi. http://www.colorado.edu/Conferences/pilgrimage/papers99/Gutschow.html.

Kumar, Bimal 2003. *District Model Land Use Plan. District-Varanasi. Uttar Pradesh. Final Report.* Sponsored by the State Land Use Board, Uttar Pradesh (Lucknow). G.P. Pant Social Science Research Institute, Allahabad. http//www.planning.up.nic.in/landuseboard/Varanasi.pdf

Friedlander, Peter 2006. Hindi in Banaras in the 1970s. A paper presented to the 16th Biennial Conference of the Asian Studies Association of Australia in Wollongong 26 June - 29 June 2006. http://www.bodhgayanews.net/hindi/FriedlanderASAA2006.pdf

Ramseier, Yves 2001. *A Bibliography on the Kashikavtti.* Gaidai, Osaka (Japan). 13pp. http://hin.osaka-gaidai.ac.jp/~ramseier

Rao, P.S.N. (2006, 12 October). *JNNURM CDP Appraisal Report - VARANASI.* Accessed on 15 January 2007, Web: http://www.jnnurm.nic.in/cdp_apprep_pdf/CDP_Appraisal_IIPA/Varanasi_IIPA.pdf

Searle-Chatterjee, Mary 2002. *Islamicization in a Globalizing Context.* [Modified and updated version of her earlier paper, 1994]. Website: www.svabhinava.org/friends/MaryChatterjee/Wahabi2.htm <accessed: 03 April 2008>

Singh, Rana P.B. 2005. *Ghats and Palaces of Banaras.* http://www.staedteforum.at/Probe/ISGM4_06/RANA%20P%20Singh.doc

——— 2005. *Life in Historic Urban Landscape of Varanasi, a Heritage City of India.* Presented in, 'Life in the Urban Landscape', International Conference for integrating Urban Knowledge and Practice. Gothenberg, Sweden: May 29-June 3. http://www.urbanlife2005.com/proceedings/A/34_Rana_Singh.pdf

——— 2006. *Varanasi as Heritage City (India) on the scale the UNESCO World Heritage List: From Contestation to Conservation.* 19th European Conference on Modern South Asian Studies. Leiden University, Leiden (The Netherlands): 27-30 June, Panel 27. SASNET, Lund University. http://www.sasnet.lu.se/EASASpapers/46RanaSingh.pdf

——— 2007. Urban Planning of the Heritage City of Varanasi (India) and its role in Regional Development. *12ᵗʰ International Conference on Urban Planning and Regional Development in the Information Society. REAL CORP 007 Proceedings*. Tagungaband, Viena (Austria), 20-23 May 2007. Web: <www.corp.it>. ISBN: 978-39502139-2-8 (CD Rom), ISBN: 978-39502139-3-5 (Print); editors: Manfred Schrenk, Vasily V. Popovich, Josef Benedikt; pp. 259-268.
http://programm.corp.at/cdrom2007/archiv/tagungsband/CORP2007_proceedings.pdf

J. Films (English)

Bau, Christian and Gutschow, Niels 2006. *Shiva's Places. Lingas and Rituals in Benares.* [In English and German]. 120pp, 80 colour photographs, and 83 minutes 4:3 DVD by Thede Filmproduction Hamburg. Verlag Peter Hess, Uenzen (Germany). ISBN: 3-938263-05-9.

The book (with DVD) contains (English and German, side-by-side) short backgrounds to the themes selected and narrated, that refer to General remarks, Longing for India, Visual work in Benares (Banaras), Place and stones, Place and its history, Picture maps of the 18th to 20th centuries, Tilabhandeshvara temple, Panchakroshi temple, Antargriha-'inner house', Avimukteshvara, Panchakroshi pilgrimage, Group of temples, Dialogue between authors and film-makers, Listing the sequences of films, and Select literature. The earlier part showing scenes and narration is very informative and innovative. However, the later part that is claimed as 'pilgrimage' with photographs only, without voice and narration turns to be tough and lacking message. For those not fully knowledgeable about this holy city, the later part does not give any impression.

Gardner, Robert 1985. *"Forest of Bliss"* (a film on Banaras). University of Wisconsin Film Archive, Madison, WI, USA. Harvard Film Archive Production, Harvard University, Cambridge MA, USA.

This is an early documentary film on the religious life of Banaras, with the wonderful contrasts of scenes, activities and perspectives.

Gardner, Robert and Östör, Åkos 2001. *Making 'Forest of Bliss': Intention, Circumstance and Chance in Non-fiction Film: A conversation with Robert Gardner and Åkos Östör.* Harvard Film Archive Production, Harvard University, Cambridge MA, USA. 135pp. Pb book: ISBN: 0-674-00787-5, Price: $ 39.95, with DVD-9. For numerous articles and reviews on this film, see: www.filmstudycenter.org/makingforestofbliss

This film is a contemporary classic of non-fiction cinema. Recalling the conditions of its filming in Banaras in 1985 and presenting their moment-to-moment impressions upon watching it several years later, Gardner and the anthropologist Åkos Östör probe questions of what it means to capture life — and death — on film. The resulting cross-section is a lively exploration of issues philosophical, anthropological and — above all — artistic. *Making Forest of Bliss* presents this dialogue, together with an introduction by the philosopher Stanley Cavell and a newly mastered DVD of the film. It is the first in Harvard Film Archive's series 'Voices and Visions in Film'.

Katz, Marc J. (producer and director) and Winbergh, Staffan (photography) 1996. *Holi Hey, A Festival of Colour, Love and Life.* 53 minutes. DVD+R 4.7GB 1-4X speed, maxell. Available from The Center of South Asia, University of Wisconsin-Madison, U.S.A. © Marc J. Katz.

This 'personalised' film documents the importance, symbolism and functionalism of Holi, a Hindu spring festival of communal inclusion, which annually unites the community, reminding everyone of the eternal interconnection of life that breaches all community barriers, e.g. age, gender, caste, social and religion at various degrees, which is not always the reality. Somehow the lower masses of people are represented in a passing way.

—— (producer and director) and Winbergh, Staffan (photography) 2001. *Tulsidas and the Fire of the Veda.* 120 minutes. DVD+R 4.7GB 1-4X speed, maxell. Available from The Center of South Asia, University of Wisconsin-Madison, U.S.A. © Marc J. Katz.

This film documents the performance of 'Sat Chandi Yagya' that was first time arranged at the Sankat Mochan Temple of Banaras in July-August 1999 for this purpose, with the support and sponsorship of the director. As the director wished, the film successfully attempts to integrate the Vedic tradition of fire ritual and the medieval tradition of Bhakti, and further succeed to superimpose the ideas of saint-poet Tulsidas who himself was unable to do so in his times. This Yagya had never been performed in the compound of the Sankat Mochan Temple, except the arranged one that was filmed in a beautiful manner. This film is a wonderful example of an outsider's love, respect and projection of a Hindu festival which leaves the inner realities, but intensionally highlights several spots of the superficial scenes. The festival of Holi is no way related to the 'Fire of the Veda', but the director has succeeded to project this message to please himself and the Western mind.

—— (producer and director) and Winbergh, Staffan (photography) 2004. *Banaras Muharram and the Coals of Karbala*. 70 minutes. VHS. Available from The Center of South Asia, University of Wisconsin-Madison, U.S.A. © Marc J. Katz.

This film documents the celebration of a Muslim Shia festival called Muharram that conveys the message of collective spiritual/mystical experience insuring communal harmony, peace, love and brother-hood among the various sects and groups of Muslims. In fact, the reflection of this film is more hyperbolic and idealistic to say that even Hindus (including Brahmins) participate actively. Of course, Shias and Sunnis frequently fight during this festival. This film completely neglected to project this situation. The film completely ignores to mention that for this celebration the police and other administrative authorities consistently make all sorts of tedious preparations during at least six weeks before the celebration so that this festival passes peacefully.

Mehta, Deepa (writer and director) 2006. *Water* [videorecording] / Fox Searchlight Pictures presents; Mongrel Media presents in associa-tion with Telefilm Canada, Noble Nomad Pictures, Echo Lake Productions; a David Hamilton production. *Imprint*: 20th Century Fox Home Entertainment, Beverly Hills, CA. Originally released in 2005 as a motion picture.

Description: 1 videodisc (*ca* 117 min.): sd., col.; 4 3/4 in. Special features: director Deepa Mehta commentary; "Behind-the-scenes" featurette; "The story behind the making of 'Water'" featurette. Music: Mychael Danna; editor: Colin Monie; director of photography: Giles Nuttgens. DVD, region 1, widescreen (2.35:1) presentation; Dolby Digital 5.1. Surround: Hindi dialogue, with optional English or Spanish subtitles; closed-captioned *Actors:* Sarala, Lisa Ray, Seema Biswas, John Abraham, Manorma, Raghuvir Yadav, Kulbhushan Kharbanda, Waheeda Rehman, Raghuvir Yadav, Vinay Pathak. Note: MPAA rating: PG-13. Genie Awards, 2006: Best performance by an actress in a leading role (Biswas); Best achievement in cinematography; Best achievement in music-original score. ISBN/ISSN: 024543266143 00.

Summary: Often, a Hindu widow in 1938 could throw herself on her husband's funeral pyre, marry her husband's younger brother or live in poverty and self-denial from then on. When eight-year-old Chuyia is widowed, she is sent to a home in the holy city of Varanasi where Hindu widows live in penitence. Her feisty presence affects the other residents, forcing each to confront their faith and society's prejudices, especially a young woman who has fallen in love with a follower of Gandhi.

Parashar, Pankaj (Director) 2006, August. *Banaras, A Mystic Love Story*. Starring: Urmila Matonkar, Ashmit Patel, Naseeruddin Shah, Dimple Kapadia, Raj Babbar. Language: Hindi; Studio: Rainbow. Run time: 165 mins.

The film is set in the mystic land of Banaras. The film is about relationship — relationship of humans with God and about the relationship of great men like Buddha, Kabir, Tulasi and Shankaracharya with Banaras. Shwetambari (Urmilla Matondkar), the bright young daughter of rich Brahmin parents (Dimple Kapadia and Raj Babbar) studies science at the local university in Banaras. Soham (Ashmit Patel), a low caste mystic and a protégé of Babaji (Naseeruddin Shah), teaches music at the University. When the two fall in love, hell breaks loose in Banaras. The orthodox and conservatives surface to the fore, threatening to take away everything from the young lovers. When her powerful parents try to ignore the social strictures for the happiness of their daughter, the dark forces and destiny take complete control. "It turned out much better than expected. It is a serious but sweet love story with a mystical component. The performances by all-Urmila Matondkar and Asmit Patel, and needless to say Naseeruddin Shah were good. Ashmit Patel was the surprise — he suited the role well and did a good job. The mystical part was very well done as well, not overdone. It was slightly hard to digest Urmila Matondkar as 'Ma' (spiritual Ma types), but she gets away with it. One of the problems that plagues all Hindi films is the length, and this is not different. They would be much 'crisper' if they were shorter. But "good watch, in any case", says a reviewer.

Rawail, H.S. (Director, Producer) 1968. *Sangharsh* ('struggle'). Based on a Bengali novel by Mahashweta Devi; screenplay: Anjana Rawail; dialogs: Gulzar, Abrar Alvi; choreography: Gopi Krishna; lyrics: Shakeel Badayuni; music: Naushad; playback singers: Lata Mangeshkar, Mohammed Rafi, Asha Bhonsle; art direction:

Sudhendu Ray; costumes: Anjana Rawail; cinematography: R.D. Mathur. Starring: Jayant, Dilip Kumar, Balraj Sahini, Sanjeev Kumar, Vyjayantimala, Dilip Dhavan. SKY Entertainment DVD. Run time: 158 minutes.

http://www.uiowa.edu/~incinema/Sunghursh.html

This beautiful and unusual film, set in the background of Banaras during the 19th century, belongs to the uncommon genre of 'historical' film and contains substantial religious subject matter. It tells the story of a great Hindu pilgrimage center — as the backdrop for a complex tale involving such thematic staples as a multi-generational family feud, conflict between love and duty (centering on a 'fallen woman'), and the glories of self-sacrifice for the sake of *dosti* (male friendship), but also introducing the tension between the ritual violence of Shakta religion (requiring periodic blood sacrifice to a powerful mother goddess), and a non-violent religious path of love and compassion. The film implicitly subscribes to the upper-middle class critique and endorsement of the legacy of a colonial discourse, though it complicates this picture somewhat through its allegiance to family tradition (apparently, even a serial murderer has to be tolerated if he's your grandpa). However, its ultimate concern to reunite two sundered brothers (actually, as in the *Mahabharata*, first cousins, and played by a Muslim and a Hindu actor) suggests a subtext that isn't really about Hinduism at all, but about the communal divide that haunts post-Partition India, here projected into the past and disguised within an exclusively Hindu milieu. Perhaps because both the story and the screenplay are by women, the film displays an unusual sensitivity to the sufferings imposed on women by men's obsession with honor and revenge. As the one man who tries to break the cycle of violence by assuming a pacifist, Gandhian role, Dilip Kumar delivers a performance of extraordinary range, restraint, and conviction. Everything else about the production shows similar quality. Though a few scenes are shot in Banaras and environs, most of the outdoor locations utilize a Deccan pilgrimage site close to Bombay (recognizable by architectural details and the dark stone typical of Maharashtra), but with similar temples and ghats.

Talwar, Bhavna (Director) 2007. *Dharm* ('the religious code'). Producer: Sheetal Vinod Talwar; script: Vibha Singh; dialogues: Varun Gautam; cinematography: Nalla Muthu; sound: Dileep Subramaniam; costumes: Shehnaz Vahanvati. Starring: Pankaj Kapoor, Supriya Pathak, K K Raina, Hrishita Bhatt, K K Raina, Krish Parikh, Daya Shanker Pandey.
http://sify.com/movies/bollywood/review.php?id=14467780&ctid=5&cid=2425

It is a known fact that caste dominates the social spectrum of India. Also known is the truth that the inherent biases of caste and the notion of pollution-purity prevails even 60 years post Independence. This beautifully narrated film is set against the backdrop of the holy city of Banaras and the river Ganga. In an age where cinema has crossed shores and continents, *Dharm* takes the viewer on a journey of spirituality and the Brahmanical way of living. It is a film about Pandit Ram Narayan Chaturvedi (Pankaj Kapoor), a Hindu Brahmin priest of Banaras who lives by his belief in the 'true Hindu way of life'. Almost a religious fanatic, Pandit Chaturvedi practices the chores of his religion, precisely as prescribed by ancient Hindu scriptures. Although he's married, this family man devotes more time to his daily prayers and rituals than to his wife (Supriya Pathak). Naturally, he asserts his adamant beliefs of casteism on everyone around, and being a Brahmin, he proclaims himself to be a part of the most superior caste in human society. But as is the case with life, even a wise man can be taught a lesson. His life, beliefs and perceptions go topsy-turvy when he meets and adopts an abandoned child. It is then that he realises the true meaning of Hinduism and the way of living a righteous life. "The journey of the protagonist Pandit Chaturvedi from ritualism to realisation has a universal message", the Director says. There are no songs in the movie. The background score by Sonu Nigam, which plays through the movie, has a soothing effect. The picturisation and cinematography are also worth a mention. More so, unlike most films on similar lines, this one does not drag and keeps the viewer hooked on. However, glitches remain. A movie which says it is dedicated to those who lost their lives in riots should have delved deeper into the hardships faced by the victims. True, the movie shows the hatred that communal forces have for the minorities, but should not the director have drawn the camera to the other side of the fence as well?

K. JAPANESE SOURCES (in Japanese)

Hasebe, Ryutei 1923. A Buddhist monument at Sarnath-Past and Present. *Mikkyo,* 2-4,3-1.1923.2, 4.

Hironaka, Seiji 1992. *Ramanagar. The Mythological City Devoted to God. City Construction as Described in Ramalila.* Unpub. B. Arch. dissertation, Hosei University, Tokyo. No. 8945138.

Ito, Chuta 1929a. The Durga temple at Benares. *Sekai Bijutsu Zenshu,* 26: 50-51. 1929. 11.

—— 1929b. A Hindu temple at Benares: *Sekai Bijutsu Zenshu,* 26: 51.

Nakamura, Hajime 1968. Ed. *Buddhist Monuments and Hindu temples in India.* Sekai no Bunka Shiseki, 5. Kodansha, Tokyo.

Oya, Toko 1992. *Varanasi. The Sacred City of Hindus' Described through Religious Space and Ghats.* Unpub. B. Arch. dissertation, Hosei University, Tokyo. No. 8945028.

Masai, Yasuo 1969. A note on Benares. *Chin,* 14-17: 36-41.

Sakata, Teiji 1993. That which pilgrims want to seek. Group pilgrimage of Hindus. *Sinica* (Taishukau- Shoten, Tokyo, 4 (no. 9; Sept.): 44-49.

Sekino, Tei 1913. Dhameka at Sarnath. *Sekai Bijutsu Zenshu,* 7: 58.

Takahashi, Yuku 1992. *City Housing in Varanasi: Summary and Discussion.* Unpub. B. Arch. dissertation, Hosei University, Tokyo. No. 8945093.

Yanagisawa, Kiwamu 2001. *A Study on the Principles of the Urban Space Formation of Varanasi (India).* Unpub. M. Arch. dissertation in Architecture and Environmental Design, Kyoto University, Kyoto. Supervisor: Prof. Shuji FUNO.

—— 2008. *A Study on the Formation and transformation Process of Urban Structure and Residential Space in Indian traditional City: case studies of Varanasi and Madurai.* Unpub. Ph.D. dissertation in Architecture and Environmental Design, Kyoto University, Kyoto. Supervisor: Prof. Shuji FUNO.

L. UNPUBLISHED DISSERTATIONS (selected)

Ahmed, Sara 1991. *Questioning Participation: Culture and Power in Water Pollution Control — The Implementation of the Ganga Action Plan at Varanasi*. Unpublished Ph.D. dissertation, Dept. of Geography, University of Cambridge, Cambridge.

Akhtar, Jamal 1992. *Muslims in Varanasi City. A Study in Cultural Geography*. Unpublished Ph.D. dissertation, Dept. of Geography, Banaras Hindu University. [Supervisor: Rana P.B. Singh].

Ashthana, Bandana 1997. *Folk Deities of Kashi and their associated Worship and Religion*. (in Hindi). Unpubl. Doctoral Dissertation, Department of History of Art, Banaras Hindu University, Varanasi. 225pp. + 78 plates, and bibliography. [Supervisor: D.B. Pandey].

Bandhu, Desh 1971. *A study of the productive structure of tropical dry deciduous forest at Varanasi*. Unpublished Ph.D. thesis, Department of Botany, Banaras Hindu University, Banaras, India. [Supervisor:. R. Mishra].

Blackford, Frank R. 1979. *Belief and Psychotherapy in Banaras*. Unpublished Doctoral dissertation in Psychology of Religion, University of Pennsylvania, University Park. 360pp.

Barrett, Ronald L. 2002. *Aghor Medicine. Pollution, Power, and Healing in Banaras, Northern India*. Ph.D. dissertation, Dept. of Anthropology, Faculty of the Graduate School of Arts and sciences, Emory University, U.S.A. 13 figs, 282pp. [Committee Chair: Peter J. Brown]. Revised and updated form published as book, 2008.

Bermigin, Isabella 1998. *The Fifty Six Vinayakas (of Kashi)*. Unpublished Ph.D. dissertation, Dept. of Study of Religion. School of Oriental and African Studies (University of London), London. [Supervisor: Simon Weightman].

Bhartiya, Suryakant 2002. Integrated Rural Development of Sakaldiha Block (District – Chandauli). (in Hindi). Unpublished Ph.D. dissertation, Dept. of Geography. Banaras Hindu University. [Supervisor: Rana P.B. Singh].

Brinkmann, Ruth 2002. *'It is not true, but we believe it'. Pilgrims' views on Varanasi's sacred space.* Unpubl. M.A. thesis in Comparative Study of Religions and Indian Art History, University of Leiden (The Netherlands). 90pp. [Supervisors: G.A. Wiegers and K.R. van Kooji; Tutor, Varanasi: Rana P.B. Singh].

Caixeiro, Mariana Cândida 1977. *O Sacrifício-final em Banaras. Tradição, continuidade e inovação no Hinduísmo ena sociedade indiana.* [The Last Sacrifice in Banaras. Tradition, Continuity and Innovation in Hinduism and Indian Society]. Tese submetrida para obtenção do grau de doutoramento em Antropologia, Departmento de Antropologia da Faculdade de Ciências Sociais e Humanas. Universidade Nova Lisboa, Portugal; [in Portuguese]. Lvii + 500pp. [Orientadores: António Bracinha Vieira, Undel, and Christopher Fuller, LSE London].

Choudhary, Vandana 2008. *Population Growth and Socio-economic Development in Varanasi City: A Geographical Analysis.* Unpubl. Ph.D. dissertation, Dept. of Geography, Banaras Hindu University, Varanasi. [Supervisor: T.D. Singh].

Cocari, Diane M. 1986. *The Bir Babas of Banaras: An Analysis of a Folk Deity of North Indian Hinduism.* Unpubl. Ph.D. thesis in South Asian Language and Literature. University of Wisconsin, Madison.

Dashrath 2002. *Urban settlements of Sant Ravidas Nagar Bhadohi District: A Geographical Study.* (in Hindi). Unpublished Ph.D. dissertation, Dept. of Geography. Banaras Hindu University. [Supervisor: Rana P.B. Singh].

Denton, Lynn Teskey (late: 1949-1995) 1988. *Purity and Power: Dimensions of Female Asceticism in the Hindu Tradition.* Unpubl. D.Phil. thesis, Dept. of Anthropology. Oxford University, Oxford. [Published as book by SUNY Press, see Denton 2004].

Derné, Stephan David 1988. *Culture in Action: Hindu Men's Talk about Women, Marriage, and Family.* Unpubl. Ph.D. thesis, Dept. of Sociology. University of California, Berkeley. [Published as book by SUNY Press, see Derné 1995].

Desai, Ms. Madhuri 2007. [*Published on: Jul 08, 2005*]. *Resurrecting Banaras: Urban Space, Architecture and Religious Boundaries.* Unpublished Ph.D. Dissertation. Program in Architecture, University of California, Berkeley.

Doron, Assa 2005. *Sons of the Ganga: The Boatmen and the Riverscape of Varanasi.* Unpublished PhD thesis, School of Social Sciences, La Trobe University, Melbourne, Australia.

D'Souza, A.W. 1933. *Warren Hastings and Raja Chait Singh of Benares.* 4. Parts. Unpublished MA thesis in History. Indian Historical Research Institute, Bombay.

Dwivedi, Jyotsana 1992. *Rural-Urban Fringe in Indian Cities: a Case Study of Varanasi.* Unpubl. Ph.D. thesis, Dept. of Geography, Banaras Hindu University, Varanasi. [Supervisor: K. K. Dube].

Eck, Diana Louise 1976. *Banaras City of Light: the Sacred places and Praises of Kasi.* 2 Parts. Ph.D. Dissertation in Comparative Religion. Harvard University, Cambridge. [Published in a revised form as *Banaras, the City of Light*; see Eck 1982].

Gautam, Atul 2007. *How to Design Good Residential Developments in the Indian Context of Varanasi.* 100 pp, 75 illustrations, 2 tables. Submitted on 06 December. Unpublished M. Arch. (Urban Design) Dissertation, Joint Centre for Urban Design, Oxford Brookes University, Oxford.

Gengnagel, Jörg 2007. *Visualised Texts-Sacred Spaces, Spatial Texts and the Religious Cartography of Banaras.* Habilitationsschrift, South Asia Institute, Heidelberg. [Supervisor: Axel Michaels].

Gupta, Ms Roxanne Poormon 1993. *The Politics of Heterodoxy and the Kina Rami Aghoris of Banaras.* Unpublished Ph.D. dissertation in Humanities Doctoral Program, Syracuse University, Syracuse NY.

Hashmi, Meraj 2001. *Faith Healing among Muslims: A Sociological Study of the Traditional Values, Norms and Behaviour Pattern of the Muslims in the Changing Social Context of Modern Society.* Unpubl. Ph.D. thesis, Dept. of Sociology, Faculty of Social Science. Banaras Hindu University, Varanasi. xv + 238pp. [Supervisor: A.L. Srivastava].

Huberman, Jennifer 2006. *Working and Playing Banaras: A Study of Tourist Encounters, Sentimental Journeys, and the Business of Visitation.* Unpublished Ph.D. dissertation, Dept. of Anthropology (major: South Asia), University of Chicago, Chicago IL. USA.

Jameson, A.S. 1976. *Gangaguru: the Public and Private life of a Brahman Community of north India*. Unpubl. D.Phil. thesis, Dept. of Social Anthropology, University of Oxford, Oxford.

Karnitis, Catherine Sofia 2002. *The Dhundhi Vinayaka Form of Ganesha and his Fifty-Six Emanations at Varanasi: Text, History, Image*. Unpubl. M.A. thesis, History of Art, The Ohio State University, Columbus, USA, 170pp. [Advisors: Susan L. Huntington and John C. Huntington].

Kaushik, Meena 1979. *Religion and Social Structure: A case study of the Doms of Banaras*. Unpublished Ph.D. thesis, Dept. of Sociology, Delhi School of Economics, University of Delhi, Delhi. [Supervisor: Veena Das].

King, Christopher R. 1974. *The Nagiri Pracharini Sabha* (Society for the promotion of the Nagari Script and language) *of Benaras, 1893-1914: A Study in Social and Political History of the Hindi Language*. Unpbl. Ph.D. thesis, Center of South Asian Studies. University of Wisconsin, Madison.

Köckman, Uwe 1980. *Revivalismus in Indien: Zur Politischen Geschichte Varanasis*. Geographische Institut der Ruhr-Universität, Bochum. Unpubl. Ph.D. thesis. xii + 325pp. [in German].

Kohili, Sujata 1986. *Varanasi: A Study in Landscape Architecture*. (With special reference to Ghats). Unpubl. M.Arch. thesis, Dept. of Landscape Architecture, School of Planning and Architecture, New Delhi.

LaDousa, Chaise P. 2003. *Teaching Complexes: Education and Language in Banaras*. Unpub. Ph.D. dissertation. Department of Anthropology, Maxwell School of Citizenship and Public Affairs, Syracuse University, Syracuse NY, U.S.A.

Lee, Christopher R. 2002. *Banaras, Urdu, Poetry, Poets (India)* [*Poetics, Politics and Performance among Everyday Poets of Urdu in Varanasi, India*]. Unpub. Ph.D. dissertation. Department of Anthropology, Maxwell School of Citizenship and Public Affairs, Syracuse University, Syracuse NY, U.S.A.

Pandey, P.C. 1992. *Rural-Urban Symbiosis in Varanasi District: a Geographical Analysis*. Unpubl. Ph.D. thesis, Dept. of Geography, Banaras Hindu University, Varanasi. [Supervisor: Bechan Dubey].

Protopapas, Janice 1996. *The changing face of Sanskrit education: a case study of traditional schooling in Varanasi, India*. Unpublished Master of Arts dissertation in Literature, University of Maryland, Baltimore.

Pugh, Judy F. 1981. *Person and Experience: The Astrological System of North India*. Unpubl. Ph.D. thesis in South Asian Civilisations, University of Chicago, Chicago.

Rai, Narmadeshvara 1977. *Varanasi ka Abhinay Parampara aur Rangamancha*. (Tradition of Theatrical Play and Stage of Varanasi). Unpub. Ph.D. dissertation. Magadh University, Bodh Gaya. [In Hindi].

Rai, Km. Seema 1993. *Environment and Health: A Geographical Study of Varanasi Urban Agglomeration*. Unpubl. Ph.D. thesis, Dept. of Geography, Banaras Hindu University. [Supervisor: R.B. Singh].

Rana, Pravin Singh 2003. *Pilgrimage and Ecotourism in Varanasi Region: Resources, Perspectives and Prospects*. Unpublished Ph.D. Dissertation, Department of Public Administration & Institute of Tourism Studies, University of Lucknow, Lucknow (UP, India). [Supervisor: Dr. Manoj Dixit]

Ranke, Ingrid 2006 (April 19). *Everyday Movement Patterns of Women in Assi (Varanasi) : A socio-spatial approach*. Human Geography, Master Class C-level Thesis, Faculty of Human Geography and Planning, Karlstad University, Sweden. 64pp. [Supervisors: Gerhard Gustafsson (Karlstad) and Rana P.B. Singh (Varanasi, India), Examinor: Bertil Lindberg].

Rashmi, Kumari 2006. *Industrial Growth and Environmental Quality: A Study of Varanasi Urban Agglomeration using GIS*. Unpub. PhD dissertation in Geography, Utkal University, Bhubaneshwar, Orissa. 69 tables, 34 figures, 32 maps, xvi + 297pp. [Supervisor: P.K. Kar]

Roberts, Simon W. 2000. *'Another member of our family': Aspects of television culture and social change in Varanasi, North India*. Unpubl. Ph.D. thesis, Department of Social Anthropology, Centre for South Asian Studies, University of Edinburgh: Edinburgh.

Schmalz, Mathew N. 1998. *A Space for Redemption: Catholic Tactics in Hindu North India*. Unpublished Doctoral Dissertation in History of Religions from the University of Chicago, Chicago. [Supervisor: Wendy Doniger].

Shepherd, Frances 1976. *Tabla and the Benaras Gharana.* Unpublished Ph.D. dissertation in Indian music and ethnomusicology, Wesleyan University, USA.

Shukla, Pravina 1998. *The Bejeweled Body: Beauty and Ornamentation in Banaras, India.* Unpublished Ph.D. dissertation in Folklore and Mythology, University of California, Los Angeles, USA. Revised and updated version published as book, 2008.

Shukla, Km. Manisha 1993. *Environmental Pollution and its Impacts on Varanasi City.* Unpubl. Ph.D. thesis, Dept. of Geography, Banaras Hindu University, Varanasi. [Supervisor: Onkar Singh].

Singh, Ajay Kumar 1981. *Monolithic Miniature Shrines of Varanasi.* Unpubl. Doctoral Dissertation, Department of History of Art, Banaras Hindu University, Varanasi. Plates, and bibliography. [Supervisor: Rai Anand Krishna].

Singh, Amar Nath 1971. *Varanasi: A Study in Urban Sociology.* Unpubl. Ph.D. thesis, Dept. of Sociology, Banaras Hindu University, Varanasi. [Supervisor: G.S. Nepali].

Singh, Arvind Kumar 1999. *Dimensions of Environmental Degradation in Varanasi City.* Unpubl. Ph.D. thesis, Dept. of Geography, Banaras Hindu University, Varanasi. [Supervisor: D.N. Singh and M. Agrawal].

Singh, Bhagya Lakshmi 1990. *Socio-economic Conditions of Slum dwellers in Varanasi City.* Unpubl. Ph.D. thesis, Dept. of Geography, Banaras Hindu University, Varanasi. [Supervisor: V.K. Kumra].

Singh, Jai Ram 1979. *The City of Varanasi, 1947-72.* Unpubl. Ph.D. thesis, Dept. of History, Banaras Hindu University, Varanasi. [Supervisor: Hira Lal Singh].

Singh, Madhuri 1990. *Varanasi in History: A Geographical Study.* Unpubl. Ph.D. thesis, Dept. of Geography, Banaras Hindu university, Varanasi. [Supervisor: K.N. Singh].

Singh, Mohan 2002. *Health Care Facilities: A Geographical Study of Varanasi District.* Ph.D. thesis, Dept. of Geography, Banaras Hindu University, Varanasi. [Supervisor: V.K. Kumra].

Singh, Pratibha 2002. *Kashi ke Shaiv Sthal: Aitihasik Bhugol evam Adhyayan* (Shaiva sites of Kashi: A Study in Historical Geography). Unpub. Ph.D. dissertation, Dept. of History, M.G. Kashi Vidyapith, Varanasi. 197pp. + 35 Figs/maps; in Hindi/ Devanagiri script. [Published as "*Shiv-Kashi*", 2004].

Singh, R.B. 1965. *Gangaputra Pandas of Varanasi*. Unpubl. Ph.D. thesis, Dept. of Sociology, Kashi Vidyapith, Varanasi.

Singh, Ravi S. 2000. *Goddesses in India: A Study in the Geography of Sacred Places.* Unpublished Ph.D. dissertation, Dept. of Geography. J.P. University, Chapra (Bihar); 211pp, 39 figures. Chapter 3 "Goddesses in Varanasi (Kashi)". [Co-Supervisors: B.L. Sinha, and Rana P.B. Singh].

Singh, Sandhya 2000. *Urban Housing Problems and Planning of Varanasi City: A Geographical Study*. Unpubl. Ph.D. thesis, Dept. of Geography, Banaras Hindu University, Varanasi. [Supervisor: S.B. Singh].

Singh, Shashi Bala 1992. *Socio-Demographic structure of Linguo-Cultural Group in Varanasi Urban Agglomeration: A Geographical Analysis.* Unpubl. Ph.D. thesis in Geography, Banaras Hindu University, Varanasi. [Supervisor: K.N. Singh].

Singh, Shyam Bahadur 2003. *Varanasi City: Urban Environmental Problem of Solid Waste Disposal and its Management.* Unpublished Ph.D. dissertation, Dept. of Geography. Utkal University, Bhubaneshwar, Orrisa. [Supervisor: S.K. Mohanty].

Singh, Vijaya Prakash 1990. *Kashi ke Mandir* (*Murtiparak Adhyayan*). (Temples of Kashi: A Sculptural Study). Unpublished Ph.D. dissertation, Dept. of the History of Art, Banaras Hindu University, Varanasi. In Hindi. [Supervisor: D.B. Pandey].

Singh, Vinay Kumar 2007. *Bénarès vu par les Voyageurs Français.* Unpublished Ph.D. dissertation, Dept. of French Studies, Faculty of Arts, Banaras Hindu University, Varanasi. In french. [Supervisor: S.K. Mishra and S.K. Dasmahapatra].

Singha, Radhika 1990. *A 'Despotism of Law': British criminal justice and public authority in North India, 1772-1837.* Unpub. Doctoral dissertation. University of Cambridge. Faculty of History,

University of Cambridge. BLDSC number: D60075; PhD.16407. [Supervisor: Christopher A. Bayly]. <revised and updated form published as book, 1998>

Smith, Travis LaMar 2007. *The Sacred Center and its Peripheries: Saivism and the Varanasi Sthala-Puranas.* Unpublished doctoral dissertation, Dept. of Religion, South Asia Institute, Columbia University, New York.

Stewart, Rebecca Marie 1965. *An Examination of the Banaras School of Tabla Performance.* Unpublished M.A. thesis in History of Music. University of Hawaii, Honolulu.

Tiwari, Reena 2003 (June). *Space-Body-Ritual: Performativity in the City* (of Varanasi). Unpubl. Ph.D. dissertation in Architecture, Faculty of Built Environment, Art and Design, Curtin University of Technology, Perth, WA, Australia. 240pp. + 2 CD: Mappings, & Tracings.

Whitemore, Luke 1999. *Pilgrims Maps and Vastushastra in Haridwar and Varanasi.* Unpublished M.A. thesis, Harvard Graduate School, Cambridge MA, USA.

Wodak, Josh 2002. *The Interrelationship between Life-Death in Benares, and Form-Content in Robert Gardner's Forest of Bliss.* Unpubl. B.A. (Hons.) thesis, Dept. of Anthropology, Sydney University, Sydney. 80pp. Ref. Code: 9832054.

Yadava, Satya Narayan 2000. *Socio-Economic Survey of the Workers in the Universities of Varanasi.* (In Hindi). Unpublished Ph.D. dissertation in Sociology, M.G. Kashi Vidyapeeth (university), Varanasi.

Zeiler, Xenia 1998. *Der Viresvara-Tempel Vârânasî.* Magisterarbeit Humboldt-Universität Berlin (Germany). [In German].

M. Unpublished Reports

Jal Nigam 1976. *Master Plan Report on Drinking Water Supply Problems in Varanasi District*. U.P. Jal Nigam, Varanasi.

—— 1980. *Master Plan Report on Rural Water Supply Schemes in Varanasi District*. U.P. Jal Nigam, Varanasi.

Sharma, Alakh N. and Raj, Nikhil 2002 (10 March). *Child Labour in Sari Units of Varanasi (Draft Report)*. Human Rights Watch interview with the author, report and statistics. Institute for Human Development, and V.V. Giri National Labour Institute, New Delhi.

Trudget, R. Dudley 1950. *Outline of a Master Plan of Banaras, India*. Town & Village Planning Office, Uttar Pradesh (India), by Banaras Improvement Trust, Varanasi. 142pp.

TCPO 2000. *Varanasi Master Plan (Frame)-2011*. (in Hindi). Town & Country Planning Organisation, UP, Varanasi. Varanasi Development Authority, Varanasi. iv + 24pp + 4 folded maps, released on 26 February 2000.

TCPO-VDA 2001. *Varanasi Master Plan, 1991-2011*. (in Hindi). Town & Country Planning Organisation, UP, Varanasi. Varanasi Development Authority, Varanasi. xii + 187pp, enclosures 61pp. + a folded map, released on 11 July 2001.

VDA 2001. *Varanasi Master Plan, 1991-2011*. (in Hindi). Varanasi Development Authority, Varanasi. ii + 49pp., enclosures 2 pp. + a folded map, released on 25 July 2001.

—— 2004 (February). *Varanasi Vision 2025, Draft Final Report*. Varanasi Development Authority, Varanasi. Prepared and submitted by ICRA Management Consukltibg Services, A division of ICRA Ltd., New Delhi. vii + 57pp., 29 tables, 12 figures.

—— 2006 (February). *Varanasi Vision 2025, Draft FINAL Report (Appendix)*. Varanasi Development Authority, Varanasi. Prepared and submitted by ICRA Management Consulting Services, A division of ICRA Ltd., New Delhi. 12pp., 7 tables, 4 figures.

VDA & DLA (UI) 1990. *Sarnath: Design Guidelines and Case Studies for Tourism Development*. Dept. of Landscape Architecture, University of Illinois, Urbana Champaign; jointly with Varanasi Development Authority, and Govts. of U.P. and India.

N. Unpublished Reports

(Varanasi: Inscribing Heritage Zones for WHL UNESCO)

[1]. Singh, Rana P.B. (chairman and editor) and Dar, Vrinda (associate & co-editor) 2002a (March 20). *Varanasi: Heritage Zones and Sites.* [Details of 53 sites and properties]. Varanasi Development Authority, Varanasi (India). 110pp + 18pp appendices + 70 figures/ maps (locational, site plans, cross sections), 45 plates of photographs, including historical outline and Selected Bibliography. 1st Report. © Rana P.B. Singh.

[2]. —— 2002b (April 1). *Varanasi: Heritage Zones and Sites. Nomination proposal for Inscription in the UNESCO World Heritage List.* [Details of 40 sites and properties]. Varanasi Development Authority, Varanasi (India). 78pp + 26 figures/ maps (locational, site plans, cross sections), including historical outline and Selected Bibliography. 2nd Report. © Rana P.B. Singh.

[3]. —— 2002c (April 25). *The Riverfront and Old City Heritage Zone of Varanasi. Nomination proposal for Inscription in the UNESCO World Heritage List.* [Details of 73 sites and properties]. Varanasi Development Authority, Varanasi (India). 174pp + 70 figures/ maps (locational, site plans, cross sections), 70 plates of photographs, including historical outline and Selected Bibliography. 3rd Report. © Rana P.B. Singh.

O. UNPUBLISHED FIELDWORK PROJECTS (Undergraduate) 1962-63 - 2005-06

The University of Wisconsin Program: College Year in India

Indian Office, 1965-2002: Vijayanagaram Bhavan B 20 / 44 Bhelupura, Varanasi, UP 221010. IndiaPresent Office, since 2005: 17, Kaivalyadham Colony, Durgakund Rd., Varanasi, UP 221005. Ph.: (0542)-2311009.
US OFFICE: The Center for South Asia, University of Wisconsin, 1242 Van Hise Hall, Madison, WI 53706, USA.

[Citation: author's surname, first names. Year. Title. Session-Year and -code]

Allen, Michael 2000. *The Rhythms of the Sacred.* 1999-2000-4.

Anders, Max 2005. *Street Sleepers & Outstretched Hands: An Attempt to Locate Varanasi Amidst India's Climate of Poverty.* 2004-05-5.

Anderson, Sidsel S. 1992. *The Ganga River and Her Ecological History.* 1991-92-1.

Asua, Vivek 1995. *An American Born Confused Deshi in Banaras.* 1994-95-3.

Askari, Jed 2000. *North Indian Classical Music Pedagogy.* 1999-00-3.

Atherton, Carolyn 1968. *The Effects of Education on Untouchable Boys in an Urban Basti.* 1967-68- 1.

Bachrach, Emilia 2003. *An Excuse to Meet with Krishna: Aspects of Devotional Singing and Storytelling in Banaras.* 2002-03.

Bacrania, Jay 2004. *Finding the Real Liberation in Kashi.* 2003-04.

Barisas, Mary L. 1969. *Banaras Textiles: The Evolution of an Art Form.* 1968-69-2.

Barr, W. Cameron 1985. *The Disco and the Darshan: Ramalila Beyond Ramnagar.* 1984-85-2.

Baughman, Donald 1967. *Religious Practices in Agriculture near Varanasi.* 1966-67-1.

Beben, Daniel Joseph 2005. *Gyanvapi Masjid in Varanasi: Analysis of a Controversy.* 2004-05-3.

Benjamin, Elisabeth Ryden 1984. *Some Access and Participation: A Case of Agricultural Information Channels in Varanasi District.* 1983-84-3.

Beecher, Allison 1992. *Annapurna Kshetra and Amriteshwar Temple: Continuity and Tradition.* 1991-92-2.

Berg, Erik 1988. *Currents of Thought and Flowing Water; The Ganga in Banaras.* 1987-88-3.

Bhalla, Anu Anchal 1990. *Marriage for Love, or Love for Marriage. 'Love Marriages' in Banarasi Society.* 1989-90-2.

Biebel, Jill A. 1979. *On Death and Dying in Kashi.* 1978-79-2

Boies, Robert 1974. *A Study of Birha Singing: A Timeless Tradition.* 1973-74-3

Bollom, Michael W. 1988. *Masti: The Laid Back Lifestyle of Banaras.* 1987-88-4

Bonifaz, C. John 1986. *Women of Sevapuri.* 1985-86-12.

Bonifaz, John C. 1986. *Images of America from Varanasi, India.* 1985-86-11.

Bottorf, Evelyn E. 1974. *Varanasi. A Socio-Ecological Study.* 1969-70-4.

Bradney, D. Michael 1968. *Christian Life in Varanasi.* 1967-68-1.

Brockschmidt, Kristin 1966. *Rajghat Excavations.* 1965-66-4.

Brooks, Douglas R. 1978. *Navratri and Sakta Tradition.* 1977-78-4.

Bunce, Laurel M. 1980. *The Tradition of Flute in Kashi.* 1979-80-1.

Burger, Kristin 1989. *Life around Death in Benaras.* 1988-89-14.

Camertini, Michael 1969. *Banaras (a film in B & w):* 22 min. BAVI 7621. 1968-69-3.

Clyne, Naresh 1987. *Some Aspects of Rickshaw Driving in Benaras.* 1986-87-3

Coccari, Diane M. 1974. *Jai Siya Ram, Jai Jai Siya Ram.* 1973-74-4.

Congress, Carol A. 1963. *Social and Economic Attitudes of Hindus and Muslims in Kakarmatta (Varanasi), India.* 1962-63-1.

Connerney, Richard D. 1991. *The Mazars of Banaras. A Look at Grave Veneration in Northern India and Relevant Theology.* 1990-91-5.

Cort, John E. 1974. *Jainism in Banaras.*1973-74-5.

Crane, Leilani S. 1979. *Some Aspects of Krishna Worship In Banaras.* 1978-79-3.

Cranswick, Amanda 1997. *Desire of Dead Souls: A Study of Sannyas in Benaras.* 1996-97-1.

Cunningham, Cynthia R. 1980. *The Brocades of Banaras.* 1973-74-5.

Custer, Caroline 2003. *Unity in Diversity: Baha'i identity in Banaras.* 2002-03.

Cutshall, Steven James 1994. *The Rainbow Connection: Social Services In Varanasi.* 1993-94-1.

D'amato, Carl 1980. *The Various Faces of Hanuman: A Study of Hanuman Bhakti in Varanasi.* 1979-80-4.

Delong, Trudy 1996. *Whores, Harlots, and other Deviants: A Study of Prostitution in Banaras.* 1995-96-10

Eck, Diana L. 1966. *Hinduism and the Indian Intellectuals.* 1965-66-6.

Edmundson, Eileen Ellen 1970. *A Study of Some Dashnami Sadhus.* 1969-70-1.

Fallon, Jayne P. 1971. *Observation and Experiences with Muslim Families in Madanpura.*1970-71-2.

Federer-Jyoti, Diana 2002. *Understanding Maternal and Child Malnutrition in North India: An in-depth Look at Nutritional Factors and Practices in Uttar Pradesh, and Programs Working to Combat Undernutrition in Varanasi District.* 2001-02.

Feibel, Carolyn 1997. *My Illness, Your Ghost: A Study of Traditional Healing and Spirit Possession in Benaras.* 1996-97.

Ferguson, Robert Andy 1982.*Wrestling with the Kali Yuga — Banaras Akharas, Copy # 2.* 1981-82-9.

Frame, Mariko 2001. *The Position of Islamic Women in Varanasi.* 2000-01-1.

Fuller, Cordelia J. 1981. *The Social Position of Women in Benaras Area.* 1980-81-1.

Glickman, Sherry 1989. *Pass the Salt: Family Conflict In Banaras.* 1988-89-12.

Goldberg, Jay 1971. *The Basics of Astrology.* 1970-71-3.

Grunwald, Maury D. 1977. *Bhutavaidya: The Practitioners and the Practice of Exorcism.* 1976-77- 9.

Hager, Gilbbert P. 1970. *The Holy City of Banaras.* 1969-70-9.

Halpenny, Philip 1967. *The Dimensions of Ganesha Worship in Banaras.* 1966-67-1.

Hardee, Karen Ann 1980. *.A Study of the Performance of Urban Family Welfare Centres in Varanasi.* 1979-80-5.

Hardy, Kathryn 2003. *Anticow: The Life and Death of a Water Buffalo in Banaras.* 2002-03.

Hayes, Courtney 1988. *Sati Shrines in Varanasi: A Historical and Anthropological Analysis.* 1987-88-14. [242pp; Honors paper presented to Macalester College (Religious Studies Dept.)

Heberlein, Joan Marie 1985. *On Perspective of Women in Daily Ritual in Hinduism in Varanasi.* 1984-85- 16

Hegg, Lea Anne 2002. *Banaras: A Case Study in Muslim Leadership.* 2001-02-3.

Herntz, Mary 1987. *The Muslims of the Shivala Community in Benaras, India: Women's Perspectives.* 1986-87-23.

Herrington, Margaret H. 1984. *The Durga Temple; A Study in Text and Context.* 1983-84-4.

Hiebert, Horace W. 1979. *Wall Hangings of the Banaras Weaving Institute.* 1978-79- 13.

Hildreth, Hooker W. 1978. *A House Divided: A Study of the Hindu Muslim Riot that Occurred in Benaras in 1977.* 1978-79-4

Hollenbach, Margaret 1963. *Human Factors in Community Development: Lahartara, One case in Point.* 1962-63- 2.

Hubert, Joyce 1983. *A Socio-Anthropological Micro-Study of Sarojini Vidya Kendra: An Experimental School in Varanasi.* 1982-83-7

Hufnagal, Karen E. 1989.*Modem Forms of Epic Images: The Nuances of Hindu Women Worshipping the Goddess.* 1988-89-11.

Husted, Wayne 1977. *Holi (Varanasi).* 1976-77-10.

Kapera, Connie 1965. *Sri Sri Kali: A Study in Two Parts — the Original Hypothesis and Attitudes Toward the Goddess.* 1964-65- 7a.

King, Dennis L. 1970. *Bhojpuri Folk Songs.* 1969-70-12.

Knipe, Jennifer 1992. *Modern Theatre in Banaras: Women Actors.* 1991-92-3.

Korom, Frank J. 1983. *The Pancakrosi Yatra.* 1982-83-8.

Latker, Richard 1993. *The Nagwa Educational Access Project.* 1984-1985.

Lindabury, Lance R. 1966. *The Scheduled Castes of Varanasi (Banaras) District.* 1965-66-1.

Lollar,Daniel 2002. *An Indian's Guide to Dying Phenomenologically: A Look at How Interpretations of the Self in Indian Systems Determines the Death Experience.* 2001-02.

Lowry, Julie 1999. *Muslim Women of Benaras.* 1998-99-3.

Luthra, Sangeeta 1987. *Understanding Religion: A Study of Sikh Institutions in Varanasi.* 1986-87-18.

MacDonald, James J. 1969. *A Study of Uses of the Bathing Ghats of Banaras.* 1968-69-17.

Madhu, Kalyani K. 1984. *A Collection of Short Stories Set in Banaras.* 1983-84-5.

Malin, Nadav 1985. *The Merits of Pilgrimage.* 1984-85-9.

McConeghey, Kevin W. 1980. *The History, Organization and Practices of Dasnami Naga Sadhus.* 1979-80-6.

McCrary, D. Campbell 1992. *The Muslims of Banaras and the Ahmed Family.* 1991-92-4.

Merrill, Chrisri A. 1986. *Holi in Banaras: A Threshold in Tradition.* 1985-86-3.

Michalik, Emily 1989. *Toward a Stable Future: Three Methods of Caring for Anath Children in Varanasi.* 1988-89-6.

Miller, Barbara D. 1970. *Hippie Culture in Banaras.* 1969-70-18.

Moayyad-Sanandadji, Shirin 1985. *Dance and Devotion: A study on the Interface of Dance and Religion in Banaras.* 1984-85-10.

Mohabir, Paul 2004. *The Ramayana in Bhojpuri Folksong: The Colloquial Interpretation of the Ramayana Narrative in Varanasi.* 2003-04.

Molzan, Janet P. 1984.*Environmental Health along the River Ganga.* 1983-84-6

Moore, Fred L. 1963. *Comparative Study of the Carpet, Khadi and Silk Industries in certain areas of Varanasi.* 1962-63- 4.

Morrow, Charley 1985. *Sadhus and Change: The Udasin Sampradaya.* 1984-85-23.

Nachowitz, Todd 1981. *Religious Ritual Implements; A Study of the Puja Ceremony of Benaras.* 1980-81-2.

Nakano, Ako 1987. *Waves of the Ganga (Photos).* 1986-87-8a.

Navkal, Vaishali 2000.*The South Asian Refugee Dilemma; A Study of Hindu East Bengalis in Varanasi.*1999-00-4.

Nedley, Harry 2004. *Puja, Gundas, and Ghats: An Analysis in Decline.* 2003-04.

Neelis, Jason 1989. *Techniques in Ancient and Modern Banaras.* 1988-89-8.

Noble, Christopher 1965. *Indulgence and Insight: Sacred and Profane Aspects of Intoxicants in Banaras.* 1964-65- 9.

Offerman, Joni 1996. *Contemporary Artists of Banaras.* 1995-96-11.

Palshikar, Shriyash 1994. *Westernization and Modernization as it relates to Sanskrit Scholarship in Varanasi.* 1993-94-3.

Palta, Monica 1999. *Sources of Pollution in Ganga: A Study of Varanasi.* 1998-99-5.

Petty, George 1986. *Cottage Industries in and Around Varanasi.* 1985-86-5.

Pimplaskar, Lima 1994. *The Forms and Worship of Ishvara.* 1993-94-4.

Powers, Penelope 1964. *A Limited Bacteriological Study of the Ganges.* 1963-64-1.

Pugh, Judy 1967. *Dasaswamedh Ghat of Banaras.* 1966-67-14.

Rader, Allison 1985. *Banaras Women: An Experience.* 1984-85-12.

Raducha, Joan A. 1972. *Internationality & Hanuman: Some Thoughts & Images.* 1971-72-1.

Rao, Avantika J. 1997. *Discussing Ganga: Perspectives on River Quality Issues, Women and Technology.* 1996-97-10

Regan, Rachel A. 1998. *Bengalis in Banaras: An Anthropological Study.* 1997-98-9.

Robinson, Margaret L. 1979. *Santoshi Ma: The Development of a Goddess.* 1978-79-6.

Rodgers, Charles A. 1984. *Farm Size, Input Use, and Agricultural Technique: A Micro Study, Umraha Village, Varanasi District.* 1983-84-7.

Roger, Jeffrey P. 1991. *An Exploration into the Increase in Popularity of Sankat Mochan Mandir.* 1990-91-8.

Saini, Arvind 1998. *Ayurveda and Promotive Health: A Textual And Anthropological Study in Varanasi.* 1997-98-5.

Samaraweera, Piyumi 1998. *Reasons of Hindu Muslim Confluence in Benaras: Past, Present and Future.* 1997-98-6.

Scaglione, John E. 1984. *Ayurvedic Medicine: Ancient Philosophical Concepts and Current Therapeutic Practices.* 1983-84-17.

Scheel, Nicole 1965. *Destitute Women in Banaras.* 1963-64-6.

Schrenk Matthew O. 1998. *"Creation from Destruction": Use of Indigenous Resources to Lessen the Pollution of Ganga.* 1997-98-7.

Sears, Tamaral 1995. *The Varanasi Temple: An Architectural History.* 1994-95-1.

Seedoriff, L.M. 1993. *Death and Spirits, Possession and Exorcism: Pisach Mochan Mandir.* 1992-93-4.

Seiden, R. Schuyler 2000. *Oral Banarsi Folklore*. 1999-00-5.

Sharma, Anupama 1986. *The Effects of Age, Education and Residence: Factors on Cognitive Test Performance of Indian Children.* 1985-86- 16.

Sheckles, Janet M. 1967. *Bits and Pieces of Buddhism in Banaras.* 1966-67-17.

Shaw, Kate 2000. *Hijras of Banaras.* 1999-00-6.

Sinha, Anashua 1986. *Bengalitola: A Community in Transition.* 1985-86-8.

Sinha, Ritu 1987. *A History of Swacha Ganga; Copy # 1 and # 2.* 1986-87-17.

Skarie, Mary E. 1968. *A Study of a Saint: Mata Anandamayi and the Religious Experiences of her Devotees.* 1967-68- 19.

Smart, Ellen 1965. *Vegetable Markets of Banaras.* 1964-65-2

Smith, T. Daniel 1972. *Ideas, Truth and School— The Teaching of J. Krishnamurti and the Rajghat Besant School.* 1971-72-26.

Smucker, Celeste 1968. *The Effectiveness of Education as a Medium of Change in an Urban Harijan Basti.* 1967-68-20.

Snodgrass, Keith 1988. *Aiye Aur Bahati Ganga Mein Hath Dhoiye.* 1987-88-8.

Sopher, Deborah Lynne 1988. *The Pusapati Family Lineage of Vizianagaram.* 1987-88-7.

Stern, Linda 1968. *Upon the Dancer by the Dreamless Wave: An Essay on Aspects of Shiva Puja.* 1967-68-21.

Stevens, Dennis 1989. *Muslim Shrines of Benaras.* 1988-89-4.

Swift, Kenneth 1974. *Children's Street and Playground Games of Varanasi.* 1973-74-19.

Taylor, Cole Hawkins 2005. *Creating Worlds and Identities: A Study of the Panchakroshi Yatra in Kashi.* 2004-05- 6.

Thorne, Steven L. 1987. *Kashike Bhojpuri.* 1986-87-19.

Thornton, Mae 2004. *Aapka Tana Mera Bana: Your Warp My Weft.* 2003-04.

Upadhyaya, Saurabh H. 2000. *Hindu-Muslim Relations in Varanasi: A study of Historical, Political & Religious Perspective.* 1999-00-7.

Vansadia, Preeti 2001. *The Personal Hygiene Study: A Look at the Hygienic Practices of Harijan Women in the Villages Surrounding Varanasi, India.* 2000-01.

Velde, Josh Vander 1997. *Idlers, Nostalgia, and other Demons: Perceiving Change at a Banarasi Paan Stall.* 1996-97-8.

Virgill, David 1999. *The Worship of Shiva in Banaras.* 1998-99-7.

Wadsworth, Cindy 1985. *Kashivasi Widows.* 1984-85-16.

Ward, Andrew 2000.*Dirty: Political and Religious Forces Undermining the Efforts to Clean the Ganges.* 1999-00.

Warner, Catherine 2002. *Hamar Matir Bhasa: A Study of Bhojpuri Usage in Benaras.* 2001-02-5

Webber, Rachel N. 1988. *Female Migrant Construction Workers (Varanasi).* 1987-88- 6.

Weber, Krista 2001. *Widows from the Margins: Representations of Indian Women.* 2000-01-4.

Welch, Claudia M. 1989. *The Idiots Guide to Banaras Hindu Winter Festivals.* 1988-89-3.

Wellford James B. 1983. *Glimpses at the Boatmen of Banaras.* 1982-83-9.

Wells, Alan 1995. *Magico-Religious Healing and Schizophrenia in India. A Case Study from Bala-Ji Mandir.* 1994-95-5.

Werrell, Melissa L. 1990. *Writing in Benaras: Two Authors.* 1989-90-1.

White, David 1975. *Bhairava.* 1974-75-3.

Willey, Kamala 1984. *Pandey Ghat.* 1983-84-11.

Williams, Donna-Marie 1979. *Institutionalized Anath Children & Their Re-Entry into Indian Society.* 1978-79-7.

Wimberger, Karin G. 1980. *Ganga Ma. A Study of an Emerging Saint.* 1979-80-27.

Womack, Julie 1983. *Ravidas and the Chamars of Banaras.* 1982-83-10.

Appendix 1

Historical and Cultural Happenings in North India and Banaras, AD 1000 – 2008.

Year	Major Power in North India	Local Power in Banaras	Religious / Cultural	Architectural
1000	-Invasion of Mahamud of Ghazni and defeat of the Gurjara-Pratiharas, 1018.	-Karnadeva, son of Gangeyadeva, ruled the city, 1041-1072. -Rule of Chandradeva, foundation of Gahadavala dynasty and Varanasi as their capital, 1090-11.	-Al-Biruni, who came with Mahmud of Ghazni, visited the city and studied Sanskrit, 1021-25.	-Karnameru temple built, 1060. -Ahmad Nialtgin plundered the city and demolished many Hindu temples, 1033.
1100	-Gahadavala dynasty, 1090-1194.	-Gahadavala kings: Madanapala, Govindrachandra, Vijaichandra, Jaichandra.	-Visit and stay of Ramanujacharya, 1116-1137. -First invasion, 1194, and second invasion by Qutb-u-ddin Aibak, 1197.	-Temples of Vishveshvara, Avimukteshvara and Vindu Madhava demolished, and Adhai Kangura mosque built, 1194.

1200	-Sultanate rule of Qutb-u-ddin Aibak (1206-1210), having Delhi as capital.	-Banaras came under the control of Iltutamish, 1210-1236.	-Saint Jnaneshvara visited the city, 1294.	-Reconstruction of the Vishveshvara temple, 1230. Padmeshvara temple, 1296.
1300	-Allauddin Khilzi (1296-1316). -Ghiyasuddin Tughluq (1320-24). -Muhammad bin Tughluq (1324-51).	-Banaras under Khilzi and Tughluq rule.	-Visit of Jina Prabhu Suri, a Jain saint, 1320.	-Building of Vireshvara and Manikarnikeshvara temple, 1300-02. -Shrine of Sayyed Fakhruddin, Bakaria Kund; Parshvanatha Jain temple.
1350	-Firuz Shah Tughluq (1351-88) extends the sway of the Delhi kingdom across North India. -Sharqi rulers of Jaunpur break away from the Delhi Sultanate, 1393.	-Banaras under the direct rule of Sharqi rulers of Jaunpur founded by Khwaja Jahan Malik Sarwar (1393-1399).	-Brahmins protest against Firuz Shah Tughluq for *Zazia* tax, 1353. -Firuz Shah Tughluq demolished many temples, 1375. -*Kashi Khanda*, a Sanskrit compendium of information about the *tirthas* and deities. Kabir (c. 1398-1448).	-Ardhai Kangura mosque, repairing and extension.
1400	-Sharqi dynasty at Jaunpur (1402-1458).	-Sharqi rulers of Jaunpur: Mubaraq Shah Sharqi (1399-1402). -Shamsuddin Abrahim Khan Sharqi (1402-36); Mahmud Shah Sharqi (1436-56).	-Mahmud Shah Sharqi demolished the Padmeshvara and Visheshvara temples, 1447-48.	-Chaukhamba mosque, 1447-48. -Bibi Raziyya mosque erected by Mahmud Shah Sharqi on the site of the Vishveshvara temple.

1450	-Lodi dynasty established in Delhi in 1451. -Hussain Shah (1458-76), last independent ruler of Jaunpur. -Bahlul Lodi (1451-89) annexes Jaunpur in 1479. -Banaras comes under the direct rule of Delhi. -Sikandar Lodi (1489-1517).	-Sharqi rulers of Jaunpur: Muhammad Shah Sharqi (1457-1458); Hussain Shah Sharqi (1458-1476). -Ghulam Amina, Jaunpur governor of Banaras, c. 1470. -Banaras under direct rule of Delhi after 1479. -Banaras taken by Sikandar Lodi in 1496.	-Vachaspati Mishra composed *Tirthachintamani*, 1460. -Guru Nanak visited Banaras, 1473. -Sikandar Lodi invades the city and demolishes many temples, 1494.	-Tomb of Jaunpur governor (?) at Bakaria Kund.
1500	-Ibrahim Khan Lodi (1517-26). -Babur (1526-30) defeats Ibrahim Khan and establishes the Mughal empire. -Mughal empire expands under Humayun (1530-40), but Humayun is defeated by Sher Shah Suri in 1538 and is expelled from India. -All of north India comes under the control of Sher Shah Suri (1540-55) and his son Islam Shah Suri (1545-54).	-Humayun, son of Babur, occupies Banaras in 1527, and again in 1528. -Banaras under the control of Sher Shah from 1538. -The Grand Trunk Road, passing throughBanaras, developed by Sher Shah.	-Babur invaded the city, 1529. -Chaitanya in Banaras, 1530. -Humayun halted in the city, 1532.	-Caravanserai of Sher Shah Suri. -Humayun defeated by Sher Shah Suri, took shelter at Sarnath near Chaukhandi Stupa, 1538.

1550	-Humayun returns to India in 1555 and successfully re-establishes Mughal power; dies soon after. -Akbar (1556-1605) consolidates the expanding Mughal empire of north India. -Mughal provincial headquarters shifted to Allahabad in 1584.	-Khan Zaman, Akbar's commander, captures Banaras in 1559. -Akbar's visit to Banaras, 1565. -Khan Zaman rebels, provoking Akbar to plunder Banaras in 1567. -Akbar erects fort at Allahabad, 1584. -Raja Todar Mal, commander at Jaunpur, 1589-1591. -Raja Man Singh, commander, 1591-1599.	-Sanskrit scholars in Banaras, including Narayana Bhatta, contribute to the revival of Vedanta and Mimansa philosophy. -Tulasi (c. 1552-1623), author of *Ramacharitamanas*, popular Hindi version of the Ramayana. -Akbar defeats the king of Banaras, and establishes a mint, 1567. -Akbar's three-day stay in Banaras, 1574. -Visit of Ralph Fitch, an English traveller, 1583-91.	-Ibrahim Shah Shah Suri establishes a mint, 1555. -Panchaganga and Adi Vishveshvara Ghats reconstructed, 1580. -Vishvanatha temple erected in 1585 by Raja Todar Mal, advised by Narayana Bhatta; the same patron builds Draupadi Kund, 1589. -Raja Man Singh builds Man Mandir at Dashashwamedha Ghat, 1586. -Pavilion at the summit of Chaukhandi Stupa erected by Govardhana, an employee of Akbar, 1589.
1600	-Jahangir (1605-27). -Shah Jahan (1627-58).	-Muzaffar Begh, commander in Banaras.	-Plague in the city, death of Tulasi, 1623. -Dara Shikoh, helped by pandits of Banaras, translates the principal *Upanishads* into Persian; completed only in 1656-57. -Varadaraja's *Girvana Padamanjari*, c. 1600-50, lists the different ghats.	-Raja Man Singh erects Bindu Madhava Temple and adjacent Sanskrit college on Panchaganga Ghat, c. 1600. -Bundi king Surjan Singh builds a palace and a *ghat*, Bundi Parkota Ghat, 1611. -Narayan Das builds Chakrapuskarini Kund, 1623.

1650	-In the civil war after Shah Jahan's death, Shuja occupies Banaras in 1558; but succumbs to Aurangzeb (1658-1707).	-Dara Shikoh, eldest son of Shah Jahan, absentee governor of Allahabad, in Banaras in 1653-57. -Shivaji seeks short refuge with the Brahmins of Banaras in 1666; in punishment, Aurangzeb orders the destruction of the city's temples, April 1669.	-Demolition of c. 76 temples under construction by Haidar Begh, 1632. -Visit of Peter Mandi, 1632. -Jean-Baptiste Tavernier visits Banaras, 1665. -Rajput rulers visit Banaras.	-Jnanavapi and Dharahara (Panchaganga Ghat) mosques built after 1669 at the orders of Aurangzeb on the sites of the demolished Vishvanatha and Bindu Madhava (1673) temples. -Raja Jagat Singh of Udaipur erects a palace on Rana Mahal Ghat, 1670, Raja Savai Jai Singh builds Ram Mandir at Panchaganga Ghat, 1699.
1700	-At the death of Aurangzeb in 1707 the Mughal empire begins to disintegrate. -Nawab Sadat Khan Burhan al-Mulk(1724-39) of Lucknow rules over the Mughal province of Awadh; gradually it became an independent state. -Nawab Safdar Jang (1739-53) mostly at the Mughal court in Delhi.	-Banaras lies within Awadh province of the Mughal Empire; but in 1719 Muhammad Khan gave Banaras to Murtaza Khan, the Nawab of Awadh. -Mir Rustam Ali (1730-38) appointed by Nawab Sadat Khan as governor of Banaras. -Mansa Ram of the Bhumihar family of Gangapur seizes the	-Rajput presence continues. -Dhundhiraja's *Vanga-manjari*, 1702-04, describes the Brahmin's life. -Maratha Peshwas contributes to the city's religious and cultural life. -Mir Rustam Ali, great patron of music and literature.	-Sawai Jai Singh of Jaipur builds an observatory at Ram Mandir, 1697-1710. -Peshwa Bajirao I rebuilds Annapurna Temple, 1725. -Peshwa Bajirao I erects riverside palace, renovates Manikarnika 1730. -Panchganga Ghat repaired by Sripat Rao, 1730. -Mir Rustam Ali constructs Mir Ghat, 1735; and lays out

	governorship of Banaras on 10 June 1738 with approval of Nawab Sadat Khan. -Raja Balwant Singh (1740-70), son of Mansa Ram, remits revenues to Sadat Khan.	-Tailanga Svami, illustrious ascetic, in Banaras 1737-87.		gardens and *havelis* at Gangapur and Bhaironath. -Balwant Singh erects fort at Gangapur, 1740-42. -Temples of Lalita Devi and Rajarajeshvari, 1745-50. -Adi Vishveshvara temple built by unknown Maratha patron.
1750	-Suja ud-Daula (1753-75) rules Awadh from Faizabad; asserts his independence from Delhi. -Triumph of East India Company army at the Battle of Plassy in 1757; British extend their influence across North India. -Shuja ud-Daula surrenders to theEast India Company after being defeated at the Battle of Buxar in 1764; restored to the throne by the British in 1765.	-Sindhia and Holkar Maratha rulers consider taking control of the city's temples, c. 1750. -Raja Chet Singh (1770-81) succeeds to the Banaras throne; compelled to pay a heavy subsidy to the East India Company as a war contribution. -Chet Singh rebels in 1781 and is deposed by Warren Hastings, Governor of Bengal; British troops occupy the city.	-Peshwas, Sindhias, Holkars and Bhonsles embark on extensive building programmes. -Warren Hastings visit to Banaras, 1773.		-Balwant Singh builds the fort at Ramnagar, 1750-52. -Rani Bhavani of Bengal built *kunds* at Kandwa and Bhimachandi on Panchakroshi pilgrimage route, and a temple at Manikarnika Ghat, 1755-56. -Trilochana temple built by Nathubala, 1760. -Balwant Singh shifts his headquarters to fort at Ramnagar, 1763; lays out garden residence at nearby Ramgarh. -City palace of Ausanganj family. -Peshwa Baji Rao II builds Dashashvamedha Ghat. -Peshwa Balaji Baji Rao II erects Annapurna temple, 1770.

-Shuja ud-Daula accepts British suzerainty in 1773 in a bid to withstand the Marathas; signs a treaty in 1775 transferring districts controlled by Chet Singh to the East India Company. -Nawab Asaf ud-Daula (1775-97). -Banaras becomes part of British-controlled India in 1794.	-Raja Mahipnaraian Singh (1781-95) installed on the Banaras throne; surrenders revenue and judicial administration to the British. -Jahandar Shah Jawan Bakht, son and heir of the Mughal emperor, flees to Banaras in 1784 and dies here in 1788. -Raja Uditnaraian Singh (1795-1835). -Anwar Bakht, son of Tipu Sultan is caught by British Army and dies here, 1799.	-William Hodges, an English artist, visits the city, 1781-82. -British artists Thomas and William Daniell pass through Banaras, 1788-1789. -Sanskrit College opens in 1791. -Nadesar Palace built by the British, 1796.	-Projects of Rani Bhavani of Natore; Durga temple, c. 1760, repair of Lolarka Kund; structures along Panchakroshi route. -Tomb of Lal Khan, prime minister of Balwant Singh, 1773. -Cremation site at Manikarnika Ghat built, 1775. -Bindu Madhav temple re-built by Maratha king, 1775. -Chet Singh builds riverside city palace and Sumeru Devi temple at Rammnagar. -Royal Shiva temples at Ramnagar, Bhaironath and Chakia. -Ahilyabhai Holkar erects Vishvanatha Temple, 1777, Indore State Ghat and Shiva temple, 1785, and Tarakeshvara temple, 1792. -Jagannath Temple, Asi ghat, 1794. -Bhonsle Palace, Lakshminarayana and Raghurajeshvara temples and Ghat, 1795. -Shitala and Dashashva-medheshvara temples.

1800	-Lord Wellesley annexes Awadh in 1801; Banaras part of the United Provinces.	-Raja Uditnaraian Singh (1795-1835). -Visit of Lord Valentina, 1804. -Hindu-Muslim riots, 1805 and 1809.	-Banaras becomes a chief trade centre. -The city attracts pandits from all overIndia; Sanskrit colleges supportedby grants from the Peshwas; AmritRao, younger brother of PeshwaBaji Rao II, exiled to Banaras, 1803. -Christian missionary activity in the city.	-Civil Lines and Cantonment laid out; cemetery, Chauka Ghat. -Adi Keshava Temple, 1806. -Brahmins' refectory and Annapurna, Lakshminarayana and Shiva temples, at Raja Ghat, 1807. -Queen Kumar Devi of Potia (Bengal) builds Prayageshvara Temple, 1810. -Radhakrishna Baga, a merchant, builds Satyanarayan Temple, 1811. -Ram and Narayana temples, Munshi Ghat, 1812. -Jai Narayan Ghoshal of Bengal builds Gurudham Temple, 1814. -Marathas sponsor Trilochaneshvara Temple, 1815-17; Kalabhairava Temple, c. 1825; Sindhia Ghat, 1830. -St Mary's, 1812; London Mission church, 1840s; St Paul's, 1847. -Mint House, 1821. -Suparshvanatha Svetambar Jain Temple, 1825.

	-Uditnaraian Singh's powers curtailed, 1828. -Raja Ishwariprasad Narain Singh (1835-89).	-James Prinsep (1799-1840), Assay Master of Banaras Mint, 1819-30; prepares first map and census of the city, 1822 and 1829; *Benares Illustrated* appears in 1833. -Raja Ishwariprasad Narain Singh assumes a leading role in the intellectual and cultural life of the city.	-Renovation and re-building of Jnanavapi by queen Baijabai, 1828. -Tomb of Jahandar Shah Jawan Bakht (Badshah Bagh), 1837. -Ranjit Singh of Lahore adds gold covering to spire of Vishva-natha (Golden) temple, 1839. -Samarajeshvara Temple at Lalita Ghat, 1841-43.
1850	-Ishwariprasad Narain Singh awarded thirteen-gun salute, 1862. -Raja Prabhu Narain Singh (1889-1931).	-Schools of music known as *gharanas* flourish in the city. -Opening of rail link between Mughalsarai and Banaras, 1862. -Ishwariprasad Narain Singh sponsors learning and culture; patronises Ramlila festival. -Shri Ramakrishna in Banaras, 1868. -M.A. Sherring's *Benares, The Sacred City of the Hindus*, 1868; first monograph on city's history, religion and culture.	-Sanskrit College, 1853. -Suparshvanatha Digambar Jain temple, 1855. -Amethi temple at Manikarnika Ghat, 1857. -Nadesar Palace purchased by Ishwariprasad Narain Singh, 1863. -Radhakrishna temple, Ganga Mahal ghat, 1864. -Town Hall, 1875; King Edward Hospital, 1877; Dufferin (Malaviya) railway bridge, 1887; Bhadaini and Bhelupura waterworks, 1898.
	-Revolt of the sepoys (mutiny) in Awadh and elsewhere in North India, 1857; soon after, the possessions of the East India Company are taken over by the British Government.		

Decade	National Polity	Rulers of Kashi / Major Events	Eminent Persons & Institutions	Temples & Constructions
			-Gorji Dikshita's *Kashiyatra-prakasha*, directory of holy sites of the city, 1883. -Banaras branch of the Theosophical Society, 1896.	-Manokameshvara T., 1895. -Gautameshvara temple, 1888.
1900	-British Government established at Calcutta. -British capital shifted to New Delhi, 1911. -India's Independence, 15th August 1947.	-Raja Prabhu Narain Singh (1889-1931). -Prabhu Narain Singh invested with full ruling powers, 1912. -Raja Aditya Narain Singh (1931-39). -Raja Vibhuti Narain Singh (1939-2000). -Vibhuti Narain Singh hands over his territories to the newly formed Government of India, 15 Oct. 1948.	-Madan Mohan Malviya, great pandit and reformer, begins campaigning for a modern Hindu university, 1904. -Shivaprasad Gupt, philanthropist and patron. -Vibhuti Narain Singh, active promoter of culture and learning.	-Lakshminarayan temple at Assi Ghat/Civil Courts, 1913. -Banaras Hindu University (B.H.U.), founded 1916. -Sayaji Rao Gaekwad Library (B.H.U.), 1927-41. -Reconstruction of Sindhia Ghat. -Bharat Mata Temple, 1936. -Vishvanatha Temple at B.H.U., 1936-1962.
1950	-26 Jan. 1950, India declared as a democratic Republic.	-Destruction of Babri mosque at Ayodhya, resulting in disturbances all over north India, 6 Dec. 1992.	-Central Institute of Higher Tibetan Studies opened at Sarnath, 1967; and declared as Deemed University, 1988. -Flood disaster in the city, 1948 and 1978.	-Svami Karpatri builds a New Vishvanath Temple at Mir Ghat, 1958. -Renovation of Trilochana Temple, 1965. -Krishnalal Sureka, a merchant, builds Tulsi Manas temple at Durga Kund, 1966. -Kamakotishvara T., 1968.

Year			
		-Vajra Vidya Samsthan at Sarnath opened on 29 Oct. 1999. -Intach Chapter Varanasi formed. -Fourth '*Master Plan of Varanasi*' (1991-2011) prepared in 1996, approved by the State Government of Uttar Pradesh, 10 July 2001.	-Thai Temple at Sarnath opened, 1976. -Renovation of Sangameshvara Temple, Asi Ghat, 1987. -Dharmachakra Indo-Japanese Society's Temple opened at Sarnath, 1991. -New Hindu astronomical observatory built in the Sanskrit University, 1992.
2000	-Formation of three new states. -Congress Party with coalition forms central government, April-May 2004.	-Vibhuti Narain Singh, the last king of Banaras, died at the age of 73 years on 25th December 2000. -The Ganga declared as "National River" by the Govt., 4 Nov. 2008.	-Consecration ceremony of Parshvanatha temple, Bhelupura, 17 Nov. 2000. -Movement for inscribing Riverfront Ghats of Varanasi in the UNESCO WHL, 2002. -Declaring the city under JNNURM and preparation of CDP, 2007. -New Transport system policy (Flyover bridges) and plans prepared, 2008.

Note: Information for this historical chart was mainly drawn from the following works:

Michell, George and Singh, Rana P.B. eds. 2005. *Banaras, the City Revealed*. Marg Publications, Mumbai.
Motichandra, 1962. *Kashi ka Itihas*. (*History of Kashi*). Bombay. 2nd ed. 1985, 3rd ed. 2003, Vishvavidyalaya Prakashan, Varanasi.
Singh, Rana P.B. (eds.) 1993. *Banaras (Varanasi). Cosmic Order, Sacred City, Hindu Traditions*. Tara Book Agency, Varanasi.
Singh, Rana P.B. and Rana, Pravin S. 2002/ 2006. *Banaras Region. A Spiritual and Cultural Guide*. 2nd. ed., Indica Books, Varanasi.
Sukul, Kubernath 1974. *Varanasi Down the Ages*. K.N. Sukul, Patna.

Appendix 2

BANARAS/ KASHI : NOTABLE DATES IN HISTORY

I. Ancient Period, BCE 1000 – CE 1000.

BCE / B.C.

———	Suparshvanatha, the 7th Jaina Tirthankara born in Singhapur (near Sarnath), Varanasi.
9th cent.	First layer of excavation at Rajghat.
———	Till the 9th cent. Kashi was an independent estate.
800-500	Existence of urban settlements in Rajghat as archaeologically evident.
8th cent.	Birth of Parshvanatha, the 23rd Jaina Tirthankara.
7th cent.	Hermitage of sage Kapila at Shivalaya/ Shivala Ghat.
6th-4thcent.	Annexation of Kashi to Koshala, Magadha and Kaushambi; the rule of Nanda.
599-527	Influence of Mahavira, the 24th Jain Tirthankara.
528	First sermon of the Buddha at Sarnath, "Turning the Wheel of Law", *Dhammacakraparavartana Sutta.*
535-485	Several visits and stays of the Buddha at Sarnath; he preached the following *Suttas*: Panca, Paccetana, Dopasa, Samaya, Katuvijaya, critique of Parayana's Mettayanjah, and Dhammadinna.
5th cent.	Sanskrit Grammarian Panini composed the *Asthadhyayi.*
272-232	Emperor Ashoka, a great Mauryan king ruled the country.
240	Emperor Ashoka paid a visit to the city.
2nd cent.	Rule of Pushyamitra, king of Shunga dynasty.
ca 81	Rule of Kanishka over Varanasi.

CE / A.D.

ca 170	Rule of Kushana, later replaced by King Bharashiva of the Naga dynasty who performed a Ten-horse sacrifice at Dashashvamedha Ghat.
3rd cent.	Establishment of the Buddhist township of Ishipattana, later called Sarnath.

ca 275	Rule of the king Nava of Kaushambi over Kashi.
4th cent.	Kashi and Koshala both fell victim of Magadha under Chandra Gupta Maurya I (*ca* 305-325).Samudragupta (c. 330-370) performed a horse sacrifice at Dashashvamedha Ghat.
ca 405	Fa-Hien, the Chinese pilgrim, visited the city.
455-467	Rule of Skandagupta Vikramaditya, who defeated the Hunas in 456.
467-472	Rule of Purugupta, a brother of Skandagupta and follower of Buddhism.
473-477	Kumaragupta II, son of Narasimhagupta, ruled the city.
477-495	Rule of Buddhagupta, a Buddhist king.
500-508	Building of the Vishveshvara (Vishvanatha) temple (perhaps for the first time) in the reign of Vainya Gupta, the Shaiva king.
510-544	Rule of Bhanugupta, who defeated the invader Hunas in 530.
6th cent	Opening of Virasaiva monastery, Jangamabadi Math as the headquarters.
7th cent.	Rule of Harsha (*ca* 606-648)
ca 635	Hsüan-tsang, the Chinese pilgrim, visited the city, during the reign of Harsha.
648-673	Rule of Adityasen, the king of Magadha.
725-752	Rule of Yashovarman of Kannauja.
752-794	Rule of Dharmapala, a king of the Pala dynasty of Bengal.
8th cent.	Shankaracharya stayed in Kashi (first came in *ca* 716), composed the *Brahmasutra Bhasya* (7.1), and built Tilabhandeshvara Temple.
9th cent.	[mid to late] rule of the Gurjara-Pratiharas.
950-1000	Dhanga, of Jejakabhukti, controlled Kashi.

II. Medieval Period, CE 1000 – 1750.

1018	Invasion of Mahamud of Ghazni and defeat of the Gurjara-Pratiharas.
c 1021-1025	Al-Biruni, who came with Mahmud of Ghazni, visited the city and studied Sanskrit.
1033	Ahmad Nialtgin plundered the city and demolished many Hindu temples.
1030-1041	Rule of Gangeyadeva Kalachuri.

1041-1072	Karnadeva, son of Gangeyadeva, ruled the City and built Karnameru temple.
1090-1100	Rule of Chandradeva, foundation of the Gahadavala dynasty, having Varanasi as their capital.
1100-1114	Rule of Madanapala.
1116-1137	Visit and stay of Ramanujacharya.
1114-54	Reign of the Gahadavala King Govindachandra.
1154-1170	Rule of the Gahadavala king Vijayacandra, son of Govinda-chandra.
1170-1194	Rule of the Gahadavala king Jayacandra, who was killed by Shahabuddin Ghori in 1194.
1194	Qutb-u-ddin Aibak (Ahmed Bin Muhammad) demolished the Vishveshvara and Avimukteshvara temples, and Vindu Madhava Vishnu temple — converted into Arhai Kangura Mosque.
1197	Second invasion by Qutb-u-ddin Aibak.
1206-1210	Sultanate rule of Qutb-u-ddin Aibak, having Delhi as capital.
1226	Banaras came under the control of Iltutamish (1210-1236).
ca 1230	Reconstruction of the Vishveshvara temple.
1248	Invasion of Shahabuddin Muhammad Ghori.
1294	Saint Jnaneshvara visited the city.
1296	Construction of Padmeshvara temple by Svami Padmananda.
1296-1316	Rule of Alauddin Khilji, who demolished one thousand temples.
1302	Construction of the temple of Manikarnikeshvara by noble man Vireshvara.
1320	Visit of Jinaprabha Suri, a Jaina saint.
1320-1351	Rule of the Tughlaqs: Ghiyasuddin (1320-24), Muhammad Bin (1324-51).
1353	Brahmins protested against Firoz Shah Tughlaq for *Zazia*-tax, but later they paid it.
1374-75	Firoz Shah Tughlaq (r 1351-1388) demolished many temples, including Bakri Kunda Temple, and built nearby Fakharuddin Alawi Dargah.
1299-1411	Life of Ramananda, who lived and taught at Panchaganga Ghat, and founded a subdivision of Vaishnavism.
1393-1518	Life of Raidasa/ Ravidasa, a cobbler-saint, born in Sirakarahia, who was a disciple of Ramananda.

1398-1518	Life of Kabir, a great social reformer, saint and poet, who preached Neo-Vaishnavism.
1400-1456	Rule of Mubaraq Shah Sharqi (1399-1402), Shamsuddin Ibrahim KhanSharqi (1402-36), and Mahmud Shah Sharqi (1436-56).
1447-48	By the order of Mahmud Shah Sharqi, destruction of the grand temples ofPadmeshvara and Vishveshvara, where later Bibi Raziyya mosque was built by him; also Chaukhamba Mosque built in 1447-48.
1460	Vachaspati Mishra composed the *Tirthachintamani*.
c. 1470	Ghulam Amina, Jaunpur Governor of Banaras.
1473	The Sikh Guru, Nanak (1469-1539) visits and stays at Gurubag, and later has religious discourses with pandits of Banaras.
1489-1517	Reign of Sikandar Lodi, a bigoted Muslim, who destroyed most of the temples of Banaras; Banaras taken by him in 1496.
1479-1531	Vallabhacharya, a great saint of Krishna devotion, was living here. Bahlul Lodi (1451-89) annexed Jaunpur in 1479.
1485-1533	Chaitanya, a great saint of Krishna devotion, lived here.
1494	Sikandar Lodi invaded the city and plundered the Hindu temples.
1529	The Mughal king Babur invaded the city.
1532	The Mughal king Humayun (1530-40) paid a visit to the city.
1535	Afghan king Shershah Suri subjugated the city together with Chunar fort.
1538	Humayun took shelter at Chaukhandi (Sarnath), after this defeat by Shershah Suri (1540-55), who renovated and redeveloped the Grand Trunk Road.
1540-1623	Madhusudana Sarasvati lived at Chausatthi Ghat.
1545-1550	Narayana Bhatta composed the *Tristhalisetu*, and contributed to the revival of Vedanta and Mimansa philosophy.
1555	Establishment of a mint by Ibrahim Shah Suri (1545-54), son of Shershah Suri.
1556	The Governor of Varanasi, Abdul Rahim Khanekhana, visited the city.
1559	Khan Zaman Shah, a military general of Akbar, conquered the city and rebelled (1567) against his master, which provoked Akbar to plunder Banaras.

1567	Emperor Abkar (1556-1605) defeated Jayachandra, king of Kashi, and partly plundered the city and established a mint.
1580	Panchganga and Adi Vishveshvara ghats reconstructed.
1552-1623	Tulasi, the sage poet of Rama devotion, author of the *Ramacharitamanasa*, lived here and composed his works, and died at the bank of the Ganga at Asi Ghat.
1583-1591	Visit of Ralph Fitch, an English traveller.
1584-85	Restoration and repairing of the Vishveshvara temple by Todaramal (Raghunatha Pandita!), a famous minister of Akbar, under the direction of Narayan Bhatta who also patronised Draupadi Kund in 1589.
1586	Raja Man Singh (of Jaipur) built Man Mandir at Dashashvamedha Ghat.
1588-89	Construction of Chaukhandi Stupa at Sarnath by Gobardhana, as ordered by King Akbar.
1589	Building Draupadi Kunda at Shivapur (NE part of city) by Govinda Dasa, with the permission of Akbar.
16th cent.	Composition of the *Kashi Rahasya*, and the *Kashi Kedara Mahatmya*.
1600	Construction of Bindu Madhava temple and adjacent Sanskrit College on Panchaganga Ghat by Raja Mana Singh of Jaipur (Rajasthan).
1605-58	Reign of Mughal rulers, Jahangir (1605-27) and Shah Jahan (1627-58).
1611	Bundi King, Surjana Singh built a palace and a Ghat; he died here in 1641.
1620	Mitra Mishra composed *Viramitrodaya*.
1623	Plague in the city; Tulasi and Madhusudana Sarasvati died. Chakrapushkarini Kunda (Manikarnika) was built by Narayana Dasa, son of Narenu Ravata (a minister of king Vasudeva).
1627-1755	Saint Kina Rama, the founder of the Aghor cult of Tantra and Shaktism, lived and died in Banaras.
1630	Renovation and reconstruction of Pishachamochana Kunda by Gopala Shahu. Varadaraja's *Girvana Padamanjari*, lists the different ghats.
1632	Haidar Begh, by the order of Mughal Emperor Shah Jahan (1627-1658), demolished about 100 temples, newly constructed or under construction.

1642	Restoration and reconstruction of the temple of Veni Madhava by Jai Singh, King of Jaipur; the temple was defaced and destroyed in 1194 by Aibak.
1653-57	Mughal king Dara Shikoh translated the *Upanishads* in Persian with the help of 150 Pandits of Varanasi.
1658-59	The city came under the rule of Emperor Aurangzeb (1658-1707), a bigoted Muslim, who demolished the temple of Krittivasheshvara and built a temple over the debris.
1660	Visit of Francois Bernier, a French scholar and medical doctor.
1664	Battle at Jnanavapi between the Dashanami Naga ascetics and the army of Aurangzeb.
1665	December 12-13, visit of Jean-Baptiste Tavernier, a French Jeweller and traveller.
1666	Shivaji found refuge with the Brahmins of the city (near Panchaganga Ghat) on his flight from the imperial court of Aurangzeb.
1669	Vishveshvara temple demolished and converted into a mosque by the order of Emperor Aurangazeb.
1670	Rana Jagat Singh of Udaipur erected a palace on Rana Mahal Ghata
1673	Veni/Vindu Madhava temple (at Panchaganga Ghat) demolished and converted into mosque by the order of Aurangazeb.
1697-1710	King Savai Jai Singh of Jaipur built a Hindu Observatory at Mana Mandira Ghat.
1669	King Savai Jai Singh of Jaipur built a Rama temple at Panchaganga Ghat.
17th cent.	Guru Tegh Bahadur, the 9th Guru of the Sikhs, visited the city; also Pandit Jagannatha composed the *Ganga Lahari*.
1712	Rule of Jahandara Shah, son of Bahadur Shah I.
1719	Emperor Muhammad Shah gives Banaras together with Ghazipur and Jaunpur to the Nawab of Awadh, Murtaja Khan, who became the first Nawab ruler.
1724-39	Nawab Saadat Khan Burhan al-Mulk (Muhammad Amin) of Lucknow ruled the Awadh province.
1725	Baji Rao Peshva-I rebuilt Annapurna Temple.
1730	Baji Rao Peshva-I erected a riverside palace, renovated Manikarnika Ghat. Panchaganga Ghat repaired by Sripat Rao.

1734	End of the rule of the Nawabs of Awadh (1719-1738); the last in-charge governor was Mir Rustam Ali, appointed by Saadat Khan, in whose honour was named Mir Ghat in 1735.
1734	Sheikh Ali Hazim (1697-1766), a great Sufi saint, philosopher and Persian poet from Iran, visited the city and settled here.
1737-87	Tailanga Svami, illustrious ascetic, lived in Banaras.
1739	Balwant Singh (r. 1739-1770), son of Mansa Ram, received a certificate of kingship from Muhammad Shah, the Emperor at Delhi, thus establishing Kashi Raj (kingship)
1740-42	Death of Mansa Ram (1740); construction of the fort at Gangapur (Thitharia) by Balwant Singh.

III. The Modern & British Period, 1750 – 1947

1750-52	The Fort at Ramanagar was built by Balwant (Baraband) Singh, who shifted the headquarters from Gangapur to Ramanagar.
1755	A new Vindu Madhav temple was built by the Maharashtrian king.Repairing and construction of Kardama Kupa, near Kardameshvara temple (village Kandwa) by queen Rani Bhavani of Natore (Bengal).
1755-56	Repairing and re-construction of water pools at Kandwa, and Bhimachandi by queen Rani Bhavani of Natore (Bengal). In c. 1760 she also repaired and renovated Durga Kund and Lolark Kund.
1764	The East India Company gained control over the city.
1766	Death of Sheikh Ali Hazim (1697-1766), the Persian poet and philosopher who settled in the city in 1734.
1770	Balwant Singh died (21 August), and Chet Singh ascended to the throne on 10 October.Peshwa Balaji Baji Rao II erected Annapurna temple.
1773	Warren Hastings visited the city. Tomb of Lal Khan, prime minister of Balwant Singh, built.
1775	Cremation site at Manikarnika Ghat constructed.On 21 May Treaty of Faizabad, the sovereignty of Banaras ceded.
1776-77	Ahilyabai Holkar, the Queen of Indore, built the present Vishveshvara/ Vishvanatha temple. She also erected Indore State Ghat in 1785, and Tarakeshvara temple in 1792.
1781	On 16 August Chet Singh's conflict with Warren Hastings' army, and Chet Singh escaped from prison. On 19 August Hastings

flew in female garments. Later expulsion of Chet Singh by Warren Hastings and end of the autonomy of Banaras; since then Banaras never came under the kings of Ramanagar Fort.

1781-82   Visit of William Hodges, an English artist.

1784   Mirza Jahandar Jawan Bakht, heir and son of the last Mughal king, Shah Alam, got refuge here and died at Shivala Ghat in 1788.

1785   Queen Ahilyabai of Indore extended and constructed Dash-ashvamedha Ghat, and also renovated many temples of Varanasi, including Vishveshvara. Construction of a bridge over the Godaulia drain at the street going to Visheshvara temple by Dedhamala Ji, known as Dedhasi ka Pul.

1787-95   Jonathan Duncan, Resident of the East India Company in the city.

1788-89   British artists Thomas and William Daniell passed through Banaras.

1791   Foundation of Sanskrit Pathshala (School) by Jonathan Duncan, later it became a university.

1794   By the order of Babu Jagat Singh, a local zamindar, the Dharmarajika Stupa at Sarnath was demolished in search of bricks for making his neighbourhood in Varanasi city. Banaras came under the British administration on 27 October.

1795   The king of Bhonshala state, Maharashtra, built Bhonshala Ghat.

1799   Anwar Bakht, son of Tipu Sultan, died in Banaras.

1799-1833   Demetrius Galanos (b. 1760- d. 1833), a Greek scholar of Sanskrit lived here for 34 years and died on 3 May 1833.

1801   Lord Wellesley annexed Awadh, and Banaras became part of United Provinces.

1803   Protest by city dwellers against the catastrophic rise of the price of grains.

1804   Visit of Lord Valentia, accompanied with Henry Salt, an artist.

1807   Amritrao Vinayaka Peshva built the Brahmins' Refectory at Agnishvara Ghat, later called Raja Ghat.

1809-10   The Hindu-Muslim riot for land possession between Jnanavapi mosque and the temple; further religious conflict at Gai Ghat Muhalla.

1810   Introduction of House Tax.

1811	Death of Chet Singh at Gwalior (10 April). Protest against *Ghora-gari* ('horse-cart') tax. Construction of Satyanarayana temple by Seth Radhakrishna Baga at Bansphatak, near Adi Visheshvara temple.
1812	St Mary's Church built, and Christian missionary activities started.
1814	King Jayanarayan Ghosal (of Bengal) built the Tantric Gurudham temple.
1815	Renovation of Trilochana Temple by Nathu Bala of Pune.
1816	The Baptist Society opened its mission in the City.
1817	The Church of England built a church at Sigra and also another at Godaulia.
1816-17	King Jayanarayan Ghosal (of Bengal) opened the first English school, named after him as Jayanarayan School.
1817	Construction of the present temple of Kala Bhairava by Baji Rao Peshva-II.
1818	Birth of Maharani Lakshmibai in Peshva Bhavan, in Assi area.
1820	Construction of the building of Collectorate.
1822	James Prinsep (1799-1840) made the first census and map of the city; he was Assay Master of Banaras Mint, 1819-30.
1824	Construction of Shreyansanatha Jain temple at Sarnath.
1824-25	Visit of Bishop Reginald Heber of Calcutta; also artists Lt. Colonel C.R. Forrest and Capt. Robert Elliot.
1827	The Persian poet Mirza Ghalib (1797-1869) visits and stays in the Ghugharali Gali.
1828	Queen Baijabai of Gwalior renovated and re-built Jnanavapi Kupa. Raja Udit Narain Singh's (1795-1835) power curtailed.
1830	Openings of grain market and godowns at Visheshvarganj. Visit of Capt. Robert Elliot.
1832	Visit of Emma Roberts.
1833	James Prinsep's (1799-1840) great work, *Benares Illustrated in a Series of Drawings*, appeared.
1835	Enthronement of Ishvariprasad Narain Singh (1835-89) as king of Kashi; he died in 1899.
1837	Tomb of Jahandar Shah Jawan Bakht (Badshah Bagh) built.
1839	The Vishveshvara (Vishvanatha) temple was gilded by Maharaja Ranjit Singh of Kashmir.

1841-43	Samarajeshvara Shiva (Nepalese) temple at Lalita Ghat was built.
1843	Foundation of Ranavira Sanskrit School.
1845	Foundation of Marwari Hindu Hospital.
1850-85	Life of the founder of the modern Hindi, Bhartendu Harishachandra.
1851	'*Kali Andhi*' (Black Storm) in the city.
1852	Gauraiya Shahi protest under the leadership of Bhauji and Visheshvar Jani, to stop breaking city-gates for making roads; however the 12 gates (*phatakas*) were demolished.
1853	The main building of Sanskrit College (University) built in Gothic style.
1855	Wajid Ali Shah visited the city.
1857	The Mutiny.
1860	Devasting fire in 'Purani Chauk'.
1862	Opening of rail link between Mughalsarai and Banaras.
1866	Establishment and organisation of Municipal Board.
1867	Toll-tax introduced. Visit of Louis Rousselet, a Frenchman.
1868	Visit of Sri Ramakrishna Paramahansa, a great Bengali saint. Sherring's *Benares, The Sacred City of Hindus*, released.
1869	On 22 October, Svami Dayananda Sarasvati, the founder of Arya Samaj, visited the city and took part in religious debates in Raja Madhava Singh's garden at Durgakund on 17 November.
1871	Visit of Edward Lear, an English artist-traveller.
1872	The first official census of the city.
1875-76	Foundation of the Town Hall.
1877	Prince of Wales, Edward VII, visited the city; King Edward Hospital built.
1882	The Nagari Pracharini Sabha established.
1883	Establishment of the District Board. Gorji Dikshita's *Kashiyatraprakasha*, directory of holy sites of the city, released.
1885	Establishment of the Congress Committee. Foundation of the Theosophical Society of India.
1887	Opening of rail-cum-road bridge on the Ganga river, called Duffrin Bridge; in 1950 this is renamed as Malaviya Bridge.

1888	Foundation of the Church Missionary Society.The temple of Gautameshvara built.
1889	Prabhu Narayan Singh became king, who died in 1931.
1891	On 8 April, demolition of the Rama temple in Bhadaini to build Water Pump, which resulted in the Ramahalla protest movement. On 15 April the demolished temple was reconstructed overnight by the city dwellers.
1891	Opening of Water Works at Bhadaini, completed by 1898.
1895	Visit of Mark Twain, a writer from the U.S.A.
1897-98	The Hindu College (Central Hindu School) founded by Mrs. Annie Besant.Bishop Johnson built churches at Sigra and Godaulia.
1902	Svami Jnanananda established the Bharat Dharma Maha Mandala
1903	Brahmana-Guru Charana Shukla of Kanpur built the Rama temple in the Sankatmocana temple compound.
1905	Foundation of Svadhyaya Mahavidyalaya.
1906	King George V, Prince of Wales, visited the city.
1909	Foundation bill for the Banaras Hindu University passed.
1910	Construction of Svami Bhaskarananda Samadhi at Ananda Bag, Durgakund. Establishment of Hindi Sahitya Sammelan.
1914	The first Archaeological Site Museum in India was opened at Sarnath.
1912	Visit of Count Hermann Keyserling, the noted German thinker.
1915	King Rameshvar Singh (Bihar) built Darbhanga Ghat and Nilakantha temple.
1916	Foundation of the Banaras Hindu University by Lord Hardinge, the Viceroy of India.
1917	The first political speech of Mahatma Gandhi in the Banaras Hindu University. Gandhi also visited the city in 1920, 1921, 1929 and 1936.
1918	Construction of the first cinema theatre at Bansphatak by Baijnath Das Shahpuri, named Madan Theatre. The first aeroplane was seen in the city.
1920	Foundation of Kashi Vidyapith by Mahatma Gandhi.
1921	The Prince of Wales visited the city.

1928	Electrification introduced.All India Conference of Brahmins under the presidentship of Rameshvar Singh, the Brahmin king of Darbhanga. The Simon Commission visited the city; citizens' protest against their meeting.
1930	Purushottam Das Khattri built the Rama Mandir near Annapurna temple. Mahatma Gandhi launched 'Civil Disobedience' movement in the city. Hindu-Muslim riot.
1931	Subhash Chandra Bose, the great patriot and leader of the independence movement, visited the city, and established the Nava Bharata Sabha; he again visited the city in 1940.
1934	Earthquake on 15th January at 14.30hr.
1935	Viceroy Lord Irwin visited the city.
1936	Shivprasad Gupt built the Bharat Mata Mandir ('Mother India Temple'), which was inaugurated on 26 October by Mahatma Gandhi.A great number of casualties due to plague.
1941	Establishment of the Dharma Sangha by Svami Hariharananda 'Karpatri-Ji'.
1942	'Quit India' movement.
1944	'Koti Maharudra Yajna' performed by Karpatri-Ji, near Asi Ghat at Nagwa.
1947	On 15 August, India became an independent country.

IV. Post-Independence Period, since 1947

1947	On 15th August India became independent from the British rule.
1948	Flood disaster in the city.On 15th October, Kashi-Raj merged into the Indian Republic.Varanasi District was formed and the Varanasi City became the district headquarters.
1950	On 26th January India declared itself as a sovereign independent state, 'Republic'.
1951	The first 'Master Plan of Banaras' (1951-61) was prepared, but never implemented.
1958	Conversion of the Sanskrit College into a University. On 16th February, the New Vishvanatha temple (with Narvadeshvara Linga) built at Mir Ghat by Svami Hariharananda 'Karpatri-Ji'.
1961	Seven-corpse incidence (*Sata Lasha Kanda*): seven pilgrims from South India were killed during boating by giving them poison.The Diesel Locomotive Works (DLW), a factory making railway engines, was opened.

1966	Construction of Tulasi Manas temple by Krishna Lal Sureka.
1967	The Central Institute of Higher Tibetan Studies opened at Sarnath, which in 1988 was declared as Deemed University.
1969	On 27th January the Mrigadayavana Mahavihara Society was established at Sarnath.
1976	The Thai Temple at Sarnath was opened.
1978	Flood disaster in the city.
1981	The 5th World Sanskrit Conference: 21-26 October, held.
1982	The Cleaning Ganga Campaign (Swatch Ganga), a NGO was established.
1986	Central Ganga Authority (CGA) was formed and the Ganga cleaning programme started.
1990	On 30th December, Kala Cakra Tantra Abhisheka at Sarnath by the 14th Dalai Lama Tenzing Gyatso.
1991	Dharmacakra Indo-Japanese Society's temple opened at Sarnath.
1992	The Udai Pratap P.G. College was declared an autonomous institution. A Hindu Astronomical Observatory was opened in the compound of Sampurnananda Sanskrit University.
1996	The fourth 'Master Plan of Varanasi' (1991-2011) was prepared and submitted.
1999	Vajra Vidya Sansthan at Sarnath was opened on 29 October.
2000	Consecration ceremony of Parshvanath temple, Bhelupura on 17 November. Death of Raja Vibhuti Narayan Singh (1939-2001), the last king of Banaras, on 25 December.
2001	On 10 July, the Fourth 'Master Plan of Varanasi' (1991-2011) prepared in 1996, was approved by the State Government of Uttar Pradesh.
2002	Movement for inscribing Riverfront Ghat of Varanasi in the UNESCO WHL.
2007	Declaring the city under JNNURM and preparation of CDP.
2008	New Transport system policy (Fly-over bridges) and plans prepared. On 4 November 2008, the Ganga is declared as "National River" by the Government of India.

Appendix 3

BANARAS / VARANASI / KASHI:
LIST OF DIVINITIES & LOCATIONS

No.	Shrine's / Divinity's name	Location
1.	Abhaya Vinayaka	Shulatankeshvara Temple, D 17/111
2.	Achakka / Achanaka Devi	Siddheshvari, near Sankatha Devi, CK 2/34
3.	Adi Bhairava	Kamachha, Adi Bhairava, B 31/126
4.	Adi Gadadhara Vishnu	Rajghat, lower part of Adi Keshava, A 37/51
5.	Adi Keshava	Adi Keshava, House No. A 37/51
6.	Adi Mahadeva	Trilochan, Adi Mahadeva, A 3/92
7.	Adi Manikarnika	near Kedar Ghat, worship the Ganga, perceiving the site
8.	Adi Varaheshvara	Dashashvamedha Ghat, near Rama Mandir D 17/111, in ruins
9.	Adi Varahi	Man Mandira, Tripurabhairavi, D 16/84
10.	Adi Vishveshvara	Bansphataka, Adi Vishvanatha
11.	Aditya Keshava	Rajghat, close to Adi Keshava, A 37/51
12.	Aditya Keshava Tirtha	in the Ganga, close to Adi Keshava Ghat
13.	Agastya Kunda	Agastakunda, near Godaulia; lost
14.	Agastya Tirtha	in the Ganga, near Chausatthi Ghat
15.	Agastyeshvara/Agastishvara	Agastakunda Muhalla, Godaulia, D 36/11
16.	Aghoreshi	near Kameshvara, A 2/21 under tree in niche (Madhi (niche))
17.	Aghoreshvara	near Kameshvara, A 2/21 under tree in niche (Madhi (niche))
18.	Aghorodha Kupa	in the northeast of Omkareshvara; now lost
19.	Agni Tirtha	at Agnishvara Ghat, called Ganesha Ghat
20.	Agnidhreshvara	Jageshvara, in Math, Ishvargangi, J 66/4
21.	Agnijihva Vetala	near Vriddhakala, K 53/32, as Shiva Linga

22.	Agnishvara – 1	near Agnishvara Ghat, Patni Tola, CK 2/1
23.	Agnishvara – 2	near Svarlineshvara, A 12/2
24.	Agnishvara Kunda	assumed to be the present Ishvargangi Talab
25.	Aindri	Indreshvara, Manikarnika Ghat, near CK 9/2
26.	Airavata Kunda	southeast of Vriddhakala Temple, K 52/39, now lost
27.	Airavateshvara	in Vriddhakala Temple compound, K 52/39
28.	Aishvareshvara	Kachori Gali, K 34/60 facing Durmukha Vinayaka
29.	Aitarini Tirtha	Aitarini Pokhra, Lat Bhairava
30.	Akareshvara	near Omkareshvara, Pathani Tola, A 33/25
31.	Akrureshvara	Vachchhraj Ghat, Bhadaini, near Ganesha
32.	Amardakeshvara – 1	backside of Kath Ki Haveli, K 34/4
33.	Amardakeshvara – 2	near Kath Ki Haveli, K 32/33, Kalamardaneshvara
34.	Amareshvara	near Lolarka Kund, on steps, B 2/20
35.	Ambarisha Tirtha	in the Ganga river, near Adi Keshava
36.	Ambarisheshvara	Sonarpura, back to Kalibari, B 13/95
37.	Ambika	Pishachamochan Akhada, C 21/55
38.	Amnatakeshvara	near Siddheshvara, Jaitpura, J 6/84
39.	Amrita	in Nilakantha Temple, CK 33/28
40.	Amriteshvara – 1	village Aswari, Panchakroshi Road
41.	Amriteshvara – 2	Svargadvari, Nilakantha, CK 33/28
42.	Amriteshvari	Amriteshvara, Nilakantha, CK 33/28
43.	Ananda Bhairava – 1	near Vriddhaditya, Mir Ghat, D 3/14
44.	Ananda Bhairava – 2	Jaitpura, in front of Skandamata, J 6/33
45.	Ananda Bhairava – 3	Mir Ghat, near Hanuman Temple, D 3/14
46.	Anantavamana	another name of Vindu Madhava, K 22/37
47.	Angaraka Tirtha	near Agnishvara Ghat, south part, in the Ganga
48.	Angareshi – 1	called Panchakaudi Mata, Nababganj, B 27/20
49.	Angareshi – 2	at Kamachchha, called Anjani Devi
50.	Angareshvara – 1	porch of Atmavireshvara Temple, CK 7/158

51.	Angareshvara – 2	near Rinamochana – Gwalgadhah, Temple in south
52.	Angirasheshvara – 1	Jangambari, attached to main Road, D 35/79
53.	Angirasheshvara – 2	Svargadvari, CK 10/16
54.	Annapurna Devi – 1	Annapurna Gali, Jnanavapi, D 9/19
55.	Annapurna – 2	in Kedara Temple compound, B 6/102
56.	Annapurna – 3	north of Annapurna Chauraha, K 53/46
57.	Antakeshvara	in Vriddhakala Temple compound, K 52/39
58.	Anusuya Devi	Narad Ghat, upper side, Dattatreya Math, D 25/11
59.	Anusuyeshvara	Narad Ghat, upper side, Dattatreya Math, D 25/11
60.	Apamrityuhareshvara	Mrityunjaya Shiva, Vriddhakala, K 52/40
61.	Apasarasa Kupa	called Gauri Kupa, well south of the Kashi Devi in Kashipura
62.	Apastamba Kupa	the well on the mound, near Bade Ganesha
63.	Apastambeshvara – 1	called Burhe Baba, in Madhyameshvara, K 53/116
64.	Apastambeshvara – 2	south of Madhyameshvara, nearby, huge linga
65.	Apsareshvara	Radhakrishna Dharmasala, CK 30/1
66.	Arka Vinayaka	Lolarka Kund, near House No. B 2/17
67.	Aruna Aditya	Trilochaneshvara Temple, backside, A 2/80
68.	Arundhati Tirtha	north side of the Chausatthi Ghat, in the Ganga river
69.	Asankhyatirthani Linga	across the Varana, 80 m west from Rameshvara
70.	Asha Vinayaka	Mir Ghat, Hanuman Mandir, D 3/79
71.	Ashadhishvara – 1	Kashipura, Rani Betia Kothi, big *linga*, K 63/53
72.	Ashadhishvara – 2	Machharhatta Fatak, Govindapura Khurd, CK 54/24
73.	Ashapuri Devi	north of Maidagin Tank, K 59/16 (near the north lane)

74.	Ashoka/ Viloka Tirtha	an ancient waterpool that filled in, now is Bulanala
75.	Ashu (Mohana) Bhairava	called Mohan Bhairava, Lala Lajpat Road
76.	Ashvarudha	in the Vagishvari Devi temple, Jaitpura, J 6/33
77.	Ashvatareshvara (Ketu)	Gomath, Brahmanal, CK 8/14A
78.	Ashvineyeshvara	near Ganga Mahal, CK 2/26
79.	Asi Sangama Tirtha	Asi confluence point of the Asi and the Ganga
80.	Asi Madhava	Tulasi Ghat, in Tulasidasa shrine chamber, B 2/15
81.	Asi Sangameshvara – 1	close to steps, Asi Ghat, B 1/169, Hariharbaba Ashram
82.	Asi Sangameshvara – 2	Asi Ghat, upper side lane, B 1/174
83.	Asi Sangameshvara – 3	Asi Ghat, Hotel Ganga View, B 1/175 (family temple)
84.	Asitanga Bhairava	in Vriddhakala Temple, near Sarveshvara, K 52/39
85.	Asthitkshepatadageshvara	along the Beniabag-Haraha Sarai lane, a huge *linga*, CK 48/45
86.	Atmavireshvara	Scindhia Ghat, near Sankatha-Ji, CK 7/158
87.	Atrishvara – 1	Kodai Chauki, D 50/33, lost; now at Narad ghat
88.	Atrishvara – 2	Narad Ghat, Dattatreya Math, D 25/11
89.	Attahasa Linga	Kashmirimal Haveli, near Shitala, CK 7/92
90.	Attahasa (Amba)	Kashmirimal Haveli, near Shitala, CK 7/92
91.	Atyugra Narsimha	Gomatha, Abhayananda Ashram, CK 8/21
92.	Avadhuteshvara	near Pashupateshvara, CK 13/85
93.	Avasana Bhairava	south gate of Tripurabhairavi, D 5/24
94.	Avimukta Vinayaka	(old one lost), presently in wall, Jnanavapi mosque
95.	Avimukteshvara – 1	northern gate of Jnanavapi, lost but site worshipped
96.	Avimukteshvara – 2	Radhakrishna Dharmashala, CK 30/1 Jnanavapi: see from the window

97.	Avimukteshvara – 3	Manikarnika Road, outside CK 10/22 A, Brahmanaleshvara
98.	Avimukteshvara – 4	Vishvanatha Temple compound, CK 35/19, Southern direction
99.	Avimukteshvara Tirtha	at Manikarnika Ghat, in the Ganga river
100.	Ayogandha Kunda	now called Pushkara, in Assi east to Mumukshu Bhavan
101.	Ayogandheshvara	at Pushkar Talab, Assi, east to Mumukshu Bhavan
102.	Ayutabhuja	Rambag compound, Chaitaipur, on Panchakroshi Road
103.	Baglamukhi	Pitambara Devi, Siddheshvari, CK 2/38
104.	Bala	Vriddhakala, in Satishvara Temple, K 46/32
105.	Balacandreshvara	old Talakarneshvara, Ausanganj, K 56/114
106.	Balishvara (Bandishvara)	in Vriddhakala Temple compound, K 52/39
107.	Balishvara Kunda	Gadhi Muhammad Shahid, now lost
108.	Balivamana Vishnu	Adi Keshava Temple, outside, A 37/51
109.	Bandi Devi	Dashashvamedha Ghat, upper side, D 17/100
110.	Baneshvara – 1	near Lolarkakunda, known as Lolarkeshvara
111.	Baneshvara – 2	in the Siddheshvara temple
112.	Baneshvara – 3	Maidagin, near Harishchandra School, D 58/96
113.	Baneshvara – 4	Prahlad Ghat, Panchagni Akhara, K 11/30
114.	Baneshvara – 5	in Asi Sangameshvara Temple, B 1/169
115.	Baneshvara – 6	Sukhlal Shah Muhal, CK 13/17; (also Banasura's statue)
116.	Baraka Devi	known as Pancakaudi Devi, B 27/20
117.	Batuka Bhairava – 1	Batuka Bhairava, Kamachha, B 21/126
118.	Batuka Bhairava – 2	Shitala Ghat, Rajmandir, K 20/6
119.	Batuka Bhairava – 3	Chowkhambha, near Gopal Mandir, CK 34/22
120.	Bhadra Vinayaka	Bhadaini, near House No. B 2/17 (in Arka Vinayaka)
121.	Bhadradoka (Hrida)	near Nageshvara, at Bhonshala Ghat; now lost

122. Bhadrakali – 1	Madhyameshvara, Daranagar, K 53/63; lost
123. Bhadrakali – 2	close north of Madhyameshvara T, K 53/107
124. Bhadrakarna Hrida	near Rameshvara, in Village Bhuili, on Panchakroshi Road
125. Bhadrakarneshvara	near Rameshvara, in Village Bhuili, on Panchakroshi Road
126. Bhadreshvara	old at Bhadaun; Patni Tola, in Upashantishvara, CK 2/4
127. Bhagiratha Linga	south of Manikarnika, facing house CK 10/49
128. Bhagiratha Vinayaka	Lahori Tola, near Phute Ganesha, CK 1/40
129. Bhagirathi Devi	Lalita Ghat, D 1/67
130. Bhagirathishvara	Svargadvari, Manikarnika Lane, CK 11/11
131. Bhairava – 1	in Harsons (near 1.5 km right to Panchakroshi Road)
132. Bhairava – 2	in Kedara Temple compound, B 6/102
133. Bhairava Tirtha	Lata Bhairava Talab
134. Bhairaveshvara	west corner of Kala Bhairava, K 32/7
135. Bhairavi – 1	Tripurabhairavi, Man Mandir, D 5/24
136. Bhairavi Devi – 2	village Harsons, Panchakroshi Road, with Bhairava
137. Bharabhuteshvara	Rajadarwaja lane, Gobindapura, CK 54/44
138. Bharateshvara – 1	Rameshvara Temple, Panchakroshi Road
139. Bharateshvara – 2	Hanuman Ghat, Sri Krishna Nivas, B 4/9A
140. Bhardvajeshvara	in Vashishtha-Vamadeva, Sankatha Ghat, CK 7/161
141. Bhashmagatreshvara	south of Kashi Karvat, CK 31/15
142. Bhavani	Annapurna, Vishvanath Gali, D 8/38
143. Bhavanishankara	as Bhavanishvara, near Annapurna and Rama temples, D 8/38
144. Bhima	Panchaganga, near Bala-ji, K 22/24
145. Bhimachandi Devi	village Bhimachandi, on Panchakroshi route
146. Bhimashankara	as Bhimeshvara, Kashikarvat, CK 31/12
147. Bhishana/Bhuta Bhairava	called Bhutabhairava, Kashipura, K 63/28

148.	Bhishma Keshava	in Vriddhakaleshvara Temple, K 52/39
149.	Bhishmachandi	Pashpani Temple II, Sadar Bazaar
150.	Bhishmeshvara – 1	Sadar Bazar, in Chandishvara
151.	Bhishmeshvara – 2	Trilochan Ghat, close to the bank, in a niche
152.	Bhishmeshvara – 3	Kabutar Bazar, Kashipura
153.	Bhishmeshvara – 4	in Vishvanatha, near Shanaichareshvara, CH 35/19, Vrihaspati
154.	Bhrigu Keshava	Nandeshvara Ghat, Nandu Phadia, steps, A 4/13
155.	Bhrigu Narayana	Saptasagar, in Pavaneshvara Temple, K 63/14
156.	Bhringiriti Gana	village Deura, on Panchakroshi Road
157.	Bhringisheshvara	as Dhanavantarishvara, in Vriddhakala Temple, K 52/39
158.	Bhurbhuvah Linga	Bhutabhairava, K 63/26; (Ganadhip, lost)
159.	Bhuta/Bhishana Bhairava	Bhuta Bhairava, K 63/28
160.	Bhutadhatrisha	Sukhlal Shah Phatak, CK 13/15
161.	Bhuteshvara	Dashashvamedha, D 17/50
162.	Bhutanatheshvara	Village Dindaspur, on Panchakroshi Road
163.	Bhutrishvara	Kashipura, Rani Betia Temple, near Ashadhishvara
164.	Bhuvaneshvari	Patni Tola, Agnishvara Temple, CK 2/1
165.	Bibhandeshvara	Tilbhandeshvara Math, in the well
166.	Bindu Vinayaka	Panchaganga, Vindu Madhava Temple, K 22/37
167.	Brahamishvara	Sakarkand Gali, D 7/6
168.	Brahma (image)	steps to Brahma Ghat, eastern side, a 13th century image
169.	Brahmacharini	Durga Ghat, K 22/72
170.	Brahmanaleshvara	Brahmanal, CK 10/53
171.	Brahmapadapadeshvara	near Batuka Bhairava (70), in north veranda
172.	Brahmavarta Kupa	Dhundhiraj Lane, Aparanath Math, CK 37/12
173.	Brahmeshvara – 1	Brahma Ghat, K 22/82
174.	Brahmeshvara – 2	Brahma Ghat, K 22/89, on the steps

175. Brahmeshvara – 3	Balmukund Chauhatta, Khalispura, D 33/66
176. Brahmeshvara – 4	near Prayaga Ghat, 4-headed Siva
177. Brahmeshvara – 5	Kashi Karvat, in Durmkha Vinayaka, CK 34/60
178. Brahmi / Brahmani	Khalispura, Brahmeshvara-well, D 33/66
179. Brahmishvara	Shakarkanda Gali, D 7/6
180. Brihaspatishvara (Jupiter) – 1	facing Atmavireshvara Temple, Scindhia Ghat, CK 7/133
181. Brihaspatishvara (Jupiter) – 2	near Dedhasi ka Pul, D 12/79, Traylokyamohaneshvara
182. Budheshvara (Mercury)	Atmavireshvara Temple, CK 7/158
183. Chakrapushkarini	called Manikarnika Kunda, at Manikarnika Ghat
184. Chamunda – 1	village Aware, Panchakroshi Road
185. Chamunda (Devi) – 2	known as Mahishasuramardini, B 2/18, Lolarka
186. Chanda Bhairava	Durga Temple, Durgakund, near Kali, B 27/2
187. Chanda Gana	in Kedara Temple compound, B 6/102
188. Chanda Vinayaka	in Bhimachandi Temple, on Panchakroshi route (as Bhimacanda)
189. Chandi Devi – 1	Sadar Bazaar, Orderly Bazar
190. Chandi Devi – 2	Kalika Gali, D 8/26
191. Chandicandishvara	Kalika Gali, D 8/27
192. Chandika	Pashpani Vinayaka II, Sadar Bazar, in a Math
193. Chandikeshvara	Kalika Gali, D 8/27, i.e. Chandichandishvara
194. Chandishvara – 1	Sadar Bazar, in Chandi Devi temple
195. Chandishvara – 2	in Kalika Temple, Kalika Gali, D 8/26
196. Chandra Kupa	Siddheshvari, in Siddheshvari Temple, CK 7/124
197. Chandreshvara (Moon)	near Scindhia Ghat, in Siddheshvari Temple, CK 7/124
198. Charcika	near Mangla Gauri Ghat, K 23/74
199. Charmamunda Devi	Lolarka Kund, Munnar Panda, B 2/62
200. Charumukha Gana	village Chaukhandi, Panchakroshi Road

385

201. Chatuhshashthi Devi   Chausatthi Devi, Rana Mahal, D 22/17

202. Chaturdanta Vinayaka   Nai Sarak, Sanatandharm School, D 49/10

203. Chaturhsagaravapi   road to Kashipura, a well, near to K 63/46

204. Chaturmukheshvara – 1   inside Vriddhakala, K 52/39

205. Chaturmukheshvara – 2   Prayaga Linga, Adi Keshava, A 37/51

206. Chaturvakratreshvara   Sakarkand Gali, D 7/19

207. Chausatthi Devi (Yogini)   Chausatthi Yogini, Rana Mahal, D 22/17

208. Chhagaleshvara   Pitarkunda, C 18/52

209. Chhagavakreshvari   eastern wall of Vrishabhadhvaja, Kapildhara

210. Chhappano Vinayaka   at Kapiladhara, near Vrishabhadhvaja

211. Chhinnamasta Devi   Teliana, Jangambari, D 35/221 A; also in the compound of Sumer Devi Temple, Ramnagar

212. Chintamani Vinayaka – 1   Scindhia Ghat, gate of Vashistha-Vamadeva, CK 7/161

213. Chintamani Vinayaka – 2   Ishvargangi Talab, Ausanganj, K 56/43H

214. Chintamani Vinayaka – 3   Kedar Ghat road, Avadha Kedar, Pitambarpura, B 7/208

215. Chintamani/Chintaharana – 4   Adi Keshava, southern shrine, K 37/51

216. Chitraghanta   Lakhi Chabutara, Chandu Nau Gali, CK 23/34

217. Chitraghanta Vinayaka – 1   Ranikuon, Chandu Nau Gali, CK 23/25; in marble temple

218. Chitraghanta Vinayaka – 2   Jagannathdas-Balbhadradas shop, CK 39/74-76, on platform

219. Chitragriva   near Kshemeshvara Ghat, Kumarsvami Math, B 14/118

220. Chitragriva Devi   Kedara Ghat, Kumarsvami Math, B 14/118

221. Chitragupteshvara   Machchharhatta Phatak, CK 57/77

222. Chitrakupa   in Chitreshvara, Rajadarwaja, near CK 57/77

223. Chitrangadeshvara   near Kshemeshvara Ghat, Kumarsvami Math, B 14/118

224. Chitrangadeshvari   near Kshemeshvara Ghat, Kumarsvami Math, B 14/118

225. Dadhi (Yogurt) Vinayaka   Dudha Vinayaka, K 23/65

226. Dadhi Madhava   Asi Ghat, Tulasidas Ashram

227.	Dadhichishvara	Kedar Ghat, huge size *linga*
228.	Dakshayinishvara	as Satishvara, road to Vriddhakala, K 46/32
229.	Daksheshvara	north of Vriddhakala Kupa, huge *linga*, K 52/39
230.	Dakshinamurti	in Kedar Temple compound, B 6/102
231.	Dalabheshvara	Man Mandir Ghat, D 16/32
232.	Damanakeshvara	at gate, in Madhi (niche), Makareshvara
233.	Dandakhyata Tirtha	Piyala Shahid ka Kund (Kupa); lost
234.	Dandapani (Bhairava) – 1	Dhundhiraja Gali, bazaar area, Jnanavapi, CK 36/10
235.	Dandapani – 2	backside of Kala Bhairava, K 32/26, called Kshetrapala
236.	Dandapani – 3	Kala Bhairava, Dandapani Gali, K 31/49 (re-established)
237.	Dandapani – 4	west to Vaikuntheshvara, in Vishvanatha court, CK 35/19
238.	Dandapani – 5	in Kedara Temple compound, B 6/102
239.	Dandishvara	near Adi Keshava, A 37/51
240.	Dantahasta Vinayaka	Lohatia, in Bade Ganesh, K 58/101
241.	Dashahareshvara	Dashashvamedha, Shitala Temple, D 18/19
242.	Dashashvamedha Tirtha	Dashashvamedha Ghat, perceived at the bank
243.	Dashashvamedheshvara	Shitala Temple, Dashashavamedha Ghat, D 18/19
244.	Dattatreyeshvara – 1	Bhagvan Ashram, copper image, Hanuman Ghat, B 5/276
245.	Dattatreyeshvara – 2	Adi Keshava, outside of the temple gate, near A 37/51
246.	Dattatreyeshvara – 3	Gai Ghat, close to the Ganga's bank
247.	Dattatreyeshvara – 4	Brahma Ghat, K 18/48
248.	Dattatrayeshvara – 5	Scindhia Ghat, upper part, CK 7/156
249.	Dattatrayeshvara – 6	Agastakunda, Agastishvara temple, D 36/11
250.	Dattatrayeshvara – 7	Narada Ghat, upper part, Math, B 25/12
251.	Dattatrayeshvara – 8	Kinarama Aghor Ashram, Ravindrapuri, B 3/335

252.	Dattatrayeshvara – 9	Panchaganga Ghat, Shankaracharya Math, K 22/11
253.	Dattatrayeshvara – 10	Dattatrayeshvara Math, CK 34/36
254.	Dattatrayeshvara Tirtha	in the Ganga, near Raj Ghat fort
255.	Dehali Vinayaka	Dehali Vinayaka, on Panchakroshi route
256.	Devadeva	Dhundhiraja Gali, in Sanyasi College, CK 37/12
257.	Devaleshvara	Saptasagar, Bhutabhairava, K 63/30
258.	Devasangheshvara	village Karoma (near 600 m right to road), on Panchakroshi road
259.	Devayanishvara	as Nakulishvara, in the root of Akshaya Vata, CK 35/20
260.	Dhanavantarishvara	in Vriddhakala Temple, K 52/39
261.	Dhanvantari Tirtha	Dhaneshra Tala, now Kupa in Math, J 4/91
262.	Dhanvantishvara	As Dhanadeshvara, Pilikothi, Dhaneshra Math, J 4/91
263.	Dharani Varaha	Dashashvamedha, outside near house D 17/111
264.	Dharma Kupa	near Vishalakshi, Mir Ghat, Dharmakup, near D 2/21
265.	Dharmeshvara – 1	Mir Ghat, Dharmakup, D 2/21
266.	Dharmeshvara – 2	in the south of Kameshvara, A 2/9, lost
267.	Dhruveshvara	Kodai ki Chauki, in Sanatan Dharm College, D 49/10
268.	Dhumavati Devi	Nati Imli, Dhupachandi temple, J 12/134
269.	Dhundhiraja (Vinayaka) – 1	at the gate of Annapurna Gali
270.	Dhundhiraja – 2	in Rani Bhavani Temple, Annapurna Gali, CK 35/28; 5 headed image
271.	Dhundhiraja – 3	near Rani Bhavani Temple, CK 37/18
272.	Dhautapapeshvara	at Panchaganga Ghat, in the porch
273.	Dilipeshvara	Devanathpura, Shivala
274.	Dipta/Diptashakti	near Sambaditya, Surajkund, D 51/90
275.	Divodasa	Bhikharidas Lane, near Parashurameshvara, in CK 14/43

276.	Divodaseshvara – 1	Mir Ghat, Dharmakupa, in Vishvabhuja Gauri, D 2/15
277.	Divodaseshvara – 2	Pashupateshvara Gali, CK 13/76
278.	Draupada Aditya	near Vishvanatha Temple, CK 35/20
279.	Draupadi	near Draupada Aditya, near Vishvanatha Temple, CK 35/20
280.	Drimicandeshvara	Jaitpura, south of Nagakuon, known as 'Mallu Halwai ka temple', J 11/148
281.	Dugdha (Milk) Vinayaka	Dudha Vinayaka, K 23/66
282.	Duli Tirtha	east of Vriddhakala, Duligadahi, now lost
283.	Durga Devi (Kushmanda)	Durgakund Temple, Durgakund, B 27/1
284.	Durga Kunda	Durgakund, attached to B 27/1
285.	Durga Vinayaka	Durgakund, southeastcorner, Durga Kund, B 27/1
286.	Durmukha Vinayaka	Kashi Karvat, CK 34/60
287.	Durvasa	in Dvarakadhisha Temple, B 22/195
288.	Durvaseshvara – 1	in Rani Betia temple, near Ashadhishvara
289.	Durvaseshvara – 2	in Kameshvara Temple, A 2/9
290.	Dvadasheshvara	near Chauk, Panchakroshi Temple, Gola Gali, CK 5/32
291.	Dvara Bhairava	in Vishvanatha Temple, southwest corner, CK 35/19
292.	Dvara Vinayaka	Saptavarana Vinayaka's gate, CK 28/10
293.	Dvarakanatha	Dvarakadhisha, Shankudhara, B 22/195
294.	Dvarakeshvara	at Shankudhara, in temple compound, B 22/195
295.	Dvareshvara	south of Durga Temple, Durgakund, B 27/1
296.	Dvareshvari	as Jarahareshvari, in Dvareshvara, south of Durga-Ji, B 27/1
297.	Dvavabhumishvara	Rameshvara temple compound, on Panchakroshi route
298.	Dvimukha Vinayaka	Surajkund, in western wall Sambaditya, D 51/90
299.	Ekadanta Vinayaka – 1	Bengali Tola, Pushpadanteshvara, D 32/102

300. Ekadanta Vinayaka – 2	Sankatha Temple's south wall, near Vairochaneshvara
301. Ekadanta Vinayaka – 3	Bansphatak, in Adi Vishveshvara
302. Ekapada Gana	village Kachnar, on Panchakroshi Road
303. Gabhastishvara (Sun)	Panchaganga Ghat, Mangalagauri, K 24/34
304. Gada Tirtha	near Adi Keshava Ghat, in the Ganga River
305. Gaja Vinayaka	Rajadarwaja, Bharbhuteshvara, K 54/44
306. Gajadhara Vishnu	Rajghat, Adi Keshava, A 37/51, outside
307. Gajanana/Gajasya	Gajanana, Rana Mahal, D 21/22
308. Gajarakna Vinayaka	Kotwalpura, Ishaneshwara, CK 37/43
309. Gajasya (Yogini)	Gajanana, Rana Mahal, D 21/22
310. Gananatha Vinayaka	Jnanavapi, Aparnath Math, CK 37/1
311. Gananatheshvara	village Bhatauli, on Panchakroshi Road
312. Ganapati	in Kedara Temple compound, B 6/102
313. Ganapriya	village Gaura, on Panchakroshi Road
314. Gandharva Sagar	village Bhimachandi, water pool, on Panchakroshi Road
315. Ganesha Vinayaka	north of Company Bagh, Ganeshganj, K 53/44
316. Ganeshvara	village Chaukhandi, Panchakroshi Road
317. Ganga Aditya	Lalita Ghat, upper side, CK 1/68
318. Ganga Keshava	a shrine, Lalita Ghat, upper part, CK 1/68
319. Ganga Keshava Tirtha	in the Ganga, near Ganga Mahal Ghat II, upstream
320. Gangeshvara – 1	Jnanavapi, under Pipal (holy ficus) tree; near CK 35/1
321. Gangeshvara – 2	east of Pashupateshvara, CK 13/79
322. Gargeshvara	east of Shramodaka Kupa, now lost
323. Garuda	Jangambadi-Teliana, D 31/43
324. Garuda Tirtha	in the Ganga, near Adi Keshava Ghat, south of Gada Tirtha
325. Garudeshvara – 1	near Kameshvara, in Khakholkaditya mini temple, A 2/9

326. Garudeshvara – 2	Jangambari, Teliana (Devnathpura) D 31/39 A
327. Gatiprati Tirtha	near Arka Vinayaka, in the Ganga; lost
328. Gauri Kunda	Kedara Ghat, close to the Ghat, stone fenced
329. Gauri Kupa	Kashipura, south of Kashi Devi, called Apsarasa Kupa
330. Gautameshvara	Godaulia, near Kashi Naresh Shivala, D 37/33
331. Ghantakarna Gana	south of Ghantakarna, inside CK 13/79, now lost
332. Ghantakarna Tirtha	Karnaghanta Talab, K 60/67
333. Ghantakarneshvara	Karnaghanta, K 60/66
334. Ghantankara	Shulatankeshvara, D 17/111
335. Ghrinishvara	Ghushrinishvara, Kamachha, in B 21/123
336. Ghrita (Butter) Vinayaka	Dudha Vinayaka, K 23/57
337. Ghushmeshvara	Ghushrinishvara, in Kamachha, B 21/123
338. Giri Nrisimha	inside Dehli Vinayaka temple, Panchakroshi Road
339. Godavari Tirtha	Godaulia, now lost
340. Gokarna Kupa	Kodai Ki Chauki, Dailu Gali, D 50/33
341. Gokarneshvara	Dayalu Gali, Kodai ki Chauki, D 50/34A
342. Gopal Mandir	Chowkhambha, Gopal Mandir, CK 34/22
343. Gopi Govinda Vishnu	Lal Ghat, A 4/24
344. Gopratara	Gopreksheshvara, Gopi Govind, Lal Ghat, A 4/24
345. Gopreksheshvara	in Gopi Govind Temple, Lal Ghat, A 4/24
346. Govyaghreshvara	Shitala Temple, Dashashvamedha Ghat, D 18/99
347. Halisheshvara	near Dhanvantishvara, J 30/22
348. Hamsa Tirtha	Hartirath Pokhara, now filled up, lost
349. Hamsheshvara	Manasarovara, lost
350. Hanumadishvara – 1	lower side, Hanuman Ghat, in Madhi (niche) B 5/19

351. Hanumadishvara – 3   Rama Ghat, Jagannath Temple, K 24/13

352. Hanumadishvara – 2   Hanuman Ghat, B 4/42

353. Harampapa Tirtha   Kedar Ghat, along the Ganga,

354. Harampapeshvara   & Nishpapeshvara, Kedar Ghat, in the Madhi (niche)

355. Harasiddhi   back of Siddhi Vinayaka, Manikarnika, CK 9/9

356. Harikesheshvara   Janganbari, Kharikuan, D 35/273

357. Harishachandra Mandapa   in Harishachandreshvara, CK 7/166

358. Harishachandra Vinayaka   Sankatha Ghat, in Madhi (niche), CK 7/165

359. Harishchandreshvara – 1   Sankatha Ghat, CK 7/166

360. Harishchandreshvara – 2   near Pataleshvara, D 32/118, outside

361. Harishchandreshvara – 3   Harishchandra Ghat, open space, called Shmashaneshvara

362. Hastipaleshvara   in Vriddhakala T.compound, K 52/39

363. Hatakeshvara – 1   Dalmandi, Gudari Bazar, CK 43/189

364. Hatakeshvara – 2   Haraha Sarai, CK 43/189

365. Hatakeshvara – 3   Manasarovara, B 1/151

366. Hatakeshvara – 4   Dudha Vinayaka, K 23/41

367. Hatakeshvara – 5   Scindhia Ghat, upper side, CK 7/136

368. Hayagriva Keshava   Bhadaini, near Anandamayi Hospital, B 3/25

369. Hayagriveshvara   near Anandamayi Hospital, Shivala, B 3/25

370. Hayakanthi   Kalimath, Lakshmi Kunda, backside

371. Heramba Vinayaka   Maldahia, Valmiki Tila, C 21/14; now shifted to nearby house

372. Hetukeshvara   Haraha Talab, now lost

373. Hiranyagharbheshvara   Haraha Talab, now lost

374. Hundana-Mundana Gana – 1   Shailaputri, Varana's bank, Madhi (niche) a Ghat, A 40/11

375. Hundana-Mundana Gana – 2   Dhupachandi Devi Temple, backside, J 12/134

376. Ikshvaku Tirtha   southern part of Rama Ghat, in the Ganga river

377. Indradhyumna Tirtha   in the Ganga river, near Rama Ghat

378. Indradhyumneshvara   Coochbihar, backside of Kalibari, B 13/98

379.	Indreshvara – 1	near Karkotakavapi (Naga Kupa); now lost
380.	Indreshvara – 2	near Tarakeshvara, Manikarnika Ghat, under Pipal tree
381.	Ishaneshvara – 1	Kotwalpura, CK 37/43 (near cinema)
382.	Ishaneshvara – 2	called Daneshvara, at Prahlada Ghat
383.	Ishvaragangi Tirtha	Ishvaragangi Pokhara, Ishvargangi
384.	Jagannatha – 1	southern side of Assi Ghat, B 1/151
385.	Jagannatha – 2	Dashashvamedha Ghat, D 17/101
386.	Jagannatha – 3	near Annapurna Temple, Ram Mandir, D 8/38
387.	Jagannatha – 4	Nilakantha, CK 33/54
388.	Jagannatha – 5	Rama Ghat, K 24/11
389.	Jagannatha – 6	Rajmandir, in Hanuman Temple, K 20/159
390.	Jagannatha – 7	Nati Imali
391.	Jagannatha – 8	Lohatiya, Bade Ganesha, outside K 58/105
392.	Jageshvara/Jogeshvara	Ishvargangi, Narharipura, J 66/4
393.	Jaigishavya Guha	Narharipura, near Jageshvara Math, J 66/3
394.	Jaigishvyeshvara – 1	at the gate of Jaigishvya Guha, Jageshvara Math, J 66/3
395.	Jaigishvyeshvara – 2	Saptasagar, Bhutabhairava, K 63/28
396.	Jamadagnishvara	east of Kala Bhairava, K 32/57
397.	Jamadagnishvara – 1	near Madhyameshvara, K 53/63, compound
398.	Jamadagnishvara – 2	Scindhia Ghat, gate of Vashishtha-Vamadeva, CK 7/161
399.	Jambukeshvara – 1	Lohatia, in Bade Ganesha, K 58/103
400.	Jambukeshvara – 2	Bade Ganesha, K 58/103
401.	Janakeshvara – 1	upper part of Tulasi Ghat
402.	Janakeshvara – 2	in Vriddhakala, K 52/39
403.	Janakeshvara – 3	inside Sankatha Temple, near Sankatha ji, CK 7/159
404.	Janakeshvara – 3	west of Durgakund, in Shukulpura, in a group of old images
405.	Janaki Kunda	called Sita Kunda, in Luxa

406. Jangalishvara	in Durga Temple, Durgakund, B 27/1
407. Jarasandheshvara	Tripurabhairavi, D 5/101, in wall; (lost: house, D 3/79)
408. Jatishvara	Called Pataleshvara, gate of house D 32/117
409. Jayanta Linga	near Kedar Ghat, at Lali Ghat, in the niche close to the bank
410. Jayanteshvara – 1	north to Mrityunjaya Temple, Vriddhakala, K 52/39
411. Jayanteshvara – 2	Bhuta Bhairava, K 63/27
412. Jnana Keshava – 1	Khowa Bazar, in Langlishvara, CK 28/4
413. Jnana Keshava – 2	Rajghat, Adi Keshava, A 37/51
414. Jnana Madhava – 1	Vishvanatha court, near Kapila, CK 35/21
415. Jnana Madhava – 2	Jnanavapi, Panchapandava Temple, CK 28/10
416. Jnana Vinayaka	near the Jnanavapi Kupa, Jnanavapi
417. Jnanadeshvara	village Asawari, Panchakroshi Road
418. Jnanavapi (Kupa/ well)	Jnanavapi Kupa in the Mandapa
419. Jnaneshvara	Lahori Tola, D 1/32
420. Jvala (Jvalamali) Narsimha	village Kotwa, on Panchakroshi Road
421. Jvalamukhi	Gola Gali, Jalpa Devi, CK 54/134
422. Jvarahareshvara	near Vagishvari, Jaitpura, J 6/85
423. Jyeshtha Gauri	Bhuta Bhairava, Kashipura, K 63/24
424. Jyeshtha Vinayaka – 1	Bhuta Bhairava, Kashipura, K 62/44
425. Jyeshtha Vinayaka – 2	near Kedar Ghat, Lali Ghat, in the niche close to Ghat
426. Jyeshtheshvara	Bhuta Bhairava, Saptasagar, Kashipura, K 62/44
427. Jyotirupeshvara	near Manikarnishvara, Kakaram Gali, CK 8/10
428. Kacheshvara	small *linga* in Shukreshvara, Kalika Gali D 8/30
429. Kaholeshvara – 1	Jyesthasthana, K 63/22
430. Kaholeshvara – 2	north of Kamachha Devi Temple, Kolhua, B 21/123
431. Kaholeshvara – 3	Bhelupur, well of Mangala Prasad, B 19/50

432.	Kala Bhairava	Kala Bhairava, K 32/22
433.	Kala Kupa	Kala Bhairava, Dandapani Gali, K 31/49
434.	Kala Madhava	Kath Ki Haveli, backside, K 34/4
435.	Kala Vinayaka	at the steps of Ram Ghat, K 24/10
436.	Kalakeshvara	Hanuman Ghat, B 4/44
437.	Kalakuta Gana	village Deura, on Panchakroshi Road
438.	Kalanatha	village Janasa, on Panchakroshi Road
439.	Kalanjareshvara	Kshemeshvara Ghat, Kumarsvami Math, B 14/10; people mostly worship this divinity in Kedara Temple
440.	Kalaraja/ Kala Bhairava	Dandapani Gali, Kala Bhairava, K 31/49
441.	Kalaratri – 1	Kali, Kalika Gali, D 8/17
442.	Kalaratri – 2	in Durga Temple, Durgakund, B 27/1
443.	Kalasha Kupa	Kalasheshvara Ki Brahmapuri, CK 7/101
444.	Kalasheshvara	Kalasheshvara ki Brahmapuri Phatak, CK 7/101
445.	Kaleshvara – 1	in the Vriddhakala, K 52/39; called Vriddhakaleshvara
446.	Kaleshvara – 2	near Kala Bhairava, in Dandapani Temple, K 31/49
447.	Kaleshvara – 3	across the Varana confluence, in ruins, established by Kala Gana
448.	Kali	Kalika Gali, Dashashvamedha, D 8/17
449.	Kalipriya Vinayaka	Manahprakameshvara Temple, D 10/50
450.	Kaliyugeshvara	in Siddheshvari Temple, CK 7/124; called Kalikaleshvara
451.	Kalodaka Kupa	well in Vriddhakaleshvara, K 52/39
452.	Kamaksha Devi	Kamaksha, near Batuka Bhairava, B 21/123
453.	Kamaksha Tirtha	Kund near Kamaksha Devi, now lost
454.	Kamala	Mahalakshmi, Lakshmi Kund, D 52/40
455.	Kambalashvatara Tirtha	north spot at Manikarnika Ghat, in the Ganga river
456.	Kambalashvatareshvara	Gomath, Kakaram Gali, CK 8/14A

457. Kambaleshvara/ Kamaleshvara (Rahu)	Gomath, Brahmanal, CK 8/14A
458. Kameshvara – 1	village Chaukhandi, on Panchakroshi Road
459. Kameshvara – 2	Machhodari, Kameshvara, A 2/9
460. Kameshvara – 3	Ghasi Tola, in the lane at the corner K 30/1
461. Kanchana Vata	banyan under which is Savitri, Dharmakupa, near D 2/15
462. Kandukeshvara	Saptasagar, Bhutabhairava, K 63/29
463. Kankala Bhairava	Manikarnika, near Jyotirupeshvara, CK 8/180
464. Kapala (Lata) Bhairava	Alaipur, Lata Bhairava, A 1/123
465. Kapalamochana Tirtha	Kapalamochana Talab, Lat Bhairava
466. Kapaleshvara	at Lata Bhairava Talab, A 1/123
467. Kapali Bhairava	at Lata Bhairava Talab, A 1/123
468. Kapardi Vinayaka	near Pishachamochan Kund, C 21/40
469. Kapardishvara	village Janasa, Panchakroshi Road
470. Kapilahrida	Kapiladhara Tirtha, water pool (Kunda)
471. Kapileshvara – 1	Kapileshvara Lane, Dudhvinayaka, K 23/14
472. Kapileshvara – 2	Known as Vrisabhadhvajeshvara, Kapiladhara
473. Kapileshvara – 3	in the ditch, near Nikumbha, in Vishvanatha Temple, CK 35/19
474. Karavireshvara	Lakshmikund, along the lane, D 52/41
475. Kardama Kunda	village Kandwa, famous water pool
476. Kardama Kupa	near Kardamatirtha, Kandwa, on Panchakroshi Road
477. Kardameshvara	Panchakroshi Road, village Kandwa
478. Kardhameshvara	near Chamunda, B 2/17, also called Karandhameshvara
479. Karkotaka Vapi/ Tirtha	Naga Kunda, Jaitpura, Bari Bazaaar, J 23/206
480. Karkoteshvara	on steps to Naga Kunda, J 23/206
481. Karna Aditya – 1	Ram Mandir, Dashashvamedha, D 17/111
482. Karna Aditya – 2	Raj Mandir, K 20/147
483. Karpadishvara	Temple at Pishachamochana Talab, CK 21/40

396

484. Karuneshvara – 1	village Aware, on Panchakroshi Road
485. Karuneshvara – 2	Lahoritola, Lalita Ghat, in Phute Ganesh CK 34/10
486. Karuneshvara – 3	Varneshvara, Dhundhiraj Gali, CK 36/10
487. Kashi Devi	Saptasagar, Kashipura, Jawahar Katra
488. Kasyapeshvara	Jangambari Road, D 35/79
489. Katyayini	Scindhia Ghat, Atmavireshvara, CK 7/158
490. Kaumari	Bhadrakali, Kashmirimal, Kalash Kup, CK 7/102
491. Kaurmishakti	Bhishmacandi, Pashpani II, Sadar Bazar
492. Kedareshvara – 1	in Kedara Temple, B 6/102; half-Shiva & half-Vishnu
493. Kedareshvara – 2	Kalika Gali, in Kali-Ji, D 8/17
494. Kedareshvara – 3	Agastakunda, Agasteshvara, D 36/11
495. Kedareshvara – 4	Scindhia Ghat, Brihaspatishvara, CK 7/133
496. Keshava Aditya	Adi Keshava Temple, Raj Ghat, A 37/51
497. Khakholka Aditya	(Vinita A.) Kameshvara T., backside, A 2/9
498. Kharva Narasimha Tirtha	in the Ganga near Durga Ghat
499. Kharva Narsimha – 1	Durga Ghat, in Brahmacharini Temple, K 22/53
500. Kharva Narsimha – 2	Durga Ghat, in Brahmacharini Durga, K 22/71
501. Kharva Vinayaka	southwest from Adi Keshava, Raj Ghat area
502. Kikasheshvara	Rajadarwaja, Narayandas Katra, CK 52/15
503. Kiraneshvara	near Mangala Gauri, in the lane, K 23/83
504. Kirateshvara – 1	near Bharbhiteshvara, CK 52/15, called Gupteshvara
505. Kirateshvara – 2	near Jayanteshvara, at Lali Ghat
506. Koka Varaha Vishnu	Siddheshvari Temple, CK 7/124
507. Kolahala Narsimha	Siddha Vinayaka, in Matha, CK 8/189
508. Kotilingeshvara	Sakshi Vinayana, Jangam Katra, D 10/49
509. Kotishvara – 1	reestablished in Trilochana Temple, A 2/80
510. Kotishvara – 2	near Sakshi Vinayaka, D 10/49

511. Krimi Kunda	Kinaram Ashram, Ravindrapuri, B 3/335
512. Krishna Gopal	Rana Mahal, D 21/19
513. Krishna Rukmini	Dvarakadhisha Temple, Sankudhara, B 22/195
514. Krishna: Vishnukrishna	Agastakunda, D 36/170; four handed image with Radha-Rukmini
515. Krishna: Yogiraja Krishna	Panchaganga, Tailanga Math, K 23/95, established by Naraharidasa
516. Krishneshvara	wall of Sankatha Devi, facing Harishchandreshvara, CK 7/159
517. Krittivasheshvara	road to Vriddhakala, Dara Nagar, K 46/23
518. Kritvishvara – 1	Javavinayaka, on steps, CK 33/36
519. Kritvishvara – 2	across Koniya Ghat at the Varana river, under fig tree
520. Krodhana Bhairava	Kamachchha, in Batuka Bhairava, B 31/126
521. Kshemaka Gana	in Kshemeshvara, Kumarasvami Math, B 14/12
522. Kshemeshvara	Kshemeshvara Ghat, Kumarasvami Math, B 14/12
523. Kshetrapala Bhairava	backside to Kala Bhairava Temple, in Madhi (niche)
524. Kshipraprasadana Vinay.	Pitarkunda, in Pitreshvara Temple, C 18/47
525. Kshoni Varaha	Dashashvamedha Ghat, near Ram Mandir, D 17/111
526. Kubereshvara – 1	in the court of Vishvanatha, northern side
527. Kubereshvara – 2	in the temple of Annapurna, in the northeast corner
528. Kubja	Kashmirimal Haveli, Prapitamaheshvara, CK 7/92
529. Kubjambareshvara	in Pitamaheshvara, CK 7/92
530. Kukkuteshvara – 1	Ranamahal, near Vakratunda Vinayaka, D 21/22
531. Kukkuteshvara – 2	near Jyestheshvara, Bhutabhairava, now lost
532. Kukkuteshvara – 3	Kalabhairav, in Dandapani Bhairava, K 31/49
533. Kukkuteshvara – 4	near southern gate of Durga Temple, Durgakund, B 27/1

534.	Kulasthambha	the pillar in Lat Bhairava
535.	Kundodareshvara	Asi Ghat (reestablished); upper part of Lolarka Kund
536.	Kunitaksha Vinayaka	Lakshmikund, old Lakshmi Temple, D 52/38
537.	Kuntishvara	Konia Ghat, across the Varana river
538.	Kurukshetra Tirtha	Kurukshetra Kunda, Asi, B 2/283
539.	Kusheshvara & Tirtha	Luxa, Rama Krishan Hospital, opposite Gali, D 53/48
540.	Kusmanda (Durga)	Durga-Ji, Durga Kund, B 27/2
541.	Kusmanda Vinayaka	near Chandishvara, Phulwaria village
542.	Kusmandeshvara	at Svargadvari
543.	Kutadanta Vinayaka	Kinaram Ashram, Ravindrapuri, B 3/335
544.	Lakshmaneshvara – 1	Hanuman Ghat, Shastri-House, B 4/44
545.	Lakshmaneshvara – 2	on Panchakroshi route, in Rameshvara Temple, Rameshvar
546.	Lakshmi Nrisimha	Rajmandir, Hanuman T., K 20/159
547.	Lakshmi Nrisimha	Rajmandir, K 20/159
548.	Lakshmi Nrisimha Tirtha	at Raj Ghat, western side in the Ganga
549.	Lakshmikunda Tirtha	Luxa, Lakshmikund, also called Lakshmi Tirtha
550.	Lakulishvara	at gate of Mahapashupateshvara (Nepali Temple), Lalita Ghat, D 1/67; re-established
551.	Lalita Gauri/Devi	Lalita Ghat, in Madhi (niche), D 1/67
552.	Lalita Tirtha	at Lalita Ghat, in the Ganga
553.	Lambodara Vinayaka	Lali Ghat, at bank, in the Madhi (niche) Chintamani Vinayaka
554.	Langlishvara	Khowa Bazar, CK 28/4
555.	Laveshvara	Laxa, in Ramakrishna Hospital, at gate, D 45/5
556.	Laveshvara & Tirtha	Luxa, Ramakrishna Hospital, D 45/5
557.	Lolarka Aditya	Lolarka Kunda, Bhadaini, the disc on the steps
558.	Lolarka Tirtha	Bhadaini, Lolarkakunda, water pool and Sun image
559.	Lolarkeshvara	huge Shiva *linga*, Lolarka Kunda

560. Lomalesha	in the compound of Vriddhakala, K 52/59
561. Madaleshvara	as Madalaseshvara, on easten lane, Kalika Gali, D 5/133
562. Madhu (Honey) Vinayayaka	Dudha Vinayak, K 23/63
563. Madhyameshvara	Dara Nagar, Madhyameshvara, K 53/63
564. Maha Kali	Lakshmikund, Kali Math, D 52/42
565. Maha Kali (Kalaratri)	Kalika Gali, D 8/17
566. Maha Lakshmi Devi	Lakshmi Kund, D 52/40
567. Maha Lakshmi Tirtha	Lakshmi Kund, Misir Pokhra
568. Maha Sarasvati	in Maha Lakshmi Temple, D 52/40
569. Mahabala Narsimha	in Kameshvara Temple, A 2/9
570. Mahabala Nrisimha	Machchhodari, Adi Mahadeva T., A 2/9
571. Mahabhaya Nrisimha	in Pitamaheshvara, wall, CK 7/92
572. Mahabhayahara Narsimha	west of Pitamaheshvara, Shitala Gali, CK 7/92
573. Mahabhima	village Harpur, on Panchakroshi Road
574. Mahadeo (Adi)	Adi Mahadeo, Trilochan, A 3/92
575. Mahadeveshvara	village Deura, on Panchakroshi Road
576. Mahagauri	Annapurna, Vishvanath Gali, D 8/38
577. Mahakaleshvara – 1	southeast corner of Jnanavapi pavilion, under fig tree
578. Mahakaleshvara – 2	Mahamrityunjaya, Vriddhakala Temple, K 52/39
579. Mahakaleshvara – 3	east of Kala Bhairava, K 32/24
580. Mahalakshmi – 1	south of Kedareshvara, B 6/99
581. Mahalakshmi – 2	Lakshmikunda, D 52/40
582. Mahalakshmi – 3	also called Shridevi/Adi Lakshmi, Lakshmikund, D 52/38
583. Mahalakshmi Kunda	Lakshmikund
584. Mahalakshmishvara	Lakshmikund, (Sorahianatha), D 52/54
585. Mahamunda	Vagishvari, Jaitapura, J 6/33
586. Mahanadeshvara	in Adi Mahadeva, A 3/92
587. Mahapashupateshvara	as Pashupathinatha of Nepal, Lalita Ghat, D 1/67

588. Maharaja Vinayaka — as Bade Ganesha, K 58/101

589. Maharunda Devi — Lolarka Kund, Munnar Panda house, B 2/62

590. Mahashmashana Stambha–1 — upper part as Chakrapani Bhairava, Kala Bhairava, K 32/6

591. Mahashmashana Stambha–2 — symbolic pillar as Dandapani Bhairava, K 31/49

592. Mahasiddhishvara — near Kurukshetra, Asi, B 2/282

593. Mahendri/Maheshvari — in Vishvanath court wall, CK 35/19

594. Maheshvara – 1 — open space, at the bank, Manikarnika Ghat

595. Maheshvara – 2 — southwest corner of Jnanavapi pavilion

596. Maheshvari — in the court hall of Vishvanatha Temple, CK 35/19

597. Mahotkateshvara — in Kameshvara Temple, A 2/9

598. Makareshvara — near Omkareshvara, Pathani Tola, A 33/47

599. Malatishvara/ Matalishvara — Mrityunjaya Temple, Vriddhakala, K 52/39

600. Mallikarjuna — Tripurantakeshvara, Sigra (Sivapurva/ Shivagiri) Tila, D 59/95

601. Manadhateshvara – 1 — near Sulatankeshvara, Prayaga Ghat, below surface

602. Manadhateshvara – 2 — Lahoritola, CK 34/14

603. Manahprakameshvara — near Sakshi Vinayaka, Vishvanath Gali, D 10/50

604. Manasarovara Tirtha — Manasarovar, Andhra Taraka Ashram, D 14/92

605. Manasarovareshvara — Manasarovar, at the corner of turning, D 14/20

606. Manda Vinayaka — Lakshmikunda, D 52/38

607. Mandakini (Ashapuri) — northeast corner of the Maidagin Tank, K 59/15

608. Mandakini Tirtha — Maidagin Tank

609. Mandhateshvara — Lahori Tola, Phute Ganesha, CK 34/14

610. Mandhatrishvara — near Mokshadvareshvara, CK 34/14

611. Mangala Gauri — Panchaganga Ghat, Mangala Gauri, K 24/34

612. Mangala Tirtha — in the Ganga, close to Lakshmana Bala Ghat

613. Mangala Vinayaka — inside Mangala Gauri temple, K 24/34

614. Mangaleshvara (Mars) — Atmavireshvara Temple, CK 7/158

615.	Mangaloda Kupa	in a house K 23/89
616.	Manikarni Vinayaka	Satuababa Ashram, Manikarnika Gali, CK 10/48
617.	Manikarnika (Ghat)	Manikarnika Ghat
618.	Manikarnika Devi – 1	Manikarnika Kunda, inside
619.	Manikarnika Devi – 2	Kakaram Gali, Brahmnal, CK 8/11
620.	Manikarnikeshvara	Manikarnishvara, Gomath Ashram, Brahmanal, CK 8/12
621.	Manipradipa Naga	Naganatha Muhalla, lost
622.	Marichishvara	Nagakuan, Marichi Kunda; Mirasagar D 25/11
623.	Markandeshvara	Dhundhiraj Gali, bazaar, CK 36/10
624.	Markandeya Tirtha – 1	in the Ganga at Panchaganga Ghat
625.	Markandeya Tirtha – 2	south of Lalita Ghat and north of Chausatthi Ghat, in the Ganga
626.	Matalishvara/Malatishvara	in the Vriddhakala Temple compound, K 52/39
627.	Matarah	Dashashvamedha Ghat, Devis in the Shitala Temple
628.	Matri Kunda	Lallapura, near Pitarkunda
629.	Matsyodari Tirtha	Machchhodari Tank
630.	Mayukha Aditya	Mangala Gauri Temple, in pillar, K 24/34
631.	Mayureshvara	Asi Ghat, B 2/174
632.	Mayuri	Rana Mahal, Chausatthi Ghat, on steps
633.	Mitra Vinayaka	Scindhia Ghat, Atmavireshvara, CK 7/158
634.	Moda Vinayaka	Kashi Karvat, CK 31/12
635.	Modadi Pancha Vinayaka	in Vishvanath Temple, backside court, CK 35/21
636.	Modakapriya Vinayaka	Trilochan, Adi Mahadeva Temple, A 3/92
637.	Mokshadeshvara	village Aswari, on Panchakroshi Road
638.	Mokshalakshmi	Kakaram Gali, Brahmanal, CK 8/11
639.	Mokshadvareshvara	near Lalita Ghat, CK 34/10
640.	Moksheshvara – 1	Panchakroshi Road, village Aware
641.	Moksheshvara – 2	west of Jnanavapi mosque, lost
642.	Mrigalochana	as Pishachaghanta, Lalita Ghat

643. Mrityavisha	old Apamrityuhareshvara/Mahamrityunjaya, K 52/39
644. Mrityunjayeshvara	Mahamrityunjaya, near Vriddhakala, K 52/39
645. Muchakundeshvara	called Baradeva, Godaulia, D 37/40
646. Mukhanirmalika	Gai Ghat, Hanuman Temple, K 3/42
647. Mukhaprekshani	near Mangala Gauri Temple, K 24/34
648. Mukti Tirtha	near Manikarnika Ghat, in the Ganga
649. Muktimandapa (Vishnu)	Jnanavapi Muktimandapa
650. Mukuta Kunda	Govabai Pokhara, Nababganj, now in ruins
651. Mukuteshvara – 1	near Govabai Pokhra, Temple, B 27/20
652. Mukuteshvara – 2	near park, Tilabhandeshvara, B 17/99
653. Munda Vinayaka	Sadar Bazar, near Chandi Devi
654. Nadeshvara	near Akareshvara, under Pipal tree, a lying *linga*
655. Naganatha	village Amra, on Panchakroshi Road
656. Nagesha Vinayaka – 1	Bhonshala Ghat, in Nageshvara Temple, CK 1/21
657. Nagesha Vinayaka – 2	in Nageshvara Temple, Matha Ghat, A 1/72
658. Nageshvara – 1	*linga* in the water, Naga Kunda, J 23/206
659. Nageshvara – 2	Matha Ghat, A 1/72
660. Nageshvara – 3	Bhonshala Ghat, CK 1/21
661. Nageshvara – 4	big Shiva *linga* at the bank, Gai Ghat
662. Nahusheshvara	Rameshvara Temple, on Panchakroshi Road
663. Nairiteshvara	west of Puspadanteshvara, D 32/107
664. Nakshatreshvara	Adi Keshava, A 37/51
665. Nakulishvara	near Vishvanatha, in Akshayavat Temple, CK 35/20
666. Nalakubera Kupa	Facing the Kameshvara Temple, A 2/9
667. Nalakubareshvara – 1	Ghasi Tola, K 30/6; (earlier as Panchaleshvara, lost)
668. Nalakubareshvara – 2	near Manikarnishvara, in Pitamaheshvara, CK 7/92
669. Nandikesha Gana	village Deura, on Panchakroshi Road

670. Nandikeshvara – 1	Raja-Nadeshar Kothi, Maldahia, S 18/240
671. Nandikeshvara – 2	east of Jnanavapi, the Great Bull
672. Nandishvari	Raja-Nadeshar Kothi, Maldahia, S 18/240
673. Nara Narayana (Keshava)	Badri Narayana, Matha Ghat, A 1/73
674. Narada Keshava	facing Prahlada Ghat, A 10/80
675. Naradeshvara	Narada Ghat, Tailanga Math, D 25/12
676. Narakarnavataraka Siva	In the compound of Bhimachandi, Panchakroshi Road
677. Naranarayana Keshava	Matha Ghat, Badri Narayan, A 1/72
678. Narasimhi	Manikarnika Gali, near Sureka building, CK 33/43
679. Narayani Devi – 1	west of Gopigovinda, as Shitala, K 20/19
680. Narayani Devi – 2	Gauri Shankar Temple, Lal Ghat, K 4/24
681. Narmada Tirtha	in the Ganga, near Chausatthi Ghat
682. Narmadeshvara	east of Trilocana Temple, A 2/19
683. Narvadeshvara	Rana Mahal, Chausatthi Ghat, eastern side, D 21/8
684. Nava Bhairava	at Lata Bhairava Talab
685. Nava Graha	Nava Graha in Kala Bhairava Temple, K 32/22
686. Navagraheshvara	Kalabhairava, Dandapani Gali, K 31/50
687. Nigadabhanji	as Bandi Devi, Dashashvamedha, D 17/100
688. Nikumbheshvara	in Vishvanatha Temple, inside Parvati Temple, CK 35/19
689. Nila Gana	village Deura, on Panchakroshi Road
690. Nilakantheshvara – 1	Bhelupura, B 20/15
691. Nilakantheshvara – 2	Bhumananda Ghat, Kedar Ghat, Tahirpur Palace, B 6/99
692. Nilakantheshvara – 3	Brahmanal, Nilakantha, Manikarnika Marg, CK 33/23
693. Nilakantheshvara – 4	Prahlada Ghat, A 10/47
694. Nilakantheshvara – 5	north road along Krimikunda, Shivala, B 10/32
695. Nilakantheshvara – 6	Kadameshvara, Kandawa, Panchakroshi Road
696. Nirvana Keshava	Bhadaini, *ca* Waterpump, B 2/64

697. Nirvana Nrisimha (Vishnu)	near Pulasthishvara, Svargadvareshvara; lost
698. Nishkalankeshvara	Dhundhiraj Gali, bazar, CK 35/34
699. Nishpapeshvara	close to Gauri Kunda, Kedar Ghat, near Nilakantha
700. Nivasheshvara	Bhuta Bhairava, K 63/27
701. Omkareshvara / Pranaveshvara	Omkareshvara, Pathanitola Tila A 33/23; other attached are: Akareshvara and Makareshvara. Ukareshvara and Bindu lost
702. Padma Tirtha	in the Ganga, near Adi Keshava Ghat
703. Padmasureshvara	near Hanuman Temple, B 13/14
704. Panchaganga	Panchaganga Ghat at the Ganga
705. Panchagangeshvara	as Panchanadeshvara, Panchaganga Ghat, K 22/21
706. Panchaksheshvara	as Rudraksheshvara, Trilocana area, A 2/56
707. Panchamukhi Ganesha – 1	near Annapurna, in Rani Bhavani Temple
708. Panchamukhi Ganesha – 2	near Annapurna lane, CK 37/18
709. Panchamukhi Hanuman – 1	Pandey Howli, B 31/302
710. Panchamukhi Hanuman – 2	Rajmandir, K 20/161
711. Panchamukhi Hanuman – 3	Rajghat (Rambagh), A 26/36
712. Panchanadeshvara	near Tailanga Math, to Vindu Madhava, K 22/11
713. Panchanadya Tirtha	at the Panchaganga Ghat, in the Ganga
714. Panchasya Vinayaka	Pishachamochan, near Tank, C 21/40
715. Pandaveshvara – 1	Panchapandava, Khowa Bazar, CK 28/10
716. Pandaveshvara – 2	southern lane to Sankatha Devi
717. Pandaveshvara – 3	in Dandapani Bhairava, K 31/49
718. Papabhaksheshvara	south of Kala Bhairava Lane, K 32/37
719. Papamochana Tirtha	called Nauwa Pokhra, near Pathani Tola, A 34/34
720. Papamochaneshvara	Upper part of Pokhara, near A 34/34
721. Paradravyeshvara	Dhundhiraj Gali, bazar, CK 35/34
722. Paranneshvara	Dhundhiraj Gali, bazar, CK 35/34
723. Parashareshvara – 1	Bhadaini, Lolarka, B 2/21

724. Parashareshvara – 2	At Karnaghanta Talab, South of Vyasheshvara; K 60/66, now in water
725. Parashurama Vinayaka	Nandan Shah Lane, CK 14/53
726. Parashurameshvara	Nandan Shah Lane, CK 14/16
727. Parvateshvara	Scindhia Ghat, CK 7/156
728. Parvati – 1	in Kedara Temple compund, B 6/102
729. Parvati – 2	Adi Mahadeo Temple, Trilochan, A 3/92
730. Parvatishvara	Trilochan, Adi Mahadeva T. A 3/92
731. Pashapani Vinayaka – 1	on Panchakroshi route, Sadar Bazar lane
732. Pashapani Vinayaka – 2	Sadar Bazar, Dakshinamurti Math
733. Pashupateshvara – 1	Maldahiya, CK 30/40, in iron market
734. Pashupateshvara – 2	Pashupateshvara Gali, Nandan Sahu lane, CK 13/66
735. Pashupateshvara – 3	Lalita Ghat, D 1/68, established by King of Nepal
736. Pashupati Tirtha	in the Ganga, near Manikarnika Ghat
737. Pataleshvara	Bengali Tola, at the gate D 32/118
738. Pavaneshvara	Bhutabhairav, K 63/14
739. Pichindila Vinayaka	Prahlad Ghat, under banyan tree, A 10/80
740. Pilippila Tirtha	north of Trilocana (bazar), A 3/87, now a Kupa
741. Pingaleshvara	as Nakuleshvara, Pishachamocan, C 21/39
742. Pishachamochana Tirtha	Pishachamocan Talab
743. Pishacha Vinayaka	Pishachamochan, C 21/40
744. Pishacheshvara	Pishacamochan, near the Kunda, C 21/40
745. Pitamaheshvara/ Prapitamaheshvara	Kishanlal Yajnika house, Shitala Gali, CK 7/92
746. Pitrikunda	Pitarkunda Talab, Lallapura
747. Pitrishvara	Pitarkunda, C 18/47
748. Prachanda Nrisimha	Asi Ghat, in Jagannath Temple, B 1/151
749. Prahlada Keshava	Prahlad Ghat Temple, A 10/80
750. Prahladeshvara	Prahlad Ghat, A 10/81
751. Pramoda Vinayaka	Kashi Karvat, Nepali Khapra, CK 31/16

752. Pranava Vinayaka	Trilochan Ghat, in Hiranyagarbheshvara
753. Pratigraheshvara	Dhundhiraj Gali, bazaar, CK 35/34
754. Prayaga Keshava	Prahlad Ghat, A 10/80
755. Prayaga Linga – 1	in sangameshvara, Adi Keshava, 4-headed
756. Prayaga Linga – 2	near Shulatankeshvara, Dashashvamedha, as Brahmeshvara
757. Prayaga Linga – 3	between Madhia and Kakarha Ghat, reestablished
758. Prayaga Madhava – 1	Manmandir, as Lakshiminarayana, D 16/21
759. Prayaga Madhava – 2	upper side, Dashashvamedha Ghat, Ram Mandir, D 17/111
760. Prayaga Tirtha	Prayaga Ghat, in the Ganga river
761. Prayaga-Sanjnaka Linga	near Varana Sangam (confluence); in Shaileshvari temple
762. Prayageshvara – 1	Dashashvamedha, in Bandi Devi, D 17/100
763. Prayageshvara – 2	Prayaga Ghat temple, built by Digpatia Estate queen
764. Prithvishvara	village Khajuri, Pishanharia Kupa, on Panchakroshi Road
765. Pritikeshvara	backside of Sakshi Vinayaka, D 10/8
766. Pulaheshvara	Facing Pulastyeshvara, CK 10/16 on platform
767. Pulastyeshvara – 1	Jangamabadi Math, at gate, D 35/77
768. Pulastyeshvara – 2	Javavinayaka, Svargadvari, Sureka Building, CK 33/43
769. Pushpadanteshvara	Bengali Tola, Devanathpura, D 32/102
770. Rajaputra Vinayaka	Raj Ghat road to Adi Keshava, A 37/48
771. Rajarajeshvara – 1	Ghughurali Gali road, CK 39/57
772. Rajarajeshvara – 2	Dhundhiraj Gali, bazar,CK 35/33
773. Rajarajeshvara – 3	Kotwalpura, CK 38/20
774. Rajarajeshvara – 4	Svargadvari, under platform, CK 10/16
775. Rajarajeshvari	Siddhagiri Math, Lalita Ghat, D 1/58
776. Rama (Ayodhya) Kunda	Rama Kunda, Luxa
777. Rama Mandir	Kanganvali Haveli, K 22/25

778. Rama Tirtha	Near Rama Ghat, in the Ganga
779. Ramakunda Tirtha	Ramakund tank, near Rameshvara, D 54/45
780. Rameshvara – 1	temple in Karaunan/Rameshwar village on Panchakroshi route
781. Rameshvara – 2	near Someshvara Temple, Man Mandir, D 16/2
782. Rameshvara – 3	Rama Ghat, K 24/10; called Vira Rameshvara
783. Rameshvara – 4	(Ramachandra) Rama Kunda, Luxa, D 54/45
784. Rameshvara – 5	Hanuman Ghat, Juna Akhara, B 4/42
785. Rameshvara – 6	Dandapani Gali, K 32/46; estb. by Raja Jaipur
786. Ranadakeshvara	In Kedara Temple compound, B 6/102
787. Ranasthambha Linga	big *linga* near Kurukshetra Tank
788. Rataneshvara – 1	along road to Vriddhakala, K 53/40
789. Rataneshvara – 2	shrinked temple at Manikarnika Ghat (it was built in 1828)
790. Raviraktaksha Gandharva	in the compound of Bhimachandi Devi, on Panchakroshi Road
791. Renuka Devi	Belvaria Colony, B 27/77
792. Reva Tirtha	Revari Talab; now lost
793. Revanteshvara	on steps at Vindu Madhava Ghat, in small Shiva shrine
794. Rinahareshvara	along road to Vriddhakala, K 53/47
795. Rinamochana Tirtha	Laddu Talab, near Hanuman Phatak, A 31/159
796. Rinamochaneshvara	Laddu Talab, Hanuman Phatak, A 31/159
797. Rudrani Devi	a shrine, 500 m west from main road, Parsipur
798. Rudrasarovara Tirtha	Dashashvamedha Ghat, in the Ganga
799. Rudravasa Kunda	Suggi Gaddhi, north of Matsyodari; now in ruins
800. Rudravasa Tirtha	Manikarnika Ghat, in the Ganga
801. Rudravasheshvara	Manikarnika, close to Chakrapushkarini Kunda under sand
802. Rudreshvara	Near Tripura Bhairavi Temple, D 5/21
803. Rukmangdeshvara	Chauki Ghat, Hanuman Temple, B 14/1

804. Ruru Bhairava – 1	Hanuman Ghat, in Madhi (niche), near to B 4/18
805. Ruru Bhairava – 2	Manikarnika, in wall of Gomatha, CK 8/21
806. Sagareshvara – 1	in Sankatha Temple, CK 7/159
807. Sagareshvara – 2	east of Sankatha Temple, close to Saptarshi Temple
808. Sakshi Vinayaka	Vishvanatha Lane, D 10/7
809. Samba Aditya	Suraj Kunda, east of Kunda, D 51/90
810. Samhara Bhairava	Gai Ghat, Patan Darwaza, A 1/82
811. Samudrakupa	Kashipura, Saptasagara Kupa, K 62/28
812. Samudreshvara	south of road to Bansphatak, near CK 37/32
813. Samvartteshvara	Panchapandava, near Jnanavapi, CK 28/10
814. Sangameshvara (Varana)	Adi Keshava, lower side, A 37/51
815. Sangameshvara – 1 (Asi)	Asi, Harihar Ashram, B 1/169
816. Sangameshvara – 2	close to Asi Ghat
817. Sangameshvara – 3	inside Hotel Ganges View, Asi Ghat
818. Sankatha Devi	Sankatha Ghat, CK 7/159
819. Sankha Vishnu	Dvarakadhisha Temple, Sankudhara, B 22/195
820. Sankhudhara Tirtha	Sankudhara Kunda, Khojwa Bazar
821. Saptavarna Vinayaka	Known as Java Vinayaka, CK 28/10
822. Sarasvati	near Gomath, CK 7/109, called Nila Sarasvati
823. Sarasvatishvara	near Hiranyagharbheshvara, at Trilochan Ghat
824. Sarveshvara	Pandey Ghat, near Baithaka Lakshminarayana, D 25/32
825. Satishvara	Vriddhakala road, Ratneshvara Temple, K 46/32
826. Satrughaneshvara	Rameshvara Temple, on Panchakroshi Road
827. Saubhagya Gauri	Adi Vishvanath, verandah, CK 38/8
828. Savitri	image under Banyan tree, Dharmakupa, near D 2/15
829. Sena Vinayaka	close to Saptarshi Temple, towards Sankatha-ji

830. Shadanana – 1	east of Tarakeshvara, at Manikarnika Ghat; now lost
831. Shadanana – 2	earlier in Satishvara, now ruined image in Kala Bhairava
832. Shailaputri/ Shaileshvari	Madhia Ghat at the Varana river, A 40/11
833. Shaileshvara	Madhia Ghat at the Varana river, A 40/11
834. Shakreshvara	called Indreshvara, upper side at Manikarnika Ghat
835. Shalakatankata Vinayaka	Maruadih Bazar, near Kakarmata Tank
836. Shanaishchareshvara (Saturn)	inside Vishvanatha compound, in brass tank, CK 35/19
837. Shankari/ Shantikari	Konia at Varana's bank, A 38/301
838. Shankha Madhava – 1	Rajmandir, K 20/137 (now lost)
839. Shankha Madhava – 2	steps of Shitala Ghat, in the niche (Madhi)
840. Shankhoddhara Tirtha	Shankudhara Talab, Khojwa, B 22/194
841. Shankukarneshvara – 1	Shankudhara, front of B 22/196
842. Shankukarneshvara – 2	Shankhudhara, near Kunda, near B 22/120
843. Shantanavishvara	Shanteshvara, in niche at steps to Trilochan Ghat
844. Shantikari/ Shankari devi	Durga, Konia at Varana's bank mound, A 38/301
845. Sharkara (Sugar) Vinayaka	Dudha Vinayak, K 23/53
846. Shashibushana Linga	Hanuman Ghat, B 4/44
847. Shatakaleshvara	Thatheri Bazaar, lower side, K 17/24
848. Shatrughneshvara – 1	Hanuman Ghat, near Dharmashala, B 4/44
849. Shatrughneshvara – 2	in Karoma, Panchakroshi road, in Rameshvara Temple,
850. Shava Shiva Kali – 1	Devanathpura, D 30/66 (a Tantric image)
851. Shava Shiva Kali – 2	Prahlad Ghat, A 10/39
852. Shesha Madhava – 1 (Vishnu)	Shitala Ghat, Vishnu in lower Madhi (niche)
853. Shesha Madhava – 2	Raj Mandir, K 20/137
854. Shikhicandi	in Maha Lakshmi Temple, D 52/40, at the gate
855. Shitala – 1	Dashashvamedha Ghat, D 18/19

856.	Shitala – 2 (Badi Shitala)	near Shitala Ghat II, down stream, K 20/19
857.	Shitaleshvara	Dashashvamedha Ghat, D 18/19
858.	Shivaduti – 1	Panchagni Akhada, Prahlad Ghat, A 11/30 (attached to Svarlineshvara temple)
859.	Shivaduti – 2	Mir Ghat, Hanuman Temple
860.	Shiva-Ganga Tirtha	Ishvaragangi Talab
861.	Shiveshvara – 1	Vriddhakala, K 52/39, southeast of Amritakunda
862.	Shiveshvara – 2	Vishveshvarganj, K 44/33
863.	Shiveshvara Kunda	known as Halu Gadha; filled up around CE 1822
864.	Shodasa Vinayaka	backside wall, Dehali Vinayaka, 67
865.	Shosanadristi (Trijata)	Raj Mandir, Hanuman T., K 20/159
866.	Shrikantha Linga	Lakshmikunda, D 52/38
867.	Shrimukhi Guha	near Omkareshvara; now deserted
868.	Shringara Gauri	Jnanavapi Mosque, backside
869.	Shringeshvara	Lakshmikund, Kalimath, D 52/35; only statue; *linga* lost
870.	Shrishti Vinayaka	Kalika Gali, out of a house D 8/3
871.	Shrutishvara	near Ratneshvara, road to Vriddhakala, K 53/40
872.	Shubhodaka Kupa	near Omkareshvara, at the eastern lane; now deserted
873.	Shukika (Shyeni)	Dhyodhiya Bir Temple, Bhelupur, B 19/68
874.	Shukra Kupa	Kalika Gali, D 8/30
875.	Shukresha	near Kashi Goshala, western gate, in a room, K 40/20
876.	Shukreshvara (Venus)	Kalika Gali, D 8/30
877.	Shulatankeshvara	Dashashvamedha Ghat, near D 17/111
878.	Shurpakarneshvara	at the gate, in Durga Temple, Durgakund, B 27/1
879.	Shushkeshvara	Asi Ghat, B 1/185 – Kashi Ashram, locally Shukreshvara
880.	Shuskodari	Vriddhakala, Daranagar, K 46/23

881. Siddha Gana	older one lost; near Vagishvari, J 6/84
882. Siddha Vapi	older one lost; near Vagishvari, J 6/84
883. Siddhakuta	high ground around Vagishvari temple, Jaitpura
884. Siddhalakshmi	Jagadhatri, east of Siddha Vinayaka, CK 8/1
885. Siddhayogeshvari	known as Siddheshvara, near Sankatha Ghat, CK 7/124
886. Siddheshvara – 1	Siddheshvarai, Siddheshvari Temple, CK 7/124
887. Siddheshvara – 2	Bengali Tola, in Pataleshvara, D 32/118, outside
888. Siddheshvara – 3	Jaitpura, near Vagishvari, J 6/84.
889. Siddheshvara – 4	Assi, Goyanka school, Asi, B 2/282
890. Siddheshvara – 5	Kinaram Ashram, B 3/335
891. Siddheshvara – 6	Bade Ganesh, Lohatiya, K 58/101
892. Siddheshvari	as Parvati in Siddheshvara, Goyanka school, B 2/282
893. Siddhi	Manikarnika, Brahmanal, CK 9/1
894. Siddhi Vinayaka	Manikarnika Gali, CK 9/1
895. Siddhidatri	Siddhamata Gali, CK 60/29
896. Siddhyastakeshvara	Bade Ganesha, K 58/103
897. Sima Vinayaka	in the route to Sankatha-ji
898. Simhatunda Vinayaka	Khalispura, Brahmeshvara, D 33/66
899. Sindhusarovara Tirtha	water pool, Dindaspur, on Panchakroshi Road
900. Siteshvara	Prachin Hanuman Ghat, southern room in B 4/42
901. Skanda (Karttikeya)	in Kedara Temple compound, B 6/102
902. Skandamata	known as Vagishvari, Jaitpura, J 6/33
903. Somanatheshvara – 1	near Kardameshvara, Kandawa, on Panchakroshi Road
904. Somanatheshvara – 2	near Langotia Hanuman, Dindaspur, on Panchakroshi Road
905. Someshvara – 1	Rameshvara Temple, Panchakroshi Road

906.	Someshvara – 2	near Manmandira Ghat, D 16/34
907.	Someshvara – 3	Pandey Ghat, D 25/34, on the steps
908.	Someshvara – 4	near Vagishvari, Jaitpura, J 6/85
909.	Srishthi Vinayaka	Kalika Gali, in outside wall, D 8/3
910.	Sthanulingeshvara/ Sthanu	near Kurukshetra Tank, B 2/247, also at Tank
911.	Sthuladanta Vinayaka	Manamandir, at the gate of Someshvara, D 16/34
912.	Sthulajangha Vinayaka – 1	Ranikuwan, near Chitraghanta Vinayaka, outside CK 23/25
913.	Sthulajangha Vinayaka – 2	in Pasupatishvara Temple, CK 13/66
914.	Sukshmeshvara	back of Dhupachandi Temple, near Vikatadvija Vinayaka, J 12/134
915.	Sumantishvara	Hanuman Phatak, A 31/91
916.	Sumantva Aditya	Hanuman Phatak, A 31/91
917.	Sumukha Vinayaka	Kashi Karvat, CK 35/7
918.	Sumukheshvara	at Trilochan, near Padodaka Kupa, A 3/87
919.	Surabhandheshvara	called Tilabhandeshvara, Math, B 17/42
920.	Sureshvara	Manasarovar, in lane, B 13/17
921.	Surya Kunda	Suraj Kund
922.	Svapaneshvara – 1	Shivala, Hanuman Temple, B 3/150
923.	Svapneshvara – 2	north of Lolarka, B 2/33
924.	Svapneshvari Devi	Hanuman Temple, Shivala, B 3/150
925.	Svargabhumi	Sarang Talab, on Panchakroshi Road
926.	Svargadvareshvara	Svargadvari, Brahmanal, CK 10/16
927.	Svarlineshvara	Prahlad Ghat, Panchagni Akhara, A 11/30
928.	Svarnaksheshvara	Dhundhiraj Gali, in Dandapani, CK 36/10
929.	Svayambhu Linga	Luxa, near Mahalakshmishvara, D 54/114
930.	Sveta Madhava	Mir Ghat, Hanuman Temple, D 3/79
931.	Sveteshvara	Panchapandava Temple, Jnanavapi, CK 28/10
932.	Takshaka Kunda	near Augharanath ki Takiya; now lost
933.	Takshakeshvara	at Augharanath ki Takiya, outside to gate, K 64/113

934. Takshrya Keshava	Rajghat, Adi Keshava, A 37/51
935. Tamra Varaha Tirtha	in the Ganga between Mangala Gauri and Ram Ghats
936. Tamra Varaha Vishnu	Nilakantha, Brahmanala, slope: CK 33/57
937. Tapobhumi	village Hirampur (Gauri temple), on Panchakroshi Road
938. Tara Devi – 1	Bengalitola, D 24/4, established by Rani Bhavani
939. Tara Devi – 2	at steps of Lalita Ghat, D 1/58, in Madhi (niche); called Tapini
940. Tara Devi – 3	Kalika Gali, at gate of Kali-Ji, D 8/17
941. Tara Devi – 4	Brahmanal, CK 32/15; established by Rani Padmavati
942. Tara Tirtha	near Omkareshvara, Pathani Tola, A 33/23, a pond at the lower side; now filled up and lost
943. Taraka Tirtha	in the Ganga, at Manikarnika, close to Tarakeshvara
944. Tarakeshvara – 1	Jnanavapi, niche of Gaurishankara
945. Tarakeshvara – 2	near Vishvanatha, Ganapatarai Khemaka Temple, CK 35/17
946. Tarakeshvara – 3	at Manikarnika Ghat, in open space, uncovered
947. Tarakeshvara – 4	at Kedar Ghat, close to the Ganga's bank
948. Tatvesha	Dharmakupa, D 3/97
949. Tilabhandeshvara	Pandey Haveli, B 17/42
950. Tilaparneshvara	near gate of Durga Temple, Durgakund, B 27/1
951. Tvashtrisheshvara	as Vishvakarmeshvara, in Brihaspatishvara, CK 7/133
952. Trayambakeshvara	Baradeo, Godaulia, Trilokinatha, D 38/21
953. Tribhuvana Keshava – 1	Dashashvamedha, Bandi Devi Temple, D 17/100
954. Tribhuvana Keshava – 2	in the veranda of Vriddhakala Temple, K 52/39
955. Trilochaneshvara	Trilochana Ghat, upper part, A 2/80

956. Trilokanatha/ Trayambaka	Badadeva, Godaulia, D 38/21
957. Trilokyasundari	Shitala Gali, gate of Pitamaheshvara, CK 7/92
958. Trimukha Vinayaka	Sigra Tila (Shivagiri), Tripurantakeshvara, D 59/95
959. Tripurabhairavi Devi	Man Mandir, Tripurabhairavi, D 5/24
960. Tripurantakeshvara	Sigra (Sivagiri/Shivpurva) Tila, D 59/95
961. Tripurasundari/Shodashi	near Pitamaheshvara Temple, Siddheshvari, Shitala in Madhi (niche), CK 60/92
962. Tripureshvara	Tripurabhairavi temple, D 5/24
963. Trisandheshvara – 1	Lahoritola, in Phute Ganesha, CK 1/40
964. Trisandheshvara – 2	Lalita Ghat, D 1/40
965. Trisandhya Vinayaka	Lahori Tola, Phute Ganesha Temple, CK 1/40
966. Trivikrama Vishnu	Trilochaneshvara Temple, A 2/80
967. Tungeshvara – 1	near Vedeshvara, Adi Keshava, A 37/51
968. Tungeshvara – 2	Called Dhanvantarishvara, in Vriddhakala Temple, K 52/39
969. Tvarita/(Chatpati)	Ravindrapuri, near Lane 3, house A 33
970. Udanda Vinayaka	on Panchakroshi route, in Bhuili village
971. Udandamunda Vinayaka	backside in courtyard of Trilocana temple, A 2/80
972. Uddalakeshvara - 1	near Lolarka Kund, B 2/20
973. Uddalakeshvara - 2	Rajmandir, Hanuman Temple, K 20/159
974. Ugra Linga	at Lolarka Kunda
975. Ugreshvara	in Lakshmikund, near Lakshmi, D 52/40
976. Uma Devi (Amba Devi)	Manikarnika, CK 7/102
977. Unmatta Bhairava	in Deura village, on Panchakroshi Road
978. Upashanteshvara	Agnishvara Ghat, Patani Tola, CK 2/4
979. Urdhvradrika/ Urdhvrareta	Phulwaria-Maduadih, Kushmanda Vinayaka
980. Urvashishvara	Ausanganj, Golabag, J 56/108, near Pipal tree
981. Utajeshvara	in Gola Dinanatha
982. Utakaleshvara	village Hirampur, on Panchakroshi Road
983. Utathya Vamadeva	at Scindhia Ghat, in Vashishtha-Vamadeva

984.	Uttararka Aditya	Bakaria Kund, Jaitpura, Alaipur J 17/13
985.	Uttararka Kunda	Jaitpura, Alaipur, Bakaria Kund
986.	Vagishvari Devi	(Skandamata), Jaitpura, Vagishvari, J 6/33
987.	Vaidyanatheshvara – 1	Baijnattha, Kamachchha, B 37/1
988.	Vaidyanatheshvara – 2	Kodai ki Chauki, D 50/20 A
989.	Vaikuntha Madhava	near Harishachandreshvara, CK 7/165
990.	Vairochaneshvara	near Sima Vinayaka, Siddheshvara, in the lane close to wall
991.	Vaishnavi/ Narayani	Lal Ghat, Gauri Shankara Temple, K 4/24
992.	Vaitarini Tirtha	Vaitarini Pokhara, Lat Bhairava
993.	Vakratunda Vinayaka - 1	Lohatia, Bade Ganesh, K 58/101
994.	Vakratunda Vinayaka - 2	Chausatthi Ghat, Rana Mahal, D 21/22
995.	Valmikeshvara – 1	Bhelupur, near Nilakantha, big *linga*, B 20/15
996.	Valmikeshvara – 2	Maldahiya, Valmiki Tila, CK 21/14; now lost
997.	Valmikeshvara – 3	Pishachamochana Kunda, CK 21/39
998.	Valmikeshvara – 4	in Trilochaneshvara, A 3/80, the big *linga* in the back
999.	Vamadeveshvara	Sankatha Ghat, CK 7/161
1000.	Vamana Keshava	Trilochan, called Madusudana, A 2/29
1001.	Varada Vinayaka	Rajghat area, Prahlad Ghat, A 13/19
1002.	Varaheshvara – 1	in the Siddheshvari Temple, CK 7/124
1003.	Varaheshvara – 2	Dashashvamedha, Ram Mandir, D 17/111
1004.	Varahi	Man Mandira, Tripurabhairavi, D 16/84
1005.	Varana Sangama Tirtha	confluence of the Varana with the Ganga
1006.	Varana Tirtha	at Madhia Ghat along the Varana river
1007.	Varana Tirtha (river)	bank, near Rameshvara temple, on Panchakroshi Road
1008.	Varanasi Devi – 1	in Lalita Devi Madhi (niche), CK 1/67
1009.	Varanasi Devi – 2	Trilochaneshvara, Trilochan, A 2/80
1010.	Varatika Devi	Panchakaudi Devi, Nababganj, B 27/20
1011.	Varuneshvara – 1	in the upper part of Siddhi Vinayaka, CK 8/8
1012.	Varuneshvara – 2	as Karuneshvara, Dhundhiraj Gali, CK 36/10
1013.	Vashishtha-Vamadeva	Sankatha Ghat, CK 7/161

1014. Vashishtheshvara – 1	Lalita Ghat, near Gangaditya, D 1/67	
1015. Vashishtheshvara – 2	Sankatha Ghat, Vashishtha-Vamadeva T., CK 7/161	
1016. Vasuki Kunda	near Vasukishvara; now lost	
1017. Vasukishvara – 1	near Atmavireshvara, Scindhia Ghat, CK 7/155	
1018. Vasukishvara – 2	Narad Ghat, facing Naradeshvara, D 25/11	
1019. Vedeshvara	in Adi Keshava, A 37/51	
1020. Vibhratakeshvara	Narad Ghat, Dattatreya Math, D 25/11	
1021. Vidara Varaha Vishnu	Prahlada Ghat, A	10/82
1022. Vidhi Devi – 1	near Vidhishvara, in Agatyeshvara Temple, Godaulia, D 36/11	
1023. Vidhi Devi – 2	Vindhyavasini near Sankatha Temple, CK 2/33	
1024. Vidhishvara	southwest side in Agatyeshvara Temple, Godaulia, D 36/11	
1025. Vidyeshvara	Nimwali Brahmapuri, CK A2/41	
1026. Vighnaraja Vinayaka	Chitrakuta Talab, J	12/32
1027. Vijaya Linga	compound of Vishvanatha, near Nikumbha, CK 35/19	
1028. Vijayeshvara/ Vijaya Linga–1	Maruadik, Kakarmatta, near Shalakanta Vinayaka	
1029. Vijayeshvara/ Vijaya Linga–2	near Moti Jhil, in the garden; now lost	
1030. Vikata – 1	near Svarlineshvara, Prahlad Ghat, A 11/30; now lost	
1031. Vikata – 2	Sankatha Temple, CK 7/ 159	
1032. Vikata – 3	Scindhia Ghat, Katyayini in Atmavireshvara, CK 7/158	
1033. Vikata Narsimha	Kedarareshvara, in Madhi (niche) B 6/102	
1034. Vikatadvija Vinayaka	Nati Imli, Dhupachandi temple, J 12/134	
1035. Vikataksha Durga	village Delahna (also called Vikata Durga)	
1036. Vikatalocana	Madhyameshvara Temple, Daranagar, K 53/63; now lost	
1037. Vikatanana/ Vikata	Scindhia Ghat, Atmavireshvara, CK 7/158	
1038. Vimala Aditya	Jangambari, Khari Kuwan, D 35/273	

1039. Vimala Durga	village Deura, on Panchakroshi Road
1040. Vimala Tirtha	Pishachamochan Tank
1041. Vimaleshvara – 1	Naya Mahadeo Muhalla, called Nilakantha, A 10/47
1042. Vimaleshvara – 2	village Payagapur, on Panchakroshi Road
1043. Vimalodaka Kunda	in Omkareshvara, Nauguturi Gadahi; ruined condition
1044. Vinateshvara	gate of Kameshvara, near Khakholaditya, A 2/9
1045. Vindhyavasini Devi	Siddheshvari, near Sankatha-ji, CK 2/33
1046. Vindu Madhava – 1	Panchaganga, Veni Madhav, K 22/37
1047. Vindu Madhava – 2	Lal Ghat, Buchai Tola, K 4/4
1048. Vindu Madhava – 3	Bhat ki Gali, K 33/18
1049. Vindu Madhava – 4	in the Math at Brahma Ghat
1050. Vindubishvara	near Nadeshvara, a broken Linga
1051. Vira Madhava	Atmavireshvara, at gate Madhi (niche), CK 7/158
1052. Virabhadra Gana	village Chaukhandi, on Panchakroshi Road
1053. Virabhadreshvara – 1	village Delahna (as Virabhadra Gana), on Panchakroshi Road
1054. Virabhadreshvara – 2	northwest of Jnanavapi mosque, CK 35/1; now in ruins
1055. Virabhadreshvara – 3	south of Madhyameshvara, Shivala facing K 53/63
1056. Viramadhava	outer wall of Atmavireshvara, CK 7/158
1057. Virarameshvara	Rama Ghat, K 24/10
1058. Vireshvara	known as Atmavireshvara, CK 7/158
1059. Vireshvara-Samsthanam	north of Prahaladeshvara, Prahlad Ghat
1060. Virupaksha – 1	village Mataladai Chak, on Panchakroshi Road
1061. Virupaksha – 2	in compound of Vishvanatha, big *linga*, CK 35/19
1062. Virupaksha – 3	near Kardameshvara temple, Kandwa, on Panckakroshi Road

1063. Virupakshi	Vishvanatha Temple compound, CK 35/19
1064. Visantimaccharupa Vishnu	Sankudhara Temple, B 22/195
1065. Vishala Tirtha	near Vishalakshi, in the Ganga
1066. Vishalakshi	Mir Ghat, near Dharmakupa, D 3/85
1067. Vishalakshishvara	Mir Ghat, in Vishalakshi Temple, D 3/85
1068. Vishnu	Vishvanatha Temple, in Virupakshi, CK 35/19
1069. Vishnurupa Vishnu	Rama Ghat, K 24/25
1070. Vishva	backside of Siddhi Vinayaka (Manikarnika), CK 9/9
1071. Vishvabhuja/ Vishvabahuka	Mir Ghat, Dharmakup, D 2/15
1072. Vishvakarmeshvara – 1	near Gwalagadha, A 34/106
1073. Vishvakarmeshvara – 2	in Brihaspatishvara, Siddheshvari, CK 7/133
1074. Vishvakaseneshvara – 1	near Asitanga Bhairava, Vriddhakala Temple, K 52/39
1075. Vishvakaseneshvara – 2	in Karamjitpur village, on Panchakroshi Road
1076. Vishvanatha/ Vishveshvara	Jnanavapi, Vishvanatha Temple, CK 35/19
1077. Vishvavashvishvara	called Vishvavasulinga, Agatyeshvara, Sutikshna, D 36/11
1078. Vishvedeveshvara	south of Madhyameshvara, K 53/63
1079. Vishveshvara (1st old site)	in Vishveshvaraganj, crossing, K 44/33; old site lost
1080. Vishveshvara (2nd old site)	Bansphatak, Razia Mosque, CK 38/5
1081. Vishveshvara (3rd old site)	the Jnanavapi Mosque (present)
1082. Vishveshvara (4th site, today)	Jnanavapi, Vishvanatha Temple, CK 35/19
1083. Vishveshvara – 2	Chitreshvara, called Vishveshvara, Daranagar, K 54/133
1084. Visvakaseneshvara	village Karmaitapur (right turn lane), Panchakroshi Road
1085. Vitanka Nrisimha	in Kedareshvara Temple, B 6/102
1086. Vriddha Aditya	Mir Ghat, way to Dharmakupa, D 3/15
1087. Vriddhakala Kupa	Daranagar, in the Vriddhakala Temple, K 52/39
1088. Vriddhakaleshvara	Mrityunjaya Temple, Vriddhakala, K 52/39

1089.	Vrishabhadhvaja Shiva	Kapileshvara, Kapiladhara
1090.	Vrishabheshvara	as Vrisheshvara, Gorakh Nath Tila, Maidagin, K 58/78
1091.	Vrisharudra	western part in Haratirath, a temple, K 46/147
1092.	Vyaghreshvara	Saptasagar, Bhutabhairava, K 63/16
1093.	Vyaseshvara – 1	Karnaghanta, Vyasakupa, K 60/67
1094.	Vyaseshvara – 2	inner compound in north corner, Vishvanatha, CK 35/19
1095.	Yajna Varaha Keshava	Prahlada Ghat, Svarlineshvara, A 11/30
1096.	Yajna Varaha Tirtha	North of Raj Ghat, near Fort, in the Ganga
1097.	Yajnavalkyeshvara	Sankatha Temple, CK 7/159; between Sima and Sena Vinayakas
1098.	Yaksha Vinayaka	Kotwalpura, CK 37/29
1099.	Yaksheshvara	village Mataladai Chak, Panchakroshi Road
1100.	Yama Aditya	Sankatha Ghat, on steps, near CK 7/164
1101.	Yama Tirtha	Yama Ghat, at the bank
1102.	Yameshvara	Yama Ghat, near Sankatha Ghat, at bank on the steps
1103.	Yamuneshvara	in Trilochan Temple, A 2/80
1104.	Yantreshvara – 1	gate of Annapurna Temple, D 9/1, established by Acharya Bhaskararai
1105.	Yantreshvara – 2	Panchaganga Ghat, called Pataleshvara, K 22/24
1106.	Yantreshvara – 3	Hanuman Ghat, B 4/55, established by Sant Muthu Svami
1107.	Yogini Pitha	Rana Mahal, where were 64 Yogini images; a few are there
1108.	Yogini Tirtha	north of Chausatthi Ghat and south of Ganga Mahal Ghat, in the Ganga
1109.	Yupa Sarovara	Sona Talab, Dindayalpur

References:

Kkh, *Kashi Khanda* of the *Skanda Purana*;
KR, *Kashi Rahasya* of the *Brahmavaivarta Purana;*
KKT, *Krityakalpataru* of Lakshmidhara's;
TvK, *Tirthavivecanakandam*; MtP, *Matsya Purana*.

Prepared & © *by* Rana P.B. Singh

Appendix 4

Shiva Lingas (324):
Total List as They Exist Today

Alphabetical Index of *Kāśīkhaṇḍa*, KKh

Se.	Siva Linga name	Ref. KKh (Kāśīkhaṇḍa)	Location in Varanasi
1.	Agastīśvara	61.177; 100.81	Agastakunda Muhalla, Godaulia, D 36/11
2.	Aghoreśa	97.87	near Kameshvara, A 2/21 under tree in niche (Madhi)
3.	Āgneyeśvara	97.120	near Svarlineshvara, A 12/ 2
4.	Agnīdhramīśvara	100.63	Jageshvara, in Math, Ishvargangi, J 66/4
5.	Agnīśa / Agnīśvara	84.73; 97.119; 100.85. 11. 157-9, 161	near Agnishvara Ghat, Patni Tola, CK 2/1
6.	Agnivarṇeśvara	65.14	near Svarlineshvara, A 12/2
7.	Airāvateśvara	67.179; 97.134	in Vriddhakala T.compound, K 52/39
8.	Aiśvaryeśa	81.47-8	Kachori Gali, K 34/60 facing Durmukha Vinayaka
9.	Amareśa	69.118	near Lolarka Kund, on steps, B 2/20
10.	Ambarīṣeśa	77.69	in Kedara Temple compound, B 6/102, now lost
11.	Ambikeśvara	67.219	near Ratneshvara (road to Vriddhakala), near K 53/ 38
12.	Amṛteśa / Amṛteśvara	73.45; 94.1; 100.32. 70.53; 94.14-9	Svargadvari, Nilakantha, CK 33/28
13.	Aṅgārakeśāna	17.15	south of Rinamochana tank, *now lost*

14.	Aṅgārakeśvara	17.12	near Mukutakunda, *now lost*
15.	Aṅgāreśa Aṅgāreśvara	86.103.17.21; 84.74	in porch of Atmavireshvara Temple, CK 7/158
16.	Aṅgiraseśa Aṅgiraseśvara	97.249.18.20	Jangambari, attached to main Road, D 35/79; also: Svargadvari, CK 10/16
17.	Antakeśvara	68.69-70; 97.132	in Vriddhakala Temple compound, K 52/39
18.	Ānusūyeśvara	97.21	Narad Ghat, Dattatreya Math, D 25/11
19.	Āpastambeśvara	97.157	called Burhe Baba, in Madhyameshvara, K 53/116
20.	Apsaraseśvara	66.3; 100.92	Radhakrishna Dharmasala, CK 30/1
21.	Āṣāḍhīśa Āṣāḍhīśvara	100.64.55.27; 97.177	Kashipura, Rani Betia Kothi, big big, K 63/53; also: Machharhatta Phatak, Govindapura road, CK 54/24
22.	Aśvatareśa	97.203	Gomath, Brahmanal, CK 8/14A
23.	Āśvineyeśvara	97.44	near Ganga Mahal, CK 2/26
24.	Atrīśvara	18.14; 97.12	Kodai Chauki, D 50/33, lost; now at Narad Ghat; also: Narad Ghat, Dattatreya Math, D 25/11
25.	Aṭṭahāsa	97.30, 32-3	Kashmirimal Haveli, near Shitala, CK 7/92
26.	Avadhūteśvara	97.181	near Pashupateshvara, CK 13/85
27.	Avimukta	39.75; 64.116; 73.35	Vishvanatha Temple compound, CK 35/19, southern direction
28.	Avimukteśa Avimukteśvara	39.90-7; 40.1-3. 61.117; 100.16. 10.93; 39.76; 39.80-6; 55.4; 61.116; 100.47, 94.	(1) north Phatak of Jnanavapi, lost, site worshipped; (2) Radhakrishna Dharmashala, CK 30/1 Jnanavapi: see from the window; (3) Manikarnika Road, outside CK 10/ 22 A, Brahmanaleshvara
29.	Avimukteśvareśvara	79.92	Vishvanatha Temple compound, CK 35/19, southern direction
30.	Ayogandheśvara	69.20	at Pushkara Talab, Assi, east of Mumukshu Bhavan
31.	Bālcandreśa	97.121-3	old Talakarneshvara, Ausanganj, K 56/114

32.	Balīśa	97.37	in Vriddhakala Temple compound, K 52/39
33.	Bandīśvara	97.136 compound, K 52/39	as Balīśa: in Vriddhakala T.
34.	Bāṇeśa / Bāṇeśvara	97.38, 206.33.139; 53.80; 69.92	(1) Prahlad Ghat, Pancagni Akhara, K 11/30; (2) Sukhlal Shah Muhal, CK 13/17,(also Banasura's statue)
35.	Bhadrakarṇeśa	69.105	near Rameshvara, in village Bhuili, on Panchakroshi Road
36.	Bhadreśa / Bhadreśvara	97.238.97.47-8	old at Bhadaun; Patni Tola, in Upashantishvara, CK 2/ 4
37.	Bhāgīrathīśvara	61.158	Svargadvari, Manikarnika Lane, CK 11/11
38.	Bhairaveśa	97.141	west corner of Kala Bhairava, K 32/7
39.	Bhārabhūta / Bhārabhūteśa/ Bhārabhūteśvara	74.45.55.27. 10.91; 55.13-4; 69.158; 100.64	Rajadarwaja lane, Gobindapura, CK 54/44
40.	Bhāradvājeśvara	65.9	in Vashishtha-Vamadeva, Sankatha Ghat, CK 7/161
41.	Bhasmagātra	69.121-2	south of Kashi Karvat, CK 31/15
42.	Bhavānīśa	10.96;	as Bhavanishvara, near Annapurna Temple, D 8/38
43.	Bhava / Bhaveśvara	69.99.69.100	near Bhimacandi, in temple compound
44.	Bhīmeśa Bhīmeśvara	69.122.69. 119-20; 70.72	as Bhimeshvara, Kashi Karvat, CK 31/12
45.	Bhīṣmeśa	75.78	(1) Trilochan Ghat, close to the bank, in niche; (2) in Vishvanatha, near Shanaichareshvara, CH 35/19, Vrihaspati
46.	Bhṛṅgīśvara	33.129	as Dhanavantarishvara, in Vriddhakala Temple, K 52/ 39
47.	Bhūrbhuvaḥ	69.148	Bhutabhairava, K 63/26; (Ganadhip, lost)

48.	Bhūtadhātrīśa	74.51	Sukhlal Shak Phatak, CK 13/ 15
49.	Bhūtīśa	97.176	(1) as Bhuteshvara, Dashasvamedha, D 17/ 50; (2) Kashipura, Rani Betia Temple, near Ashadhishvara
50.	Brahmeśa / Brahmeśvara	10.90; 70.32; 73.46; 74.45; 97.239, 242.52. 73, 96, 99; 83.97; 100.81	(1) Brahma Ghat, K 22/82; (2) Balmukund Chauhatta, Khalispura, D 33/66; (3) near to Prayaga Ghat, four headed Siva
51.	Brāhmīśa	100.89	Sakarkand Gali, D 7/6
52.	Bṛhaspatīśvara (or Vibhāṇḍeśvara)	10.90; 17.59, 61, 64; 97.95	facing Atmavireshvara Temple, Scindhia Ghat, CK 7/133
53.	Budheśvara	15.48, 50, 67	Atmavireshvara Temple, CK 7/158
54.	Caṇḍīśa / Caṇḍīśvara	69.57-8; 73.47. 97.169; 100.90	Kalika Gali, D 8/27
55.	Candra	86.108	near Sindhia Ghat, in Siddheshvari temple, CK 7/124
56.	Candreśa / Candreśvara	10.87; 14.25; 69.107; 100.45, 85.14.35, 41, 46, 49, 56, 59, 66, 69,76; 15.67; 17.62; 73.33; 79.105; 84.76; 97.38, 116	near Sindhia Ghat, in Siddheshvari temple, CK 7/124
57.	Catuḥsamudrakūpa	97.168	in well at Kashipura road, near K 63/46
58.	Caturmukheśa Caturmukheśvara	55.10.55.9	(1) inside Vriddhakala, K 52/39; (2) Prayaga Linga, Adi Keshava, A 37/51
59.	Caturvaktreśvara	100.89	Sakarkand Gali, D 7/19
60.	Chāgaleśa	53.128	Pitarkunda, C 18/52
61.	Citragupteśvara	70.38-9; 97.200, 202; 100.84	Machchharhatta Phatak, CK 57/77
62.	Citrāṅgadeśvara / Citraṅgeśa	70.43; 77.67, 72.97.249	near Kshemeshvara Ghat, Kumarsvami Math, B 14/118
63.	Dākṣāyaṇīśvara	67.218	as Satishvara, Road Vriddhakala, K 46/32

64.	Dakṣeśa / Dakṣeśvara	97.131; 100.49. 87.4-5; 89.134, 137-9; 94.36; 97.129; 100.30	north of Vriddhakala Kupa, huge linga, K 52/39
65.	Damaneśa	97.87	at gate, in Madhi (niche), Makareshvara
66.	Daṇḍī / Daṇḍīśvara	69.101.69.103	near Adi Keshava, A 37/51
67.	Daśahareśvara	52.95	Shitala Temple, Dashashavamedha Ghat, D 18 /19
68.	Daśāśvamedheśa	52.71, 91-2	Shitala Temple, Dashashavamedha Ghat, D 18 /19
69.	Dattātreyeśvara	33.142; 61.13; 97.233	(1): Adi Keshava, outside of temple gate, near A 37/51, (2): Brahma Ghat, K 18/48, (3): Agastakunda, Agastish vara temple, D 36/11
70.	Dehalivighneśa	57.72	in Dehli Vinayaka Temple, on Panchakroshi Road
71.	Devadeva	69.11	Dhundhiraj Gali, in Sanyasi College, CK 37/12
72.	Devaleśvara	97.171	Saptasagar, Bhutabhairava, K 63/30
73.	Devayānīśvara	97.227	as Nakulishvara, in the root of Akshaya Vata, CK 35/ 20
74.	Dhanvāntarīśvara	97.137	in Vriddhakala Temple, K 52/39
75.	Dharmeśa / Dharmeśvara	10.89; 73.33; 81.15, 23, 31, 44-6; 83.101; 86.109; 100.28, 88.69.37; 78.47, 52-3, 55; 79.25; 80.3; 81.47, 74-7; 100.46	(1): Mir Ghat, Dharmakup, D 2/21, (2): in the south of Kameshvara, A 2/9, lost
76.	Dhautapāpeśvara	33.156	at Panchaganga Ghat, in the porch
77.	Dhruvakuṇḍa / Dhruveśa /	97.234.97.236; 100.82.21.128; 97.234	Kodai ki Chauki, in Sanatan Dharm College, D 49/10 Dhruveśvara
78.	Dilīpeśa	97.242	Devanathpura, Shivala

79.	Divodāseśvara	58.214	Mir Ghat, Dharmakupa, in Vishvabhuja Gauri, D 2/15
80.	Dṛmicaṇḍeśvara	53.124	Jaitpura, south of Nagakuon, as 'Mallu Halwai temple', J 11/148
81.	Durvāseśa	97.177	in Kameshvara Temple, A 2/9
82.	Durvāseśvara	85.74	in Rani Betia temple, near Ashadhishvara.
83.	Dvāreśvara	97.256	south of Durga Temple, Durgakund, B 27/1
84.	Gabhastīśa / Gabhastīśvara	33.154; 84.61; 97.183, 185-6, 193; 100.50.49. 27; 49.77-9	Panchaganga Ghat, Mangalagauri, K 24/34
85.	Gaṇādhyakṣa	69.128-9; 97.58	village Bhatauli, on Panchakroshi Road
86.	Gandharveśvara	66.21-3	west of Nagakunda (Bhiran Sagar), at the kunda, *now lost*
87.	Gaṇeśvara Gaṇeśvareśvara	10.88.97.231	village Chaukhandi, Panchakroshi Road
88.	Gaṅgeśa Gaṅgeśvara	10.91; 97.207; 100.31, 50, 93. 91.1, 5-7, 10-1	(1): Jnanavapi, under pipal tree, near CK 35/1
89.	Gargeśa	97.87	east of Shramodaka Kupa, now lost
90.	Garuḍeśa Garuḍeśvara	10.88; 83.96.50.142	(1): near Kameshvara, in Khakholkaditya mini Temple, A 2/9, (2): Jangambari, Teliana, D 31/39A
91.	Gautameśvara	97.238	Godaulia, near Kashi Naresh Shivala, D 37/33
92.	Ghaṇṭākarṇeśvara	53.33	Karnaghanta, K 60/66
93.	Gokarṇa / Gokarṇeśa / Gokarṇeśvara	74.45.10.88; 53.81; 97.233. 53.82; 100.83	Dayalu Gali, Kodai ki Chaki, D 50/34A
94.	Goprekṣa	100.55; 73.60; 97.9, 11, 13, 21, 25	in Gopi Govind Temple, Lal Ghat, A 4/24
95.	Graheśa	97.201	Kalabhairava, Dandapani Gali, K 31/50

96.	Halīśeśa	97.140	near Dhanvantishvara, J 30/22
97.	Hanumadīśvara	97.43 in Madhi, B 5/19	lower side, Hanuman Ghat,
98.	Harikeśeśa Harikeśeśvara	97.233.10.95	Janganbari, Kharikuan, D 35/273
99.	Hariścandra / Hariścandreśa Hariścandreśvara	100.86.97.248. 10.95; 61.78; 69.80	(1): Sankatha Ghat, CK 7/166, (2): Near Pataleshvara, D 32/118, outside
100.	Hastipāleśvara	97.133	in Vriddhakala Temple compound, K 52/39
101.	Hāṭakeśa Hāṭakeśvara	69.149, 69. 151.100.83	(1): Dalmandi, Gudari Bazar, CK 43/189, (2): Haraha Sarai, CK 43/189
102.	Hetukeśa	97.174	Haraha Talab, now lost
103.	Hiraṇyagarbha Hiraṇyagarbheśa	73.60.100.54	near Trilocana Ghat, in the niche (Madhi)
104.	Huṇḍaṇeśa	66.32	(1) Shailaputri, Varana's bank, Madhia Ghat, A 40/11; (2): Dhupachandi Devi T., backside, J 12/134
105.	Indradyumneśvara	77.70; 84.68	Coochbihar estate, backside of Kalibari, B 13/98
106.	Indreśa / Indreśvara	10.95; 70.28; 97.117.81.41-3	(1): Near Karkotakavapi (Naga Kupa); now lost, (2): Near Tarakeshvara, Manikarnika Ghat, under pipal tree
107.	Īśāna / Īśāneśa / Īśāneśvara	10.88; 73.60; 100.55.14.6-7, 9-11; 69.94; 97.214; 100.89.69.93	(1): Kotwalpura, CK 37/43 (near cinema), (2): called Daneshvara, at Prahlada Ghat
108.	Jaigīṣavyaguhā-liṅga	97.170	at the gate of Jaigishvya Guha, Jageshvara Math, J 66/3
109.	Jaigiṣavyeśvara	10.87; 63.80, 85	(1): Ishvargangi, Narharipura, J 66/4, (2): Saptasagar, Bhutabhairava, K 63/28
110.	Jalaliṅga	69.161	near Manikarnika, Jalashayi Ghat, in water
111.	Jamadagnīśvara	97.141	east of Kala Bhairava, K 32/57

112. Jambukeśa Jambukeśvara	10.87; 73.61; 97.159; 100.60. *65.19	(1): Lohatia, in Bade Ganesha, K 58/103, (2): Bade Ganesha, K 58/103
113. Janakeśa	68.70; 97.253	(1): in Vriddhakala, K 52/39, (2): inside Sankatha Temple, near Sankatha ji, CK 7/159
114. Jāṅgaleśa	97.258	in Durga Temple, Durgakund, B 27/1; (2) at Mukutkunda, Nababganj
115. Jarāharaliṅga	97.204	near Vagishvari, Jaitpura, J 6/85
116. Jarāsandheśa Jarāsandheśvara	83.103.97.240; 100.80	Tripurabhairavi, D 5/101, in wall; (lost: house, D 3/79)
117. Jaṭī, Jaṭīśvara	69.78	called Pataleshvara, gate of house D 32/117
118. Jayanta / Jayanteśa	69.72.97.135	(1): north of Mrityunjaya Temple, Vriddhakala, K 52/39, (2): Bhuta Bhairava, K 63/27
119. Jñāneśa / Jñāneśvara	61.141; 73.45. 81.47; 84.58	Lahori Tola, D 1/32
120. Jyeṣṭha / Jyeṣṭheśa / Jyeṣṭheśa / Jyeṣṭheśvara	73.61.*13.2910. 87; 65.2, 82.63. 10-3, 20; 65.1, 37, 44; 66.1-2, 7, 164; 97.166	Bhuta Bhairava, Saptasagar, Kashipura, K 62/44
121. Jyotīrūpeśvara	73.47; 94.30-1, 34	Bhuta Bhairava, Saptasagar, Kashipura, K 62/44
122. Kaceśa	97.228	small linga in Shukreshvara, Kalika Gali, D 8/30
123. Kaholeśa	65.18; 97.256	(1): small linga in Shukreshvara, Kalika Gali, D 8/30, (2): north of Kamachha Devi Temple, Kolhua, B 21/123
124. Kāla /Kālakeśa	97.221.97.209	Hanuman Ghat, B 4/44
125. Kālañjareśvara	77.71	Kshemeshvara Ghat, Kumarsvami Math, B 14/10; people mostly worship in the Kedara temple
126. Kālarāja	31.150; 67.164; 69.107; 97.199	Dandapani Gali, Kala Bhairava, K 31/49

127. Kalaśeśa Kalaśeśvara	97.201.10.86; 61.193; 84.75; 100.85	Kalasheshvara ki Brahmapuri Phatak, CK 7/101
128. Kāleśa / Kāleśvara	10.86; 53.58; 97.129.53.57	(1): in the Vriddhakala, K 52/39, called Vriddhakaleshvara, (2) near Kala Bhairava, in Dandapani Temple, K 31/49
129. Kambalāśvatareśa	61.81	Gomath, Kakaram Gali, CK 8/14A
130. Kaṃbaleśa	97.203	Gomath, Brahmanal, CK 8/14A
131. Kāmeśa / Kāmeśvara	10.87; 73.34; 85.78; 86.109; 97.96; 100.29. 33.122; 69.23; 85.75-6; 97.97; 100.46	(1): Machchhodari, Kameshvara, A 2/9, (2): Ghasi Tola, in the lane at the corner K 30/1
132. Kandukeśa / Kandukeśvara	10.96; 65.38-43, 85; 100.24. * 65.37	Saptasagar, Bhutabhairava, K 63/29
133. Kapāleśa / Kapālīśa	97.65, 108. 69.112	at Lata Bhairava Talab, A 1/123
134. Kaparoadīśa / Kaparoadīśvara	10.96; 54.1, 5, 56, 79-80; 55.2; 69.68.69.67	village Janasa, Panchakroshi Road
135. Kapileśa / Kapileśvara	33.158; 73.157; 97.217.73.158; 83.67; 97.77; 97.82-3	Kapileshvara Lane, Dudhvinayaka, K 23/14; (2): in the ditch, near Nikumbha, in Vishvanatha Temple, CK 35/19
136. Karandhameśvara	97.252	Lolarkakunda, near to Camunda, B 2/17.
137. Karavīreśvara	97.115	Lakshmikund, D 52/41
138. Karkoṭakeśvara / Karkoṭeśa	66.23; 97.117.66.26	on steps to Naga Kunda, J 23/206
139. Karuṇeśvara Karuṇeśa	73.45; 94.20-8.97.223; 100.88	Lahoritola, Lalita Ghat, in Phute Ganesh CK 34/10; (2): Varneshvara, Dhundhiraj Gali, CK 36/10
140. Kaśyapeśa	100.82	Jangambari Road, D 35/79
141. Kātyāyana Kātyāyaneśa	97.258.68. 66.65.12	near Scindhia Ghat, in Atmavireshvara Kātyāyaneśvara Temple, CK 7/158

429

142. Kedāra / Kedāreśa	55.8; 73.33; 77.1-5, 25, 46, 60, 62-7; 86.109; 97.250; 100.27, 45. 10.87; 77.9-10	Kedara Ghat, B 6/102; half-Siva & half-Vishnu; (2): Kalika Gali, in Kali-Ji, D 8/17, (3): Agastakunda, Agasteshvara, D 36/11, (4): Scindhia Ghat, in Brihaspatishvara, CK 7/133
143. Kīkaseśvara	100.83	Harahasarai, CK 48/45
144. Kiraṇeśvara	33.155	near Mangala Gauri, in lane, K 23/83
145. Kirāteśa	55.8; 69.157-8	near Bharbhiteshvara, CK 52/15, called Gupteshvara, (2): near Jayanteshvara, at Lali Ghat
146. Koṭīśa / Koṭīśvara	97.63-4.97.62	Re-established in Trilocana Temple, A 2/80, (2): near Sakshi Vinayaka, D 10/49
147. Kratvīśvara	18.21	Koniya Ghat, across Varana, under holy fig, (2): Javavinayaka, on steps, CK 33/36
148. Kṛṣṇeśa	97.34	wall of Sankatha, facing Harishchandreshvara CK 7/159
149. Kṛttivāsa / Kṛttivāsas / Kṛttivāseśvara	24.81; 68.59, 62, 72; 69.3; 100.45.68.67-8; 69.55; 73.32; 86.108; 100.25. 10.86; 33.166-7; 68.29, 34-5, 38-45, 49, 60, 84-5	road to Vriddhakala, Dara Nagar, K 46/23
150. Kṣemeśa Kṣemeśvara	97.249.77.72	Kshemeshvara Ghat, Kumarsvami Math, B 14/12
151. Kubereśa Kubereśvara	55.11.13.162-3	in the court of Vishvanatha, north side, (2): in the temple of Annapurna, in the NE
152. Kubjāmbareśvara	70.60	in Pitamaheshvara, CK 7/ 92
153. Kukkuṭeśa Kukkuṭeśvara	66.4.53.59; 69.75	Ranamahal, near Vakratunda Vinayaka, D 21/22, (2): Kalabhairav, in Dandapani Bhairava, K 31/49, (3): near southern gate of Durga Temple, Durgakund, B 27/1

154.	Kuṇḍeśa Kuṇḍodareśvara	97.105-6.53. 78-9	Asi Ghat (re-established); upper part of Lolarka Kund
155.	Kuntīśvara	97.18-9	Konia Ghat, across the Varana river
156.	Kūṣmāṇḍeśa	97.206	at Svargadvari, CK 10/16
157.	Lakṣmīśa	97.113	Lakshmikund, (Sorahianatha), D 52/54
158.	Lāṅgalīśa / Lāṅgalīśvara	10.93; 55.21; 97.214; 100.64, 91.55.20	Khowa Bazar, CK 28/4
159.	Lomaśeśa	68.67	in Vriddhakala Temple, K 52/59, Lomaleśa
160.	Madālaseśvara	97.230; 100.65	As Madalaseshvara, on eastern lane, Kalika Gali, D 5/133
161.	Madhyameśa Madhyameśvara	97.149, 153-4. 10.90; 67.177-8; 73.60; 97.151; 100.54	Dara Nagar, Madhyameshvara, K 53/63
162.	Mahādeva (ādi)	10.96; 51.21; 55.12; 69.27-35, 117; 73.32; 74.120; 79.99; 86.108; 97.7, 9, 26; 100.45	Adi Mahadeva, Trilochan, A 3/92
163.	Mahākāla Mahākāleśa	69.20; 97.131. 97.131 53.29; 100.39,93	Mahamritunjaya, Vriddhakala Temple, K 52/39, (2): east of Kala Bhairava, K 32/24, (3): southeast corner of Jnanavapi pavilion, under Fig tree
164.	Mahālakṣmīśvara	10.91; 69.124; 97.109	Lakshmikund, (Sorahianatha), D 52/54
165.	Mahāmuṇḍeśvara	97.69	in Vagishvari Temple, Jaitapura, J 6/33
166.	Mahānādeśvara	69.22	in Adi Mahadeva, A 3/92
167.	Mahāpāśupateśa	97.213	as Pasupathinatha of Nepal, Lalita Ghat, D 1/67
168.	Mahāsiddhīśvara	97.254	near Kurukshetra, Asi, B 2/282
169.	Maheśa / Maheśvara	100.94.51.70; 69.130; 70.30; 73.47; 100.38	open space, at the bank, Manikarnika Ghat, (2): southwest corner of Jnanavapi pavilion

170. Mālatīśa/ Mālatīśvara	68.68.97.135	Mrityunjaya Temple,Vriddhakala, K 52/39
171. Manaḥprakāmeśa Manaḥprakāmeśvara	100.89.100.65	near Sakshi Vinayaka, Vishvanath Gali, D 10/50
172. Manīkarnīkā	100.79.	Manikarnika Ghat, open, uncovered
173. Maṇikarṇeśa Maṇikarṇikīśa Maṇikarṇikīśvara Maṇikarṇīśa Maṇikarṇīśvara	12.97.61.104.61. 105.10.92; 73.35; 74.45; 97.204. 61.112; 86.109; 100.46.	Manikarnishvara, Gomath Ashram, Brahmanal, CK 8/12
174. Marīcīśvara	18.17	Nagakuan, Marichi Kunda; Mirasagar D 25/11
175. Mārkaṇḍa Mārkaṇḍeyeśa Mārkaṇḍeyeśvara	10.92.100.92. 61. 165, 170	Dhundhiraj Gali, bazar, CK 36/10
176. Marukeśvara	69.159	called Nairittishvara, near Pushpa- danteshvara, Devanathpura, D 32/102
177. Matrīśvara	18.16	near Pitrikunda, at bank of Matrikunda, now lost
178. Mayūreśa Mayūreśvara	53.80. 53.79	Asi Ghat, B 2/174
179. Mokṣadvāreśvara	73.46; 94.20; 94.29	near Lalita Ghat, CK 34/10
180. Mokṣeśa Mokṣeśvara	10.91; 97.223; 100.94. *61.115	west of Jnanavapi mosque (lost)
181. Mṛtyvīśa	97.129	Mahamrityunjaya, K 52/39
182. Mucukundeśa	97.238	called Baradeva, Godaulia, D 37/40
183. Mukhaprekṣeśvara	97.188	near Mangala Gauri Temple, K 24/34
184. Mukuṭeśvara	97.258	near Govabai Pokhra, Temple, B 27/20, (2): near park, Tilabhandeshvara, B 17/99
185. Muṇḍaneśa	66.23	Shailaputri, Varana's bank, Madhia Ghat, A 40/11; (2) Dhupachandi Devi Temple, backside, J 12/134
186. Nādeśa / Nādeśvara	73.164; 97. 79-80.73.156, 159, 74.104	near Akareshvara, under Pipal tree, a lying linga

187. Nāgeśvara	100.86	Bhonshala Ghat, CK 1/21, (2): linga in the water, Naga Kunda, J 23/206
188. Nahuṣeśa	97.239	Rameshvara Temple, on Panchakroshi Road
189. Nairṛteśa Nairṛteśvara	97.249.69.160	west of Puspadanteshvara, D 32/107; same called Marukeshvara
190. Nakṣatreśvara	15.9, 16, 19	Adi Keshava, A 37/51
191. Nakulīśa Nakulīśvara	97.217.69.116, 120; 100.63, 91	near Vishvanatha, in Akshayavat Temple, CK 35/20
192. Nalakūbaraliṅga	70.58, 60; 97.97-9	near to Manikarnishvara, in Pitamaheshvara, CK 7/92
193. Nandīśvara Nandikeśa	97.29.10.89; 73.47; 100.39, 93	Raja Nadeshar Kothi, Maldahia, S 18/240, (2): east of Jnanavapi, the Great Bull
194. Nāradeśvara	97.56-7	Narada Ghat, Tailanga Math, D 25/12
195. Narmadeśa / Narmadeśvara	61.172; 75.11; 92.1, 27, 30; 93.1; 100.31, 50.10.91; 92.24	east of Trilochana Temple, A 2/19
196. Nikumbheśa Nikumbheśvara	97.225-6.55.11	in Vishvanatha Temple, inside Parvati Temple, CK 35/19
197. Nīlakaṇṭha Nīlakaṇṭheśvara	69.59-60; 77.68.61.197	Bhelupura, B 20/15, (2): Brahmanal, Nilakantha, Manikarnika Marg, CK 33/23
198. Niṣkalaṅkeśa	100.92	Dhundhiraj Gali, bazar, CK 35/34
199. Niṣpāpeśvara	83.82	close to the Gauri Kunda, Kedara Ghat, near bank
200. Nivāseśa / Nivāseśvara	10.89; 63.16-7; 97.167. * 73.61	Bhuta Bhairava, K 63/27
201. Oṃkāra / Oṃkāranātha 10.86/ Oṃkāreśa 33.118;73.73-6./ Oṃkāreśvara 73.147, 155, 162-3; 74.106-7	61.189, 167; 73.32, 166-71, 174-6; 74.58, 74, 80, 82, 95, 100, 117-8;121; 75.24, 60; 76.156; 86.108; 87.2; 94.36; 100.26-7, 44.	Omkareshvara, Pathanitola, Tila A 33/23; other attached are: Akareshvara and Makareshvara. Ukareshvara and Bindu lost

219.	Pratigraheśvara	100.92	Dhundhiraj Gali, bazar, CK 35/34
220.	Prayāga / Prayāgeśa / Prayāgeśvara	97.17. 61.36, 39, 44. 61.203	in Sangameshvara, Adi Keshava, four headed, (2): near Shulatan keshvara, Dashashvamedha, as Brahmeshvara, (3): between Madhia and Kakarha Ghat, re-established, (4): Dashashvamedha, Bandi Devi, D 17/100
221.	Prītikeśa/ Prītikeśvara	97.218; 100.65. 10.89	Backside of Sakshi Vinayaka, D 10/8
222.	Pṛthvīśvara	83.74	backside of Sakshi Vin., D 10/8
223.	Pulaheśa	18.19	facing Pulastyeshvara, CK 10/16 on platform
224.	Pulastīśvara Pulastyeśa	61.188. 18.19	Jangamabadi Math, at gate, D 35/77, (2): Javavinayaka, Svargadvari, Sureka Building. CK 33/43
225.	Puṣpadanteśvara	97.246-7	Bengali Tola, Devanathpura, D 32/102
226.	Rājarājeśa	100.90	(1) Ghughurali Gali road, CK 39/57; (2): Dhundhiraj Gali, bazar, CK 35/33; (3): Svargadvari, under platform, CK 10/16
227.	Ratneśa / Ratneśvara	67.28-32,164-5, 194-5, 200, 203; 73.33; 86.108; 93.38; 100.25, 45.* 10.92; 33.165; 66.148; 67.1, 3, 17-8, 36, 43-4, 46, 51, 54, 61, 63, 130, 137, 150, 161, 184-5, 211-7; 221-3; 79.96	along road to Vriddhakala, K 53/40
228.	Revateśa	97.194.97.190 Revateśvara	on steps at Vindu Madhava Ghat, in small Shiva shrine
229.	Rudreśa / Rudreśvara	97.89. 69.90-1; 97.91	near Tripura Bhairavi Temple, D 5/21
230.	Ṣaḍānana	67.220	Adi Mahadeva Temple compound, A 3/92

231.	Sagareśa Sāgareśvara	83.64; 97.41	in Sankatha Temple, CK 7/159; (2): east of Sankatha Temple, close to Saptarshi Temple
232.	Śaileśa / Śaileśvara	66.142-8, 149; 73.60; 94.37; 97.62; 100.52.33. 135; 66.124; 67.7; 69.86; 70.37; 100.25	Madhia Ghat at Varana river, A 40/11
233.	Śakreśa	97.210, 213	called Indreshvara, upper side at Manikarnika Ghat
234.	Śālakaṭaṃkaṭa	69.61	Maruadih Bazar, near the Kakarmata Tank
235.	Saṃgameśvara	70.77	(1): close to Asi Ghat; (2): Adi Keshava, lower side, A 37/51
236.	Śaṃkukarṇa	69.44	Shankudhara, front of B 22/196
237.	Samudreśa	97.214	south of road to Bansphatak, near CK 37/32
238.	Saṃvarteśa	97.198	Panchapandava, near Jnanavapi, CK 28/10
239.	Śanaiścareśvara Śanīśvara	17.127.10.94	Vishvanath Temple compound, CK 35/19
240.	Saṅgameśa Saṅgameśvara	61.6; 73.60; 84.2. 10.95; 15.9; 97.16; 100.53	(1) Asi Sangam : Asi, Harihar Ashram, B 1/169; (2), Varuna sangam: Adi Keshava, lower side, A 37/51
241.	Śaṅkukarṇeśvara	53.27-8; 97.86	Shankhudhara, close to Kund, near B 22/120
242.	Śāntanavaliṅga	75.77	Shanteshvara, in niche at steps to Trilochan Ghat
243.	Sarasvatīśvara	75.9	near Hiranyagharbheshvara, at Trilochan Ghat
244.	Śaśibhūṣaṇa	69.17	Hanuman Ghat, B 4/44
245.	Śatakāla	97.172	Thatheri Bazar, lower side, K 17/24
246.	Satīśvara	93.1-2, 30, 33, 37-8; 100.32, 50	Vriddhakala Road, Ratneshvara Temple K 46/32

247. Śaunakeśa	97.158	near Bade Ganesh, K 58/103, existed till 1822, then lost.
248. Siddhayogīśvara	14.64	in Siddheshvari Temple, CK 7/124
249. Siddheśvara	67.176; 97.164; 97.254	in Siddheshvari Temple, CK 7/124
250. Siddhyaṣṭakeśvara	67.173	in Bade Ganesha, K 58/103
251. Śivaliṅga	51.65; 53.21; 69.104	so common, difficult to identify
252. Skanda / Skandeśvara	61.120. 33.125; 69.25; 70.29; 97.26	near Adi Mahadeva, A 3/92; lost
253. Somanātha	100.81	near Karoadameshvara, Kandwa, on Panchakroshi Road
254. Someśa / Someśvara	97.197. 10.95; 83.95	near Manmandira Ghat, D 16/34; (2): Pandey Ghat, D 25/34, on the steps; (3): near Vagishvari, Jaitpura, J 6/85
255. Śrīkaṇṭha	69.65-6	Lakshmikunda, D 52/38
256. Sthāṇu	69.7	near Kurukshetra Tank, B 2/247
257. Sukeśa / Sukeśeśvara	97.142.53.126	near Kashi Goshala, western gate, in a room, K 40/20
258. Śukreśa /	16.124, 126, 128; 17.128; 61.135; 73.61; 97.227-30.	Kalika Gali, D 8/30
Śukreśvara	16.128; 100.58	
259. Sūkṣmeśa Sūkṣmeśvara	69.69. 69.70	Back of Dhupachandi Temple, near Vikatadvija Vinayaka, J 12/134
260. Śūlaṭaṅka	69.39	Dashashvamedha Ghat, near D 17/111
261. Sumukheśa	55.25-6	at Trilochan, near Padodaka Kupa, A 3/87
262. Śuṣkeśvara	97.253	Asi Ghat, B 1/185 Kashi Ashram, locally Shukreshvara
263. Svapneśvara	70.93	Shivala, Hanuman T., B 3/150
264. Svargadvāreśvara	73.46; 94.29	Svargadvari, Brahmanal, CK 10/16
265. Svarlīna	10.95; 69.24; 73.60.	Prahlad Ghat, Panchagni Akhara, A 11/30
Svarlīneśvara	84.31	

266. Svarṇākṣeśa	97.224	Dhundhiraj Gali, in Dandapani, CK 36/10
267. Svayambhūliṅga	69.124	Luxa, near Mahalakshmishvara, D 54/114
268. Śveteśa	97.198	Panchapandava Temple, Jnanavapi, CK 28/10
269. Takṣakeśvara	66.11	at Augharanath ki Takiya, outside to gate, K 64/113
270. Tārakeśa / Tārakeśvara	53.120; 73.45; 81.41; 97.210; 100.39, 50, 93. 10.89; 53.121; 61.119, 121; 69.153-4	(1): Jnanavapi, niche of Gauri shankara; (2): near Vishvanatha, Ganapatarai Khemaka Temple, CK 35/17; (3): at Manikarnika Ghat; (4): at Kedar Ghat, close to the Ganga's bank
271. Tṛreśa (= Praṇaveśa?)	97.236	Omkareshvara, Pathanitola, Tila A 33/23; other attached are: Akareshvara and Makareshvara. Ukareshvara and Bindu lost
272. Tattveśa	81.45	Dharmakupa, D 3/97
273. Tilaparṇeśvara	53.122; 100.65	near gate of Durga Temple, Durgakund, B 27/1
274. Trilocana	100.27; 69.23; 73.2, 6, 32; 75.5, 11-2, 15, 25-9, 32, 38, 57, 64-8, 71; 76.14, 98, 153, 157, 162, 165-8	Trilochana Ghat, upper part, A 2/80
275. Tripurāntaka	69.73-4; 97.232; 100.64	Sigra (Shivagiri/ Shivpurva) Tila, D 59/95
276. Tripureśa	33.138; 69.91	Tripurabhairavi temple, D 5/24
277. Trisandhyeśa Trisandhyeśvara	10.96; 100.88 61.173, 175	Lahoritola, in Phute Ganesha, CK 1/40; (2): Lalita Ghat, D 1/40
278. Tryambaka	69.79	Baradeo, Godaulia, Trilokinatha, D 38/21
279. Tuṅga / Tuṅgeśvara	97.140.97.138	Near Vedeshvara, Adi Keshava, A 37/51; (2): called Dhanvantarishvara, in Vriddhakala Temple, K 52/39

280. Tvaṣṭrīśa	97.189	as Vishvakarmeshvara, in Brihaspatishvara Temple, CK 7/133
281. Uddālakeśvara	70.78; 97.83	near Lolarka Kund, B 2/20; (2): Rajmandir, Hanuman Temple, K 20/159
282. Ugra /	69.97-8.	at Lolarka Kunda
283. Ugreśvara	97.113	in Lakshmikund, near Lakshmi, D 52/40
284. Upaśāntaśiva	10.96; 73.61; 97.49; 100.56	Agnishvara Ghat, Patani Tola, CK 2/4
285. Ūroadhvaretas	69.63-4	Phulwaria-Maduadih, Kushmanda Vinayaka
286. Urvaśīśa	100.63	Ausanganj, Golabag, J 56/108, near pipal tree
287. Uṭajeśvara	65.86	in the Gola Dinanatha
288. Utathyavāmadeveśa		97.202 Sankatha Ghat, Saptarshi Temple, CK 7/161
289. Vāgīśvara	67.168	Jaitpura, in Vagishvari Temple, J 6/33
290. Vaidyanātha	21.126; 97.236; 100.82;	Baijnattha, Kamachha, B 37/1
291. Vaidyeśvara	97.138	Kodai ki Chauki, D 50/20 A
292. Vairocaneśvara	33.140; 61.184; 97.37	near Sima Vinayaka, Siddheshvara, in the lane close to wall
293. Vālmīkeśvara	75.82	Maldahiya, Valmiki Tila, CK 21/14, now in ruins; (2): Bhelupur, near Nilakantha, big *linga*, B 20/ 15; (3) in Trilocaneshvara, A 3/80, the big *linga* in the back
294. Vāmadeva Linga / Vāmadeveśvara	100.87.65.12	Sankatha Ghat, Saptarshi Temple, CK 7/161
295. Varāheśa	10.94; 97.196	Dashashvamedha Ghat, near Rama Mandir D 17/111, now in ruins
296. Varuṇeśa	10.94; 12.97-8, 100; 97.206	in the upper part of Siddhi Vinayaka, CK 8/8; (2): as Karuneshvara, Dhundhiraj Gali, CK 36/ 10

297. Vasiṣṭha /	61.171.	Sankatha Ghat, Saptarshi Temple,
Vasiṣṭheśa /	10.94; 61.166;	CK 7/161
	97.34.	
Vasiṣṭheśvara	18.21; 61.170	
298. Vāsukīśa	100.79.	near Atmavireshvara, Scindhia
Vāsukīśvara	66.7	Ghat, CK 7/155; (2): Narad Ghat, facing Naroadeshvara, D 25/11
299. Vedeśvara	97.14-5	in Adi Keshava, A 37/51
300. Vibhāṇḍeśa	97.256	in Tilabhandeshvara Temple, B 17/99, in the well
301. Vidhi /	70.46.	in Agatyeshvara Temple, southwest
Vidhīśa /	10.94; 97.243.	side of Godaulia, D 36/11
Vidhīśvara	70.46	
302. Vidyeśa /	100.85.	Nimwali Brahmapuri, CK A2/41
Vidyeśvara	97.38	
303. Vighneśa	57.82	Vighnaraja Vinayaka Temple, Chitrakuta Talab, J 12/32
304. Vijayaliṅga	69.61	in Vishvanatha T., near Nikumbha, CK 35/19
305. Vijayeśa	69.62	Maruadih, Kakarmatta, in Shalakanta Vin.
306. Vimaleśa	97.73.	Naya Mahadeo Muhalla,
Vimaleśvara	69.24	called Nilakantha, A 10/47
307. Vīrabhadreśa	97.155.	S of Madhyameshvara, Sivala facing
Vīrabhadreśvara	55.4; 100.94	K 53/63; (2): NW of Jnanavapi mosque, CK 35/1; now ruined
308. Vīrārāmeśvara	84.69	Rama Ghat, K 24/10
309. Vīreśa /	10.121; 17.62;	known as Atmavireshvara,
	51.106; 61.185;	CK 7/158
	82.3; 83.111-23;	
	84.115; 97.39;	
	100.46, 85.	
Vīreśvara	10. 103, 105, 109, 112-3;	
	11. 160; 73.34;	
	82.1; 83.54; 84.77;	
	86.109; 100.29	
310. Virūpākṣa	69.130; 97.226	in compound of Vishvanatha, big *linga*, CK 35/19

311. Viśālākṣīśa Viśālākṣīśvara	10.93. 97.240	Mir Ghat, in Vishalakshi Temple, D 3/85
312. Viśvakarmeśa Viśvakarmeśvara	86.10; 100.30. 73.34; 86.1-2; 97.69; 100.46	in Brihaspatishvara, Siddheshvari, CK 7/133
313. Viśvaliṅga	11.130	backside of Siddhi Vinayaka (Manikarnika), CK 9/9
314. Viśvāvasu	97.243	called Vishvasulinga, Agatyeshvara, Sutikshna, D 36/11
315. Viśvedeveśvara	97.154-5	south of Madhyameshvara, K 53/ 63
316. Viśveśa	9.52; 13.163; 17.128; 21.113; 33.17; 35.51; 38.107; 42.43; 48.55; 51.101; 53.28; 55.20; 61.145; 69.74; 75.54; 95.41; 96.5-6; 97.225; 100.33, 47, 77, 102, 104.	Jnanavapi, Vishvanatha Temple, CK 35/19 (as Vishvanatha)
Same as 316. Viśveśvara / Viśvanātha	3.86-7, 89, 91; 10.93; 11.119, 121; 21.42, 109-10, 123, 127; 22.37; 26.130-2; 32.126; 34.36, 66; 49.15; 73.35; 74.46; 97.124; 99.15, 42; 96.97. 3.26-7; 5.31; 61.113; 100.95	Jnanavapi, Vishvanatha Temple, CK 35/19 (as Vishvanatha)
317. Vṛddhakāleśa Vṛddhakāleśvara	10.86; 55.9; 61.24. 24.72-3, 80-1; 67.180; 73.46; 97.124	Mritunjaya Temple, Vriddhakala, K 52/39
318. Vṛṣabhadhvaja / Vṛṣadhvaja	70.74; 73.60; 100.56. * 62.85	Kapileshvara, Kapiladhara, on Pancakroshi route, across the Varana river
319. Vṛṣabheśvara	66.19; 97.25	as Vrisheshvara, Gorakh Nath Tila, Maidagin, K 58/78

320.	Vyāgheśvara /	65.82-83.*	Saptasagar, Bhutabhairava, K 63/16
		65.75, 85-6;	
	Vyāghreśa /	100.24, 59.	
	Vyāghreśvara /	10.94; 97.165.	
	Vyāghraliṅga	73.61; 97.169.	
321.	Vyāseśa /	10.94;	Karnaghanta, Vyasakupa, K 60/67;
		97.143, 145.	(2) inner compound in north,
	Vyāseśvara	53.37;	Vishvanatha Temple, CK 35/19;
		95.68, 71-4;	(3) Vyasanagar (Vyasapur),
		97.178	Sahupuri, Ramanagar
322.	Yājñavalkyeśa	97.34	near Sankatha Temple, CK 7/159;
			between Sima and Sena Vinayakas
323.	Yameśa /	51.106, 108, 110.	Yama Ghat (Sankatha Ghat),
	Yameśvara	51.107, 115	near bank on the steps
324.	Yamuneśa	10.93; 75.10	in Trilochan Temple, A 2/80

Note:

Out of 524 Shiva Lingas enlisted in the KKh,
200 are not known or identified, or may be lost.
It means presently only 324 Lingas exist in Kashi.

Prepared and © by Prof. Rana P. B. Singh

Shiva Lingas (200) :
Not Known, unidentified, or Lost.

Alphabetical Index of *Kāśīkhaṇḍa*, KKh

Se.	Shiva Linga name	Ref. KKh (Kāśīkhaṇḍa)
1.	Aditīśa	97.208
2.	Āhutīśa	97.103
3.	Ājyapeśvara	97.162
4.	Akrodhaneśvara	65.17
5.	Akṣapādeśa	97.174
6.	Alarkeśa	97.230
7.	Analeśvara	69.165
8.	Anānteśvara	61.198
9.	Anārakeśvara	97.59
10.	Aśvatthāmeśvara	75.80
11.	Autathyeśvara	65.12
12.	Avabhrātakeśvara	97.57
13.	Bābhraveyeśvara	65.16
14.	Bāṣkulīśa	97.84
15.	Bhṛgu	97.75
16.	Bhuvaneśa	97.72
17.	Brahmarāteśvara	97.161
18.	Caitraratha	97.193
19.	Cakreśa	97.50-1, 107, 208
20.	Caturvedeśvara	69.81
21.	Cyavaneśa Cyavaneśvara	68.66; 97.101.65.16
22.	Dadhikalpeśvara	97.185
23.	Damicaṇḍeśa	97.118
24.	Dārukeśa	70.80
25.	Deveśa Jayanta	69.71

443

26.	Dharaṇīśa	81.44
27.	Dharmaśāstreśvara	33.133
28.	Dhāteśa	97.197
29.	Dhiṣaneśa	17.62
30.	Dhundhumārīśvara	66.26
31.	Dīpteśa	69.114
32.	Dṛḍheśa	97.200
33.	Dṛkkeśa	10.88
34.	Droṇeśa	75.79, 81
35.	Drumicaṇḍeśa	10.88
36.	Gadādhareśvara	66.6
37.	Gālaveśvara	65.13
38.	Gaurī	49.28
39.	Gayādhīśa	97.241
40.	Gāyatrīśvara	97.112
41.	Gobhileśa	97.182
42.	Hareśvara	69.80
43.	Haridīśa	97.258
44.	Harikeśavana	100.82
45.	Hārīteśvara	65.13
46.	Harṣitaliṅga Harṣiteśvara	69.87.69.88
47.	Hastīśvara	97.135
48.	Himastheśa	69.131
49.	Hiraṇyakaśipu	97.23
50.	Hiraṇyākṣaliṅga Hiraṇyākṣeśvara	97.241.97.29
51.	Īśa	86.67
52.	Īśvara	51.45; 89.124
53.	Jābālīśvara	65.5
54.	Jaiminīśa	97.194-5
55.	Jālakeśvara	65.19
56.	Jaleśa	65.19

57.	Jālmeśa	65.19
58.	Jāmbavatīśvara	97.44
59.	Jārudhīśa	65.19
60.	Jātūkarṇeśvara	65.19
61.	Jīmūtavāhaneśa	97.182
62.	Kāliṅga	69.107-8
63.	Kalindameśvara	65.17
64.	Kāmada	85.73
65.	Kaṇādeśa	65.15; 97.175
66.	Kanakeśa	97.197
67.	Kaṅkeśa	65.17
68.	Kaṇṭheśvara	65.18
69.	Kaṇveśvara	65.12
70.	Kapileśāna	73.165
71.	Kapotavṛttīśa	65.17
72.	Kaustubheśvara	97.84-5
73.	Kausumeśvara	65.13
74.	Khaṭvāṅgeśa	97.71-2
75.	Khurakartarīśa	61.163
76.	Kiṭīśvara	61.205
77.	Kṣetrajña	97.15
78.	Kumbhi	65.13
79.	Kuntaleśvara	65.17
80.	Lāṅgala	73.46
81.	Likhiteśvara	97.178
82.	Lokapāleśvara	81.43-4
83.	Lokapeśa	97.211
84.	Mādrīśvara	65.9
85.	Magadheyeśvara	65.18
86.	Mahābala	69.11
87.	Mahālayaliṅga	97.92

88.	Mahāliṅga	69.84
89.	Mahātejas	69.44-7
90.	Mahāvrataliṅga	69.25
91.	Mahāyogīśvara	69.48
92.	Mahodareśvara	53.35-6
93.	Mahotkaṭeśvara	69.23
94.	Makheśvara	10.96; 84.62
95.	Maṇḍaleśa	97.100
96.	Māṇḍavyeśa / Māṇḍavyeśvara	97.196.65.3
97.	Mantreśvara	69.88
98.	Manuliṅga	97.237
99.	Marutteśa Marutteśvara	10.91; 65.18; 97.210. *84.71
100.	Mataṅgeśa	65.18; 97.160-1
101.	Mitrāvaruṇeśa	10.97
102.	Muṇḍāsureśvara	97.25
103.	Muṇḍeśa	97.243
104.	Naidhruveśvara	65.14
105.	Naigameyeśvara	97.27
106.	Naimiṣa Naimiṣāraṇya	69.10.69.11
107.	Naleśvara	69.165
108.	Nandiśeṇeśvara	53.56
109.	Nirjareśa	97.205
110.	Paiteśvara	97.204
111.	Pañcaśikheśvara	97.103
112.	Pañcakeśa	55.12
113.	Pañcavaktra	81.48
114.	Parjanyeśa	97.239
115.	Parṇādeśvara	65.14
116.	Patrīśa	10.89
117.	Pavamāneśvara	13.28, 30
118.	Phāguneśa	97.213

119.	Piṅgalākhyeśa	55.2
120.	Piṅgaleśvara	53.58
121.	Pitṛliṅga	33.174
122.	Prabhāmaya	53.124-5
123.	Pracaṇḍeśa	97.196
124.	Prahasiteśvara	85.22; 97.167
125.	Prasannavadaneśa	97.30-31
126.	Priyavrateśvara	33.159; 97.237
127.	Purāṇeśvara	33.132
128.	Purūraveśvara	66.27
129.	Rākṣaseśa	97.207
130.	Rambheśa	81.43; 97.211
131.	Rāvaṇeśvara	97.195
132.	Rudrāvāseśvara	61.111-2
133.	Śacīśa	81.42
134.	Sahasrākṣaliṅga	69.85, 86
135.	Śailādīśvara	61.143
136.	Śailādaja	97.221
137.	Śākheśa	97.27
138.	Saktuprastheśvara	65.15
139.	Śalaṃkāyanakeśvara	65.16
140.	Śambhu	12.90; 10.142; 13.136, 139; 16.83; 17.31; 50.138; 51.61-2; 53.68; 54.2; 55.2; 58.15
141.	Sanakeśa	97.101
142.	Sanandeśa	97.102
143.	Sanatkumāra	97.102
144.	Śāṇḍiyeśa	97.107
145.	Śaṅkara	17.126; 83.43; 100.90;
146.	Śaṅkareśa	65.4
147.	Śaṅkhacūḍeśvara	67.169

148.	Śaṅkheśvara Sāṅkhyeśvara	97.178.84.30
149.	Saptasāgara	33.136
150.	Sārasvataliṅga	33.134.
151.	Śarva	69.81-2
152.	Sarvatīrtheśvara	33.134
153.	Śaśāṅkeśa	97.193
154.	Śaśīśvara	97.211
155.	Śātātapeśa	97.173
156.	Satyavatīśvara	97.112
157.	Sāvitrīśvara	97.112
158.	Siddhīśa / Siddhīśvara	97.247.97.100
159.	Śilādeśa	97.29
160.	Śilāvṛttīśvara	65.16
161.	Śiva Jñāneśvara	61.140
162.	Śiveśa /Śiveśvara	97.141.97.140
163.	Somanandīśvara	53.55
164.	Śreṣṭha	69.163-4
165.	Śrīliṅga	33.43
166.	Sthalaliṅga	69.161
167.	Sthūlakarṇeśvara	53.123
168.	Śubheśvara	97.76
169.	Sugrīveśa	97.43
170.	Śūleśa /Śūleśvara	97.52-3.97.54
171.	Supratīkeśvara	66.28-9
172.	Svaīnaliṅga / Svaīneśvara	97.36.100.53
173.	Tāra	97.221
174.	Triviṣṭa /Triviṣṭapa	75.72-4.50.2; 69.166; 73.6-7; 75.4, 7, 9, 12-5, 17, 21, 23, 31, 49, 59; 76.85; 79.97; 86.108; 92.16; 100.45
175.	Tryakṣeśvara	55.15

176.	Umāpati	69.113-5
177.	Upajaṅghani	65.8
178.	Upamanyu	97.192
179.	Vadanaprekṣanā	97.188
180.	Vāḍavya	97.255
181.	Vairāgyeśa	81.46
182.	Vaivasvateśa	97.208
183.	Vājasaneya	65.11
184.	Vājimedhaka	97.243
185.	Vālakhiyeśvara	75.81
186.	Vālīśa	97.42
187.	Varaṇeśa	97.60
188.	Vatseśvara	65.14
189.	Vijvara	97.13
190.	Vināyakeśvara	33.126; 69.47
191.	Vindatīśa	53.127
192.	Virādheśvara	55.22-4
193.	Viśākheśa	97.27
194.	Vṛddhavasiṣtha	97.33
195.	Vṛṣeśa /Vṛṣeśvara	69.92; 73.47.66.21
196.	Vṛttīśa	97.189
197.	Vyāghrapādeśvara	97.192
198.	Yadṛccheśa	97.202
199.	Yajñeśvara	33.131; 69.83
200.	Yogeśa	97.196

Note:

Out of 524 Siva Lingas enlisted in the KKh,
200 are not known or identified, or may be lost.
It means presently only 324 Lingas exist in Kashi.

Prepared and © Rana P. B. Singh

Appendix 5

VARANASI / KASHI:

THE 84 *GHATS* ALONG THE GANGA RIVERFRONT

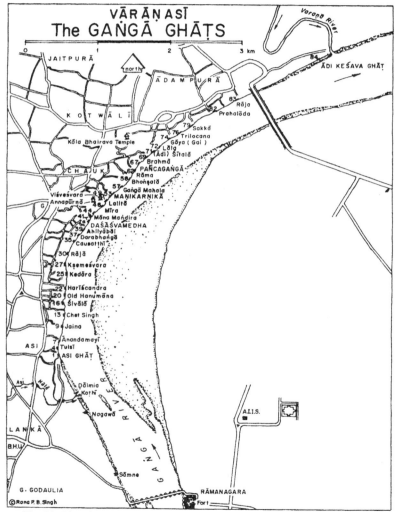

Fig. 32. Riverfront Varanasi: the Ghats along the left bank of the Ganga river.

(from the south to the north; see Fig. 32, cf. Singh and Rana 2002/ 2006)

— Ramanagar Ghat	30. Raja	61. Mehta
— Samne Ghat	31. Khori	62. Rama
— Nagwa Ghat	32. Pande	63. Jatara
1. Asi (*Assi*) Ghat	33. Sarveshvara	64. Raja Gwaliar
2. Ganga Mahala (I)	34. Digpatia	65. Mangala Gauri
3. Rivan (Riwan)	35. Chausatthi	— Balaji
4. Tulasi	36. Rana Mahala	66. Venimadhava
5. Bhadaini	37. Darbhanga	67. Panchaganga
6. Janaki	38. Munshi	68. Durga
7. Anandamayi (Akrura)	39. Ahilyabai	69. Brahma
8. Vaccharaja	41 a. Dashashvamedha	70. Bundi Parkota
9. Jaina	42. Prayaga	71. (Adi) Shitala
10. Nishadaraja	41 b. Dashashvamedha	72. Lal
11. Panchakota	43. Rajendra Prasad	73. Hanumangarhi
12. Prabhu	(early name *Ghoda*)	74. Gaiya / Gai
13. Chet Singh	44. Mana Mandir	75. Badri Narayana /
14. Niranjani	45. Tripura Bhairavi	Matha
15. Mahanirvani	46. Mira	76. Trilochana
16. Shivala	47. Yajneshvara / Naya	77. Gola
17. Gularia	48. Nepali	78. Nandeshvara /
18. Dandi	49. Lalita	Nandu
19. Hanuman	50. Bauli / Umraogiri	79. Sakka
20. Prachin Hanuman	51. Jalashayi	80. Teliya Nala
21. Karnataka/Mysore	52. Khiraki	81. Naya / Phuta
22. Harishchandra	— Cremation Ghat	82. Prahlada
(Cremation Ghat)	53. Manikarnika	— Nishada
23. Lali	54. Baji Rao	— Rani
24. Vijayanagaram	55. Scindhia	— Tikeshvara
25. Kedar	56. Sankatha	— Ravidas/hainsasur
26. Chauki	57. Ganga Mahala (II)	83. Raj
27. Kshemeshvara	58. Bhonshala	— Lakshmana
28. Manasarovara	59. Naya	84. Adi Keshava
29. Narada	60. Ganesha/Agnishvara	— Varana Sangama

Appendix 6

Varanasi / Kashi: 96 Jala Tirtha Yatra
('Pilgrimage to Waterfront Sacred Spots')

Ghat	Ghat name	Attached Jala Tirtha
1.	Asi (*Assi*) Ghat	Asi Sangameha Tirtha
22.	Harishchandra	Adi Manikarnika Tirtha (Prachin Parampapa Tirtha)
25.	Kedar	Parampapa Tirtha
29.	Narada	Prabhasa Tirtha
32.	Pande	Ganga Keshava Tirtha
34.	Digpatia	Agatsya Tirtha
35.	Chausatthi	Yogini Tirtha
41 a.	Dashashvamedha	Dashashvamedha Tirtha, Rudra Sarovara Tirtha
42.	Prayaga	Khurkartari Tirtha, Markandeya, Vashishtha, Arundhati, Prayaga Tirtha
41 b.	Dashashvamedha	Narmada Tirtha, Visandhya Tirtha
43.	Rajendra Prasad	Prabhasa Tirtha
46.	Mir	Jarasandheshvara Tirtha
47.	Yajneshvara / Naya	Vishal Ganga Tirtha
48.	Nepali	Bhagirathi Tirtha
49.	Lalita	Lalita Tirtha, Bharirathi Tirtha
50.	Bauli / Umraongiri	Pitamah Tirtha, Brahmanala, Jnana, Shailad Tirtha
51.	Jalashayi	Vishnu Tirtha
—	Cremation Ghat	Pashupati Tirtha, Rudravasa, Vishvamukti Tirtha
53.	Manikarnika	Manikarnika Tirtha, Chakrapushkarini, Avimukteshvara, Tarak, Skanda, Dhundhi, Bhavani, Ishana Tirtha
56.	Sankatha	Harishachandra Tirtha, Parvata Tirtha

452

57.	Ganga Mahala (II)	Kambalashvatara Tirtha, Sarasvata, Uma Tirtha
58.	Bhonshala	Angara, Kala Tirtha, Chandra Tirtha
59.	Naya	Vira Tirtha
60.	Ganesha/ Agnishvara	Vighnesha Tirtha, Ikshvaku, Marutta, Menavaruna, Agni Tirtha
62.	Rama	Rama Tirtha
64.	Raja Gwaliar	Piplada Tirtha, Tamra Varaha Tirtha, Kala Ganga Tirtha
65.	Mangala Gauri	Mayukharka Tirtha
66.	Venimadhava	Vindu Tirtha
67.	Panchaganga	Jnanahrida Tirtha, Panchanada Tirtha
68.	Durga	Markandeya Tirtha, Kharva Nrisimha Tirtha
69.	Brahma	Bhairava Tirtha
71.	(Adi) Shitala	Karnaditya Tirtha
73.	Hanumangarhi	Nageshvara Tirtha
76.	Trilochana	Pilapipla Tirtha
77.	Gola	Pinshegila Tirtha
78.	Nandeshvara	Hiranyagarbha Tirtha, Pranava Tirtha
81.	Naya / Phuta	Gopratara Tirtha, Sankha Madhav Tirtha
82.	Prahlada	Bana Tirtha, Svarnilina, Sankhya, Uddalaka, Nilagriva, Shesha Tirtha
83.	Raj	Mahishasura Tirtha
84.	Adi Keshava	Lakshmi Nrisimha Tirtha, Gopi Govinda, Vihar Nrisimha, Yajna Varaha, Nara Narayana, Vamana, Pranava, Aditya Keshava, Dattatreyeshvara Tirtha
—	Varana Sangama Ghat	Padodaka Tirtha, Shvetadvipa, Khsirabdi, Shankha, Chakra, Gada, Padma, Maha Lakshmi, Garuda, Narada, Ambarisha Tirtha

* Those Ghats not possessing any Jala Tirtha are not mentioned.
For the full list of Ghats, see Appendix 5.

References : Kkh, *Kashi Khanda* of the *Skanda Purana;* KR, *Kashi Rahasya* of the *Brahmavaivarta Purana;* KKT, *Krityakalpataru* of the Lakshmidhara's *Tirthavivecanakandam*, TvK; MtP, *Matya Purana.*

Appendix 7

HINDU FESTIVALS WITH TITHI & ROMAN DATES

Festival	Hindu Date/*Tithi*	2006	2007	2008	2009	2010
Makara Samkranti	Always on 14th January, when the Sun leaves the zodiac-house of Capricorn and enters Aquarius					
Pausha Purnima	Pausha, L-15, F	14 Jan	3 Jan	22 Jan	11 Jan	31 D.'09
Magha Amavasya	Magha, D-15, N	29 Jan	19 Jan	7 Feb	26 Jan	15 Jan
Vasant Panchami	Magha, L-5	2 Feb	23 Jan	11 Feb	31 Jan	20 Jan
Magha Purnima	Magha, L-15, F	13 Feb	2 Feb	21 Feb	9 Feb	30 Jan
Maha Shivaratri	Phalguna, D-14	27 Feb	16 Feb	6 Mar	23 Feb	12 Feb
Holi / Dhuraddi	Chaitra, D-1	15 Mar	4 Mar	22 Mar	11 Mar	1 Mar
New *Samvata* starts, Vasant Navaratri	Chaitra, L-1	30 Mar 2063	19 Mar 2064	6 Apr 2065	27 Mar 2066	16 Mar 2067
Rama Navami	Chaitra, L-9	6 Apr	26 Mar	13 Apr	3 Apr	24 Mar
Mahavira Jayanti	Chaitra, L-15, F	13 Apr	2 Apr	20 Apr	9 Apr	30 Mar
Buddha Purnima	Vaishakha,L-15,F	13 May	2 May	20 May	9 May	27 May
Ganga Dashahara	Jyeshtha, L-10	6 Jun	25 Jun	13 Jun	2 Jun	21 Jun
Ratha Yatra	Ashadha, L-3	27 Jun	16 Jul	4 Jul	24 Jun	13 Jul
Guru Purnima	Ashadha, L-15, F	11 Jul	30 Jul	18 Jul	7 Jul	25 Jul
Naga Panchami	Shravana, L-5	30 Jul	17 Aug	6 Aug	26 Jul	14 Aug
Raksha Bandhana	Shravana, L-15, F	9 Aug	28 Aug	16 Aug	5 Aug	24 Aug
Krishna Janmasthmi	Bhadrapada, D-8	16 Aug	4 Sep	24 Aug	14 Aug	2 Sep
Haritalika / Tija	Bhadrapada, L-3	26 Aug	14 Sep	2 Sept	22 Aug	10 Sep
Lolarka Shashthi	Bhadrapada, L-6	29 Aug	17 Sep	5 Sep	25 Aug	13 Sep
Ananta Chaturdashi	Bhadrapada,L-14	6 Sep	25 Sep	14 Sep	3 Sep	22 Sep
Jivitaputrika/ Jiutia	Ashvina, D-8	15 Sep	26 Sep	15 Sep	13 Sep	2 Oct
Pitri Visarjana	Ashvina, D-14	22 Sep	10 Oct	29 Sep	18 Sep	7 Oct
Navaratri, NR 1	Ashvina, L-1	23 Sep	12 Oct	30 Sep	19 Sep	8 Oct
Lakshmi Puja, NR 8	Ashvina, L-8	30 Sep	19 Oct	7 Oct	26 Sep	15 Oct
Dashahara, NR 10	Ashvina, L-10	2 Oct	21 Oct	9 Oct	29 Sep	17 Oct
Kojagiri / Purnima	Ashvina, L-15, F	7 Oct	26 Oct	14 Oct	4 Oct	22 Oct
Karva Chautha	Karttika, D-3	10 Oct	29 Oct	18 Oct	7 Oct	26 Oct
Dipavali / Divali	Karttika, D-15, N	21 Oct	9 Nov	28 Oct	17 Oct	5 Nov
Annakuta	Karttika, L-1	22 Oct	10 Nov	29 Oct	18 Oct	6 Nov
Surya Shashthi	Karttika, L-6	28 Oct	16 Nov	4 Nov	24 Oct	12 Nov
Prabodhini Ekadashi	Karttika, L-11	2 Nov	21 Nov	9 Nov	29 Oct	17 Nov
Karttika Purnima	Karttika, L-15, F	5 Nov	24 Nov	13 Nov	2 Nov	21 Nov
Margasirsa Purnima	Margasirsa,L-15,F	4 Dec	24 Dec	12 Dec	2 Dec	21 Dec
Lunar Eclipse	Full Moon (F)	7 Sep	3 Mar	16 Aug	31 Dec	—
Solar Eclipse	New Moon (N)	29 Mar	19 Mar	1 Aug	—	15 Jan

Festival	Hindu Date/*Tithi*	2011	2012	2013	2014	2015
Makara Samkranti	Always on 14th January, when the Sun leaves the zodiac-house of Capricorn and enters Aquarius					
Pausha Purnima	Pausha, L-15, F	19 Jan	9 Jan	27 Jan	16 Jan	5 Jan
Magha Amavasya	Magha, D-15, N	3 Feb	23 Jan	11 Feb	30 Jan	20 Jan
Vasant Panchami	Magha, L-5	8 Feb	28 Jan	15 Feb	4 Feb	24 Jan
Magha Purnima	Magha, L-15, F	18 Feb	7 Feb	25 Feb	14 Feb	3 Feb
Maha Shivaratri	Phalguna, D-14	3 Mar	20 Feb	10 Mar	1 Mar	17 Feb
Holi / Dhuraddi	Chaitra, D-1	20 Mar	8 Mar	28 Mar	17 Mar	6 Mar
New *Samvata* starts, Vasant Navaratri	Chaitra, L-1	4 Apr 2068	23 Mar 2069	11 Apr 2070	31 Mar 2071	21 Mar 2072
Rama Navami	Chaitra, L-9	12 Apr	1 Apr	20 Apr	8 Apr	28 Mar
Mahavira Jayanti	Chaitra, L-15, F	18 Apr	6 Apr	25 Apr	15 Apr	4 Apr
Buddha Purnima	Vaishakha, L-15, F	17 May	6 May	25 May	14 May	4 May
Ganga Dashahara	Jyeshtha, L-10	11 Jun	31 May	18 Jun	8 Jun	28 May
Ratha Yatra	Ashadha, L-3	3 Jul	22 Jun	10 Jul	29 Jun	18 Jul
Guru Purnima	Ashadha, L-15, F	15 Jul	3 Jul	22 Jul	12 Jul	31 Jul
Naga Panchami	Shravana, L-5	4 Aug	24 Jul	11 Aug	1 Aug	19 Aug
Raksha Bandhana	Shravana, L-15, F	13 Aug	2 Aug	21 Aug	10 Aug	29 Aug
Krishna Janmasthmi	Bhadrapada, D-8	22 Aug	10 Aug	28 Aug	17 Aug	5 Sep
Haritalika / Tija	Bhadrapada, L-3	31 Aug	18 Sep	8 Sept	28 Aug	16 Sep
Lolarka Shashthi	Bhadrapada, L-6	3 Sep	21 Sep	11 Sep	31 Aug	19 Sep
Ananta Chaturdashi	Bhadrapada, L-14	11 Sep	29 Sep	18 Sep	8 Sep	27 Sep
Jivitaputrika/ Jiutia	Ashvina, D-8	21 Sep	9 Oct	28 Sep	17 Sep	6 Oct
Pitri Visarjana	Ashvina, D-14	27 Sep	15 Oct	4 Oct	23 Sep	11 Oct
Navaratri, NR 1	Ashvina, L-1	28 Sep	16 Oct	5 Oct	25 Sep	13 Oct
Lakshmi Puja, NR 8	Ashvina, L-8	4 Oct	22 Oct	12 Oct	2 Oct	21 Oct
Dashahara, NR 10	Ashvina, L-10	6 Oct	24 Oct	14 Oct	4 Oct	23 Oct
Kojagiri / Purnima	Ashvina, L-15, F	12 Oct	29 Oct	18 Oct	8 Oct	27 Oct
Karva Chautha	Karttika, D-3	15 Oct	2 Nov	22 Oct	11 Oct	30 Oct
Dipavali / Divali	Karttika, D-15, N	26 Oct	13 Nov	3 Nov	23 Oct	11 Nov
Annakuta	Karttika, L-1	27 Oct	14 Nov	4 Nov	24 Oct	12 Nov
Surya Shashthi	Karttika, L-6	1 Nov	19 Nov	8 Nov	29 Oct	17 Nov
Prabodhini Ekadashi	Karttika, L-11	6 Nov	24 Nov	13 Nov	3 Nov	22 Nov
Karttika Purnima	Karttika, L-15, F	10 Nov	28 Nov	17 Nov	6 Nov	25 Nov
Margasirsa Purnima	Margasirsa, L-15, F	10 Dec	28 Dec	17 Dec	6 Dec	25 Dec
Lunar Eclipse	Full Moon (F)	15 Jun 10 Dic	—	25 Apr	—	4 Apr
Solar Eclipse	New Moon (N)	—	—	—	—	—

Lunar month: D, Dark Fortnight (waning), L, Light Fortnight (waxing); F, Full Moon; N, New Moon. This is protected by copyright, and can be used strictly and only with written permission. *By & © Rana P. B. Singh.*

The Author

Prof. Rana P.B. Singh (b. 15-XII-1950), PhD (1974), Professor of Cultural Geography & Heritage Studies since January 1999 at Banaras Hindu University, has been involved in studying, performing and promoting heritage planning, sacred geography & cultural astronomy, peregrinology, eco-tourism and development in the Varanasi region for the last three decades, as consultant, project director, collaborator and organiser. He has been Visiting Professor of Geography at Virginia Tech (USA), Japan Foundation Scientist at Okayama, Indo-Swedish Visiting Professor at Karlstad University, Ron Lister lecturer at University of Otago, NZ, Linnaus-Palme Visiting Professor at Karlstad University, Sweden, Indo-Japanese Exchange Professor at Gifu University, Japan, and Indo-Swedish Visiting Professor at Gothenburg University. As visiting scholar he has given lectures and seminars at many universities in Australia, Austria, Belgium, Denmark, Germany, Finland, Italy, Japan, Malaysia, Nepal, Netherlands, New Zealand, Norway, Philippines, Singapore, Spain, Sweden, Switzerland, Thailand, USA (including Hawaii), and USSR (since 1990 Russia). During 1976-1988, he served as Assoc./ Secretary and Co-chairman of the IGU Com./WG on 'Rural Habitat in Developing Countries'. He is member of the IGU Initiative: Cultures and Civilisations for Human Development. He is the *Founding President* of the (a) Society of Pilgrimage Studies, SPS (1989), (b) Society of Heritage Planning & Environmental Health, SHPEH (1989), (c) Indo-Nordic Cultural Association, INCA (1992), and (d) Indo-Japanese Friendship Association, IJFAB (fd. 1989). He is also Member, UNESCO Network of Indian Cities of Living Heritage (- representing Varanasi), and Chief Advisor & Member: INTACH, Indian National Trust for Art, Culture and Heritage (chapter Varanasi).

Prof. Rana is a member of the SASNET (Sweden), and of the Executive Board, the International Research Forum, IRF, for SAARC, Tokyo; Member, IGU Initiative: Culture and Civilisations for Human Development; and a Life Member of INTACH, NAGI, NGSI, SPS, and Kautilya Society. During 1985-95, he has served as Assoc./ Executive

Editor of the *National Geographical Journal of India*. He has also served as Chief Co-ordinator to several international projects, like (a) UNO-CHBP, New York on 'Rural development in Indian Environment; case of Varanasi, 1977, (b) Japan Foundation, Tokyo on 'Changing Japanese and Indian Rural Habitat', 1980; (c) Imperial College (UK) project on 'Impact of Air Pollution on the Vegetable Farming System and Socio-economic Characteristics and its Policy Implications', 1999-2002; (d) SAI Heidelberg (Germany) project on 'Visualising Sacred Space and Religious Cartography of Varanasi', 1999-2002; (e) 'Xerox Co. Project on Crossings: Kashi and Cosmos', 2000-01, and (f) 'University of Colorado, Boulder – Cultural Astronomy of Banaras Project', 1999-2001.

Under the supervision of Prof. Rana 8 students have received Ph.D. degrees. His publications include 11 monographs, 23 books, and 177 research papers, including articles in internationally reputed journals like Erdkunde, GeoJournal, Geoscience & Man, Architecture & Behaviour, Pennsylvania Geographer, The Ley Hunter, Place, International Journal of Heritage Studies, Asian Profile, and also in series from Routledge, Ashate, Longman, and Oxford. His recent publications include *Environmental Ethics* (1993), *Banaras (Varanasi): Cosmic Order, Sacred City, Hindu Traditions* (1993), *The Spirit and Power of Place* (1994), *Banaras Region: A Spiritual & Cultural Guide* (2002/2006, with P.S. Rana), *Towards the Pilgrimage Archetype* (2002), *Where the Buddha Walked* (2003), *Cultural Landscapes and the Lifeworld* (2004), *Banaras, the City Revealed* (2005, ed. with George Michell), *Banaras, the Heritage City of India: Geography, History, Bibliography* (2008), *Uprooting Geographical Thought in India: Toward Ecology and Culture in 21st Century* (2009), and *Sacred Geography of Goddesses in South Asia* (2009). He is presently working on *Kashi & Cosmos: Sacred Geography and Ritualscape of Banaras*.

Contact address:

New F-7, Jodhpur Colony; Banaras Hindu University, Varanasi, UP 221005.
Tel: (0542)-2575843 (Res.). (0542)-6701387 (chamber). Cell: (0)-9838 119474.

E-mail: ranapbs@gmail.com

Pilgrimage and Cosmology Series

1. *Banaras Region. A Spiritual and Cultural Guide*
    Rana P. B. Singh and Pravin S. Rana, 2002, 2006

2. *Benares, A World Within a World*
    Richard Lannoy, 2002

3. *Towards the Pilgrimage Archetype.*
    The Pancakrosi Yatra of Banaras
    Rana P. B. Singh, 2002

4. *Banaras in the Early 19th Century: Riverfront Panorama*
    Text by Rai Anand Krishna, 2003

5. *Where the Buddha Walked:*
    A Companion to the Buddhist Places of India
    Rana P. B. Singh, 2003, 2009

6. *Cultural Landscapes and the Lifeworld: Literary Images of Banaras*
    Rana P. B. Singh, 2004

7. *Luminous Kashi to Vibrant Varanasi*
    K. Chandramouli, 2006

8. *Banaras, the Heritage City of India.*
    Geography, History and Geography
    Rana P. B. Singh, 2008

Also published by **Indica Books**

*   *A Pilgrimage to Kashi. Banaras, Varanasi, Kashi*
    colour comic by Gol

*   *The Ganga Trail. Foreign Accounts and Sketches of the River Scene*
    by Jagmohan Mahajan

*   *Varanasi Vista. Early Views of the Holy City*
    by Jagmohan Mahajan